Canada

SINCE 1960

A PEOPLE'S HISTORY

A Left Perspective on 50 Years of Politics,
Economics and Culture

Edited with an Introduction by
CY GONICK
founder of *Canadian Dimension* Magazine

James Lorimer & Company Ltd., Publishers
Toronto

Notice to educators:

This book is available for purchase in print and ebook form. Copies can be purchased from our website at www.lorimer.ca. Copies of individual chapters or portions of the full text in print or digital form are also available for sale at reasonable prices. Contact us for details at rights@lorimer.ca.

The publisher and the author of this work expect that portions of this work will be useful for education, and expect reasonable compensation for this use. This can be readily achieved by arranging to purchase these portions from the publisher. Contrary to the view of university administrators and their legal advisors, it is unlikely that use of a chapter or 10% of this work for educational purposes with no payment to the publisher or author would be found to be fair dealing under the Canadian Copyright Act.

James Lorimer & Company Ltd., Publishers acknowledges the support of the Ontario Arts Council. We acknowledge the support of the Canada Council for the Arts which last year invested $24.3 million in writing and publishing throughout Canada. We acknowledge the Government of Ontario through the Ontario Media Development Corporation's Ontario Book Initiative.

 Canadä Canada Council   Conseil des Arts
for the Arts   du Canada

Cover design: Tyler Cleroux, Adam Hartling & Naoli Bray
Cover image: Alamy

Library and Archives Canada Cataloguing in Publication

Canada since 1960 : a people's history : a left perspective
on 50 years of politics, economics and culture / Cy Gonick, editor.

Includes bibliographical references.
Issued in print and electronic formats.
ISBN 978-1-4594-1113-5 (paperback).--ISBN 978-1-4594-1114-2 (epub)

1. Canada--History--1963-. 2. New Left--Canada.
I. Gonick, Cy, 1936-, editor II. Title: Canada since nineteen sixty.

FC600.C285 2016   971.064   C2016-900196-2
                                          C2016-900197-0

James Lorimer & Company Ltd., Publishers
117 Peter Street, Suite 304
Toronto, ON, Canada
M5V 2G9
www.lorimer.ca

Printed and bound in Canada.

CONTENTS

THE CULTURAL DIMENSION

THE INSTITUTIONAL DIMENSION

THE GLOBAL DIMENSION

DIMENSIONS OF POLITICAL ECONOMY

THE REGIONAL AND URBAN DIMENSION

FOREWORD
Mel Watkins

History, in my experience, is what happens before you are born. It is the terrain of the historians and other moulders of memory and keepers of the flame. I was born so long ago that there is for me no history in this book. I was there when it happened — I can remember reading the first issue of *Canadian Dimension* (hereafter sometimes *CD*) fifty years ago, and still counting — and I can assure you that it's as good as it gets when it comes to the truth.

It is published in Winnipeg, in the province of Manitoba. That province, to quote an ad by the government of Manitoba that ran in the *New York Times* in the 1950s when I was a graduate student in economics at MIT, encouraged companies to move to Manitoba because it was "strategically situated half way between the Atlantic and the Pacific." But the economics we were learning said that, transport by land being much more costly than by water, this was precisely the place not to locate.

Unless, apparently, you were publishing a leftie magazine and wanted to be in the place where east meets west and there was an established culture of protest, up to and including a general strike. And it was the home of Cy Gonick, a youthful, entrepreneurial professor at the University of Manitoba, freshly back from graduate studies at Berkeley, the mecca of the New Left.

In the seventh decade of the twentieth century, a.k.a. "the sixties," the last truly great decade for progressives (too bad if you missed it, for there is no reason to think it will ever happen again), the gods and goddesses, aided and abetted by Gonick, created *Canadian Dimension*. In its early days the magazine became a voice of an emerging Canadian left nationalism that challenged the staid conventional wisdom of the times. More enduringly, it has been a voice of the New Left, of anti-capitalism, of anti-imperialism, and latterly of ecosocialism. When the self-styled Waffle movement for an independent socialist Canada was created within the NDP at the end of the sixties, *CD* was the first to publish its manifesto in full. While the Waffle collapsed far too soon, *CD* lived on, down to the present day.

For *Canadian Dimension* partakes of a long socialist tradition in Canada and elsewhere that bears witness to the damage to body and mind and soul wrought by capitalism and insists that there are democratic alternatives, more democratic than capitalism will contemplate. It likewise reports on the struggle of unions at a time when the mainstream media have made the unions a part of business history, and hence subject to a business point of view, or have simply ignored them.

The sixties was a primal scream against the war in Vietnam, against American imperialism, against colonialism, against Canadian complicity, against oppression of the poor, against exploitation of workers, against capitalism as we knew it. Briefly there was a hole in the sky and if you looked up you could see everything that was wrong with the world.

There was an equally long list of what dissenters wished for, a mixture of the new and of retrievals, revivals, from the past. Women's liberation, beyond equality. The rights of aboriginal people, treaty rights and beyond. The right of Quebec to self-determination. Canadian unions for Canadian workers. Public enterprise, informed by a public enterprise culture, not just state ownership. Public control over foreign takeovers of Canadian companies. Workers' control. Respect for nature, and environmental regulation. Gay and lesbian rights. The Canadianization of Canadian universities. Industrial policy to create a mature and diversified Canadian economy.

The range of the topics in this book reflect the wide and imaginative coverage of *CD*. *Canadian Dimension*. Would you believe the great athlete Bruce Kidd, on sport, his own insider, gutsy writing? Who thinks writing from a socialist perspective is just wishful thinking? Who is more grounded, more in touch with the grass roots, than a runner?

So what happened? Why did the seventies become the decade of transition to the neoconservatism era, globally, with the election of Thatcher and Reagan? Was the sixties decade too good to be true? No, but it was too good to last.

The sixties cast a long shadow forward in matters cultural, in the broadest sense of that term, but it failed to change capitalism; its mindless greed, its commodification of everything, the extraordinary power of the global corporation to impose globalization corporate-style, the relentless diminution of democracy.

While the good things of the sixties happened, there were bad things as well. The birth of the New Left was paralleled by that of the New Right and, not surprisingly, the powerful — the elites — chose the right over the left. When extremist US Senator Barry Goldwater won the Republican nomination for the presidency in 1964 and was roundly whipped, there were some, myself included, who imagined the future could not lie with the right. We were wrong, terribly wrong. The right grew as it moved to the far right, from the conservative to the neoconservative. The economy, essentially freed from democratic control, forced society into its mould. The language of business became the common discourse.

To take a case in point, universities have been bureaucratized, corporatized, their faculties depoliticized and immobilized. David Naylor, the immediate past president of my own university, the University of Toronto, is now on the board of Barrack Gold, which is busy pulverizing the Earth and its peoples in the search for gold. In the new norm, it's simply another career move. Canadian universities compete to see which can have the best business school; ironically, while Canada does well in global ratings of world-class schools of management studies (for whatever they're worth) its business class remains stolidly second-rate, a culture of complacency. Think of it as the Toronto Maple Leafs writ large.

At the recent annual shareholders' meeting of Scotiabank, chief executive Brian Porter called for building pipelines to move oil, that from the tar sands included. He called debates about this "bickering," said dithering was detrimental to Canada's "brand" (as if countries were just companies), and that economic prospects were being put in jeopardy "for all Canadians" (as if a banker knows what's good for everybody). He made the customary reference to sustainability, that infinitely flexible word that can mask the worst of behaviour.

Keynesianism, which the powerful had never taken seriously and the Left saw as necessary but insufficient, instead of being morphed into industrial policy was declared dead, replaced, in the name of globalization, by helping the corporation with free-trade agreements, deregulation, privatization and union busting. Keynes was slain to make way for Hayek and Friedman, who praised the market that they imagined to be self-regulating.

Capitalism has never been a thing of beauty. It must deliver the goods or imprison the people. We know how that is working out today. Workers' wages have stalled and inequality has thrived. The regular invention of new means of speculation led to the financial crisis of 2007/8 and the world skated very close to the sort of crash that created the Great Depression of the 1930s. Small countries, like Greece presently, are pushed to the wall; crippled by austerity, they are told to swallow even more. Yet if the Left is forced to fail, might not fascism, which has plagued Europe, now manifesting itself in hatred of immigrants by the extreme right, be back on the table?

Worst of all, a triumphant capitalism has created an endgame of global warming/extreme climate change/species extermination including that of humankind itself. Canada, with its tar sands and its indifference to the control of carbon emissions, has become a shameful place. Canada is stuck in a staples trap while miring the world in a carbon trap. This country has become a world-class menace.

Remember though: we haven't created only Stephen Harper. We've also created Naomi Klein — along with *Canadian Dimension*! The day may be coming, the sooner the better, when there still may be time, where power has so undermined its legitimacy it has no choice but to heed the truth.

Pockets of resistance, of dissent, have survived. Just to hang in, be around, be here, are achievements in themselves. *Canadian Dimension* is a survivor. It has rolled with the punches. It has called for alternatives. It has met the test of the worst of times. Unlike other magazines it did not have charitable status and was immune to Harper's letting loose the government auditors.

Economists — both Cy Gonick and myself are members in bad standing of that profession — talk of path dependency. Well, in March 2015 a conference was held in Ottawa with the mind-numbing title "North American Competitiveness: A Future Role for Canada." It sounds like endless conferences that have been held since the 1950s. We've got in the mess we are presently in because of them. No sensible person would put his or her hopes there.

This is a book about how hope has been kept alive. It had, and has, a resonance with the times. Read it and heed it. There is much to be done and little time left to do it. We need the voice of *Canadian Dimension*, loud and clear.

INTRODUCTION
Keeping the Spark Alive
Cy Gonick

When I began producing *Canadian Dimension* back in the summer of 1963 it never occurred to me that it would still be around more than fifty years later. In point of fact, it should never have lasted beyond that first issue. I had no money, no funding, no business experience or knowledge of how to produce a magazine, and I knew very few writers I could call on. Somehow, though, we managed to beat the odds and go on to become the longest-lived magazine of the independent Left in Canada — and indeed among the longest lasting magazines ever published in this country. Without corporate advertising or political sponsorship, with few government grants and despite a dismal financial history, *Canadian Dimension* survived to celebrate its fiftieth anniversary, and as of this writing we are planning our 316th issue.

The opening chapter of this book is my version of the history of *Dimension* from 1963 to 2013. I don't even try to take the measure of the magazine's contribution and impact over the years — only what we were trying to do and why. Each subsequent chapter revolves around a particular theme that *Dimension* focused on throughout its history. The only instruction I gave to contributing authors is that I wanted their unvarnished evaluation of how well, and specifically how insightfully, the magazine dealt with the theme assigned to them. As you will see, few held back.

Over all, *CD* published over three hundred issues in this period, about fifty thousand pages. An average of seventy-five to a hundred authors contributed articles to the magazine each year. More important than the sheer numbers is that they comprise a large portion of the intellectual Left active in English Canada in the past fifty years. So *CD* can been seen as a piece of Canadian social and intellectual history from a left perspective.

In the magazine's fiftieth year, out of curiosity, we asked members of the *CD* collective, our editorial board, to tell us how they would identify themselves politically. Most said "anticapitalist." Many said "ecosocialist." A few said "communist." None said "social democrat." Had we conducted this internal survey thirty or forty years earlier my guess is that categories like "socialist," "new left," "left social democrat," or "left nationalist" would have been most commonly volunteered.

Dimension has always been committed to socialist values of equality and participatory democracy — extending democracy throughout all dimensions of life, but it has never been officially or informally associated with any political party. To be sure, some of its editors have been members of one political party or another over the years, but *Canadian Dimension* per se has always been fiercely independent, beholden to no institution and financed almost entirely by its subscribers.

The magazine's founders and earliest contributors were young men — mainly in their twenties and a few in their early thirties. I have managed to stay actively engaged in the magazine throughout its fifty-plus years. But each decade or so a small cohort of *Dimension* editors emerged that helped shape the concerns and character of the magazine. In the early years that cohort included David Sheps, Gad Horowitz, John Warnock, Bruce Kidd, and Alvin Finkel. In the middle years it broadened to include the likes of Jim Silver, Paul Graham, Fred Gudmunson, and Henry Heller. More recently Andrea Levy has joined me in steering *CD*. And as declining health conditions inevitably sap some of my energy, I hope she will be accompanied by both stalwarts and newcomers in determining the current and future direction of the magazine.

Certain themes have recurred with striking regularity in *Dimension*: what role Canada plays in the world, and particularly in the American Empire, and what role a more independent Canada could play; how imperialism works and how to build a movement to defeat it; how to give full and sustained recognition of *deux nations*, Canada and Quebec, either in one state or two; how the capitalist system produces social injustice, income insecurity, and growing inequality; how liberal and social democratic reforms can never yield workable remedies; what alternatives to capitalism might look like; and what strategies are necessary to build movements to effectively challenge capital.

Of course, much has changed since *Dimension* was founded: the movement for Quebec self-determination and years later the movement for First Nations sovereignty; the rise of feminism and gay liberation; the environmental crisis and the urgent need to stop climate change; the internet and social media; the surveillance state. On the world scene, the disintegration of the Soviet Union and the consolidation of American global dominance; then the unexpected rise of twenty-first-century socialist governments in Latin America; the upheaval in Arab countries; and the outbreak of new wars in Iraq, Libya, and Afghanistan. Many of these were anticipated and all of them were reflected and dissected in *CD*'s pages and, more recently, on our website.

How is it that a magazine with such flimsy finances has managed to survive for over fifty years when, in the same period, dozens of publications were founded, flourished briefly, floundered and then expired — some with massive advertising and circulation rates five and ten times larger than *CD*'s? Perhaps part of the explanation is that I have never been concerned with commercial success. Profit was never a consideration. Our business model consisted largely of soliciting left academics and activists to write for us as an act of solidarity and as an expression of their practical political engagement. We offered meagre pay to part-time staff, to those contributors who had no other source of income, and to designers. Whatever was left was ploughed back into the magazine for extra pages or colour. Further, no magazine has enjoyed a more stable or a more loyal readership. Through most years, up to a third of our readers have contributed a sum beyond the subscription price.

In our fiftieth anniversary issue (March/April 2013), some of our veteran writers volunteered their thoughts on how *CD* managed to survive for over five decades.

"No one has its hooks in *CD*. It stuck to its independence from vested interests on the Left, including the NDP and the labour bureaucracy. It has not been afraid to criticize, very sharply at times." — *Stan Gray*

To this observation I would add that it's true, *Dimension* has managed to piss off, at least once, just about every participant in civil society. But being independent has allowed us to take our shots and give activists the space to take theirs. Of course there have been times that we've paid a steep price for this independence. We've been boycotted, lost our charity number, sued and threatened with lawsuits.

"Today's *CD* is far more willing to [put] front and centre the perspective of Aboriginal peoples, women, environmentalists, gays and others who barely figured in the journal's worldview in the early days — while maintaining, indeed even being more forceful in its critique of the market economy which threatens the existence of humanity and all other species." — *Alvin Finkel*

"Historically, the pivotal role played by many *CD* contributors in the feminist struggles taking place in the economic, political and cultural spheres renders their contributions of particular significance, and the magazine truly provides a living archive of a vibrant and dynamic era." — *Stephanie Ross*

"*Canadian Dimension* has not managed to change the world decisively — a rather tall order for one small publication in one particular corner of the globe — but it has provided a forum, especially in Canada, in which those who are committed to this project can discuss what needs doing and how to do it. This necessarily involves debate, exchange and at times heated disagreement. It entails sharing information and keeping old insights alive, as well as being willing to entertain and learn from new ones. For 50 years *Dimension* has been doing all this and more. Few magazines of the Left have had this kind of continuity." — *Bryan Palmer*

On a personal note, *Canadian Dimension* has been my daily preoccupation for fifty-three years; apart from my children it has been the one constant in my life. I am very grateful to all the comrades who have worked alongside me over the years to produce *Dimension*, and I want to extend my thanks to all those who have contributed chapters to this book.

In an exclusive interview in Montreal on the occasion of his benefit lecture to mark *CD*'s fiftieth anniversary, Noam Chomsky was asked what kind of role he thought a small left-wing magazine like *Dimension* could play. He replied that it was pretty impressive how *CD* had been helping to keep activism alive for more than fifty years, encouraging interaction and stimulating organizational efforts, especially in the absence of the kind of lively working class culture and vibrant left press that had thrived prior to the 1950s. "Someone has to keep the spark alive," Chomsky remarked.

That is a badge I wear with pride.

— Cy Gonick, December 2014

PART I

THE CANADIAN DIMENSION

BARBECUED MONK

TEST-BAN TREATY

THE BLACK NEGRO

CHAPTER 1
The Canadian Dimension
Cy Gonick

Introducing ourselves

Canadian Dimension *is a new and independent journal of fact and opinion. It is the product of the post-nuclear generation of leftish thinkers. Despite the terrifying (and terrified) world in which we were born, we are not without hope for a better future. We have not become so disillusioned, so swamped by commercialism, so paralysed by the bomb that we have halted the search for "the good society" and the use of reason as a guide to action. But we are tired of the old frame of reference, of the old clichés and of the superficiality of the mass media. We intend to challenge the assumptions of the cold war and of the free enterprise economy . . .*

— *On the cover of the first issue*

I. 1963–1974: BEGINNINGS

Canadian Dimension was conceived in the dead of winter in the prairie city of Saskatoon in 1963. With family in tow, I landed in Saskatoon after having accepted a teaching post at the University of Saskatchewan. Though I was born in Winnipeg and grew up there, I attended university in the USA and had not resided in Canada for the better part of six years. The politics I brought with me were the politics of the US student movement in the earliest days of the then New Left.

As an undergraduate at the University of California at Berkeley in the late 1950s, I was active in a student organization called Slate, which organized around issues like civil rights, migrant labour, the death penalty, the House Un-American Activities Committee and the CIA-sponsored invasion of Cuba. Then, when I returned to Berkeley as a graduate student in 1960, I joined a small Marxist study circle that met weekly and out of which was born one of the first New Left publications in the US: *Root and Branch*. Only three issues of *Root and Branch* were published and I had articles in two of them. In retrospect, I think that experience inspired my desire to publish a magazine — although I had no such plans when I first arrived in Saskatoon.

These were action-packed years prefiguring the Free Speech era when Berkeley students occupied the administration building and were hauled off to jail. In the spring of 1960, I was in the rotunda of City Hall in San Francisco on Black Friday, as it came to be called, when police dumped thousands of gallons of water from fire hoses on student demonstrators trying to attend hearings of the House Un-American Activities Committee. Some days earlier, I was part of the vigil on the eve of the execution of Caryl Chessman at San Quentin. Chessman had spent eleven years on death row though he had not been convicted of any crime involving the killing of another human being. That fall, I was at Sather Gate on the Berkeley campus listening spellbound to the impassioned speeches of Maurice Zeitlin and Robert Scheer, who had recently returned from a summer in Cuba. Scheer and Zeitlin were part of our Marxist circle and key figures in *Root and Branch*. Speeches about the Cuban revolution and American foreign policy were given for hours at a time, drawing thousands of students every day. Street-corner orators were commonplace in Berkeley during those years, but I had never seen anything like this.

In truth, I found Saskatoon a boring place to be — although to be fair, back in those days few cities anywhere in the world could match the intellectual ferment of Berkeley. At twenty-six years of age, I felt that I had just begun to find a place for myself in the world of ideas. I wanted and needed the stimulation of intellectual debate and exchange. Where could I find that in Canada? I remember searching the periodicals section

23

of the U of S library and finding nothing that could be described as even vaguely inspiring. I tested the idea of putting out a new journal among my new colleagues. I had taken it into my head that if I launched a magazine I could find the people with ideas with whom I needed to engage. By then I had made a few friends and many enemies by speaking out on campus about the Cuban Missile Crisis at a rally. I had no takers save one; that was G. David Sheps, a boyhood friend from Winnipeg's North End, also marooned that year in Saskatoon, where he was beginning a teaching career in English literature.

David and I became fast friends and allies. He had a wide-ranging mind and was remarkably articulate about subjects in which we shared a common interest and other subjects about which I knew next to nothing. David was intrigued by the idea of starting a magazine and he had better contacts than I did.

We mused over what form it should take. A journal of ideas, certainly, oppositional, vaguely socialist, analyzing current issues and events from a left-wing but independent perspective. Beyond that I don't recall intense discussions about content, let alone marketing, financing, design and everything else that producing a magazine entails. There was no plan and no planning back then. Until a decade or so ago, what planning there was at *CD* simply aimed at getting out the next issue. One issue at a time has been *CD*'s operational basis for most its existence. The possibility of lasting a quarter of a century, let alone a half a century, never crossed anybody's mind — certainly not mine. I do recall discussing possible names back in that winter of 1963. "Rally" was the name favoured by Fay, my first wife. It was David who suggested *Canadian Dimension*.

I left Saskatoon that summer for Winnipeg, taking the first issue of *Canadian Dimension* (*CD*) with me — all one thousand or so copies. It had been printed up in Saskatoon. I don't recall the name of that printer but he was a godsend. He chose a banner for us and designed that first issue including its cover. While that banner would disappear from the *CD* masthead, dropped by subsequent designers and replaced by several other banners over the years, it was rediscovered in 2005 and adopted by Zab, a revolutionary designer who undertook a total remake of *CD* that year.

The cover of that first issue features the short paragraph I wrote titled "Introducing Ourselves" which appears above as this chapter's epigraph. For content, I mainly invited articles from a few Saskatoon colleagues. Paul Phillips, then a MA student who would become one of Canada's top political economists and a frequent contributor to *Dimension*, wrote about the just released Norris Report. This was a government ordered investigation of the disruption of shipping and racketeering on the Great Lakes. I asked a law student and student journalist by the name of William Deverell to write about the coming provincial elections in BC. Deverell, now best known for his superb mystery novels, returned to *CD* only a few years ago with an article analyzing the unique character of Canadian suspense novels. An award-winning English prof, Carlyle King, surveyed recent Canadian fiction. I asked Scott Gordon, an Ottawa-based economist I had read, to write an article on foreign investment in Canada, a topic that was just beginning to be debated. And I wrote three short articles: "Nuclear Arms for Canada," "The Crisis in South Vietnam" and "The Little World of Walter Gordon."

Around the time I had arrived back in the country, Canada was smack in the middle of a political crisis over the Diefenbaker government's refusal to arm the Bomarc missile with nuclear weapons. "We shall not have Canada used as a storage dump for nuclear weapons," Dief thundered. So a new US-made Bomarc, accepted by Canada years earlier and designed for atomic warheads, was rendered useless just as American President John Kennedy called on Canada to join the US in preparing for a Soviet counterattack against the US naval blockade of Cuba then in progress to prevent Soviet weapons from reaching Cuban soil. An irate John Kennedy blasted Diefenbaker, contributing to an internal revolt within the Tory caucus that ended in a Liberal victory in the April 1963 federal elections. One of the first acts of the Lester Pearson government was to accept the nuclear warheads. In my comment I said that "the Canadian assumption of a nuclear defense cannot be justified on any legitimate grounds. Pearson has traded away an independent foreign policy for Canada for various economic concessions from the US government." And I challenged the peace movement to question the assumptions of the Cold War, NATO and the strategy of deterrence. These were to be recurring themes in *CD*, as was Vietnam, where the US undertook its first combat mission in the spring of 1962.

Being at the helm of *CD* demanded that I bring myself up to speed on the issues of the day. The biggest challenge was that I came at it with scant knowledge of Canadian history and institutions. This shortcoming was remedied in short order, but not soon enough to enable me to avoid at least one very damaging faux pas. Early on, I wrote an article about the crisis in Canadian trade unions, arguing that trade unions had become little more than organizations selling a service to their members, not unlike other service industries, and that they were led by grossly overpaid officials who had more in common with bosses than with workers (1:3, December/January 1963-4). Here I drew on the writings of US sociologist C. Wright Mills — one of my intellectual heroes. Applied to Canada, however, this portrait was exaggerated, one-sided, and dismissive of what was still one of the more democratic organizations in the country. It would take a few decades to overcome the labour movement hostility spawned by that and similar articles.

I mailed the first issue of the magazine to a list of potential authors I had compiled, with a short note asking them to subscribe, spread the word, and contribute articles. And I convinced a few newsstands in Winnipeg to stock it on commission. Altogether, I distributed about three hundred copies within a few months. Along with working on my thesis, I was able to devote that first year in Winnipeg to *Canadian Dimension*. In the spring of 1964 I was hired to teach economics at the University of Manitoba, a post I held for the next three and a half decades. It provided me with the income that enabled me to remain the magazine's unsalaried publisher and editor.

I have to admit, the next few issues were not pretty. I did my best to patch things together, forcing things in with a shoehorn where necessary to make them fit. While I learned a few things about layout, I would never be a designer. But soon thereafter *CD* underwent a magical transformation. I had been invited to address a Voice of Women meeting in Winnipeg, where I circulated copies of my ugly duckling. A note was passed up to me by someone offering to contribute artwork. That someone turned out to be June Sherwood, arguably Winnipeg's most accomplished graphic artist, who happened to have a strong progressive background. She generously agreed to take over the entire design and layout of the magazine — for free. Voila! *Canadian Dimension* was now the most interesting-looking magazine on the newsstands.

My basement became *Dimension* central for the next several years. Knowing next to nothing about journalism, running a business, or laying out a magazine, I simply plunged ahead — found a local printer, took out a post office box, made more lists of contacts, sent out magazines and pleas for help. Somehow, it was sufficient. Articles began to come in, a few subs, offers to help and a little money to boost the small sums I was able to contribute to pay the printing bills.

By the end of that first year, we had a paid circulation of about six hundred. Come mailing time, family, friends, and neighbours gathered together in our basement to address and bundle the magazine. One neighbour, Elaine Halliday, volunteered to keep track of subscriptions and newsstand sales. Elaine soon became indispensable, and after she left to take up paid employment I brought in a series of part-time paid clerical workers to run the office. Somehow, through these early years we managed to publish eight issues a year — a feat we cannot duplicate today.

While I soldiered on with *Dimension,* some of my friends in the Bay area with whom I had worked to produce *Root and Branch* were involved with a magazine project that was truly extraordinary. By late 1964 *Ramparts* had morphed from a staid Catholic monthly into America's most radical publication — slick, irreverent, bold, sophisticated in design, muckraking in content with a promotional flair and financial support in the millions of dollars that allowed it to reach a circulation of 229,000 by 1967 — more than half of it newsstand. I was green with envy. But by 1975 *Ramparts* flamed out. Like the New Left, it reached the zenith of its influence by the close of the sixties. In the end, it was brought down by raging egos, political divisions and flagrant overspending, in addition to new publications competing for the same media niche. But in its heyday, *Ramparts* made journalistic history.

CD had smaller triumphs starting out. That first year saw four breakthroughs. First, mainly due to the recruiting efforts of Associate Editor

David Sheps, by then living in Montreal, we were the first English-language publication to analyze the rise of the new Quebec nationalism. That included publishing a translated version of the document written by Michel Chartrand, Jacques-Yvan Morin and André L'Heureux calling for a new two-nation Confederation (1:4-5, February/March 1964). Second, at a time when many Canadians were becoming aware of our status as a branch plant of the US, we were the first to explore what an independent Canadian foreign policy and defence policy might look like and what it would take to develop a more independent economy and cultural life (1:3, December/January 1963-4). Third, *Dimension* threw the spotlight on the American assault on Vietnam at the very outset of the conflict (1:1-2, September/November 1963). We persisted in analyzing this war most every issue through to the Paris peace talks in 1975, while drawing attention to Canada's hypocritical role. And fourth, we contributed greatly to bringing socialism out of its Canadian closet when, in defiance of Cold War venom, we began a series we called "Socialism in the 20th Century" (1:6, May/June 1964).

In subsequent years, we linked up these themes — American imperialism, Canadian independence and socialism and self-determination for Quebec. But *Dimension's* ultimate validation came as young authors, a new generation of activist writers and public intellectuals, found a space in the magazine to exchange ideas about how to change the world, define their own thinking and in so doing redefine what Canada was becoming and what it could become. By 1965–66 young professors like Charles Taylor, Gad Horowitz, George Grant, John Warnock and Mel Watkins; graduate students like James Laxer, Stan Gray, Jim Harding, Leandre Bergeron; and labour journalists like Ed Finn had found in *Canadian Dimension* a space to share and debate their ideas. James Petras, a fellow Berkeley grad student, sent articles to *Dimension* from day one, a practice he kept up long after he had become one of the most celebrated radical writers in the US.

James Laxer, then a graduate student at Queen's University, rehearsed in those early issues of *CD* many of the themes he would take up throughout his writing career: "The Search for Canadian Nationalism" (5:7, December/January 1968–69), "The Student Movement and Canadian

Independence" (6:3-4, August/September 1969), "The Socialist Tradition in Canada" (6:6, December/January 1969-70), "Continental Energy" (6:8, April/May 1970), "The Alienation of Canadian Resources" (7:7, January/February 1971).

The eminent Canadian philosopher Charles Taylor, having just recently returned to Canada from his studies at Oxford University where he encountered the British New Left, was recruited to *Dimension* by David Sheps. They met during the 1965 federal election when Sheps campaigned door to door for Taylor when he ran for the NDP against Pierre Trudeau in the Mount Royal riding. Taylor's earliest *CD* essays included "Alternative to Continentalism" (3:5, July/August 1966), "Nationalism and Independence" (4:3, March/April 1967), "René Lévesque's New Party" (5:4, April/May 1968), "A Socialist Perspective on the 70s" (5:8, February 1969), and "Marcuse's Authoritarian Utopia" (7:3, August/ September 1970). In this latter essay, Taylor registered his growing unease with New Left thought as expressed by its most heralded philosopher. "The real political disaster for left politics in Marcuse's vision," he wrote, "is that it encourages undiscriminating support of any movement which proclaims strident opposition to the system," while displaying a "blithe unconcern for what the rebellion is for." Moreover, in his view, by "writing off the affluent working class as irrational victims of manipulation," Marcuse was helping only to drive a wedge between the affluent working class and the disadvantaged, weakening any chance for an alliance between them which, he maintained, was "the only basis of progress in our society."

By the end of the decade still other young writers found their way to *Dimension* — essayist Herschel Hardin, Olympian long-distance runner Bruce Kidd, poets Dennis Lee, Al Purdy and Richard Sommer, art historian Barry Lord and professors Clark Blaise, Ian Lumsden, Louis Greenspan and Henry Heller. The magazine featured a lively letters section, drawing exchanges from the likes of NDP leader Tommy Douglas, former leader M.J. Coldwell, poet Irving Layton, *Globe and Mail* editorial writer Anthony Westell, Professors George Grant, Ed Broadbent, Laurier Lapierre and Ramsay Cook. Cook, already a distinguished Canadian historian, sent this note: "Two of the best discussions of Canadian politics and political thought I have read in a long time were both printed in *Canadian Dimension* magazine" (2:5, July/August 1965). *Dimension* also attracted favourable reviews in the *Montreal Star* and the *Toronto Star* and, as a frequent guest of the CBC's new show "Cross Country Checkup," hosted then by Betty Shapiro, I was able to draw further attention to *CD*. Wherever I travelled — to Montreal for "Cross Country Checkup" or to Toronto or Vancouver to appear on panels — I made a point of finding newsstand outlets for *CD*. By 1966 *CD*'s circulation had climbed to over twelve hundred, and by 1970 it was close to four thousand, including three thousand paid subscribers. The results of a 1970 survey of our readers showed that nearly a quarter of *CD* readers were under twenty-five years of age and another 40 per cent between twenty-five and forty. Over half were students, school teachers and professors. Every year 150 to 200 subscribers made small donations that added up to a quarter or so of our annual revenue. Ads were scarce and there were no government grants.

Our circulation was still paltry, our finances precarious and our organization crude, but the magazine had found its voice, identified its causes and joined the battle of ideas.

Canadian Dimension and "the sixties"

For me the decade of "the sixties" refers to the tumultuous years between 1964 and 1974, ten years that shaped the political history of *Canadian Dimension*. It was a crowded decade that encompassed a youth rebellion against middle class conventions of respectability; the sexual revolution; the civil rights movement in the US, the student movement and the rise of a New Left; a workers' revolt — as much against the labour movement's own leaders as against the bosses; the global revulsion against American imperialism; a movement in English Canada to gain greater economic and cultural independence from the US; a movement in Quebec for self-determination; the first stirrings of a First Peoples' movement; and the beginning of a movement for women's liberation and gay rights.

The Canadian peace movement came alive the moment Lester Pearson signed Canada on to nuclear weapons in 1963. *CD* carried articles by renowned political scientist C.B. Macpherson on the folly of nuclear deterrence (1:3, December/January 1963–4) and by peace activist Dan

Daniels on the civil disobedience action at the Bomarc missile base at La Macaza, 110 miles north of Montreal (1:7, July/August 1967). In December of 1964 I attended the founding conference of Student Union for Peace Action (SUPA). I described the 150 students that attended the Regina conference as "perhaps the most impressive group of young Canadians that has yet been assembled in any one place" (2:2, January/February 1965). Modeling itself on the American Students for a Democratic Society (SDS), SUPA concentrated on antipoverty work, community organizing and what was called student syndicalism — a theory of students as catalysts of social change. Future *CD* contributors Myrna Wood and Joan Newman (later Kuyek) were among the pioneers of community organizing in urban settings. Jim Harding, federal Chairman of SUPA, wrote "The Powerless Minority," a *CD* article in which he was one of the first to describe First Peoples as "a colonial people who have been ruled by outside authorities over which they have no direct control" (3:2, January/February 1966). John Conway sent *CD* an article about the conditions he found on Carry-the-Kettle, an Indian reserve in Saskatchewan he was assigned to report on by SUPA (5:2, January/February 1968). *CD* also focused on the first rumblings of opposition to what was then called "the multiversity." In an article I contributed (3:3-4, March/June 1966) I wrote:

> *The university may be regarded as a business enterprise which manufactures B.A.'s and B.Sc.'s. The students are goods in process . . . The workers who fabricate the goods in process are the professors. The professors in turn are supervised by the plant foremen — the deans; the general manager of the plant is the university president . . . The goods in process are tested periodically in the various stages of production — to ensure that they conform to the minimum standards and specifications. Exceptional quality is duly rewarded. After the final stages of fabrication have been completed, the finished commodity is available for sale to the highest bidder. The best markets today seem to be large corporations, government bureaucracies, the*

31

professions, but the most rapidly expanding market appears to be graduate schools.

Such critiques were of course only a prelude to student revolts that would erupt around the world a few years later. And university campuses were by no means the only sites of revolt. A wave of wildcat strikes in the mid sixties had ended a long period of labour complacency following important union breakthroughs at the end of World War II. Though Canada was a noncombatant in the Vietnam War, the Canadian economy was working to capacity supplying the US with strategic war materials. The resulting labour shortage emboldened Canadian workers. Ed Finn was the first to notice. In a *CD* article titled "The New Militancy of Canadian Labour" (3:1, November/December 1965), Finn wrote: "Rank and File apathy has been replaced by an activism so intense that it has shaken the entire labour movement, and indeed the entire economy of the nation." He argued that the wildcat strike could be regarded as the trade union equivalent of the student sit-in. Led by a new cohort of workers that were coming to doubt the willingness of their elected officials to provide the decisive, militant leadership they sought, Finn labelled them the labour movement's New Left. Noting that they were recruited from the same generation as the university's New Left, he observed: "Both share the same discontent with the status quo, the same willingness to engage in civil disobedience to dramatize their feelings." A frequent contributor to *CD*, Ed Finn was then editor of *Canadian Transport*, the Canadian Brotherhood of Railway, Transport and General Workers newspaper, a post he held for several years before taking on a similar function with the Canadian Union of Public Employees and subsequently with the Canadian Centre for Policy Alternatives.

Most of us were familiar with the Port Huron Statement, the 1962 manifesto of Students for a Democratic Society, but it was an article by Stan Gray published in *CD* in 1965 (3:1, November/December 1965) that first articulated the thinking of SDS in Canada. Stan was then a McGill University student and SUPA activist. A red-diaper baby, he grew up in the Montreal Jewish St. Urbain Street neighbourhood immortalized by Mordecai Richler. After attending Oxford University in England on scholarship, Stan returned to McGill as a lecturer in political science and ended up, in 1969, as leader of McGill Français, a movement to force this bastion of Anglo Canadian privilege to teach in French, for which effort he was fired from his teaching post. Stan became an activist with the Front de Liberation Populaire (FLP), a mass movement organized by Michel Chartrand and the Montreal Labour Council of the Confederation of National Trade Unions (CSN). Though never involved with the FLQ, Stan was one of the hundreds arrested following the 1970 kidnappings. Released from jail after three weeks, he left Montreal and moved to Hamilton to become a Westinghouse assembly line worker. Within a few years he was elected as a shop steward and union health and safety representative and in the 1980s began sending CD groundbreaking articles from the shop floor of Westinghouse.

In his 1965 New Left article, Gray made several points. First, the new movement must be oriented towards grassroots organizing and look to "the dispossessed and powerless groups in society as important components of a new radical coalition." Second, leadership must come from youth and particularly from university students. Third, the organization should be local and community based, oriented to immediate issues that preoccupy people, opposed to bureaucratic power structures and governed by principles of participatory democracy rather than from the top down. Fourth, while not opposed to involvement in parliamentary politics, a radical movement can only be built outside the NDP, which is irrevocably committed solely to parliamentary politics "which leads it into the trap of social change via electoralism." CD embraced a lot of this. We have always been attracted to New Left notions of participatory democracy, an emphasis on extra-parliamentary politics, community organizing and personal liberation. We were less convinced that "the disposessed," while essential in any mobilization, could take the lead as agents of change, a point I will return to later.

It's true, as Jim Harding complained in a letter to CD, that Dimension was never part of the counterculture. But he was wrong in his dismissal of us in that same letter as "a magazine for academic socialists." If Jim meant that literally, our reader surveys show that academics have never been more than a small component of our subscription base. If, as more likely, he was dismissing us as a bunch of armchair socialists, he was wrong on that count too. True, many of us — Jim Harding included — take on the role of public intellectuals, but we have always understood public intellectuals as a vital component of any movement for social change. We paid a little attention to the counterculture with articles on Bob Dylan, the yippies and urban communes, but for us the sixties was more about the emergence of the New Left, stirrings in the working class, the anti-Vietnam war protests, Canadian independence, Quebec sovereignty and the beginning of Red Power.

For an independent and socialist Canada

Through the fifties and early sixties I think it's fair to say that most Canadians looked to the US as a model. As a society, we tended to welcome all things American — their cars, the suburbs, Hollywood, their radio sitcoms. Our pop heroes were all American — Joe DiMaggio, Sinatra, Bob Hope, Elvis, Nat King Cole, Muhammad Ali, John F. Kennedy. With rare exceptions, there was certainly no conception of America as an imperialist state, and expressions of concern for Canada's growing dependency on it were rare. In almost all quarters, nationalism was a dirty word. But the escalation of the war against Vietnam begun under JFK and pursued by Lyndon Johnson changed everything. More than any other event in these years, it was the Vietnam war that provoked a sense of revulsion toward the US. *Canadian Dimension* was very much a product of the wave of anti-imperialism that covered the globe. For our generation, Vietnam was clearly the defining event. It forever changed the way we saw the United States and it forced us to reexamine our perception of Canada.

The US had been involved in Vietnam ever since the French colonial forces had been routed by Communist nationalists in 1954, with the Communists holding the northern half of the country. The subsequent peace conference that produced the Geneva Accords called for democratic elections within two years that would unify the two halves. Canada was named as Western representative on the three-member International Control Commission established to supervise the ceasefire and to ensure the elections. The Kennedy administration sent in special forces and poured in millions to support the unpopular president of South Vietnam, Ngo Dinh Diem. It was determined to prevent an election from occurring, claiming the Communists were violating the ceasefire. Canada, faithfully supported the US in the ICC, pretending the violations of the Accord were entirely the work of the North. The Americans eventually tired of the corrupt and brutal Diem regime and, according to some accounts, arranged for his assassination in 1963. It was after the August 1964 Tonkin resolution in the US Congress, giving President Lyndon Johnson carte blanche to "take all necessary measures," that things really heated up.

I tracked these developments in a three-part series beginning in May 1965 (2:4) called "What Every Canadian Should Know about Vietnam," which we then turned into a pamphlet. Beginning in that same issue, John Warnock wrote a series of articles on Canada and Vietnam.

As in the United States, Canadian public protest against the war mounted in 1967–68. Canadian rocker Burton Cummings howled his critique of the Republic: "I don't want your war machine, I don't need your ghetto scene. American woman, stay away from me." *Canadian Dimension* was very much part of this tide of anti-American sentiment. A poem titled "1966" in our September/October 1966 (3:6) issue provides an early indication:

America you bastard
murderer of dreams
(and dreams are your
most innocent murders)
seed blaster
harvest ghoul
America America
the burnt seed lies by the side
of your turnpikes
autograveyards
motel cities
military camps
the heaped-up contempt

of every dream of paradise on earth
stinking your greens
the burnt seed
shines darkly
blasting out
the sun

In a widely quoted article titled "Why I am Anti-American" (5:1, November/December 1967), US-raised John Warnock condemned the US as a "sick society" worshipping property and profit, dedicated to inequality and founded on violence, its economic empire maintained by direct and indirect use of armed force. "I am a Canadian nationalist or as the liberals prefer, anti-American," Warnock concluded, "not because I support some state-worshipping philosophy but because I am a universalist. Today the alternative to being a Canadian nationalist is nothing but absorption into the empire of the United States, and I do not desire such a fate for Canada."

Anti-American sentiment on the Left reached its peak in the campaigns led chiefly by Robin Mathews. *Dimension* chose not to join his crusade against the hiring of American professors, but when he sent us an article opposing Canadian support for American draft dodgers, arguing that they contributed to the colonization of Canada, we decided to publish it (6:7, February/March 1970). I remember thinking at the time that this was an outlandish opinion but that it should be aired to provide a space for discussion. From that point forward, *Dimension*'s policy has been to publish articles if we think they represent points of view that need to be discussed, even though editors might disagree with them. As expected, there were critical responses to Mathews's views and we printed them in subsequent issues.

Such expressions of ultrapatriotism never sat well with me. How could they, given my history? Besides, the contributions of expatriot American intellectuals were hugely important in those early years of *Dimension*, as they would be throughout our history, to say nothing of those expatriates' contributions more broadly to left discourse and activism in this country.

In March of 1967, *Canadian Dimension* celebrated Canada's Centennial by holding a conference on "Canada and the American Empire." It took place in Montreal at what was then Sir George Williams University (now Concordia) with papers presented by Charles Taylor, Andre Gunder Frank, Jacques-Yvan Morin, Dimitri Roussopoulos, Evelyn Dumas, Gad Horowitz, myself and several others. The keynote address was delivered by Tommy Douglas. The proceedings were published over two issues of the magazine in the spring of 1967 (4:3 and 4:4).

Gad Horowitz called his presentation "On the Fear of Nationalism: A Sermon to the Moderates" (4:4, May/June 1967). In it he maintained:

> *The nationalism that has bathed the world in blood is not the nationalism that seeks to prevent the integration of Canada into American society. There are, to begin with, crucial distinctions to be made among the nationalism of expansionist great powers, the nationalism of small states struggling to preserve some degree of independence and the nationalism of colonized people seeking self-determination. The first of these is never justifiable. The other two, nearly always are. Canadian nationalism is clearly that of a small state: our relationship with the United States is analogous to the relationship of Finland with the Soviet Union . . . [Further,] there is a difference between racist nationalism and other types of nationalism . . . Canadian nationalism has nothing to do with race, nothing to do with blood and soil . . . [It] does not lead to Auschwitz. It simply leads away from Washington.*

Horowitz also took aim at those on the Left who accused those socialists who were also Canadian nationalists of betraying socialism. "Canadian socialists are nationalists," he argued, "because they are socialists . . . We are nationalists because, as socialists, we do not want our country to be utterly absorbed by the citadel of world capitalism."

One of the points I emphasized in my own presentation, "The Political Economy of Canadian Independence," published in that same issue, was the distinction between economic nationalism of the liberal persuasion and economic nationalism of the Left. Economic nationalists like Walter Gordon were less interested in creating a more independent Canada than in strengthening Canada's position within the continental economy and creating more space within it for Canadian business. I argued that "self-determination for Canada vis-à-vis the US would be of little value if it merely involved the shifting of effective decision making from the USA to corporate boardrooms in Toronto and Montreal . . . The implementation of a serious programme of Canadian independence would doubtless require public ownership of the leading links of the economy." These distinctions may seem like ancient history, but to this day some friends on the left who have consistently sneered at anything smacking of nationalism refuse to acknowledge the distinctly socialist argument for Canadian independence we put forward in *Canadian Dimension*.

In retrospect, I can see that "The Open Letter to Canadian Nationalists" we published in the same May–June 1967 issue was partly to blame for blurring this distinction. Though signed by Horowitz, David Sheps and myself, it was a Horowitz initiative and to my recollection mainly, if not entirely, written by him. It was essentially a proposal to form a common front in the form of a Movement for Canadian Independence:

> . . . *Canadian nationalists differ from each other in many important ways . . . [But] if we cannot agree on a common minimum program to halt the tide of integration and if we cannot create a vehicle for promoting that program then it is most likely that none of our visions of a future Canada will be realized. We will all be smothered by America.*

Dozens of (mainly supportive) letters poured in and many volunteered to help organize the Movement for an Independent Canada. But the three of us who penned the proposal had never discussed actually undertaking it ourselves, and we did not have the capacity for doing so. Elsewhere on the political spectrum, however, concrete organizing got underway. In the fall of 1970, Walter Gordon, Peter Newman and Abraham Rotstein launched the Committee for An Independent Canada. The CIC came up with its own common minimum program and with ten thousand members and forty-one chapters no doubt influenced the spate of nationalist legislation passed by the Trudeau government in the early 1970s: the Canadian Development Corporation that promoted Canadian ownership; Petro-Canada; the Foreign Investment Review Agency; the elimination of tax privileges for *Time* and *Reader's Digest*; the CRTC's 30 per cent rule for Canadian content on radio. None of us joined the CIC, although it came pretty close to the kind of organization proposed in our open letter. I was more comfortable being part of the Waffle movement within the NDP, a group whose 1969 "Manifesto for an Independent Socialist Canada" clearly drew upon the political analysis anchored by *Canadian Dimension*.

Pierre Trudeau took over the reins of government in June 1968, was re-elected with a minority government in 1972, lost the 1979 election to Joe Clarke's Conservatives and regained power in 1980. He was one of the "three wise men" Lester Pearson attracted to Ottawa in 1965 to stave off the nationalist revolt in Quebec. The other two were Jean Marchand and Gerard Pelletier. Trudeau, immediately named Justice Minister, was widely trumpeted as a great civil libertarian and free thinker. Peter Newman praised his "hidden dimensions." It was CD's David Sheps who may have provided the most astute assessment of Trudeaumania (5:6, September/October 1968): Standing up to Quebec was Trudeau's main attraction for English-Canadian voters, he wrote. For them, Trudeau was "the knight that could slay the Quebec dragon." According to Sheps, with his extraordinary popularity Trudeau could have communicated the realities and aspirations of French Canada to the rest of the country. But he chose not to seize this historic opportunity, thereby forcing the Québécois to choose between a separate state of their own and a federalism unwilling to accommodate their national aspirations. "Is it too much to hope," Sheps asked, "that we will have heard the last of the nonsense which finds Trudeau 'radical' or 'progressive' and which sees the electorate as having opted for his 'just society'?"

Gad Horowitz, Red Tories and Deux Nations

Of all the writers who contributed to *Dimension* early on, there was none whose influence on the magazine's politics was greater than Gad

Horowitz, who was then teaching political science at McGill University. He grew up in Calgary, and came to Winnipeg to attend United College. Horowitz had a strong attraction for John Diefenbaker back then, something I never understood until I read his first article in *CD*, "Tories, Socialists, and the Demise of Canada" (2:4, May/June 1965). That is where he popularized the expression "red tory" in reference to George Grant, who had just published his famous *Lament for a Nation*. Canada was dying, said Grant, because the only remaining nationalists were Conservatives of the Diefenbaker stripe — and because of their ties to free enterprise, they were incapable of using the powers of the state to build an independent nation.

Horowitz demurred: "The existence of Canada was in the past guaranteed by the nationalism of our economic elite. They have abandoned nationalism, and are therefore twice cursed: for being an economic elite and for being anti-national. If Canada is to remain in existence, the nation building role must now be played by forces other than those of entrenched wealth — popular forces with democratic socialist leaders who know where they are going. In English and French Canada as in all small nations, socialism and nationalism require one another."

These ideas were echoed and further developed in everything Horowitz contributed to *Canadian Dimension* in those early days, culminating in his bold "two-nations" analysis and in his call for a Canada independent of the United States, a socialist Canada. In his argument for an asymmetrical federalism, "The Future of English Canada" (2:5, July/August 1965), Horowitz wrote:

> *There is no way of avoiding an autonomous Quebec.*
> *Quebec demands and deserves autonomy. She will have*
> *autonomy within confederation, or there will be no*
> *confederation. But there is no reason to strengthen other*
> *provincial governments. On the contrary, there may be good*
> *economic and political reasons, and good English Canadian*
> *nationalist reasons for strengthening the federal government*
> *in its relationship with the English-speaking provinces.*
> *The obvious solution . . . would appear to be a federal*

*government which is weak in relation to Quebec but strong
in relation to the other provinces — in other words a 'special
status' for Quebec within confederation.*

Canadian Dimension was born in the midst of the Quiet Revolution,
the series of reforms that brought in new labour laws supporting unions;
took Quebec's hospitals, social services, educational system and universities out from under Church control and into the public sphere; and negotiated the surrendering of federal pensions, job training and family allowances to Quebec City. When René Lévesque failed in his efforts to push
the Liberal Party further to accept his vision of Sovereignty Association,
he formed the Movement for Sovereignty Association and announced his
intention to establish a new political party. It was just at that moment
that *CD* published a "Symposium on René Lévesque" (5:2-3, January/
March 1968). Led off by Gad Horowitz, it included contributions from
David Lewis, Evelyn Dumas, Robert Cliche, Ed Finn and Charles Taylor.

"Why has René Lévesque become a separatist?" Horowitz asked.
"Because the interminable dialogue continues, and we are as far as ever
from reaching its conclusions, and René Lévesque is an impatient man.
The 'special status game,' while it would never achieve special status
would, bit by bit, win a slowly growing autonomy for Quebec over a
period of many years — within an increasingly decentralizing Canada.
The result? While this game goes on, French Canadians everywhere will
slowly be assimilated into the surrounding North American homogeneity
. . . That is what Lévesque is afraid of. That's why he stopped playing the
special status game."

"In a way, we have the same problem," Horowitz added. "By the time
we will have regained control of our economy, we will have nothing but
American thoughts in our heads. Control of our economy — for what?"

Horowitz returned to this theme in a two-part review of John Porter's
classic *The Vertical Mosaic*. Prior to the 1960s, most Canadians thought of
their country as English, the rest being contemptuously lumped together
as foreigners, frenchies or Indians. But after the sixties, English Canada
discovered and Trudeau promoted multiculturalism — the Canadian
mosaic, as it came to be known — which dovetailed nicely with the

denial of the French-English duality. As Horowitz saw it (3:1, November/ December 1965):

> The mosaic . . . is the absence of a sense of identity, the absence of a common life which can be shared by the English-speaking regions and tribes of Canada . . . [I]n the absence of a Canadian identity, we identify . . . with the American national community. Its media absorbs us . . . [W]e participate vicariously in the affairs of the American community, without power over those affairs . . .

Horowitz lamented our obsession with national unity and the resultant absence of class politics. Ordinary people, he maintained, cannot use politics to change the conditions of their lives when politics is not based on class, but rather on regional or ethnic divisions. Fixating on national unity puts the existence of the nation perpetually in question so that political debate is never centred on "who gets what, when and how. It takes for granted that those who have the most will keep it and get more, the only question being whether they will get it in one nation or several, through the provincial governments or the federal." Class politics, Horowitz suggested, could unite the country by uniting its various non-elites across ethnic and regional barriers. But class politics could only emerge by settling the national question — and that meant granting a special status for Quebec within confederation.

Altogether, Horowitz contributed a total of sixteen articles to *Dimension* from 1964 to 1970. In his contributions — whether in the form of articles, reviews, dialogues (with the likes of Charles Taylor and George Grant), or "sermons" — he mostly dealt with the same themes: class, socialism, nationalism and Canadian independence.

Of course we published other writers on these themes. The issue of US ownership and control was heating up in the early sixties. The Liberal government of the day had just been forced to withdraw provisions in Finance Minister Walter Gordon's 1963 budget that imposed a 30 per cent takeover tax on shares in Canadian corporations sold to nonresidents. In a special issue we called "Is Canada Possible?" (1:8, September/

October 1964) economist H.C. Pentland outlined a plan for a Canadian-owned economy; Ed Finn speculated about the prospects for an autonomous labour movement; Canadian literary scholar Neil Compton lamented Canada's cultural void. Earlier that year political theorist C.B. Macpherson argued for an independent foreign policy including withdrawal from NATO (1:3, December/January 1963-4). Charles Taylor, then federal vice chairman of the NDP, worried about how Quebec nationalism was splitting Quebec's left and labour movement (1:7, July/August 1964). These were important contributions, but in my opinion none surpassed the boldness, clarity and edge of Gad Horowitz.

Horowitz shifted his interests after 1970 but his affiliation with CD would be renewed decades later when he returned to the magazine in the late 1980s to offer an exceptionally insightful personal/political advice column and again in the new millennium with "the Horowitz Paragraph," a pithy and quirky short column on the affairs of the day and yesterday.

1968

"The earth moved. It was one of those rare moments in history when all that had been solid (and stultifying) seemed to melt into air." So wrote Bryan Palmer in "May 1968, an Appreciation," his article in CD commemorating the events of forty years earlier (42:3, May/June 2008).

The signal year 1968 exploded in student-led antiwar protests across the world. Workers occupied factories. Students seized university administration offices. In France, student demands for university reforms soon led to radical critiques of entire academic disciplines as bastions of bourgeois thought. Workers joined students in massive demonstrations in the streets of Paris demanding the resignation of President Charles de Gaulle. Unions mounted a general strike. With the country at a standstill, revolution was in the air. In Germany, three hundred thousand students in a hundred universities protested against American imperialism and the role their institutions were playing in the military-industrial-university complex. There were rumblings in the Soviet empire too, especially in Czechoslovakia where students, artists and intellectuals were demanding democratic reforms and cultural freedoms.

In the summer of 1968 I took my first-ever trip to Europe to learn what I could about these events and to gather material for the magazine. The September/October 1968 (5:6) edition included transcriptions of speeches by Herbert Marcuse on France and Rudi Dutschke on Germany. I pulled together my reflections in "The New International Left" and wrote another piece based on my trip to Prague, where I met with members of the political underground just ten days before the Soviet invasion.

Campus revolts came to Canada too, although they were rarely as incendiary. The flashpoints were Sir George Williams (now Concordia), McGill and Simon Fraser. *Canadian Dimension* covered all three.

David Sheps, our Associate Editor who taught at Sir George Williams, wrote a blistering account of the actions of black students who demolished the university computer centre, destroying vital student records and the research of several university professors (5:8, February 1969). The action began when word got out that a biology professor, Perry Anderson, was allegedly failing all the black students in his class. The university formed a committee to look into the allegations, but there was no agreement on how the members of that committee should be selected. Angered by the lack of progress, some students took matters into their own hands and occupied the computer centre. When police arrived to force them out, someone set fire to the office and the computer mainframe was destroyed. The professor's transgressions were never determined since no evidence was publicly brought against him. Rosie Douglas, who would ultimately be elected Prime Minister of Dominica, the tiny Caribbean country of his birth, was one of ninety-six students arrested. He spent sixteen months in jail and was finally deported. In an interview with the McGill student newspaper decades later, Douglas described the humiliations he and other black Caribbean students suffered in finding work and rental accommodations in Montreal in the 1960s. Taking a united stand against Anderson and the university's intransigence in getting to the bottom of the allegations would, he thought, be a good example for black Canadians of how to fight discrimination.

Across Canada the media denounced the students as "thugs," "rampaging criminals" and a "gang of hooligans." For his part, Sheps was outraged that these students chose to target Sir George Williams, "an extraordinarily liberal university with a marked community service orientation . . . and a very large number of markedly left-wing professors . . . most of whom criticized the students and the muddle-headed and guilt ridden liberals who encouraged them and welcomed their every disruptive action." He maintained that while the black students "may have had an understandable, if undifferentiated, sense of frustration and anger towards the white world, the white students acted in terms of the purest nihilism . . . and nihilism is no ally of socialism or of genuine social revolution . . . Perhaps," he concluded, "it is time the political left in Canada realized that in the slow and painful process of building a viable socialist movement, we must do so without the romantic incendiarism and apocalyptic messianism of many segments of the student and new left."

An even more biting critique of "mythmakers of revolutionary barricades" by Eugene Genovese (6:1, April/May 1961), a radical historian who landed at Sir George Williams after being hounded out of several American universities, brought a stout defense of the New Left from Philip Resnick, then a University of Toronto grad student — with a rejoinder from Genovese (6:2, July 1969). It was around this time David Sheps departed from *Dimension* and ultimately the political Left.

Down the road from Sir George Williams, Stan Gray was heading a fifteen-thousand-strong demonstration outside the gates of McGill, chanting "McGill français! McGill aux Québécois! McGill aux travailleurs!" *CD* published the text of a speech Gray made explaining Operation McGill and what he described as a convergence of two movements in Quebec that had not before been linked — "the national liberation struggle against Anglo-American colonialism and the militant rise of the Quebec working class led by Michel Chartrand and the CSN" (6:6, December/ January, 1969–70). Stan was by now a figure of much controversy in Quebec, having been fired from his post as a lecturer in political science, then heading up the Front de Liberation Populaire and playing a prominent role in establishing a Quebec Committee for Solidarity with the Black Panthers. *CD* received mail about Stan Gray and the situation at McGill, not all of it complimentary. Aside from some scurrilous personal attacks — "allied with fascists," "a puppet of the nationalists," "he wants so badly to live in a revolutionary situation he has made up a never-never

45

land which he insists is today's Quebec," and more — the brunt of it consisted of critiques of New Left politics. For his part, Stan wrote CD a letter asking us to remove his name from our list of contributors with a note to me saying that he could not stomach our social democratic politics (6:8, April/May 1970). Our dispute was never personal and we were able to resume a close and productive relationship a decade or so later. By then, Stan had relocated to Hamilton and had become chief shop steward in charge of health and safety at the vast Westinghouse plant.

Simon Fraser was the site of the third campus revolt. It involved a six-week strike in the fall of 1969, a purge of the seven striking faculty members and termination of one of the most exciting experiments in university education in this country's history — the Politics-Sociology-Anthropology interdisciplinary department. Mordecai Briemberg, who would later become a member of the CD collective, was the elected chair of the PSA Department and was one of the purged faculty members. Twelve teaching assistants involved in the strike were also dismissed. One of them was Jim Harding, a frequent contributor in the magazine's early days.

In a CD review of a book published on the occasion of the fortieth anniversary of the founding of Simon Fraser University (40:2, March/April 2006), Briemberg recounted some of the unique features of PSA, such as its commitment to democratic and egalitarian decision-making, critical thinking, including a recognition of the possibility of transcending the social order, and a commitment to serving the interests of working people, Native people, the poor and the youth.

He went on to say that "The university president took on the task of crushing us, declaring that, 'the society and economy is capitalist and the university serves that system.' Given the opposing orientations, expressing conflicting class interests, it is not surprising the full range of state institutions were mobilized to crush the radicals."

Sharon Yandle, a student at SFU at the time, wrote an account of the conflict in the February/March 1970 issue (6:7) of CD that remains to this day among the most insightful and balanced analyses available. Yandle was totally supportive of the aims of the PSA, but she did not hold back on some of its shortcomings. The article described "a tendency to engage in bitter internal holy wars [within the Department] and to alienate outside support [on campus] . . . While publicly stating again and again its assumptions, beliefs, values, orientations and goals, PSA's word did not become flesh. The 'PSA idea' remained exactly just high ideals which bobbed around helplessly in a sea of dialogue. Had PSA truly developed and effected its ideas in the community — had it truly placed itself in service to the disadvantaged and to labour — it might have been able to develop the allies it so desperately needed to counteract its isolation on campus."

The era of the New Left in Canada was now almost over. SUPA had imploded at the end of 1967. Some of its leaders were enticed into the Company of Young Canadians, which had been established precisely to draw them away by offering them a comfortable substitute amply financed by government funds. Some SUPA activists went on to take leadership roles in the Canadian Union of Students. Others would become active in the Waffle movement within the NDP. Relatively few went on to participate in the proliferation of Trotskyist, Maoist and other groups.

James Laxer offered one explanation for SUPA's demise in "The Student Movement and Canadian Independence" (6:3-4, August/September 1969). He argued that being an offshoot of the American New Left and of SDS in particular, adopting its ideology, issues and lifestyle, SUPA and Canada's New Left in general had been "unable to formulate a political strategy relevant to Canadian society." He suggested that American radicalism was not a suitable guide for Canadian radicals because "it is conceived out of the conditions of the heart of the empire rather than the conditions of a dependent country like Canada . . . Unlike Quebec student radicals who experience imperialism as the degradation of their own society, the Canadian New Left does not prefer its own country over the United States. Without a personally experienced anger about the takeover of Canada, how can leftists seriously consider themselves part of an anti-imperialist movement? Not understanding Canadian history and lacking a useful historical theory of society tends to reduce radicals to plunder and sabotage in its dealings with the rest of the community."

There were other explanations for the demise of the New Left. In a small book published in 1973 that didn't get as much play as it should have, Margaret Daly wrote: "Had Art Pape (a SUPA leader) and Doug Ward (president elect of the Canadian Union of Students) decided to stay clear of the CYC the history of the New Left in Canada would have been entirely different . . . Without the split down the middle of SUPA whether or not to cooperate with the CYC, and without lucrative CYC consulting jobs to drain off the talent of so many SUPA members who knows what sort of independent New Left organization might have risen from SUPA's ashes?"[1]

This position was endorsed in *Dimension* a few years later. Martin Loney stated in the lead article of the April 1977 issue (12:2), "Bankrolling the Revolution": "Government financing [of the volunteer sector] simply serves to keep potential dissidents participating in the mainstream of society, to buy off the more militant of the poor to provide opportunities for expressive but non-threatening deviancy . . . Divisions emerge between permanent paid staff and volunteers. The organization begins to operate on a scale which cannot conceivably be sustained by its own members, peoples' livelihood begin to depend on government largesse, grantsmanship replaces strategy and responsibility replaces militancy. It is fundamental, after all; you do not bite the hand that feeds you."

No doubt there is some merit to both these explanations. My own view, written in the earliest days of the New Left, questioned the New Left's core notion that the poorest and most dispossessed have no stake in the status quo and are therefore the most likely agents of radical change. I noted that their dependency on the state made them unlikely candidates to lead the struggle to overthrow capitalism. Instead of avoiding established organizations, I advocated the opposite — penetrating "the major institutions where people are — trade unions, churches, teachers' societies, student organizations, the NDP — to create within them constituencies which can be harnessed to a political movement aimed at national independence and socialism . . ." "Strategies for Social Change" (4:1, Nov/Dec 1966). Finding a way to expand and deepen our base while retaining our militancy was easier said than done, but the New Left was a student movement without wider social connection and, except for its forays into the ghettoes and First Nations reserves, seemed happy, even determined to stay that way. Besides, the system was too strong back then. It delivered the goods and had the wherewithal to keep a grip on society's poor and outcasts. Capitalism was not in crisis. The conditions were not ripe for widespread revolt. Further, what did Frantz Fanon, Che Guevara, Regis Debray and the other heroes of the New Left have to say that was relevant to making change in a country like Canada? There are lots of reasons why the New Left flame extinguished so quickly.

"In the hearts and minds of all those who abhor capitalist injustice . . . the sixties will never die," mused Bryan Palmer in an article he wrote, "May '68, An Appreciation": "*Dimension* put it well in a 1988 commemoration when it declared defiantly: 'We were brazen and brave and we shook them badly despite our mistakes. We'll do it again.'" (42:3, May/June 2008)

The October Crisis

In June of 1969 I was elected to the Manitoba Legislature as an NDP member of the Schreyer government. I had never been interested in a political career and this would be a very short one. As I wrote in "Strategies for Social Change" a few years earlier, I had no illusions about the NDP being an agency of radical change but I thought the experience could be worthwhile. It complicated things at *Dimension*, however, especially as I also became heavily involved in the Waffle movement, I was partnering in raising a family that would number four children with the birth of Noam in March 1970, and continued teaching on a part-time basis at the University of Manitoba. It was a crazy time. To help out at *CD* I hired a part-time assistant, Alvin Finkel. A prodigious researcher and an amazingly swift writer, Al was then a grad student in history and past editor of the student newspaper, *The Manitoban*. Today, he is one of Canada's pre-eminent historians. When Al began turning up wearing gloves while working the typewriter in our basement office that winter, I knew it was time to move out of the house. That's when *CD* joined up with Kelly Clark on the ninth floor of the Ryan Building in Winnipeg's downtown Exchange district. Kelly had taken over as *Dimension*'s art director after June Sherwood moved out to British Columbia. Kelly, clearly of the Beatnik generation, was an artist of some notoriety who had designed

Winnipeg's short-lived underground paper, *Omphellous*. We would work together for many years.

Incidentally, one of the first visitors to our office was Fred Kelly, a young Ojibway from the Lake of the Woods. Fred was then assistant to the president of the National Indian Brotherhood and vice-president of the Union of Ontario Indians. Trudeau had just introduced the 1969 White Paper on Indian Affairs that proposed the abolition of the *Indian Act*, the rejection of land claims, and the assimilation of First Nations people into the Canadian population with the status of an ethnic minority. The White Paper was part of Trudeau's idea of the "just society." Fred brought with him a portfolio of clever cartoons he wanted us to publish. They mainly targeted Jean Chrétien, then Minister of Indian Affairs. The White Paper fanned the flames of native consciousness, of recognizing land claims and entrenching Aboriginal rights in the constitution. We published Fred's cartoons in the October/November 1969 issue.

Not long after we had other visitors to the office, uninvited ones and ones we had no interest in entertaining. Arriving for a meeting early one Saturday morning in late December 1970, we were surprised to find the office door opened and even more surprised when some burly figures rushed past us making for the stairs. We had caught federal agents in the act of rifling through our records. Their interest in *Dimension* at this time likely stemmed from a special issue we had just published on the October Crisis (7:5, December 1970). We called it: "WAR DECLARED ON QUEBEC." Our printer was so concerned about the issue that it insisted on us posting a disclaimer on the contents page disassociating it "from the opinions, articles and content of this issue."

"What is happening to us?" popular writer-broadcaster Laurier Lapierre asked in a letter to *CD* in that special issue. "Here's a Trudeau — with that record in Asbestos, in *Cité Libre* and so many other issues involving government overkill — behaving as if he were a modern Mussolini? Or Jean Marchand, all his life he has fought repression, distortion and political manipulations. And now he talks as if he had become an incarnation of Maurice Duplessis." Lapierre recounted that since 1963 Quebecers had lived through two hundred bombings and six resulting deaths as well as countless bank robberies. "We have known that evil" and learned to cope with it. But now Trudeau brings in the *War Measures Act* and it is accepted without evidence and without question. "Are we so tormented with the spectre of separatism that it dominates our lives and works its way into all our decisions and our silences? Must we maintain Canada together by means of blackmail, intimidation, war measures act and political terrorism?"

For that special issue, Al Finkel pulled together interviews with Front de libération du Québéc (FLQ) lawyer Robert Lemieux, labour leader Michel Chartrand, self-proclaimed Quebec revolutionary Charles Gagnon and spokesman for the Committee for the release of political prisoners during the trial of the FLQ Jacques Larue-Langlois. Charles Taylor sent us his take on the crisis, "Behind the Kidnappings: Alienation Too Profound for the System to Contain." Daniel Latouche, political scientist and former executive assistant to René Lévesque, sent us "Political Violence in Perspective." We were the first to publish a translation of the FLQ Manifesto. And we published excerpts of Pierre Vallières's *White Niggers of America*, a book Bryan Palmer would describe as "Canada's most quintessential New Left text . . . that spoke to a working-class Québécois audience in languages of sentimentality and rage."[2]

Some of the contributors to this issue were among the five hundred arrested under the *War Measures Act*. Chartrand, Vallières and Gagnon were cellmates. In the following issue, the writer David Lewis Stein, who collaborated with us for a time, made a case for a *Canadian Dimension* Quebec Trials Fund. Early in the spring of 1971 Al Finkel interviewed Michel Chartrand on his swing through English Canada (7:8, April 1971).

The War Measures Act reached into Winnipeg. One of the volunteers who helped manage a bookstore *CD* had opened a few months earlier had put a sign in the window "Free the FLQ," which was immediately spotted by the media. When they called to ask me, as an elected official, if I approved that sign, I answered something to the effect that I was not a supporter of the FLQ but I opposed the imposition of the *War Measures Act* as an infringement on the civil liberties of all Canadians. And I added that declaring Quebec to be in a "state of apprehended insurrection" was a deliberate falsehood propagated to halt the spread of separatist sentiment and to garner electoral support in the rest of Canada. It was totally out of proportion to the actions of this tiny clandestine organization. Perhaps because I was the first in Manitoba to publicly oppose the measure the story got headline treatment in the local media. I received several threatening phone calls that week and found myself an object of public scorn as perfect strangers would openly curse me and shout at me in anger in the streets of Winnipeg. Somehow the police got wind of what was happening and offered me and my family police protection. I was mightily relieved when, some weeks later, Tommy Douglas stood up in the House of Commons to challenge Trudeau: "The government, I submit, is using a sledgehammer to crack a peanut" were his words and the local spotlight soon shifted away from me.

For some, the October Crisis spelled the end of the sixties. But there was much more to come. In the winter months of 1972 the three Quebec union centrals — the Fédération des travailleurs et travailleuses du Quebec (Quebec Federation of Labour), the Confédération des syndicats nationaux (Confederation of National Trade Unions) and the Corporation des Enseignants du Quebec (Quebec Teachers Corporation) formed a common front that launched a 210,000-worker general strike. The strike reached into every corner of Quebec and evolved in an increasingly radical direction. Each of the union centrals produced a manifesto the likes of which had never before been seen. *CD* published one of them in the March/April 1972 issue.

Waffle days

CD was centrally involved in the emergence and all too brief life of the Waffle movement within the NDP. The purge of the Waffle in 1972 marked the end of our close, if often strained, relationship with the NDP.

In those early years *Dimension* acted as a sort of conscience of the NDP, harkening back to the socialism of the Regina Manifesto. We even bawled out Tommy Douglas once for not taking a stronger stand on Vietnam. NDP conventions were always important events for *CD*. We covered them all, while hawking the magazine. No doubt NDP members and supporters made up a significant portion of our readers in those years.

I was not among the handful of individuals who met in Toronto in the spring of 1969 to write the Manifesto for an Independent Socialist Canada — the Waffle Manifesto, as it came to be called. But from the beginning the Waffle received vigorous editorial support from *CD*.

The Manifesto, which *CD* reproduced in the October/November 1969 issue, argued that Canada's cultural and economic survival is threatened by American control of the economy, that the central reality for Canadians is the American Empire, which has reduced Canada to a captive resource base and consumer market. From these main objectives followed others. A more autonomous Canadian capitalism does not offer a route to independence because it is weak and in any case too closely intertwined with the continental economy. So "independence is not possible without socialism and socialism is not possible without independence" — the slogan articulated in *CD* some years earlier. The Manifesto called for "nationalization of the commanding heights of the economy such as the key resource industries, finance and credit, and industries strategic to planning our economy." But public ownership was not a sufficient condition of socialization. There had to be some form of workers' control in the management of industry. And if industry and government were to be socialized and become more democratic, the party that heads that government must also become more democratic. Thus emphasis was placed on internal democracy and linkages of the party to social movements outside the walls of parliament. The Party must become "the Parliamentary wing of a movement dedicated to fundamental social change, not just an electoral party striving for success at the polls." And finally, if Canada were to seek greater independence from the USA, it had to extend the same right to nations within its territory. Thus the Waffle supported Quebec's right to self-determination, up to and including the right to separate.

Tommy Douglas welcomed the new movement. In a *CD* interview (7:8, April 1971) he told grad student Stephen Langdon that "the party needs pioneers who break trail for them." The Waffle played a useful role in shaking up the party and saying to its members "just a moment, these are our long term objectives. We haven't reached them yet and we're not moving fast enough." Not all leading figures in the party shared Douglas's tolerance for dissent. As the Waffle grew stronger, sprouting provincial groups throughout the country and a Waffle labour caucus, not only challenging philosophy, policy and objectives and party structure but also running slates for party executive positions, producing its own monthly newspaper, organizing its own conferences and eventually employing some full-time organizers — party leaders and officials accused it of being a party within a party. Pressed by party-affiliated union heads, they were determined to crush it. After much manoeuvring and attempted compromise, the Waffle was purged from the Ontario NDP in 1972 and other Waffle groups soon joined them.

Dimension published a special issue in April 1971 with the coverline "The NDP and The Waffle, the Inside Story." Besides the interview with Tommy Douglas, the issue included an article by Krista Maoets that laid out a socialist-feminist program, a brief history of the CCF-NDP by Alvin Finkel, a short profile of the Waffle and a comparison of the views of Wafflers and non-Wafflers within the party. The comparison was based on a unique survey *CD* sent to seven hundred Waffle members and seven hundred non-Waffle NDP members across the country.

Things really heated up as the April 1971 federal leadership race approached with the Waffle's James Laxer among the five candidates alongside Ed Broadbent, John Harney and Frank Howard and the eventual winner David Lewis. In "Sour Winners," an article we published in June 1971 about that convention, John Warnock and I described how "union muscle intimidation was let loose throughout the convention floor" and portrayed the scuffles at the microphones between Wafflers and unionists. This nastiness would reach a fever pitch following Laxer's surprisingly strong finish, garnering nearly as many constituency delegate votes as Lewis in the final ballot. But it was the Waffle's daring labour intervention in January 1972, organizing an Auto Pact conference in Windsor right in the heartland of the United Auto Workers, that brought matters to a head. Distributing a pamphlet at the Ontario Federation of Labour convention denouncing the "right-wing establishment" of the unions as a partner of big business and calling for "completely independent Canadian unions" was the last straw.

The three months leading up to the June 24 Ontario NDP Council meeting in Orillia that finally purged the Waffle were as intense as any in the history of the party. I wrote an editorial, "The Lewises Versus the Waffle," which argued that:

> . . . to say in one breath that dissent is tolerated in the NDP
> — and in the next breath that dissenting groups shall be
> denied the means that are necessary to make their dissent
> effective — borders on the hypocritical. Nor is it the case
> that there are no other organized groups within the party —
> the most powerful one being the unions.
>
> The Waffle group is no artificial creation of a few
> alienated intellectuals. It is part of the radicalization
> of Canada. It was initiated by NDP members who
> had become frustrated by the drift of the party towards
> liberalism and away from socialism and by the inability
> and refusal of the party leadership to come to grips with
> American imperialism. It grew in strength because it
> touched responsive chords in thousands of other NDPers and
> attracted hundreds of new members to the party.
>
> Should the Waffle be forced to leave the party in
> Ontario thousands of New Democrats from coast to coast
> will terminate their membership, not only those who are
> Waffle supporters but rank and file members who, while
> disagreeing with Waffle policies, have come to see the
> existence of the Waffle as a healthy development in the
> party.

Does this editorial stand the test of time? Only partly so. Thousands did drop out and while some returned, in my view the NDP was never again such a vital political force, so alive to new thinking and attractive to young people. I regret only that part of the editorial that personalized the conflict, arguing that David and Stephen Lewis were using the Waffle as a handy scapegoat for the party's poor showing under their leadership.

Was the Waffle episode a hopeless adventure? Of course it was, and while some of the acrimony brought about by its aggressive behaviour could have been avoided, the NDP could never have been converted into the anticapitalist anti-imperialist party we wanted.

Waffle stalwarts in Ontario attempted to sustain their efforts in something they called Movement for an Independent Socialist Canada (MISC). MISC did valuable research and educational work but its brief foray into electoral politics was a disaster. The Saskatchewan Waffle, which was also strong, went a different route but also ended in disarray. Once the Waffle was removed from the NDP, all the divisions within the Waffle, some personal and some ideological, played themselves out in full force. Acrimony and venom shifted from the bigger NDP arena to the smaller post-Waffle one. All of this was played out in the pages of *Dimension* as articles by James Harding and Leo Panitch, among others, stirred up pages and pages of letters in issue after issue.

Assessing the first decade

This discussion finally petered out by the end of 1974. No doubt it disgusted some readers and exhausted still more. Our readership had climbed to its all-time peak of six thousand subscribers and over a thousand newsstand sales. But the collapse of the antiwar movement, the New Left and the Waffle and the 1973 CIA-led sabotage and defeat of Allende's Chile — much analysed in *CD*, all had a dampening effect on the Left. Radical movements wither as radical change seems increasingly unachievable. It was inevitable that *Canadian Dimension*, always located on the left margins of this country, would see its readership fall off. When people are in motion the margin stretches and magazines like *Dimension* thrive. When they are discouraged, quiescent and demobilized we suffer. This is our political cycle.

For those of us in the independent Left not attracted to one or another of the proliferating far-left organizations, it was now beginning to feel like we were treading water, waiting for the next wave of radicalism. And it would be a long, long wait, over a quarter of a century. But in the meantime there was still much to talk about and new priorities to explore. The so-called "new political economy" emerged out of the growing awareness of Canada's dependence on the USA. Though never a theoretical journal, *Dimension* made some significant contributions to the growing literature, especially in the form of debates involving some of the pioneers like Tom

Naylor of McGill University and some of the opponents of dependency theory in the Trotskyist movement. Canada was at the beginning of a severe economic crisis, which came to be called stagflation, that would end with a wage-control regime brought in by Trudeau, followed over the ensuing decades by monetarism and deficit phobia and a whole series of fundamental reforms that we now call neoliberalism. Among them was the Canada-USA Free Trade Agreement. These reforms signalled hard times. Analyzing them and the crisis that ushered them in would fill our pages for years to come.

* * *

But in an April 1974 editorial statement marking our ten-year anniversary, I indicated that, in my opinion, *Dimension* had to become more diverse and eclectic: paying more attention to feminist perspectives, incorporating the newly developing ecological movement, examining the experiences of First Peoples, expanding the cultural presence in *CD* and embracing a personal-is-political approach. "We only distort who we are when we confine our definition of politics to matters of state and economy. A politics that ignores daily existence can never develop a vision of a new way of life. A socialism that promises to revolutionize society on the basis of institutional changes that do not touch the inner life of people is a sham."

Back in 1963 we didn't write about feminism, the environment, human rights, the rights of gays and lesbians, and the physically and mentally impaired or about how we live our lives in relation to the politics we espouse. The scope of what is considered political has expanded enormously since then. For a variety of reasons, until the mid-eighties our capacity to move in these directions proved to be partial, but we did persist with this change in accent.

One of *Dimension's* distinguishing features is that we have always been a magazine of advocacy journalism as opposed to a magazine of detached commentary. This has never changed. If anything, our writers are more involved as social activists now than when the magazine was founded. This is one of the main reasons why *Dimension* has endured. Activists need a forum and for much of our fifty years *CD* has been one of the few spaces available for serious discussion and debate. From time to time some readers have complained that too much space in the magazine is taken up with what seems like interminable debates. But that's to argue against what *Dimension* is largely about — which is not to say that we couldn't have wielded a sharper blue pencil to curtail the long-windedness of some of the comrades.

II. 1975–1994: NEW DIRECTIONS

With Al Finkel having left Manitoba, I was again looking for help in the *CD* office. In fact, to give me additional time to write a book about the coming economic crisis, I looked for a full-time managing editor. For the first time in our ten-year history our financial situation allowed for it. I hired John Gallagher of Regina for the job. Gallagher had plenty of experience in student journalism and his politics matched ours. Soon after he arrived, John and I took off for Kenora where a group of young native people were occupying Anishanabi Park in protest against Indian Affairs and the dismal state of living conditions, especially housing on reserves, the high death rate, police repression and humiliation. We wrote a first-hand account of the occupation, interviewing its remarkable young leader, Louis Cameron, the town's mayor and numerous others. That experience convinced me that I had made a very good choice in hiring Gallagher. At first the arrangement seemed to work well enough but within a year or so troubles began to emerge, especially between Gallagher and Kelly Clark. Kelly was a profoundly heavy drinker and now he found a ready partner in Gallagher. But, unlike John, Kelly could handle his liquor. He was a meticulous and highly productive artist who never missed a deadline and had zero tolerance for anyone who messed up his work schedule. By summer 1975 Gallagher was missing assignments and meetings. When I approached him about it, he tried to make it a personal issue between himself and me, at which point I established an advisory committee to help us through our difficulties. Early in the fall months Kelly threatened to resign as artistic director unless we did something about Gallagher. I remember calling an 11 a.m. Saturday meeting of the advisory committee to confront him. Gallagher showed up at 1:30 p.m.

That was the end of his short tenure at *CD*. Shortly after that incident we converted the advisory committee into a collective.

Canadian Dimension goes collective

The *CD* collective has taken a variety of forms over the years. In its early days, the collective met weekly and took responsibility for all aspects of the magazine from determining content, copy editing and proofreading to finance and circulation. Within this collective, however, there was little interest in the mundane tasks of winning new subscribers and raising money. We never even tried to bring in ads or to promote the magazine in the mainstream media. Meetings were long and boisterous, sometimes rancorous. But by and large, the collective process has been quite effective. There have been various points of conflict of course. The worst ones were not over politics and content but over process, personality, responsibility, division of labour and work style. Whenever the collective got too large, the division of labour resembled Adam Smith's pin factory — but without the coordination, let alone supervision. There were always plenty of volunteers, all with good intentions. Sometimes experience or requisite skills were in short supply, however. In some years, most of the work was left to me, which rankled especially on those occasions when my ideas for content were shot down for lack of support among what I considered the unproductive minions.

In the pre-Internet era the collective was entirely Winnipeg-based. This constituted a fairly severe limitation since it was not easy to find a group of people who shared roughly the same politics and could work in a give-and-take environment of criticism and self-criticism. But in addition to those already challenging criteria, collective members also needed to be familiar with magazine culture or able to adapt to it pretty quickly. Working with the constraints of deadlines and word counts, avoiding academic and political jargon, understanding the need for content diversity, working to develop a national network of contacts for articles all seem simple enough and recruiting people with the necessary background would likely not have been a problem in metropolitan centres like Montreal, Toronto and Vancouver — but they proved to be daunting requirements in the confines of a smaller city like Winnipeg. Once the collective went electronic in 1999 they were more easily met.

The original crew, comprising the likes of Ester Reiter, Fred Gudmundson, Ken Hughes, John Loxley, Gisele Toupin and Leona McEvoy, worked together particularly well and various others were integrated into the collective with ease in the early eighties: Ustun Reinart, Jim Silver, Paul Graham and, later, Henry Heller. Graham and Silver were particularly energetic collective members and served for a decade. Henry Heller remains on the collective to this day.

Fred Gudmundson came to Manitoba from Saskatchewan where he had worked as a farmer, and was instrumental in organizing the National Farmers Union. Fred, along with his partner, Carole, was very active in the Saskatchewan Waffle. Fred hadn't finished high school but he was widely read and an original thinker and he developed a unique prose style — acerbic, profane and often hilarious. He was a prolific writer on a staggering range of topics. His column, "Fred's File," comprised a unique blend of peasant wisdom and political satire that assured it a prominent place in the magazine for years. Once in a while Fred landed us in trouble. A month after Ed Schreyer accepted Trudeau's invitation to become Governor General, someone came to our weekly meeting busting to tell us his latest idea. "You remember that British working class saying: 'The working class can kiss my ass, I've got the foreman's job at last'? Well, that's what Schreyer is saying: 'the working class can kiss my ass, I've got the governor general's job at last.'" Fred burst into laughter, and Fred had a lusty and infectious laugh. "We gotta put that in the magazine, a big picture of Schreyer saying just that." As usual, Freddy convinced the rest of us and we did just that on the back page of the first issue of 1979. A dozen or so NDP stalwarts instantly cancelled their subscriptions. Tragically, Fred died of a heart attack in 1996. We paid him homage by putting his photograph on the cover of our January/February 1997 issue.

Ester Reiter (then Koulack) came to Winnipeg from her native Bronx, New York, in the sixties. Ester, a feminist activist, had a background in old left politics. Ester was feisty, fun, opinionated and loud. Hardly a meeting would go by without her and I ending up yelling at each other at the top of our lungs about something or other. At first, the rest of the collective was aghast at how we went at each other — thinking quite understandably that these two must hate each other's guts. But that was never the case at all. It was just our way of relating to each other and we carried on in that fashion for years, loving every minute of it.

Ken Hughes brought a new dimension to *CD*. David Sheps's earlier efforts notwithstanding, literature and the arts were never our strong point. Ken was a Brit who came to Manitoba to teach English literature at the University of Manitoba. But Ken had a background in history and was steeped in working-class culture. When he threw himself into the study of Canadian fiction such as the novels of Margaret Laurence ("Divining the Past, Present and Future" 10:7, March 1975), his particular bent was to understand them in terms of their class content and the political and historical context in which they were written. He did the same when he devoted his boundless energy to studying the visual art being produced by contemporary artists in Manitoba like Don Proch (13:3, August/September 1978) and Jackson Beardy (14:3). Ken's work appeared quite regularly in *CD* from the mid 1970s to the mid-eighties and from that point on we maintained a sustained interest in culture. For instance, we asked Milton Acorn to become our house poet in the late 1970s. Acorn, Canada's People's Poet, so named by other poets when he was passed over for a Governor General's award, gave *CD* many poems over the next decade (see, for example 15:8/16:1, December 1981), as well as contributing several articles and profiles — like the affectionate one he wrote of Joe Wallace (12:4-5, September 1977). Milton passed the mantle of *CD* house poet on to Tom Waymen in the mid 80s and when Brenda Austin Smith joined the collective in the nineties we resumed our tradition of publishing poetry. In the meantime Ustun Reinart had broadened *CD*'s coverage of the culture front with her reviews of films and popular theatre after she came onto the collective. So Ken Hughes started a tradition that continues to this day.

This was a brilliant group, but, in some ways, standing out even in that exceptional company was Henry Heller. Born and raised in the Bronx, Henry also came to Manitoba in the sixties. He is a historian, now of world renown. But for the purposes of the *CD* collective what has always been more important even than his encyclopedic and acute mind has been his consistently good sense, fairness, steadying influence on the rest of us and his willingness to pitch in. Henry remains an invaluable member of the collective.

Paul Graham and Jim Silver both served ten years on the collective (1982–1992). Over those years Jim often played the role of catalyst in discussions about the political direction of the magazine as well as relentlessly pursuing authors in every corner of the country. Paul Graham served as the business mind behind *Dimension*. During his tenure the Magazine and Periodicals Association named *Canadian Dimension* the best-managed little magazine in the country. Paul was a jack-of-all-trades. At one time or another he served as managing editor, designer and Doctor Dimension, the author of the column we call "This Dimension" that appears at the beginning of every issue.

Before the collective went virtual, the work of soliciting and editing articles was divided up among the various members by section. In the early eighties for instance, John Loxley handled "the world" and Jim Silver "the nation," while Brenda Austin Smith did "poetry," Ester and Leona did "women," Don Sullivan did "environment," I did "labour" and so forth. Copy deadline meetings seemed interminable as each of us fought for space for "our" section articles. Then, once all the compromises and trades were made, the copy editing would proceed. More often than not, however, at the post–copy deadline meeting someone, usually Jim Silver, the most zealous and tireless pursuer of articles in the history of *Dimension*, would come up with a new article that demanded consideration. During his time as editor of "the nation" section, Jim was likely responsible for at least half the articles that finally appeared in the magazine.

Editorials were a joint effort. An evening was set aside to discuss possible editorial themes. Once a topic was agreed upon, one member was cajoled into writing a first draft. Discussion of that draft at a subsequent meeting could be quite brutal for weak egos.

There were years when the size of the collective was particularly large, numbering a dozen or more — far more than a small bimonthly magazine could effectively use — especially since few had an interest in the business and circulation side, which could have used far more input. As chair, Jim Silver, followed by Paul Graham, did his best to develop a healthy process, but meetings could be quite fractious, resulting in hard feelings that sometimes took years to overcome.

Radical trajectories: Marxism, left nationalism, feminism

In his brilliant book *Canada's 1960s*, Bryan Palmer wrote that three "radical trajectories" emerged from the final days of the New Left: Marxism, left Nationalism and Feminism.[3] Not surprisingly these three themes pervaded the pages of *Canadian Dimension* through the 1970s and into the next decade.

The first signs of the close of what came to be known as the golden era of American capitalism brought a steady stream of Marxist analysis to *Dimension*. *CD* authors, myself in particular, homed in on the economic crisis of stagflation and on the Trudeau government's sudden conversion to wage and price controls. We understood that this attack on collective bargaining and retrenchment of the welfare state was not a momentary blip: it was the beginning of what would come to be known as neoliberalism.

Dimension also held the inside track in exposing the dangers and folly of the Canadian Labour Congress's response to this new policy direction — its now-forgotten flirtation with corporatism, or tripartism as it was called then. This fantasy of a full partnership arrangement with representatives of business, labour and government engaging in a system of "national, social and economic planning" was laid out in a document called "Labour's Manifesto for Canada" presented to the CLC annual Convention in 1976. I believe that *Dimension*'s investigation of the ramifications of this proposal along with our relentless dissection of the workings of wage and price controls gained the magazine as much notice within the Canadian labour movement as it would ever enjoy (11:5, June 1976; 12:4-5, September 1977; 12:1; 12:3; 15:3 December 1980).

A second facet of *Dimension's* Marxism turned to class conflict at the point of production, a theme explored in a variety of ways over a decade and a half. Joan Kuyek had been working as a service representative for two and a half years when she and another Bell employee anonymously wrote "Working for Ma Bell" (8:7, June 1972):

Ma Bell keeps her workers down in a variety of ways. She makes sure that we feel every error or misunderstanding is our fault; she exploits our need for income and job security; and she makes sure her employees are divided among themselves.

"Working for Ma Bell" was the lead article of a *Dimension* focus in 1972 we called "This Issue is All About Work." We continued this theme in the 14:3, December 1979, issue that we called "Battle for the Workplace." There, labour historian Graham Lowe described when and how scientific management was introduced to Canada. Another young labour historian, Craig Heron, showed how and why the time clock was first introduced here. A few years later in another work-place theme issue that we called "Dying for a Living," the focus shifted to the health hazards of everyday work situations, including not only injury but illness arising from working with toxic materials like asbestos and lead, and the stresses and strains found in most workplaces (14:7, June 1980). A year later a fourth workplace issue explored the impact of computerization on factory, office and service work (15:8-16:1, December 1981).

Then, in 1983, after an absence of over a decade, we finally heard from Stan Gray; now, as it turned out, employed by Westinghouse in one of its plants in Hamilton. Over the next few years Stan contributed three stunning articles, the most frequently reprinted articles in the history of *CD*. He was the health and safety representative of Local 504 of the United Electrical, Radio and Machine Workers when a barrel exploded on the shipping floor, blinding twenty-two-year-old worker Terry Ryan. "The Case of Terry Ryan" (16:7-8, January 1983) exposed how Ontario's Ministry of Labour collaborated with Westinghouse in covering up this and other incidents of company negligence. Gray also castigated his own union for failing to support him and other safety reps fighting for the health and safety of workers. His explanation of that failure goes to the heart of class conflict on the shop floor and the union leadership's often ambiguous role.

Conservative union leaderships have never been comfortable
with the health and safety struggle because it challenges
the company at a very basic level and because they can't
control it very easily. Safety is a shop floor battle, constantly
challenging management's right of control over the
production process. Corporations highly value their power
to design and alter the work process as they see fit — to
decide what chemicals to put into the product, to arrange
work tasks, to bring in new machines and control the pace
of technological change. But the safety struggle is precisely
over these daily conditions and so it conflicts with that
management right.

At a much-publicized hearing before the Ontario Labour Relations Board, Gray presented extensive evidence of government cover-ups, refusal to recognize safety hazards, refusal to issue orders and enforce orders, inadequate testing procedures and misleading reports. In its decision the Board substantiated Gray's case in almost every detail but in the end weaselled out of taking a stand that would put the provincial government on the spot.

I consider Gray's second article from the shop floor among the very best pieces of journalism *Canadian Dimension* ever published. At sixteen pages it was also the longest article we ever published; our articles seldom exceed four pages. "Sharing the Shop Floor" (18:3, June 1984) told the story of what happened at a Westinghouse plant when closure of one division forced the company to transfer women workers protected by seniority to another division, one that had always been a male preserve. Gray, a shop steward in that division, described his campaign against the sexist culture of men enraged at the idea of women coming into their male sanctuary. The strength of this article lay in his analysis of male workplace culture and how management uses male sexism as a divide-and-conquer tactic to foster splits that would weaken shop floor union organization.

Manly factory culture becomes an outlet for accumulated
danger and frustration against tedious work and
subordination to the boss. It's a form of rebellion against

civilized society's cultural restraints. In this manly atmosphere they could be vulgar and obscene, talk about car repairs and football. No need to be polite. You could yell and scream, throw things at each other . . . The women's invasion is threatening because they are robbing us of our haven and also the one badge of our superiority, our manly work.

John Calvert was a member of the research staff at the national office of the Canadian Union of Public Employees when he wrote "Reflections of the Labour Movement's Malaise" (17:6, December 1983). "Malaise" turned out to be among the most influential articles about the state of the unions since the mid-sixties writings of Ed Finn.

Instead of working with local community groups, supporting other progressive organizations, encouraging union members to become local activists . . . and instead of being a movement which attempted to satisfy a broad range of workers' needs and interests . . . unions came to be viewed as merely one of literally hundreds of organizations competing for members' attention. They sold a service, negotiating and enforcing contracts, like many other organizations and business firms . . . The excessive concern with bargaining and servicing contracts has blinded unions to the importance of creating an alternative culture for their members. They did not provide a vision of a better and more humanely way to live which could be contrasted to the mass consumerism being prompted everywhere by capitalist enterprises. The result was that unions became a marginal force in the lives of most members, fostering low attendance at meetings and a general sense of apathy.

Like Ed Finn, Joan Kuyek and Stan Gray, John Calvert's insights about work and unions arose out of direct experience and observation. Today, their contributions may appear commonplace but that's because in their wake so many academics and graduate students followed up these first-hand analyses with books, theses and journal articles that failed to acknowledge the source of those original insights.

Turning to Bryan Palmer's second radical trajectory, *Dimension* was a bit slow off the mark in recognizing the immense importance of women's liberation as it emerged out of the sixties. Our earliest connection arose from within the Waffle with contributions from Jackie Larkin, Krista Maoets and Varda Burstyn (then Kidd) but also from community organizers Myrna Wood and Joan Kuyek, journalist June Callwood and track star Abbie Hoffman. Sporadic articles did not spark the response we were looking for so our newly formed collective decided to publish a special women's issue (10:8, June 1975). At eighty-four pages this was and remains the biggest issue *Canadian Dimension* ever published. The cover, our first full-colour cover, featured the classic representation of Queen Nefertiti of Egypt's Eighteenth Dynasty. It was appropriate for women's liberation, we explained, because "as queen she was at least the equal of the men of her time" and because "she contributed to the demystification of royalty by permitting the secularization of even the most important acts of the royal family, including their private lives."

In the introduction to the issue, *Dimension* editors explained:

> *This issue of* Dimension *on women's continuing struggle toward liberation is a timely one, if not a little overdue. The fantastic effort of women in Canada and the world to come to terms with their oppression has tremendous importance to all who seek the end of exploitation and a better future for all of humanity. The very intimate oppression of women has forced new definitions of what is personal and what is political.*
>
> *By giving expression to the silent frustrations of women whose work is unrecognized in the home and exploited in the workplace, who carry subordination in their souls from earliest childhood, this revolt has unleashed a new species of anger.*

In the eighties *Dimension* launched its first feminist column, "Half the Sky And Then Some," with Dorothy Smith and Jackie Larkin. Despite these efforts, including several special women's issues over the decade, *Dimension* never became a favoured venue for this era's explosion of feminist writing. The reality is that most feminists were mainly interested in conversing among themselves and therefore sought out separatist venues. Except for Marxist feminists, magazines like *Canadian Dimension* with their mainly male readerships were understandably not a high priority. In our experience this only began to change towards the end of the century with the resistance to the cutbacks imposed by neoliberalism and the challenges of globalization, and especially after the economic crisis of 2008 and the climate crisis brought about a convergence of class, gender and environmental issues. One of the ways this would work itself through *CD* is a partnership we formed in 2010 with a movement of young feminists called RebELLEs who defined themselves as anticapitalist, anticolonialist and antipatriarchy. In 2010 RebELLEs edited a special issue of *CD* we called "The New Feminist Revolution" (44:6, November/December 2010).

In her contribution to *CD*'s fiftieth anniversary issue, Stephanie Ross wrote this account of *CD* and feminism:

> *CD's engagement with feminism since the late 1960s reflected the struggles that characterized the impact of feminist ideas and practices in the academy, in progressive movements, and in personal lives and relationships. Because feminism sought to undo centuries-old patriarchal practices that implicated all our institutions and our own subjectivities, the process of that undoing inevitably involved conflict and controversy. The articles and debates that appeared in CD's pages provide a chronicle of a movement defining itself, and often at odds with itself. Historically, the pivotal role played by many CD contributors in the feminist struggles taking place in the economic, political and cultural spheres renders their contributions of particular significance, and the magazine truly provides a living archive of a vibrant and dynamic era.*

For Bryan Palmer's third post–New Left trajectory, economic nationalism, in this period *Canadian Dimension* concentrated its attention on the resources and energy question, its connection to the American Empire but also to colonialism within Canada. This focus was sparked by the energy crisis in the fall of 1973 when oil-producing Arab countries proclaimed an oil embargo in response to the US decision to resupply the Israeli military during the Yom Kippur war. John Warnock and Rob Dumont predicted that the year 2000 would likely "mark the peak in world oil production" with the US becoming more and more dependent on oil imports, increasingly so from Canada (9:7-8, November/December 1973). A quarter century or so later (40:4, July/August 2006) *Dimension* published a special issue on peak oil: "Oil Sucks! Getting Ready for When the Well Runs Dry."

By the mid 1970s *Dimension* had already zeroed in on what would become, over the next half century, the most damaging of schemes to harness Canadian energy resources. As early as October 1972 (9:1), John Warnock warned that the Mackenzie Valley Pipeline the Trudeau government was about to explore would be "a $5 billion disaster," enabling the United States to "win access to Canada's northern reserves" [of energy] and "pose problems of environmental damage and exploitation of the area's native people."

Larry Pratt was an early critic of the Athabasca tar sands. He wrote that the Syncrude deal consummated in February 1975 "stands in the great traditions of Canadian state capitalism . . . The use of huge sums of public money to underwrite the cost of massive resource extraction projects controlled by foreign capitalists is not exactly a historic innovation: essentially we are putting up well over a billion dollars to facilitate the expansion of the American petroleum industry into a new and costly energy source, the Athabasca tar sands. In addition, Syncrude probably marks a major turning point in the oil industry's campaign to resolve the so-called "energy crisis" on its terms. It is the most striking testimony we have yet witnessed to the political muscle of the oil lobby" (10:7, March 1975).

While these articles explored Canada's role as a resource-exporting hinterland to the American metropolis, a young anthropologist, Peter Usher, contributed several articles calling for the need to come to terms with the problems raised by the metropolis-hinterland relationship within Canada:

> *The growth of metropolitan Canada is largely dependent on*
> *the extraction of resources from the hinterland. Consciously*
> *or not, metropolitan Canada is now in a position to dictate*
> *the terms on which the hinterland population will live*
> *("Hinterland Culture Shock," 8:8, August 1972).*

On that point, another anthropologist, Harvey Feit, examined how the James Bay Development Corporation set up in July 1971 "has begun a transformation of the land and its resources that will have significant effects on the lives of native peoples without their consent or even their involvement. The determination of the JBDC to push on with the project despite the clearly expressed opposition of the native peoples . . . makes one point clear to those peoples, that they are no longer going to be allowed to control the resources critical to their lives" ("Plugging James Bay into New York," 8:8, August 1972).

A parallel analysis of the Churchill River Diversion announced by the Schreyer government in Manitoba was denounced in *CD* as "ecological blindness." It would affect over five hundred miles of rivers and lakes, the largest diversion ever attempted in North America, "What happens to the 20 million acre feet of Churchill water?" asked engineering Professor Cass Booy, who was released as chairman of the Manitoba Water Commission as a result of his opposition to the diversion. "It will be flushed into South Indian Lake, destroying its 300 square miles of shoreline and raising the lake's level by 12 feet. Crumbling clay, tree trunks, floating peat moss and sunken debris will turn the beautiful lake and its surrounding area into an oozy brown swamp in which the quality whitefish will not survive, nor the fur animals which together comprise the livelihood of a highly successful Indian community." All the power generated by the diversion was for sale to mid-west USA since it would not be needed in Manitoba for at least another twenty years ("Is This Diversion Necessary?" 9:6, July 1973).

As I pointed out at the time, none of these schemes to move Canadian resources to the US was exactly foisted on the Canadian state:

> *A powerful alliance of vested interest groups has emerged to actively campaign for each and every project that aims to sell Canadian resources to the USA. These include multinational corporations who sponsor the projects; the banks and finance companies that help finance them; the railway and pipeline companies that carry the resource products to American markets; the local businessmen and chambers of commerce in northern communities that profit from any new activity in their region; the provincial and federal governments who are prepared to invest vast amounts of public money to support private developers ("The American Empire . . . The Long Descent," 9:7-8, November/December 1973).*

Searching for a sense of direction

The years between 1975 and 1995 were especially hard on the Left — here in Canada, as everywhere. We didn't know it then, but the new directions in state policy would amount to a revolution of sorts, and it wasn't our revolution: the move from activist economic policies to monetarism that made inflation rather than unemployment the key policy target; the attack on trade unions, legislating controls on wages, legislating striking workers back to work and jailing union leaders — all of which was aimed at shifting the balance of class forces back to capital after years of something close to full employment had strengthened workers' power at the bargaining table but also in the workplace. The revolution in state policy also included the free-trade agreements that gave multinational corporations the right to sue governments to block regulations they don't like, undermining democracy and national sovereignty; deficit phobia and the obsession with balanced budgets, a cover for cuts in government spending that by 2013 sent the share of federal government spending in the economy to as low as it had been seventy years earlier; the reshaping and retrenching of welfare programs and unemployment insurance to suit the needs of a more flexible labour market, compelling people to accept whatever jobs the market offers; the transition from social citizen-ship and universal benefits to niches of mainly means-tested programs that individualizes risks; the privatization of crown corporations that had denied some very substantial pieces of real estate and industry from private enterprise.

This transition to what would eventually be known as neoliberalism pulled all politics to the right. It was just getting going in the seventies and eighties and we had no way of knowing it would have another thirty years and counting. It was impossible then to think that the Reform Party would be as successful as it has been and that someone like Stephen Harper, a former Reform Party leader and president of the right-wing National Citizens' Coalition would wind up Prime Minister for more than a decade. At *CD* we watched the continued movement of the NDP to the centre. In Manitoba, the home province, the Schreyer and even the Pawley governments appeared quite progressive compared to the minimalist NDP governments that followed. We made a decision to hitch our wagon to the emerging popular movements because they were so grassroots and so energetic. But there were weaknesses in those movements as well, particu-larly their tendency to focus on a single issue, seriously eroding the holistic approach to social change.

If we felt like we had been on the offensive in the sixties and early seventies, we were now clearly on the defensive, rocked by one political and economic assault after another, battered at every turn, simply trying to hold onto the gains of the immediate post-WWII period. In retrospect, *CD* in the eighties and early nineties was involved in a search, trying to find a place in the changing landscape of the Left in Canada.

Internal debates and conflicts

Although the period from the sixties through the seventies was marked by cataclysmic events, from an institutional perspective *Dimension* sailed through it pretty well unperturbed. The eighties and nineties were, by comparison, filled with internal strife and intense debate among our writers and readers. One likely reason for the difference is that whereas in the sixties era the Left was on the ascendant, challenging American imperialism and the capitalist system, in the decades that followed we were frustrated with our inability to respond effectively to the drastic policies being introduced worldwide to undo the gains of the early post-WWII period and to restore business profitability. We turned our aggression inwards, sniping at each other, desperately trying to hold onto our respective domains — no matter how small they had become. Differences were exaggerated while commonalities were played down. Identity politics would emerge that further weakened our ability to work together.

Quebec sovereignty

The quick rise to power of the Parti Québécois in 1976, leading to the first referendum, in 1980, sparked an intense debate in CD that included some prominent voices within the Quebec Left, both Francophone and Anglophone. In introducing Jean-Marc Piotte to *Dimension* readers, political scientist Philip Resnick described him as "the most influential Quebec Marxist of his generation." In his March 1975 article that Resnick translated for CD, Piotte argued against the prevailing two-stage strategy within the Quebec Left — first win an independent state, then the campaign for socialism can begin. Piotte wrote that an independent state brought into being by the Lévesque-led Quebec *bourgeosie* would only "reinforce American imperialist domination over both Canada and Quebec . . . We must understand clearly: no liberation, no revolution is possible here unless American imperialism is destroyed on its own continent" and this requires that the Quebec working class be united with the Canadian working class and not divided. He declared that Quebec socialists should throw in their lot with the anti-US imperialist movement in English Canada rather than supporting Quebec nationalism.

Immediately following the PQ victory, another Quebec Marxist, Gilles Bourque, expressed similar views in CD (13:1). But Henry Milner, who would soon join the PQ and serve on its executive council, effectively rebutted these and other articles in CD with detailed counterarguments (13:6, March 1979). In our contribution to this discussion in the same issue, Fred Gudmundson and I argued that Canadian socialists needed not only to support the right of the people of Quebec to determine their own future, but to explain to workers in English Canada that the struggle for independence is not a struggle against them but to end centuries of national oppression. Like socialists in Quebec, we said, we should be using the referendum debate to develop our own campaign for a different kind of state. We were shouting into the wind, as it turned out.

The question of Quebec sovereignty surfaced again and again in *Canadian Dimension*, the last time in our fortieth anniversary issue (September/October 2003) when we asked our several contributors: Is Quebec Nationalism Still a Galvanizing Force?

Direct action

In October 1982 Litton Systems, a Toronto plant manufacturing guidance system components for the cruise missile, was bombed by a group representing itself as Direct Action. *CD's* January 1983 issue reprinted two statements from the group responsible for the action, including its explanation as to how a Litton security guard came to be unintentionally killed in the explosion. Five of its members were arrested and charged with various offenses. A few months later, we carried an investigative article by Tom Hawthorn, then a freelance journalist, about the rabid way the media covered the trial and how this made it impossible to obtain a fair jury trial. On our collective at the time were two new members we barely knew, Michelle Pujol and Joe Dolecki, who it turned out were strong advocates of the Direct Action group and insisted that *CD* carry an editorial supporting its action. None of the rest of us were prepared to go along but we invited them to prepare a draft that we could discuss. Very reluctantly, they agreed to do so. At a subsequent meeting when the collective decided it could not accept the draft, very angry words were exchanged and they both resigned. One of our members, Mark Gabbert, wrote the draft that would be the basis of our editorial statement (17:4, September 1983).

The editorial started off by noting that while the media savages the violent actions of this group, it ignores the far greater violence "systematically carried out by the capitalist state itself: massacre in Lebanon, assassination in El Salvador, counterrevolution in Nicaragua, the arms race, environmental destruction . . . It is a measure of the success of its psychological warfare against us all that that the state's official, orderly, institutionalized terror goes largely unrecognized and uncondemned, while acts of resistance are greeted with shock and dismay." The editorial then went onto say that *CD* supports various forms of direct action like strikes, sit-ins and demonstrations but that all political activity must be evaluated on the basis of whether or not it contributes to "the radicalisation of Canadian workers, their involvement in mass organizations and their alliance with other oppressed and discontented groups in a struggle for state power . . . building a movement to create a socialist Canada . . . Isolated acts of sabotage do nothing to build or defend such a movement . . . Undertaken by small, secretive groups cut off from any responsibility to mass political organizations, such sectarian adventures politicize no one, defend no one's interest, do nothing to increase collective strength, and threaten the safety of the innocent. More, they invite repression from the state: whatever its limits, and they are many, the civil and political liberty provided by bourgeois democracy is of enormous value in the struggle for socialism."

It is interesting that our editorial statement, "Once More Around the Bloc," about the actions of the Black Bloc during the G20 protests nearly thirty years later, advanced much the same analysis (44:5, September/October 2010).

The New Democratic Party

With the defeat of the Waffle most, but not all of us at *CD* chose to move on, looking for a politics outside the NDP. Beyond the NDP's unwillingness to tolerate serious debate, *Dimension* criticized the party's rejection of what used to be called "extra-parliamentary" politics, and took issue with the kind of parliamentary politics it actually engaged in — channelling social discontent into lobbying for meagre reforms rather than demanding radical changes to the basic structure of capitalist society. In wrapping up the discussion of this issue after forty years of sometimes quite heated debate, Sam Gindin put it succinctly — the NDP's project aims to moderate capitalism, not transform it. We need a different project (34:2, March/April 2000).

A September 1983 editorial statement, "The Left and Popular Movements," signalled our intention of shifting gears. It explored how people become involved in political action, acknowledging that it is peoples' consciousness of their racial oppression or gender and sexual oppression that is just as likely to galvanize them into political action as their experience of economic exploitation. "We can't pretend that popular movements proceed to socialism or revolution or any such," the statement went on. "But without them, there is no hope for socialism. The role for socialists in these struggles is to modestly and soberly work to inject in them a 'sense of the whole,' to show links . . . and to provide a sense of alternatives . . ."

In the mid-1970s *Dimension* had launched a discussion about building a new socialist movement. A special issue on Euro-Communism, then in vogue, was one of the early highlights of this discussion (November/ December 1978). Not long after it appeared, the office received a call from Bill Ross, Manitoba leader of the Communist Party of Canada, requesting a first-ever meeting with the *CD* collective. First thing Ross did when he showed up with a few of his associates was to dramatically plunk down a pile of books and pamphlets — the sacred Marxist texts. The meeting was remarkably formal with presentations followed by responses and it lasted the better part of an afternoon. Nothing much happened beyond this respectful exchange, but in the magazine itself the Euro-Communist issue elicited a number of commentaries ("The Canadian Left Debates its Future," 13:8, June 1979), from, among others, Joe Levitt of the NDP, Danny Goldstick of the Communist Party and Charles Gagnon of In Struggle. "A New Dimension," an editorial statement that emerged from long hours of discussion within the *CD* collective and elegantly composed by Ken Hughes finally closed that particular debate. But the wider debate inside our pages had barely begun!

Leo Panitch's reflections in the June 1984 issue, "The Need for a New Socialist Movement," sketched out a multidimensional process that could lead to the founding of a new movement, possibly a new party. An editorial in the follow-up issue, "Where We Stand," outlined the core principles of Canadian socialism as we saw them: economic democracy and equality through social ownership and workers' control; women's liberation; national self-determination — "Quebecois and native peoples will freely define their relationship to Canada and together we will gain independence from US economic and cultural domination";

international cooperation, solidarity and peace. A year later in an issue devoted to examining the performance of the only NDP government at the time, that being Manitoba, the editorial ("The NDP and the Left") enunciated our evolving position: "This is not a new call for socialism in the NDP . . . It will not challenge capitalism or the authoritarian state. But within these limitations, the NDP can be forced to defend existing gains and used to win new ones." Not at all satisfied with this stand, *Dimension's* labour columnist, Marvin Gandall, called us out when he challenged the "non-aligned Left" to take the plunge back into the NDP, the only game in town (19:4, September/October 1985). This brought a vigorous riposte from Donald Swartz (19:6, January/February 1986) and for the next few years nothing more was heard on the topic.

In September 1987, beginning with an editorial, "NDP Must Act Now," *Dimension* began to revert to its old practice of advising the NDP on how it must act to hold up the left positions in Parliament. We were back at it again following the 1988 Free Trade election, "What Should We Do About the NDP? And What Should the NDP Do About Us?" (23:3, April/ May 1989) entreating the party to get back to its roots: "For better or for worse, it's the NDP that carries the banner of the hopes, struggles and achievements of several generations of working people. That's why no one on the Left — whether we are card-carrying members in unions, farm organizations, the women's movement, or green politics — none of us can ignore the question of where the NDP is going. We all need a national party that voices our concerns and mobilizes our collective voices."

We were finally challenged by one of our long-time readers, Ulli Diemer: "Let's Stop Kidding Ourselves About the NDP" (23:8, November/ December 1989). Quoting editorial after editorial going back to 1967, Diemer concluded that, like Canadian socialists in general, we had been terribly reluctant to give up our illusions about the NDP: "The NDP of the real world, as opposed to the NDP of our fantasies, was conceived, founded and has always functioned as an organization that seeks to tame or improve the capitalist system, not to overturn it." I think it is fairer to say that for all but one small band of Trotskyists, this delusion had died and lay forever buried with the Waffle. But there were still a few on our collective who held that with a broad socialist party nowhere on the horizon, there was no place else to go. Their judgment? Work in the social movements alongside the NDP for the limited reforms that could be won with NDP governments. Ulli Diemer came to a conclusion more in line with what we had expressed in our 1983 statement: work to build alliances of existing social movements with the aim of creating "a social movement that goes beyond single-issue organizing to work towards an integrated vision of a fundamentally different society."

Sam Gindin picked up this thread a decade later. In "The Party's Over" he advanced the idea of a "structured movement against capitalism" — something more than a coalition and less than a party. Originally published in *This Magazine*, *CD* invited several activists to discuss this idea (33:2, March/April 1999 and May/June 1999). The movement Gindin imagined would not be socialist, but it would create a space for socialists. Similar to Diemer's notion, it would be broad-based and, unlike single-issue coalitions, it would define itself as a movement for overall social change incorporating a wide range of issues and developing its own ideological perspective. It would have a national structure with local chapters and a dues-paying membership. It would engage in popular education with internal debates and develop a capacity to respond to appeals from ongoing struggles. It would not contest elections or endorse any party.

What came of this idea? A Rebuilding the Left conference in the fall of 2000 attracted several hundred activists (35:1, January/February 2001). Despite the appearance of a hopeful start, in the end most participants in the meetings that followed seemed content to stay within their own organizations rather than build a common movement. Toronto established the Socialist Project and Winnipeg the Structured Movement Against Capitalism (SMAC). Both were mainly educational groups that attracted small active memberships whose efforts to build wider movements met with only small successes. Interesting enough, these projects and others spawned across the country resurfaced in 2015 with the expectation that that a decade of widespread activism would create a more fertile environment in which to build a pan-Canadian socialist formation. As for *CD*, the NDP has long since lost its status as a vital force for change. No doubt about it, this shift in our politics lost us many readers over the years. This is something of which we were always aware but we never allowed it to alter our direction.

Free trade

Greater independence from the US behemoth emerged very early on in the life of *Dimension* as one of our lasting missions. So it should be no surprise that as soon as a Canada-US free trade agreement was mooted in the fall of 1985 *CD* jumped on it and our pages quickly filled with articles condemning the idea. "Free trade may be the single most important policy issue of our generation," I wrote in our January/February 1986 issue, "not only because it will increase our trade and investment dependency on the USA, but because it is bound to touch nearly every thread of the social and cultural fabric of this country." Our editorial that issue was the first to beat the drum for a free trade referendum: "*Dimension* believes that oppositional groups should be demanding a national referendum on free trade before any agreement is signed. We must have a public debate, but more than that a debate whose results will be democratically recorded."

As negotiations got underway in 1986, the newly formed Council of Canadians established the Pro-Canada Network to lead the fight against free trade. The agreement was finalized on October 4, 1987, and signed a year later but the opposition forces did manage to turn public opinion against it and to force a federal election on the issue. In the 1988 election the Mulroney Conservatives won a majority of the seats, but only because the Liberals and NDP split the anti-free trade vote.

CD was highly critical of some aspects of the anti-free trade campaign. Leo Panitch chided that, contrary to the near-apocalyptic refrain that the agreement would mean "the end of Canada as we have known it, shifting our economic axis southward, imposing the rule of business in our society, destroying our welfare state, undermining our culture, subverting our national sovereignty," the FTA was rather "a punctuation mark on a very long historical sentence of business predominance in Canada alongside economic and cultural integration with the United States" (21:8, January 1988). The campaign also erred, he maintained, in "mythologizing the Canadian state as if [until now] it had always . . . been a repository of

Canadian independence and social justice." An alternative to free trade, Panitch insisted, would require a sharp break with the past and radical new directions. Enhanced Canadian independence and expanded social justice could not happen without "the socialization of investment decisions," beginning with "taking the banks into the public domain." But these and other ideas floating around at the time were not brought into the campaign for fear that they would drive away business support.

Panitch's article echoed an earlier contribution by Donald Swartz and Greg Albo, then a grad student at Carleton University. "Why the Campaign Against Free Trade Isn't Working" argued that the campaign offered no viable economic alternative to free trade (21:5, September 1987). Since the free trade agreement was being introduced at a moment when the old Keynesian welfare-state model was widely thought to have brought the Canadian economy to a standstill, a program that offered little more than a return to this failed model would be unconvincing to workers as well as to most everybody else. Same for subsidizing businesses to protect jobs, another ingredient of the failed recipe for managing the economy. Further, they added, proposed trade diversification that "would have Canadian workers competing not only against their increasingly unorganized American counterparts but against their counterparts in South Korea, Taiwan and Brazil etc. . . . would hardly likely arouse the enthusiasm of Canadian workers!"

Swartz and Albo made reference to a policy of a more self-sufficient, diversified and democratically controlled economy as an alternative to free trade.

Should the free trade agreement be consummated without a clear notion of an alternative direction, Swartz and Albo presciently warned, the anti–free trade coalition would dissolve without having built an agenda to fight against a strengthened capitalist class that would seek still deeper integration into the US orbit.

In an article we wrote evaluating the campaign against free trade in the April/May 1989 issue, Jim Silver and I started off by saying that the campaign to defeat the Canada-US Free Trade Agreement "represents the greatest mass movement this country has seen since the dirty thirties," involving labour, church people, environmentalists, women's groups,

80

farm organizations, peaceniks and still others. Nevertheless, our evaluation, based on a survey we conducted with on-the-ground participants in the campaign, while lauding the tireless and effective work of some individuals, ended up being quite critical of most of the organizations in their less than stellar efforts to mobilize their members. (Most of the thousands of people that joined local coalitions did so as individuals rather than as members of this or that organization.) Our purpose in writing the article was to discover our strengths and weaknesses to better enable us to carry on the fight. But as Swartz and Albo predicted, the fight would collapse after the agreement took effect in January 1989, so our effort was in vain.

In the meantime, we learned from personal contacts that our article won *CD* no friends among the leadership of the left/popular movements — though none voiced their concerns to us directly. However, as expected we did hear from the national organizer of Citizens Concerned about Free Trade who called us "vicious, biased, unprincipled" among other epithets. The CCAFT were tireless organizers, as we acknowledged, but they were divisive, tightly controlled and, as we said, "overly centred around the cult-like figure" of its national chairman, David Orchard, who later went on to run for the leadership of first the Conservative Party, then the Liberal Party.

The sharpest response to *CD's* approach to the free trade debate followed an open letter signed by several (but not all) members of the *CD* collective urging the Liberal Party and the NDP to enter into a tactical alliance in the 1988 election, dividing up the 295 ridings between them so as not to split the anti–free trade vote. In the likely event that they would not agree to take this step, we urged our readers to adopt a policy of strategic voting. We were careful to add that we were not advocating a merger of the two parties, but only a one-time measure to turn back the agreement while continuing our work building and uniting the popular movements. We received letters from every Trotskyist faction in Canada expressing disgust that we would "cross the class line" and weaken Canada's working class party, all to the end of promoting our "pro-imperialist nationalism" (22:7, October 1988, 23:1, January/February 1989). This is the same message we received from these voices twenty years earlier when *CD* first outlined our critique of Canada's growing economic and cultural dependence on the USA.

Dimension has never relinquished this theme. We attempted to revive it in 2002 in the midst of the antiglobalization era when we called for building a popular sovereignty movement "not to defend the Canadian state — which is so thoroughly integrated into the American imperial project — but to confront it; and to challenge the rule of transnational capital by demanding new institutions for popular democratic control of the economy, resource development and social expenditures." This would involve recognizing the existing sovereignty claims of francophone and indigenous peoples within a reformed Canadian state." Our appeal went largely unanswered.

Dimension debates madness

While the free trade debate was heating up three others broke out. In our June 1988 issue antipsychiatry activist Don Weitz wrote an article we titled "Manufacturing Madness" in which he argued that psychiatric institutions "drive the sane crazy and make the mad madder" and followed this with "Chemical Lobotomies," which laid out some horrifying effects of drug therapies (25:3, April/May 1991). A decade-long debate ensued, much of it drawing on the personal experiences of the contributors.

The relative importance of biological or social factors in human evolution and individual development has been a perennial subject of political debate since the time of Thomas Malthus. The Left has always been wary of arguments tending toward biological determinism. In particular, the disgraceful history of racism and the eugenics movement provoked ongoing suspicion against establishment science and medicine.

In this context, the roots of mental illness has been a topic of heated discussion in *CD*. Reflecting the views of Thomas Szasz, Michel Foucault and R.D. Laing, Weitz argued that psychiatric institutions were totallizing and dehumanizing. In "Chemical Lobotomies" he painted psychiatric institutionalization as a mechanism of social control, like drug therapy.

In her article of June 1990 (24:4) titled "Madness," Angela Browne also attacked the use of drug therapy and the deinstitutionalization of mental patients as a neoliberal technique for reducing costs in lieu of providing social support and the possibility of self-help. It was the tragic consequences of the social abandonment of the mentally ill that Agnes Grant highlighted in "Schizophrenia on Our Streets" (29:5, October/November, 1995). Following the case of a young schizophrenic, Grant traced the not-uncommon trajectory from mental illness to destitution on the streets. But, contrary to the more common view in *CD*, she held civil libertarians who insist on the rights of mental patients responsible for such abandonment, rather than deinstitutionalization. In the same issue, Irit Shimrat reflected a more typical perspective, concluding "consider the possibility that kindness, respect, patience and free responsible choices can be more helpful to a crazy person than incarceration, force, electroshock and potent chemicals."

Throughout this debate that extended over more than a decade, *CD* reader Joe Levitt contributed several letters taking on both Weitz and Browne. Levitt argued that schizophrenics like his son suffered from a physical disorder of the brain and, while conceding that psychiatric drugs can sometimes have harmful side effects, he insisted that drugs can relieve the most extreme symptoms of paranoia, enabling schizophrenics to live outside of psychiatric hospitals. Levitt also made the point that those who insist that there is no such thing as mental illness — that it is hospitals and psychiatrists that make people insane — unwittingly fall into league with neoliberal ideology that says society has no responsibility for those who cannot take care of themselves.

What causes AIDS?

The issue of the social versus the biological also surfaced in a debate over the causes of AIDS, in some respects a modern version of 1800s debate between the contagionists, the extremists of whom argued that diseases were due to single germs, and the anticontagionists, who said diseases were caused by a combination of economic and social factors. In their October 1989 article (23:7) "Aids: Modern Medicine's Achilles' Heel," investigative journalists Bruce Livesay and Ellen Lipsius took up the cause of the anticontagionists. Following the work of Peter Duesberg of the University of California, they argued that the HIV virus is not the cause of AIDS but rather that the disease is the result of multiple cofactors such as poor nutrition, poverty and reckless sex and drug lifestyles that lower resistance to a host of already existing infections.

Their article provoked several responses including an article, "Germs and Politics," written by community health consultant Ronald Labonte (24:3, April/May 1990). Labonte argued that while the germ theory is inadequate to explain the totality of disease, this did not make it wrong. As regards the obsession with HIV in AIDS, he said it was neither the germ theory nor the modern medical monopoly that eclipsed the multiple-factor explanation for AIDS, but the domination of a particular elite within the scientific medical community and the economic windfalls for drug treatments such as AZT. In the final analysis, he concluded, contrary to Livesay/Lipsius, that HIV is necessary for AIDS, but that it is not sufficient. Five years later precisely the same debate was recycled, this time between Brian K. Murphy's "AIDS Obscures Injustice and Medicalizes Poverty" and another article by Ron Labonte (29:3, June/July 1995).

CD also published several articles on the politics of fighting AIDS, beginning in September 1989 (23:6) with Jeff O'Malley's "Building Solidarity in the Fight Against AIDS." Cindy Patton's "Aids Bureaucrats Ignore Women" noted the overwhelmingly male bias to the medical and social analysis and treatment of the disease. Tim McCaskell's "Aids Activism: The Development of a New Socialist Movement" described the transformation of the fight against AIDS into a political movement in North America led by the organized gay community.

The personal is political

Within the collective the most acrimonious debate took place around the advice column called "Personal/Political" launched by Gad Horowitz in the October 1987 issue. "Personal/Political is not an advice column like the others," Horowitz wrote in his introduction. "The purpose of this column is not just to dispense free advice about personal problems, but to do so, whenever possible, from a radical point of view concerned to develop a psychology helpful to people who want to (or want to want to) bring about a socialist feminist transformation of society." At the time Horowitz was still teaching political theory at the University of Toronto, but when I learned that he had also established a select therapy practice,

I suggested he write this advice column for *CD* and he readily accepted. The results exceeded my expectations. Here is a sampling.

ENGELS WAS A FACTORY OWNER (21:6, October 1987): "I am a socialist. I am wealthy. I have a big house and a big car and I even like big cigars. Contribute a lot of money to progressive causes. My 'comrades' think I am a hypocrite."

GH: "Frederich Engels was a factory owner. He did not sell his factory and divide the proceeds among the workers. If not for the money he gave Marx, Marx could not have written *Das Kapital*. Marx didn't think Engels was a hypocrite. He knew that capitalism was full of contradictions."

OTHER MASCULINITIES (21:6, October 1987): "A few weeks ago I saw a political graffiti stenciled on a wall: 'Men, Why Do We Rape?!' Since then I have no desire whatever to make love. I have become extremely disgusted and depressed with my sexuality. It offends me as a feminist man. When I have intercourse with my lover I feel that male sexuality is animalistic and impersonal, objectifying women rather than relating to them as unique intelligent persons worthy of respect."

GH: "It is natural, but unfortunate, that certain feminist discourses have become thoroughly mixed up with hatred of 'male sexuality' (and in some cases of all sexuality). There is no 'male sexuality' per se. What you call 'animalistic' and 'impersonal' is at bottom the inherently passionate and ecstatic quality of sexual experience: you can forget about your precious unique personhood, become the pre-person, the transpersonal, the animal, the child and last but not least, the 'woman' in you."

TWO KINDS OF PEOPLE (21:7, November/December 1987): "I have just completed my PhD dissertation on Marxist Theories of the State but I can't bring myself to hand it in because I fear I will be judged a mediocre scholar. The thought of my mediocrity has always been very depressing to me. The deadline for submission is getting close."

GH: "Mediocrity is a pejorative, contemptuous, classist way of talking about worthwhile human activities that do not happen to be superlatively outstanding. Every individual has endured experiences of shaming and humiliation and so becomes more or less driven by a desperate need to win over others in order to disprove his worthlessness and validate his own existence. From now on, every time the thought of mediocrity comes to mind, you might find yourself thinking about this: Every time you thus direct contempt toward yourself you are strengthening the capitalist system. You might find yourself thinking about converting your contempt for yourself into hatred for the system that has taught your grandparents, your parents, your brothers and sisters, your teachers, your friends and yourself to hate yourselves, consciously and unconsciously, as real or potential 'failures', 'losers', and 'non-entities'."

The column initially attracted the occasional letter of disagreement, but with "Amazon Fantasy Trouble" (22:3, May 1988) the floodgates really opened. Letters poured in, most of them critical — as in "this column is an affront to feminism"; give Gad "an unceremonial heave ho and get a feminist to write about socialist feminist issues." On the other hand Varda Burstyn, in response, wrote a long article "Fantasy and Desire, Patriarchy and Progressive People" (23:2, March 1989) that talked about "how corrosive a force women fear their own sexual desire is," observing that "Gad does a good job understanding the specificities of sexuality, its characteristics, its components and its dynamics," and praising *Dimension* for having "the intelligence and courage to publish his column." Women in the collective disagreed. At a meeting devoted to discussing the column, they complained about the advice Gad was offering to women, questioning his ability as a male to understand the context of women's reality ("Assessing Gad's Column" 23:2, March 1989). Horowitz replied to the collective and ended the column.

There has never been another time when I came so close to resigning. Among other things I was disgusted by all the men on the collective who sat stone silent through this discussion, so intimidated were they by the female sentries among us. In retrospect I realized that some may have just disagreed with Horowitz or just found his column distasteful, but at the time I interpreted their silence as intimidation. And I still think we lost lost a gem to identity politics.

Greenpeace

Because it targeted Canada's best known, largest and widely respected environmental organization, Bruce Livesey's 1994 article "The Politics of Greenpeace" proved to be the most controversial exposé ever published in *CD*. Greenpeace was famous for its battles with multinational corporations, dramatic direct action media spectacles, refusal to accept corporate and government funding, and its success in putting environmental issues on the public agenda — all reasons why *CD* readers expressed "shock" and "astonishment" after reading Livesey's article.

What sparked Livesey's investigation was Greenpeace's effort to break its staff union, firing or laying off most of its campaign staff and activists and spending money on expensive union-busting lawyers. "Once upon a time Greenpeace did some great work," he acknowledged in response to his critics, "but the organization that captured the public's attention in the 1970s and 1980s no longer exists. Today, Greenpeace is disinterested in devoting resources to grassroots environmental campaigns that connect with those people truly affected by ecological destruction. The campaigns that it does fund, such as the one on Clayoquot Sound, are designed to garner media coverage in the hopes that the public will give Greenpeace money . . . Up to 95% of the money it raises is spent on administration and fundraising."

"Self-righteous sectarian politics" wrote noted sociologist and feminist Dorothy Smith. "I take the strongest exception to the author's personalist attack" on Greenpeace director Jeanne Moffat, blasted John Foster, national secretary of Oxfam Canada. "A vicious, unfair hatchet job on our most effective environmental organization," declared another critic. "Couldn't we leave the task of discrediting progressive organizations to publications like the *Toronto Sun*"?

But the article found as many supporters among *CD* readers as it did critics.

Ann Chiu wrote: "Congratulations on a very bold article on Greenpeace. As a former employee I found the article to be blunt but truthful. Many present and former staff who read it were taken aback because the issues it raised were tabooed and silenced internally for such a long time."

Kim Goldberg wrote in: "I have always believed that a just cause will not be hurt by the truth. So you won't hear any howls from this quarter over Bruce Livesey's insightful and provocative exposé on Greenpeace. The argument that we shouldn't engage in honest appraisal of left institutions because it plays into the hands of the Right does us more harm than good, although it has been used many times to suppress internal criticism of everything from the NDP to Castro. And now Greenpeace. The task of exposing contradictions and failings within the Left is simply too important to grassroots democracy to be left to the corporate press. Good job, *CD*."

Dimension editors closed the discussion on whether *CD* should be scrutinizing the behaviour of progressive organizations with this comment:

"This focus on Greenpeace has provoked as much debate as we have seen in the pages of *CD*. Yet, long-time readers of *CD* know we have never hesitated to take on the NDP, unions and other organizations of the Left and the popular movements — to say nothing of the Establishment— sometimes at considerable cost to the magazine. This we shall continue to do."

The Palestine-Israel conflict

The Palestine-Israel conflict has long been a stormy issue in left circles. In *Canadian Dimension* a battle erupted late in the game and was centred not on the conflict itself but on the influence of the Israel lobby on American policy in the region.

Before the occupation of the West Bank and Gaza became the main concern, the issue of note was the more general one of the legitimacy of Israel's right to exist versus the national aspirations of the Palestinians. Though in hindsight it appears balanced, *Dimension's* position when it first entered the discussion back in 1968 was considered unacceptable by the vast majority of Jewish opinion makers:

> *For Jews the establishment of the state of Israel was the Great Return. For Palestinian Arabs it was the Great Invasion. The struggle in the Middle East is ultimately a struggle between two legitimate nationalisms over the right to a small strip of land. Neither a Jewish state nor an Arab state can satisfy both national aspirations. Only a mutual compromise, a bi-national state can do that. And neither side is willing to seriously consider the prospect.*

That position, reiterated again in 1973 at the time of Israel's twenty-fifth birthday, supplemented by critical analyses of Israeli policies, cost *Dimension* many of its Jewish subscribers. Unambiguous opposition to the occupation and acknowledgement of the apartheid character of the Jewish state removed still more from our subscription rolls. But within the *CD* collective none of this had been viewed as controversial. That awaited an analysis put forward by collective member James Petras in 2002 about the preeminent role of the Israel lobby in determining American policy in the Middle East. In her argument against the decision of the *CD* collective to publish Petras's article, collective member Abbie Bakan accused Petras of shifting the focus of the Left away from the strategic interests of US imperialism in the Middle East and fuelling anti-Semitism by the focus on the role of "rich Jews" in the formulation of US foreign policy: "Don't blame US imperialism; don't blame the oil or arms industries; don't look to US geo-political or military interests; blame the Jews — especially the rich ones. A left cover for anti-Semitism can only increase the resolve of the far right." Upon making this statement in the magazine, Bakan and an associate of hers stormed out of the collective, publicly condemning *CD*'s editorial process (36:3, May/June 2002).

In "Unusual Sensitivities" (36:4, July/August 2002), *CD* collective member Mordecai Briemberg attempted to explain why serious criticism of Israeli state policies arouses such emotional responses:

> . . . *criticism that can disengage people from the long established pro-Israeli framing of the conflict merges into anti-Semitism and anti-Semitism in turn merges into the Holocaust; the Holocaust merges into annihilation of Jews world-wide; and the final bar that imprisons all reasonable discussion: the existence of the Israeli state alone can prevent the total annihilation.*" So criticism of it risks "*promoting an abominable horror* . . . Concerns about fuelling anti-Semitism should be addressed to the Israeli government," Briemberg concluded, "not directed against progressives who wish to analyse the structures and practices of Israeli state lobby forces within our own political system. To commit, as the Israeli state does, morally indefensible acts, to arrogate unto itself the claim that it acts in the name of all Jews, and then to foreclose any serious and sustained criticism of its repugnant acts with threats of slander or loss of job and office* . . . *is to fuel real anti-Semitism.*

Several other *CD* articles caused a storm of protest or at least heated controversy. John Warnock wrote a sharp rebuke to an article by Ken Hanly that defended genetic engineering of plants and animals (34:6, November/December 2000). Ravi Malhotra's defence of the jailing of Robert Latimer for the second-degree murder of his twelve-year-old quadriplegic daughter, Tracy Latimer, brought arguments from Svend Robinson, Richard Fidler and Margaret Assels with a spirited rejoinder by Malhotra (35:3, May/June 2001; 35:4, July/August 2001). Collective members James Petras and Andrea Levy engaged in a sharp exchange about what Levy described as "the draconian measures taken by the Cuban government against a group of individuals deemed enemies of the state . . ." and what she described as Petras's "scurrilous attack on a group of very decent American left intellectuals, including Chomsky, who signed a very balanced statement opposing summary executions" (37:4, July/August 2003). An article describing sex work as sex slavery drew letters of rebuke from several sex workers (45:1, January/February 2011). A CD editorial criticizing the politics of Black Bloc actions at the G20 protests attracted letters both pro and con from CD readers (44:6, November/December 2010).

The range of disagreement has been wide. No institution, no political, economic or social arrangement has been spared "ruthless criticism." If anything, movements on the Left have come under even greater critical scrutiny — without constraint, but also without sectarianism.

CD's financial crunch

In 1977 our accountant helped us apply for charitable status by establishing a foundation we called the Manitoba Foundation for Canadian Studies whose purpose would be to promote educational activities. The application was accepted, securing the magazine much-needed revenues. We immediately set up a Second Decade Fund that brought in nearly $20,000 from a total of 350 donors.

It didn't take long for Revenue Canada to realize its "error" and in 1980 our charitable status was revoked. "On the basis of the material contained in the Canadian Dimension magazine," they wrote, " it would appear that its goal is not to educate the reader in the sense of training the mind in matters of political science, but to promote a particular ideology."

The case attracted immediate attention. In a column for the *Financial Post* ("Political Activities: A Charitable Dilemma"), tax lawyer Arthur Drache noted that this was the first time a charitable organization had ever lost its status on account of political activities. He called it "a threat to free speech" and mused that "Revenue Canada had selected as a test case an organization which would not command broad political support." NDP MP Bob Rae brought the issue to the House of Commons, demanding to know how the Trudeau government could defend this action against *Canadian Dimension* when the Fraser Institute, "a front organization for our largest corporations is able to claim charitable status." Letters of support poured in from many corners, including the likes of novelist Margaret Laurence, poet Earle Birney, cleric Gregory Baum, ex-Liberal cabinet minister Walter Gordon and the United Church of Canada. Fund raising events were organized in Ottawa, Toronto and Winnipeg. An appeal to our readers brought in $15,000. While *CD* never did regain its charitable status, the campaign we fought stopped the government of that day from taking on other organizations whose political leanings it disagreed with. Thirty years later the Harper regime showed no such restraint in cutting off charities whose political expression it sought to silence.

Into the eighties *Dimension*'s circulation fell as rapidly as it had risen in the seventies. While our annual expenditures never exceeded $75,000, still a paltry sum, revenue from subscriptions and newsstand sales now fell short. Other sources of funding had to be found and new efforts deployed to win back readers.

In 1985 we came up with the *CD* 400 Club. We calculated that if we could convince four hundred readers to sign up for a preauthorization payment plan with a contribution averaging $10 a month we could work our way towards becoming a monthly publication. Within the first year a hundred joined and it inched forward from there. Though we never did reach four hundred, this structure gave the magazine the stability it had always lacked. By the end of the eighties we were once again able to hire a managing editor and for some years we did increase our production to eight issues a year. By that time we were finally starting to increase our subscription base, ending a twelve-year slide.

There were other fund raising schemes, including art auctions and chess tournaments. Most important, in 1988 CUPE founding member Gil Levine organized *CD*'s twenty-fifth anniversary celebration dinner in Ottawa. This became an annual event which, for the price of a dinner and a subscription, brought together hundreds of Ottawa activists each year. Over the next twenty-five years the Ottawa benefit would raise nearly $60,000 for the magazine and recruit a few thousand subscribers.

Who reads *Dimension*?

A mid-80s survey of subscribers showed that teachers and professors made up 22 per cent of *CD* readers, and students another 8 per cent. Office workers comprised 13 per cent and manual workers another 10 per cent. As many as 27 per cent reported being active in the NDP; 23 per cent in unions; 14 per cent in the women's movement; and another 8 per cent on environmental issues.

Nearly 10 per cent of *CD* subscribers then were under twenty-five years of age and 36 percent were between twenty-six and thirty-five. Another 25 per cent were between the ages of thirty-six and fifty with 29 percent over fifty. A survey ten years later, however, confirmed a troubling trend to which we had not paid sufficient attention: The average age of *Dimension* subscribers was climbing. Nearly half were over fifty; less than 20 per cent were under thirty-five. Solutions would be forthcoming, but they were still a few years away.

Socialist angst

Every decade or so, *Canadian Dimension* would suffer a bout of socialist angst: Capital is clobbering working people and the poor; where is the resistance? Where is the socialist alternative? What is the socialist alternative?

A June 1988 editorial, "Taking Stock," acknowledged that "we live in something like a state of siege. While capitalism is in crisis, transnationals are working around the clock turning the world upside down. They're revolutionizing the workplace, invading just about every corner of what's left of the public realm, and pushing the State to dismantle the services we fought so hard to build. Meanwhile the New Right has grabbed the ideological terrain, setting the legislative agenda and the terms of the debate. Instead of moving beyond the welfare state and the limited victories of the past, Leftists find themselves in the ironic position of defending the status quo."

Eighteen months later, an editorial titled "A New Popular Consensus" (23:8, November December 1989) took up the questions of the sources of resistance and the nature of the socialist alternative. It saw the seeds of a vital opposition among environmentalists, feminists and peace, labour and anti-poverty activists. And it identified the elements of an emergent popular consensus in: "a desire for more sustainable forms of production and consumption"; "a shared responsibility for the future of the environment"; "democratization of power relations between men and women at work and in the home" and within the Left itself; "disengagement from the cold war and fortress America and support for liberation struggles"; organizing against homelessness and poverty and "renewal of the ethic of social citizenship"; "humanizing the workplace and creating better and more stable jobs"; and "fuller democratization with new forms of popular control, accountability and community ownership."

We admitted up front that for the most part the leadership of this opposition and its inspiration was not coming from socialists and socialism. "Organizationally, we are its weakest link and we have at least as much to learn from the environmentalists and the feminists as they do from us. But we have a special contribution to make . . . Environmental struggles, for one, have the potential to become radically anticapitalist . . . Sustainable development within capitalism is a contradiction in terms. Uncontrollable growth destroys the environment. Yet some environmentalists continue to believe that their concerns can be met within capitalism. But until we develop our own local and national forums to help us work out socialist perspectives on concrete problems . . . our contribution to the process will be minimal."

A few years later the socialist angst had not dissipated. On the occasion of our thirtieth anniversary, our editorial compared the *CD* of 1993 with that of 1963:

The Canadian Dimension of 1993, in many ways, is the
same as the CD of 1963 — an alternative mirror of our

*life and times, a sharp stick in the eye of authority, a cry
for justice, an attempt to illuminate the often murky way
forward. [But] in 1963 we didn't write about feminism,
the environment, human rights, gay and lesbian liberation,
and the connection between the politics we espouse and the
way we live our lives. Leftish thinking and socialism for that
matter, hadn't considered these issues much less understood
their importance. Faithful* Dimension *readers know . . .
they are standard and welcome fare in today's Canadian*
Dimension.

True, but oversimplified. In "A New Popular Consensus" we had
written that the vision embodied in our new concerns and the agenda
it produces are not a mere updating of old ideas. They amount to a
fundamental reformulation of the meaning of social progress. But while
socialists had acknowledged the new concerns, we had incorporated it
only partially and unevenly. For example, Varda Burstyn observed in
a *CD* article addressed to the male Left, "Marxists who thought their
Marxism absolved them from further self-examination and change in
personal behaviour, will have to be willing to change themselves if they
want to change the world." ("The Uneasy Alliance of Women and the
Left," 17:4, September 1983). The same might be said about the Left's
attitude to the environmental crisis.

"*CD* at 30" concluded that "*Canadian Dimension*'s renewal is a reaffirma-
tion of the philosophy that has guided us over the past 30 years. We cherish our pluralism because we think it is an integral part of the struggle to
replace capitalism. We prize our independence because it gives us the freedom to maintain that pluralism, to question left orthodoxy, to challenge
our allies and heap abuse on capitalist pigs everywhere. And we remain
an alternative because those capitalist pigs hold sway almost everywhere,
brutalizing the Earth and all of her creatures. What we need to renew is the
way we implement our vision of what an alternative magazine should be.
It is not enough to say that *CD* is a voice for a broad range of progressive
activists and thinkers. We have to actually publish those voices and reach
those activists."

In large part that would be the challenge for *CD* in its fourth decade.

PART III: PUSHING 50, 1995–2013

For me, this period in *Canadian Dimension*'s history has been the most satisfying since the first decade of our founding. Through most of it we have been able to employ a part-time Associate Publisher, which relieved me of the burden of day-to-day management, enabled the magazine to meet publishing deadlines more consistently and to develop better routines and procedures. As well, having finally retired from my teaching position at the University of Manitoba, I was able to devote much more time to the magazine. This allowed me to introduce several new editorial features and projects that I had been wanting to develop, to recruit a new generation of writers and collective members and to help shape *Dimension* into a more activist institution on the Left. With a new design, superb young designers and much more attention paid to both the aesthetics of the magazine and the quality of its writing, I believe *Canadian Dimension* evolved into a far better-looking and much more interesting magazine than it had ever been. For a very brief few moments we even managed to break out of the red and enjoy a positive bank account. That was when, in 2004, Noam Chomsky filled the University of Toronto's Convocation Hall to speak at a *CD* benefit event. In 2013, on the occasion of *CD*'s fiftieth anniversary, Chomsky filled the Université de Montréal's Salle Claude Champagne, once again moving us into the black.

In 1999 we reorganized. The collective went virtual, using the Internet to bring together members from across the country. The work of our Winnipeg collective group was trimmed down considerably. Most of the editorial work, including the planning of issues and the writing of editorials could be done online. While the meetings in our offices at the Emma Goldman Centre atop the Mondragon Café/Bookstore became shorter, less raucous and much less frequent — my role as coordinating editor actually grew. Among the earliest recruits to our expanded collective were Eric Shragge and Andrea Levy in Quebec, Greg Albo and Geoff Bickerton in Ontario, Mordecai Briemberg in BC and John Warnock in Saskatchewan. Other outstanding members were added along the way: Joyce Green, Dennis Pilon, Peter Kulchyski, Sam Gindin, Corvin Russell, Brenda Austin-Smith, Judy Deutsch, Ian Angus, Clayton Thomas-Müller, David Hugill, Saul Landau and James Petras among several others. Besides Henry Heller, several stalwarts from the old regime, like Ed Janzen, Kevin Mathews and Krishna Lalbiharie continued as members. By 2012 the *CD* collective was thirty-two strong.

A 2002 subscriber survey showed that the advancing age of our readers remained a stiff challenge. We attempted to counter this by attracting younger members to the collective, recruiting younger columnists and soliciting articles from younger writers. One very positive change from the earliest days of the magazine, when we had to draw mainly on academics for articles, is the rising number of young freelance radical journalists like Yves Engler, Dawn Paley, Stephan Christoff, Martin Lukacs, Anthony Fenton, Derrick O'Keefe, Tonya Davidson, Chris Arsenault, Angela Day, Lia Tarachansky, Macdonald Stainsby and Harsha Walia. All of these and many others made their way onto the pages of *Dimension* in the last decade.

CD also welcomed the contributions of front-line activists and organizers like Clayton Thomas-Müller, then with the Indigenous Environmental Network; Barbara Legault and Sarah Granke of the young feminist movement RebELLEs; Elle Flanders of Queers Against Israeli Apartheid; Judy Da Silva of Grassy Narrows Reserve; Richard Sanders of Coalition to Oppose the Arms Trade; Ugo Lapointe, cofounder of the Coalition pour que le Québec ait meilleure mine and Kim Cornelissen of the Association québécoise de lutte contre la pollution.

For a few years each issue of the magazine profiled "activists changing the world" nominated by their peers in education, labour, the environmental movement, the feminist movement, the indigenous movement. A new feature we introduced, "Sixty Days Around the Left," provides readers with contact information about events taking place between issues of the magazine. For a few years each issue carried a story about a "pathbreaker," an organization making strides to change our world.

"The Personal Dimension" was yet another innovation. We asked a number of people, not all of them well known, to tell their stories or some part of it — how they came to their politics; what events,

experiences, people, authors or films shaped their lives; what twentieth-century political movements most inspired them or disillusioned
them; what they believe to be their major achievement as a public
intellectual or activist, as a private citizen and in their personal lives;
how they have come to describe themselves politically; how their views
have changed over time. Among the personal dimension pieces we
published were those of the theologian Gregory Baum, feminist and
Québec solidaire co-leader Françoise David, historian Bryan Palmer,
feminist Varda Burstyn, indigenous author Taiaiake Alfred, workplace
health and safety activist Stan Gray, political economist Mel Watkins,
and young Filipino activist Melissa Gibson.

While *Dimension* has always had an interest in culture and the arts, that
now began to occupy a more central place in the magazine. As collective
member Kevin Mathews expressed it in introducing a special issue on
Artists and Politics (41:1, July/August 2007):

> *If society has an imagination to express its desires and fears,*
> *it is activated through art. If society is to experiment with*
> *change, with new forms, with its power structures, with*
> *ways of seeing and with language itself, it must be through*
> *art. If social change is the agenda, then art must make up a*
> *large part of the toolkit.*

Jazz and politics, visual art, Canadian theatre, the Canadian film industry, political crime fiction, science fiction, indigenous literature, and the
activist lens are among the art forms explored in recent years.

As Brenda Austin Smith remarked, in her contribution to *CD*'s fiftieth
anniversary issue (47:2, March/April 2013):

> *What I noticed more than anything else in CD in the last*
> *20 years is an important shift in the magazine's coverage*
> *of culture. Far from occupying merely its own section of the*
> *magazine, culture — understood broadly as the network of*
> *lifeways, institutions, practices and expressions in which and*
> *through which we live — permeates the magazine's pages.*

It is not just that CD *reviews books and films, or provides a space for poetry or photo essays or that it profiles artists, it's that these reviews and profiles are embedded in a more generous and flexible notion of culture that now animates the magazine."*

The format of the magazine changed radically, with part of every issue being devoted to a specific theme: Cities, Indian Country, Arts and Politics, Food, Pensions in Peril, Queer, Remembering 1968, Immigration, the Criminal (Justice) System, Precarious Work, Big Media, Canada Mines the South, the New Feminist Revolution, Our Winnipeg, Today's Student Activism, Climate Change, Peak Oil, Degrowth. This format, which required much planning and coordination, a capacity we did not have until now, allowed the magazine to explore these topics in some depth.

One of the major disadvantages of a magazine that appears only bimonthly is the time lapse between issues. With the development of the *Canadian Dimension* website and a weekly radio show ("Alert"), this limitation was largely overcome and in some ways allowed us to expand our reach to audiences and readers that would otherwise not have access to the magazine or are more attuned to other media.

A new political phase

Towards the end of the nineties *Dimension* asserted "a new political phase is opening up in Canadian politics, and a revitalized socialist project must be placed on the agenda." Ontario's Days of Action against Mike Harris's Common Sense Revolution, and the anti-globalization mobilizations against the Multilateral Agreement on Investment, the WTO meeting in Seattle, the Summit of the Americas meeting in Quebec City and other actions in Europe opened up what seemed to be a new momentum for the Left in Canada and around the world. As Jason Zeidenberg put it in his *Dimension* article describing the mass demonstration that brought over two hundred thousand protesters to Queen's Park on October 26, 1996: "It's not that Queen's Park felt like Paris in 1968 or Winnipeg in 1919, but for the people who turned out on October 26 this was an entirely new feeling . . . The sense that things may change is out there and it is leading people back to activism in a big way" (January/February 1997).

Metro Toronto's Days of Action was the high point of a mobilization that began from the very first sitting of the Harris legislature and continued through numerous demonstrations, rallies, teach-ins, strikes and seven city-wide political strikes. Like the federal Liberal government and the other provinces, Harris's Tories were driven by deficit dementia, but theirs went further and deeper, and displayed a kind of missionary zeal not found elsewhere.

Combining one-day strikes with demonstrations that included a wide assortment of community groups and social movements was a new and important development. Trade unions had to find a way of working with coalitions of pensioners, feminists, artists, environmentalists, students and welfare recipients. Union leaders had to persuade their members to go on an illegal strike, lose a day's pay and risk their employer's discipline.

Grasping the importance of this mobilization, *Dimension* covered it like no other media. From the beginning, however, we recognized that these actions would lead nowhere if they did not prepare the way for a general strike. Our January/February 1997 editorial said it plainly: "The objective must not be merely to scare Harris, but to make Ontario ungovernable. Days of Action will not accomplish this . . . The only thing that will bring his 'common sense revolution' to screeching halt is an unlimited general strike."

That did not happen, of course. A raging war inside the labour movement between those unions favouring radical action and those that would have nothing to do with political strikes and saw the election of NDP governments as the only way forward had from the beginning weakened Days of Action and guaranteed that a general strike was not on the agenda. Still, with mammoth actions in Seattle, followed by the events in Quebec City to defeat the Free Trade Area of the Americas, left momentum continued to build.

In the spring of 1999 *Dimension* organized a discussion around an article by Sam Gindin originally published in 1998 in *This Magazine*. The article was titled "The Party's Over." Taking aim at the rightward drift of the NDP, Gindin argued that it was time to discuss creating a new party. While any attempt to form it was premature, the ground for it needed to be readied, wrote Gindin. He called for the building of a "structured movement . . . something more than a coalition and less than a party." The discussion in *Dimension* carried on for a full year, mirroring meetings held in several cities. This culminated in a Rebuilding the Left Conference in October 2000. While the conference was hugely attended and raised much excitement, it failed to achieve its goal. The Ontario Coalition Against Poverty continued to put up a fight against cutbacks in that province, but demonstrations everywhere fell off dramatically in size.

At the global level, Bush's war against terrorism gave imperialist aggression an unprecedented licence. Many new free-trade agreements were signed. China entered the WTO. Even though the World Social Forum made its debut in 2001 and carried forward in growing numbers in subsequent years, the Seattle moment slipped away. *Dimension* writers took aim at the summit-hopping tendencies within the antiglobalization movement. "We need to focus on local struggles first and foremost," argued Macdonald Stainsby. Commenting on the G8 demonstrations in Calgary and Kananaskis in 2002, Tom Keefer poked fun at "protest porn": "ordinary working people can see pretty clearly that a movement made up of naked, grunting, mud-covered middle class 'earth people' had little concrete to offer them in overcoming the oppressive conditions of their lives" (36:5, September/October 2002).

In *Dimension* the discussion about globalization took its own spin. A series of insightful articles by Sam Gindin challenged the conventional wisdom that in a globalized world the nation state was rendered powerless ("Challenging Globalization," 36:4, July/August 2002; "Sovereignty and Empire," 37:4, July/August 2003). In particular, he challenged the view of some currents on the Left that political struggles on a national level had become irrelevant and should be abandoned in favour of "internationalism." As Gindin put it ("The Fight against Globalization Must Begin at Home," 38:6, November/ December 2004):

Internationalism begins at home. Accumulation may
increasingly be international in scope but the social
foundation of its power — property rights, contracts, the
credibility of currencies, labour rights and labour markets —
are established and reproduced at the level of nation states
. . . Resistance cannot be separated from place; concrete
and sustained mobilization can only occur within historical
communities that must be built nationally before they can
aspire to an effective internationalism.

This was another round of a debate carried on in *Dimension* from its earliest days.

Economic slump

Two momentous crises marked the opening decade of the twenty-first century: climate change, and the financial meltdown and global economic slump of 2008–2009.

For *Dimension*, the economic slump was a crisis waiting to happen. Our analysis of the collapse of Enron and Worldcom and the crash of 2002 indicated that the signs of a world crash of historic proportions were already present (36:5, September/October 2002). All the elements eventually assigned by critics of the 2008–2009 crisis had come into play by then: deregulation of financial markets, explosion of speculative activities, massive industrial overcapacities, huge debt loads. We noted that the crash of 2002 was an early result of the neoliberal regime of the eighties and nineties introduced to counter the economic stagflation of the seventies — free trade to force greater competition, deregulation and privatization to open up new outlets of profit opportunities, attacks on trade unions to counter their successes in advancing wages and benefits, ending universalization and trimming the welfare state. While we did not anticipate that the trigger for the next global crisis would be the bursting of a US housing bubble, we were right in doubting that the pressure for regulatory reform would be sufficient to clear the way for a long period of prosperity.

Similarly, for the slump of 2008–2009 we were skeptical that the bailouts, fiscal stimulus, quantitative easing and new financial regulations introduced in the US, Europe and the rest of the world would break the slump and usher in a full recovery:

> *With industry awash in excess capacity, investment will be meager for some years to come. With a huge oversupply of housing, office and retail space, residential and commercial construction will also stagnate. Consumption spending is crippled by unprecedented levels of household debt and by crushing unemployment rates.*
>
> *By means of bailouts and fiscal stimuli — measures that socialize the cost of capitalism's crisis — public debt has largely replaced private debt as the engine of the capitalist economy. Without it, the global economy is likely to go back into the tank. Yet deficit fetishism is inducing governments to roll back public expenditures by trimming staff and programs and freezing or reducing public sector wages and benefits, including pensions. This is capitalism's dilemma: it can't live with ever rising public debt and it can't live without it. (44:3, May/June 2010)*

Since this editorial was written, recovery from the Great Recession has indeed stalled. Only continuous rounds of both public and household debt and extraordinarily high growth rates of India and China have enabled the global economy to avoid actual shrinkage.

Dimension raised a full array of alternative policies, but as Gindin and Panitch rightly insisted, "a coherent alternative is not just a set of economic policy proposals, but a political movement that can develop the popular appreciation and capacities for radical democratic control over investment" (42:4, July/August 2008). Unfortunately, except for momentary upsurges such as the protests in Wisconsin in 2011, the Occupy Wall Street movement, Quebec's Maple Spring, and the more sustained Indigenous resistance movement, there were few signs at least in North America of building the "infrastructure of resistance" they were calling for. Even in Europe, where austerity-escalated unemployment has risen to staggering rates of up to 25 per cent in some countries and far higher for young workers — a terrifying 60 per cent in Greece, 53 per cent in Spain and 40 per cent in Italy — widespread public anger has so far only produced sporadic and ineffective explosions from below. This does not take away from the fact that the eruption of class politics with people out in the streets in huge numbers in various parts of the world is something we have not seen in a very long time.

The mass mobilizations in the global South have been especially momentous. In 2000, for example, a popular uprising in Bolivia blocked water privatization and helped launch a revolt that brought down three presidents and swept Evo Morales and the Movement Towards Socialism into office. Hugo Chavez was elected president of Venezuela in 1998 and over the next decade or so introduced a series of democratic and anticapitalist reforms as part of a social project that came to be known as the Bolivarian Revolution. These are examples of mass-based structured movements with a long history of struggle. In North America in particular, however, there has been a decided absence of and even a deliberate avoidance of anything smacking of structured opposition arising from potentially movement-building struggles for reforms around housing needs, food and water security, a living wage, free tuition, universal childcare, free public transit, expansion of public pensions, nationalizing the banks, stopping the tar sands, fracking, coal mines and offshore drilling. Instead, episodic protests and promising movements leave no structures behind once their moments have passed. Largely as a result, protests here are rarely sustained, movements are quickly exhausted and organizational capacities are left underdeveloped.

Any left analysis of the first decade of the twenty-first century and the prospects for far-reaching social change must contend with the crucial weakness of the labour movement, which has historically played a central role in transformative politics. Not only has union density substantially dropped in virtually all sectors, but unions are in addition mainly engaged in defensive actions to hold onto past gains for their members and too often see their future tied to the success of the ruling class even to the extent of joining in their efforts to seek government funding for their industries. This undermines their commitment to fighting for the kinds of structural reforms mentioned above. That said, we need to acknowledge the efforts of some unions to reach out to support community-based actions and social movement mobilizations that potentially define more of a class-based politics that transcends their more narrow membership-based concerns. It's also important to recognize the assault on organized labour mounted in the USA and advancing steadily in Canada. Dozens of anti-union legislative changes have been passed in recent years that, combined with a propaganda war, has seriously weakened labour's strength.

Indian country, climate crisis and ecosocialism

Over the past decade or so CD has stepped up its coverage of two issues in particular: the recolonization of Indian Country and the ecological crisis, especially in the guise of climate change.

In this country, as in parts of Latin America, the most active and effective resistance to capital has been coming from grassroots movements of Indigenous peoples. From the beginning the Canadian state has been engaged in clearing the land of its original inhabitants so that it could be settled by farmers and eventually by urban dwellers. But no matter to what distant corners they were pushed the Indigenous peoples remained targeted for extinction whenever and wherever their presence collided with the advance of capitalist development. It is evident that the conquest, that process of dispossessing First Peoples to allow others to accumulate wealth, is still going on. It is equally evident that Aboriginal peoples are living on the frontiers of the front lines of the anticapitalist struggle.

All through its fifty years, beginning with the struggle over Trudeau's White Paper that at its core aimed to eliminate Aboriginal rights, *Dimension* focused attention on the key mobilizations and battles: the occupation of Anishinabe Park in Kenora, the cross-Canada caravan to Ottawa, the conflicts over the James Bay power project and northern Manitoba's Churchill River Diversion, the Mackenzie Valley pipeline proposal, the conflict on Oldman River in southern Alberta, the murder of Dudley George, the blockade at Gustavson Lake in BC, the fight over fishing rights at Burnt Church and against clear-cut logging at Grassy Narrows. Until the battles over the tar sands and the pipelines to carry oil and bitumen, these were sporadic and uncoordinated struggles. But *Dimension* attended and reported on the historic gatherings of Defenders of the Land in Winnipeg (2008) and Vancouver (2009), the first convergence of Indigenous leaders from communities engaged in direct, nonviolent opposition to resource capital and the state. As Peter Kulchyski suggested, "there is a sense that, perhaps for the first time, it may be possible to build a sustained mass movement in support of indigenous struggles in Canada" (44:2, March/April 2010). The Idle No More movement may be proving him correct.

Dimension also began to focus more than ever before on the environment, and particularly on the phenomenon of climate change. While economic crises, however severe, are cyclical, the climate crisis is cumulative with devastating losses assured should it surpass the frightful tipping points first exposed by climate scientist James Hanson. Unless there is a drastic diminution of the transfer of carbon from below ground to the atmosphere, planet earth will be made unlivable for billions of human beings as well as nonhuman animals.

Contrary to mainstream environmentalists, *Dimension* has maintained that the climate crisis cannot be fixed by changing business behaviour through market incentives, nor by technological breakthroughs or personal lifestyle changes. It arises from rising atmospheric carbon spawned by the relentless economic growth intrinsic to the capitalist system and driven by fossil fuels — oil, natural gas and coal. Capitalism cannot accept limits on its growth any more than a person can cease to breathe, Joel Kovel wrote in *CD*, and therefore the climate crisis can be vanquished only by deep structural changes in the way production and distribution are organized and resources allocated. As Kovel declared in the lead article prior to the UN Climate Change Conference in Copenhagen (43:6, November/December 2009): "Basically, a simple choice looms. We can have either capitalism with no hope for the future, or get rid of capitalism and have a fighting chance for a future."

Kovel espoused a new paradigm that he called ecosocialism and *Canadian Dimension* was an early adopter. As he described it in *CD*, "ecosocialism incorporates all prefigurative practices whose common ground is the inhibition of the transfer of carbon from earth to sky, and that also work against the regime of accumulation. This would extend from struggles in the global South to block the life destroying extraction of petroleum from Indigenous lands, or the ravages of the 'Clean Development Mechanisms' imposed by Kyoto; to struggles in the global North against militarism and imperialism, alongside those that break the power of the energy, oil and automobile giants so that ecologically sane modes of transportation, energy production, etc., can arise" (41:6, November/December 2007).

A few years later, talking about the growing climate justice movement springing up on every continent around the time of Copenhagen, Kovel expanded on this theme: "We can build a movement of movements from below, harbingers of a transformed world — a movement to reveal the murderous betrayal of life by the capitalist class, and centred around the principle of keeping the sources of carbon in the ground as we build ecologically socialist ways of production" (43:6, November/December 2009).

The sequel to Copenhagen, the World People's Conference on Climate Change and the Rights of Mother Earth, brought over thirty-five thousand people to Cochabamba. As reported by *CD* collective member Terisa Turner who attended the gathering, this alliance of Indigenous groups, climate justice activists, trade unionists, socialists and sundry other fighters for social change may be the early sign of a global mass anticapitalist green movement (44:5, September/October 2010).

Of course, within broad environmental discourse, ecosocialism is only a minor current. Mainstream environmentalists are still wedded to market ecology and other business-friendly approaches to climate change, species loss and other processes of ecodisintegration. One important explanation in addition to their like-minded ideological dispositions was advanced by *Dimension* contributors Petr Cizek (40:4, July/August 2006) and Macdonald Stainsby (45:4, July/August 2011). All but a few mainstream environmental organizations are being funded by the world's biggest polluters. They had evidently decided to stop fighting against environmentalism and instead co-opt it. They have been establishing foundations that provide substantial funding for environmental organizations that join them in front groups and partnerships that greenwash their activities and policies and that promote shockingly timid policy prescriptions.

With a large roster of ecosocialist activists on its collective — Terisa Turner, Roger Rashi, Peter Kulchyski and Judy Deutsch (in addition to Andrea Levy who contributes a left biocentric perspective to the magazine) — CD is well equipped to remain at the forefront of the ecosocialist movement.

Looking back, looking ahead

So much has happened since *Canadian Dimension* was founded fifty years ago. Vietnam and a new anti-imperialist consciousness; a new identity for Canada as the northern resource-based extension of the American Empire; the ascent and the fall of the New Left; the collapse of Soviet-style communism and the disintegration of the Soviet Empire; neoliberalism and the attack on the welfare state; the globalization of corporate capitalism and the incorporation of China and the global South; feminism and the growing acceptance of gay and transgender rights; the discovery that the personal is political; the assault on nature and the looming crisis of climate change. In recent years we have seen the financialization of the capitalist economy; the doctrine of "humanitarian intervention," a cover for good old-fashioned imperialism right up there with "the white man's burden"; a revival of austerity fiscalism that shifts the burden of bank bailouts and other kinds of corporate welfare onto the working class; the emergence of Canada as a mining superpower in the global South and the rise of a militaristic Canadian state that has become "empire's ally" to the USA.

All these developments have been reflected and dissected in the pages of *Canadian Dimension*.

By all measures of commercial success CD should never have gotten off the ground let alone survived for fifty years: without political affiliation, corporate advertising, government grants or any source of funding other than from its readers, with a small readership and an unorthodox organizational structure. Renewal, commitment and loyalty have been the keys to *Dimension*'s endurance. Over the decades we have been able to attract exciting new writers and to retain and expand our readership. And with very limited advertising revenue and government grants, it has been our readers who have kept the magazine afloat with donated funds over and above the price of a sub. Further, despite paltry pay and limited hours we have managed to hire committed and capable staff.

One critical factor underlying *CD*'s endurance has been our independence, a factor underscored by Stan Gray in his contribution to the anniversary issue (47:2, March/April 2013):

> *No one has its hooks in* CD. *It stuck to its independence from the institutional vested interests on the Left, including the NDP and labour bureaucracy. It has not been afraid to criticize, very sharply at times.*

Bryan Palmer offered another explanation for *Canadian Dimension*'s endurance:

> *Canadian Dimension has not managed to change the world decisively — a rather tall order for one small publication in one particular corner of the globe — but it has provided a forum, especially in Canada, for those who are committed to this project to discuss what needs doing and how to do it. This necessarily involves debate, exchange, and, at times, heated disagreement. It entails sharing information, keeping old insights alive as well as being willing to entertain and learn from new ones, and refusing to succumb to the onslaught of hegemonic hype. For 50 years* Dimension *has been doing this and more.*

Through all the ups and downs, my commitment to radical politics and to this project of *Canadian Dimension* has rarely wavered. *CD* has been for me an unfailing vehicle for meeting exciting thinkers, exploring new ideas, confronting current developments, and developing the skills and the grit to survive in a tough industry on a tiny budget. As the founder of *CD* I was very pleased to have been able to celebrate its fiftieth birthday. Indeed, the spirited events in Winnipeg and Montreal marking the fiftieth, along with the publication of the special anniversary issue (47:2, March/April 2013), have given *Dimension* revived energy and renewed commitments. While I intend to continue to play a hand in planning and coordinating the magazine, this function is already being shared with other members of the *CD* collective. I have come to call upon one of these, Andrea Levy, for advice on just about all decisions I'm required to make. Andrea's superb editing skills are displayed in every issue of the magazine. I doubt very much that I could carry on in my role in *CD* without her assistance. As well, Andrea is responsible for connecting *CD* with like-minded comrades in Quebec, including Les nouveaux cahiers du socialisme, with whom we teamed up to organize and sponsor the People's University at the August 2014 People's Social Forum. With her involvement in both worlds she is enabling Quebec socialists and Canadian socialists to work together on a level unprecedented in our fifty-plus years.

My concluding note is this: Capitalism is crisis-prone, driving a relentless assault on nature and humankind. There has to be a better way, call it what you may, to organize ourselves and live together. I am convinced that magazines like *Canadian Dimension* are essential in charting that course.

PART II

NATIONAL DIMENSIONS

CHAPTER 2
Canada and the American Empire
Joseph Roberts

Independence is a priority for socialists because without it we cannot control our economy and our resources and our basic institutions to remake our society.

— Cy Gonick Editorial, "Liberal-izing Continentalism"
(7:4, October 1970)

The theme of Canadian identity permeates the contents of *Canadian Dimension* from start to present. Those responsible for the journal have continually sought strategy to build a movement, and a system of ideas to achieve an autonomous country, based on social solidarity, enjoying peaceful relations with the rest of the world. In the process the journal has brought to view over half a century a significant number of voices commenting on that important theme.

During the first three decades of its existence *CD* was a focal point of efforts to build strategic thinking toward a more explicit independence from the American leviathan. While the magazine continues to reflect that outlook with information and debate, it's fair to say that no major political formation has emerged to campaign on behalf of that inchoate popular sentiment.

For Europe, North America and Japan the sixties marked the high point of the post–World War II "golden age" of Keynesian economic prosperity, recovery from depression and war. That era had seen the establishment of US dominance in the capitalist world under the umbrella of the Bretton Woods Agreement enshrining US economic hegemony, and the North Atlantic Treaty Organization guaranteeing US-enforced cooperation of former European combatants mobilized under the banner of collective defence against declared Soviet aggression. The era also ushered in the beginning steps leading to European unification and stabilization of global hostilities between superpower leaders of communist and capitalist blocs.

But the sixties also saw national liberation revolts in the Third World, the rise of the civil rights movement in the US, the anti-Vietnam war movement and reinvigoration of the women's movement. All of this animated US politics with stimulating reverberations in Canada and Europe.

For the Left there was excitement over the Cuban Revolution and, more broadly, the turbulent anticolonial struggles in the Third World. Independent European imperialism was finished after the French military defeat at Dien Bien Phu, in North Africa and the failed intervention in the Suez Canal seizure. Such events ushered in a decade of youth-led "New Left" radicalism in the US, Canada, Quebec, Britain and Europe.

There was no radical periodical in English Canada in the early sixties. *Canadian Dimension* determined to provide such a vehicle, the likes of which had emerged after World War II in Europe, Britain and even in the United States.

The theme of US domination of Canada, its economy, its foreign policy and its culture played an important part in the original content. Of course, it loomed large in Canadian political awareness in the 1960s. The very first issue of *CD* (1:1-2, September/November 1963) featured an article about benefits and burdens of foreign investment, and, still in its first year (1:8, September/October 1964), the magazine chose as its theme "Is Canada Possible" with articles on the economy ("A Plan for a Canadian Owned Economy" by H.C. Pentland), on culture ("Canada's Cultural Void" by Neil Compton) and the labour movement ("Prospects for an Autonomous Labour Movement" by Ed Finn). An editorial on the 1965 federal election (2:6, September/October 1965) condemned the

113

Liberal Government's ". . . quiet step by step sell-out of Canadian sovereignty to the United States." It spoke of the "price to be paid for every special privilege the United States government bestows upon Canada."

The editorial listed four recent examples of Canadian policy capitulation to Washington. While governments worldwide condemned the US role in overthrowing the government of the Dominican Republic in 1963, Canada remained silent. Second, in its role on the three-member nation International Control Commission in Vietnam, Canada consistently rejected the majority position of India and Poland on responsibility for continuation of the war, while absolving the US of responsibility. The third sell-out was the exemption allowed *Time Magazine* and *Readers' Digest* from a Canadian law designed to promote domestic ownership of printed-word publications. But "the most outlandish sell-out" was Canadian acceptance of Bomarc nuclear missiles. The editorial acknowledged there were no easy solutions to the problem of economic and therefore political dependency on US domination, "but there are solutions and they are to be found in policies which aim at the gradual but radical change in the structure of the Canadian economy."

For the emerging character of *CD* and the debate in liberal and left opinion during the sixties, the discussion about nationalism initiated in 1969 by Gad Horowitz commanded greatest attention. For Horowitz the focus was on Canada's fading affiliation with Britain and the increasing bond with the United States in an era when that country consolidated its role as the dominant imperialist force in the world.

A national strategy for independence

Canada had ceased being a colony, in the conventional meaning, by stages beginning with Confederation and culminating in patriation of the *British North America Act* in 1982. But in 1963 the extent of American influence over Canadian defence policy was vividly displayed when Conservative Prime Minister Diefenbaker refused to arm American-supplied Bomarc missiles with nuclear warheads and American official criticism, echoed by Diefenbaker's own caucus, resulting in the fall of his government and loss of the ensuing election.

The concept Horowitz employed to galvanize the generally felt unease about the relation with the US was nationalism. He was aware that for some liberals and others on the Left the appeal to nationalism constituted a dangerous parochialism open to fruitless disputes and irrational populist digressions at best, and degeneration into right-wing political movements at worst. In his essay "On the Fear of Nationalism" (4:4, May/June 1967), Horowitz retorted that "this view is false because it is based on a model of nationalism which is not applicable in Canada. The nationalism that has bathed the world in blood is not the nationalism that seeks to prevent the integration of Canada into American society." Horowitz drew a distinction between the nationalism of expansionist great powers and the nationalism of small states trying to preserve some degree of independence.

In an editorial as early as 1970 (7:4, October/November), *CD* formulated the gist of its left nationalist position:

> *Foreign ownership is an issue in Canada only because Canadian capitalism is totally integrated into American capitalism, because the key decisions affecting Canada are not made in this country, but in the USA; because Canada has been made into a resource colony for American industry and a consumer market for American manufacturers. The fifty-one percent Canadian ownership formula [promoted by mainstream economic nationalists] will not change any of this. Canada would still remain a resource colony for the US, exporting jobs and importing finished goods; key decisions would still be made in private US boardrooms; there would be no less distortion between public goods and private goods, no less poverty or inequality; oppression of working men and women, students and farmers would not have diminished. Independence is a priority for socialists because without it we cannot control our economy and our resources and our basic institutions to remake our society.*

At the end of the 1960s a socialist faction developed within the New Democratic Party, whimsically calling itself a "Waffle" movement. It sought to restore the NDP as a vehicle for socialist change. The policy components of that movement included attempts to put forward a position on "the national question," to heal the enduring conflict between Quebecois and Anglo-Saxon identity and power. But more strategically, its nationalism focused on the economy. It advocated recovering control over the economy from the engulfing power of American corporate influence, asserting Canadian cultural preeminence in broadcasting and publishing, wresting control over labour unions from American internationals, and shaping resource development strategy based upon Canadian economic needs and prospects including recognition of wasting resources and environmental considerations. There was even the beginning of recognition of the long-ignored need to confront the internal colonialism of aboriginal apartheid. The whole of this platform had been developed in the pages of *Dimension*.

In the atmosphere of nationalism associated with the Waffle movement, *CD* carried a host of articles devoted to foreign ownership of the Canadian economy and responses to it. In 1971 (7:7, February/March) a series of essays entitled "Alienation of Canada's Resources" introduced by James Laxer, titular leader of the NDP Waffle faction, included individual analyses of worrisome developments in the Maritimes, British Columbia, Ontario, Manitoba and Saskatchewan, and articles on water, pollution and cities.

In 1972 (8:4-5, January) John Richards, a Saskatchewan MLA and activist in persuading the NDP government to create SaskOil, wrote "Plant Shutdown: Taking Over Imperial Oil." Economist Kari Levitt, author of the path-breaking book *Silent Surrender*, provided an argument for socialism advising going "Beyond Foreign Ownership" (8:6, March/April 1972). And Stephen Hymer, early scholar of the emerging multinational corporation phenomenon, wrote "The Multinational Corporation; Your Home is our Home" (8:6, March/April 1972).

In 1973 (9:7-8, Nov/Dec) Rob Dumont and John Warnock described "The ABCs of Oil," which provided an early consideration of the newly beckoning Athabasca tar sands. Larry Pratt (10:7, March 1975) provided further analysis in "Syncrude: the Canadian State as Agent of Foreign Corporations."

The discussion of imperialism, present at *Dimension*'s beginning as opposition to America's Vietnam War, gradually took on a more comprehensive and introspective dimension and acquired a more Marxian political economic analysis. Cy Gonick's "Metropolis/Hinterland Themes" (8:6, March/April 1972) was an early exploration of what was to become known as "The New Political Economy," a fusion of Marx, iconic Canadian economic historian Harold Innis, along with work by contemporary academics Andre Gunder Frank, Kari Levitt, Thomas Naylor, Mel Watkins, Wallace Clement and others. The New Political Economy aimed to discover the roots of Canada's unique position as a "rich dependent state" — importing US capital and exporting resources to the US market with a stunted manufacturing sector, mainly assembling products for the domestic market, developed and designed in the US. An even earlier article by Gonick, "The Political Economy of Canadian Independence" (4:4, May/June 1967), laid out the basis of what was to become a widely accepted explanation of the contradictory nature of the Canadian economy:

> *Canada is a small regional economy within the continental North American economy . . . [Its] function . . . is to supply staple commodities as substitutes for the increasingly depleted resources of the US American corporate ownership of Canadian resources and Canadian manufacturing industries guarantees and perpetuates this branch-plant regional economy: resource industry is developed to supply US industry with raw materials; manufacturing industry is developed to supply the limited domestic market. The so-called Staple Theory [first developed by Innis] which is commonly used to explain economic growth in Canada is really a pseudonym for a kind of imperial relationship.*
>
> *Trade ties and US ownership of Canadian industry are the twin components of branch plant regional economy . . . They are the leading links which integrate the two economies into one continental exchange network. It is important to recall that economic integration is inevitably*

accompanied by ideological integration and the major
vehicle for ideological integration is the multinational
corporation. For with American corporations come American
business methods, American trade unions, American
values, goals and tastes. As this infiltration pervades our
schools, universities, mass media, professions, trade unions,
offices and factories it draws us deeper and deeper into the
American system, destroying the will to be different.

As the Canadian economy became more and more a northern extension of the US economy, the Canadian business class saw its interests
bound up with promoting unlimited trade and investment ties and, in its
commercial trade and regulation policies, the Canadian state facilitated
that integration.

Gonick distinguished this analysis from what was being advanced by
nationalists of the Walter Gordon stripe who urged greater ownership
for Canadian corporate interests: "self-determination for Canada vis-a-
vis the US would be of little value if it merely involved the shifting of
effective decision-making from US corporate boardrooms to Canadian
boardrooms . . . Where economic power and through it political power
is concentrated in the hands of the few, *whether American or Canadian*,
the scope of real democracy is necessarily very limited" (4:4, May/June
1967). In any case, Canadian capitalists had no interest in leading, let
alone capacity to lead, the building of an east-west national economy.

Not quite all voices of the Left accepted this view of Canada with a
weak capitalist class and a dependency of the US with a truncated economic structure, overly reliant on resources for export while having to
rely on imports for virtually all its advanced technology products. An
early example of a diametrically opposing point of view was a short book
by two young Trotskyists, Steve Moore and Debi Wells, titled *Imperialism
and the National Question in Canada*. They argued that Canada was not
uniquely integrated to the US — no more so than European countries
— and that Canada was not at all a dependency of the US. On the contrary, Canada was itself a fully fledged imperialist power on par with
European imperialist countries like France, Britain, Germany and Japan

— with Canadian capitalists, backed by the Canadian state, engaging in independent imperialist action.

Shortly after its appearance, John Warnock wrote a detailed critique of this work in *Canadian Dimension* (11:4, March 1976). As he noted, the quality of this book did not warrant such a lengthy review: "It is poorly organized, repetitive, full of obvious distortions, errors and contradictions. There are inadequate and misleading statistics as well as major theoretical shortcomings." Nevertheless Warnock, a prodigious researcher and serious scholar spent page after *Dimension* page subjecting this work to the most thorough review it would ever receive. Why? "Despite these serious shortcomings, it is the only substantive publication by any of the anti-nationalists on the Left in Canada. For that reason it should be analyzed rather than simply dismissed." Interestingly and importantly, this perspective, however inadequate and badly presented in this treatment, did not disappear. Twenty-five years later it surfaced again, sometimes repeating the same faulty methodology but, on the whole, argued in a much more sophisticated manner. This time it would be Cy Gonick that refuted its conclusions — while at the same time conceding that Canadian capitalism had matured over this period and that in a few sectors Canadian corporations had emerged as global players (40:6, November/December 2006).

The free trade battle

During the decade 1984 to 1994 a battle raged to stop both free-trade agreements and, once they were adopted, to "scrap the deal." The campaign was the last in an era of nationalist resurgence that had begun in the 1950s during the administration of John Diefenbaker. The campaign marshalled forces of centre and left political opinion organized nationally in action groups such as Pro-Canada Network, Council of Canadians, The National Action Committee on the Status of Women, The National Farmers Union, GATT-Fly, Citizens Concerned about Free Trade and in many local organizations. In this decade *CD* was the leading vehicle of analysis and debate, developing a strategy of opposition to Canadian governmental policy covering all aspects of trade — historically the defining strategy of Canadian development.

As the push toward a continentalist agreement gained momentum CD produced a plethora of articles examining the likely consequences of such an agreement with the US. In "Free Trade: The Real Agenda" (20:5, September/October 1986), Fred Gudmundson wrote: "What excites the Tories is that by eliminating tariff barriers they'll ultimately eliminate non-tariff barriers, including much of the progressive legislation won by women, workers, farmers and other groups over the last half century . . . Non-tariff barriers — marketing boards, social programs, sound labour practices, cultural programs, regional development programs may not be on the bargaining table, but they'll be cut anyway, by us, as part of the 'harmonization' process of matching the competition so as to attract capital and keep our jobs."

With the campaign against the Free Trade Agreement gaining momentum in 1987 CD produced a comprehensive review of what the proposal said and implied for many sectors of Canadian society. In "The Free Trade Agreement; What it Says And What It Means" (21:6, October 1987), several authors contributed pieces covering the binding dispute settlement mechanism, the idea of harmonizing social and economic policies, governance of investment, liberalization of financial services, culture, energy, automobile production, trade in services, jobs, prices, forest products, fisheries, and agriculture.

In "Culture and Free Trade" (21:5, September 1987), the text of a speech given at the Manitoba Legislature, Rick Salutin argued "If anyone wants to know what the effects of a free trade deal with the United States are likely to be — the best possible test case is the area of culture. We have had virtual free trade in culture for most of our history. The result is that culture in Canada is more or less an alternative culture. Mainstream culture in English Canada is and always has been dominated by either Britain or the United States."

"Free trade is not about Trade" is the title of a useful article by Sid Shniad (36:3, May/June 2002) examining the spate of agreements that come under the name "free trade." Sid Shniad revealed that these agreements were much more than about trade. By permitting corporations to sue governments they believe have passed laws or regulations that in any way limit their profits, they severely constrain governments' ability to regulate corporate behavior, let alone establish government-run businesses or social services. Any government that pursues policies that conflict with corporate priorities faces the threat of massive legal suits or international trade sanctions. Corporate rights take precedence over citizen rights. Further, in a special clause uniquely imposed on this country, Canada is prohibited from restricting exports of energy to the US no matter what effect that might have on its ability to serve domestic needs.

Despite sharp public opposition Prime Minister Mulroney and President Reagan signed an agreement on January 2, 1988, to conclude a free-trade agreement. In its first issue that year (22:1, February) *CD* discussed strategies for seeking abrogation of the agreement. Most significantly it endorsed a declaration entitled *A Time to Stand Together, A Time for Social Solidarity* issued in the fall of 1987 and endorsed by "most major union, church, women's, farm, anti-poverty and aboriginal organizations." Mobilization of popular opposition rather than simply relying on parliamentary parties was the preferred course of resistance.

Despite spontaneous and organized public opposition, it became evident even before the trade deal was enacted that the campaign was deficient. In the heat of the anti–free trade campaign, Greg Albo and Donald Swartz argued that the alternative to free trade promoted by the Council of Canadians and other opponents amounted to little more than a defense of post-WWII industrial and employment policies that had failed to produce anything like full employment and income security, let alone reducing class, gender and regional inequalities. Meanwhile, the proponents of free trade were speaking to the widespread understanding that the old recipes for managing the economy hadn't been working and that changes were necessary. "There is no escaping the need to restructure the opposition to free trade around a more clearly anticapitalist pole," they argued. "A less export oriented, more self-sufficient Canada in a more diversified and democratically controlled economy" was the basis of the alternative to free trade they espoused. Pulling the campaign left in this manner could not happen, however, so long as the campaign strategy aimed to avoid "class polarization" including confrontation with business (21:5, September 1987). That same issue of *CD* included an essay by GATT-Fly, a global justice project of Canadian churches. Titled "Building

Self-Reliance," it outlined the principles of a more self-sufficient economy and offered a concrete picture of what it would look like.

Appealling for support from Canadian business was futile, Leo Panitch argued in a follow-up article (22:4, June 1988) entitled "The Only Way Out of the American Empire":

> The monolithic support that spokespeople for Canadian business have given this deal is remarkable indeed. And what it demonstrates is that the attempts by previous governments to address our dependency — from the Gray report, to the establishments of the Foreign Investment Review Agency, to tax breaks for investing in Canadian films, to the national Energy Program — failed to achieve their main purpose of encouraging the development of a national bourgeoisie in this country. A national bourgeoisie is one that takes as its goal the accumulation of capital with a distinctive Canadian polity, economy and culture as its base. What the Free Trade deal shows above all is that any attempt to develop a strategy for national independence that relies on inducing Canadian capitalists to become nationalists must fail. Without such a national bourgeoisie, no capitalist society or political regime can escape dependency.

Panitch went further, saying there could be no substantive independence for Canada without socialism and no socialism without independence, repeating the formula expressed in the "Waffle" manifesto of 1969.

The North American Free Trade Agreement of 1992 crowned the achievements of the Mulroney Conservative regime. CD responded by trying to organize a movement to "Scrap the Deal." But the tide had turned. By 1990 the neo-liberal rationale had become hegemonic in political economic discourse.

Since the terrorist attack in Manhattan of 2001, not only foreign policy but much else in the nature of Canadian state structure, policy and economic processes have undergone refinement and reorientation to accommodate to American requirements to create "Fortress North America." These adjustments and processes were catalogued in Greg Albo's comprehensive *CD* article "Canada and World Order after the Wreckage" (41:2, March/April 2007), and have since been extended in such events as the "Beyond Borders Agreement" signed by Prime Minister Harper and President Obama in December 2011:

> *Since the 1980s, the Canadian state and ruling classes have pulled Canada closer into the U.S. sphere, symbolized initially by the spineless decision of the Trudeau government to allow cruise missile testing in Canada. Since then, Canada has given consistent support, in the form of peace-keeping operations or military deployments, to US military and diplomatic interventions— as in Somalia, Haiti, and elsewhere. Canada has also played a pivotal role in the "quartet" of countries setting the SWTO trade agenda, and as the staunchest supporter of U.S. policies towards Latin America.*
>
> *While the Chrétien Liberals kept Canada out of the Iraq war, they also contributed to making Canada the third largest participant in the American "War on Terror" since September 2001. The subsequent joint Smart Borders Agreement and the triparte North American Security and Prosperity Partnership further integrated Canada into American geopolitical strategies. Together, these measures have all but dissolved whatever independence Canadian foreign policy had once exercised (41:2, March/April 2007).*

CD's editorial, "The Final Takeover" (41:5, September/October 2007), addressed the subject of the Montebello, Quebec, conference between US president G.W. Bush, Mexican president Felipe Calderon and Canadian Prime Minister, Stephen Harper. This meeting ratified the Security and Prosperity Partnership of North America (SPP). Under the post-9/11 priority of security the US imposed nontariff barriers against select imports from Canada and Mexico and pressed these governments to align their policies and regulations with those of the USA. The editorial declared that to these impositions "the response of both Canadian and Mexican governments has been to beg the Americans for more of the same — offering up more and more of their sovereignty in exchange for illusory trade benefits, which always seem to be just around the next corner."

These developments led Cy Gonick to return to the question "Is Canada an Imperialist State?" (40:6, November/December 2006). Reviewing the changes in the state of our economic dependency on the US as reflected in various statistics of ownership and trade flows, the editor observed, "The degree of Canada's integration with the US remains unique in the world." Over a half century since the founding of *Canadian Dimension*, there has not been a decisive change in the structure of the economy and extent of that economic integration. While there had been some progress in moving away from being an economy based on resource extraction, in the past decade the economy has reverted back towards being staples-driven. In a 2012 report prepared for the Centre for Policy Alternatives, economist Jim Stanford points out that "in July 2011 unprocessed and semi-processed resource exports accounted for two-thirds of Canada's total exports, the highest in decades."[1]

Of course, there have been some extensive changes since 1963. Canadian capitalists have been far more resilient than many anticipated. Canada is still the recipient of a large amount of US direct investment though significant amounts are now flowing the other way. Yet, while US capital remains dominant in a number of Canadian industries, Canadian capital in the US is of marginal importance by comparison. Since the signing of the free-trade agreement, Canada is even more dependent on exports to the US, exports remain disproportionally resource-based and Canada is still dependent on the US for advanced technology and for high-tech manufactured goods. Though most Canadian foreign investment is located in the US and secondarily in Europe, Gonick conceded that in recent years there has also been significant Third World investment activity, especially in mining. But "imperialism loses its meaning if it is simply read as instances of foreign investment . . . Imperialism must also be seen as a form of extended political rule, even though rule may be of an informal type, as has been typical of American imperialism

. . . To date, Canada does not possess the military and diplomatic levers to protect the investments of its multinational corporations [operating abroad]." It is true Canada has exercised increasing military collaboration with US military aggression — mainly as "part payment of Canada's dues to maintain our good standing in the American empire — something our leaders thought they might have lost for refusing to join with the US invasion of Iraq."

"So, finally, is Canada an imperialist state? Yes," says Gonick, "but only as a second-tier member of US-led collective imperialism. The American empire works through other states, including the Canadian state, and in this sense the Canadian state is complicit in imperialism and Canadian capital certainly benefits from imperialism."

Plainly "Canada does not have the capacity to act as an independent imperial power." On the other hand, "If . . . Stephen Harper's Conservatives continue to expand our military machine, it is plainly possible that Canada's role could evolve into something like that of Uncle Sam's deputy sheriff" (40:6, November/December 2006). That 2006 hypothetical by 2011 became a concrete reality with Canadian military action to bring down the Ghadaffy regime in Libya.

Foreign policy

Themes of opposition to Canadian participation in cold war political/military strategy, autonomy in international relations and aversion to the collaboration of Canadian politicians in the imperialism of the US informed *Canadian Dimension* policy throughout its existence. Throughout the sixties and into the seventies scarcely an issue of *CD* lacked comment on the Vietnam War, on diplomatic and foreign policy information and analysis.

Back in the second issue of the magazine (1:3, December/January 1963–64), C.B. Macpherson, the internationally respected scholar of the theory of political liberalism, wrote a lengthy article, "Beyond the Nuclear Arms Issue," proposing a foreign policy for Canada as a contribution to peace, independent of American Cold War strategy. Considering the consequences of military use of nuclear weapons by the US and Russia, he said, "it follows that every country which still has some choice in its foreign and defense policy should direct its policy toward counteracting those beliefs [regarding the aggressive intentions of one another by the US and Russia] and diminishing world tensions and increasing the possibility of general disarmament."

At the time, when the overwhelming volume of North American published utterance on the cold war rationalized US foreign/military policy and demonized the USSR/communism, Macpherson's article was a careful, balanced, realistic analysis and outline of the steps the Canadian Government might take to exercise a peaceful influence in the Western community. Specifically he proposed a "general line of policy" which stressed the importance of maintaining a clear independence of US policy to increase Canadian influence and promote multilateral disarmament. Lessening tensions, he argued, and raising the prospects for disarmament would be helped by the existence of nonaligned nations and by increased Canadian aid to underdeveloped countries. The best course would be for Canada to withdraw from NATO. But, since that was unlikely, Canada should play a non-nuclear role in NATO and remain within the organization if the US should take some new initiative breaking the disarmament negotiations stalemate.

Macpherson's policy line would remain CD's for the next fifty years. For example, in 1987 (21:3, May/June), Leo Panitch picked up the issue of NATO once again. In "The NDP and NATO" he said "[t]here is nothing more dramatic or useful that Canada could do . . . than to leave NATO and NORAD while developing a fully independent . . . stance towards US as well as Soviet policy. Canadians may well be ready, if not yet for a political move toward democratic socialism, then at least for assenting to a strategy for achieving an independent international role which would allow us to be a far more effective force for peace than we can possibly be within the military framework of the United States empire."

Direct Canadian involvement was avoided in such overt US interventions as Cuba, Guatemala, Dominican Republic, Nicaragua and Grenada. Refusal to join in prosecution of the Vietnam War and cautious provision of haven for American war resisters helped preserve the domestic ideal of Canada as an "honest broker." But Canadian diplomatic support was never denied the US in the United Nations and Canadian armaments industries prospered in supplying the US military. This ambiguous and self-deceptive semi-avoidance of direct involvement in the most flagrant expressions of US imperialism was corrosive of national values and practices. As a result, when the Cold War ended and US global dominance could no longer be rationalized as protecting the world from Soviet aggression, it became easier for more right-wing forces in both Liberal and Conservative governments to take active, unambiguous roles in the Afghanistan debacle and the Iraq War, and then a leading role in the NATO intervention in the 2011 Libyan civil war, as well as aggressive posturing in support of Israel and against Iran.

By 1975, with the Vietnam War concluded in American defeat, *CD* carried fewer articles on foreign policy. However, in 1977 (12:1, January) *CD* devoted an entire issue to Southern Africa, a realm of conflict and imperialism virtually invisible to Canada. Among the most notable articles in that issue, "Canada and Southern Africa" by John Saul, provided a lengthy catalogue of official hypocrisy: Throughout the crucial era of decolonization in the region, emerging countries were everywhere awash in violence. Official Canadian diplomacy condemned the white minority regimes while denying aid to the liberation forces. At the same time a blind eye was turned to the Canadian mining and trading corporations conducting business as usual with the target regimes. Often that included a range of diplomatic and trading benefits extended by Canada to those corporations profiting in the midst of open liberation struggle against an *ancien regime*.

Saul concluded, "a great deal of self-education about Southern Africa — the present issue of *Canadian Dimension* representing one important contribution to that process — will be necessary if the Canadian Left is to realize the latter goal [of helping the growing number of left sympathizers sort through the complexities], and succeed in staying the Canadian government from doing the worst that it might otherwise do in Southern Africa in the continued service of 'Western Interests'."

In "US: Get Out of Grenada!" (17:6, December 1983), after a sketchy description of the limited information about the cause of the invasion and its effects in smashing the socialist New Jewel Movement, this *CD* editorial focused on the post-invasion role, urging that no Canadian troops or police participate in the pacification process. It went on to locate the US aggression in Grenada within the wider intrusion in the Caribbean and Central America. "Those of us who believed that Vietnam taught US imperialism a lesson must not be complacent . . . 'Vietnamization' of Central America is firmly underway. Fresh blood is being shed daily in Nicaragua, as an army of Honduran-based contras numbering an estimated 8,000–10,000, carry out their bloody work."

Throughout the eight-year Reagan regime in the United States *CD* campaigned against the reignition of Cold War militarism. Ernie Regehr documented "The Military Industry in Canada: Street Vendor to the Global Arms Marathon" (19:4, September/October 1985), and "Holding Hands with the Nuclear Monsters: Canadian Complicity with Reagan's Strategy" (21:7, November/December 1987). Regehr concluded that "there is in Canada a substantial military production capacity that is dependent upon decisions made in the Pentagon. For the Pentagon to continue making the 'right' decisions for that industry, Canada must demonstrate a general demeanour of co-operation and solidarity with US military initiatives. The result is that there is both a conscious and unconscious predisposition against independent Canadian initiatives that directly challenge US policies and interests." At the same time, "in an effort to reduce reliance on the Pentagon, Canadian firms and their government agents are anxious to break into new markets. These are largely in the third world and almost inevitably lead to choices between sales and human rights, with growing pressures to downplay the latter."

Twenty-four years later Richard Sanders, coordinator of the Coalition to Oppose the Arms Trade, was giving a detailed description of Canadian military exporters that equip US weapons systems used in Gaza, Iraq, Afghanistan and elsewhere. He reported that the Canadian Association of Defence and Security Industries, an organization representing 540 military companies and heavily subsidized by the federal government, organized a "mission" in 2004 to advance partnerships between Canadian and Israeli military companies (43:3, May/June 2009).

In 1990 *CD* published a powerful indictment of Canadian complicity in the tragedy of East Timor by Elaine Briere and Dan Devaney, "Canada — Partner in Genocide. East Timor: the Slaughter of a Tribal

Nation" (24:7, October). The authors stated that "Canada is among the top 5 foreign investors in Indonesia, which includes 300 Canadian companies looking for cheap labour without the problems of unions — banned in Indonesia." Further, they detailed CIDA funding intended for East Timorese but channelled through the Indonesian central government, Canadian military sales to Indonesia to be used against the East Timorese, university contracts, multinational corporate development funding ultimately benefiting the central government in its repression campaign. Their conclusion was that in adopting the position that "the Indonesian takeover, although unfortunate, is a 'fait accompli' . . . Canada plays a major role in sabotaging the right of the Timorese to a nation of their own."

As President Bush prepared for the first war against Iraq, *CD's* editorial "Bring the Troops Home" (25:1 January/February 1991), identified "the hypocrisy too blatant to be overlooked" — Saddam was to be punished for invading Kuwait while the US goes unpunished for aggression against Grenada, Panama and Nicaragua; Hussein is punished while US ally Israel violently occupies the West Bank and Gaza. Meanwhile "Canada tags along faithfully beating the American war drum, while conveniently ignoring both our opposition to self-determination for East Timor, and Indonesia's massive human rights abuses in that country."

Haiti claimed increasing attention. In 2004 Canada joined with French and American forces to oust democratically elected Jean Bertrand Aristide. Since that time Canadian troops, police and aid agencies have participated in the manipulation of politics of that poorest of hemispheric countries. A *CD* editorial "Haiti — The Job of Nations" (44:2, March/April 2010) noted that after participating in the kidnapping of Aristide, Canada provided financing as well as diplomatic and "security" support to the installed government of Gerard Latortue, who was carrying out illegal mass detentions, numerous disappearances and summary executions of Aristide supporters.

In two separate editorials appearing in 2006, *CD* summarized Canada's more aggressive militaristic role in world affairs. In "Canada Out of Afghanistan and Haiti" the editors declared:

Currently Canada is participating in two operations — in Afghanistan and Haiti — that have absolutely nothing to do with peacekeeping, despite the repeated use of the word to describe these operations . . . Whatever the Canadian government's motive in committing Canadian troops to these military actions, the fact remains that in doing so, a decades-long policy of non-participation in aggressive combat actions by Canadian forces has been overturned without even the nicety of a debate in Parliament, let alone a real discussion by Canadians.

Afghans and Haitians do not differentiate between American and Canadian occupiers. Nor is there any reason to. Canada's involvement in the occupation of Afghanistan and Haiti serves no worthwhile purpose. It only commits Canada as an active participant in the imperialist system known as the American Empire. (40:3, May/June 2006)

In "Imperial Agendas: The New Canadian Militarism," the editors explained:

The 9/11 events gave the U.S. state the opportunity to openly declare a new set of security doctrines, extending its overseas military capabilities to secure oil supply routes in the Middle East and Asia. It views Canada's energy resources in the same way. Tightly linked with the Calgary oil crowd, the Harper Tories are acutely aware that their role in the new international order is to keep feeding the ravenous U.S. war machine, and their foreign policy reflects this view (40:6, November/December 2006).

Continuing its historical role of galvanizing those who actively commit to a Canadian tradition of peace this editorial urged "building a peace movement and mobilizing popular forces against American imperialism and Canada's new militarism must be given first priority in the months ahead." It identified trade union involvement, the Israel boycott, disinvestment and sanctions campaign, union, university and church pension fund investment policies as targets in a fightback campaign.

In "Empire's Ally: Canadian Foreign Policy" (40:6, November/December 2006) Greg Albo showed how the Canadian state was thoroughly reorganized and redesigned with greatly enhanced military and security capacities to keep pace with post-9/11 US priorities. These changes bolstered Harper's goal of deeper integration with the US. Albo contended that "defense of the general economic interests of Canadian capital, which [now] necessarily includes the American capital invested in Canada and Canadian investment in the U.S., has recast the entire foreign policy apparatus of the Canadian state . . . Harper has pushed even more strongly [than Paul Martin] . . . defining Canadian foreign policy interests as tied to U.S. security concerns and imperial agendas to ensure Canadian capitalists' access to U.S. markets for their goods and capital."

As if to echo Albo's *CD* article, *Globe and Mail* columnist Lawrence Martin declared:

> *Rarely, if ever, has a country's image been altered so much so quickly. Under the Conservatives, Canada is a country that venerates the military, boasts a hardened law-and-order and penal system, is anti-union and less green. It's a government that extols, without qualms of colonial linkage, the monarchy, that has a more restrictive entry policy, that takes a narrow view of multiculturalism, that pursues an adversarial approach to the United Nations. In a first, Canada's foreign policy, its strident partnership in the Middle East being a foremost example, can be said to be to the right of the United States.[2]*

Conclusion

Cy Gonick's conclusion in his article "Is Canada an Imperialist State?" (40:6, November/December 2006) underlines the ancient principle that foreign policy is an extension of national domestic policy. "[T]he drift of Canadian politics toward an imperialism-complicit posture is one upshot of the loss of the kind of Canadian-centred political economy we were attempting to build in the 1970s. It also highlights how the current drift toward militarism pulls us away from the kind of internationalism most Canadians cherish."

The primacy of security criteria has made it more untenable for the small, independent space for foreign policy that Canada had opened for itself during the post–World War II period. In that era Canada projected itself as a middle-range power seeking to work through the United Nations. Canada had sought, as an American ally, to emphasize cooperative negotiations for security among capitalist powers and fostering international positions with Third World countries. That view of Canadian foreign policy is over.

Canadian Dimension's focus on national independence, foreign policy and relations with the United States during the past fifty years has remained remarkably consistent. From its beginning the argument has been that Canada is vulnerable to the elephantine proximity of the US. Governed by two dominant political parties that primarily express the interests of a class of capital aligned with evolving American imperialism, Canada is pulled ever deeper into the vortex of economic, political and military subordination. Public opinion polls and articles, editorials, opinion columns, and letters-to-the-editor of major newspapers today reflect much of the critique to be found in *Canadian Dimension*. *CD*, for all its continuity is anything but irrelevant — but it has yet to ignite a sustained broad national movement for independence and socialism.

CHAPTER 3
Balancing the Claims of Nation and of Class: Fifty Years of Covering Quebec

Peter Graefe

For who among us has not argued the right of Quebec to self-determination, and how many of us have not taken the next logical tsep [sic] supporting the case for an independent Quebec (hopefully socialist, but we are realistic enough to recognize this as unlikely, at least initially) side by side with an independent English Canada (hopefully socialist).

— Philip Resnick, *"Strategy and its Discontents"* (10:7, Mar 1975)

Building an effective Left in a multinational state requires spaces of dialogue and exchange, but these are hard to sustain when the logic of national autonomy pushes towards doing things separately. The pages of *Canadian Dimension* captured failures of the classic left organizations to do so, detailing the inability of the new NDP of the 1960s to catch the wave of Quebec's Quiet Revolution in the 1960s, and the splits between the Fédération des travailleurs et travailleuses du Québec (FTQ) and the Canadian Labour Congress leadership in the 1970s. But to what extent has *Canadian Dimension* itself served as a meeting place for independent socialists in Canada? It has played the crucial role in providing a platform for the open presentation of the views of left currents in Quebec, despite the discomfort such views create for many on the Canadian Left who have embraced a fairly unreflective Canadian nationalism.

Fifty years after its founding, *CD* continues a proud tradition of non-ethnocentric coverage of Quebec politics, but some strategic limitations persist: *CD* seems to have catalogued parallel social projects which have but rarely considered how, by being crossed strategically, they might spark some new possibilities for social change.

Promising beginnings

Canadian Dimension started publishing just as the Quiet Revolution was taking shape in Quebec, and when the political situation was highly in flux. It captured the development of a new nationalism in those years, and the rapid shift of this nationalism towards a fundamental restructuring of the Canadian federation. In 1964, the question was whether the shiny new NDP, formed in part to appeal to Quebec voters, could find the magic recipe on the constitutional question so as to permit the founding of a provincial party. This no doubt reflects in part the presence of Charles Taylor on the board in the magazine's first couple of years, and his own attempts to square this circle for the NDP. Only three years later, Taylor was still trying to square this circle for the NDP, but *Canadian Dimension* had come to entertain what was then a fairly controversial support for a new Canadian union.

The ability of *CD* to quickly arrive at a defensible position on the national question that parsed Quebec nationalist rhetoric without falling into anglo-Canadian ethnocentrism is remarkable. By 1967, just as Lévesque was putting together the forerunner of the Parti Québécois, the main outlines of the *Canadian Dimension* analysis of Quebec were taking form. These were shaped by an engagement with thinkers on imperialism, such as at *Dimension*'s 1967 conference in Montreal on "Canada and the American Empire." The magazine's position caught something fundamental about Quebec nationalism and the Canadian political community, and in many ways remains the guiding premise of its analysis of the Quebec situation to this day.

The magazine's line crystallized in 1968, with editorials on "The Canadian Union" (5:2-3, January/March 1968) and "English-Canada and Special Status" (5:5, June/July 1968): Strengthening the central government would push Quebec out of Confederation "unless we restructure the federal framework by giving Quebec a special status."

It is worth noting that this position was largely based on the conviction that English-Canada (as it was then called in the magazine) needed to be more centralized in order to deal with pressing issues of economic and social development and to resist the pressures of continentalization. From there, the continued refusal of Quebecers to melt into such a centralizing project, coupled with *CD*'s respect for self-determination (for Cameron Nish, "pan-Canadianism is the modern rendition of assimilation" (6:2, July 1969), led to an openness to considering complex solutions that today we might call multinationalism. As Gonick wrote in January 1968 (5:2-3, January/March 1968), "English Canada needs Quebec, even an 'independent' Quebec, in our own struggle for national survival."

That this accommodation was fairly utilitarian also had its purposes: rather than ascribe Quebec nationalism with some sort of transcendent historical purpose of bringing socialist change (or, more modestly, wide-ranging social justice), it allowed both a critical analysis of that nationalism and continued conversations with the Quebec Left. In other words, one could accept the legitimacy of Quebec's national demands, particularly as their recognition might speed a centralization in the rest of the country, even while criticizing Quebec's nationalist movement for being insufficiently socialist and anti-imperialist. Or, to take the words of a contributor like Gad Horowitz, national recognition could spark a creative politics of left versus right both in Canada and in Quebec, or as the Waffle Manifesto had it, "two nations, one struggle."

This view came out in Gonick's remarkable piece, "Conversations with René Lévesque" (5:2-3, January/March 1968). Even before the PQ was launched, Gonick captured Lévesque's common appeal and lack of politician skills, but even more so the extent to which what was to become the dominant strand of Quebec nationalism was hobbled by its continentalism. Thus, its limited horizons in terms of challenging American imperialism, leading Gonick to note that Lévesque could only see Quebec as another Finland, and that Lévesque "may despise Ontario, but he really wants Quebec to emulate that province." Or as Jean-Guy Loranger concluded in May 1971 (6:8, April/May 1970), Lévesque's strategy would mean "Canadian vassalage to Washington would be divided into two American sub-vassalages, rival or complementary."

This stance was controversial, and *CD* opened its pages to divergent viewpoints. Some were wary of any entanglement with Quebec nationalism, which a young Julius Grey seemed willing to tar with the brush of fascism. For others, it was politically unsalable. Michel Chartrand criticized the Waffle for pushing the NDP on the two-nations question: "You don't ask the master to break the chains for the slave. And, meanwhile, you're hurting the chances for building socialism in English Canada by worrying about us" (7:8, April 1971).

Perhaps the most provocative critique was Stan Gray's "The Battle of Quebec," (6:6 December/January 1969–70) which painted Quebec as on the verge of revolution given the increasing fusion of nationalist and class demands and organization. When the magazine raised critical questions about the real reach of such sentiment, Gray wrote angrily, "your attitudes and articles on Quebec are uninformed, usually reactionary and typical of hypocritical English Canadian misunderstanding and smugness" (6:8 April/May 1970). Three decades later, *CD* would name Stan Gray "Canada's greatest shit disturber." But in the moment, it accepted Gray's resignation and stuck to its position: national oppression was an important issue, but did not make national movements bearers of socialism in and of themselves.

The magazine's cautious realism may have displeased some looking for fiery analysis, but it would be difficult to treat the response to the 1970 October crisis as anything but brave (7:5-6, December 1970). Filled with stories trying to make sense of both the particularities of the situation of Quebec, but of political violence and its uses more broadly, it included interviews with individuals with ties to the felquistes, such as Charles Gagnon and FLQ lawyer Robert Lemieux, as well as left activists such as Michel Chartrand. For someone born after the events, the interviews and stories present a far more ambiguous sense of how the Quebec Left viewed the FLQ and violence than is usually retold in the present. They also show a more critical take on the Montreal municipal FRAP party as an elite debating society as opposed to a vehicle for organizing the working class, than tends to be aired today.

As *CD* moved into the 1970s, then, it could proudly look to a defensible position on the national question and an admirable willingness to publish critiques in its pages. This open position allowed the magazine to remain on the cutting edge of developing political questions in Quebec, be it Harvey Feit's exposé of Hydro Quebec's James Bay development plans and the Cree response (8:8, August 1972), or analyses of political divisions within the CSN and FTQ over political strategy, including linkages with the Parti Quebecois (e.g., Lizée in 10:1, April 1974 or Lipsig in 9:1, 1973).

The PQ, the referendums, and the constitutional interlude

The *CD* position on the national question was first phrased in a programmatic context: what sort of relations between nations would be appropriate in building a socialist Canada? The advances of nationalism in Quebec, the strengthening of the Parti Québécois, and Trudeau's interest in constitutional change all signalled that ideas like "self-determination" would need to be concretized in tricky political situations that did not always hold clear promise for socialist progress. As Henry Milner pointed out (13:6, March 1979), "no political analysis is possible if based on the premise of supporting only that which will overthrow capitalism," but that held the corollary of needing to choose between nonrevolutionary options.

As a result, a good deal of attention in the late 1970s was given to discerning the class character of the Parti Québécois, so as to inform a proper referendum strategy for the Canadian Left. This included both more general and theoretical reflections, such as Gilles Bourque's class analysis of the PQ (13:1, 1978), and specific analyses of how the post-1976 Lévesque government related to the labour movement (e.g., Pauline Vaillancourt on changes to the Labour Code, 12:6 and 12:8, 1977) and the women's movement (e.g., Stephen Schecter interviews Léa Cousineau, 13:1, 1978). Whether the PQ ultimately was a petty-bourgeois party, or instead was the vehicle for a Quebec bourgeoisie to renegotiate its place under American imperialism, the general thrust of analyses was that the PQ retained an openness to the Left as it sought to construct a coalition for the referendum. While this attempt to hegemonize the broader Left was problematic, it also opened possibilities for radical projects in a sovereign Quebec.

This led *CD* to embrace a form of "critical yes" as its referendum stance. In July 1977 (12:3), Philip Resnick had pushed for a strong prosovereignty stance on the grounds that it would allow English Canada to work out its own sense of nationhood. Cy Gonick agreed that the push for "national unity" was "the particular expression of bourgeois nationalism adopted by the ruling class of Canada to dampen class struggle and discourage class polarization," but remained worried that this might lead to decentralization in English Canada, weakening the capacity to resist American imperialism.

By March 1979 (13:6), this crystallized into a referendum strategy. Making the point that as early as 1965 *CD* had held the view that the national question needed to be cleared up so as to get to class politics, Fred Gudmundson and Cy Gonick argued for the yes. However, this was not an unconditional yes, which was seen as foolish because it meant surrendering any bargaining leverage. Instead, what was required was an autonomous campaign that went beyond the PQ and started to organize people for struggles after the referendum. This nevertheless was a bit vague.

CD's stronger register for the 1980s referendum was instead that of the right to self-determination, which came out strongly in its June 1980 (14:7) editorial against the "People to People" campaign. The editorial was skeptical that separation would end the exploitation of the working class, and noted the interests of Quebec capitalists in separation, but concluded, "we believe that there are genuine broadly-based national aspirations in Quebec that should be allowed free expression."

The post-referendum post-mortem of August 1980 (14:8) suggests why self-determination was *CD*'s stronger suit. When Leo Panitch and Philip Resnick suggested that a "yes" would have been good for the English Canadian working class, Pauline Vaillancourt noted that this argument was not really made during the referendum. Perhaps it was not made because it spoke to a somewhat mythical sense of solidarity, where the separate development of the working classes instead made a form of respectful parallelism the most realistic option. Indeed, Panitch concluded, "in the last two decades of the 20th century, we are not going to achieve solidarity between the two working classes themselves. We have to look to building the solidarity of the Quebec working class in Quebec and of the English working class in English Canada."

Post-referendum, *CD*'s coverage focused heavily on PQ-labour movement tensions, as the recession pushed the PQ to break public sector contracts and impose draconian penalties on the teachers who defied the legislation. There are also glimmers of recomposition within the Left, with coverage of the implosion of the Marxist-Leninist parties and the internal battles within the CSN. Throughout these articles, a couple of themes are repeated: first, a recognition that demands for women's equality needed to be given more space and prominence, and second, that unions had to do more to develop community alliances. The patriation of the Canadian Constitution without Quebec's consent received relatively slight mention, although Pauline Vaillancourt captured how union-PQ tensions affected mobilization against Trudeau's machinations (15:5, April 1981), and how the Mouvement socialiste saw the PQ's participation in the negotiations as further sign that its "aim was to preserve the autonomy and rights of the fledgling Quebec bourgeoisie" even at the cost of legitimating "the whole undemocratic process" (16:3, May 1982).

Following the patriation of the Constitution in 1982 and the defeat of the PQ in the 1985 Quebec election, there were a series of reflections on the future of the nationalist and separatist movements in those years. The conclusions were cautious. Certainly, the PQ was in decline, in part because of its success in reducing visible discrimination, and in part due to disunity in its coalition (Vaillancourt, 18:5, October/November 1984; Sher, 19:5, December 1985; Molnar and Slater, 20:7, January 1986). On the other hand, Vaillancourt noted how the fact of the referendum now made the concept of calling Confederation into question entirely legitimate, and Molnar and Slater quoted Gilles Bourque as saying, "national oppression may take different forms but it doesn't disappear. You don't have to scratch a francophone in Quebec very deeply to find a nationalist."

Perhaps what was missed in this period was the decline of the Left as a force shaping the sovereignist coalition, and indeed within Quebec politics as a whole. An exception would be Vaillancourt's throwaway line that "Marxism itself is as out of fashion in certain Quebec left intellectual circles as it is in Paris!" (18:5, October/November 1984). Indeed, it is only with the launch of *À bâbord* in 2003 that a viable magazine that was something approaching a Quebec equivalent of *Canadian Dimension* returned to the scene, complemented by *Les nouveaux cahiers du socialism* in 2009.

It is not that all the radical academics suddenly gave up critical class analysis for either mainstream rewards or the romance of postmodernism, although many did, but many others were burnt out. The wave of radicalism unleashed by the Quiet Revolution washed onto the beach of the 1980s, leaving a failed referendum, the denial of Quebec's national rights with the 1982 constitutional imposition, and the neoliberal landscape of Thatcher, Reagan and Mulroney. The energy likewise fell out of *CD*'s coverage: for instance, Meech Lake was largely ignored until the risk of its passing came on the radar.

Dimension came out strongly against the accord with its editorial "Reject Meech Lake" (24:1, January/February 1990), arguing that the Accord would "irreparably damage Canada" by "permanently weakening the powers of the federal state." Indeed, with the Accord, "Canada will be reduced to a loose collection of provincial fiefdoms, and will be all the more susceptible to the power of multinational capital." The problem was the recognition that a no to the Accord meant the non-recognition of Quebec and potential secession. The solution for *CD* was to scrap the Accord and to take the Constitution to the people. This ultimately left the magazine looking flat-footed, applying long-held values (strong central government, Quebec's right to self-determination) to a *fait accompli* where they could be held together only with the most general of solutions (public consultation, which *CD* portrayed more in terms of a special Parliamentary committee, as opposed, say, to a constituent assembly).

In retrospect, the lack of Quebec voices on Meech Lake was unfortunate. A key claim of *CD*'s rejection of Meech Lake involved the spending power provisions, which were seen as preventing future universal social programs. Ultimately, the Quebec Left rejected these same provisions on the opposite grounds: namely that they recognized and legitimized the use of the spending power and thus made it easier to use. In some ways, this debate was never joined in the pages of the journal, although Joe Levitt's impassioned letters did raise the relevant issues. Reading with the benefit of twenty-five years of hindsight, one wonders if the opposition to everything Brian Mulroney drove the analysis too strongly here.

As debate then shifted to fashion what became the Charlottetown round, CD attempted to elaborate a forward-looking vision on the Constitution so as not be boxed in, as it had been with Meech. The fundamental building blocks, according to the March 1991 editorial "Remaking Canada — this time for the people" (25:2) remained "a strong federal state, national treatment for Quebec and the First Nations, and a fair share for the 'regions'." Around this, CD added a need to strengthen democracy (referendum, recall, proportional representation), to which it later added the Social Charter (25:8, December 1991), although its readers might have anticipated some stronger beer. Not surprisingly, the Charlottetown Accord fell short, with particular emphasis on the erosion of the federal government's ability to manage the economy or maintain a Canada-wide safety net (26:7, October 1992).

The 1995 referendum arrived largely as a non-issue. Indeed, the debate about the referendum was published after the vote itself! CD maintained its long-standing position of defending Quebec's right to self-determination, albeit with a preference for asymmetrical solutions, immediately following the failure of Charlottetown (27:1, January/February 1993). But if in the 1980s it came to a position close to that of a "critical but independent yes," in 1995 it was a more grudging and hedged assessment, noting that the class nature of the PQ project conflicted with CD's commitment to social justice (28:5, October/November 1994).

The magazine ran two pieces on support for the yes, specifically by Monique Simard (25:5, July/August 1991) and Pierre Paquette (29:6, December 1995), which really testified to the loss of left influence on the national question through the 1980s. Clearly, there was still social democratic promise in the "yes" camp, phrased largely in terms of progressive competitiveness: a yes would allow Quebec to pursue a more egalitarian course by taking a more inclusive high-skill/high-wage path in the global economy. This reflected the largely unconditional support provided for the yes by Quebec progressives, especially by the union federations. The failure to develop an independent positioning with respect to the project, or to obtain some *quid pro quo* for support, meant that there was far less to warm the heart of the democratic social-ist. For *CD* it was time to "decolonize, not dismantle, Canada" (29:6, December 1995), which later in the decade led to *CD* taking a lead role in organizing English Canadian opposition to the *Clarity Act* in the name of support for Quebec's self-determination (32:4, July 1998).

Assessing *CD*'s position on the national question

In surveying the arc of the national question, one cannot ignore Serge Denis's extensive critique of *Canadian Dimension* on this point.[1] For Denis, *CD*'s analysis remained blocked through the late 1970s and the 1980s. On the one hand, it adopted a form of parallelism, supporting the right of Quebecers to determine their own constitutional future, while the Left in the rest of Canada pursued its own strategies. On the other, while this meant tacitly supporting the greatest threat to the integrity of the Canadian state, *CD* continued to stand for the strengthening of that state as the means of advancing a radical project in Canada. The possi-bility of a radical reimagining of the political community in the case of Quebec sovereignty appeared off the table.

By the time of Meech Lake and Charlottetown, Denis portrays this project as increasingly empty: the defence of the Canadian state against the balkanization of decentralization becomes the defining principle, with little else behind it. In dealing with Meech Lake, for instance, the magazine is willing to see promise in the suggested changes put forward by the Manitoba and Newfoundland govern-ments, on the one hand, or to call for wide-ranging popular consul-tation, on the other. But in terms of a proactive vision of what the Constitution should be in terms of socialist strategy, *Dimension* was strangely short of prescriptive radical imagination.

There is some strength to Denis's critique. The possibility of the

Quebec and Canadian Lefts to be more creative around the national question by breaking out of their parallelism and crafting joint strategies was rarely proposed or developed. In this, of course, *CD* was not much different from the women's and labour movements, who likewise tended to default to a respectful parallelism in order to prevent a complete nationalist schism in their ranks. Moreover, when it came to envisaging how Quebec sovereignty might open substantial possibilities for reforming the Canadian social and political order, *CD*'s imagination was surprisingly modest.

On the other hand, Denis perhaps undersells the depth of *CD*'s understanding of the state: the point was not to simply reproduce a stronger version of the federal state, but to create a different kind of state. This seems implicit in the various treatments of the national question over the years, and would be made explicit in the debates about popular sovereignty in the early 2000s. In other words, while the defense of a strong central government is a bit limiting (indeed, Philip Resnick likewise argued that this was bad strategy as a slightly more decentralized Canada might actually be a stronger, more legitimate one), it was the result of taking imperialism seriously. Denis's critique itself never came to suggest what alternative political form might provide a bulwark to imperialism, at least in a manner that would allow for a fuller assertion of democratic control in America's northern reaches.

While *CD*'s editorial stance received this critique for not laying out a more radical stance, it also opened its pages to interventions questioning its willingness to give much play to national claims. These indeed grew more numerous as radical pressures on the sovereignist movement waned in the 1990s. Some of these remained quite general, rejecting nationalism per se for being necessarily exclusivist, compared to a true socialist internationalism (e.g., Alison Hayford, 27:3, May/June 1993; Brenda Austin-Smith, 30:1, February/March 1996). It is not surprising that this did not move the *CD* position: the same cautious realism that led the magazine to question claims (like Stan Gray's) that the national and class questions were inseparable no doubt asked whether adopting said internationalism was really a means of negating an engagement with national inequality in the here and now.

More challenging have been the grounded challenges by Eric Shragge and Andrea Levy, who ask how helpful nationalism is in terms of organizing working people, especially in a diverse city like Montreal. In a number of communities, nationalism is seen as a marker of exclusion and division, or perhaps just simply seems beside the point when faced, say, with Québécois owners and managers. Ultimately, for Shragge, organizing around cross-class identity comes at the cost of being able to advance organizing campaigns grounded on class, race/ethnicity and gender.

Quebec and structured movements against capitalism

As the magazine provided space in its pages in the early 2000s to pursuing Sam Gindin's idea of a "structured movement against capitalism," it was natural that it would look to developments in Quebec, where the melding of left political groups and the anti/alter-globalization movements first into the Union des forces progressistes (UFP) and then Québec solidaire (QS), has provided the most successful example of a new sort of movement-party. In the process, it provided a regular column ("Quebec Communiqué") to Pierre Dostie, a spokesperson for the UFP. For an "independent socialist" magazine, this was a bit of a departure.

But even in the early 2000s, this was a difficult perch to occupy. In reading Dostie's columns, there is a consistent disjuncture: when analyzing Quebec politics, we get a complex analysis of social movement and labour movement positioning around the neoliberalisms of the Liberal Party and the Parti Québécois, yet when we turn to Canada-wide issues like the Liberal sponsorship scandal or the enduring success of the Bloc Québécois, Quebec is described in far more monolithic terms.

The critical sociologist and sometimes *CD* contributor Gilles Bourque has written that it now sounds odd to use the language of national oppression to describe Quebec-Canada relations, and yet the continued and deliberate refusal of recognition of Quebec's national status ultimately must boil down to that.[2] In this context, strategic dialogue between the Canadian and Quebec Lefts is perhaps ever harder.

Much as the welfare state and postwar union rights led to some class abatement and the erroneous claim that class struggle was passé, so the strengthening of a Quebec capitalist class and the end of flagrant anti-francophone linguistic discrimination has made it easy for the English Canadian Left to be complacent about Quebec national struggles. How often do progressives outside Quebec point to particular aboriginal-Quebec flashpoints or to some xenophobic pronouncement by Pauline Marois, not as a means of engaging debates about strategies for working together for justice, but as a means of ignoring national inequality in Canada with a clear conscience? The reaction for Quebec progressives like Dostie is often to rally to the national flag. The mutual incomprehension is probably no less than when *Canadian Dimension* was launched, nor still the need for places like *CD* where some exchange of views is still possible.

That said, even as Québec Solidaire is slowly shedding its "structured movement" characteristics to become more of a political party, Quebec politics as a whole has continued to capture *CD*'s attention given the strength of a series of protests (and their underlying social movements), ranging from the large union protests in the first years of the Charest government, to the traction of antiwar and climate justice organizing, through to the recent Maple Spring, which reminds us that student protest can still engage the fuller horizon of social justice.

Nationalism in a new millennium

Having said as much, the development of Québec Solidaire as a kind of modern left party raised again the question of nationalism. As in the past, *CD* continued to recognize the importance of the national question, while opening its pages to voices critical of the power relations bound up in nationalism. For instance, around Quebec's commission on reasonable accommodations, Aziz Choudry, Gada Mahrousse and Eric Shragge raised the question of whether nationalism is a help or hindrance: "Take a walk in Côte-des-Neiges or Parc Extension in Montreal. New immigrant communities have a stake in basic social transformation, but can only play that role when the Left understands that its worn-out Nationalist vision blocks building that base" (42:3, May/June 2008; see also Shragge and Levy, 37:2, March 2003).

145

The magazine nevertheless stuck to its long-standing analysis. This included reflections on the state of Quebec nationalism in *CD*'s fortieth anniversary issue. Three separate pieces by Daniel Salée, Jocelyn Couture and Pierre Dostie and Molly Alexandre (37:5, September/October 2003) differed in their takes on the extent to which Quebec nationalism had been tamed by both the progress of francophones and neoliberalism, but none felt that national claims could be avoided in building progressive politics. Part of this was *realpolitik* of where the Left was at, but part of it too was recognition that national inequality still shaped the world of political action.

Behind this position was also the rephrasing of the traditional position in renewed debates about imperialism. The initiative around popular sovereignty was crucial in this respect (36:4, July/August 2002). It enabled the magazine to rephrase its anti-imperialist message in a manner that made the recognition of national self-determination less of a secondary and procedural step in reaching the primary goal of building the strong central state needed for socialism. The task at hand, "involves building a multi-national movement of popular sovereignty that unites various non-elite groups across ethnic, racial and regional boundaries . . . to challenge the rule of transnational capital by demanding new institutions for popular democratic control of the economy, resource development and social expenditures." The initiative on popular sovereignty was critical of certain localist tendencies of the antiglobalization movement and continued to see crucial roles for nation states in enabling meaningful democratic control.

However, with the position that, "a popular sovereignty movement cannot be about defending the Canadian state, but confronting it and changing it — radically — to accommodate a variety of sovereignty claims," more space was given to those holding competing sovereignty claims (including Quebec nationalists) to engage in the project as a joint one, rather than a purely parallel one. In retrospect, it is this vision that was missing at the time of Meech and Charlottetown, and that could have provided for more innovative proposals for democratizing political institutions when the Constitution was open for debate. It is also the openness of this vision that has allowed *CD* to reopen channels of exchange with the Quebec Left around questions of climate justice, such as its linkages with Alternatives for the "Coachamba plus one" conference in Montreal in 2011.

Conclusion

When a magazine develops a line in 1965 and sticks to it for half a century, it has either developed a dogma, or shown an uncommon perception of the deeply rooted fault-lines of the political community. In the case of *CD*, it is the *absence* of dogma that accounts for the longevity of this line; it understood that national inequality existed and constituted a source of injustice, but that nationalism itself was shot through with inequalities. To prize one over the other or to claim that both were the same would be to misunderstand these forces.

The other wise step was to leave the question of how national struggles and social struggles fit together in particular times and places to a nonsectarian debate. These are ultimately questions that are too big to be solved deductively: they require strategic reflection in concrete circumstances, reflecting the power and potentials of the social forces in the moment. This is especially the case since socialists, or even social democrats, have not been driving the bus over the past half-century. They have had influence by shaping the terrain for more dominant actors, as opposed to being in a position to implement their values directly.

All told, this has allowed *CD* to take a productive position through the years. It has stood apart from the Canadian Left that acritically sees Quebec as a progressive vanguard, on the one hand, while reminding others that there is a social justice dimension to national inequality. It has also been a place where readers outside Quebec can follow the unique political conversation with a degree of sophistication in terms of the divisions of opinion within the Left itself.

Nevertheless, the non-dogmatism does come at the price of a certain "parallelism," of recognizing two parallel lefts but having little to say about what projects they could pursue together, or how one's struggle might open spaces for the other. This is too much of a responsibility to put on a magazine: it is the lefts themselves that must engage this, and frankly both sides seem at a loss as to where to start. Fifty years of *CD* is also fifty years of largely autonomous development for these lefts, to say nothing of the diminished horizons in terms of what social change might look like.

That *CD* continues to devote space to be a place for exchange is in itself an achievement. That it works to open promising paths, such as linkages with the Green Left in Quebec on climate justice, should inspire further linkages. That that exchange must be expanded substantially for a Left that wishes to shape the diverse Canadian political community should also be clear.

CHAPTER 4
Fifty Years in Indian Country
Peter Kulchyski

*The Left more broadly could stop seeing indigenous rights as the issue
of the week, and instead focus its energies here, on the understanding
that in Canada this is the defining issue of our generation.*

— Canadian Dimension Editorial (47:2, March/April 2013)

Canadian Dimension has had a long and illustrious history covering
Aboriginal issues from a critical standpoint. Its pages have featured
some of the leading Aboriginal critics — from Howard Adams or Emma
Laroque to Winona LaDuke and Joyce Green — as well as anthropolo-
gists the calibre of Michael Asch or Harvey Feit, historians like Stanley
Ryerson or Tony Hall, social scientists or social science–oriented
journalists like John Warnock or Heather Robertson, and of course
activists, many activists, from Stan Persky and Fred Gudmundson to
Corvin Russell and Clayton Thomas-Müller, with editor Cy Gonick
himself weighing in at important moments. Although in its very early
years coverage of Aboriginal issues was somewhat sparse, *Canadian
Dimension* devoted increasing levels of attention over the decades and
in the last twenty years can be seen as almost a paper of record, giving
attention to all the major battles, issues and events that have defined
Aboriginal political conflict in Canada.

This chapter will review *Canadian Dimension*'s coverage by decade in order to show the sweep of its coverage. This narrative also allows for showing the development of a distinctive consciousness around Aboriginal issues in the magazine. In general, early issues focused on Aboriginal poverty or militancy; slowly a growing awareness of the specificity of Aboriginal and treaty rights as issues sinks in, and eventually many around the magazine come to see Aboriginal politics as, rather than a sideshow, a central political struggle within Canada.

The eighties

Coverage of Aboriginal issues in the sixties was comparatively sparse, but a few very striking pieces did appear. It is notable that nothing at all appeared on Aboriginal issues from 1963 until 1966; although there was much reflection on Canadian identity and culture, Aboriginal people were largely absent from this discourse. Two pieces appeared in 1966. The first, by James Harding, a student activist, was called "The Powerless Minority" and focused largely on poverty issues. Harding referred to Michael Harrington's *The Other America* in order to argue, presciently enough, that "there is increasing evidence that 'Another Canada' exists" (3:2, January/February 1966). Although he saw colonial control by the Department of Indian Affairs as a critical issue, Harding tended to see Aboriginal peoples as a racial minority: the sort of argument that would underlie Trudeau's proposed White Paper policy prescription of a few years later. Another early article, by P.S. Barry on "Our Northern Colony," argued for increasing self-government in the Northwest Territories at the time of the Carrothers Commission then examining the issue. Although there was a good deal of attention specifically given to Aboriginal peoples, this was muted somewhat by the notion of a "northern" sociality and by some surprisingly conservative notions ("the RCMP have a fairly honourable record in the NWT" 3:6, September/October 1966). Both of these pieces, and a third published in 1968, focused on poverty as the main issue facing Aboriginal people. "Notes from Carry-the-Kettle" by John Conway in early 1968 was a first-hand account of a new teacher's life on reserve, filled with quite interesting anecdotes (for example about the corruption of the local Indian agent or how a nearby bar was segregated).

The next three major pieces published by *Canadian Dimension* in the sixties accomplished a great deal in terms of establishing its position as a venue for critical voices around Aboriginal issues. These were an interview with Métis activist Howard Adams, an article on hydroelectric development in northern Manitoba by Cy Gonick, and an analysis of the White Paper by James Duran. "Red Power: An Interview With Howard Adams" by long-time *Canadian Dimension* contributor John Warnock remains rewarding reading to this day, with Adams near the outset noting that "it is extremely important that we organize and unite as a racial group and that we operate from a base of political power" (5:4, April/May 1968) and arguing that the Canadian government, like any "typical imperialist" state, "is prepared only to let us have certain meaningless and irrelevant discussions and concessions but not to grant us the constitutional and political rights we so urgently need in order to help ourselves." Adams is eloquent about why Aboriginal peoples want to stay in their communities, about the impact of church-run residential schools, and about the creation of "comprador" elites among Aboriginal peoples.

Cy Gonick's insightful "The Tragedy of South Indian Lake" reviewed the proposed Churchill River Diversion project then on the drafting tables of Manitoba Hydro, concluding that "there is no just compensation possible in the case of the Indian-Métis community at South Indian Lake. They cannot be shoved about once more at the whim of the white man without destroying their self-respect as individuals and their sense of achievement as a community," adding that "over a century ago we took away the livelihood of the native peoples; we cheated them and robbed them not only of their resources, but of their way of life and their dignity as human beings. We are properly critical of our ancestors in their callous treatment of the red man. Now we are about to relive that horrible history" (5:8, February 1969). This could be written today about the next wave of proposed hydroelectric dams in northern Manitoba, in Quebec, in Labrador, about uranium mining projects near Baker Lake in Nunvaut, about tar sands development in northern Alberta and pipeline projects in northern BC.

* * *

At the very close of the sixties *Canadian Dimension* published an article by James Duran called "The New Indian Policy: Lessons From the U.S.," which accurately compared the "Statement of the Government of Canada on Indian Policy, 1969" (known commonly in Indian country as the White Paper) to the Eisenhower-sponsored "Termination Policy" attempted in the United States almost two decades earlier. The article skewered the White Paper thoroughly, concluding that "the aims of integrating Indian communities with the larger Canadian community, of removing all legal distinctions in the name of equality, and of terminating federal responsibility by transferring to the provinces the duty to provide services on the same basis as to any other citizen merely means assimilation to the Indians" (6:6, December/January 1969–70). Although the ultimately successful battle over the White Paper was in its initial stages, *Canadian Dimension* was able to show leadership over the mainstream media by positioning itself as not buying into the "equality" rhetoric that underpinned the proposed policy. There was little in the way of follow-up, and although *Canadian Dimension* does not appear at the time to have grasped the overall historic significance of this struggle and its dénouement, it did give voice to a strong, accurate, politically valuable refutation of the proposal.

The seventies

In the seventies *Canadian Dimension* began to pay serious, systematic and ongoing attention to Aboriginal issues in a way that it had not in its first decade. In fact it becomes impossible to give space to every article published in this or the following decades, but a few themes became consistent through the seventies: attention to the major resource development projects was probably the dominant theme; analysis and discussion of resistance movements also resulted in some very strong pieces. The narrative of Aboriginal poverty ("poor Indians") disappeared and was replaced by narratives of resistance to colonial exploitation and calls for respect for Aboriginal or treaty rights (and cultural difference). In the seventies *Canadian Dimension* also began publishing pieces that educated its readers (and itself!) on the historical context to Aboriginal people's struggles.

Two articles early in the decade offered strong historical analyses: one by Stanley Ryerson on the Manitoba resistance of the Métis, the other by Heather Robertson on treaties in northern Manitoba. Interestingly, both emphasize Aboriginal values that coincide with the values of democratic socialists. Ryerson wrote of "the intervention in history 'from below' by some hundreds of Métis buffalo-hunters and boatmen, carters and farmers, in defence of their rights. They created and maintained for the better part of a year, against all odds, their own popular democratic state" (7:1-2, June/July 1970).

Heather Robertson, inadvertently echoing James Harding, noted that "we can . . . no longer continue to believe that Indians consider themselves to be part of the province or even part of the nation," adding that while some Aboriginal people have "disappeared into what the government is pleased to call 'the mainstream'," there still remained "the traditionalists; they speak their own language, try to live off the land and secretly worship the spirits. They are against affluence, against progress, against education, against law and order, against organization, against everything white Manitobans consider important" (7:1-2 June/July 1970). Her analysis of the treaties left much to be desired (she saw them as "terms of capitulation" and doesn't pay them much substantive attention) but she does at least acknowledge their existence.

A third historical piece, called "100 Years of Making Indians in B.C.," by Mike Kew, presented a quite extensive history of the *Indian Act*, focusing on the provisions regarding Indian status. Kew also discussed the fact that there were few treaties in BC, noting that the Nisga'a land issue was moving to the Supreme Court of Canada.

Howard Adams, at nearly the same time, wrote a review of three now "classic" books on Aboriginal politics. Of Heather Robertson's *Reservations Are for Indians*[1] he wrote "this is the most comprehensive and instructive book on the Indians of Canada, to date" though later he also suggested that "perhaps the entire book could have been put into a historical, political perspective of capitalist Imperialism" (7:3, August/September 1970). Of *The Unjust Society* by Harold Cardinal[2] he wrote "it is not only new; it is a history making document. It is a sign that native people of Canada are awakening to their plight and proof that they have the intellectual leadership needed; they are able to analyze and record their own story from their own point of view." Adams was quite critical of *Native Rights in Canada*,[3] on the other hand, arguing that "the Indians have never regarded the judicial system as a protector or as a liberator, and they are not likely to change now. All in all, the judicial system is part of the oppressor's machinery, and this book, 'Native Rights in Canada,' does little to change this concept." Perhaps *Canadian Dimension* as a whole subscribed to this latter view, as it gave little attention to the historic legal battles at that time, which included the Calder and Lavell/Bedard cases, and in later decades — really until the late nineties — continued to largely ignore the legal side of the struggle for Aboriginal rights.

Three major megaprojects arguably dominated political discussion in Canada — James Bay and northern Quebec hydro development, the Mackenzie Valley pipeline and the Churchill River diversion and Lake Winnipeg regulation hydro development. Writing about the first of these in a nuanced historical and cultural analysis, Harvey Feit concluded in part that "the corporations" activities are supported by well-intentioned experts who have not recognized that processes of management and control already exist in these communities, in part because there are no supra-ordinate authorities in the communities vested with the planning function" (8:7, June 1972). Feit's article on "The Waswanipi of James Bay" recognized the resilience and value of the local hunting culture and outlined arguments that would inform the struggles of northern indigenous communities through to the present. Although Feit clearly provided a strong analysis of the culture and history that were essential for understanding the decades-long struggle in the region, there was little in the way of follow-up. The dramatic events around the injunction granted to the Cree, the hurried negotiation of a land claim settlement, the even more rushed implementation of that settlement and the way these ultimately laid a foundation for decades of conflict were not covered, though Feit's article remains a gem. Later, in the eighties and nineties, coverage of the struggle of the Cree in the region would return.

The Mackenzie Valley pipeline was featured in several pieces in the 1970s. A few articles written early on in the decade, including one by John Warnock, who called the project a "$5 Billion Disaster," questioned the economics of the project. Geographer Peter Usher wrote an anthropologically inflected piece, very much in the vein of Harvey Feit's, called "Northerners and the Land," in which he noted, "to native people, the land is more than just a source of food or cash. It is the permanent source of their security and of their sense of well-being" (11:2, October 1975) and that "native peoples' concern for their land has been increasingly articulated in terms of aboriginal rights" (11:2, October 1975). Two additional articles focused on the famous Berger report, *Northern Frontier, Northern Homeland*, released in 1977.[4] In "Berger Day" Larry Sanders noted that "the Left's earlier dismissal of the Berger process as merely a sop to native interests, or a revisionist attempt to reconcile the contradictions of northern colonial polities of the past and present governments, is impolitic. Instead, the report should be seen as a thorough, albeit Liberal, documentation of Canadian capitalism's exploitation of the north" (12:3, July 1977). A few months later, in "Post Berger Blues," Cy Gonick wrote that "self determination became the rallying cry for the Dene because only by controlling their lands can they protect their material interests" (11:4, March 1976). He thought that "there is every reason for [the fledgling] alliance [of southern urbanites and farmers with Dene and Inuit] that grew out of the struggle against the Mackenzie Valley pipeline to become a permanent one." But that was not to be. An even later article, on the church-sponsored "Project North," by Hugh McCullum and Russ Hatton, began with a statement that *Canadian Dimension* readers could by then clearly appreciate: "the most oppressed people in Canada today are the Native people — Indian, Inuit, Métis — and particularly in the North they are demanding a change in their arrangement with Canada" (13:5, January/February 1979).

Meanwhile, the fallout from the failed White Paper had created an opening for demanding a more positive policy framework. While significant events, like the "Indian Control of Indian Education" policy document of the National Indian Brotherhood,[5] and the Red and Brown papers proposed in response to the White Paper, were not covered by *Canadian Dimension*, it did have extensive coverage of the Aboriginal activists who inspired an early seventies uprising. Writing in a lengthy article on "The Occupation of Anicinabe Park" John Gallagher and Cy Gonick argued that "the warriors represent a new, young and aggressive leadership among Indians. They seized the initiative in Kenora, took the risks they felt necessary, and demonstrated themselves to be skilled tacticians during negotiations" (10:5, November 1974). The piece included a strong review of the colonial history of western Canada. It was part one of a two-part special issue called "Racism: The New Indian Wars?" The second part, called "Welcome to Ottawa," was written by David Ticoll and Stan Persky and dealt with the Native caravan of 1974. This also lengthy article provided a first-person account of the alliances and events that led to the violent deployment of RCMP riot police on Parliament Hill against a diverse crowd of Aboriginal activists, and remains perhaps the definitive account of that event. Together these articles established *Canadian Dimension* as a place where Aboriginal activists could be fairly represented, and in which stories of grassroots struggles could be told. In the seventies *Canadian Dimension* also published Leonard Pelletier's statement to the Canadian court at his extradition hearing, in which he powerfully states "when colonial white society invades and occupies our territories these are not called criminal acts, but when the native people stand up and resist, these acts are considered criminal" (11:6, Summer 1976), and an article about the death of activist Anna Mae Aquash.

* * *

Coverage of Aboriginal issues in the eighties was regular with some very strong articles, but also sporadic. It was a time of some intricate political negotiations at the institutional level, and contributors to *Canadian Dimension* did not seem compelled to pay too much attention to the establishment of sections 25 and 35 in the Constitution, the follow-up constitutional conferences on Aboriginal rights, or even the Neilsen Report[6] that recommended a "minimal standards" approach to driving First Nations people off reserves. Attention was paid to the Aboriginal Justice Inquiry in Manitoba; resource conflicts continued to be covered; and social issues such as child welfare made it onto the *Canadian Dimension* horizon; there was some reflection on "the good old days" of native activism in the seventies, and there was enough of a knowledge base that even some debate around how to theoretically position this form of politics started to emerge. In the middle of the decade a very strong theme issue on "Indian Country" ensured that the magazine continued to play a strong role in reporting and critically analyzing events. By this time *Canadian Dimension* was showing interest in the wide variety of areas in which a new Aboriginal politics were being articulated, from child welfare and education to funding for band councils or a visit to reserves by the then South African (apartheid) ambassador.

The decade began with a very nice review, "Discovering an Indian Proletariat," by Stan Persky, of the Rolf Knight book *Indians at Work.*[7] Persky made some strong theoretical points, noting that "the present state of affairs is hardly satisfactory to historical materialists and other reasonable persons, since the current version does little to explain the precise relationship between an incursive mode of production (capitalism, which itself is subject to transformations over time) and a communal mode, nor how the producers of the latter are subjugated by (or is the current phrase "articulated into"?) the workings of the former" (14:7, June 1980). Persky was especially struck by the fact that during the century from 1850 to 1950, in British Columbia, "those heretofore not-very-visible native people were logging, fishing, fishpacking, cartaging, longshoring, farming, mining, sailing, and railroad building in more or less the same fashion as were non-native workers at the time." Persky saw this as a "simple, great and (for the anthropology business) cosmic discovery." While Knight's book is indeed worthy, and the question posed by Persky about the "precise relationship" between modes of production is to my mind the critical question to ask, the search for an Aboriginal proletariat became a theoretical dead end that would only attract some on the Canadian Left in the decades to come.

Canadian Dimension in 1981 editorialized about the smaller-scale Mackenzie pipeline that was eventually built from Norman Wells in the NWT to northern Alberta, being one of the few Canadian publications to pay attention to Trudeau's betrayal of Thomas Berger and his recommended ten-year moratorium on any pipeline. A few years later, as that pipeline was completed, Fred Gudmundson would write a detailed historical analysis of the Norman Wells oil fields, with interesting information about how John Rockefeller created Imperial Oil in order to avoid the antitrust decisions of the US Supreme Court and a narrative that reached all the way to the approval of the pipeline to Alberta in 1980, Trudeau's retaliation for the defeat of the Mackenzie Valley pipeline.

Three other resource-based conflicts that *Dimension* gave some attention to were the Lubicon struggle in northern Alberta, a salmon fishery struggle in Quebec, and the struggle against the logging of Clayoquot Sound. The Lubicon conflict provoked a sharp debate within the magazine, as Fred Gudmundson sharply criticized a Bruce Kidd editorial which had suggested that the Olympics should still be celebrated while acknowledging the boycott sponsored by the Lubicon. Writing about the draconian use of force by the Quebec government in a fisheries dispute, Rita Dagenais presciently observed that "what the Quebec government has on its hands is not a problem of a few thousand salmon, but a full-scale political debate which threatens its most basic political and economic interests" (16:2, March 1982). It is a statement that could be repeated to this very day about every resource-based struggle with Aboriginal peoples in Canada. The 1989 article on "The Battle for Clayoquot Sound," written by "The Friends of Clayoquot Sound," prominently mentioned Aboriginal support for the struggle against logging of old-growth forest in the area, but paid little attention to Aboriginal rights as a foundation of resistance.

The special volume devoted to Aboriginal issues in 1985 can be said to reflect a "mature" *Canadian Dimension* approach to the topic, with strong pieces from Murray Dobbin, Emma LaRoque, and Micheal Asch among others, and a powerful collection of articles that look at international indigenous contexts and issues. In his guest editorial "Why Pardon Riel?" Dobbin argued that pardoning Riel would not accomplish anything because "Riel and all those who rebel against repression will always be 'guilty' in the eyes of the state, regardless of what any politician or government declares" (19:5, December 1985). Michael Asch's review of the Penner Report, *Indian Self Government in Canada*,[8] is also an important piece. He was generally quite favourable about the report and its recommendations, though he firmly rejected delegated models of Aboriginal self-government, even on an interim basis as had been recommended by Penner, arguing instead that the answer "lies in keeping pressure on the constitutional table for it is only through constitutional change that real self-government can be achieved" (19:5, December 1985). Emma LaRoque's "Reflections," is a riposte to the poet Earle Birney's comment that there are no ghosts in Canada. She wrote, "if non-native Canadians are haunted by a lack of ghosts, it is because they have not looked into their historical and ideological closets. Perhaps this is why a disturbing number of white Canadians do not see us when we play, work, shop, attend classes or cry beside them," adding that "I am haunted by many ghosts. The ghost of twisted history and ideologies. The ghost of oppression. The ghost of lakes, rivers, prairies, and mountains that once whispered a thousand native names and legends now lost to Parks Canada's pale explanations. I am haunted by the day to day suffering of Native Peoples across this land of wealth and opportunities" (19:5, December 1985).

Two articles on the problem of child welfare appeared in the early eighties, one called "Stop Stealing Our Children" and the other "Our Children Are Dying." The former piece, written in 1982 by Richard Thatcher, observed that "social workers are . . . caught between the silent middle class which wants them to do the dirty work and be quiet about it, fiscal strangulation, and the objects of the dirty work who refuse any longer to tolerate mistreatment" (16:2, March 1982). The latter, written a year later by Ustun Reinart, reported on how First Nations in Manitoba were taking control of child welfare, noting optimistically that "Native Family Services has been able to keep at least one hundred native children out of care and with their families over the last year" (17:4, September 1983). Reinart became something of a regular contributor to *Canadian Dimension*, among other pieces adding one of the first for the magazine devoted specifically to Aboriginal women. Entitled "How Powerful We As Native Women Really Are" and co-written with Doris Young, the article reported on the emergence of a new organization from northern Manitoba called the Indigenous Women's Collective. Young and Reinart reported on the issue of status and discrimination among First Nations women and made it clear that "the women who founded the IWC had experienced the triple jeopardy most Indigenous women face daily: racism, sexism and discrimination.

They felt Indigenous women as a group remained at the bottom of the socio-economic scale, yet were burdened with an overwhelming share of responsibility for their families and communities" (22:2, March/April 1988).

Three other mini-masterpieces were sprinkled through *Canadian Dimension*'s writings in the eighties. Métis historian Ron Bourgeault used the occasion of a much publicized and controversial visit to several reserves by then apartheid South African ambassador Glen Babb to compare that country's policies with Canada's. This allowed him to present the most detailed history of Canadian Aboriginal policy yet published in the magazine, and to make the point that "the fundamental difference between Canada and South Africa was that Canada was interested in segregating and managing, as cheaply as possible, a population of people it did not need or want as an important source of labour. South Africa was interested in the same type of relationship, but for a people whose labours it needed and wanted cheaply" (21:8, January 1988). Earlier in the decade economics professor John Loxley, in an article called "Indians Organize Around the Budget," made a strong argument for Aboriginal self-government by observing that "Indian aspirations are constantly being conditioned and frustrated by the financial control that the state exercises over these institutions [of 'devolved government']" (17:6, December 1983). If anything, the politics of using financial levers as a political tool has actually grown worse in the last decade and a half. Finally, an interview with George Erasmus by *Canadian Dimension* regular Fred Gudmundson provided readers with a variety of historical and political insights. Erasmus echoed Loxley's point about funding control issues and noted that "in the later 60s and throughout the 70s it became clear that we were working on a band aid operation" (18:5, October/November 1984). Hence the turn to a need for structural change, such as achieving a meaningful form of Aboriginal self-government.

All this work clearly had an impact on the editors of *Canadian Dimension*. In a striking editorial near the end of the decade, regarding the Mulroney-inspired cutbacks to postsecondary education for First Nations students which had provoked a large and energetic student-led resistance, the editors did not simply applaud the activists and decry the poverty, as might have been the case ten or twenty years earlier. Instead, the editorial entitled "Native Education: Paid in Advance. Paid in Full" argued that "for Aboriginal organizations, the issue goes beyond revisions to the Post-Secondary Educational Assistance Program (a.k.a. E-12). It strikes the heart of century-old treaty rights" (23:4, June 1989). *Canadian Dimension* had clearly picked up the language of Aboriginal and Treaty rights, supported the movement for self-government, and was in a position to provide a strong and continuing venue for the new generation of Aboriginal activists that had begun to emerge.

The nineties

This came to fruition over the next two decades. The number and variety of articles on Aboriginal issues increased again in the nineties. By then *Canadian Dimension* took on board the whole spectrum of political, legal, historical and cultural issues circulating around Indian country. The constitution, court decisions, cultural politics, urban issues and so on joined the discussions of resource-based conflicts and activist moments. The magazine was well positioned to provide a critical voice on the conflicts at Kanesatake, Gustavson Lake, the Oldman River and Stoney Point; it discussed the failure of the Meech Lake constitutional accord, the Royal Commission on Aboriginal Peoples, and the appalling Delgamuukw decision eventually reversed by the Supreme Court; it dwelt on issues of stereotyping and urban Aboriginal presence; it published work by Tony Hall, Priscilla Settee, Winona LaDuke, and an interview with Ward Churchill. There was something in nearly every issue and the magazine can claim to be one of the few consistent sources outside the soon-to-be nearly silenced Aboriginal print media — a paper of record, as it were — on Aboriginal political struggle. It becomes impossible to review even a majority of these pieces so instead a representative sample must suffice.

Then Native American Studies professor Tony Hall's two-part series in 1991 reflected the newer and far more nuanced understanding of the issues at stake. In the first part, called "Putting Aboriginal Issues on the Canadian Political Agenda," he noted that "the reality is that Aboriginal groups have all along been treated as existing outside the primary structures of Canadian democracy" and went on to argue that in meeting the challenge of an Aboriginal "politics of inclusion," "non-Natives in Canada will be facing the challenge of bringing their own political institutions more in line with the structures of decision making with the deepest heritage in this land. The process almost certainly will draw fresh sources of nutriment to a national political system becoming parched by intolerance" (25:4, June 1991). Hall thereby raised the stakes of the conflict, ensuring that people on the left would see Aboriginal struggles in Canada not as a sideshow, not as a part of a rainbow coalition of more "ands" to the growing list of causes, but rather as integral to a meaningful socialist vision of Canada. This is made even clearer in the second part, which focused on Aboriginal conflicts in Quebec and pointedly argued, "old patterns can be perpetuated that relegate Aboriginality to a marginal and diminishing feature of Canada's emerging identity . . . Or, alternatively, Aboriginality can be embraced as a fundamental characteristic of Canada" (25:5, July/August 1991). In 1993 Hall wrote about the failure of the Charlottetown Accord that stressed the emerging divisions within and among the Aboriginal leadership, with a strong historical analysis of the various blocks and shifting alliances within the Assembly of First Nations.

The year of Kahnesatake (Oka) provoked much reflection in Canada around broad issues of Native-newcomer relations. A very interesting piece by Paul Ogresko called "Reflections on Oka" emphasized how much the media had downplayed and ignored Quebecois solidarity with Mohawks, writing for example that "the night I arrived in Montreal last fall there was a demonstration of Quebecers in support of the Mohawks. In what had become a weekly occurrence, more than a thousand Montreal residents marched from a downtown park to Quebec Hydro where, quite appropriately, Robert Bourassa has his Montreal offices" (25:1, January/February 1991). This facet of the response to Kahnesatake within Quebec is still largely unknown in English Canada.

In all, these statements of support for indigenous peoples and growing awareness of the centrality of their struggles to Canadian politics were not empty rhetoric, and had significant political implications. When an editorial endorsed Quebec's right to separation, but added a qualifier supporting "Aboriginal peoples' right to self-determination" within the province (28:5, October/November 1994), no less a luminary of the Canadian left than Leo Panitch weighed in by noting angrily that "there is, in the end, a profound difference between the aspirations currently being articulated around self determination by the First Nations and that by Quebec. The latter is about statehood; the former is not (nor could it be, if you retain any political economy perspective on the material base of geo-political entities)" (28:5, October/November 1994). Panitch remained, and remains, devoted to working-class struggle in Canada as the primary political moment of opposition and would not recognize the degree to which Aboriginal struggles raise the profoundest questions of property ownership, challenging the values of capitalist colonialism and thereby fundamentally challenging the Canadian project in its current, profoundly elitist, form. An earlier editorial on "The Year Before Columbus" had already implicitly repudiated Panitch's view, by emphasizing the values embedded in Aboriginal cultures: "striking was the tolerance of these people given the rich diversity of their religious beliefs"; "the land was not the strict property of individuals but was considered to be the flesh of the community"; "sharing and co-operation were essential to the way of life." The editorial concluded "it is still not too late for us to learn something of how to live from these survivors. They deserve a party. Better yet give them land and autonomy" (25:5, July/August 1991).

Dimension continued and increased its coverage and analysis of Aboriginal women's issues with a number of powerful articles, including "Breaking the Silence" in 1992 by Marilyn Fontaine-Brightstar, which stated bluntly that "we have found it necessary to speak out against the violence and the sexism within our community even though it means breaking ranks with the Chiefs" (26:2, March 1992). Winona LaDuke, at that time co-chair of the Indigenous Women's Network, had her formal statement to the United Nations Fourth World Conference on Women in Beijing published in the magazine. In her powerful statement she asked "what gives these corporations . . . a right which supersedes or is superior to my right to live on my land, or that of my family, my community, my nation, our nations, and to us as women?" (30:1, February/March 1996). She also wrote a lovely compilation of women's stories she had gathered at the Conference called "I Fight Like A Woman" (30:2, April 1996).

As in the previous decade, *Canadian Dimension* excelled in its coverage of resource use/"development" conflicts through the nineties. During an interesting interview with Ward Churchill on the Lubicon Cree struggle against oil development he was asked about healing and reconciliation. Churchill responded by noting the complexity of the problem but also: "the dominant population, the settler society, 'Canadians,' the settler populations anywhere in the world, must begin to obey the law. You hear a lot of rhetoric, especially conservative rhetoric in Canada, about law enforcement. Well then — obey the law. The big laws, like the legal compacts which govern Canada's relations with other nations, including the treaties and aboriginal rights. And if the little laws can't be made to conform to big laws, then the little laws shouldn't count" (32:2, March/ April 1998). An article by O.A. Rosenkrantz reporting on the phase two James Bay hydro project called "Quebec Cree Face Catastrophe" wrote that "the irresponsibility and callous disregard for human and environmental suffering that lies behind this project is mindboggling" (25:4, June 1991).

Not every article "toed the line" on the value of Aboriginal culture and Aboriginal rights. In "Rethinking Environmental — First Nations Relationships" David Orton looked at indigenous leaders who were promoting development projects and called into question notions of an inherent or essential "ecological Indian": "In building alliances with Native peoples in Canada on a basis of equality, everything is up for critical discussion, including basic assumptions. The ecological shortcomings of contemporary Indigenous world views need to be discussed frankly and fairly, even while recognizing that our main preoccupation must remain with the sicknesses of contemporary industrial society" (29:1, February/March 1995). Orton noted presciently enough that "corporations and governments can wear Native masks," something that would become increasingly common. There were many more resource-based conflicts covered over the decade, with strong descriptive reporting and analysis informing the *Canadian Dimension* approach to these issues.

CD collective member Phil Lancaster's comments on the final report of the Royal Commission on Aboriginal Peoples[9] can close out discussion of the nineties. Lancaster weighed in with a judicious and balanced review, concluding with words that resonate with the government's ultimate sidestepping of the recommendations that flowed from RCAP: "Eventually, it will not be possible for government to express concern and do nothing. The RCAP is a step along the way. No more. The real work of politics, organizing, must continue" (31:1, January/February 1997).

The new millenium

As the nineties gave way to the naughts, *Canadian Dimension* continued to increase its coverage, analysis and debate around Aboriginal issues. Over the next decade and up to the present (2013), the voices of Taiaike Alfred, Kahntineta Horn, Nahanni Fontaine, Ardith Wakem, Ramona Neckoway joined those of previous indigenous activists published in the magazine. Richard Wagamese wrote a series of quite lovely, reflective, memory pieces over the course of the period. A wide variety of issues were foregrounded, including the "lobster" wars on the east coast, the Nisga'a land claim, the standoff at Gustafsen Lake, the emergence of the Defenders of the Land and Idle No More and the then Indian Affairs Minister Robert Nault's proposed "governance act." More recently, Harper's determined inaction on Aboriginal issues has become a theme, with the poverty and immiseration it enables gaining traction. The Alberta tar sands development, and First Nations opposition to it and to the pipelines it wants to spawn, has also been a central topic in recent years. Many of the writers who contributed in the past, such as Tony Hall, continued to submit work; I myself was among those who "joined the stable" and began to contribute regularly through this period. Each year "Indian Country" became a feature focus and, as with the previous decade, there were far too many pieces published to be able to exhaustively review them here.

The year 2000 began with a sparkling debate about the recently signed Nisga'a Final Agreement. In an article subtitled "Negotiating Space in the Master's House" Ardith Walkem, an Aboriginal lawyer and activist working in BC, was sharply critical of the deal, noting that "the overall result of these sections is that the agreement solidifies the Canadian rule of law over Nisga'a territories, governments and citizens" and that "the Nisga'a treaty does not result in any restructuring of Canada, nor does it recognize the Nisga'a right to self-determination" (34:1, February 2000). This sparked a response by Phil Lancaster, arguing that "The Nisga'a Treaty is Our Treaty," as his piece was titled, and that "what the treaty offers . . . is a small place to regroup and prepare for further struggle with renewed vigour — a small, stable homeland where pride can be sustained with some self government and some economic possibilities" (34:2, March/ April 2000). In effect, it was a debate about whether indigenous peoples should settle for something less than the sovereignty and ownership of traditional territories that are due them, with Walkem asserting that to do so is to agree to continued colonization, and Lancaster arguing that to do so sometimes can be a step towards decolonization. Interestingly, a few months later Gabriel Haythornwaite would write a piece about the rejection of the Nisga'a model by other BC-based First Nations in which he strikingly argued that "there are no concerted attempts on the Left to build solidarity with Native peoples. Nor can one discern any qualitative difference in the positions of the Left, moderate or radical, from that of the liberal colonialist project of 'self-government'" (34:5, September/ October 2000).

This issue was taken up in an editorial for a *Canadian Dimension* special issue featuring indigenous art, politics and culture in 2007. The editorial, called "New Clothes, Same Old Colonial Thinking," also noted that the Left "has not in practice done very well reaching across the cultural boundary" but emphasized that there was "much to learn from Aboriginal peoples, many of whom are far more 'developed' than their Western neighbours when it comes to democratic decision-making forms; when it comes to building communities that deserve the name of community; when it comes to maintaining a sustainable balance with their ecological settings; and when it comes to asking spiritual questions in an open, curious, non-sectarian and non-institutional way" (41:1, 2007). The issue included work by Cathy Mattes on Aboriginal art (including some striking samples of cutting-edge pieces), an article on hydro development in northern Manitoba by Ramona Neckoway, a reflection on the AlterNative film festival and Aboriginal new media activists by Kathleen Buddle, a discussion of the history of Aboriginal title that I wrote and thoughtful, broad ranging pieces by Anthony Hall and Taiaiake Alfred. It also offered brief biographies of a number of community-based Aboriginal activists, an essay by James Wastesecoot on Big Bear, discussion of international indigenous issues by way of an article on the conflict in Oaxaca, another installment of Kahentinetha Horn's "Indian Country" column and more. The issue was thoughtful, dynamic, nuanced, critical and colourful; it represented the best that a mature *Canadian Dimension* could offer its readers and in effect opened a new door for the Left in Canada to think through its position around Aboriginal resistance.

Even in his Quebec column, Pierre Dostie made the argument far from earlier attempts to put indigenous sovereignty and Quebecois sovereignty in separate silos, that "the process of attaining Quebec sovereignty might well be compromised, even, if the strategy does not take into account the question of First Nations" and further that "it is the responsibility of the sovereignty movement to propose strategic alliances and a process of achieving sovereignty that would also allow for First Nations to exercise their sovereignty and make their voices heard" (41:1, January/February 2007). Meanwhile, within Indian Country, activists like Taiaiake Alfred were arguing that "we need to revive our traditional forms of government," effectively discussing the substantive form that indigenous sovereignties might assume. Alfred went on to argue that "colonization is a process of disconnecting us from our responsibilities to each other and our respect for one another, our responsibilities and our respect for the land, and our responsibilities and respect for the culture" (41:1, January/February 2007). Anthony Hall, in the same issue, while celebrating the success of the struggle to save Haida Gwai, noted that "the bright spot that this campaign represents, however, must be set against the background of human devastation that is the most striking evidence of the failure to recognize and affirm the existence of Aboriginal and treaty rights over several generations." With this issue, as well as many that came before and many that would follow, *Canadian Dimension* successfully positioned itself as a platform for critical debate and discussion within the Left and among indigenous activists around the emerging Aboriginal resistances in Canada.

Whether or not the ethnocentric fraction of the Canadian Left (which perhaps reached its apotheosis with the appalling book *Disrobing the Aboriginal Industry* by Frances Widdowson and Albert Howard[10]) liked it, through the naughts and to the present Aboriginal peoples' struggles became seen as central to a socialist project in Canada. In the naughts the investment by *Canadian Dimension* in the struggle for Aboriginal rights did not dissipate, but grew, as the conflicts escalated. Though this was in part a reflection of the magazine's taking on board an eco-socialist perspective, it clearly also was an outgrowth of the very strong historical, political and cultural smithy through which the magazine's outlook had been forged. Both the historical conjuncture — Aboriginal issues were not disappearing and, in fact, seemed to be growing in the urgency and profound level of challenge they presented — and the increasing involvement of academics and activists in the struggle made this a logical step. Hence the decade hardly featured an issue that did not have some Aboriginal content, and almost every year an "Indian Country" theme appeared. One of these dealt with the specific issues pertinent to Inuit (who had been covered through their involvement with particular struggles, but never previously featured). As new, young activists were drawn to the *CD* collective many of them were centrally concerned with Aboriginal politics. Their ranks include young Aboriginal activists like Clayton Thomas-Müller and Ben Powless, as well as a strong cohort of settler anticolonial militants like Corvin Russell, Martin Lukacs and Krishna Lalbiharie. Such a diverse and knowledgeable group will ensure that *Canadian Dimension* does not have to worry about standing on the sidelines while Aboriginal people hurl themselves at a totalizing Canadian state.

PART III

THE GREEN DIMENSION

CHAPTER 5
The Green Dimension
Andrea Levy

Canadian Dimension was launched almost exactly one year after the publication of Rachel Carson's *Silent Spring* and six months after *Our Synthetic Environment* written by Murray Bookchin under the pseudonym Lewis Herber. Neither book earned a mention in the magazine. *Dimension* was no exception to the Left's mainly dilatory reckoning with the critical importance of the ecology question, publishing next to nothing on matters environmental in its inaugural decade. Fifty years on, however, it ranks as one of the few Canadian magazines attempting to take the full measure of the mess humankind is making of its habitat.

To its credit, even in its earliest incarnation, *Dimension* did not descend to dismissing the environmental crisis as a "bourgeois" concern, and in the seventies and eighties the magazine featured occasional, often very good, articles on environmental issues. Historically, the labour movement came at environmental questions through the lens of occupational health and safety, and that is reflected to some degree in the magazine's early approach. It ran various articles on workplace environmental hazards such as asbestos, lead, sulphur dioxide and cobalt dust, and published exposés of toxic pollution in local communities, especially Indigenous communities, such as Jim Harding's 1976 reportage on mercury poisoning in northwest Ontario, as well as several discussions of the dangers of uranium mining and nuclear energy. An excellent article on the "Poisoning of Canada" by Robert

Sass and Richard Butler in May 1982 was devoted to the unprecedented release by industry in the post-World War II period of toxic chemicals solvents, pesticides and fertilizers. Like many *CD* articles on environmental issues, it was written from the perspective of environmental justice before that term gained currency, depicting the disproportionate burden of pollution placed on Indigenous communities and the process by which Indigenous peoples in Canada have been made "environmental refugees within their own land."[1] The first editorial to broach environmental questions was the March–April 1985 editorial on the Bhopal disaster, which explained that tragedy was the inevitable outcome of a system of ineffective corporate regulation, rather than an isolated accident, and pointed to the problem of the profit-driven overuse and misuse of pesticides resulting in pesticide contamination worldwide.

Still, in the first three decades of its existence, with some noteworthy exceptions such as Fred Knellman's 1971 discussion of soil, water and air pollution arising from unchecked technological development in the service of power and profit, the magazine approached the subject in a largely piecemeal fashion, focusing on polluting industries but not yet elucidating the big picture: the ecological unsustainability of prevailing human production and consumption practices as a whole.

By the 1990s, the environment was foremost among the political concerns of Canadians and it was becoming a central theme of the magazine. James Harding's "The Urgency of Environmental Politics" (23:1, January/February 1989) set the tone. Harding stressed that the environment was not a single issue but part of a larger picture of ongoing ecological degradation bound up with the system of production and consumption. And a year later *CD* cautioned readers that "Leftists Pass [the] Eco-Buck at Their Peril" (24:6, September 1990). This editorial expressed discomfort with the Left's typically sharp dismissal of appeals by the environmental movement to change consumer behaviour as naïve and pointless, while nevertheless concurring with the analysis of the problem as a structural one which no amount of electric cars and composting could remedy. Individual action, *CD* pointed out, could lead to social action and social movements are stronger if "built on a solid base of people living out their core beliefs." But for *CD* conventional environmental discourse was entirely inadequate to the burgeoning crisis, and the recognition of the urgency of the ecological question went hand in hand in the magazine with an ongoing critique of mainstream responses.

Green perspectives, red prisms

Brewster Kneen's takedown of sustainable development, also in the January–February 1989 issue, was a case in point. Kneen set about exposing the superficiality and hypocrisy of the discourse around sustainable development, which was manifest from the start, he observed, in the Brundtland Report itself, which offered no structural analysis or acknowledgement of the state as an instrument of corporate power and omitted any call for structural reform. He also cast a critical eye on the very notion of development, which "has always referred to that process whereby others are incorporated into our economy, as a source of cheap labour, as a source of cheap raw materials, or as a market." Sustainability and development thus defined are irreconcilable, he argued, and an environmentalism which fails to recognize this is limited to isolated efforts to preserve nature in the form of wilderness and iconic species. Kneen's piece also presaged *CD*'s incipient stance in relation to the environmental movement, accusing mainstream environmentalism of acquiescing in the dominant ideology of the supremacy of the laws of the market. In the absence of a structural analysis and radical systemic critique or strategy for far-reaching social and economic change, Kneen charged, environmentalists fall back on "appeals to those with the power, those who have caused the problems."

"Does the state of the environment make you see red?" *Dimension* leadingly asked its readers. And *CD* hoped that environmentalists too would come to name the system as their efforts to win the hearts and minds of the power elite failed, in the meantime attempting to foster mutual understanding between leftists and environmentalists. Conscious of the tensions and conflict that marked the relationship between organized labour and the environmental movement, for example, the magazine mainly sought to mediate and find common ground.

* * *

Kim Goldberg, who wrote one of *CD*'s longest running columns, "The Pacific Edge" (1990–2002) about BC politics, frequently discussed environmental issues, such as the conflicts between loggers and forest defenders. Time and again she pointed to the common adversary facing environmentalists and workers: the forest industry, which, she frequently pointed out, cared as little about preserving jobs as it did old-growth forests.[2] Many other contributors took the same tack, denouncing jobs-versus-environment blackmail and attempting to foster mutual understanding and solidarity between environmental activists and trade unionists. Naturally, *CD* insisted that, like all politics, environmental politics is also class politics, and it unfailingly reminded environmentalists that social justice must not be overlooked in the struggle for environmental sanity. As former *CD* columnist Doug Smith pointed out, "Reduce, Reuse, Recycle" required a fourth "R": *Redistribute*.

* * *

From the 1990s forward the magazine provided periodic coverage of environmental activism, such as the protests and blockades against clearcutting in Clayoquot Sound on Vancouver Island in the summer of 1993, which drew twelve thousand people and resulted in some nine hundred arrests — still the largest civil disobedience movement in Canadian history. And *Dimension* was also sensitive to state repression and corporate demonization of environmental activists. Goldberg was particularly strong on this score, whether she was exposing the use by MacMillan Bloedel of SLAPP suits to intimidate activists and cripple protest (26:7, October 1992) or discussing BC premier Glen Clark's demonization of environmentalists in the latter half of the 1990s (a harbinger of the Harper government's branding of environmentalists as terrorists some fifteen years later). Nor did she spare the NDP government of Mike Harcourt, which approved clear-cut logging in Clayoquot sound in 1993 and, Goldberg informed readers, was quietly ceding to pressures from mining interests to limit the land afforded protected area status by the Harcourt government.

Taking aim at environmentalism

Bridging the red-green divide didn't mean suspending critical judgment of environmentalism, of course, and the magazine took the movement to task on a variety of counts, confronting its reformism and other ideological and political failings. The most spectacular example of this was Bruce Livesey's attack on Greenpeace (28:4, August/September 1994), which Cy Gonick remembers as the most controversial article in *Dimension*'s entire history.[3] While recognizing Greenpeace's historic role in building awareness of environmental issues and acknowledging that it was continuing to contribute to campaigns on specific issues like clear-cutting in Clayoquot Sound, Livesey accused the NGO of having lost touch with the grassroots and of drifting towards corporate environmentalism. In particular, he censured it bitterly for abandoning its own campaigners when faced with a financial crunch in 1991 and for ensuing anti-union activities. Livesey relied on the testimony of former Greenpeace campaigners like former antinuclear campaigner Stan Gray, and former pulp and paper campaigner Gord Perks, both of whom had been fired in 1993 for denouncing the NGO's plans to lay off staff. He portrayed Greenpeace as an increasingly corporate, sexist, white middle-class organization, obsessed with earning media attention for the financial contributions that secured, insensitive to the rights of its own campaigners and insensitive to questions of environmental racism. The accusation of sexism was ironic because Livesey offered up an inexcusably sexist depiction of Greenpeace's then executive director Jeanne Moffat for which *Dimension* issued a sincere apology in the subsequent issue of the magazine. The article elicited a barrage of (mostly angry) letters, accusing Livesey of being misinformed and, in turn, of misinforming readers, of providing fodder to the mainstream media's efforts to discredit Greenpeace and of sectarianism, among many other complaints. These were published in the subsequent issue along with an official rejoinder from Moffat herself. Livesey was given ample space to defend his claims.

More recent and quite damning discussions of mainstream

environmental organizations appeared in the magazine in 2006 and 2011, for example, by environmental journalist Petr Cizek and anti-tar sands activist Macdonald Stainsby, respectively, pointing to the cooptation of groups like the Sierra Club of Canada and the Pembina Institute as a result of funding by right-wing American "charitable" organizations like the Pew Charitable Trusts and the Tides foundation.

More broadly, as noted earlier, *CD* continually raised questions about what many at the magazine and on the anticapitalist Left in general perceived as the rather futile reformism of the (mainstream) environmental movement; its tendency to avoid addressing the structural problems underpinning the ecological crisis and to fall back on moral exhortations and appeals to consumer behaviour. But it sought to stimulate debate and air a variety of viewpoints. In the September–October 2003 fortieth anniversary issue, for example, Keith Stewart, who was then associated with the Toronto Environmental Alliance and later worked for major environmental NGOs; political economist John W. Warnock, a founding member of Saskatchewan's New Green Alliance (the forerunner of that province's Green party); and Alberta political scientist Laurie Adkin all weighed in on the question of the environmental movement's reformism. Stewart, who had himself written a caustic critique of "ecological modernization," one of the theoretical guises of the neoliberal market-based approach to environmentalism, for the March–April 2002 issue, sought to defend environmentalism and more specifically the fight for the ratification of the Kyoto protocol, arguing that victories are necessary to build a movement, and observing that people come to the environmental movement not as political theorists but as citizens with a sense that something precious is in peril, whether locally or globally. While they may work for reforms that are functional to capitalism, he maintained, they are ultimately opposed to the system without necessarily possessing the theoretical tools to engage in a sustained critique. Adkin took the middle ground, leaning towards Stewart's position that most environmental campaigns embrace values and objectives that are inherently or potentially anticapitalist, and maintaining that when environmentalists support market-based approaches like carbon taxes they typically do so less out of conviction than as a pragmatic adaptation to the dominance of neoliberalism. Warnock took a less sanguine view, cautioning against the populist character of much green politics and condemning what he saw as the environmental movement's firm commitment to a strategy of reforming capitalism.

Some on the magazine today harbour similar reservations about the nascent degrowth movement, although *CD* offered that current a fairly extensive forum in the April–May 2012 issue, which proved, to my gratification as editor of that issue, one of the most popular in the magazine's history. It explored various perspectives on the need to emancipate the global North from the ecocidal imperative of economic growth, a compelling idea particularly at a historical juncture when growth is proving entirely compatible with spiralling inequality, the expansion of precarious employment and rising joblessness, giving the lie to the claim for growth as a rising tide that floats all boats. By implication degrowth is anticapitalist, since growth is the oxygen of capitalism's fire, but it spans a political spectrum that encompasses those who believe another capitalism is possible, a steady-state economy in Herman Daly's phrase. For *CD*, capitalism with a human face or a green heart is by definition a contradiction in terms.

Embracing ecosocialism

Indeed, a constant in *CD*'s treatment of environmental questions has been an emphasis on capitalism as the principal cause of the ongoing ecological meltdown and, consequently, the chief obstacle to any serious design to reverse it. This is the central premise of a set of ideas that goes under the rubric of "ecosocialism," with which *CD* has self-consciously identified itself in recent years. Ecosocialism represents the culmination of the evolution of the traditional Left on the ecology question, from its initial ambiguous reaction to the environmental movement and the concerns it signalled to an integration of ecological considerations and a recasting of Marx's thought not only as fundamentally compatible with ecology but providing an adequate explanation of the ecological crisis. It rests on an analysis of the inherent character of capitalism as a system predicated on a profit-or-perish ethos and a structural need for never-ending growth which reduces land, labour and

176

life itself to the status of commodities. Moreover, as a system governed by short-term interests, it eschews the long-term economic and social planning necessary for successful environmental management.

* * *

The ecosocialist current, represented today by thinkers such as Joel Kovel and John Bellamy Foster, draws on the pioneering work of left thinkers such as André Gorz and Herbert Marcuse. A young and evolving set of ideas, ecosocialism can more usefully be seen as a series of debates — about capitalism and nature, about the nature of capitalism, about Marx and ecology, about productivism and technology, about development and consumption and natural limits — than as any unified system of thought. But it is noteworthy that its foundations are being laid at a time when the larger environmental movement has flagged as a force for the kind of substantive societal change necessary to achieve its aims — this for a variety of reasons, including the institutionalization of green movements and parties, the cooptation of environmental issues by government and the corporate world, the relentless peddling of market solutions to ecological problems and an ongoing greenwashing campaign by industry.

Like the magazine's founder and publisher, many current and past *CD* editors, including Ian Angus and Roger Rashi among others, identify themselves as ecosocialists, and all are united in the conviction that only structural change, not the fiction of sustainable development or techno-fixes like geo-engineering, can begin to mitigate the ecological crisis: It is commodity production itself that must be overcome if humans are to live more lightly on the earth.

Voices in the wilderness: Interspecies solidarity

Perhaps a little surprisingly, *Dimension* has also given a voice over the decades to a current of deep-green thinking that rejects the reduction of nonhuman nature and nonhuman beings to the status of "resources" for the fulfillment of human interests, a perspective to which the Left has traditionally been quite hostile. This challenge to anthropocentrism was given expression for many years by the progenitor of left biocentrism, the late David Orton, in various articles as well as his column "The Green Web," and it is that cast of mind that informs my own "*Eco*Side" column.

Orton contributed to the magazine on a regular basis from 1989 to 1996, primarily at the invitation of Cy Gonick, whose ecumenical spirit and desire to foster productive dialogue trumped the *CD* collective's suspicions. Orton was also the object of a vitriolic ad hominem attack by Len Bush and subsequent defense by Tom Holzinger sparked by a February–March 1995 piece that respectfully broached certain tensions between ecological perspectives and support from *some* First Nations for questionable projects billed as sustainable development (such as Aboriginal-sanctioned logging in Clayoquot, support for a pipeline in Nova Scotia, support for the fur industry and commercial trapping). Orton maintained that notwithstanding the enormous pressures on Indigenous communities, they should not be treated as exempt from all criticism by the environmental movement.

In general, Orton, who was seeking to reconcile radical left politics with a version of deep ecology, professed to feel like a voice in the wilderness within *Dimension*. Like many on the Left, the majority of *Canadian Dimension* editors contend that the source of ecological degradation lies exclusively with capitalism and they find themselves at odds with radical greens who see the roots of the ecology crisis in anthropocentrism, industrialism and unchecked population growth that spells the certain death of habitat and scarcity of food sources for other species. Ultimately, though, that particular debating point is moot because even if the argument for capitalism as the singular source of all that ails us ecologically is contestable, the case for capitalism as an immoveable obstacle to reducing humanity's ecological bootprint is unassailable. Ecosocialists emphasize that the ecological crisis is not the result of greed or neglect on the part of individual capitalists who might be prevailed upon to become more socially and environmentally responsible; thus, moral exhortations and appeals to conscience, often the strategy of choice for mainstream environmentalism, are futile because they overlook the structural determinations of capitalism. As this brief retrospective aims to show, *Dimension* has made this case strongly, with regular articles on the limits of environmental reformism and the deceptions of corporate greenwashing.

What columns like "The Green Web" and "*Eco*Side" have tried to drive home is that while capitalism is inimical to ecological well-being, so is a socialism that fails to move beyond an instrumental view of the natural world. If human needs of whatever order always take precedence over the needs and interests of nonhuman beings and entities then we will replace one form of chauvinism with another and in the long run there will be no space for anything that does not immediately serve the interests of billions of bipeds.

On the question of the needs and interests of other species, *Canadian Dimension* has shown the indifference typical of a left that has failed to overcome human chauvinism to a point where the lack of regard for other beings arguably strains any claim the magazine can make to an ecological standpoint. Aside from Orton's contributions, my own column, and an article or two over the last few decades on the agony inflicted on factory-farmed animals,[4] the dominant perspective regrettably remains a perception of nonhuman sentient life as a storehouse of "resources" available for human consumption. To date, ecosocialism seems largely lacking in any "spiritually generous compassion for the needless suffering" of fellow sentient beings.[5] Nor has it put much muscle into pressing the strong ecological argument for a sea change in alimentary and agricultural practices away from meat consumption and intensive livestock farming.

A burning question

Although *CD*'s treatment of ecological issues was rather spasmodic in the first years of the new millennium, one of the issues which did command considerable attention is climate change. This was not self-evident, since, in what is probably one of the more embarrassing moments in the magazine's history, the first full article that *CD* ever published on the subject, in the April–May 1990 issue, was a denial of the urgency of global warming in which the author rejected the case for anthropogenic climate change (and disputed human impact on the ozone layer for good measure). He attributed changing climate patterns to solar variation and maintained that if it were to occur, global warming would be good for Canada!

In the last seven or eight years, however, *CD* has covered the looming catastrophe of climate change in a serious and sustained way — especially in relation to Canada's singular contribution to that catastrophe in the form of the Alberta tar sands. Several special issues have been published, such as "End Times In Copenhagen" (43: 6, November/December 2009), which pilloried the central place of the tar sands in the Canadian economic development model and offered a critique of strategies for mitigating climate change that fail to move beyond meagre emissions reductions targets and cap-and-trade schemes — all themes the magazine has returned to in subsequent issues. "Stepping Up for the Planet" (45:6, November/December 2011), an unprecedented joint production saw *CD* team up with the South African journal *Amandla* to offer a critical perspective on the Durban COP17 United Nations' meeting on climate change. In addition to commentary and reportage from a number of journalists, academics and activists, *CD* editors Cy Gonick, Ian Angus, Judy Deutsch, Terisa Turner and Clayton Thomas-Müller, among others, have all explored aspects of the devastating implications of climate change for Canadians and the world. These pieces, like many other *CD* reflections on ecological themes, have often benefited from accompanying reproductions of remarkable drawings by Cuban-born cartoonist Angel Boligán, who made his career in Mexico as one of the world's great political cartoonists and whose work evinces an acute ecological sensibility.

First Nations on the front lines

Particularly in the new millennium, it is Canada's Indigenous peoples who have been leading the efforts to combat climate change and protect the natural environment from the predation of corporate capitalism, and *Dimension* has contributed to publicizing their struggles, as members of Indigenous communities use every means at their disposal from the courts to civil disobedience to impede ecologically-destructive resource development projects such as mines, pipeline and the tar sands, which are typically located on or in close proximity to Indigenous territories. As *CD* collective member Martin Lukacs summed it up in an article for the *Guardian:* ". . . finally honouring Indigenous rights is not simply about paying off Canada's enormous legal debt to First Nations: it is also our best chance to save entire territories from endless extraction and destruction. In no small way the actions of Indigenous peoples and the decision of Canadians to stand alongside them — will determine the fate of the planet."[6]

Clayton Thomas-Müller's participation in the *CD* editorial collective since 2009 has given the magazine a privileged connection with Indigenous environmental resistance in Canada. Thomas-Müller, a Manitoba Cree, is one of the founders of Defenders of the Land, a pan-Canadian network of Indigenous communities and activists involved in struggles to protect the land and assert native rights, as well as an anti–tar sands campaigner for the Indigenous Environmental Network.

Just as the historic Left conceived the prospects for change to be strongest at the point of production, many of Canada's most powerful environmental resistance movements have taken shape at the point of extraction, from the Lubicon Cree struggle with the Alberta and federal governments against oil and gas development[7] to the successful resistance of the Kitchenuhmaykoosib Inninuwug to gold mining on their territory without their consent[8] and the emergence of Idle No More.

While *CD* has not flinched either from commenting, when relevant, on instances of First Nations' complicity with and investment in environmentally destructive projects, such as the Mackenzie Gas Project, that will pollute and imperil their territories,[9] the magazine has remained steadfast in supporting and casting light on the environmentally-charged struggles of Canada's Indigenous peoples. And the attention *CD* devotes to this resistance is consonant with *Dimension*'s abiding attention to Indigenous politics, as Peter Kulchyski underscores in his chapter in this volume.

At a historical moment when denial of the ever-narrowing limits to growth, consumption and waste is promoted by global elites, and when Canada in particular is governed by those bent on criminalizing environmental advocacy and protest, *Canadian Dimension*'s dissenting voice could not be more vital. We are part of a small but dedicated tribe of academics, journalists and activists prepared to condemn a global economic status quo that is now nothing short of suicidal and to stand in solidarity with all those who refuse to capitulate to it.

For all the weight and urgency environmental concerns are now accorded in the magazine, however, it cannot be said that ecological consciousness permeates the pages of *Canadian Dimension*. *CD* is certainly a forceful advocate for the far-reaching societal changes necessary to even make a dent in the relentless degradation of ecosystems. But the looming disaster of climate change, fresh water pollution, ocean destruction and biodiversity extinction remains compartmentalized, confined to a column here, an article there, an annual special issue. While it may be true that *CD* could not allot substantially more space to our civilization's steady advance towards ecocide without fundamentally changing its vocation, that story remains somehow one among others. The irony is that the revenge of nature is rendering nugatory the historical project of the Left in all its guises. To echo David Orton, there can be no justice for people on a dead planet.

CHAPTER 6
Natural Resources and Canadian Capitalism: The View from *Canadian Dimension* Magazine

John W. Warnock

Canadian Dimension magazine was launched at an important turning point in Canadian history. From the end of World War II to the early 1960s Canadian political discourse had been dominated by the Cold War between the United States and its allies and the Soviet bloc. The threat of invasion from the USSR had served to override any concern over the growing integration between the United States and Canada. This period also saw the increased domination of the Canadian economy by US transnational corporations and the growing dependence on trade with the United States. Canadians were becoming aware of the degree to which they were under the influence of the American mass media and culture.

The early 1960s saw the emergence of a student movement at Canada's universities and a growing concern over nuclear war and nuclear weapons. At the same time there was a revival of the Canadian tradition of political economy. For the first time since the end of World War II, academics and other researchers began empirical studies on the state of the Canadian economy and its relationship to the United States. The conclusion of Harold Innis, our most notable political economist, was that "Canada moved from colony to nation to colony."[1] A.R.M. Lower, another of Canada's premier political economists, declared that Canada was "a subordinate state" becoming a "satellite of the United States."[2] Canada's weak capitalist class faced the reality of having to compete with branch plants of large American corporations. There was no attempt to try to create an independent Canadian strategy for development.

The emphasis on continental integration

During the Great War there had been significant military and economic cooperation between Canada and the United States. But from the perspective of the US government and its people, Canada was still a colony within the British empire. A special white settler colony, of course, with a significant degree of self-government. For the loyal colonies of Canada, Australia and New Zealand, it was "Ready, Aye Ready" when called on by the imperial centre. During the Great War there was some military coordination with the United States, but it was insignificant compared to the cooperation between the two major Anglo-Saxon powers. This was to change.

As the war clouds formed, in August 1938 President Franklin Roosevelt travelled to Queen's University where he declared in a formal speech: "The Dominion of Canada is part of the sisterhood of the British Empire. I give to you assurance that the people of the United States will not stand idly by if domination of Canadian soil is threatened by any other Empire."

The Ogdensburg Agreement which followed created the Permanent Joint Board of Defence between the two countries, and planning began for continental economic and military cooperation and integration. The Hyde Park Agreement of April 1941 more specifically called for major economic integration between the two countries. The Joint Economic Committee formed in June 1941 concentrated on how best to rationalize natural resources on a North American continental basis. This was the formal recognition that Canada was moving from a British colony to an American protectorate. It also was a declaration that the Canadian economy would shift from an East-West to a North-South basis.

After Pearl Harbor, Canada was left out of the process of military and political planning. FDR talked with Winston Churchill, not with Ottawa. The Atlantic Charter was signed off the coast of Newfoundland without Canada's participation. At the end of the war Great Britain was greatly weakened while the United States was stronger than ever as mobilization had ended the Great Depression. The US government now assumed the role of chief defender of the free world against Soviet totalitarian communism.[3]

The Cold War

In November 1945 President Harry Truman asked Canada to continue the wartime cooperation indefinitely. Mackenzie King's government agreed. Joint defence plans were created, this time with the USSR as the enemy. In February 1947 it was announced that the United States and Canada had formulated a Declaration of Defence Co-operation. Cold War military activities increased in the Canadian north. In October 1950 the two countries revealed the New Hyde Park Agreement, calling for a sharing of natural resources and industrial mobilization to support the anticommunist war in Korea.[4]

As the United States government mobilized to fight the Korean War, planners discovered that there was significant evidence of the depletion of US-based strategic resources and basic raw materials. President Harry Truman created the Materials Policy Commission, commonly known as a Paley Commission after its chairman, which reported in 1952. The United States was found to be heavily dependent on the import of key materials, including nickel, manganese, tungsten, florspar, zinc, lead, bauxite, aluminum, iron ore and copper. The concern of the Commission was guaranteed access to non-hostile sources of supply.

In support of this goal, the Commission recommended that the US government encourage the investment by American corporations in the development of these resources. It was noted that US corporations were heavily involved in the development of these key resources in Canada. Twenty-nine strategic resource commodities were identified as of particular concern due to the depletion of US reserves. Of these twelve were to be safely found in Canada. The construction of the St. Lawrence Seaway was endorsed as a means of facilitating the import of raw materials to the US industrial heartland.[5]

At this time, there was little concern over petroleum resources. Production was still ample in the United States, friendly governments were being supported in Venezuela, and the US government was working with Great Britain to maintain domination over the new oil sources in the Middle East. After 1970, when it became known that the US had passed its peak in domestic oil production, the government and the oil industry began to promote a continental energy agreement with Canada.

The structure of the Canadian economy

Over the 1960s and 1970s there were many studies which dissected the shift in Canada's dependency from Great Britain to the United States. Under the domination of Great Britain, the emphasis had been on the export of natural resource staples to the mother country and other European states. Canada moved from fish, square timber and agricultural products to the new staples of pulp and paper, a wide range of minerals and petroleum products. This was documented to some degree in the 1957 Royal Commission on Canada's Economic Prospects under the chairmanship of Walter Gordon.[6]

The themes of these studies were reflected in the articles which appeared in *Canadian Dimension*. They noted the high degree of foreign ownership in general and in the resource sector in particular. In mining and petroleum it went from 37 per cent in 1948 to 59 per cent in 1960. The Twentieth Century Fund study noted that Canada was not short of capital. New foreign investment in Canada was largely financed through the generous depreciation and depletion allowances granted by the federal government to existing foreign corporations, retained earnings and borrowing from Canadian financial institutions.[7]

By 1962 58 per cent of all exports went to the United States, which in turn provided Canada with 60 per cent of our imports. Raw materials and partially finished products accounted for 62 per cent of exports and chiefly manufactured goods only 37 per cent. In contrast, 77 per cent of our imports were manufactured goods. The structure of our trade was more like that of a less-developed country than an advanced industrialized economy. This was "the new dependency." For many studying the new political economy, including contributors to *Canadian Dimension*, there were similarities to the structure of the economies in Latin America.

Mainstream economists argued that Canada had a "comparative advantage" in the area of the development of natural resources. There was still an unused capacity in the agricultural sector, with exports often limited by policies in non-Canadian markets. In the forest sector, around 40 per cent of the value of lumber, wood products and pulp and paper was exported, with the share going to the USA steadily increasing. In 1960 two-thirds of the fish caught in Canadian waters was exported. The new boom was in the mineral sector. Canada was among the top four world producers of twelve important primary products and the second largest producer of natural gas.[8]

The oil industry

On the political front, the Waffle movement within the New Democratic Party was launched in 1968 with a manifesto calling for the creation of an independent socialist Canada. *Canadian Dimension* magazine and most of its contributors were closely linked to this development. The Waffle focused on foreign domination of the economy by transnational corporations, the deepening of integration with the United States, the democratization of the Canadian political system and the promotion of a socialist alternative.

James Laxer, one of the national leaders of the Waffle movement, contributed an overview of the status of the natural resources industry in a 1971 issue of *Canadian Dimension* (7:7, January/February). He noted that "Canada has fewer controls on foreign investors than any other major country on earth." In 1969 the National Energy Board projected major increases in the extraction of oil and gas in Canada and their export to the United States. The NEB concluded that the USA "was Canada's only possible customer." US ownership was overwhelming in Canada's resource industries: 99 per cent in oil refining, 82.6 per cent in the oil and gas wells industry and 84.9 per cent in the primary metal smelting and refining. Laxer noted that "the key components of the Canadian resource sector are dominated by huge vertically-integrated American conglomerates."

This produced an overall negative impact on Canada. The terms of trade were unfavourable to resource-extracting countries and favourable to manufacturing countries. Capital invested in resource extraction produced far fewer jobs than investment in manufacturing. Furthermore, the Canadian government heavily subsidized the resource industries with tax rates well below other sectors of the economy.

Laxer argued that the Canadianization of investment in the resource sector did not change corporate behaviour. Canadian capitalists were also committed to continental integration. Our present status as a resource-producing hinterland for US capitalism could only be changed with an entirely different approach to development (7:7, January/February 1971).

The oil industry in Canada was led by Imperial Oil. Originally a Canadian-owned company, Exxon bought the company in 1899 for less than $1 million. As the leading oil corporation in Canada, it was involved in the early developments in Turner Valley, Alberta, in the 1920s and the Leduc discovery in 1947. It partnered with the federal government in the creation of Syncrude in the tar sands. For years Imperial Oil was the price leader at the retail gasoline stations. In the early 1970s it was a major supporter of a continental energy agreement. It had also been a major contributor to the Liberal and Conservative parties. Laxer argued that if Canada is to have any control over its oil and gas industry there had to be Canadian public ownership of Imperial Oil (11:8, November 1976).

Canadian Dimension took a strong stand against the development of the Mackenzie Valley pipeline. My article in the October 1972 issue (9:1) traced the history of the Liberal government's support for the building of a Northern transportation and communications corridor up the valley, beginning with an all-weather highway. A pipeline would carry Arctic oil and gas to the US market.

The environmental costs of the project had been detailed in a national conference held in Ottawa in May 1971. There had been no hearings to determine the position of the native population which lived in the area, at the time estimated to be seven thousand First Nations, five thousand Métis and thirteen thousand Inuit. They objected strongly to the federal government permitting Elf Oil and Imperial Oil to drill in the area when there had been no agreements negotiated with any of the Aboriginal groups. Reflecting the position of the Waffle and *Canadian Dimension*, I argued that any development of natural resources in the far north should be limited to Canadian-owned Crown corporations.[9]

Fred Gudmundson updated this issue in 1986. This was after the creation of the Berger Inquiry and the release of its report in 1977. The commission concluded that "no major developments be undertaken in the area for a least ten years." This would allow time for the negotiations for land claims and for the Dene to establish institutions for self-government.

Imperial Oil, a subsidiary of Exxon of the United States, had created the Northwest Company and sent them to the Fort Norman area to drill. The Normal Wells field was developed, a pipeline was built, and a refinery was established in Whitehorse. The federal government received one-third of the net returns from this oil development. The royalties paid by Imperial were set at only 5 per cent. The local Dene population received nothing. In 1980 Imperial applied to expand production and to build a pipeline to the South. The Liberal government announced that it would reopen negotiations with the Aboriginal people affected. As Gudmundson argued at the time, fraud and deception had been the rule in the history of negotiations between the indigenous populations and Imperial Oil and the Government of Canada. It was doubtful if this would change (19:6, January/February 1986).

The status of the oil industry in Canada became a major public issue in the 1970s. This was triggered by the fact that when major oil-producing areas in former colonies achieved independence and the Middle East producing countries took the initiative to create the Organization of Petroleum Exporting Countries (OPEC), they attempted to raise world prices by acting as a limited cartel. All of these new producing governments created state-owned oil corporations.

In October 1975 (11:2) Ed Shaffer wrote an overview of the world energy industry in *Dimension*. The industrial revolution had replaced the reliance on human and animal energy with fossil fuels; solar energy borrowed from the past. He described the close link between the energy industries and imperialism. Great Britain, working closely with its own oil corporations, used its world colonial empire to try to protect oil resources. The US government followed suit, giving its own transnational oil corporations "full diplomatic and military backing in their foreign ventures." Both countries supported the international oil cartel set up by the seven largest corporations, all American or British. They worked together closely to control Iraq, Iran and the Persian Gulf feudal regimes.

They convinced their puppet governments in these areas not to spend their royalties on programs to improve the standard of living for their peoples but to purchase military equipment in the West and invest the surplus in Western banks.

Shaffer, an economist at the University of Alberta, concluded that these developments would not be easy to change. The Western states are committed to private ownership of resources, which produces "the permanent inequality of incomes" which is "so essential to the function of a market society." Given this model of development, the widespread prevalence of the large segment of society who are "have-nots" requires a strong state with military and police power. Thus, the most successful market economies have also been those with a long history of militarism and "seizing property from others." Capturing cheap resources has permitted the expansion of their industrial capacity. This system also produces enormous waste and ecological destruction. The first step to real change requires the recognition that "social responsibility implies private irresponsibility. In a society based on private property, a social ethic must always be subservient to a private one. It cannot be otherwise" (11:2, October 1975).

The July–August 1982 issue of *Canadian Dimension* (16:5) featured a special focus on the oil industry. Brian O'Neill introduced readers to the issue of oil and gas extraction offshore of Nova Scotia and Newfoundland. Nova Scotia's premier, John Buchanan, predicted a major boom in oil and gas production. O'Neill argued that this was political hype as studies indicated that there was limited natural gas to be exploited. In contrast, there was a much greater potential off Newfoundland. Brian Peckford, Newfoundland's premier, had been aggressive in demanding a high share of the offshore reserves, which the federal government, which owns the resource, was loath to cede to the province. As always the development was a product of large transnational oil corporations.

Ed Shaffer (16:5, July/August 1982) analysed the impact of the controversial National Energy Program and the Ottawa-Alberta agreement of 1981. The battle between the federal government, the Alberta government and the oil industry never addressed the key issue, he argued: "how to use Canada's energy resources to bring maximum benefit to

Canadians." Indeed, the 1981 agreement would likely result in higher oil and gas prices right in the middle of a very deep downturn in the Canadian economy.

The oil industry dictated the absurd Canadian oil policy where western production is shipped to the United States and more expensive oil is imported for refiners in eastern Canada. Furthermore, the federal government paid these refiners a subsidy for imported oil to balance the difference in cost with western Canadian oil. The only way to end the stranglehold that the transnational oil companies have over oil policy in Canada is through public ownership.

Larry Pratt (16:5, July/August 1982) provided a summary of Robert Bertrand's seven-volume study on *The State of Competition in the Canadian Petroleum Industry*, completed under the *Combines Investigation Act*. While OPEC and state-owned national oil companies produced state-to-state deals which maximized benefits for producers and consumers, such was certainly not the case in Canada. Policy has been dictated by the four majors: Imperial, Gulf, Texaco and Shell. They dictated the 1961 National Oil Policy, which excluded western oil from Montreal and prevented independent Ontario refiners from buying oil from other sources, while Alberta's "pro-rationing" policy kept prices high. Bertrand documented the practices by which the four majors created monopoly power. As we all suspected, the parent oil corporations "consistently over-charged the Canadian affiliates, then skimmed the profits to their subsidiaries based in tax havens such as Bermuda." Pratt argued that the liberal view of breaking up the giant oil corporations or trying to regulate them was a non-option; only public ownership with democratic accountability could work.

The National Energy Program created a serious conflict between Alberta and the federal Liberal government of Pierre Elliott Trudeau. It also resulted in vigorous attacks on Canada by the transnational oil corporations and the US government. But it won strong support from the Canadian public. In January 1983 (16:7), Julian Sher wrote an assessment of the policy. On the plus side, there had been an increase in Canadian ownership of the oil industry, up from 6.7 per cent to 32.8 per cent, measured by industry revenues. A new crown corporation,

Petro-Canada, had taken over Petrofina. The lucrative incentives provided by the federal government to Canadian firms led to the development and expansion of new Canadian-owned enterprises, including Norcen, Nova and Dome Petroleum. Unfortunately, the policy came right in the middle of a world recession which saw a major decline in oil prices. The economy was also hammered by the high interest rates set by the central banks. The Reagan Administration denounced the NEP for discriminating against US oil corporations. As Sher stressed, this national policy was designed to aid Canadian capitalists. It came at "a fairly steep price for ordinary Canadians."

The tar sands

In the January 1977 issue of Canadian Dimension (12:1), Ed Shaffer offered a favourable review of Larry Pratt's book, *The Tar Sands: Syncrude and the Politics of Oil*. The Syncrude project would likely become the model for "new energy adventures in Canada." In this case federal and provincial governments provided 70 per cent of development costs for 30 per cent equity in this joint venture. Royalties have been virtually nonexistent. The fact that development is concentrated in large transnational corporations, most of them foreign-owned and -controlled, blocks the possibility of national sovereignty and independence. It is a classic example of how metropolitan powers exploit hinterland areas.

As Shaffer and Pratt pointed out, in the Syncrude model of private development with government minority participation, the private sector received "extremely liberal tax concessions, a no-strike agreement, huge government investments in infrastructure, exemption from export restrictions, a guaranteed rate-of-return, and a guaranteed price." The environmental damage was deemed acceptable and native communities were ignored. By renouncing the option of public ownership and development, Canadian governments "lost their sole opportunity to checkmate what we have called the oil industry's monopoly veto power — its power to block development of resources such as Athabaska sands."

In the 1990s the political concern over the oil industry shifted from the domination of US capital and continental integration to "peak oil" and the development of the tar sands. Conventional oil production was declining and around the globe the industry was shifting to the more expensive and more environmentally threatening alternate sources. In Canada that meant a major shift to production at the Alberta tar sands.

To stimulate the development of the tar sands, the Alberta government invested hundreds of millions of dollars in research and development, provided the industry with major tax breaks, and established extremely low royalty rates. There has been a united front of support for this model of development: the Alberta Conservative governments, the Liberal governments of Jean Chrétien and Paul Martin, and Stephen Harper's Reform/Alliance parties. The federal NDP did not oppose this development.

The tar sands turned into the largest megaproject in the world. The costs of development are enormous. A huge area the size of Florida will be made a "national sacrifice area," like the Hanford Nuclear Reservation in eastern Washington state. The Athabaska River system will be devastated. Many pipelines are to be built. Mining requires two tons of sand and nine barrels of water to produce one barrel of synthetic oil. Drilling for the 80 per cent of the economically feasible reserves, using steam extraction, will require all of the natural gas projected from the Mackenzie and Alaska pipelines. The Lubicon Cree, the Chipewyan nation and other Aboriginal groups will have their lands devastated. And 70 per cent of the production will be shipped to the USA (31:2, March/April 1997).

Paul Phillips stressed that the decline in oil production and higher prices brought by peak oil would have a devastating impact on agriculture and food. Modern industrial agriculture is heavily dependent on fossil fuels for production and transportation. The agri-food system in the United States uses ten calories of fossil-fuel energy to produce a single calorie of food energy. In the long run, he predicted, peak oil will require a return to more labour-intensive agriculture and local production for local consumption (40:1, January/February 2006).

There is a very good reason why human beings have become so dependent on conventional oil: it is easy to extract from the ground and has a high net energy ratio. As Jack Santa-Barbara pointed out in a special *CD* issue devoted to peak oil, in the early period of oil dependency the ratio of net energy was 100 units out for one unit of energy invested; this has now fallen to around 20:1. But that is still much better than alternative energy, which is around 10:1, and to government-subsidized ethanol, which may not even produce a net energy. The process of producing so-called "clean coal" with CO_2 sequestered is very energy-intensive, with no guarantee that the buried CO_2 will not find its way to the surface. Any real alternative to our dependence on oil will require a major shift away from growth and profits to meeting basic human needs (40:4, July/ August 2006).

Dimension took an editorial stand on this issue in its January/February 2006 edition (40:1). Canada needs a radical shift in its transportation system and "big and multiple injections of funds" into the development of alternative energy sources. To finance this transformation we would have to nationalize the oil and gas industry, which could be compensated with long-term government bonds. We would also need to abrogate NAFTA to get out of the continental energy pact. Other countries, like Venezuela, are pursuing similar policies. Public opinion polls indicate that there is solid support for such a strategy.

In his contribution to the 2006 special edition on peak oil (40:4, July/ August), a geographer by the name of Petr Cizek produced some of the best research on the tar sands. The J. Howard Pew family, owners of the Sun Oil Company (Sunoco) pioneered the development of the tar sands through Suncor. Syncrude was a joint-venture corporation heavily subsidized by the Alberta and federal governments. By 2005 fully half of Canada's oil production was coming from the tar sands. As described by Cizek, the environmental impact of the development, and its use of fossil-fuel energy and water, is almost beyond comprehension. Over the long run, the industry is planning to develop nuclear power to heat the steam for the in situ extraction of the bitumen.

All the huge international oil corporations are investing in the tar sands. They make big money since royalties and taxes are minute. The only rational alternative is to shut the industry down and follow a different path. Cizek provided groundbreaking research on the major environmental groups in Canada, showing that virtually all of them are dependent on direct or indirect grants from oil corporations. Some are even partnered with oil corporations. Most, including the Pembina Institute, receive large grants from the Pew Charitable Trusts, founded by the Pew family with its heavy investment in tar sands development. According to Cizek, this explains why the major environmental organizations normally call for modifications of the tar sands projects or at best for a moratorium on new projects. They never call for what is really needed: "Shut 'Em Down!" (40:4, July/August 2006; 43:1, January/February 2009).

The role of the major Canadian environmental groups in the legitimization of the tar sands project was further examined by Macdonald Stainsby (45:4, July/August 2011). He emphasized the special role of the US-based Tides Foundation, created by large corporations in the oil business, which has helped finance almost all the major Canadian environmental organizations and created the North American Tar Sands Coalition. The goal has been to direct political activity away from shutting down the tar sands to mitigation of the worst of the environmental impact. Partnerships were made with oil corporations; they agreed to protect water supplies, improve the tailings systems, set aside permanent conservation areas, create carbon offsets, support alternative energy projects, and look into the issue of carbon capture and sequestration. Stainsby concluded the article by arguing that once the public agrees to endorse the Canadian tar sands development project, there can be no prohibitions on developments in similar heavy-oil areas of the world.

Subsidizing the Canadian mining industry

Dimension and the new political economy focused on the domination of the mining industry by large transnational corporations, especially those from the United States. The focus was also on the close ties to the United States through the structure of trade.

A new direction was established when Eric Kierans released his report, *Natural Resources Policy in Manitoba*, prepared for the Government of Manitoba, in February 1973. Kierans, who was a distinguished professor of economics at McGill University, had also served as a Liberal Member of Parliament and a member of Pierre Elliott Trudeau's cabinet, as well as a past president of the Montreal Stock Exchange. In May 1973 (9:5), *Canadian Dimension* ran extensive extracts from this report. No editorial comment was needed.

Kierans's report stressed the monopoly power of the mining industry in Canada, the extensive subsidies granted the corporations by the provincial and federal governments, the very high profits made by the industry, and the fact that the industry was capturing the bulk of resource rents (or excess profits) from the exploitation of a resource which belonged to all the people. The industry in Manitoba was dominated by four firms: Inco, Falconbridge, Hudson's Bay and Sherritt Gordon. They held 80 per cent of the mining claims filed by the province.

The profit captured by the mining industry was far greater than other Canadian industries. This was due to the high depletion allowances granted the firms, the exemption from paying any taxes on the profits for the first three years of operation, the accelerated depreciation allowances granted by governments, and the very low royalties charged by the provincial governments. The excess profits of the private mining corporations came from their ability to capture the bulk of the economic rents, the surplus profits which should have gone to the owners of the resource, the Canadian people.

The report cited the potash industry in Saskatchewan as an illustration of the folly of giving corporations extensive subsidies and virtually exempting them from paying royalties and taxes. The result was a very significant overinvestment in the potash industry. To prevent financial collapse of the firms, which were all transnational corporations, the provincial government created a potash cartel which shared production and fixed prices. The rent from the extraction of the potash under this "free market" system of development did not go to the people but was wasted away by the inefficient private mining industry.

Using data from the federal government, Kierans calculated that the return on capital invested in the mining sector between 1965 and 1969 was a colossal 45.8 per cent. Of the net profit to the mining corporations, 14.7 per cent went to the people who owned the resource, the shareholders of the corporations received 50.2 per cent, and 35.1 per cent was retained by the corporations for expansion and growth.

What was the solution to this resource rip-off? Kierans proposed that all future mining development in the province be "firmly in the hands of the public sector." Exploration should be by a provincial Crown corporation. All mineral rights should be held by the Crown. Crown corporations should be created for the development of all new ore bodies. For the existing mines, they should be assessed a property tax on their reserves. Royalties should be assessed on the volume of ore extracted, not on net income. An additional tax should be applied to all existing leases for mining claims.

The conclusion that Kierans wrote could have been written by the Waffle or the editorial board of *Canadian Dimension* magazine:

> *To be satisfied with the new jobs created and to forego the surpluses and profits inherent in the development of its own endowment is hardly the mark of a strong and mature government. It accepts the role of "hewers of wood and drawers of water" for its people when they are capable of much more. That role provides wages and salaries and little else. The profits, which direct and finance the future, belong to those who have been invited in . . . and does nothing for Manitoban priorities in the fields of agriculture, health, education or whatever."* (9:6, July 1973)

Canadian mining corporations move abroad

The more recent concern reflected in *Canadian Dimension* has been the development of a very strong Canadian owned mining sector which is now investing extensively in less-developed countries. Toronto has become the mining finance capital of the world, where around 40 per cent of all new investment capital is raised. Canadian-based mining companies now account for around 40 per cent of the worldwide expenditure for exploration.

In a special issue devoted to examining Canadian mining in Latin America and Africa (45:1, January/February 2011), Lisa North summarized the horrendous record of Canadian mining companies in Latin America. In almost every country where they are found there is a constant conflict with local people over "air, soil, and water contamination and their impacts on environmental and human health as well as agriculture."

The government of Stephen Harper resisted all efforts to establish legislative requirements for corporate accountability. The example of Sweden and Norway show that countries can hold their companies accountable for behaviour overseas.

Canadian mining corporations were encouraged to invest abroad as the cost of production was lower than in Canada. Furthermore, the move to the neoliberal model in the less-developed countries, as imposed by the international financial institutions, produced a bonanza of incentives. In an article with a focus on Africa, Bonnie Campbell noted the privatization of local state involvement in the mining sector. Typical Canadian-style subsidies were introduced. Norms and standards were reduced, including in employment, health and environment. The Canadian government takes the position that it is up to the local government to set the standards. A classic cop-out (45:1, January/February 2011).

Honduras is a good case study in the close links between the Canadian government's political goals and the economic goals of Canadian corporations investing abroad. In 2009 the military overthrew the democratically elected government of President Zelaya. He had proposed a referendum to be held with scheduled elections to see if the public wanted to call a constitutional assembly to draft a new constitution. The existing constitution, helped along by the US government, was imposed on the people by the previous military dictatorship. The local business class and the military feared the development of another leftist regime as in Venezuela.

The new military-backed regime was expelled from the Organization of American States and was not recognized by the vast majority of its members. But the US and Canadian governments gave it full support. Stephen Harper stood by, "Ready, Aye Ready," backing President Barack Obama and the military dictatorship. Harper and his ambassador in Honduras were also quick to defend the role of Canadian mining corporations and those working of the *maquila* (free trade) manufacturing sectors.

Widespread repression occurred after the military coup. Many key leaders of the progressive alliance, the National Front of Popular Resistance, were murdered. Death squads were present across the country. Goldcorp, a prominent mining corporation based in Saskatoon, was a key mining corporation charged by locals with human rights abuses, exposure of toxic chemicals, and environmental violations. Goldcorp received significant support and assistance from the province's NDP governments. A former NDP finance minister, Eric Cline, has been employed by it. "If pressure is not brought to bear in Canada on government policy makers, investors . . . and company shareholders," concluded Grahame Russell, "then Canadian mining companies will continue to operate their profitable and harmful mines with impunity" (45:1, January/February 2011).

Conclusion

Canadian Dimension magazine was founded by Cy Gonick at a time when democratic political mobilization was on the rise across Canada and the United States. The New Left was determined to challenge and move beyond the tired old Cold War straitjacket. In the universities it was not only students but a new group of academics who branched out to provide a critique of modern imperialism and corporate-dominated capitalism. This was a period when we began to seriously look at our history and what Canada could be, beyond a loyal colony of the British Empire or a silent ally of the United States in its imperial ventures.

At this time there was also a proliferation of new alternative media sources across Canada. Several national and regional magazines were created. There was also a flowering of independent community-based newspapers. It was an exciting period in Canadian history. Most of the others have disappeared, but *Canadian Dimension* remains.

The most important political movement in Canada during this period was the formation of the Waffle group within the New Democratic Party. It was able to break into the mainstream media. All during this period of time and up to the present, activists have turned to *Canadian Dimension* for an analysis of what was happening and why.

As we look at the debate around the petroleum and mining industries in Canada, again *Canadian Dimension* has played a key role in revealing the workings of these industries. It has covered the stories and presented the analysis that has been completely absent in the mainstream media. It has also given excellent coverage to the role of Canadian governments and Canadian corporations on the international level. In the era of electronic media, *Canadian Dimension* remains available to Canadians as part of the new media and the old. Political activists and others find that it remains a vital asset.

PART IV

THE CULTURAL DIMENSION

CHAPTER 7
Becoming Ordinary: Fifty Years of Arts and Culture

Brenda Austin-Smith

If society has an imagination to express its desires and fears, it is activated through art. If society is to experiment with change, with new forms, with its power structures, with ways of seeing and with language itself, it must be through art.

— *Kevin Matthews (41:4, July/August 2007)*

In the collection *Resources of Hope*, Raymond Williams insisted that "culture is ordinary," and that the most vivid and significant considerations of culture acknowledge its double nature as both a "whole way of life" and the realm of "arts and learning." The "making of a society," he wrote, is "the finding of common meanings and directions, and its growth is an active debate and amendment under the pressures of experience, contact, and discovery." His words are an apt introduction to this chapter on cultural commentary in the pages of *Canadian Dimension* magazine. For fifty years the magazine's many contributors engaged in a version of Williams's "active debate" over culture and its connections to institutions, practices and power. Among the many topics of those debates were the politics of representation, the role of the state in producing and disseminating cultural products, censorship and control of the media, the resilience of working class culture and the meaning and value of particular cultural moments, gestures and products. Cultural institutions (galleries, museums) cultural practices (sports), and cultural media (newspapers, television, cinema, the Internet) were all sites of intense scrutiny and engaged, often provocative, commentary. But *CD* did not just analyze culture. Over its five decades of production, the magazine also published original works of fiction, poetry, cartoons and photo essays, and its covers featured the work of both new and established artists.

The variety of topics and forms covered in the magazine over such a long time is difficult to summarize in one chapter; however, there were patterns and tendencies in *CD*'s treatment of culture in the Williams sense of the word. Some of these were a function of certain columnist's interests. Other trends in theme or topic were, unsurprisingly, connected to the broad concerns of the era — e.g., how writers responded to the Vietnam War, or the effect of free-trade policies on Canadian publishing houses. Others flowed from the magazine's commitment to a certain style of left nationalism, which encouraged, especially early in its life, a rhetoric characterized more by passionate denunciation than by attentive cultural analysis. This tendency was especially pronounced in the magazine's early writing on the artifacts of popular culture, particularly when these were American television shows, movies or music. What did not change over half a century was *CD*'s commitment to cultural content; what did change was the definition of cultural content that the magazine was committed to, and the way it regarded culture and its expressions. While there was always room in the magazine for coverage of the fine arts — fiction, poetry, theatre, dance, painting — what became more prominent in the last few decades of the magazine's history were articles that discussed and explored various cultural phenomena on their own terms, rather than judging them as having achieved a political goal or expressed a political view the writer thought was appropriate.

The relationship between politics and culture, and what it meant to regard culture from a political perspective, was something *CD* persistently wrestled with. The problem the magazine faced was how to write about cultural products and events without either endlessly and repetitively criticizing novels or poems or films for failing to be somehow adequately political, or, on the other hand, offering the kind of discussion and reviews easily found elsewhere. Both of these tendencies were apparent in the magazine's writing. But there were also examples of writing that were more interesting than a mere review or a predictably scathing critique, just as there were examples of writers who subjected unusual materials to cultural analysis. The absence of a political "line" or approach to culture, especially in the absence of writers assigned to certain subjects over time, meant a lack of development in some of the magazine's analysis, and theoretical debates over reform vs. revolution rapidly became sterile when films or books served as occasions for condemnation of the current political system. Williams's notion of "active debate" certainly flourished as first one and then another writer took up the intellectual cudgels for or against a given political interpretation of an event or piece of art (like Andre Serrano's "Piss Christ"), but what was more interesting was when one writer took on film or book reviewing, or cultural writing in general, bringing to the task the sustained attention a reader came to recognize and appreciate, or when someone took seriously the expressive and pleasurable aspects of culture, and not just its role in furthering political goals. It is in this departure from an assessment approach to culture that *CD* made its most interesting and useful contributions to cultural commentary.

Identity crisis

In its very first issue in 1963 the magazine announced itself as a "product of the post-nuclear generation of leftish thinkers . . . tired of . . . the superficiality of the mass media" among other things (1:1-2, September/ October 1963). But no overall approach to the consideration of art and culture appeared in the first editorial, leaving individual writers to their own devices when it came to setting a tone for how the magazine regarded culture and its products. The absence of a governing cultural philosophy, like the absence of a consistent political "line" for the magazine's perspective more generally, gave its contributors the freedom to engage with material however they wished to. Whatever their individual takes on the topic at hand, though, a dominant issue of the magazine's first couple of decades in the realm of arts and culture was Canadian identity, often expressed as virulent anti-Americanism, and the degree to which that identity is, could be, or should be nourished and supported by both artists and the government as something distinct and valuable. Still another was the value and purpose of media itself as a political and cultural form and vehicle of expression. Though *CD* had a traditional arts focus on novels, poetry collections, dance and theatre, its earliest issues also featured pieces on comics and popular music — though judgment of fans as "the vast, Hit Parade–stupified pubescent public" (1:1-2, September/November 1963) found its way into the magazine's pages, a sign of an anti-popular bias on the part of some of the academics who were the majority of the magazine's contributors at the time.

The Canadian culture debate was set in motion by Neil Compton in the article "Canada's Cultural Void" (1:8, September/October 1964), which examined what he called the "new cosmopolitanism," revealed in "the leading arts of the mid-twentieth century, the theatre and the cinema." In the current climate of global arts, he argued, it would surely be wrong to put too much stress on the Canadianism of Canadian culture. This debate over whether the country could or should nurture a national culture, and what the qualities of such a culture were, proved a mainstay of *CD*'s culture articles. Here though, Compton dismissed the search for national essentialism in the realm of art: "Our forefathers had enough trouble keeping alive and warm in these northern latitudes without worrying about art." Given the huge influence of American culture and its various productions, "how can 'the Canadian identity' be anything but the ambiguous and uncertain thing that it is?" he asked. Instead of championing a kind of Canadian art, we should instead rejoice "at any kind of creativity wherever and however it reveals itself." He concluded with a call for the state to support "excellence" in the arts rather than the "barbarous term" Canadian content. Later writers, among them the left nationalist Robin Mathews, took issue with Compton's implicit assertion that excellence could not, in the first instance, justify government support of Canadian culture, and the matter of Canadian identity, as it is adequately or inadequately expressed in fiction, poetry (and in the hiring practices of Canadian universities), became a topic of repeated debate in later issues.

This first volume also featured film reviewing and commentary for the first time, something *CD* continued to offer over the years, and also introduced the cultural assessment mode of reviewing, in which films were criticized for what they did not do, or say, or show, with negative judgments of popular culture as the default setting for commentary. In this first film column, for example, William Marantz lambasted Hollywood films as "producer" made, contrasting them with the "director" made artistic work of Europe, while giving back-handed compliments to a number of contemporary films, calling *Doctor Strangelove* "almost inspired." In his observation of how hungry the public seemed for films consumed while on the move, Marantz conjured an unforgettably hilarious image: "Unless Darwin didn't know his apples, the man of the future will be born with wheels instead of feet, and an exhaust pipe for a rectum" (1:6, May/June 1964).

While *CD* published Canadian poets and reviewed Canadian as well as American and European films in this first decade, domestic writers, films, and artists were not necessarily treated any more gently, as when G. David Sheps, writing a negative review of Stephen Vizinczey's *In Praise of Older Women* observed of Vajda, the novel's protagonist, that he is "the Adam Smith of sex, the sexual version of economic man whose free market principles tolerate no interference" (3:2, January/February 1966). William Marantz reviewed the low-budget Canadian feature *Nobody Waved Goodbye*, and said of its improvisational style that it is "a great crashing bore of a film, with nothing worthwhile to say and saying it badly" (3:1, November/December 1965). And Richard Sommer, reviewing several books of poetry, remarked of Margaret Avison (whom he considered "this country's finest poet") that excessive hyphenation had entered her style "like a tarantula in bananas" (4:6, September/October 1967). As funny as many of these observations were, they also typified a tone of excessively critical commentary that characterized much of the writing in *CD*, in which left credibility was often established through negative assessments of the object under discussion, rather than through the analysis of complex relationships between artists, institutions, and their social, political and cultural contexts and expressions.

Bruce Kidd penned the first of his many sports columns for the magazine on "The Future of Canadian Amateur Sport," where he examined the role played by government and volunteer organizations, as well as the resistance of amateur sport to both professionals and nationalists who seek to exploit it for their political ends (4:5, July/August 1967). Kidd relished the independence of amateur sport, but saw the necessity of more formalized and permanent structures to encourage and support the development of athletes and competitive sport programs. His call for Canadians to direct their attention to more than final scores, to pay attention to "the decisions which affect sport," was much more satisfying than earlier pieces on this subject in CD, which lamented that we did not adopt British team sports (rugby, for example) that might have assisted in forging for us a stronger national identity, assuming both the masculine nature of sport (soccer, hockey, cricket and rugby are the model sports on offer), and the homology of team and nation. Kidd's columns brought to the topic of sports an analytic consistency and an internationalist spirit missing from other writing on culture and cultural institutions in CD up to this point. Kidd lapsed into romantic overstatement and assumed the gender-exclusive nature of some sports when he wrote "Hockey is . . . in our blood. An intensely physical contest waged over a frozen land, it reflects the struggles of our history and the demands of our environment. . . . Every Canadian male has played it . . . every Canadian female is familiar with its intricacies" (6:2, July 1969), and fell for the gloomy excesses of left rhetoric when he predicted the "complete integration" of Canadian football into the American version of the sport was imminent (6:5, October/November 1969) and asked "Can Canada really be Canada without the Grey Cup?" Nevertheless, the treatment of sport in CD benefitted from Kidd's careful and intelligent assessment of sport as more than an opportunity to rail at American capitalism.

CD devoted space to media — newspapers, television, radio — for the first time when Cy Gonick wrote an obituary for *This Hour Has Seven Days*, calling it "the conscience of Canada" and " a wonderful nuisance" (3:3-4, March/June 1966). CD's nationalist tendencies surfaced again in Richard Sommer's criticism of the *Georgia Straight*'s reliance on American content sourced from the Underground Press Syndicate, though he praised its connection to its community and its bravery in "fiercely attacking its enemies." In its forthrightness and energy, he wrote, it, unlike other papers in Canada, truly "belongs to its readers" (6:2, July 1969).

Growing confidence

CD's covers became more colourful in the 1970s, often featuring graphics influenced by the psychedelia craze. There were references in its pages to "beautiful mini-skirted creatures, and young men sporting their first beards," and full-page ads for collections of recently-released Danish erotica. The October Crisis and Watergate resonated through-out its pages. For the first time, there was also coverage of the effects of government austerity measures on the arts. The nationalist theme became more pronounced in *CD*, manifest most typically in articles by Robin Mathews. Mathews had already published a poem in *CD's* centennial issue (3:6, September/October 1966) in which he compared Canada — unfavourably — to "a tired prostitute beyond her prime" who "would throw her charms away less openly / would exercise more choice / than you have ever done / would charge at least a reason-able rate." This gave way to more general attacks on the presence of American culture in Canada, such as the one he launched against the first issue of the journal *Canadian Review of American Studies*, calling it a "cultural gunboat" representing the takeover of Canadian culture (and Canadian universities) by the US (7:3, August/September 1970). So influential was this sense that the formation of a Canadian identity and culture meant expunging all traces of American influence, that in a later article on his love for American folk songs (11:6, July 1976), Winnipeg musician Jim Donovan admitted that it was "not at all popular to say something pleasant about America and my romance may seem almost traitorous to some, another example of cultural imperialism." Looking back on the persistence of this anti-American animus in the pages of the magazine in the first two decades of publication, it becomes pos-sible to read it not as a thoughtless rejection of all things American, but as an expression of opposition to the US involvement in Vietnam, translated and extended from the realm of the specifically political into that of the cultural.

A more nuanced and confident approach to Canadian culture as labour process and complicated practice, rather than as the pure antithesis of all things American, also emerged in this decade. "The Fight for the National Film Board" (7:8, 1971) described the effect of government cuts on the circulation and screening of films from the NFB. The article described a bitter round of negotiations with the union representing NFB workers, who unwittingly bargained for salary increases that resulted, as soon as the agreement was signed, in the revelation that the NFB's budget was frozen, and layoffs would have to finance the increases. Near its end, the article discussed the value of NFB archives to cable-TV broadcasting, and envisioned a future in which "Each home would have a coded NFB catalogue, just as it has a telephone directory, and the viewer would be able to dial any film he wanted to see and have it fed into his TV set. As the system developed, materials other than the NFB film library would also become available." Arthur Fuller also reviewed the first Winnipeg Film Symposium, debated the wisdom of a quota system for the exhibition of Canadian films in Canadian movie theatres, and had this to say about the effect of historical and political events on Canada's persistent identity crisis: "A while ago, everyone wondered if there really was such a thing as the Canadian Identity. People don't talk about it anymore, because now we know it exists. Canadian artists do not have to create it: events of the last decade did" (10:3, July 1974).

This shift in treating culture as a field of inquiry and analysis in its own right, instead of as little more than a symptom or expression of fundamental national or economic forces, was most apparent in the articles and reviews contributed to *CD* in this period by Ken Hughes. Hughes wrote a lengthy discussion of Margaret Laurence's *The Diviners*, claiming that the book "tells us that pioneering is never finished in a society. For while the content may change, we all remain pioneers of a future that must be made and cannot just be found" (10:7, March 1975). Hughes also contributed an essay on the "Poet Laureate of Labour," transplanted Scotsman Alexander McLachlan (11:4, March 1976). But it was his essay "Eaton's Best Cellar: Would Timothy Approve?" (11:5, June 1976) that broke with the kind of cultural assessment essays *CD* tended to favour till then. Hughes's analysis of images in an Eaton's department store advertising circular was reminiscent of Roland Barthes's semiological readings of contemporary cultural phenomena in the collection *Mythologies*. Hughes didn't belabour the point that the multi-page ad for the store's products was an expression of capitalism. Rather, he provided a close reading of the images, described what he saw in detail, and offered a demonstration of how the insert's layout, copy and images worked together to produce a stylistic drama of power that invited the reader to participate in a fantasy of entitlement and privilege through the consumption of fashion. Another example of this close reading of cultural practices and forms that found unexpected connections between apparently disparate phenomena appeared in his essay on the circus, in which he wrote "A circus is a play that has not yet achieved a state of complete coherence" (13:2, n.d.). Hughes also wrote the first column on television for *CD* (11:2, 1975) about the CTV comedy *Excuse My French*, which he saw as an imitation of *All in the Family*, and criticized, because, in its desire to present typical figures, it sacrificed character and became irritatingly mechanical. Ken Hughes's pieces were wonderfully written, thoughtful and enjoyable essays, early examples of cultural studies criticism in *CD* that, instead of pronouncing judgment on "good" or "bad" aesthetic objects and their presumed salutary or pernicious effects (especially on the formation and maintenance of an identifiable national identity), paid close attention to Raymond Williams's "ordinary culture."

Michael Sotiron offered a similar treatment of popular culture in a book review when he wrote that "By now the debate about the existence of an indigenous English-Canadian culture should be over since there is ample evidence of it," at least in the realm of so-called "high-brow" culture (12:2, April 1977). But, he asked, was there such a thing as "low-brow" English-Canadian culture? He gave a qualified yes, noting the beginnings of a "local pulp industry" in books. Thus he reviewed four genre paperbacks to see what it was all about, concluding that these readable packages of sex, violence and tension "do wonders in dispelling the staid and self-effacing image of Canadians." An even more experimental example of cultural analysis was Susan Perly's poetic essay "Every Buddy and Cultural Underdevelopment" (13:2, n.d.), which mixed fragments of imagined biographies of unemployment with profiles of the Cape Breton music scene (featuring bands like Buddy and the Boys), and excerpts from song lyrics. It was an impressionistic piece of writing that used the strategies of creative nonfiction to produce a moody sense of the region's economic depression, but that didn't neglect the wry humour and creative vibrancy of those same communities for the sake of a romantic portrait of isolated working-class despair. And an interesting tempering of *CD*'s excesses of cultural pronouncement also appeared in Dennis Cooley's review of Robin Mathews' collection of polemical essays, *Canadian Literature: Surrender or Revolution*, which lauds Mathews's political analysis of Canada's position vis-a-vis the US when it comes to cultural imperialism, but criticizes Mathews as an analyst who is unable or unwilling to acknowledge the complexities of the literary works he examines (13:4, November/December 1978).

Bruce Kidd's sports columns in the 1970s began to combine gender and economic analysis in ways still tinged with anti-American feeling, as when he described how Acadia University's decision to hire American coaches and recruit athletes with scholarships disenfranchised students interested in sports other than basketball, football and hockey (6:8, April/May, 1970). He saw this trend as the "Americanization of Acadia," which brought with it "the American sporting traditions of the 1950s: authoritarian coaches with gladiatorial philosophies and deified athletes who are taught to conform to the superman stereotypes of the comic book and the breakfast cereals." But later that same year, in the column "Sportsmen or Gladiators?" Kidd's analysis was attentive to the intersections of gender and commercial sport interests in ways that indicated the effects of the second-wave feminist movement on the understanding and analysis of sport. He wrote about youth rejection of sport on the basis of its ultra-competitive reputation: "there is a general revolt among young people today against all competitive aspects of modern living" (7:4, October 1970). In his conclusion, Kidd reminded his readers that there was nothing unconditionally competitive or aggressive about all sports: "Only in commercial sport where there is a financial incentive to exploit personal vindictiveness is physical and psychological violence common." In 1971 Bruce Kidd's column "Jocks of the World Unite," described athletes going on strike to protest the authoritarianism of coaches, and the refusal of athletic departments at various American universities to negotiate with athletes, as well as the serious sanctions they faced from school authorities and others, such as beatings, and the withholding of scholarships (7:6, January/February 1971).

Over three issues, beginning with 6:8, April/May, 1970, *CD* published a brief to the Senate Hearing on Mass Media. The tension between protecting and encouraging domestic production in the face of American product, and facilitating access to global televisual content, emerged in Part II of the brief, in which *CD* "tentatively welcomes" the Canadian content requirements of the CRTC and calls out the government for deliberately underfunding the CBC, while letting private broadcasters off the hook when it comes to contributing to the public good (7:1-2, June/July 1970). These criticisms were followed by a list of recommendations, which included a 100 per cent tax "on the advertising and public relations budgets of all vendors and producers of consumer commodities and services, except for minimum-sized classified ads inserted by individuals, and perhaps a few other exceptional categories" that would go directly to an independent Crown agency for consumer research. But it is in the brief's suggestion that "either all cablevision relays of American broadcasting be disallowed," or "such cable relays be allowed everywhere" that the more interesting struggle between the wish to support national production through a closed or quota system brushed up against what the brief called a real "open policy" on broadcasting, couched in terms of resisting the dominance of American programming. Why, said the brief, shouldn't Canadians be able to listen to the speeches of Chou En-lai? "Why not have the Moscow State Circus in action, in addition to Walter Cronkite talking about some local American clown, or some Canadian trying to talk like Walter Cronkite talking about some local American clown? Why leave it at the barbarities and vast boredom of roller skating and wrestling, when we could have good football from Latin America every week of the year?" The brief also called for the dismantling of the CTV, and the preservation of a "low-cost auxiliary network" for actualities. A number of contradictions and unacknowledged assumptions coloured these proscriptive comments. The uncomfortable possibility that an open policy might introduce more, rather than less, American content into Canadian homes was not considered, any more than was the assumption that television should default to realist forms ("actualities") rather than to popular content (with football somehow escaping the condescending labels applied to wrestling and roller skating) critically examined. Anxiety over the role of media as either a corrective or corrupting force on the national population permeated the brief, often accompanied by utopian expectations that the content of a public broadcast system would be essentially progressive and somehow socially improving.

In the 1970s CD's treatment of popular culture was shot through with ambivalence over the source of the artifact under discussion, especially if the source was American. Understandable as this was, given the size of the US cultural industries, there was nevertheless an elision between worry over the dominance of the US commercial entertainment industry, and concern that the content of American popular culture was a contaminating influence. An example of this worry was Don Kerr's review of several Hollywood films in which he described "the Hollywood Massage Parlour, whose giant hands reach up across the world's longest undefended border, right through toques, ear muffs, and parka hoods, get inside the skull to the knead the soft core of public opinion north of the 49. It's the great American sit-in, and it's time to have a close look at what it wants to do to us" (12:4-5, September 1977).

Engagement

In the 1980s, the suspicion directed at popular culture generally, and American popular culture in particular, was much less apparent in CD. Perhaps the influence of British cultural studies as championed by critic Stuart Hall had an effect on some of the writers penning columns about film and television during this decade, given that many of those writers were academics whose disciplines (like English) were under pressure to adjust their notions of what constituted cultural material worthy of sustained investigation and interpretation. One sign of this shift in attitude was Kenneth McRobbie's review of the book *The Cultural Connection*, which criticized the author's view of culture as upper-class (14:4-5, February/March 1980). Another writer in the same issue whose contributions to the magazine exhibited a cultural studies attitude was Stan Persky, who wrote about the weather channel in his column "TV Season" as a "hit program" of 1979–1980, a fave, it seemed, of the under-thirty crowd in Terrace, BC, from where he wrote. Like Ken Hughes and Kenneth McRobbie, Persky engaged the popular and sometimes ephemeral texts of culture from the perspective of viewers and readers not assumed to be white, straight, male, or living in some unnamed or urban space. Persky's columns acknowledged the physical, sexual and class situation of viewers, and considered how such embodiment might shape engagements with mass cultural products like American television. Another of Persky's columns, for example, focused on Steven, the gay blond character on *Dynasty*, again shifting the content away from judging what's on the tube, to describing and exploring the situation of the viewer — someone with time to watch the shows now that he has been laid off "on account of the interest rates" (15:8, December 1981).

This shift from evaluating (and often condemning) the politics of culture to richly descriptive interpretations of how people actually interact with popular culture and make it meaningful to them was apparent too in the magazine's writing on music and theatre. Whereas Irwin Silber had once written "There is something about the vapid naturalism of most country music that is an insult to human intelligence . . . " (6:3-4, September 1969), thirteen years later Jock Macray wrote about country music in an appreciative way, making its connections to working-class hopes and fears clear to those who would dismiss it out of hand: " . . . the dynamics of working class culture must be looked at in their real historical dimensions, not merely as adjuncts to economic and political processes . . . the living tradition of country music is *historical*, and contains the frustrations and possibilities of people in time — working people in our time" (16:3, May 1982). This emphasis on the meaning and value of Canadian working-class culture — especially when produced by working people — added vibrancy to *CD*'s writing on theatre in this decade. Mary Abbott, for example, wrote in "The Burin Story" about her participation in the struggle to prevent the closing of a local fish plant in Newfoundland, and the play collectively written about that event. She said of her experience, "I end the play with a monologue of my own, about how I feel now that it's over. My feeling is that in the end we won. Our plant was to be closed completely. Instead we have refit and secondary processing . . . The people of Burin really enjoyed our play. I know I did — because there was a message in it for every small fishing community around. That message was that no one has to take anything lying down" (19:1, March/

April 1985). In another example of this approach, Cy Gonick conducted an extensive conversational interview with David Fennario following a performance of the play *Joe Beef* in Montreal (21:2, April 1987). Gonick wrote about Fennario's own attachments to, and disappointments in, various left organizations, and what Fennario saw as a common problem on the Left: "how to juggle education with entertainment, the message with the medium — and how to get the message to an audience not only sympathetic but, more to the point, one that can be moved to action." In a slightly different take on the matter of theatre's political intentions, Don Kerr wrote in the same issue that community theatre that is not obviously radical or challenging from an outsider's point of view may actually be so: "Perhaps in Canada just to say 'Hi' is a kind of politics, so inundated are we by other voices, primarily American. It may be necessary to say 'Hi' to each other before we can say 'Boo' to others."

The debate about the efficacy of culture in producing political consciousness and action surfaced again when Ken Waldhauser wrote about the late-night CBC show "Brave New Waves," praising its mix of radical music acts, spoken-word performances, interviews with singer-songwriters like Billy Bragg, and focus on national artists (20:5, September/October 1986). He also asked, "As socialists and sometime nationalists how should we view the development of this pseudo-independent radio? In what way does this show promote 'free' cultural development and encourage progressive artists to promote alternative visions?" Though he didn't answer the questions, the relevance of these measures of value in the discussion of popular culture is itself worth debating. The unargued assumption once again is that culture, especially popular culture, must be demonstrably political in some way, or that it must justify its existence by striving for, if not achieving, in some clear way, the education or enlightenment of its audience.

Meanwhile, throughout the decade *CD* continued to publish original works of poetry by Canadian authors such as Patrick Lane, Erin Moure, Miriam Waddington and Lorna Uher. The magazine also profiled literary and visual artists such as Margaret Laurence and Jackson Beardy (whose work featured in a special issue of the magazine edited by Ken Hughes). Reading the diversity of this material, as well as the debates and discussions about the state of filmmaking and publishing in the wake of the Free Trade Agreement, it is hard to give much credence to Robin Mathews's contention in CD's twentieth anniversary issue that "We have, in short, the intellectual life of a banana republic" (18:5, October/ November 1984). The assumption that Canadian movie and television viewers were vulnerable and helpless in the face of American culture, unable to respond carefully and thoughtfully to films and television programs, is the grim assumption of these comments, as is the bias against pleasure and delight as a motive for engagement with popular culture.

The call for a boycott of the Olympic Games to protest the Soviet "military intervention" in Afghanistan dominated the coverage of sports by Bruce Kidd in 1980 (14:6, May 1980). Kidd argued, "Despite its many problems, the Games have been an unsurpassed vehicle for cross-cultural understanding and human inspiration in a troubled world" and noted the danger of a renewed Cold War if a boycott was carried out. He compared the call for a boycott of the current games to previous calls for boycotts in 1936 and 1976, and said that this time, those who were calling for it were politicians who had "rarely taken an interest in sport," whereas other boycotts had been initiated by athletes and sports officials. He concludes by recounting the history of the 1936 games, as well as the efforts of the Socialist Workers Sports International and the Red Sports International to put on the People's Olympic Games in Barcelona as a counter-Olympics, a protest against what they called "the Berlin Olympiad which stands for the fascization of sport and the preparation of youth for war," games which were cancelled on the first day of scheduled competition. It's a fascinating bit of history woven into a careful analysis of the limitations of boycotts, something that Kidd treated in subsequent columns on the value of the games, flawed as they may be.

Connected culture

In the early 1990s, after writing a guest editorial and a column on the Royal Ontario Museum's controversial "Into the Heart of Africa" exhibit (24:7, October 1990), I joined the editorial collective of the magazine. For the next decade, I wrote columns for the "Connections" section of CD. I also chose and wrote introductions for the poems the magazine published several times a year, including several special issues celebrating International Women's Day and May Day. It was the start of an energetic decade — the last of the twentieth century — in which CD's attention to the national arts and culture scene was increasingly complemented by an international focus on the various intersections of representation and politics. And through it all, the bright thread of the Internet and its effects on jobs, on art, and on larger questions of global culture, wove itself into the discussion.

The 1990s began rather stormily in the magazine's pages. Censorship by the Left was vigorously debated by Richard Nobel, Ken Morrison and me, in articles and letters responding to Andreas Serrano's infamous "Piss Christ" in 1990 and 1991. Nobel wrote sharply and compellingly (24:5, July 1990) about the necessity for art that offends, and pointed out that in the absence of the state's ability to stop certain sexual activities (e.g., prostitution, sado-masochism), "they opt for what they imagine to be the next best thing: controlling representations of these practices." The value of the offensive and the ugly in art practice became something of a recurring theme that year, with my column on "What Do Socialists Really Want?" and Scott Forsyth's review of the film Bethune: The Making of a Hero, which noted the disturbing similarity between left and right responses to Hollywood films: on both sides the audience is regarded as easily duped and in need of protection from politically dubious ideas (25:2, March 1991). Forsyth departed from this predictable critique and argued for the contradictory pleasures of this film, despite its status as a bio-pic. Forsyth's reviews considered the workings of alternative popular culture on its own terms, rather than always finding fault with the products of Big Media, or holding artists to account for failing to achieve what the reviewer thought they ought to have achieved.

While CD continued to publish poetry, profile visual artists and review films, what also became more apparent was the effect of the Internet on and in popular culture. My columns for the magazine on the influence of the net on popular culture appeared over the course of several issues of the magazine. In many of these, I was a bit of a net-skeptic when it came to touting the brave wired world of harmonious interconnection. I wrote about the meaning of "community" in this new, connected, unregulated space (29:2, April/May 1995), and later that same year, about the "flight from the body" encouraged by the net, as well as the promise that cyberspace would be free of the prejudices that attend real bodies in a real space — which I characterized as a liberal fantasy in which everyone is presumed to be white and able-bodied unless they indicate otherwise. My column on computers and work commented on the job destruction wrought by technology, and about those of us who stood to be cast aside in this revolution: "Many will find themselves shrugged off as redundant and unemployable even before they graduate, unless the symbiosis between new technologies and the production of private wealth can be disrupted" (30:5, September 1996). In May/June of that year, my column Thoreau@Walden.Pond considered the growing intrusion of work into leisure and privacy, enabled by technology. My sometimes negative spin on things technological was met by net optimism in columns like Kim Goldberg's "Organizing the Net," in which she wrote about her "info safari," a zooming browse through and across the Internet to gather information, news, hobnob and otherwise participate in and partake of the political potential and richness of the net (29:1, February/March 1995). Her piece described the growing usefulness of the Internet for political organizing, and anticipated the "information wants to be free" campaigns that would later find expression in WikiLeaks.

Material culture still received its due in the mid 1990s in articles on theatre, experimental film and literature, and on the complex ways in which artists took up events and issues to which we are intensely attached. In these pieces, there was often an uneasy but painstaking combination of rigourous political assessment and aesthetic analysis not easy to sum up as either complete appreciation or critique. An excellent example appeared in 29:2 April/May 1995, where Susan Heald wrote about the east-coast playwright Wendy Lill's deep interest in the "politics of memory" in plays like *The Fighting Days*, *The Occupation of Heather Rose*, *Memories of You*, *Sisters* and *All Fall Down*. Heald wrote of her disappointment with Lill's treatment of child sexual abuse accusations, and concluded this way: "Remembering differently, remembering different things, thinking differently about memory: these are important to the struggle to understand and end child sexual abuse, as well as to the development of a Canadian culture and the changing of Canadian society. In spite of my discomfort with her latest offering, in my memories of Wendy Lill's work I want to acknowledge the ways she has kept these projects front and centre."

The intersection of power and sexuality from something other than a straight perspective received attention in Marion Yeo's piece "Last Night I Had the Queerest Dream" (31:6, November/December 1997), which reviewed *1919*, a film by Noam Gonick that reimagined a Winnipeg bathhouse as the centre of revolutionary erotic politics. The short film made sexual and working-class desire — for freedom, for choice, for respect — mutually resonant metaphors, and tacked on a revisionist conclusion in which the strikers won. In her review, Yeo observed that though Winnipeg's most famous labour strike was unsuccessful in one sense, it was a "triumph of mobilization," and this film "provides a new narrative, one that makes the victory explicit through the introduction of gay liberation values, especially those of coming out and asserting an authentic sexuality." Also in this issue was Robin Mathews's essay "Canada's Hidden Working Class Literature," which documented what Mathews called "a literature in hiding . . . in any mainstream consideration of our literature and its working-class expression." The titles he named included *Eight Men Speak, Waste Heritage, This Time A Better Earth* and *The Magpie*. This literature, he wrote, "takes the people of the working class seriously, seeing them as fundamental to society. It works out their destiny in terms of their real culture." In doing this, they were distinguished from the romanticized portraits of working-class life in novels like *In the Skin of a Lion*. The related focus of these two very different articles — class, sexuality, and the power of art — testified to the diversity of cultural topics in *CD* during this decade, and the broadening of its cultural coverage to include experimental film.

CD's first media piece of the decade was by Kim Goldberg, in the 24:5 July/August 1990 issue. In "People's TV: It's closer than you think," Goldberg imagined a world of locally-controlled broadcast television stations carrying content produced by viewers. "The programming on the local stations has become so popular that people seldom tune in to the other channels run by centralized, monolithic corporations." Though

219

Goldberg was talking about a utopia of activist cable television, democratically controlled by viewers who are also content creators, the description anticipates the invention of YouTube fifteen years later. Goldberg's vision of cable TV was positive, with all transmissions communicating socially progressive and transformative content, indulging in the flip-side of gloomy notions of media control over audiences.

For most of the 1990s Doug Smith worked the media beat for *CD*, with his back-page "Out of Bounds" column skewering corporate media barons like Conrad Black, and analyzing the absurdities and failures of Canadian journalism. For example, he criticized *Globe and Mail* columnist Jeffrey Simpson's role as an "unofficial apologist" for war, and described both the brutality of both Saddam Hussein and Syrian President Assad, and the support both regimes received from the US (25:2, March 1991). Smith also kept an eye on the Winnipeg media scene, decrying the "boosterism" that manifested itself in the "breath-taking and ultimately pathetic attempt to save the city's professional hockey team, the Winnipeg Jets," and the requirement that one maintain an "unrelenting optimism" despite the realities of Winnipeg. Smith recounted efforts to raise money for the cause that resulted in more donations in two weeks than the United Way raised in one year, and called the city out for its hypocrisy, its interest in circuses rather than in bread (29:6, December/January 1995–96).

Smith satirized the hysterical right in a hilarious column (29:5, October/November 1995) recounting another media claim that held Marxists responsible for promoting violent rap music. "I buckle over with laughter trying to imagine any of the Marxists I know chilling with Tupac Shakur" he said, and ended: "I think the stage has now been reached that Marxists should take some comfort in the idea that someone somewhere still views them as a Menace 2 Society." Soon after this Smith wrote about "suckhole journalism," the sycophantic writing of David Frum, Andrew Coyne and others: "one starts to wish that the much-heralded death of the author was something a little more literal when the children of millionaires start depicting themselves as courageous defenders of free speech who have put their careers at risk to defend the rights of millionaires" (30:3, May/June 1996).

In the background of these and other columns by Smith, Goldberg and others were the struggles of the progressive press to stay afloat in an era of corporate consolidation perfected by Conrad Black in his acquisition of the Southam chain in 1992. Brian Eng reviewed the birth, life and death of one of these, the left weekly newspaper the *New Times*, tracing its beginnings as a "transformation" of the *Canadian Tribune*, and what he sees as the fundamental flaws in the paper's "development of an organized, accountable decision-making process" (29:1, February/March 1995). "If there is a lesson from the *New Times* experience," he wrote, "it is that our internal democratic structures are a key element of our struggle. The organs and political bodies that claim to speak for us and organize us must be structured to ensure that the entire range of our voices is heard." Within a few months, Smith wrote an obituary for Winnipeg's own *Inner City Voice*. He began with a description of his mixed feelings upon receiving his first issue of it nine years earlier: he was amazed and happy to see it, but disappointed that he hadn't been involved in its birth. Since then, he had written monthly media columns for the paper, and had watched it lurch from one financial crisis to another. He ended the piece with a somberly optimistic note about the vulnerabilities of the left press published in a magazine whose own financial fortunes could, and did, swing wildly: "And in the coming year independent journalists will try again and probably fail again. It is through those failures that we will attain a voice of our own" (29:4, August/September 1995).

Millennium cultures

The presence and coverage of culture and the arts in *CD* in the 2000s reflected in many ways the general interest in new media forms, as well as the good and potentially troublesome aspects of so-called "convergence culture." While long, comparative reviews of novels and poetry collections dwindled in frequency in comparison to those that had appeared in the 1970s and 1980s (signalling, perhaps, the dominance of visual culture over literary culture in the new century, as well as the diversity of cultural events covered by the magazine), the "All That's Left" section of the magazine continued to offer capsule reviews of books and films of interest to readers. There were still poems in *CD*, and still reviews of plays like *Eight Men Speak* (34:2, March/April 2000). And film continued to receive the lion's share of attention as a media form deserving of comment and analysis. Many more of those films were non-Hollywood films, independent films or documentaries, however, than ever before. Louis Proyect's column in 35:4 July/August 2001, for example, profiled the work of Ousmene Sembene. Film writing in *CD* also departed from like-it-or-not reviews, putting films into conversation with other works, and into relevant historical, economic or cultural contexts, much as in earlier decades contributors like Myron Turner and Kenneth Hughes had treated novels and poetry collections. Rick Slye's "left Film Guide" reviewed several thematically or historically related films, like *Go Tell the Spartans*, *Full Metal Jacket*, and *84 Charlie MoPic* on the thirtieth anniversary "of the Vietnamese people over the American Wermacht" (39:5, September/October 2005). In the same issue Louis Proyect continued his contribution of individual film reviews — in this issue, of Spielberg's *War of the Worlds*, which led him into a discussion of Tom Cruise, Scientology and H.G. Wells's predilection for social Darwinism — the idea of "inferior races" the theme that ties all these together.

But some debates about the relationship between art and politics never go away. Jonathan Culp's essay on activist video confronted some of the tensions between artists and activists over the content and purpose of media (38:4, July 2004). He noted the smaller audience for the third travelling Satan McNuggit Popular Art "Recycled Cinema" tour, and realized that his own need for political video that does not conform to the "riot porn" of activist documentary contributed to this decline in spectators. He asked, "What do activists and artists have to offer each other?" It's a powerful question. Culp went on to raise, dissect, and reject old dichotomies between art and activism, as well as the idea that for artists to be political, they must be propagandists. This, he wrote, "reduces us, as human beings, to media." It is a wonderfully written manifesto for the role of the aesthetic in social movements, and the requirement for artists to make art that does not subject itself to the short-term needs of the state, or of any progressive cause (even, by implication, of a magazine like *Canadian Dimension*). It is exactly this kind of engaged and spirited articulation of art as a progressive end in itself, rather than as an instrument in someone else's toolbox, that marked a kind of argumentative continuity in *CD*'s cultural content over the decades.

Along with film, theatre, and video games, music remained in the spotlight in the new millennium. In "Rebel Yells," Rick Hesch amassed evidence that, contrary to those who lamented the retreat of music into quietism, "we appear to have entered a renaissance of broadly oppositional popular music unseen since the creation of punk during neoliberalism's infancy. This upsurge in politically progressive popular music is analogous to a recent increase in socially critical documentary film" (40:1, January/February 2006). Also on the music beat, Jim Naylor overcame his initial skepticism to give *Strike! The Musical* a good review, realizing that "it has helped resurrect the hopes and challenges of strike-bound Winnipeg in ways most earlier treatments have not. The sterile dichotomies over how 'revolutionary' the strike was fade, and other meanings open themselves" (37:3, May/June 2006). Louis Proyect's essay on "Jazz and Radical Politics" (40:4, July/August 2006) told a number of stories about the intersection of music and communism, among them, that Frank Sinatra was "close" to the party when he first performed "The House I Live in," composed by Abe Meerpol, a communist writing under the name Lewis Allen. Erin Millar profiled the gay/bi rock band Galaxy in 40:6 (November/December 2006) focusing on their song "Pink Collar Holler," about the feminization of poverty and the ghetto of working-class women's work.

The "Can Art Save the World" Issue appeared over two issues in 2007, with writers weighing in on topics ranging from vintage posters, the art of Shirley Bear, art from Port-au-Prince, to the beginnings of Winnipeg's Graffiti Gallery, to a pictorial spread on images of Palestinians living under Israeli occupation, exhibited as part of Mayworks Festival of Working People and the Arts in Toronto. In the introduction to the art and politics focus, Kevin Matthews declared, "If society has an imagination to express its desires and fears, it is activated through art. If society is to experiment with change, with new forms, with its power structures, with ways of seeing and with language itself, it must be through art" (41:4, July/August 2007). It was a powerful and inspiring introduction to a terrific set of articles and reviews, the entire focus of the issue testifying yet again to the centrality of culture and artistic expression that became an essential part of *CD*'s political approach in the most recent two decades of its life. This issue also featured a roundtable on "The Politics of Artists," gathering opinions from a number of *CD* contributors and activists on the role and value of art in the project of social change and justice. The arts focus continues in 41:8 (July/August 2007), with a feature interview with sci-fi novelist Ursula K. Le Guin, in which she talks about updating some of the ideas expressed in the classic *The Left Hand of Darkness*. One of the most startling of her comments is on the role of forgiveness in left politics: "Should a Marxist forgive Lenin and Stalin? Should a Jew forgive? Should a Palestinian forgive? Is there such a thing as political forgiveness? Russia and the US haven't 'forgiven' each other all the insults of the Cold War, they've just cozied up for whatever they can get out of each other. I think forgiveness is a word without meaning in corporate capitalism."

The wealth of writing on culture and its expression in this most recent decade was mind-boggling, and impossible to cover in any but the most cursory of ways: from a roundtable on the film *Avatar* (44:2, March/April 2010) and Warren Cariou's review of new Canadian writing in "CanLit Afterlife" (44:6, November/December 2010), to Benjamin Gillespie's article on the art/life work of Nina Arsenault, "self-proclaimed as 'Canada's most famous transsexual'" (44:4, July/August 2010). The "Our Winnipeg" issue (44:1, January/February 2010) was, of course, Winnipeg-focused, with articles like Noam Gonick's "The Ghost of John Hirsch," Ed Janzen's "The Power of Myth: How Winnipeg and its Art Became Such a Big Deal," and "Come Together: A Winnipeg Hipster Tapestry in Little Italy," by filmmaker Guy Maddin. Maddin's article takes the reader tripping along Corydon Avenue, zeroing in on Bar Italia, the café Maddin calls "the closest thing to Jazz Age–vintage *Les Deux Magots* this lively Fragile-X community can create from its gallery of demimondaine, flaneurs, artists, and professionals."

The magazine's most recent expression of art's importance to political struggle was "The Art of Protest" issue (46:6, November/December 2012). In its pages, Andrea Levy introduced the art focus with "Occupy

Canada and the Art of Protest," which explored the close relationship between the Occupy movement and street theatre, art shows and graffiti, illustrated by photos. In "Art and Politics," Carol Conde and Karl Beveridge wrote about their own art processes and influences, the way they were politicized by their success as artists whose works were sought after by collectors, their repeated run-ins with the AGO and their long association and cooperative art projects with unions. There was an interview with political cartoonist Angel Boligan, and an extended review of graphic novels. The issue also included a long discussion of *Road Movie*, a film and installation on the segregated roads of the occupied West Bank.

CD's "Big Media: Breaking the Monopoly" issue appeared in January/February 2008 (42:1). Featuring a giant, single-screen-eyed Cyclops on its cover, this issue covered the waterfront of media concerns, from fighting to keep the Internet open and free, to battling corporate control over converging technologies. Robert Hackett's article "Why Media Reform Should Be a Democratic Priority" recounted successful petitions against media consolidation in the US, and argued strenuously for the stepping up of such actions. "Media are the institutional space that concentrates society's symbolic power, a concentration that the Internet has only somewhat ameliorated." He noted that even the Internet was subject to threat "from the logic of enclosure," and was becoming in many ways a "means of neoliberal globalization." Hackett's points were expanded by Steve Anderson in "The Fight for the Open Internet" in the same issue. Using research by Michael Geist, Anderson tracked the growing hunger of Internet service providers for lucrative gatekeeper status on the net by shaping and controlling Internet traffic. He pointed out that public-interest groups, labour groups, NGOs, small business and citizens in general stand to lose if this control is allowed to dominate, and he advanced a detailed argument for net neutrality.

On the very next page David Skinner addressed foreign ownership of media, and the then-current CRTC review of rules governing media mergers. Noticeably absent from the agenda of regulators was "meaningful support for public and community sectors of the broadcasting system."

Skinner's conclusion, which echoes comments that appeared in every decade of *CD*'s coverage of media, communication, convergence and consolidation, were these: "Media are the grease in the cogs and wheels of democracy. They are the means through which Canadians come to know and understand their place in the world, celebrate the achievements of their fellow citizens and be entertained by their fellows. The people of Canada deserve to have a say in the future of their media system."

Winnipeg journalist Lesley Hughes joined the *CD* collective and published her first media column, "On the Edge," in 2003. Over the first decade of the 2000s, Hughes's column tackled a variety of issues, from bad journalists and crooked politicians to celebrity obituaries, writing sharply and compellingly about the political resonances between the near and the far in our media-saturated world. She wrote about the conversion of Paul Pritchard from everyday citizen to citizen-journalist as a result of the death of Robert Dziekanski, and about Michael Jackson as "the ultimate icon of corporate media strategy" (43:5, September/ October 2009). On this last point, she recounts asking classes of would-be journalist, "How is it that everyone knows Michael Jackson is a child molester, and nobody knows what an oligarchy is?"

While keeping a jaundiced eye on the local media and political scene, Hughes also outlined connections between Project Censored, WikiLeaks and the Steig Larsson trilogy (45:2, March/April 2011): "In fiction the truthtellers are validated, whereas in real life, we have seen Julian Assange painted as public enemy number one." "If current popular culture is any index," she observed, "the revolutionaries among us are getting restless and there is a willingness, indeed a hunger, to hear them." Hughes is, predictably, priceless on the Murdoch newspaper scandal in England. "Richard Reeves, a staffer who quit New York Magazine when Rupert Murdoch bought it, recalls that he once stood next to Murdoch at a urinal, and always regretted that he hadn't peed on him when he had the chance. There may soon be plenty of others with somewhat similar regrets" (45:5, September/October 2011).

In 2006, *CD* welcomed back a sports column, this one by Simon Black, who brought to the task a light wit and a superb analysis of the many intersections of sport and power. In 41:2, March/April 2007, for example, Black tackled David Beckham — Mr. Posh Spice — in the wake of the soccer star's signing of a mega-million contract "that stands to make any progressive weep." Black said of Beckham that his "contribution to commerce far outweighs his contribution to the sport he loves," and, mid-column, appended a "TM" superscript to the athlete's name just to make the point clear. Black also interviewed Dave Zirin, who "combines progressive politics with sports journalism, exposing the 'athletics-industrial complex' that rules professional sports" (41:4, July/August 2007). The interview ended with Zirin reacting to news that the Winter Olympics in Vancouver were three years away: "Start. Organizing. Now." Perhaps Black's most outstanding column was "The Not So Curious Case of Caster Semenya" (43:6, November/December 2009), recounting the humiliation of the South African runner who was subjected to a "gender test" after her victory in Berlin. "If Semenya is found to be intersex then she has the right to define herself and make that definition known to others when and if she so chooses to," he observed, mentioning as well the racist quality of the subjection of a black woman's body to investigation. This is why, he wrote, her "case" was really not "curious" at all, but rather the most recent of a long history of dehumanizing practices, with science, "civilization" and sport as their cover.

In "Sexism, Soccer and Struggle" (45:3, May/June 2011), Black considered the unfair working conditions of players on the Canadian women's national soccer team, and pointed out the sexism that pays them like "casual day-labourers, negotiating wages with every new job." His musings on gender, sports and aggression continued in "Would Baby Storm Riot," as he pointed out that some women caught on tape in the Stanley Cup riot had "smashed the odd window as well" (45:5, September/October 2011). But perhaps what makes Black's writing so captivating is his honesty — his willingness to make his own responses a part of his careful but incisive analysis. In his column on Penn State, and on the riot by supporters of Joe Paterno, for example (46:1, January/February 2012), Black articulates his ambivalence over the culture of violence he associates with much of sport: "while watching the footage of this frat-boy uprising, deep down inside me, in some dark authoritarian corner of my soul, I wanted to cast aside [my] principles just this once and find some joy in one of those jackass students getting a rightful smack across the head. Now, isn't that ironic?" Finally, in a roundup of sports heroes and villains in 46:5 September/October 2012, Black demonstrated that, indeed, less is more, by devoting just one line to explaining why Don Cherry appeared in his end-of-year list of sports villains: "For yet another season of being himself."

The wealth and diversity of arts and culture content — broadly defined — in the magazine was truly remarkable, achieved in part by a broadening of the editorial collective's membership, a deliberate effort to recruit new and young contributors, and a recognition of how easy it is for a well-intentioned political publication to rest on the laurels of the familiar. While men still tended to dominate as the authors or subjects of articles, *CD* became much better at covering queer artists, performance and media art, and most crucially, First Nations art and artists. The lingering notion that art and culture, however understood, was a "soft" issue for a political magazine to cover, and simply not crucial to our situated, political lives, was long gone. In its place was a magazine still full of cultural debate (as in Ed Janzen's column "Vulture" that eviscerated television comedies like *The Office* for its "misanthropic, middle-class, anti-working-class fantasy" 43:6, November/December 2009), but the essential value of art and culture to the Left was no longer in question. It became, in the best sense of the word, ordinary.

References

Barthes, Roland. *Mythologies.* Trans. Annette Lavers. London: Jonathan Cape, 1972.

Williams, Raymond. "Culture is Ordinary." In *Resources of Hope: Culture, Democracy, Socialism*, 3–14. London: Verso, 1989.

PART V
THE INSTITUTIONAL DIMENSION

CHAPTER 8
Fifty Years of Class Struggle
Larry Haiven and Judy Haiven

If we can't find ways to develop this kind of public support — especially from other sections of the working class, be they unionised or non-unionised, fully employed or precariously employed, unemployed or the poor — we won't get very far in sustaining our wage demands and benefits, raising the standards of lower paid members, or defending working conditions . . . while the primary focus of unions has been on bargaining collective agreements and resolving workplace grievances, the attack is now coming directly from the state, and it will come on many fronts at the same time — from attacking seniority rights of teachers to privatising health care services, to limiting the right to strike.

— Sam Gindin and Michael Hurley in "The Assault on Public Services," Canadian Dimension 45:6, November/December 2011

For students of Canadian labour — trade unionists, academics and leftists interested in workers and their struggles — fifty years of *Dimension* articles provide a veritable treasure trove. For many years, other than the house organs of the Communist Party and other left groups (which, while informative, concentrated on their special interests), *Dimension* was the sole source of non-sectarian left insight and reflection on the deep background of the labour movement and of changes in labour markets and workplace relations.

When *Dimension* began, industrial relations was still an issue well-covered in the mainstream media and academe, which seems a curiosity in the twenty-first century. The *Globe and Mail* had a full-time labour beat until the early 1990s. Reading fifty years of *Dimension* on labour and work makes one realize how much has changed but also how much has stayed the same. As we will see under the themes addressed in this chapter, debates which exploded and raged for a period subsided, either as major victories were won or defeats suffered, so it is fascinating to read back to when they were intense. On the other hand, certain themes persist unabated: the erosion of the post–World War II "social contract," the growing deregulation of labour markets, the challenge from women and other equity-seeking groups for justice in the workplace, the fight in the labour movement between those seeking accommodation with employers and those seeking radical transformation of the workplace, the "contested terrain" of the work floor, the struggle between jobs-at-any-price and other important objectives, like environmental stewardship, economic planning and economic independence.

Of course, *Dimension* is not like the daily newspaper, where the fabled editor shouts "hold the front page" to cover a breaking fire or assigns a team of ace reporters to an election. Its content has been dependent upon the interests, indeed the whims, of activists and experts writing mostly in their spare time. But over the long haul, most of the major issues for labour have found their way into the magazine's pages in one way or other.

Dimension was lucky to have some of the most senior and respected left trade unionists and labour academics writing in its pages. And, from the 1980s, it also had several regular labour columnists, steeped in labour lore, who ensured that the issues were covered with some expertise and regularity.

There are simply too many labour and work issues to do justice to in this chapter and so we have concentrated on a few.

Independent Canadian unions

Seen from this end of the time telescope, the amount of space devoted in *Dimension* to the struggle by Canadian trade unionists for independence from their US-based parent unions seems almost quaint. Today only 26 per cent of them are in US-based unions.[1] But it was not always thus. In 1961, 75 per cent remitted their dues and took their marching orders (and often orders not to march) from south of the border. By the time *Dimension* was born, a rash of high-profile defections had occurred. The Canadian Textile Council (CTC), the Bricklayers, Masons Independent Union of Canada (BMIU), the Pulp and Paper Workers of Canada (PPWC), the Canadian Association of Industrial, Mechanical and Allied Workers (CAIMAW) and the Canadian Union of Operating Engineers (CUOE) were among the first. And the Mine, Mill and Smelter Workers Union, practically moribund in the US from anticommunist attacks, had given its Canadian branches considerable autonomy as they geared up to fight raids by the United Steelworkers. These unions and others would help form the Council (later Confederation) of Canadian Unions in 1969, devoted to leading the independence struggle.

The initiative had two main causes: First, a new generation of trade unionists had not grown up in the Depression and had not participated in the fight to establish industrial unions in the late forties and fifties. They were not content with the postwar "social contract" among business, labour, and the state and they rankled at the straitjacket of assembly lines, industrial discipline and the "scientific management" of Frederick W. Taylor, despite growing material benefits. They were part of a new rash of industrial militancy that exploded in North America and Europe. Second, a new wind of nationalism was blowing through Canada, fanned by the centennial celebrations of 1967 and the critique of American imperialism provoked by the Vietnam War.

The fight for Canadian unions was a point of bitter contention in the Canadian Left. Many claimed that only the larger "international" unions could stand up to the might of international companies. The NDP would hardly bite the hand of American unions that fed it. Trotskyist-inspired organizations decried nationalistic tendencies in Canada, and the Communist Party of Canada, loath to anger American unions in which they were active, called timidly only for greater "autonomy" and denounced the practice of "raiding" (supplanting a US union with a Canadian one). The unallied "New Left" was also less than attentive to

the phenomenon, turning its attentions at first to community organizing. Only the Vancouver-based Progressive Workers and a few other
groups embraced the independence movement in labour, followed in
the early seventies by the Canadian Liberation Movement and the Waffle
Movement in the NDP.

Canadian Dimension, therefore, deserves credit for reporting ener-
getically on the issue from the beginning and for taking sides with the
independentists.

An early review by Ed Finn (4:4, June 1967) took the publication of
landmark *International Unionism: A Study in Canadian-American Relations*
by University of Toronto industrial relations professor John Crispo as an
opportunity to comment on the growing movement. Finn summed up
the feelings of nationalists unabashedly:

> *The continuing takeover of Canadian industry and resources
> by American interests is arousing concern among those
> citizens of Canada who wish to preserve their country's
> independence. They see quite clearly that the erosion of
> economic control leads inevitably to the reduction, and
> eventual loss, of political sovereignty.*
>
> *But it is not only Canadian industry that has been
> "taken over" by the United States. The Canadian Labour
> Movement has also been Americanized to a large extent,
> with more than 70 percent of all organized workers in
> this country now belonging to American unions. Many
> nationalists believe it is as necessary to "repatriate" the
> Canadian labour movement as it is to regain control of our
> industry, if Canada is to be saved from complete absorption
> into the American empire.*

Finn opined that even where US unions had granted Canadians some
home rule, "[t]he 'autonomy' exercised by union officials is therefore
more apparent than real." He then concluded on a pessimistic note:

> *. . . the emergence of a strictly national labour movement*

remains a theoretical possibility only. In spite of the severe limitations in autonomy granted to the Canadian sections of most internationals, there seems little likelihood of the kind of strong upsurge of nationalist sentiment among Canadian members that alone might lead to the achievement of true independence. Canadian workers, by and large, do not seem so much concerned about such abstract questions. National unionism would only command their loyalty if, in addition to being Canadian, it offered them material benefits, at least as good as those provided by the international.

To be fair, who in 1967 would have even dreamt that the vaunted United Auto Workers, then still led by the redoubtable Walter Reuther, would within a decade and a half see its Canadian members secede, and without the vicious retribution visited upon other independentists?

A short two years later (6:3-4, August/September 1969), Finn reported the beating-back of a move within his own, long-independent Canadian union, the Canadian Brotherhood of Railway, Transport and General Workers (CBRT) to merge with the US-based Brotherhood of Railway, Airline and Steamship Clerks. A US union officer admitted to Finn that "a move in 1969 to dissolve a national union and bring its members into the American ambit was 'running against the tide of nationalism now sweeping the labour movement and the nation.'"

A year later (7:1-2, June/July 1970), Gil Levine reported on a bold nationalistic reform resolution brought to the floor of the Canadian Labour Congress convention. Emboldened by the success of the Waffle Group at a recent New Democratic Party convention — Waffler Jim Laxer would give David Lewis a run for his money at the leadership race a year later — nationalist trade unionists would propose minimum standards for Canadian sections of US unions. These included: a Canadian office, Canadian officials elected by Canadians, Canadian policy conferences, Canadian staff, sufficient dues left in Canada to serve Canadian members' needs, an end to US headquarters' approvals for Canadian collective agreements, freedom of Canadian members to determine their own political activities (including affiliation to political parties) and the right to merge with other Canadian unions. Today, these seem extremely tame. But a watered-down, nonbinding version was all the establishment would allow. Still, this was a first limited victory within the "house of labour."

In the June 1971 issue (8:1), Bob Sass, writing as Robert B. Morris, reported on the previous year's disaffiliation of the Saskatchewan locals from the Retail, Wholesale and Department Store Union (RWDSU) and the defection from the Retail Clerks International Union (RCIU) a year later. He condemned the "reverter" clause in the constitutions of most American unions which allowed them to seize the assets of any local or subdivision that sought its independence, so that rebels would pay dearly.

All was not clear sailing with the new Canadian outfits, especially to some critical leftists. In the same issue, Alvin Finkel condemned the move from the US machinists union to CAIMAW at Winnipeg's Bristol Aerospace as "little more than a change in the faces of the contract negotiators," with many of the undemocratic practices of the old union continued in the new. Raided US unions staged counter-raids and in some cases, the back-and-forth struggle lasted many years. A decade after the RWDSU split, Clare Powell (14:6, May 1980) described the bitter internal rivalries in the Saskatchewan breakaways that tempted the newly-merged United Food and Commercial Workers (UFCW) to try its hand at supplanting the Canadian union (mostly unsuccessful).

Most of the new Canadian unions were considerably more radical than their US counterparts and it was not long before some very bitter strikes for their very survival ensued. An early and iconic struggle occurred at the Brantford Texpack factory organized by the Canadian Textile and Chemical Union, led by veteran independentists Kent Rowley and Madeleine Parent. In several issues during 1971 and 1972, *Dimension* reported on the dispute. In November 1971 (8:3), Marc Zwelling described how the US hospital supply company, with help from the Ontario government and the police, had tried to break the union and turn the Brantford plant into a warehouse only. This strike and several others by that union captured the imagination of young radicals in southern Ontario and embarrassed the traditional trade unions by attracting support from their own members.

"The Canadian Textile and Chemical Union" claimed Zwelling, "has now given the lie to the myth that independent Canadian unions can never win against powerful multinational corporations. Granted it did not do it alone. What was critically important was the support it was able to muster both inside and outside the labour movement But that is the real lesson. It is not the existence of international unions that gives labour its strength — but dedicated union leadership, a militant membership and strong support from the rest of the labour movement."

Kent Rowley himself appeared in the pages of *Dimension* several times before his untimely death in 1978. He took issue even with Zwelling's favourable account for describing Rowley as an "outcast" in the labour movement "pluck[ing] away like a scavenger at the malcontents and neglected membership of American-based unions." The accusation of raiding, Rowley fired back "has lost its sense and meaning as Americans have come to believe that they 'own' Canadian industry." In the March 1973 issue (9:4), Rowley wrote a long article detailing the many sins of US unions in Canada, including the busting of the Canadian Seaman's Union by Hal Banks and the Seafarers International Union and the 1971 order by the United Autoworkers that their Canadian members at Douglas Aircraft end their strike upon pain of trusteeship. As for the reverter clause, Rowley wrote ". . . in the long run, to hell with the property! The longer Canadians stay in American unions, the more we shall be bled. At some point the flow must stop or we shall die. We had better not wait long."

Dimension carried a tribute to Rowley following his death at age sixty in 1978 and cited playwright Rick Salutin's comment summing up Rowley's approach to the US-dominated labour movement — "You need not sell out."

Amid charges that US unions were labour agents of US imperialism, historian Irving Abella provided a contrarian view in the March/April 1972 issue (8:6), précising the book *Nationalism, Communism and Canadian Labour* he was writing at the same time. "It wasn't," he wrote about the 1930s and forties, "that American unions were so imperialistic and aggressive, that they moved in with greedy hands to take over an infant Canadian trade union movement to collect more dues. They were simply responding to pressing invitations sent by Canadian workers who had more confidence in the capabilities and strength of the American unions than they had in their own." A review of Abella's book by historian David Frank in the June 1974 issue (10:2), lauds the author's investigation of the anticommunist witchhunts in the unions but faults his focus on leaders and his failure to give credit to the rank-and-file.

Origins notwithstanding, US unions had some real conflicts of interest with their Canadian members and support for them in Canada was severely tested by US President Richard Nixon's moves in the early seventies to support repatriation of Canadian jobs in US branch plants and invocation of the now-perennial "Buy American" policy. With most of their members residing in the US, the international union headquarters supported the moves.

Christine Krawczyk (9:4, March 1973) described the first major blow to the United Steelworkers in Canada with the breakaway of the Kitimat smelter workers to form the Canadian Aluminum Smelter and Allied Workers Union (CASAW) and similar attempts in southern British Columbia mines and smelters (old Mine Mill locals had ceded to Steel more than a decade back). The Kitimat workers were to remain militant, holding an eighteen-day wildcat strike in 1976 over local conditions and to enforce an alliance with the then-legally-striking Alcan workers in Quebec. The company successfully sued the union for over $1 million and imposed heavy discipline upon two hundred activists, but the union persisted, later helping to initiate an international alliance of aluminum workers (16:5, July/August 1982).

Articles on the US-Canadian union question were scarce in the following four years until a tumultuous strike at Winnipeg's Griffin Steel brought the issue back to *Dimension*'s pages (12:3, July 1977), described by trade unionist D. Craig Gilchrist. The plant, enticed to Manitoba with public funds to provide jobs, had been one of the first whose workers opted for CAIMAW a decade earlier and both sides were spoiling for a fight. It came over the seemingly small issue of voluntary overtime, but it blossomed into a set-piece battle that spread to the rest of the provincial labour movement and to the NDP government. Scabs, scores of police and arrests ensued. Seeing this as an epic confrontation over labour rights, as in Texpack, rank-and-filers from CLC affiliated unions (some

237

Canadian, some US-based) joined the picket line while their union leaders hedged on official support. "It has been said," wrote Gilchrist, "that labour in Winnipeg lost its 'balls' in the defeat of the 1919 General Strike. This present situation presents them with an opportunity to regain that which they lost so long ago."

In the late 1970s *Dimension* reported on two militant independent unions that launched inspirational organizing drives and/or strikes. Dedicated to enhancing the rights of women workers the Service, Office and Retail Workers' Union of Canada (SORWUC) set out to organize hitherto neglected realms where women predominated: restaurants and offices. But it was the bank campaign that received most attention. Forced by the federal Labour Relations Board to organize branch by branch, it was initially successful at organizing several branches, but the union (and the copycat CLC-sanctioned Canadian Union of Bank Employees) was never able to achieve the holy grail — spreading its success to enough branches to negotiate a national collective agreement. Clerical and technical workers at Toronto's York University turned their Staff Association into a union, joined the Confederation of Canadian Unions and went on strike in 1978. Ellen Meiksins Wood, who covered the strike for *Dimension*, wrote words that would ring prophetic for the next thirty years and for the several York strikes that followed:

> *If one of the major functions of the state is to act as a shock-absorber for capital, there is a sense in which workers in the public sector bear the brunt of economic crisis for workers in the private sector. This may help to explain the lack of solidarity between workers in the two sectors and the weak support given to beleaguered public sector workers in what for them is a particularly bad time, when they are the direct victims of shifts in government spending and the first objects of government's political battle against labour.*

Nationalists in the labour movement had to wait until the mid-1980s for their major advance, but not before a few near misses.

Glen Wanamaker (18:3, June 1984) described how the newly-minted Canadian Mine Workers Union (CMW) attempted twice to win the Cape Breton coal miners (employees of Devco) away from the US-based United Mine Workers of America (UMWA), failing both times. Workers had been angry when a 1981 strike ended due to lack of funds in the UMWA despite the Canadians paying into its strike fund for years. The United Steelworkers were subject to a serious challenge in Local 1005 at Hamilton's Stelco works. Nationalist Cec Taylor described in the March 1984 *Dimension* (18:1) his travails against that union.

The big breakthrough came in 1984 when the Canadian section of the United Auto Workers (UAW) under leader Bob White broke with its US headquarters. According to an article by John Deverell (19:1, March/April 1985), the dispute had been festering since 1979 when the American leaders had jumped into concessions and collaboration with the auto companies (UAW President Douglas Fraser had joined the Chrysler board of directors from 1980 to 1984.) It came into the open during the 1984 bargaining round; the split was quick and, compared to other US unions, relatively free of acrimony. In the article, Deverell wondered whether or not the UAW-CAW split might mean an avalanche toward independent Canadian unions, citing the US-loyal Steelworkers (especially with Canadian Lynn Williams in the international president's chair in Pittsburgh) and several other US unions.

A year later (20:1, March 1986) Charlotte Yates lauded the emergence of the CAW as "a phoenix rising from the ashes of the Canadian labour movement," forced into retreat since the early 1970s. More than Deverell, she held hope for greater Canadianization of the labour movement following the CAW move, pointing to the merger with the Canadian Airline Employee's Association. Over the years, Yates's prediction held true as mergers with the CAW increased and other unions moved to independence.

The Auto Workers may have been the most spectacular and media-heralded breakaway, but the various elements that combined to found the Communications, Energy and Paperworkers Union (CEP) had been working away more quietly from the 1970s. The Communications Workers of Canada (CWC) gained independence from its US union in

1972. The Canadian Paperworkers Union (CPU) followed in 1974 and the Energy and Chemical Workers (ECWU) broke away from its US parent in 1980. They all combined into the CEP in 1992 and several smaller media unions joined them within a few years to form one of the largest unions in Canada.

An insightful article by Rebecca Murdock (29:6, December/January 1995–96) reviewed the "Merger Mania." The author averred that "So-called 'super unions' offer more clout and greater resources at a time when many unions are feeling pinched by rising operational costs," but warned that "members from small unions are justifiably concerned that their interests will be absorbed and potentially lost in a super union structure." She also warned that the super unions had resources so large that the importance of the Canadian Labour Congress would inevitably decline.

"The million-dollar question," concluded the author, "is: can a super union produce the economies of scale it promises while representing the needs of members in diverse job sectors across the breadth of Canada?" All the more relevant given the recent (2012) merger between the CEP and CAW to form the largest private sector (three hundred thousand members) union in Canadian history at a time when union density is under fire from employers and governments.

Workers' control and tripartism

Like the Canada-US union question, another labour issue covered especially well in the pages of *Dimension* seems almost old-fashioned amid the twenty-first–century depredations of neoliberalism and attacks by employers and the state upon the very legitimacy of trade unionism. The decline of modern industrial relations had begun in the early 1970s with the end of the long wave of post-WWII prosperity. But this was not immediately evident as the late 1960s and early seventies wave of industrial militancy (mentioned above) broke upon the shores of the developed world. An article by Ed Finn (4:2, January/February 1967) explored the question "Why Canadian Workers Are Kicking." He summed it up as follows:

240

*Canadian labour is in a state of turmoil. Unrest and
dissatisfaction among union members is now pandemic, as
intense among civil servants and other clerical employees
as it is among the most rugged blue collar workers. The
new militancy has manifested itself in the form of wildcat
strikes, defiance of elected union leaders, rejection of new
contract terms that would have been eagerly seized a few
years earlier, and general discontent with traditional union
methods and policies.*

Commissions of inquiry like the UK's Donovan Commission and
Canada's Woods Task Force (both in 1968) examined the unrest and
suggested that the poor quality of work life was a major cause. Discourse
in the next decade focused on the need for greater union and worker participation, both at the corporate and the shopfloor levels.

In Canada, the late 1970s and early 80s saw serious debates within
and without the labour movement on catchwords as varied as "tripartism," "industrial democracy," "workers' control," "corporatism," and
more micro-level schemes as "job enrichment," "job enlargement,"
and "consultation." By 1975 the federally-sponsored Canadian Labour
Relations Council had brought together labour, employers and government to discuss issues of common concern. But double-digit inflation
prompted Prime Minister Trudeau to impose wage and price controls
soon afterward, essentially suspending meaningful collective bargaining.
Pulling out of the Council and a one-day national strike by affiliated
unions in 1976 signalled the CLC's displeasure but also strengthened its
hand for the machinations of post-controls era. In the same year the CLC
produced a historic manifesto. In the aftermath of wage controls, it predicted, governments would turn away from the old laissez-faire attitude
and look for ways to more closely manage the economy and the labour
movement should be ready to seize the opportunity.

Dimension recognized quite early on how crucial this question was
for the Canadian labour movement and devoted considerable space
throughout 1977, including most of the July 1977 issue (12:3), to a
critique. Cy Gonick pointed out that the debate had to be seen in light

of the economic crisis of 1973 and the already-beginning attack on collective bargaining heralded by the anti-inflation controls program. Some in government, said Gonick, were looking to get unions to exercise voluntary restraint and to contribute to raising productivity. In return, they were willing to offer labour a place at the table on a number of tripartite boards, including a renewed Council. There would also be a federal agency to gather and publish collective bargaining information, a code of fair labour practices, and a national centre for occupational health and safety.

Gonick quotes a Rotary Club of Ottawa speech by Bryce Mackasey, a leading federal government proponent of labour inclusion,

> Instead of fighting society for a bigger slice of the pie, and thus preventing the pie from being baked, I think the unions should be fighting for a hand in the baking. They should be fighting the root cause of worker discontent. The primary need of the worker today is job satisfaction and a chance to develop his skills and abilities, his initiatives and his individuality. The unions should be fighting for a more democratic work place.

Were unions finally going to be taken seriously? Was this a real chance for unions to abandon their focus on narrow collective bargaining and finally to be brought into the realm of politics in their own right (as in some European countries)? Or was it a ploy by employers and governments to co-opt a generation of militants and their more pliable leaders? Gonick concluded that the proponents of tripartism within governments were weakly committed to it and that in any case that the tripartite proposal put forward by the Canadian Labour Congress was misplaced and dangerous:

> . . . labour in Canada is not moving in the direction of transforming society. In its Manifesto for Labour, the CLC is requesting a secure place for itself in the co-management of the existing system. Perhaps what is needed at this time is

a counter-Labour Manifesto which would directly challenge
corporate power in Canada and chart the labour movement
on the road to socialism.

The same *Dimension* issue carried a report on the National Film Board's *Temiscaming*, about the worker buyout of an American-owned pulp and paper plant to form Tembec Forest Products. Though the workers were induced to buy shares, they had no effective control and the old hierarchical structure continues. The author concludes that the film:

> . . . *is bound to raise questions about some of the schemes*
> *of job enrichment, job enlargement, worker councils, profit*
> *sharing, representation on boards, etc., etc. that are being*
> *so enthusiastically publicized these days as panaceas for*
> *improved industrial relations. This film helps us to see the*
> *limitations of all such schemes. On the other hand, we also*
> *know about the limitations of traditional trade unionism.*

Another article in the issue by Gonick examined the "West German model" of co-determination. Again, some of the Canadian trade unionists, politicians and employers were fascinated not only with the model, but also with the labour peace it delivered. While appearing to offer workers real participation in the managing of enterprises, Gonick concluded that the model:

> *shows that by accepting corporatist solutions, trade unions*
> *give up their freedom to formulate independent political*
> *alternatives. They cripple themselves as defenders of the*
> *immediate interests of the working class and they are turned*
> *into enemies of the socialist opposition that challenges the*
> *basic structures they have become part of.*

Leo Panitch concluded this very important discussion with his own examination of "a conception of workers participation and self-management that places it within the context of a revolutionary process and understands that process as involving a change in the working class itself through its struggle for *hegemony*" (emphasis added). Referring to Antonio Gramsci, the originator of that phrase, Panitch insisted that "the task of workers control was not just economic and political, but cultural, in the deepest sense of the word." Left to its own devices to participate in the management of enterprises, the working class would make "workers control" a hollow activity. The guarantor of a cultural revolution had to be a mass revolutionary party.

Dimension would revisit industrial democracy two years later in a special issue entitled "Battle for the Workplace" (14:3, December 1979) devoted to the theme, again with Cy Gonick contributing several articles. By this time, Harry Braverman's iconic *Labor and Monopoly Capital: The Degradation of Work in the Twentieth Century* had not only burst upon the scene (in 1974) but had spawned almost a firestorm among a generation of labour scholars and activists. The book is widely recognized as one of the most important contributions to Marxist theory on labour, read and appreciated not only by socialists, but by all analysts of the workplace. The issue contained probably the last public interview with Braverman, in which the author talked about the degraded working lives of the de-skilled masses of workers. He had a jaundiced view of the idea that extrinsic rewards from work could ever replace intrinsic rewards:

> *Preparing our life for leisure? It's an outrageous proposition on the face of it. The idea of sacrificing 6-7-8 hours at work so that we can enjoy the rest of our day. That, if you'll forgive the expression, is bullshit. Because it will be this nullity, this vacuum in people's lives that will more than ever shape their lives. The more working lives are emptied of content and transformed into a nullity, the more the same thing happens to life outside the job and we can already see a complete demonstration of that in modern society.*

Braverman was an American socialist, economist, writer and former skilled tradesperson, associated with the radical journal *Monthly Review.* He delved back into Marx to resurrect the concept of the "labour process,"

244

whereby the capitalist, Mr. Moneybags, goes to the labour market and hires a given quantum of what? Marx distinguished between labour power (workers' potential ability to labour) and the actual amount of labour that the worker produced. Returning to the factory, Moneybags confronts the problem of extracting labour from the hapless worker. Under modern capitalism, just how much labour can be extracted from a given amount of labour power depends on the industrial organization, discipline, work flow, machinery, training, and motivation that the capitalist can muster in his workforce. Braverman resurrected the work of the premier industrial engineer of the twentieth century, Frederick Taylor, claiming that Taylor's concepts of "scientific management" have inspired and haunted the labour process since the early 1900s, not only in factories but in offices and all other types of workplace. By separating conception (the thinking about how work would be done, to be performed by managers) from execution (the actual doing of the work, to be performed by workers), Taylor would transform American (and then world) capitalism.

Braverman also foretold of attempts by employers to disguise the dehumanizing effects of "Taylorism" by allowing limited worker autonomy, or at least the appearance of some. Once the managerial conquest of labour had been achieved, claimed Braverman, management could add back in just as much worker participation as it wished, without sacrificing the basic principle of control. Taylor predicted that once his system was in place, unions would be totally unnecessary.

The December 1979 issue (14:3) contains a tribute to the work of Katherine Stone, a scholar who investigated the introduction of incentive systems and job ladders in the US steel industry. Once Taylorism had eliminated most differentiation by skill, the tendency was for workers to realize common interests and unite. But, as Gonick said, "the owners developed strategies to convince workers that their individual interests were the same as the company's." The employer strategies postponed, but could not stop the advent of industrial unionization.

Craig Heron contributed to the issue an exploration of the importance of the punch clock in modern industrial engineering and Graham Lowe discussed how scientific management came to be adopted in early twentieth-century Canada, first in factories, then in the office and civil service. He also covered the rise of "welfare work" or the early human resources management function and joint works councils in attempting to palliate some of the worst effects of Taylorism. In the article, Lowe also introduced the ideas of Canadian deputy minister and then minister of labour William Lyon Mackenzie King (later prime minister), a strong believer, even theorist, of class collaboration between labour and capital. In 1914, King went to work as industrial relations consultant for John D. Rockefeller in the wake of the latter's involvement in the Ludlow massacre and developed "joint industrial councils," which Lowe called "a sophisticated form of company union."

In the 1990s a new challenge emerged from employers using the language of worker involvement. Known by several monikers like "team concept," "concertation," "quality of working life," and "total quality management," the drill was the same: workers (and their unions) would cooperate with management in their plant or company against the competition of workers from another plant, another company, another country. Workers (renamed "associates") would be formed into teams where they would collaborate to find ways of speeding up production, improving quality, or both. Bosses would be called "team leaders."

Unions in Canada generally opposed these moves, with greater or lesser success. One renowned experiment happened at the CAMI plant (a joint venture between Suzuki and General Motors) in Ingersoll, Ontario. In agreeing to the experiment, the CAW won the right to represent the workers, and to examine and document the process so that it could better understand team concept. The union later produced a book and a movie on the "CAW Research Project on CAMI." This involved visits by a union team to the plant, surveys of the workers, interviews with managers, team leaders and union representatives and shop-floor observation. Herman Rosenfeld, a CAW staffer later to become CD's labour columnist, wrote about it in the January 1993 issue of Dimension (27:1):

> The survey . . . found that workers sensed that a large
> chasm existed between the promises of an empowering,
> equal, democratic and caring work environment and the

246

reality of production at CAMI. By the final round of the
survey, only about one-third agreed that they were actively
involved in making decisions at work; this was down from
one-half in the first round. When asked to describe what
those decisions were, the majority referred to their ability to
decide upon how to perform their immediate job.

Workers also began to suffer from debilitating repetitive stress injuries from the hard work and yet experienced the tyranny of the group, feeling guilty for abandoning their teams when they were absent.

So troubled did relations become that in 1992, three years after the plant opened, the union members went on strike for five weeks. A wildcat strike ensued in 1995. Rosenfeld summed up the lessons learned (30:3, May/June 1996):

First, the essence of the lean production model is surely
cost reduction and work intensification, just as its critics
have asserted. Second, the very institutional forms that
management sets up in order to manufacture commitment to
its corporate goals are themselves vulnerable to contestation
and struggle by the workers. The strategy and tactics for this
type of struggle are still in their infancy. Perfecting them
will present great challenges to unions.

Third, a union can play a critical role in modifying the
effects of lean production. Indeed, the existence of a union
providing an alternative pole of reference to that of the
company's ideological apparatus can allow the workers to
gain the space to develop their own perspective.

The challenge from women workers

One more theme well covered by *Dimension* is the rise of equity-seeking groups and their challenge to employers and the labour movement. One of this chapter's authors remembers well working for a UAW-organized factory in Toronto in the early 1970s where the collective agreement contained, for several classifications, two separate wage scales — one for men and one for women. It was not until the 1980s that a new generation of feminists finally made a significant dent in the male power structure of workplace and union. The aforementioned coverage of SORWUC and the York University Staff Association in the late seventies did, by association, deal with women and unions. Articles about general issues of women's liberation had appeared earlier in *Dimension* but it was not until the 1980s that serious coverage began.

A thoughtful article by Judy Darcy (someone with deep experience in both the women's and the labour movements and later national president of CUPE) in the November 1983 issue (17:5), considered "women's issues" in the labour movement and took the brothers to task. "The predominantly male union leadership," wrote Darcy, "despite statements at times more progressive than its members might support, is fundamentally threatened by the power and demands of trade union women and the women's movement."

". . . [T]he crux of the matter," continued Darcy, "lies in the distinction between support for 'women's issues' and *women's liberation*. That distinction has come home to me in numerous discussions with people in my own local and in other union bodies over the issue of abortion, women's right to choose."

Darcy warned presciently that until the labour movement understood the nexus between capitalism and patriarchy, "the danger is very real that women's 'economic' issues will still be the first to go when the bargaining gets tough. And until that consciousness exists, the labour movement will not be a solid ally of the women's movement and all its demands. It will not use its enormous power and strategic position in society in the interests of all oppressed and exploited social groups."

An article by Marlene Kadar in June 1984 (18:3), discussed unions and sexual harassment. Kadar cited union research that shocked members. The British Columbia Federation of Labour passed a policy statement in 1980 after learning that 90 per cent of the respondent women had experienced sexual harassment. In 1982, 80 per cent of Winnipeg women in trades reported being harassed at work and similar numbers came from a survey by Alberta's provincial employees union. Kadar quoted author Lin Farley about what had to change:

by condemning the abuse, rather than the objection; by
acceptance of the damage as real, rather than trivial; by
ceasing to presume women's accusations to be gratuitous and
false; and by recognizing the enormous effort it takes for
working women to overcome their socialization to passivity
in order for them to complain.

The hardest nut to crack was the rank-and-file. A long and introspective essay by Stan Gray in the same issue, "Sharing the Shop Floor," examined the sexual battleground in the workplace with special emphasis on his personal experiences advocating for his union sisters at Hamilton's Westinghouse plant. He affirmed the prevalence of regarding women's complaints as frivolous and how he fought a long battle against ignorance and prejudice among his male colleagues. His description of the introduction of women to a department long male-only, "the invasion," is particularly insightful, recounting the changes not only in the brothers' attitudes, but in his own as well.

Westinghouse was not the only Hamilton factory to experience the influx of women blue-collar workers in the early 1980s. Gray also recounted the story of Bonita Clark, who was hired, along with several other women, in 1979 after a group called Women Back in Stelco pressured the company (20:3, May 1986). Six years later, after all of the women had either left, been dismissed or been laid off in a recession, only Clark was left. She filed at the Labour Relations Board against the company over sixty charges of sexual and other harassment, one of the early cases of a "poisoned work environment" after having her complaints sidestepped at the Human Rights Commission. Not only was she touched, prodded and propositioned, she was also singled out for humiliation, made to ask over the plant intercom for permission to go to the bathroom and faced with open displays of pornography.

Bonita Clark's case galvanized the Ontario labour movement and pushed the cause of women workers' rights forward qualitatively. But women's fight was not only against the employers and the male rank-and-file. The labour movement was also a terrain of struggle. An article by Marg Ball (19:4, September/October 1985) tackled the question. She pointed out that it was only at the beginning of the 1980s that paid child care began to be provided at union conventions. Once in front of a union audience, the women were routinely disparaged for being overly shrill and aggressive. Even after inroads had been made, women regarded the breakthroughs as bittersweet:

> It proved ironic and painful, after hours of heated and often sexist debate on convention floors, to watch male labour leaders . . . announce proudly (after acceptance of affirmative action) "Who says the labour movement discriminates?" Male leaders saw it as a victory. Female unionists knew that, if true equality existed in the union movement, affirmative action would never have been needed at all.

Ten years later (31:5, September/October 1997), CAW leader Peggy Nash could write of the experience within her union:

> A CAW national women's department was essential to fight for and coordinate women's programs in the union. Also key was the national women's committee made up of leadership women who knew what was needed and were prepared to organize and build support. The union's internal strategy has been to reach out to women. For 20 years in the CAW, local union women's committees have been mandatory under the national constitution. CAW women activists are encouraged to form networks in their community as a less formal, more community-based approach to the union. Local committees and networks are not just forums for a few women to meet.

The labour front from 1995

While the number of CD feature articles on labour declined after the nineties, Geoff Bickerton's labour column more than made up for it in consistency of analysis. In issue after issue, Bickerton wrote on important themes and threads in the Canadian labour movement. The value of his column was that it was a first-hand diary of Canada's labour movement and its relations with the Left over nearly twenty years. Bickerton recently retired as the Research Director for the Canadian Union of Postal Workers (CUPW).

Bickerton noted the division in the labour movement as the CLC refused to become involved in the 1995 Days of Action, the mobilization of workers for the massive rotating work stoppages in eleven Ontario cities. Instead the Canadian Auto Workers (CAW) and public sector unions were at the helm, while the "Pink Group" — the Steelworkers, the UFCW and the CEP hung back.

In the winter of 1997, a hundred postal workers, CUPW members, descended on Preston Manning's Ottawa home, when he, representing the Reform Party, sat in Parliament as the leader of the Opposition. In a thoughtful article on the advisability of demonstrating or picketing outside managers', owners', or right wing politicians' homes, Bickerton noted:

> *It was a surreal sight, a hundred post officer workers in workers' winter clothes marching outside the grandeur of the mansions of Rockcliffe Park, singing a rather off-key version of "we are the posties in your neighbourhood." Still there was a sense of pride in invading foreign territory to embarrass the man who had led the crusade for the legislated denial of our right to strike.*
> *"Are the Bosses' Homes Out of Bounds?" (32:2, March/April 1998)*

Though Bickerton agreed that taking the struggle to people's homes is "not neat and tidy," he thought unions tended to be too polite. He believed that picketing homes should be done as a last resort, when workplace actions could not be organized.

Some issues in the last twenty years have all but dropped off the agenda. For instance, Bickerton admonished labour to stop being so defensive and to address major important issues such as socialism and

251

how to change the capitalist system. In the May/June 1998 issue (32:3) he argued quite persuasively that since there was no more "Soviet bogey-man," no more Cold War, a "wider scope of political discussion may be possible within unions.

Bickerton took a historical lens to the issue of Canadian versus US-based "international" unions. In "Canadians Must Decide Labour's Future" (34:6, November/December 2000) he asked why Canadian unionists should have tolerated Andy Stern, the international president of the Service Employees International Union (SEIU), intervening in Canadian union politics. Earlier in 2000, Stern had attended a meeting of leaders of the CLC, the Canadian Auto Workers (CAW) and the Canadian section of the SEIU. In what was labeled a "raid," eight Canadian SEIU locals had jumped from the US-based parent union to join the CAW. This was not the first time Stern had intervened in Canadian union affairs. According to Bickerton, in 1999, Stern had stopped a merger between the Quebec wing of the SEIU and the Canadian Union of Public Employees (CUPE), which had been sanctioned by the Quebec Federation of Labour "When Canadian workers are prohibited from assuming the responsibility to run their own affairs," Bickerton asserted, "it is the entire labour movement that suffers."

Bickerton also shed light on new and important issues. In "Labour Must Act Against War" (37:2, March/April 2003), he wrote strongly and passionately about the importance of the labour movement opposing Canadian involvement in the US's war on Iraq:

> This war is about racism and militarism, imperialism and
> nationalism. It's about fear and insecurity and ignorance
> and hatred. It is also about the American bourgeoisie
> extending its economic, political and military domination in
> the Middle East.

Prime Minister Chrétien pulled away from that war, only to enmesh Canadians in another aspect of the US War on Terror a year later when Canadian troops were sent to Afghanistan. Bickerton called the Canadian Labour Congress's opposition to Canada's involvement in Afghanistan clear and unequivocal ("Labour Stands up Against War," 40:4, July/August 2006).

> *Now, in 2006, the CLC and the labour movement have taken a strong position against the deployment of Canadian troops in a foreign country. It has done so at a time when none of the major political parties and not one MP (prior to the May 17 parliamentary vote on extension of Canada's commitment in Afghanistan) had been prepared to call for the withdrawal of our troops. Sometimes it takes guts to do the right thing, and the CLC and the affiliate leadership should be commended for their stand.*

In the same vein Bickerton wrote about the value of the CUPE Ontario resolution on Palestine that called for the union "to support the international campaign of boycott, divestment and sanctions until Israel meets its obligation to recognize the Palestinians people's inalienable right to self-determination" ("Labour Should Follow CUPE Ontario on Israel," 39:5, September/October 2005). This was a major initiative for CUPE, which garnered a virtual hailstorm of criticism from the media and Israel apologists. Bickerton talked about the union movement needing to raise the issues of the Palestinian human rights and the need for education for trade union members on this huge battleground.

In a series of columns over several years, Bickerton examined a question central to the labour movement — how to develop good leaders. As early as 2000, he observed that the best union leaders were usually marginalized people, people of colour, aboriginals, gays and lesbians, the disabled and women because they are ready to take more risks to enable full participation, than traditional white men who (to a large degree) had benefited from the status quo.

Bickerton also wrote about leadership when analyzing labour's role at the Quebec "Summit of the Americas" in 2001 ("Labour and Violence," 36:3, May/June 2002). Sixty thousand labour and other activists, led in part by trade union leaders, turned away from battling directly with the police at the "Wall of Shame" and instead marched far away from the action. The leaders had promised the marchers it would be a "peace-ful" march, and Bickerton thought it would have been "dishonest and irresponsible" to lead them into a possibly violent confrontation with the police. The sticking point for labour would be agreeing to "diversity of tactics" which meant, in essence, countenancing violence:

> . . . *doubtful that the labour movement will organize in*
> *support of the actions organized on the basis of 'respect for*
> *diversity of tactics.' There is simply too much bad history*
> *and too little trust in the leadership of the groups that*
> *promote these tactics.*

In the last five years of *Dimension*, a number of writers have made valuable contributions to current issues such as teachers' and public ser-vice workers' struggles, plant closures, pensions, and precarious labour. Sam Gindin and Michael Hurley (45:6, November/December 2011) linked the attacks on public sector workers to increasing privatization. Governments are restructuring how "services are organised and delivered so they can, piecemeal if necessary, be privatised." They contended that the only way to save these services and jobs is to get the public onside and that trade unions have been remiss due to "debilitating cultures of bureaucratisation to thin and ineffective democracy, inadequate expres-sions of class solidarity and little strategic sense of how to respond to the great changes that have occurred over the past three decades."

Mick Sweetman (63:3, May/June 2012) wrote about two major recent lockouts as capital's response to the economic crises. A smelter, Alcan, in Alma, Quebec, and a factory, Electro Motive Diesel (EMD), in London, Ontario, had been recently sold to giant international corporations — the former to Rio Tinto Alcan (RTA), and the latter to Caterpillar. In both cases, the companies wanted to slash costs and ratchet-down wages. The Steelworkers (at RTA) and the CAW (at EMD) each organised massive days of action in which workers bused in to demonstrate. The CAW also sought support from Occupy London (Ontario) and other community groups. But after a month Caterpillar announced EMD was moving to Muncie, Indiana, a right-to-work state. Workers in Muncie would have their wages cut by at least one-third, and there would be no requirement to pay union dues.

Conclusion

The themes addressed in this chapter have several things in common.

First, they are not just "labour" issues but relate strongly to issues in the broader political economy. The struggle for Canadian unions echoes the larger struggle for Canadian political and economic sovereignty. The subject of worker control is a subset of the larger topic of democratization. And, of course, the travails of women in gaining justice in the workplace and their trade unions echoes the larger contention for justice in society, not only by women, but other equity-seeking groups.

Second, they presented a bracing challenge to the conventional "ways of thinking" of the labour movement as it had evolved since the end of the Second World War. Modern Canadian (and North American) industrial relations is a creature of the intersection of "Fordism" (the regime marked by mass production, mass consumption and mass income-distribution which characterized the middle of the twentieth century) and American imperialism (the hegemony of US industry, products and culture, including trade unions). The fight for Canadian unions was a revolt against both of these. A key feature of Fordism and the "social contract" among labour, employers and the state was the tradeoff between growing worker prosperity and absolute managerial control of the workplace. But as the Fordist compromise eroded in the 1970s and eighties, a new system of regulation and a new relationship among the three players was, for a while, up in the air. Would labour gain a "seat at the table" as it had in Europe? Or would it be relegated even further to the margins? We can see the answer now, but it was far from decided in the middle years of *Dimension*'s life. A further key feature of Fordism was the privileging of a white, male work force. Confronted with rising labour costs and increasing competition, North American firms could continue that white male privilege only by increasingly segmenting the labour force, relying on female and non-white labour on the periphery. The demand for justice by equity-seeking groups has challenged that trend.

Third, the themes embodied a striking challenge to "business as usual" for the leadership of the trade unions, rooted as it had been since the turn of the twentieth century in the United States, in modest and apolitical workplace collective bargaining and in a white male body-and-mindset. While few truly international trade unionists could understand how one country's union movement could control that of another, to most Canadian union leaders it was unquestioned. This was true not only among labour conservatives, but also for those who looked to the US for their left radical inspiration in the 1930s and forties and even fifties. The debate over industrial democracy, too, was well beyond the imagination of the old guard in the unions, who felt they could happily go on negotiating workplace collective agreements and handling grievances forever. But perhaps, the most challenging was the demand of women workers for them to abandon the way their sense of "maleness" was inextricably bound up in industrial work and trade unionism.

CHAPTER 9
Rebelling Youth: Universities and Students
James Naylor

The university may be regarded as a business enterprise which manufactures B.A.'s and B.Sc.'s. The students are 'goods in process'; the manufacturing process generally takes three to four years after which the student emerges as a finished product — a B.A. (B.Sc.). The workers, those who fabricate the goods in process to the finished commodity stage, are the professors. The professors in turn are supervised by the plant foremen — the deans; the general manager of the plant is the university president. His function is to ensure that the enterprise runs smoothly and efficiently, to utilize the plant at maximum capacity, to ensure that the workers concentrate on what they are being paid to do — which is to fabricate the raw material. The goods in process are tested periodically in the various stages of production — to ensure that they conform to minimum standards and specifications. Exceptional quality is duly rewarded. After the final stages of fabrication have been completed the finished commodity is available for sale to the highest bidder. The best markets today seem to be large corporations, government bureaucracies, the professions, but the most rapidly expanding market appears to be graduate schools.

— Cy Gonick, "Self-Government in the Multiversity," Canadian Dimension 3:34, March/June 1966

Overwhelmingly young scholars and activists themselves, those who edited and wrote for *Canadian Dimension* in its early years were well aware of, and were deeply engaged in, a wide range of campus-based activities. At the same time, *Dimension*'s attitude towards the emerging student movement was informed by its broader political project, to reinvigorate political debate and link together the disparate sites of activism, from the campuses, to the unions, to the NDP, and beyond. This would result in a constructive engagement with activists who were emerging on the campuses and looking outward at a vast multitude of social issues.

Consequently, the magazine engaged the emerging student New Left in a manner that challenged its shortcomings and sought to push it in a direction that would allow it to develop wider linkages. In January/ February 1965 (2:2), Cy Gonick reported on the organizations that would come to signify the emergence of the student-based New Left — the Combined Universities Campaign for Nuclear Disarmament (CUCND) and its successor, the Student Union for Peace Action (SUPA). The language was typical of the cut and thrust of 1960s debates on the Left. Despite his regard for several of the participants, "it was clear" this student New Left "knew nothing about the power structure of this country and who makes them."[1]

Gonick would expand on this critique in the November/December 1966 issue in a wide-ranging programmatic and strategic statement in which he was highly critical of Canadian "New Leftism" — "more of a myth than a reality" — for its programmatic weakness and strategic naïveté. He painted a picture of a New Left that rejected the established structures of the Left like unions and the NDP, considering them "too corrupt, authoritarian and manipulative to work in," and instead isolated itself among "counter communities" of students and the marginalized. The critique was much more than a plea for the New Left to return to the structures of the old Left, but to recognize (and he drew on Perry Anderson) the importance of socialists inhabiting civil society more widely and developing strategies appropriate to the real problems of people in their workplaces, schools and neighbourhoods. More specifically, he contrasted the rootlessness of SUPA members to the commitment and effectiveness of those active in American organizations of the New Left, such as the Students for a Democratic Society, the

Student Nonviolent Coordinating Committee and the movement against the Vietnam War. [2]

Certainly SUPA was, as Gonick put it, on "shaky" ground; it would collapse within months. Notably, though, the Canadian university-based New Left that survived and grew out of the ashes of CUCND and SUPA was much more successful than the American in developing roots in a number of areas, particularly the labour movement. The solution to this puzzle is perhaps best explained by John Cleveland, who noted that the first Canadian New Left was much more closely associated with universities than was the case in the US, since the catalysts for the American movement — civil rights and then the Vietnam War — quickly drew students off of campuses and into much broader social struggles. In contrast, Cleveland notes, the English-Canadian student movement "took place in a relative vacuum," leading them to a "Change the University First" perspective.[3] There seemed to be little happening, at least until the very late 1960s, to draw students into the kinds of broader struggles that Gonick envisaged.

Except, perhaps, for Quebec. The Quebec student movement had a substantially different history and developed an ideology of "student syndicalism" through its connections with European student movements as well as from Quebec nationalism in the 1950s and early 1960s. It spoke to exactly the kind of broader social solidarity that Gonick has seen as lacking in the English-Canadian movement and responded quickly, publishing Serge Joyal's explanation of student syndicalism (2:3, March/April 1965), immediately after it served as a background paper at a CUCND conference in Regina, and a founding document of the *Union générale des étudiants du Québec* (UGEQ). *Dimension* circulated it widely as an offprint. Student syndicalism defined students as workers in training, part of a productive process, with economic and social interests in the society as a whole. Most significantly, "the student union must relate itself to other dynamic forces in society" and particularly labour unions, to transform the nation as a whole.[4]

Student syndicalism spoke to the emerging confluence of class and national struggles in Quebec and the explosion at McGill University that stretched from 1967 to 1969 can be seen in this light. Surprisingly, for an institution so closely identified with Montreal's Anglophone elite, McGill's Students for a Democratic University's campaign for student syndicalism convinced McGill's students to vote to join the UGEQ. As McGill Political Science lecturer Stan Gray explained (5:2-3, January/March 1968), "Essential to the syndicalist orientation is the combination of student unions with workers' trade unions for action at the political level, since it recognizes that student problems are part of national and social problems and that the university itself cannot be basically altered until society as a whole is radically changed." Gray reported to *Dimension* about an opening round in this struggle, which occurred over the attempted penalization of students for "obscene libel" related to a satirical article in a campus paper and culminated in arrests (including Gray's) at a sit-in; within a year Gray was a central figure in the much broader Opération McGill. This campaign for the "socialization of McGill," attacked many symbols at once: the legacy of colonialism, the injustices of capitalism, the present-day dominance of the English language, Anglophone control over the Quebec economy, and the inadequacy of the francophone education system.[5]

Gray was fired, ostensibly for his role in disrupting a Board of Governors' meeting, in spite of support from the *Confederation des syndicats nationaux* (CSN), an important centre of radicalism in 1969. The McGill campaign was assessed in extraordinarily negative terms in the October/November 1969 *Dimension* (6:5) by Julius Grey, a student and future McGill law professor, who assailed Stan Gray and the New Left for its assault on university culture and standards under the guise of "anti-elitism," and its alliance with "fascists," (meaning "French-Canadian nationalists"). Martin Loney, until recently president of the Canadian Union of Students, came to Stan Gray's defense in the following issue (6:6, December/January 1969–70), decrying Gray's blanket condemnations. Surely, "*Dimension* should have more important things to publish." For his part, Stan Gray's own trajectory was reflected in a Toronto speech published in that same *Canadian Dimension*. Now representing the *Front de libération populaire*, his attention was focused on the increasingly proletarian character of the national movement in Quebec under the influence of the CSN; universities and colleges were cited only as scenes of official repression rather than as potential sources of revolutionary energy.

Universities were increasingly the sites of huge confrontations and, by 1968, students seemed to be in the forefront of social struggles internationally. The year opened with the first installment of a series on "The University Explosion" (5:2-3, January/March 1968) and ended with a long segment on student power that looked far beyond Canada, examining developments in Latin America, China and Japan (5:7, December/ January 1968-69). In 1969, exploration of two of the significant conflicts of the era provoked debate in CD's pages. The first took place in Montreal. The product, in part, of the growing mobilization of the city's Black community and conflicts at Sir George Williams University (now part of Concordia) over West Indian students' charges of racism against a biology professor, about two hundred protestors occupied the university's ninth-floor computer centre. When the city's riot police invaded, a fire broke out, computers were destroyed, and about two million dollars damage done.[6] The response in the February 1969 *Dimension* (5:8) was surprisingly hostile. Sir George Williams English professor (and CD's associate editor) G. David Sheps wrote a long and detailed attack on "student nihilists" who were "always at war with the idea of civilization itself — socialist civilization as well as bourgeois civilization." On one hand, Sheps appeared enamoured of Sir George Williams, an "extraordinarily liberal university," while on the other he was specifically concerned with a stream of "sentimentality and romanticism" on the Left which he saw as developing within the American SDS (presumably the Weathermen) and, in Canada, in a stream of Maoism.[7]

Sheps's critique was narrowly focused on the events at Sir George with only a passing reference to anticolonial and Black Power movements in which the activists considered themselves grounded. He also suggested that Eugene Genovese, the prominent Marxist historian of African-Americans who taught at Sir George Williams from 1967 to 1969 before moving on to the University of Rochester, held similar views. Indeed, he did. In a substantial article (5:4, April/May 1968) Genovese acknowledged much of the New Left critique of universities but attacked what he saw as the "half-truth" of seeing them as "merely bourgeois institutions involved in a conspiracy to brainwash students and to serve the Establishment," considered it reductionist to see the universities as simply analogous to capitalist workplaces, and called for the concerted defense of university autonomy. More broadly, he too saw within the student New Left a nihilist current marked by "obscurantism, egocentric pseudo-existentialism, and abstract moralizing," with which socialists had nothing in common. This was a harsh assessment, to be sure, but the critique had much in common with *Dimension*'s earlier dismissal of the student New Left's isolation from potentially wider movements. Whatever the strengths of this argument, it was a difficult debate that was posed, in the late 1960s, in a manner that seemed to do little to advance the debate. Julius Grey's and David Sheps's contributions were dismissed by some activists as liberal or social democratic defenses of the status quo (a taste of the times could be seen in a debate over Sheps's report that invoked Gustav Noske, Rosa Luxemburg and debate over "Left-wing Communism" in Germany after World War I in issue 5:4, April/May 1968. When Stan Gray finally wrote in anger against the "reactionary" *CD* articles by Sheps and Genovese (6:8, April/May 1970), Gonick pointed out that he saw *Dimension* as a forum for just such discussions, and articulated his consistent view that "[t]he hostilities of Blacks and the alienation of middle class youth are not sufficient ingredients for revolution" and pointed out that the explosions that had occurred were signs of "desperation and hopelessness." As always, the task was to build a mass movement of those who had the social weight to affect change. At the same time, those whose own struggles were seen simply as signs of "desperation" had every reason to feel slighted. Nor did *Canadian Dimension*'s orientation towards broader connections with the Left-wing of the NDP through the Waffle movement, or to labour, hold out much appeal to activists whose struggles were remote from these arenas. The magazine was, in short, out of tune with student struggles as defined by campus-based activists.

The second conflict occurred at Simon Fraser University — British Columbia's "instant university" that opened in 1965. SFU attracted a considerable number of radicalizing faculty and students who soon challenged an autocratic administration that had had a free hand in its initial establishment. *Dimension* had not reported on struggles there until events dramatically culminated in a faculty/student strike in SFU's Political

Science, Sociology and Anthropology (PSA) department in the autumn of 1969. The department had been constructed, largely, by British Marxist sociologist Tom Bottomore, and had developed a particularly engaged pedagogy and a democratic structure that empowered faculty and students equally. The conflict ended in defeat for the PSA department; the department was broken up and faculty dismissed in what has been described as "likely the largest political purge of faculty in North American history."[8] Sharon Yandle, a student radical leader who had come out of SUPA, assessed the entire struggle with considerable insight (6:7, February/March 1970), explaining "the PSA idea" of a participatory democracy that included real power sharing between faculty and students, a politically challenging array of guest speakers, and a rejection of ties to government and business. At the same time, she drew a balance sheet that clearly recognized the movement's shortcomings: "Had PSA truly developed and effected its ideas in the community — had it truly placed itself in service to the disadvantaged and to labour — it might have been able to develop the allies it so desperately needed to counteract its isolation on campus."[9]

As Genovese had lamented, some such as George Haggar seemed to entirely dismiss the university as "a place which seduces virgin minds with the values of capitalism, produces unquestioning slaves to augment the economic system and supplies the high priests to expound the morality, religion and manners of the bourgeois order" (5:4, April/May, 1968).[10] The conflict at SFU certainly spoke to the critique of the university in capitalist society but at the same time saw the institution as a site of struggle and posed the possibility of a new pedagogy that emphasized the development of learning and community. In the same vein (and in the same issue), Anthony Mardiros targeted the academic credential of the Ph.D. degree, the proliferation of which was detrimental to both critical inquiry and effective teaching as universities fought to oversupply the academic labour market with new graduate students who were forced to jump through regimented and meaningless "hoops." An article by Errol Black that appeared a decade and a half later (17:2, May 1983) spoke to precisely this issue of reifying academic credentials to the detriment of useful knowledge. In 1981, Brandon University had refused to hire Pat Mooney as a sessional lecturer to teach a single course. Mooney was both an activist on agricultural issues, specifically issues of biodiversity and the challenges of agribusiness, and had written the important and prescient book *Seeds of the Earth*.[11] But he did not have a university degree; nor, argued Black, was he acceptable to the local elite in a mostly rural community. But he did bring to the university experience and critical thinking. Indeed, rather than dismissing the university, writers such as Ken Morrison (7:3, August/September 1970) and Arthur Schafer (14:3, December 1979) thought about how to encourage critical pedagogy, both in terms of specific questions, such as Cold War texts, or more broadly. The intellectual consensus of the magazine was that the university opened up space for debate and action, but constraints that ranged from corporate control of funding to an alienated student body "socialized to passivity, and deferential to hierarchically structured authority" required analysis and action.

The goal both of student movements and *Dimension*'s academic commentators was to radically democratize the university, making it accessible to workers and the socially disenfranchised, and encouraging critical thought. In tone, and arguably in content, this radical critique of the inherited legacy of the Canadian university, however, fits awkwardly with some elements of the growing left nationalist strain in the late 1960s. In "The Americanization of Canadian Universities" (5:8, February 1969), Robin Mathews spoke to what he saw as the rapid trend toward "the extinction of the Canadian university as a viable Canadian institution." The rapid expansion of post-secondary education in Canada had led universities to turn to the United States for faculty, a process, Mathews argued, that resulted in a curriculum that ignored Canadians and Canadian issues. Moreover, the process was self-sustaining, as American-born and -trained faculty preferred to hire more Americans through "old boy networks" and gave preference to those trained in US graduate schools. Abraham Rotstein's assertion (approvingly cited by Mathews) that if "one of the university's functions is to perpetuate a society and its culture, we must ask if it is competent to do this when most of the teaching is done by outsiders," clashed with the New Left's thorough-going critique of the society they inherited, as well as their definition

264

of "outsiders," which spoke much more to issues of class. In October 1970 (7:4), regular *Dimension* contributor John Warnock similarly saw American academic immigrants to Canada as carriers of "the American ideological approach" just as Krista Maeots, a Waffle founder, worried about "the" Canadian point of view being squeezed out.[12]

The Struggle for Canadian Universities (as Mathews and fellow Carleton University professor James Steele called their edited book) was fought across the political spectrum and through various media.[13] In August/ September 1969 (6:3-4), it was James Laxer, a leader of the Waffle within the NDP, who fine-tuned the argument more along *Dimension's* lines, but it is worth noting that he chose to do so by aiming his polemical fire at the student New Left, which was not sold on the new left-wing nationalism. In keeping with previous *Dimension* critiques, Laxer argued that the student Left displayed a "rootless radicalism" that took little notice of the specific challenges or opportunities that the "unique experience" of English-Canada offered. In a tone reminiscent of Gonick's earlier criticism, albeit with a richer narrative that reflected his engagement with the student Left, Laxer argued that the lack of non-university-based issues such as civil rights and the Vietnam War left left-wing students immersed in their "unique life-style" and without links to broader movements, and left the Canadian New Left largely devoid of any strategic perspectives.

Laxer's solution was to urge the New Left to seek "an alliance with potentially radical social forces in Canada" which meant, in essence, "the traditional Canadian Left" of labour and the NDP. He acknowledged the various reasons that leftists may have given up on such allies, particularly the NDP, but he argued that they were increasingly active and drawn to Canadian nationalism, which would, he argued lead them to more radical conclusions about American imperialism. This was a two-stage process which involved the defense of "Canadian institutions," which he also noted would run afoul of the New Left's misplaced (he argued) suspicion of institutions. Such a sentiment might be appropriate in the United States but, he argued, a dependent country like Canada had to defend and rely on its institutions as a necessary refuge. All of this conflated a number of issues — nationalism, the NDP and the fate of the Waffle — which were far from specifically campus issues. It was left to former CUS president Martin Loney's assessment of the potential of the Waffle on campuses to suggest that radical students neither needed, nor perhaps wanted, the Waffle. He acknowledged the isolation of student radicals, their difficulties in communicating their messages and, at times, the "excruciatingly millennial" outlook (6:6, December/January 1969–70). At the same time, though, Loney clearly appreciated their healthy skepticism about working within the NDP and a fear that, as in the case of the British Labour Party, radicals would indeed be co-opted by the institution and the state. Moreover, university radicalism had its own victories that had to be acknowledged, such as the growing impact of the women's liberation movement on campuses. In the end he suggested that the Waffle organize elsewhere: "European and North American experience has shown that the problem lies not in radicalizing students but in ensuring that their radicalization is not paralleled by an increasing reaction from the rest of the population." Just as the issue sparked heated debate across academe, it lit up the Socialist Studies meetings at the 1970 Learned Societies meetings where the issue was "Will Canadian universities serve the nation better by hiring more qualified Canadians, as Mathews and Steele hold — or by hiring anyone (Canadian or foreign) who will assist in a root-and-branch reordering of our universities?"[14] These two options fought themselves out in the heart of the magazine.

At least briefly. After 1970, students and, for the most part, universities fell from the pages of *Canadian Dimension*. The absolute disappearance of students was the more remarkable since, although the "explosive" period of student strife passed quickly from 1968 to 1970, there continued to be considerable activity, associated with a "second" New Left, often but not exclusively associated with various Marxist organizations, which were active on campuses and which sought to address many of the strategic failings of their immediate precursors. In a telling, brief letter in 1988, Steven High wrote to suggest that *Dimension* should, in some manner, deal with youth.[15] Where *Canadian Dimension* came to focus its attention, quite effectively, has been on the political economy of universities. Analysis of the place of the university in capitalist society has been a staple of the magazine since Cy Gonick argued in 1966 (3:3-4, March/June) that "government-financed expansion of Canadian universities is being justified on the grounds of supporting the needs of our state religion — economic growth."[16] In October/November 1969 (6:5), in the midst of the Waffle era, contributors such as Mel Watkins spoke about Canadian universities in the context of continental integration and their role in producing "branch-plant intellectuals," who would serve US capital. By the 1980s and 1990s, however, contributions to the journal spoke to the new era of neoliberalism as the public sector was denigrated and all was "for sale," to cite the title of Howard Buchbinder and Janice Newson's assessment of university-corporate relations (20:1, March 1986).[17] And, by 2005, the place of the university as "a last bastion of critical thought in an age of manufactured consent" was, according to Andrea Levy, increasingly precarious. In the September/October 2005 theme issue of *Dimension* (39:5), a slate of contributors explored the corporate university and the myriad of ways in which organizations in agribusiness (Monsanto), biomedicine (Apotex) or the military (the list is too long to begin) not only shaped research priorities, but undermined transparency, academic freedom and self-governance at the university.[18]

An important corollary to all of this is the changing shape of labour at Canadian universities, a theme that has been followed relatively closely by *Canadian Dimension* over some time. In June 1979 (13:8) Ellen Meiksins Wood carefully analyzed the previous year's strike of almost a thousand clerical and technical workers at York University, rooting it in the growing industrial logic of a "rationalized" institution and the relationships between universities and the state. Similarly, the challenge of confronting self-confident Conservative governments in the 1990s in defense of academic freedom and integrity was explained in Doug Smith's account of the faculty strike at the University of Manitoba (30:1, February/March 1996). But the magazine most effectively realigned with current campus-based struggles on the issue of contingent labour. In January/February 1999 (33:1) Peter Babiak wrote about "The New Proletariat," the legions of sessional lecturers, like himself, who labour on North American campuses without benefit of full-time wages, benefits or security. The creation of "knowledge factories" where cheaper, more easily replaceable labour fills the classrooms stems from the same processes others have identified at the corporate university. The result has been union organization and, particularly at York University, a series of hard-fought strikes. The long-est (at eighty-five days) and most unsuccessful was fought there during the winter of 2008–2009. In 2009 (43:4, May/June), *Dimension* printed two assessments of the strike by Tyler Shipley and Tyler McCreary that assessed the strategy followed by CUPE local 3903 quite differently. In opening up this debate — readers were invited to comment on the articles on the *Canadian Dimension* website — the magazine was dir-ectly engaging important issues of strategy. What had made *Dimension* an important voice in student movements and the New Left in the late 1960s was its ability to mix a socialist analysis of capitalism with the debate about how to respond to the challenges activists confronted. The issues posed in these articles and, for instance, in the September/October 2010 *Dimension* editorial on Black Bloc tactics at the Toronto G20 summit, began in the magazine and continued on the website. At the same time, in its issue on precarious labour (45:2, May/June 2011), Elise Thorburn eloquently explored the ties between students, the labour market and the corporate university. Taken together, they reflect some of the issues raised in the late 1960s regarding the kinds of alliances radicals need to form. But they potentially did so in a manner, I would argue, that takes greater heed of the multiplicity of oppressions and struggles that need to be both individually recognized and strategically connected. *Canadian Dimension* has had an ongoing connection with the political economy of universi-ties and has, over time, developed analyses that can effectively inform campus-based activity.

In the new century, youth began to reappear in *Dimension*. In 2002 (36:1, January/February), prompted by the rise of a youthful antiglobal-ization movement that demonstrated massively and dramatically at the World Trade Organization meetings in Seattle in 1999 and against the Free Trade Area of the Americas summit in Quebec City in 2001, *Dimension* published an issue on the theme of youth activism. Notably, youth were not presented as students and universities were not noted as a potential site of struggle (with the single exception of a Canadian Federation of Students advertisement for demonstrations against tuition hikes). Editorially, Ed Janzen attempted to define the specific character of this new youth radicalization. He identified the extent to which "the unethical, inequitable and untenable system of global capitalist economics" and its "startling inequalities" as creating a more generalized crisis, stirring a wide range of diverse constituencies. Not surprisingly, the array of movements that mobilized youth were difficult to classify and Janzen's conclusion reflected the open-endedness of this "dark and uncertain moment" of globalization and the war on terror, when an alternate future remained uncertain. In the same issue, Joel Harden published a sweeping article on youth radicalization internationally while Elizabeth Carlyle explored the role of young women in revitalizing the National Action Committee on the Status of Women; each carefully enumerated the strengths and problems confronting this new generation entering into struggle at a particularly challenging conjuncture. Certainly, as new youth movements appeared, *Dimension* responded enthusiastically, and sought to help provide them with a forum to consider strategic and programmatic responses. The emergence of the youthful feminist movement RebELLE prompted a special issue on the "New Feminist Revolution," (44:6, November/December 2010) and the second RebELLE gathering in Winnipeg in May 2011 was carefully reported in 2011 (45:5, September/October).

Similarly, *Dimension* traced the reemergence of student movements. In 2005 (39:4, July/August), Quebec student leader Tim McSorley reported on a two-hundred-thousand-strong student strike against cuts in financial aid in Quebec. An uneven, but broadening student "re-engagement" prompted the magazine to focus on "Today's Student Activism" (42:4, September/October 2008). And, once again, Quebec was at the forefront. According to Xavier LaFrance and Chris Webb (42:4, September/October 2008), subsequent struggles demonstrated that CEGEP- and university-based organizations stretched "well beyond the usual narrow confines of student politics seen in the rest of Canada." Susan Dianne Brophy's assessment spoke of activities, both campus-focused, such as campaigns against fee hikes and the like, and broader linkages that linked students to national and international movements, including Students against Israeli Apartheid and a range of labour, environmental and antiracist activities. University administrations and the police seemed to agree that the student movement was a growing force. Noaman Ali reported the arrests of students peacefully protesting fee hikes and the commercialization of the university in Toronto and Vancouver.

Finally, in 2012, to cite the subtitle of Eric Martin and Simon Tremblay-Pepin's article in the special issue (46:5, September/October): "Québec Students Teach the World a Lesson." *Canadian Dimension* played an important role in assessing the meaning of the massive and dramatic student strike that transfixed Quebec and measured it, interestingly, with much the same yardstick as it had used decades earlier. Like the Quebec student syndicalism of the 1960s and 1970s, the 2012 strike proved a (in this case, a more successful) focal point of broader social struggles. As André Frappier and Bernard Rioux pointed out in their analysis of the 2012 events, Québécois students rose to the challenge in Quebec in a manner that highlighted the failures of the labour movement to provide leadership in the struggle against neoliberal austerity. This was, of course, an important example for activists far beyond Quebec. It is worth noting, as well, that the considerable attention *CD* paid to the *Printemps érable* builds on the magazine's long history of emphasizing the importance of Quebec's social movements, with the goal, to cite Andrea Levy and Fanny Theurillat-Cloutier, of fostering communication and "to encourage the linkage of struggles" across Canada. It was in this spirit that Hugo Bonin's assessment of the strengths and weaknesses of the Quebec student strike (47:1, January/February 2013) echoed the kind of critical reflection on important student struggles that had marked *Dimension*'s reportage in the 1960s.

By 2013, *Canadian Dimension* reflected both the reemergence of a youth movement and an analysis of its importance for rebuilding the Left. A regular "Youth Rising" column explores youth activism across a range of sectors. Tasha Peters (46:6, November/December 2012) reported the most recent Power Shift, a gathering of "under 30s" who explored, in particular, First Nations issues and the environment, the convergence of which would explode in the weeks immediately following in the dynamic "Idle No More" movement. Ongoing neoliberal assaults on education no doubt will provide the fuel for new explosions as well as new opportunities for the magazine to demonstrate its value to a whole new generation of student and faculty activists. But as Maryam Adrangi argued in the special issue on "Youth in Revolt" (47:1, January/February 2013), campus and community struggles can and should be linked. This issue of the magazine explored a range of struggles, effectively demonstrating the breadth of youthful anger, mobilization, and critical thought.

Interestingly, in 2013, *Canadian Dimension* spoke to youth in a more explicit manner than it did during the great student and youth revolt of the 1960s. The difference, of course, is that the magazine was deeply embedded in that earlier revolt, sought to cultivate a broader audience and, as much as possible, to direct it away from campuses and specifically "youth" issues, in order to participate in the construction of a larger and more effective Left. Fifty years later, an established presence in Canada, *Dimension* self-critically recognizes that new generations of activists are mobilizing with their own visions, experiences and understandings. Now a multigenerational institution, it has to be cognizant of these differences in order to establish and maintain any relevance to youth. At the same time, *Dimension*'s unique history allows it to speak across generations, as with Joan Kuyek's and Bryan Palmer's explorations of the history of youth radicalism "Youth in Revolt" issue (47:1, January/February 2013). In an important sense, *Canadian Dimension* embodies the collective experience of different generations of youth.

CHAPTER 10
Canadian Dimension and the Great Canadian Health Care Debate

Arthur Schafer

In 1946, the CCF Government of Saskatchewan brought in the *Hospitalization Act*, guaranteeing free hospital care for most residents of that province. Fifteen years later, in 1961, Tommy Douglas introduced legislation to provide universal health care for the citizens of Saskatchewan. Then he stepped down as Premier to become federal leader of the CCF.

Saskatchewan doctors, sensing that this legislation would be a threat to their incomes, launched a bitter strike in an effort to kill the infant medicare scheme in its cradle. Happily for the people of Saskatchewan, the infamous doctors' strike failed to achieve its purpose and in the summer of 1962 Woodrow Lloyd, Tommy Douglas's successor in the Premier's chair, launched a universal health insurance scheme for the province: medicare-in-one-province, so to say.

On the fiftieth anniversary of the doctors' strike, Lorne Brown and Doug Taylor reminded us (46:4, July/August 2012) that when medicare was introduced in Saskatchewan there was a heroic attempt made by grassroots activists — including trade unionists, agrarian radicals and progressive doctors — "to provide a consumer-controlled alternative to entrepreneurial fee for service medicine." Community clinics were to be the vehicle by means of which doctors became public servants rather than profit-oriented business-people. Sadly, unrelenting opposition from organized medicine ensured that the community clinic model never achieved its potential.

The year in which medicare became a reality in Saskatchewan, 1962, was also notable as the year in which "Red Tory" Prime Minister John Diefenbaker appointed his former university classmate, Justice Emmett Hall, to be chair of the Royal Commission on Canada's health care system. Ironically, it was the Canadian Medical Association (CMA), a bitter foe of national health care insurance, that had pushed Diefenbaker to establish this Royal Commission. The CMA expected that the Conservatives would appoint a Commission chair under whose guidance "socialized medicine" would be stopped in its tracks (Brown and Taylor, 2012). To their chagrin, the opposite happened.

When it reported, in 1964, the Hall Commission recommended that the federal government adopt the Saskatchewan model for the entire country. This was an important turning point in Canadian history. It speaks volumes about Diefenbaker and the Conservative Party of his time that Hall was the person chosen to head up the Royal Commission on National Health Services. Justice Hall, after all, had helped to draft the CCF government's compulsory hospital plan of 1948. He was clearly no friend of the private insurance industry, nor was he a stooge of that part of the medical profession which had set its face implacably against any kind of universal government health care system. Is it imaginable that the Harper Conservatives of our day would choose someone of Hall's progressive open-mindedness to play such a decisive role in health care policy? One need not linger long on this question to perceive its absurdity. The Harper government may sport the same "Conservative" label as the Diefenbaker government, but the contents of the party's philosophy have changed utterly.

As mentioned, John Diefenbaker selected Justice Hall to play a pivotal role in plotting the overall direction of what was to become our nation's health care system. A year after the Hall Commission published its second and final volume, CD gave Emmett Hall six pages in which to set out the case for medicare. The essence of Hall's position, as outlined in his CD contribution (2:3, March/April 1965), was that a government-funded universal health care system should be seen as a fundamental human right — comparable to the right to education. Hall's CD article mentioned humanitarian considerations as a rationale for universal access but, interestingly, the primary argument he offered in defence of medicare appealed more to enlightened prudence than it did to human compassion or fellow feeling:

> . . . *the health of Canadians is a matter of concern to us as a nation . . . no Enlightened government can ignore that the economic capacity of its citizens to be productive depends upon their health and vigour as much as upon their educational attainment. Vast expenditures are being contemplated in the field of education. These may prove ineffective if not accompanied by good health.*
>
> *Health services and education must now be regarded as twin endeavours, advancing mankind. Neither will attain its full potential for good if one is allowed to lag behind the other.*

By 1966 Prime Minister Lester Pearson's minority Liberal government moved to create a medicare system for all of Canada. The feds offered to pay 50 per cent of health care costs for a universal insurance scheme, with the provinces paying the other half.

Tommy Douglas is universally acclaimed as "the father of medicare" but it is significant that Diefenbaker and Pearson could also, with some legitimacy, have claimed at least partial paternity. At that historic juncture, medicare was everybody's baby. This claim is somewhat exaggerated, of course. Both the Conservative and Liberal whips had to work strenuously to keep their less-progressive backbenchers in line but, at the end of the day, members of Parliament voted overwhelmingly for a universal single-payer health care insurance scheme across the country.

It was precisely at this time in Canadian social history, between the introduction of medicare in Saskatchewan (1962) and the introduction of a national medicare plan for Canada (1964) that *CD* published its first issue (1:1-2, Fall 1963). Remarkably, after fifty years, both medicare and *Canadian Dimension* still exist though, it must be acknowledged, the magazine has more than once tottered on the brink of financial disaster — saved by dint of heroic life-support interventions from its dedicated readership, and by the dedication of its editor and the people he recruited as contributors. Right-wing critics are now claiming that medicare is "unsustainable" and must be radically "reformed" if it is to survive; but, significantly, almost no one dares openly to advocate its demise. That is because, over half a century, every opinion poll has shown that our public health care system enjoys overwhelming support from the Canadian public.

Nevertheless, there has been a steady, albeit surreptitious, erosion of the scope of medicare and some fear that our health care system may be facing the prospect of salami-style "death by a thousand cuts. First, the Chrétien Liberal government, with Paul Martin as finance minister, wielded a blunt fiscal axe against the health care budget. Now, Stephen Harper's Conservatives seem set to "reform" medicare in ways that could arguably be described as attempted "mercy killing" by stealth or, more accurately, merciless killing. By reducing significantly the amount of money transferred to the provinces and by attenuating federal controls that have hitherto guaranteed high and reasonably uniform standards for health care delivery across the nation, the Conservatives are opening a path for the privatization of health care or so it appears to many of the Government's critics.

Medicare as the "glue" that holds Canada together

A recent poll by Nanos Research found that support for public health care in Canada has risen to 94 per cent.[1] That is a truly amazing number, rendered even more amazing when one considers that the Canadian public continues to give its whole-hearted support to universal government health insurance in the face of an unrelenting media campaign to persuade us that our health care system is "broken" and, worse, that it is in "crisis" and simply cannot be "sustained" in anything like its present form. This hostile campaign has been organized and funded, predictably, by the insurance industry and by ideological adherents of "free market" ideology, aided and abetted by the usual suspects: media owners, editors and advertisers, not to mention industry-sponsored think-tanks such as the Fraser Institute.

Ninety-four per cent public support for medicare comes as close as makes no difference to virtual unanimity — in a society where unanimity on any other issue is almost inconceivable. This persistent and massive level of support means that people from across the entire political spectrum support medicare and that, regardless of geography, Canadian men and women of all ages and every socio-economic stratum view health care as a public rather than as a private good. Health care is seen as a fundamental right of citizenship rather than as a market service to be bought and sold according to how fat or thin one's wallet happens to be.

Based upon extensive polling research, the Romanow Commission's Interim Report, released in February 2002, neatly encapsulated the view of most Canadians, then and now: ". . . need should always be taken into account, with a majority convinced that it should be the sole factor in determining what core of medically necessary services the system should cover."[2] There is no surprise here. Canadians have been giving pollsters (and politicians) the same message for a half-century. Attacks against medicare tend to be viewed as attacks on our society's underlying core values — values such as fairness, compassion, equality of opportunity and social solidarity.

During this fifty-year period many features of Canadian society have undergone radical transformation but, remarkably, our commitment to health care equity has remained unwavering. It is not much of an exaggeration to say that medicare is the closest Canadians come to having a national religion.

The threat to medicare

Despite the enduring popularity of our universal health care system, powerful economic interests have been working to shift Canada towards an American-style free market system, one in which health care is treated as a commodity, something to be bought and sold, rather than as a fundamental human right. One of the important contributions made by CD over these decades has been to chart and critique the subtle and the not-so-subtle attempts by the enemies of medicare to undermine its popular foundations.

In 1984, for example, the magazine published articles by Victoria Braden, "Medibucks: When health care is directed toward making a profit, the medicare ideal of universality without financial deterrents, goes out the window"; Jim Silver, "The Erosion of Medicare" and Mike Wahn, "Losing Medicare: Why Worry?" (18:2, May 1984) as a counter-blast to those seeking to destroy medicare. In March, 1991 (25:2), the magazine published a piece in which Tim Sale, later to become Minister of Health in the NDP government of Manitoba, shared with *CD* read-ers his fears about "The Death of Medicare," subtitled "Killing it softly." Sale followed up, in March, 1992 (26:2), with a second article: "Health Care Alternatives." All of these articles — by Branden, Silver, Wahn and Sale — dealt, in one way or another, with the threat posed to medicare by those who want to introduce American-style market-place health care to Canada.

Jim Silver saw the prime threat as coming from deliberate under-funding by the federal government. When the feds provide insufficient money to the provinces to pay for doctors' fees and hospitals, this underfunding provides an opportunity for the more "free-enterprise-oriented" provincial governments to justify the introduction of market mechanisms such as extra-billing and user fees. Federal underfund-ing also encourages provinces to permit the provision of an increas-ing number of health care services by privately-owned for-profit corporations.

As one might expect, there is ample empirical data demonstrating that extra charges do not in practice deter middle- and upper-class Canadians from inappropriate use of the system — after all, those who are econom-ically well-off can easily afford to pay these "nuisance" fees in order to consult a physician when they have the sniffles or a headache. By con-trast, less-well-off Canadians find the extra charges burdensome, and a plethora of empirical studies shows that many are deterred from seeking timely and necessary medical help for themselves or for their children.

The *Canada Health Act* mandates the federal government to impose financial penalties on provinces when they undermine universal access by such means as the imposition of user fees. However, several provincial governments, mostly Conservative, are now actively promoting a trend towards marketplace health care. The federal government seems unwill-ing to use its financial power to reverse this trend.

What all market-oriented mechanisms have in common is that they shift health care financing away from a community pooling of risk towards a system offering more risk for the individual. It is a trend in which individual self-reliance steadily supplants social solidarity.

Silver rightly deplored "the doctor-centred curative-oriented and increasingly technologically-based system of serving the health needs of Canadians." He advocated, instead, an alternative, more radical, vision of health care in Canada. Be warned, he cautioned *CD* readers (18:1, March 1984): If one simply accepts as a given the current physician-dominated system then one will be committed, willy-nilly, to rapidly-inflating incomes for doctors and further inflated profits for the growing private-sector component of our health care system. Without radical reform of the system, increased expenditure will yield very little real benefit to public health.

Mike Wahn's article (18:2, May 1984) pointed to a related fear. Medicare effectively barred the door against any but a tiny role for the insurance industry, thereby denying the industry a lucrative source of profits. But, "as medicare erodes, middle class patients will begin to buy health insurances again, to cover that part of their medical bills not covered by the government." Gaps in medicare coverage and an ongoing process known as "delisting" [see below] have meant that the door is now at least partly ajar. Ever opportunistic, the insurance industry senses the potentiality for bold expansion.

In theory, medicare coverage is meant to extend to all "medically necessary services." But many important services have never been covered and some have been covered only partially: dental care, for example, has never been included as part of our medicare system; drug coverage varies from province to province and is nowhere as extensive as it needs to be; psychiatric services for those with mental health problems are inadequate almost everywhere across the country and home care provisions are severely limited in most provinces. This list of important omissions from the scope of our medicare system could be easily expanded: ambulance service, physiotherapy, eye glasses and hearing aids, prosthetic devices, wheelchairs and other mobility aids are not covered or are not adequately covered.

These gaps in coverage make it advisable for those, mostly middle- and upper-class Canadians, who can afford private health care insurance, to seek coverage privately. Many Canadians already have such "supplementary" health insurance through their employment. Moreover, as previously covered services are "delisted" by government fiat, i.e., no longer included under the rubric "medically necessary treatment," the private insurance industry is poised to expand rapidly to meet the increasing demand for private-sector health insurance coverage. This worrying trend towards the purchase of private health insurance is further accelerated when public provision for some services, such as MRI scans or cataract and hip replacement surgery is seen as inadequate because it often requires unacceptably long wait times. The existence (or the perception) of lengthy queues in the public sector, whether for testing or for treatment, provides fertile soil for those who seek to plant the seeds of private for-profit health care delivery.

The popularity and success of medicare has hitherto depended upon what we might call "the middle-class bargain." So long as most Canadians believe that our publicly funded medicare system will provide them with timely access to high quality care, at an affordable cost to society, then they willingly forego the right to buy health care services privately. But political support for medicare is likely to erode substantially if people come to believe that escalating costs mean that preserving equal access will undermine the quality of care available or will "bankrupt" society.

So, for example, when patients learn that there are lengthy queues for the cataract surgery they need or for a hip replacement then the result is likely to be public disaffection from medicare. Moreover, when private clinics are allowed to provide these much-sought-after services, in competition with our public hospitals, and when private clinics can siphon away key medical and technical staff from the public sector (generally by offering higher remuneration), an increasing number of middle-class Canadians will be tempted to buy private insurance coverage, thereby enabling them and their families to obtain care from profit-making medical centres.

In other words, if *universal* access comes to be seen by the middle class as conflicting with access to *high quality* care then support for universal access will be difficult to maintain.

The good news in this story is that universal government-funded health care, with the administrative efficiency that comes from having a single payer, turns out to be highly efficient. Our medicare system is vastly more efficient, for example, than the American "free enterprise" model, mostly because when you introduce a multiplicity of private for-profit insurance companies into the equation, this necessarily generates dramatically increased administrative costs. Each private insurance company has to employ its own small army of actuaries, advertising and marketing personnel, and claims assessors. The advertising and marketing departments induce as many consumers as possible to buy health insurance but then, when individual policy-holders become ill and make claims for reimbursement, the goal of the claims assessment department is to disqualify as many of these claims as possible. Moreover, at the end of the day, each company must, if its shares are to retain or increase their stock-market value, return a generous profit to investors/shareholders. In large measure, this explains why Americans spend, per capita, at least 50 per cent more for health care than citizens of other industrialized countries. It is also why they have the worst mortality and morbidity outcomes in the advanced industrialized world.

The bad news, as Tim Sale observed in his *CD* piece (25:2, March 1991), is that the federal strategy of steadily shifting costs onto the provinces may stress provincial finances to the point where underfunding results in a system that cannot meet reasonable expectations. At that point, a frustrated general public may begin to listen sympathetically to the siren call of for-profit health care.

The other bad news is that Canada's fee-for-service system of physician remuneration encourages assembly-line medical care. Doctors who organize their practice in such a way that they can see fifty patients a day will make double the income of their colleagues who see "only" twenty-five patients a day. In consequence, doctors who wish to "keep up" with their high-billing colleagues can afford to spend only a few minutes with each patient. Hence, the proliferation in doctors' offices of signs reading "Only one complaint per visit." Hence, also, a pervasive pattern of care which involves listening for a few minutes to the patient's complaint followed rapidly by the writing of a prescription for a drug or medical test.

Patients who take their medication as prescribed nevertheless may find that it confers little benefit or, worse, they may find that it aggravates rather than alleviates their health problems. Adverse effects from prescription drugs taken precisely as directed are among the top ten leading causes of death in North America.

Private clinics and entrepreneurial doctors and nurses

Canadians have been encouraged to believe that, so long as medicare pays for all "medically necessary services," it scarcely matters whether we allow private for-profit clinics to deliver those health services to us. So long as you get the cataract surgery or hip replacement that you need and so long as government insurance pays the full shot, why should you care whether the eye surgery is done in a public hospital or in a private clinic?

Many people might think that it does not matter; but, *CD* contributors have been stressing over five decades that it matters a great deal how the delivery of services is organized. As Mike Wahn pointed out (18:2, May 1984), when the delivery of health care is organized on a for-profit basis the result is a perverse incentive (to doctors and to privately-owned clinics and testing laboratories) "to over-service their patients, to perform unnecessary surgery or to write unnecessary and sometimes dangerous prescriptions to get patients out of the office quickly."

Perverse incentives doubtless explain, to a significant degree at least, the fact that throughout North America mortality and morbidity figures are far worse in for-profit private clinics and hospitals than they are in not-for-profit public facilities, a point made by Robert Chernomas in "Sustainability: Profit is not the Cure" (46:4, July/August 2012).

Chernomas pointed to a range of studies demonstrating persuasively that "for-profit health care is more costly, of lower quality, provides lower patient satisfaction and has a higher mortality rate than not-for-profit health care." This point is further developed by William Charney in "Do No Harm: The Epidemic of Medical Errors in the US and Canada: A Leading Cause of Death" (46:4, July/August 2012). Charney argued that the profit motive, which drives so much of the American health care system, contributes significantly to serious medical errors, and he cited a study from March 2000 entitled "Hospital Ownership and Preventable Events" showing that "patients in for-profit hospitals are two to four times more likely than patients at not-for-profit hospitals to suffer adverse events such as post-surgical complications, delays in diagnosis and treatment of an ailment."

Indeed, what American experience demonstrates is that as health care becomes increasingly commercialized the impact of commercial pressures on health care providers is transformational. Once physicians and nurses come to see the health-care system as "an industry," professionalism erodes and gradually transmogrifies into entrepreneurialism. Under the cover of such buzzwords as "choice" and "diversity," health care facilities become part of a medical-industrial complex and the values of business come to trump the patient-centred orientation of traditional health care ethics.

The canard of "crisis" and "unsustainability"

For the past decade or longer, critics of medicare have reiterated frequently the claim that the costs of our health care system are rising at such a rapid rate that they are already or will soon become unsustainable.

Chernomas (46:4, July/August 2012) tackled the "unsustainability" argument head-on. He pointed out that, contrary to the unsustainability mantra of right-wing ideologues, those parts of the Canadian health care system that are publicly administered — hospitals and physician services — are both cost effective and fiscally sustainable. By contrast, those parts of our system which are run in a private for-profit manner — primarily prescription drugs and medical devices — are precisely those parts of the system in which costs are escalating dramatically.

Opponents of medicare like to point out that health care takes an increasingly large percentage of provincial revenues. This is the basis for their claim that medicare is unsustainable. Alleged fiscal unsustainability is, in turn, the basis for their claim that we have no choice but to "reform" the system by introducing user fees and private for-profit clinics.

In rebuttal, Chernomas cited the doyen of Canadian health economists, Robert Evans, as having demonstrated empirically that medicare spending has been basically stable for decades. Meanwhile, the cost of drugs, medical devices and other services not covered by medicare

— such as dental services and home care — have (between 1975 and 2009) more than doubled as a proportion of health care spending. Also important to note: Even when medicare costs are basically stable over time, they can misleadingly be made to appear "unsustainable" by those who, deliberately or unwittingly, ignore the fact that governments have reduced the tax base significantly and have severely cut other public services. If the overall budget shrinks while health care costs remain stable then health care costs will seem proportionately larger even though they remain unchanged. "The sustainability issue," Chernomas wrote, "more than any other provides the ideological cover for any number of schemes to undermine political support for medicare."

What should socialists think about "mental illness"?

CD has published articles about many different aspects of mental illness, ranging from an exposé of Canadian psychiatrist Dr. Ewen Cameron and a quasi-exposé of British psychiatrist R.D. Laing to a critique of the way in which Big Pharma uses the psychiatric profession to promote dangerous but (for the companies) highly profitable drugs.

In "The Enduring Hell of Dr. Ewen Cameron" (22:7, October 1988), Lanny Beckman described the key role played by Cameron in the transition of Canadian and indeed world psychiatry from the barbarism of "the snakepit era" to what purported to be the more sophisticated treatments of "the snakeoil era." Cameron achieved his ambitious goal of building a psychiatric empire in Montreal, at the Allan Memorial Institute. His preferred treatment modality, known as "psychic driving," became internationally famous, as did Dr. Cameron himself. The treatment patients received from Cameron and his medical associates and graduate students involved frequently repeated doses of ECT, or shock treatment, as well as powerful brain-altering chemicals, with the aim of "wiping the slate clean." Patients were administered up to four ECT treatments a day for periods as long as seventy-five days. Most were also given multiple doses of LSD. The ostensible goal was to reduce patients to a blank slate on which the therapist could then reconstruct a new personality.

Cameron accepted substantial funding from the CIA, which was interested in the Cold War potential of brainwashing techniques. As summarized by Beckman, Cameron's methods were guided by a few simple principles:

> . . . *use new and untested treatments; administer them in multiple and arbitrary combinations; maintain the doses at high levels of frequency and intensity; disregard ethical guidelines requiring such things as the informed consent of subjects; ignore the distinction between treatment and research and between patients and subjects.*

Predictably, it all ended very badly. Even Dr. Cameron eventually recognized that his "miracle" cure was no cure at all but more akin to a devastating assault, and he publicly recanted — but not before he and his colleagues destroyed the lives of many unsuspecting patients. Even today, perhaps especially today, it would be no bad thing if every psychiatrist (along with the rest of the medical profession) had the Hippocratic principle *primum non nocere* — "first of all, do no harm" — engraved deeply in his/her consciousness.

British psychiatrist R.D. Laing also achieved international fame, but in his case as a leader of the so-called anti-psychiatry movement. Jim Harding, a previously staunch admirer, attended a Canadian lecture given by Laing at the University of Guelph. Harding reported on the experience in "R.D. Laing's Canadian Tour" (10:2, June 1974). In his lecture, Laing invited the audience to consider the biochemical, physiological and emotional development of the child *in utero*. Gestational development, he claimed, was the key that would unlock an understanding of the human psyche. A disillusioned Harding found the lecture "rambling" and ill-prepared. Having heard the same lecture at the University of Manitoba, I can confirm that both Laing's thesis and his "supporting" arguments were totally opaque.

R.D. Laing was famous for propounding the thesis that people with schizophrenia should be recognized not as mentally ill patients in need of treatment but as prophets, people who articulated truths that neither their family nor the wider society could tolerate. Other *CD* contributors dissented from this position. Agnes Grant, for example (30:5, September/ October 1996), argued that:

Schizophrenia is a disease of the brain that affects the
chemical messengers that translate perception around us into
appropriate thought and response. It is a biological disorder
of the brain that adversely affects a person's ability to think,
feel and interpret sensory information.

As treatment for the symptoms of this disease, Canadian psychiatrists frequently prescribe very powerful drugs to people with the illness including, these days, thousands of very young children and tens of thousands of elderly people living in nursing homes. These drugs, whose usefulness for many patients is questionable, cause an array of side effects, some of them described in horrifying detail by Don Weitz in "Chemical Lobotomies" (25:3, April/May 1991). Here is Weitz's account of one such side effect, known as tardive dyskinesia:

It is marked by abnormal, rhythmical, involuntary muscle
movements: most often of the mouth, tongue, face and jaw
. . . This condition can result in problems sitting, walking,
breathing, talking and chewing . . . There can be twisting
and jerking of the head and sometimes of the entire body
. . . The damage may also involve problems of lowered
intellectual functioning, apathy, indifference and dementia
(senility).

Readers may suspect that Weitz, who described himself as "a psychiatric survivor," was too personally involved in the issues to give a dispassionate and balanced account of the risks and benefits of psychiatric drugs. That may indeed be true. But, nevertheless, his article issued prescient warnings against the dangers of antidepressant drugs known as SSRIs (such as Prozac, Paxil and Zoloft). He flagged the concern that these drugs can induce suicide. At the time, evidence of suicidality was denied and covered up by the drug industry (along with other serious side effects). It was not until years later that drug researchers were able — as a result of discovery during litigation against the companies — to gain access to the raw data from company-sponsored clinical trials. The newly-revealed data confirmed what was already strongly suspected, viz., that the risk of suicidal ideation and suicide (for those taking Prozac-type drugs) was significantly elevated. Eli Lilly, Pfizer, GlaxoSmithKline and other manufacturers of SSRIs were eventually compelled to attach "Black Box Warnings" to drug labels and were also fined billions of dollars in civil and criminal penalties for illegally promoting the prescription of SSRI antidepressant drugs to children, for whom there was no evidence of efficacy but strong evidence of harm.

In an article on the integrity of published drug research entitled "Whose Bread You Eat, His Song You Sing" (44:1, January/February 2010), I argued that when the pharmaceutical industry funds scientific research, the consequence, very often, is the introduction of a deeply worrying bias in the published results. What purports to be "science" all too often deserves to be seen as "marketing." "If we want public science in the public interest," I concluded, "it's going to have to be paid for with public funds." Nowhere in biomedical research is the bias caused by industry funding more marked than in psychopharmacology: benefits are exaggerated, risks are downplayed.

The bogus nature of many claims made on behalf of both antipsychotic and anti-depressant drugs was described by Antony Black in "Prescription for Scandal" (34:5, September/October 2000). Black argued that we should be highly concerned about the spread, from major psychiatric institutions to the population at large, of a narrowly biological (i.e., drug-based) approach to psychiatry. In a memorable phrase, he describes this development as the "psychiatric colonization of the normal" — nowadays more commonly referred to as "the medicalization of life."

There is indeed much cause for concern. The prevailing theories of biological causation are unsubstantiated. For example, the much-touted "serotonin deficiency" hypothesis, invoked to explain depression and to justify treatment with selective serotonin re-uptake inhibitors, runs up against the inconvenient fact that many people with low serotonin levels are not suffering from depression. Equally inconvenient, many patients who are clinically depressed have perfectly normal serotonin levels. Randomized controlled clinical trials, especially those conducted by researchers who are not employees of or funded by Big Pharma, tend to show that for mild and moderate depression the SSRIs work no better than placebos. Unlike placebos, however, the SSRIs have a range of toxic side effects. Most of the people for whom these drugs are prescribed have very little awareness that the scientific evidence for effectiveness is weak and far too often they are not adequately warned about the potentially serious side effects.

Using Prozac as an example to illustrate the problem of adverse consequences, Black notes that one can find articles published in distinguished medical journals the conclusion of which is that Prozac (like the other drugs in its class) appear to induce or exaggerate "paranoia, compulsion, depression, suicidal ideation and violence." What makes the situation even worse is that Prozac and the other SSRIs are widely marketed with the promise that if you are lucky enough *not* to be suffering from depression you might nevertheless want to obtain a prescription — in order to make yourself "better than well." To describe what is happening as "the wholesale drugging of this involuntary population on the basis of totally unsubstantiated theories of biological causation" will sound, to many readers, as if it is the rant of an ill-informed "extremist." In the decade since Black wrote his *CD* article there has been an outpouring of books and journal articles, from reputable scholars, confirming that the situation is at least as bad as he describes and possibly worse.

Health is about much more than health care

Although *CD* has defended medicare since its inception, contributors have also been keenly aware that the health of Canadians is determined by much more than our health-care system. Indeed, the marked correlation between disease and poverty has been a continuous theme of *CD* contributors.

Jack Siemiatycki, in an article entitled "The Distribution of Disease: Like Income, Disease is Not Distributed Equally under Capitalism" (10:2, June 1974) tellingly quoted Norman Bethune's prescription for health: "The best form of providing health protection would be to change the economic system which produces ill-health, and liquidate ignorance, poverty and unemployment." Siemiatycki rejected the popular idea that workers could achieve equal health status if only they were able to gain equal access to health care: "Even if everybody got the same amount and quality of medical care, the incidence of sickness would still be much higher among workers and the poor. The reason: Disease and disability are directly related to social class and living conditions."

Siemiatycki considered rates of illness and death in Canada from cancer, diabetes, infectious diseases, dental disorders, mental illness and industrial accidents and disease, and he then provided data to show how social class and disease are intimately related. "All classes of people get sick. But workers and the poor get sick more often and more seriously." It follows that any government truly committed to improving population health would have to recognize that social factors such as housing, education, job security, safe working conditions and self-esteem are interdependent. Tackling any one of these problems by itself can at best have a limited effect. "It is the whole complex of poor socio-economic conditions that must be attacked." This is as true for mental illness as it is for physical illness. Unfortunately, however, the psychiatric profession has a tendency to ignore such psycho-social factors as childhood poverty, neglect and abuse in favour of exclusively biological theories.

The notion that "health problems are causally related to social problems such as poor housing, low income and alienation or lack of social cohesion in communities" is developed by Vicki Kelman in "Community Health Centres" (13:7, May 1979). Kelman argued that if we focus our attention narrowly on government intervention to guarantee accessibility of medical and hospital services then we will miss the broader point that universal health care is only one piece of the public health puzzle.

In further support of this thesis, Tim Sale pointed out in "Health Care Alternatives" (26:2, March 1992) that there is solid evidence in support of the view that "acute care medicine was not really the major factor in producing a healthy population." Sale credited pioneering epidemiologist Thomas McKeown for helping to advance the view that "public health measures, life-style, the environment and poverty levels were the most powerful determinants of health status."

In addition to Sale, many other *CD* contributors have recognized the importance of McKeown's approach. This has been noticeably true for *CD* contributors who have chosen to write about the HIV/AIDS epidemic. Brian K. Murphy, for example, in "AIDS Obscures Injustice and Medicalizes Poverty" (29:3, June/July 1995), argued that "[a] radical shift is necessary to acknowledge and address the social and economic conditions that promote AIDS." Social and political factors, rather than the biology of the immune system, are of critical importance. The issue is one of justice. Ronald Labonte, who criticized Murphy for his dismissal of the biological origins of the HIV/AIDS epidemic ("HIV/AIDS has Biological as well as Social and Political Origins" (29:3, June/July 1995), nevertheless joined with Murphy in recognizing that (in the words of Dr. Robert Scott Root-Bernstein) our prime need is "to solve the social, economic, health, education and medical care problems that create the conditions that permit AIDS to develop in the first place." Only thus can we hope to "solve" the AIDS crisis.

McKeown's approach to public health leads us inexorably to the conclusion that differences in access to medical services, drugs, surgical procedures and hospital beds have a comparatively modest effect on health. Even important differences in lifestyle, such as smoking, heavy alcohol consumption, a sedentary lifestyle and a high-fat diet, account for only a small fraction of the difference in mortality and morbidity between those at the top and those at the bottom of the socio-economic scale.

Evidence supporting McKeown's hypothesis has continued to mount over the decades, although the focus of much contemporary research has shifted from absolute to comparative poverty. As recently as the autumn of 2011, the National Council of Welfare published a report, *The Dollars and Sense of Solving Poverty*,[3] using Canadian data to demonstrate that reducing income disparities is a far more effective way to promote health (and save money) than can be achieved by providing additional chronic and acute care hospital beds. For example, type 2 diabetes and heart disease both occur much more frequently in poor than in wealthy neighbourhoods. Indeed, their report concludes that about 20 per cent of all health care spending in Canada is attributable to income disparities. One cannot easily avoid the conclusion that it is highly unequal living conditions that are the primary determinants of health rather than medical treatments or lifestyle choices.

Sale concluded that "[i]ncreasingly, we understand that poverty is the forerunner and companion of much sickness and the cure is in adequate incomes, not more doctors." A few years after Sale's article appeared in *Dimension*, David Smith reminded readers in "Community Health Alternatives" (29:5, October/November 1995) that: "When the Canada Health Act was passed in 1968 it was perfectly clear to all 10 ministers of health that providing universal sickness insurance without engaging in vigorous preventive action would send health costs through the roof." He concluded by observing that:

> *The guiding principle must be the preventive principle*
> *. . . We need a structure that enables individuals to take*
> *effective responsibility for their own health and is, at*
> *the same time, the vehicle for community action. This is*
> *essential for good health and for the growth of democracy at*
> *the community level.*

University of Manitoba health economist Robert Chernomas, writing in 1986 (20:6, November) agreed with Smith's contention that health protection requires vigorous community action but Chernomas had reservations about assigning to individuals the responsibility for their own health. Under the sub-heading "Who is your worst enemy" Chernomas wrote:

> *I consume a low fat, low cholesterol, low salt, low sugar*
> *diet of fresh fruit, vegetables, and whole grains. I am a*
> *vegetarian who jogs . . . plays tennis, racquetball, etc. Have*
> *I guaranteed myself an absence of chronic disease?*

He answered his own question unambiguously: "Certainly not. I still must breathe the polluted air, drink the polluted water, eat the gassed tomatoes, and the pesticide-laced lettuce." The wider point made by Chernomas remains as true today, twenty-five years later, as it did when he first made it in 1986. "Personal solutions can never be as effective against disease or as economically efficient as political solutions." Ironically, those who urge us to take individual responsibility for our own health may inadvertently provide cover for the corporate sector to continue adding toxic chemicals to our food, air, water and earth. More will be said later about the connection between environment and health.

In "Healthy Cities, Healthy Communities" (32:3 May/June 1998), Marcia Nozick developed the theme that when it comes to ill health, inequality rather than poverty is the prime culprit: "Studies in the developed world have discovered that absolute wealth or standard of living is not a determining factor in health . . . Nor is poverty. The determining factor is relative wealth and relative poverty." Among affluent societies, those which have less inequality of income tend to have significantly better health outcomes — apparently (though this hypothesis is somewhat speculative) "because of the prevailing quality of relationships and connectedness to others." Nozick summarized the argument as follows:

> The poor and marginalized (in a society that boasts of
> plenty), will suffer from feelings of powerlessness to affect
> their circumstances, victimization and low self-esteem,
> which will then be reinforced and mirrored back to the
> person through societal attitudes expressed as prejudice,
> exclusion and . . . low social value. Lack of self-worth leads
> to depression, inability to focus on work or school, stress,
> alienation, drug problems, violence, crime, nutritional
> deficiencies and living in the most unsafe places in a city —
> all high risk factors for personal health and social deviancy.

Some of the best current research on population health — including a recent World Health Organization report, "Closing the Gap in a Generation," and Richard Wilkinson and Kate Pickett's much-praised study, *The Spirit Level*[4] — points unmistakably to the same conclusion reached by Nozick in *CD* fifteen years ago. If we are to achieve good public health we must be willing to tackle both poverty and inequality. Poverty clearly matters. Unemployment and insecure work are associated with poor health, as are inadequate housing, poor diet and low status. But the distribution of income matters as well. A large part of the reason why generous social security systems and access to free public education and primary health care make a real difference is because they narrow the growing gap between rich and poor.

In *CD* 46:4 (July/August 2012), Jill Eisen picked up and expanded several key ideas encapsulated by the phrase "the social determinants of health" — ideas that *Dimension* contributors have been exploring for almost forty years. Eisen noted that we are surrounded by messages urging us to take responsibility for our own health. We are exhorted by frequently-repeated government advertisements to stop smoking, drink less, drive safely and exercise more. Eisen did not deny that this is good advice but, she argued (in a manner similar to Chernomas), such lifestyle advice deals with only part of the problem:

> *Healthy lifestyles are no doubt good for us, but it turns out*
> *that the social conditions in which we live and work are*
> *more important in determining our health than either the*
> *health care system or our personal habits.*

Of course it makes sense for people to eat a healthy diet and exercise regularly; but epidemiological research has been telling us for decades that "the greatest gains in health have come from . . . laws banning child labour, setting minimum wages, creating the 40-hour week, establishing social safety nets, and mandating universal access to education."

Scholars tend to measure individual and social well-being by appealing to such criteria as mortality and morbidity, crime rates, obesity, mental illness, teenage pregnancies and addictions. Wilkinson and Pickett, mentioned above, analyze masses of data from different societies. They have concluded that for societies which have made the great leap from poverty to sufficiency and then to affluence, the level of inequality matters almost more than any other factor. On the basis of virtually every criterion of individual and social well-being, affluent societies which are more equal do better than those which may be wealthier overall but are less equal. If we compare wealthy societies with each other, for example, we find that the more-equal societies (such as Sweden and Japan) do better on every measure than the less-equal societies (such as the USA, Britain and

Portugal). Canada, being more equal than America and Britain but less equal than Sweden and Japan, achieves levels of well-being roughly in the middle of the pack. As Canada has become wealthier, overall, but more unequal in the way we distribute that wealth, our levels of crime, drug addiction, disease and suicide have all risen compared to those wealthy countries which enjoy greater levels of income equality. And, as you would expect, the burden of disease is highest among those at the bottom of the socio-economic scale and lowest among those at the top. What you might not expect, however, is that even the wealthiest Canadians have worse health outcomes than their counterparts in other wealthy (but more equal) societies. This is true for virtually any disease you care to name, from cancer to stroke to diabetes to arthritis to mental illness.

The relationship of human health to ecosystem health

Two threads linking CD authors over the first fifty years of the magazine's existence are the shared conviction that individual health is inextricably linked to community health and the shared insight that both are inextricably linked to environmental health. In a 1980 editorial (15:3, December), CD appealed to the authority of cancer researcher Samuel Epstein and his seminal book *The Politics of Cancer* to support the view that up to 80 per cent of all cancers are environmentally created.

In June of that same year (14:7), Mary McArthur described how the Bendix factory in Windsor, Ontario, because of its use of asbestos in the manufacture of automobile brake linings it manufactured, exposed its workforce to asbestos-related cancer (mesothelioma). Even after local ventilation and dust collectors had been installed at the machines, the air remained thick with asbestos dust. The workers knew full well that their workplace was hazardous. For one thing, a number of life insurance companies refused to sell policies to asbestos workers. Tragically, this situation prevailed for decades. Although a minority of workers was militating for improved workplace health and safety

> [t]he majority of workers are unwilling to challenge the
> Bendix Company. This attitude stems from a combination of
> factors including denial of the danger, lack of information,

293

fear of plant closure, and misdirected loyalty towards an
uncaring employer.

Utterly inadequate health and safety standards were staunchly defended by the Ontario government, whose eagerness to please a large and powerful corporation easily outweighed its concern to protect both the plant workers and the wider community. McArthur described how a three-month strike by Bendix workers in 1977 finally forced the Ontario government to upgrade health and safety standards. Shortly thereafter the company closed one of its plants.

Over the years, *CD* writers have analyzed many similar cases. Larry Gautier warned us, based upon his experience working as a union health and safety representative (14:7, June 1980) that "[a]s with any other issue the political cannot be divorced from the work place. Occupational health and safety is no exception."

Writing in 1983 (16:7-8, January) Stan Gray described the escalating struggle by Ontario workers against workplace death and disease, including the battle of the Elliot Lake uranium miners over cancer and silicosis, revelations about the "cancer belt" around the steel mills of Hamilton, mine accidents at Inco, in Sudbury, and toxic coke at steel mills throughout Ontario. He expressed scorn for government complicity in such corporate workplace scandals and scorn for a system of justice that punished workplace injuries and deaths as mere regulatory offences, no matter the degree of employer negligence or recklessness. In his *CD* review of a film produced by the Union of Injured Workers (18:4, Summer 1984), John Marshall commented:

As long as it is more profitable to pay compensation
benefits and the occasional fine, workers will continue to
be slaughtered in mines, factories, and on construction sites
across the country.

Stan Gray's central message was that workers and communities could not rely on the goodwill of governments any more than they could rely on corporations to behave with common decency. Sadly, as he pointed out, it would also be naïve to rely exclusively on those trade unions whose conservative leaderships "have never been comfortable with the health and safety struggle because it challenges the companies at a very basic level and because they can't control it very easily."

Skeptical about the willingness of the labour movement to take effective action on workplace health issues, the Windsor Occupational Safety and Health Council argued (14:7, June 1980) that grassroots union members have little choice but to engage in self-education programs about the causes of and solutions to their many health problems and they must also seek allies among the general public through community educational campaigns.

A more positive view of trade unions as a vehicle for aggressively tackling issues of workplace pollution was expressed by Wiho Papenbrook in "Fighting for a healthy workplace in Kitimat" (16:5, July/August 1982). In the case of the Alcan Aluminum Smelter in Kitimat, the union commissioned a scientific study which exposed the shocking extent of the plant's toxic pollution to both internal and external environments. Alcan's response was what one would have expected:

> When the study was published, the Company viciously
> attacked it and tried to denigrate its findings. Alcan
> attempted to deliberately make the issue an economic and
> political one through clever use of the media and Company
> hired specialists.

It should not require enormous courage and perseverance for workers and their unions to achieve a right so basic as "the right to live and work without dying for it"; but in a world dominated by wealthy and powerful corporations and their governmental allies nothing short of courage and perseverance will do the trick.

In his article on "Environmental Hazards and Human Health" (46:4, July/August 2012), David Boyd quoted a declaration from Canada's federal, provincial and territorial health ministers, meeting in 2005, in which they set out their goal for environmental quality:

*Canada is a country where: The air we breathe, the water
we drink, the food we eat, and the places we live, work and
play are safe and healthy — now and for generations to
come.*

From an aspirational point of view, this public declaration could
scarcely be bettered. And yet here we are now, many years later, and
the Harper government is "waging a wholesale attack on the environmental safeguards intended to protect ecosystems and our health."
Environmental scientists, on whose research we depend to assess when
an ecosystem threat is serious and to come up with effective ways of
dealing with these threats, are being laid off by the hundreds. Those public service scientists who retain their jobs have been gagged and, at the
same time, legislation vital to the assessment and protection of Canada's
environment has been rendered toothless. All this has occurred rapidly,
with little or no opportunity for serious parliamentary debate and no
genuine opportunity for public participation.

As David Boyd noted, with more than a touch of frustration, it is blind-
ingly obvious that if we seek to reduce national expenditure on health
then we must address the social determinants of health "including poverty,
inequality, education, social support networks and, last but not least, our
biophysical environment." As *CD* authors have stressed for the past half
century, we cannot succeed in achieving a high level of both individual
and public health unless more resources are devoted to the prevention of
illness and accidents.

The World Health Organization estimates that, annually, in Canada,
thirty-six thousand deaths and 13 per cent of the total disease burden
are attributable, partially or entirely, to environmental hazards (such
as polluted air and water). Boyd sensibly conceded that at present such
estimates can be only approximations, since they reflect "our lack of
understanding of health-environment relationships."

What we know with certainty is that "a disproportionate burden of the
[health] costs falls on communities that are already socially and economically marginalized." Boyd acknowledged that "[i]n Canada, that often
means Aboriginal communities." Long-time *CD* readers may remember

the vivid article (11:7, October 1976) in which Jim Harding recounted the shameful saga of how Dryden Pulp and Paper and Reed Paper poisoned the Wabigoon River and the English River with high levels of mercury. In this saga, as in so many others, the Ontario government acted as the agent of wealthy corporations rather than as defender of the right to life and health of First Nations people. The "freedom" of the company to pollute clearly trumped the right of northern Ontario people, mostly natives, to a liveable environment. There is no way of avoiding the conclusion that from the government's point of view "the health of natives was a low priority."

The take-away message from half a century of *CD* articles on both medicare and health is that, at the end of the day, the story of health is largely the story of status, equality and social justice. In the domain of both health care and public health there remains a vital and continuing battle to be fought. The struggle for social justice is no less important today than it was a half-century ago when both *Canadian Dimension* and medicare were lusty infants bursting onto the Canadian scene.

CHAPTER 11
Crime and Punishment:
The More Things Change . . .

Evan Bowness and Elizabeth Comack

The government's get-tough approach isn't aimed at big ticket crooks, like large-scale drug dealers, corporations who exploit employees or the environment, or others who sustain a system of criminalized racism, poverty, homelessness and addiction. And it doesn't address the root causes of a good deal of the crime it does target: adverse social, economic, or family conditions.

— Shawn Bayes, "Harper's Crime Laws" (41:2, March/April 2007)

The opportunity to reflect on the topic of crime and punishment comes at a significant moment in the history of criminal justice in Canada. In March 2012 the Canadian Parliament passed Bill C-10, the so-called *Safe Streets and Communities Act*, a collection of nine different crime bills that had previously failed to gain force of law during the Harper government's first term of office. Among the most significant changes in this legislation are the elimination of accelerated parole reviews, mandatory minimum sentences that remove the judiciary's discretion to rule in favour of shorter or community-based sentences when appropriate, and a drastic constriction on the possibility of pardon for thousands of people with criminal records. Ironically coming in an era of decreasing crime rates,[1] the new legislation forcefully pushes forward the conservative "tough on crime" agenda — an agenda that responsibilizes disadvantaged people and punishes them for their marginalization, adds to an already overflowing prison population and recklessly spends tax dollars on prison expansion, and fails to create a social support network that can meaningfully prevent crime and invest in community-based alternatives to curb recidivism rates. The net effect of the new legislation, therefore, will be more people criminalized and incarcerated in Canada's burgeoning prison industry.

Although the "tough on crime" agenda has gained momentum with the passage of Bill C-10, the debate over whether to tweak a broken system for the worse or take a more progressive approach to crime and punishment is certainly not new. Just as significant, the political rhetoric adopted by governments to frame crime and punishment issues is not substantially different than when CD was first published in 1963. For this reason, we take as our starting point the adage, "the more things change, the more they seem to remain the same." Over the last fifty years, various federal and provincial governments in Canada have tapped into the public's fear of crime as a strategy to deflect attention away from more pressing social issues in an effort to secure their political legitimacy. So even though the economic landscape has changed, the spectre of crime and "criminals" has remained a ready scapegoat in mainstream political discourse for explaining away the ills of society.

Challenging the Conservative agenda

Over the years CD writers have endeavoured to expose the limitations of this conservative agenda as it applies to a host of crime and punishment issues. Michael Mandel's 1979 article "The Ideology of Prison Reform," could have been written several decades later, as it pre-empts the work of governmentality scholars on neoliberal responsibilization and risk-management strategies.[2] Mandel focuses on the recommendations that emerged from an all-party parliamentary committee formed in 1976 to address prison reform. Chaired by Liberal MP Mark MacGuigan, the committee advocated for giving greater control to the personnel who administer the prison system and placed the onus on prisoners to engage in their own "personal reformation" — as principle four of the MacGuigan report reads, "only the wrongdoer can bring about reform in himself since he is responsible for his own behaviour" (13:7, May 1979). The function of this stance, Mandel notes, is to locate the "cause" of criminal behaviour in the prisoner and to make him or her bear the full weight of its "cure."

While Mandel pointed to the depoliticization of crime and punishment in the MacGuigan Report, other *CD* writers have taken pains to expose the politics of imprisonment. One of the most prolific of these writers is Ruth Morris. In a 1984 article, Morris showcased the increasing costs of incarceration and the building of new prison cells as opposed to relying on community-based alternatives. An advocate of prison abolition, Morris maintained that "It is powerless people who are imprisoned everywhere. You don't cure powerlessness by punishment or therapy. It can only be cured by sharing power and resources in the wider society" (18:4, August 1984). In another article, Morris (19:3, July/August 1985) drew attention to prison overcrowding, making the point that Canada, in company with the US, has the highest rates of incarceration in the Western world. Four years later, she addressed the public's fear of crime, especially as it centres on the dangerous offender, arguing that our fears of the violent few mask the reality that they make up "much fewer than 5 percent of the prison population." Our chances of encountering a violent death from industrial accidents and drunk drivers are much higher, Morris observed, and our risk of violence is much greater from family and friends than from strangers (23:2, March 1989).

Other *CD* writers also took up the challenge of countering the conservative agenda in the 1980s. Like Morris, Keith Jobson (18:4, August/September 1984) highlighted the increasing costs of criminal justice, noting that between 1966 and 1982 estimated costs increased 750 per cent, from $0.6 billion to $1.7 billion. Similarly, Claire Culhane commented on the relationship between the growth of the prison population and social and economic conditions, saying, "they're inseparable. We now have 4.3 million Canadians living below the poverty line. If no money goes to help these people cope, where else are they going to go? There's no denying it's the poor and powerless who fill our prisons" (20:2, April 1986).

One plank of the conservative agenda on crime and punishment in the 1980s was the Mulroney government's call for a free vote in the House to reinstate capital punishment. Coming at a time when the debate over the implementation of the Free Trade Agreement was reaching its peak, the free vote was seen by many commentators as a way to deflect attention from more serious issues confronting the country. *Dimension* featured two articles on the capital punishment debate. Claiming capital punishment to be "the ultimate expression of racial hatred and economic oppression," Morris (20:3, May 1986) laid out several arguments against the use of the death penalty. Fred Gudmundson (21:4, July/August 1987) defined capital punishment as the "supreme class act. It's the best measure of the extremes to which the ruling class will go to protect the destructive values that form the foundations of privilege and power."

As the neoliberal state's cuts to social programs proceeded apace in the 1990s, *Dimension* writers again addressed the discourse of fear engendered by the conservative agenda. Commenting on the Ontario government's move to target squeegee kids with legislation aimed at "aggressive panhandling," Samir Gandesha (34:1, February 2000) noted that the preoccupation with safety has its roots in the 1970s when the welfare state showed the first signs of decline in response to the crisis of the global economy. Gandesha located the authoritarian crackdown on squeegee kids in the economic context of youth unemployment, the elimination of the social safety net and the absence of community.

Raising concerns over illicit drug use has been an enduring staple of the conservative agenda. One of the first *CD* articles to address this issue was a 1967 piece by Morton Minuck on "Marijuana and the Law." In addition to exposing the misconceptions and irrational fear that surround the use of the drug, Minuck advocated for legalization, suggesting that while marijuana users are likely persecuted by law because of their minority group status, it is also the case that "drug racketeers possess the political influence that drug users lack, and that it is the displeasure of the underworld at the prospect of legalization, in the face of the millions of dollars to be made through the illegal sale of marijuana, that is a factor behind the inappropriate and damaging laws that govern marijuana today" (4:2, February 1967).

The moral panic surrounding marijuana continued to fuel the conservative agenda several decades later. In 2000 Kim Goldberg noted that the "war on weed" was escalating in BC with a campaign that targeted grow-ops. Convicted pot growers were being sentenced to as much as two years' imprisonment. Kim Goldberg observes, "Reminiscent of Reefer Madness, Vancouver newspapers scream 'Pot industry a public threat,' while giving out handy front-page hints for spotting a grow house, and urging readers to squeal on their neighbours via the police potline" (34:5, September/October 2000).

A shared analysis

While the range of crime and punishment topics covered is diverse, the *Dimension* articles reflect a shared analysis that emphasizes the intersections of race/gender/class to understand the issues considered. More specifically, crime and punishment are situated within the broader context of colonialism, patriarchy and capitalism. Furthermore, in countering the "tough on crime" agenda and its attempt to responsibilize those people affected by racism, sexism and poverty, *CD* authors encouraged readers to question the claim that individuals merely "choose" not to obey the laws of mainstream society; rather, the "choice" to participate in criminal activity is, more often than not, one based on necessity or survival.

Several articles addressed issues relating to Aboriginal people and the criminal justice system. In relaying the story of an Aboriginal man who took a short prison sentence for his brother whose partner was expecting a baby, Morris (19:5, December 1985) describes the prison system as one that "grinds Indians through its ravenous jaws so systematically and impersonally that it doesn't even notice the substitution of one brother for another, so long as it can digest another Indian." Speaking to the over-representation of Aboriginal people in the courts and corrections, Morris notes that, "Having stolen this country from the native people, having done so much to destroy their culture, having exposed them to intolerable health conditions and the destruction of much of their family life, we solve the resultant problems by jailing them" (19:5, 1985).

The troubled relationship between Aboriginal people and the criminal justice system came more into the foreground in 1989 with the establishment of the Manitoba Aboriginal Justice Inquiry (AJI). Janet McFarland highlighted the work of AJI commissioners Alan Hamilton and Murray

Sinclair, asserting that "the evidence is strong that some natives are victimized by the system" and that "police inaction, prejudice and brutality are constant themes during the inquiry" (23:4, June 1989). In hearing submissions from hundreds of individuals and groups, the AJI was revealing systemic racism in the administration of justice in the province. It was also painstakingly investigating the deaths of Native leader J.J. Harper and Helen Betty Osborne, a nineteen-year-old student from Norway House.

In the same *CD* issue, Lisa Priest described the horrendous murder of Osborne just outside The Pas, where on November 13, 1971 four white men abducted and sexually assaulted her, and brutally stabbed her to death with a screwdriver. Even though many residents of the town knew who the assailants were, Priest demonstrated how a culture of racism and desensitization to the plight of Native people enabled a sixteen-year-long cover-up. Some years later, writing about a Saskatchewan case with a disturbing similarity to the Osborne murder, Ron Bourgeault called attention to the economic racism at play in the death of Pamela George. The two white, male university students who sexually assaulted and killed George were acquitted of first-degree murder, instead being convicted of the less serious manslaughter charge. Race, gender and class privilege were all too evident in this case; the accused were deemed to be "upstanding citizens," whereas George, in the judge's words, "was indeed a prostitute" (31:3, May/June 1997).

The ways in which race, gender and class inequalities intersect for women in the prison system are also addressed by *CD* writers. Elizabeth Comack relayed the standpoints of twenty-four women incarcerated in a provincial "correctional" institution — a term that one woman dismissed by saying, "You can't tell me that in something that they call a correctional institute that it in any way, shape or form corrects" (30:4, July/August 1996). Highlighting the "miles of problems" faced by women in prison and the conditions they endure while incarcerated, Comack makes all too clear the dismal prospect of resolving the women's troubles within prison walls. Similarly, Kim Pate (40:2, March/April 2006), Executive Director of the Canadian Association of Elizabeth Fry Societies, attributed the fact that women are the fastest-growing prison population worldwide to a system of laws and policies that "effectively criminalize poverty, disabilities and resistance to colonialism."

A common approach to raising awareness about crime and punishment issues in *Canadian Dimension* has been to give voice to those most affected by dire social and economic conditions and state interventions into their lives. Drawing upon her experience as a federally-sentenced prisoner, Ann Hansen (36:5, September/October 2002) used the metaphor of prisons as a "looking glass of society" to illustrate how the prison is a reflection of the fact that women are the most victimized in our society; they are the poorest, least educated and most racially discriminated against. Calvin White relayed the story of Stewart Donegal, a nineteen-year-old who was sentenced to the "subtle daily trauma" of prison — an experience that trains you "to be a more dangerous person, a more unpredictable person. An angrier person" (34:4, July 2000). More recently, Comack and her colleagues (42:2, March/April 2010) drew upon the knowledge of Aboriginal street gang members to address the problems of Winnipeg's inner city, concluding that the street gang members have it right: "If you want to change violence in the 'hood, you have to change the 'hood."

Beyond street crime

Dimension also worked to expand the frame of crime and punishment beyond "street crime" — the decided focus of the conservative agenda — to include state-organized crime and corporate crime. In the 1980s Lauren Chambliss and William Chambliss pointed to the role of the CIA in arms and drug smuggling to finance its agenda, noting that while President and Nancy Reagan "scream about the crimes of abortion and drug use," and the US attorney general decries youth crimes and petty criminals, "the known crimes by officials acting within the logic and requisites of agencies of the United States government reveal a pattern of criminality that is mind boggling" (21:5, September 1987). Writing about "Corporate Crime and the Westray Tragedy," Harry Glasbeek and Eric Tucker declared that the explosion at a coal mine in Pictou County, Nova Scotia, that killed twenty-six miners was not an "accident" but the result of a series of conscious decisions, "as is most occupational health and safety damage in Canada." Westray stands as "a stark example of how workers take all the risks and employers displace theirs. This is hidden through the manipulation of legal forms and by the assumption that workers and capital have a common interest in safe and healthy working conditions" (28:1, January/February 1994). More recently, commenting on the public outrage following the death of an on-duty police officer relative to the sparse media attention received by most other workplace deaths, Glasbeek (46:3, May/June 2012) noted that "the ensuing default position in law is that harms inflicted on the environment, consumers and workers in the quest for profit by private property owners are not truly criminal in nature." By calling attention to the ways in which corporations and states are able to define their own behaviour as "normal" while the political and media discourse condemns street crime and criminals as being "out of control," articles like these serve an important function in asking readers to consider how "crime" is constructed, and how "punishment" applies to only certain kinds of socially destructive actions.

Advocating alternatives

In 2007, summarizing the Left critique of the Harper government's crime laws, Shawn Bayes made the point that, "The government's get-tough approach isn't aimed at big ticket crooks, like large-scale drug dealers, corporations who exploit employees or the environment, or others who sustain a system of criminalized racism, poverty, homelessness and addiction. And it doesn't address the root causes of a good deal of the crime it does target: adverse social, economic or family conditions" (41:2, March/April 2007). Raising awareness of the problems arising from the conservative approach to criminal justice and the relationship between inequality and the law, however, is only one aspect of the work *CD* contributors accomplish when writing about crime and punishment. Equally important are their efforts in pointing to alternatives and pathways to positive change.

Commenting on gang-controlled drug trafficking in Vancouver and the escalating violence associated with it, Jerry Paradis (43:4, July/August 2009) takes a sober approach to drug-related crime reduction: "Try, but you can't cut off the supply." Paradis explains that "participation in the drug trade is a replaceable crime" in that every time we throw a drug dealer in jail another one is waiting to step up. Because of the economics of illicit drug sales, prohibition is expensive and largely ineffective in preventing addiction and gang violence. Arguing the need to "shed ideology and think creatively," Paradis proposes that we adopt a drugstore model to supply marijuana and other presently illicit drugs, much like New Zealand has done with regard to the sale of liquor. Admitting that his model is presented in "very broad strokes," Paradis maintains that it "would be a vast improvement on kids being lured into drug use by persons solely interested in their profit and in expanding their market" (43:4, July/August 2009).

More recently, building on opposition to the "tough on crime" approach and timed with the introduction of Bill C-10, *Dimension* dedicated a special issue to "Canada's Criminal (Justice) System" that was designed to not only document the ways in which the expansion of the criminal justice system has become a central part of political and economic restructuring in Canada but also to propose alternatives — and there are many on offer. Bronwyn Dobchuk-Land (45:5, September/October 2011), for instance, points to grassroots approaches, such as Winnipeg's community-created Safe Walk Corridors, where sex workers avoid working during school hours to minimize contact between johns and children, and the Circle of Courage program at Ka Ni Kanichihk, which works with Aboriginal youth to help them understand the relationship between crime and colonialism. For Dobchuk-Land, such programs have the potential to move beyond punitive criminal justice responses to fashion more inclusive forms of community organizing. Similarly, James Patterson and Ashley Titterton (45:5, September/October 2011) argue that "increasing public demand for funding for offender skill-building, post-release treatment, community supports and victims programs (all cost-effective tools to prevent crime and fight recidivism) represent a productive alternative at a fraction of the cost of incarceration." And others, like Robyn Maynard, advocate for restorative justice approaches, such as the one implemented by Onashowewin, a Winnipeg agency which aims to address the causes rather than the symptoms of youth criminality. Such programs allow for accountability "because they also involved the victims of youth offenders, as well as their surrounding communities" (45:5, September/October 2011).

Continuing the struggle for justice

That many of the crime and punishment issues considered by *Canadian Dimension* continue to persist amidst a changing political and economic landscape could reasonably give us pause to be skeptical about the prospects for transformative change. Indeed, it may be no coincidence that the Harper government's *Safe Streets and Communities Act* comes at a time when the divide between rich and poor in our society is growing ever wider. By all accounts, this "tough on crime" agenda will only exacerbate that divide. All the more reason, therefore, for progressives to continue to challenge the conservative agenda, give voice to those adversely effected by social marginalization, question the official line between "legal" and "criminal," and call for alternatives to failing approaches to dealing with social problems. In this way, *CD* has provided an important forum for fostering the kind of critical, reflexive thinking that is a precondition for realizing substantive change.

CHAPTER 12
Racism, Human Rights and Immigration
Christopher Webb

Young people need to know that their history involves the turning away of a ship with Jewish refugees from our shores at the height of the Jewish Holocaust because "none was too many," or that the Komogata Maru, *carrying South Asian immigrants, was turned away into the dangerous Pacific waters. The Chinese head tax and various legislated prohibitions against Chinese family reunion and the internment of Japanese Canadians assumed to have crossed loyalties should not remain stories told on Saturday morning heritage classes. They should be the subject of official history lessons in schools. Because these stories represent the contradiction that defines key characteristics of Canadian society . . .*

— Grace-Edward Galabuzi, "The Contemporary Struggle Against Racism in Canada," 38:1, January 2004.

In the January 2004 issue of *Canadian Dimension* Grace-Edward Galabuzi, a leading scholar of racism in Canada, pointed to the denial of Canadian racism as an underlying tension within our society. Rooted in a sense of moral superiority derived from comparisons to US racism, Canadians are quick to point to the history of the Underground Railroad or multiculturalism as evidence of greater racial harmony while relegating the nastier episodes to the dustbin of partially acknowledged but largely forgotten history. And yet the contradictions between these two narratives strike at the heart of Canadian society, as "a tension between the liberal democratic values of equality and the prevalence of workplace, social and cultural hierarchies based on superficial attributes" (38:1, January 2004). These contradictions were thrown into stark relief in the fall of 2011 when I traced the route of the Underground Railroad through Southern Ontario with a group of migrant farm workers and migrant justice activists from Latin America and the Caribbean. The lives of these ostensibly free workers were juxtaposed against the history of escaped slaves who found a safe haven in Canada. Unlike those escaped slaves, migrant workers will never find a home here. For them Canada is a place of hard labour; their dreams must be lived elsewhere.

The Canadian record on racism includes a legacy that indigenous people have to live with on a daily basis. The importance of these issues warrants a separate chapter, so I will restrict myself to other matters of race, human rights and immigration in the magazine's catalogue. I would like to stress though that any serious discussion of contemporary racism and human rights cannot be separated from Canada's colonial policies, particularly its crimes against Indigenous people which include genocide, residential schools and forced relocations.

Canadian Dimension's 50-plus years of coverage of racism provides insight into the Canadian Left's response to struggles around the world and racial politics at home. While it made significant contributions in these areas, these debates often took a backseat to the magazine's primary areas of interest in political economy, left strategy and trade union politics. Its embrace of left nationalism somewhat limited its coverage of these issues until the early 2000s, as evidenced by its exchange with Nandita Sharma (37:3, May 2003). The magazine's struggle to reconcile competing claims of identity and difference with the political imperatives of socialist unity was a reflection of the internal crises of the New Left during these years.

Dimension's roots in the US alternative press movement caused it to focus on the civil rights struggle from its inaugural issue in 1963.[1] Donald Warden, a young black lawyer and civil rights activist, wrote of the limitations of the civil rights struggle in emancipating African Americans. Much like Frantz Fanon's psychology of colonial oppression, Warden explained how "the black man in America . . . has been divested of his cultural heritage, and given in its stead a system of values which relegates him to inferior status" (1:1, September 1963).[2] The mind of the South, as he put it, remains the mind of the nation, and desegregation would not address the "real Negro problem," where black youth live in an environment of "self-hatred and fatalism." The piece also satirized the coffee-shop culture of the sixties where "the white participants are liberals, and the black, just plain 'sick.'"

The escalation of the civil rights struggle, the death of Malcolm X the previous year, and the birth of the Black Panther Party led to further coverage of Black Power struggles. Bayard Rustin, a socialist, civil rights activist and editor of *Liberation Magazine*, penned an article in 1966 on the Watts Riot in which he too argues that while civil rights "ameliorates some of the misery, it has not yet frontally attacked the basic economic problems" (3:2, January 1966). The manifesto of the Watts' rioters was written "in the burnt buildings and smashed stores . . . if things don't change, these young people were saying they would do it again."

And they did just that the following year, with riots against immiseration, poverty and racism hitting major US cities in the North and South. The magazine ran a special issue titled "Explosions 67" with a focus on the "Black Rebellion." While its timing was appropriate, the articles could not keep pace with a movement that was rapidly evolving, splintering and challenging both the old and new Left. The urgency that characterized previous coverage was missing, as the magazine chose to reprint Warden's 1963 piece on "The Black Negro" under the title "The Roots of Black Power." For *Globe and Mail* reporter Loren Lind the riots could not be pacified by the civil rights leaders, much less by piecemeal policies that promised jobs and welfare (4:6, September 1967). Yet many leftists would have little time for the adventurism of the Black Power movement and its dismissal of the integrationist approach of the civil rights leaders. In a July-August 1968 review of Stokely Carmichael and Charles Hamilton's *Black Power: The Politics of Liberation in America* Norman Klein chastises them for ignoring the organization and discipline advocated by Martin Luther King Jr. while advocating a utopian politics that "concedes economic independence yet assumes political liberation and independence as an end result" (5:5, July 1968). As the sixties waned the Left, in its many variations, struggled to make sense of political formulations that began to emphasize identity and interrelated oppressions above class struggle.

Following the upheavals of the late 1960s and the assassination of Martin Luther King Jr. the magazine turned its gaze elsewhere for a time. While it continued to cover the antiwar movement and student politics south of the border, it primarily concerned itself with the direction of the women's movement, the changing shape of Canada's economy and the state of the Left in the Trudeau years. This is not to say that the magazine entirely abandoned its coverage of racism during this time. In fact, its coverage of the struggle against white minority rule in Southern Africa was extensive. Debates among Canadian anti-apartheid activists were covered in some depth in the magazine; notable among them are those pieces by *Southern African Report* editor and long-time ally of African liberation struggles John Saul. The piece that stands out, however, is Ron Bourgeault's *Canada Indians: The South African Connection* published in 1988. In the mid 1980s the apartheid regime sponsored a number of fact-finding missions by Saskatchewan's indigenous leaders, which they used to point out Canada's hypocrisy in condemning South African apartheid while doing little for indigenous people at home. Beyond the rhetoric, the rationale behind the trip was a great deal more sinister. South African ambassadors to Canada had been exploiting the plight of indigenous communities for years, visiting reserves in Manitoba and Saskatchewan and utilizing conservative and opportunist chiefs to further apartheid's international propaganda campaign.

As a publication that was outwardly socialist in orientation, the issue of "human rights" was of central importance. Yet in order to delineate itself from the liberal hubris that often surrounds the term, the magazine's writers rarely framed issues in this light. To them feminist, indigenous and anti-imperialist struggles were more reflective of what Immanuel Wallerstein termed "anti-systemic movements" that were part of a broader emancipatory effort.[3] The introduction of the *Charter of Rights and Freedoms* in 1981, however, prompted a wider-ranging discussion among the magazine's editors on a socialist interpretation of human rights and whether these should be enshrined in the constitution. For the editors the *Charter*

311

failed to recognize the sovereignty of Quebec and indigenous nations within Canada, dealt narrowly with civil rights while ignoring economic rights, and was seen as a skirmish between Eastern and Western finance and energy capital (15:4, January 1981). The editors were also critical of the "opt-out clause," which they insisted was "large enough to drive several War Measures Acts through." Abuses of *Charter* rights, particularly domestic spying and surveillance operations against activists, received substantial coverage in subsequent years. Toronto lawyer Jeff House exposed the ongoing surveillance and intimidation of left-wing activists by the RCMP and the 1981 McDonald Commission, which allowed senior RCMP officers and politicians to escape public scrutiny. House raised important questions at the heart of Canadian civil liberties, such as what statute authorizes the RCMP to prepare detention lists, and what does the state consider "legitimate dissent"?

It is hard not to notice the glaring omission of black Canadian history in the magazine's first few decades. Black Canadians remained absent from its pages until the 1990s. In 1996 St. Mary's University graduate student Sheridan Hay argued that the black community's contribution to Canadian society is repeatedly ignored as blacks are "relegated to 'visible minority' status, where they are cast off to blend into a sea of shades and cultures" (30:6, November 1996). Hay scrutinized mainstream media stories in order to demonstrate how the media, and Canadian society more broadly, invisibilizes the black community. One notable case was known as the Ringma affair, in which Reform MP Bob Ringma said that blacks and homosexuals should be moved to the back of the store if they cause an employer to lose business. Major newspapers substituted black with "visible minority" and "ethnic groups," reframing the story as an instance of Canada's troubled multiculturalism rather than a case of racism. "But then again," wrote Hay, "Racism against blacks is an American problem, not a Canadian one."

In its fortieth anniversary issue (38:1, January/February 2004), the editors argued that multiculturalism has been a political project, allowing the state to maintain hegemony by appealing to various subaltern and ethnic groups. And yet below state discourse lies the truth about Canada: a nation built upon settler colonialism, unequal coexistence between

English and French Canada, and the targeted policing and criminalization of immigrant communities throughout the nation's history and particularly so after 9/11. In this issue Grace-Edward Galabuzi pointed to the fact that pronouncements of Canadian equality, "continue to come up against the legacy of 'the white settler colony,'" particularly at a time when racialized minorities become more relevant statistically. During the war on terror, racial discrimination took on added dimensions as it intersected with national security interests. This racialization of the state's security apparatus follows in the footsteps of the criminalization of racialized communities by police forces across Canada. For Galabuzi, the changes to Canada's political economy also exacted enormous pressure on racialized communities, as "racialized Canadians are ghettoized in contingent employment." This argument was fundamentally different from the magazine's position in 1966, where the editors argued that "25% of the population . . . the old, unemployed, Indians and Negroes" were in fact not part of the economy, but "neglected rather than exploited" (3:2, January 1966). Galabuzi called for a more thorough examination of racism in the Canadian workplace and the need for the labour movement to adopt an explicitly antiracist politics.

Canadian multiculturalism also bred a vicious form of racism and xenophobia that exploded in the early nineties in the form of far-right racism. In 1993 Helmut-Harry Loewen and Mahmood Randeree, two members of the Manitoba Coalition Against Racism and Apartheid, appeared before a Human Rights Tribunal investigating the rise of the KKK and other white supremacist groups in Manitoba (27:2, March 1993). The rise of far-right groups in the 1990s was alarming, with the neo-Nazi Heritage Front drawing hundreds to their Toronto meetings as they rapidly made inroads into Toronto's public schools. Another obscene episode of far-right violence covered by the magazine was the murder of Cree trapper Leo LaChance by Carney Nerland, a KKK member and a leader of the Aryan Nations in Saskatchewan. For Ron Bourgeault, the RCMP clearly interfered in the case, using witness protection laws to get Nerland a lighter sentence, as he was their insider in the world of prairie neo-Nazism (28:2, March 1994). The racism propagated by white supremacist groups during this time is but one element of more complex patterns of structural racism. As Loewen and Randeree pointed out: "It can be viewed as a distant early warning signal that registers tensions, tremors and fissures which could, under a certain coalescing of conditions, become an even greater threat to the lives of aboriginals, people of colour, immigrants, refugees and other targeted groups" (27:2, March 1993).

Interestingly, the first real discussion of Canadian immigration policy comes from an article about nuclear weapons and Japanese internment during the Second World War. In his article, Stephen Salaff reminds us of Prime Minister Mackenzie King's diary entry following the bombing of Hiroshima and Nagasaki: "It is fortunate that the use of the bomb should have been upon the Japanese rather than upon the white races of Europe" (13:3, August 1978). Along with his "none is too many" statement, Mackenzie King systematically constructed those deserving of asylum and those unfit for Canada's shores. These racial discourses remain with us today in the state's denunciations of "bogus" refugee claimants, "queue jumpers" and those not acquainted with Canadian values. Official multicultural histories also offer a sanitized version of the immigrant experience, as Paul Peters argued in his review of Ukrainian-Canadian immigrant narratives: "The happy legend about those who came to Canada, seeking wealth and freedom does justice neither to the complexity nor the painful facts of what really happened" (14:7, June 1980).

Immigration and refugee policy during the Cold War was an ideological battleground, as Jeff House argued in December 1979: "Our humanitarianism serves not humanity, but the self interest of our ruling class" (14:3, December 1979). House was referring to refugee policy surrounding the arrival of "boat people" fleeing Vietnam, Cambodia and Laos after the fall of Saigon. Canadian immigration policy, he argued, "weeds out socialists and communists, in the name of humanitarianism, and greets anti-socialists and anticommunists like long lost brothers and sisters." The arrival of 490 Sri Lankan migrants on board a ship off the coast of British Columbia in 2010, and the scrutiny surrounding their alleged "terrorist" connections, should remind us that Canada's immigration policy remains wedded to our broader imperial policies, political alliances and trade interests.

The collapse of Communism and the onset of neoliberal globalization brought major changes to Canadian immigration policy. In 2006 Liz Fekete of the Institute of Race Relations noted that the difference between past migrations and today is the sheer scale of displacement occurring around the world (40:2, May 2006). As a combination of wars, economic misery and environmental catastrophe restructured the planet's population on a scale previously unheard of, Canada began to erect ever more insurmountable barriers to those considered undeserving of status or protection. Canada's immigration policies have always been tailored to the demands of an expanding capitalist economy. Yet the assaults on previously sanctioned refugee and immigrant protections by Steven Harper's Conservative government, bolstered by post-9/11 Islamophobic rhetoric, have been dramatic.

The immigration system was effectively overhauled to provide those with money and desirable skills permanent residency while relegating all other immigrants to temporary residency tied to precarious forms of contract labour. In a piece on migrant worker organizing in Montreal, Jill Hanley and Eric Shragge describe the barriers facing those immigrants from the global South whose qualifications and credentials are rarely recognized, trapping them in a cycle of low-wage service jobs (42:3, May 2008). According to a 2011 report on immigration, race and labour in Canada, racialized Canadian workers earned only 81.4 cents for every dollar paid to nonracialized Canadian workers.[4] Trapped within this system, workers desperately need the resources for collective action, but trade unions have been slow to reach out to them. Shragge, Henaway and Hanley outlined the work done by Montreal's Immigrant Worker's Centre as an example of the new community-oriented unionism that is urgently needed to help vulnerable workers.

In the very same issue I argued that Canadian immigration policy entails much more than managing economic and population growth (43:5, September 2009). Rather, it is a powerful tool in shaping the geopolitics of global capitalism. Canada's support for imperialist wars, free trade policies and various international agreements are ways of inserting itself into networks of global capitalism in which human labour is the most valuable resource. Canada's demand for ever-more flexible forms of labour has prompted a range of "designer neoliberal" immigration policies of temporary, contract and seasonal work, increasingly performed by immigrants from the global South. This workforce is highly precarious, as Greg Shupak noted in his article on the thousands of migrant workers who were deported as a cost-cutting measure during the 2008 economic crisis. The increasing prominence of migrant workers to the economy has led to a number of important articles in the magazine in recent years. Tonya and Katherine Davidson paint a multigenerational portrait of life, labour and immigration in Leamington, Ontario, where thousands of Mexican farmworkers toil in fields and packhouses each year. Unlike the Davidsons' ancestors, who migrated to Leamington generations ago, these workers are transients, often treated with hostility and suspicion (43:5, September 2009). The rise of Canada's precarious migrant workforce has also been accompanied by sweeping changes to refugee policy. Angela Day points to the rise of Mexican refugees fleeing the war on drugs and Canada's crackdown on Mexican asylum seekers. As she so cogently argued, the rising number of refugee cases is a direct outcome of NAFTA: "Mexico wasn't always a haven for drug traffickers, nor was it the source country for so many asylum seekers" (43:5, September 2009).

In a 2003 article, scholar and activist Nandita Sharma took *Canadian Dimension* to task for allegedly considering "Canadian nation-building, or the struggle for strong Canadian sovereignty, as reflective of all that is good in the world" (37:3, May 2003). Sharma's sharp opposition to the magazine's discussion of a renewed left nationalism reveals much about the ideological positioning of the magazine over time and the substantial debate this has created among the Canadian Left. For Sharma all nationalist practices are inherently exclusionary, and within the current phase of globalization reproduce a system of global apartheid. As an exclusionary project, nationalism should be firmly rejected in favour of decolonization, which, for Sharma, involves a rejection of all nation states. This criticism of the magazine's ideological manoeuvrings seems well placed, especially given its limited coverage of antiracist and immigrant struggles in previous decades. Yet, to the magazine's credit, its response to Sharma was not a complete dismissal, but an attempt to engage with what decolonization as a practice might look like. The magazine has always been somewhat more pragmatic in this sense. In their response, the editors rejected Sharma's assertion that a multinational

Canadian sovereignty, comprised of different autonomous groups within a Canadian state, is contradictory. Rather, the editors emphasized the unity of these competing claims that must be accommodated within the borders of Canada "on the basis of equality and democracy" in a concrete attempt to "dismantle the colonial state" (37:3, May 2003).

While heated, this discussion appears to have had some impact on the type of material published in the magazine after, which has stressed the pertinence of antiracist and migrant worker struggles. The magazine's roots in a mostly male and white working-class culture have been the subject of trenchant criticism and debate, which is precisely what is needed if any decolonial praxis is to be transformative. Indeed, the changing nature of Canada's working class along with the increasingly brazen role of Canadian capital abroad have already caused some ideological repositioning within the magazine, which will undoubtedly be driven further by new generations of writers, scholars and activists.

PART VI

THE GLOBAL DIMENSION

CHAPTER 13
Revolution and Imperialism: A North American Internationalism

Henry Heller

For the truth about Vietnam, which to this day has remained essentially indigestible to the mainstream political culture of the West, is that the United States of America, armed with the most powerful military machine that had ever existed on the face of the Earth, attacked a helpless, peasant society and visited upon it a conflagration of such savagery that it left upwards of four million of its people dead . . . Though it is fair to say that the Vietnam War sensitized the American public with respect to further military commitments abroad (the so called "Vietnam Syndrome"), and drove U.S. hegemonic strategy away from open aggression towards the use of covert subversion and proxy forces, it is equally fair to say that, today (following Panama, Somalia, Iraq and Yugoslavia), these ideological "setbacks" have been essentially overcome.

— Anthony Black, "The Vietnam War, 25 Years Later" 34:4,
July/August 2000

The Vietnam Years

The first issue of *Canadian Dimension* appeared in 1963 in the midst of the Cold War. The ultimate showdown of that war, the Cuban nuclear missile crisis, had passed the year before. Meanwhile the shockwaves of revolution in Cuba continued to reverberate throughout Latin America and the rest of the underdeveloped world. French colonialism had recently been defeated in Vietnam (1954) and Algeria (1962). In the United States the civil rights movement that began in the south spread northward and increasingly young people — white and black — were seized by the music of rock and roll and the seductions of sex and drugs. In Canada the torpor of British Victorian ideology and the repression of the Cold War was lifting, challenged by a restless new generation while there were signs of growing nationalist and labour unrest in Quebec and among the indigenous people.

This was the context in which *Canadian Dimension* magazine was born. The struggle against US imperialism in Vietnam was central to the concerns of the new magazine and its editor Cy Gonick, freshly returned to Canada from Berkeley, California. A major insurgency had broken out in that country which would topple the puppet regime of President Ngo Dinh Diem. Young Gonick wrote a feature article in the first issue of the magazine introducing Canadians to the historical background of the Vietnamese conflict, describing growing American involvement, especially the attempt to stave off complete rural revolution through the strategic hamlet program. Taking account of the ongoing Buddhist crisis Gonick presciently forecast the overthrow of Diem and concluded that "most objective observers agree that only a full scale invasion of American troops can stem the tide of Viet Cong victory" (1:1-2, September/November 1963).

On the eve of that American invasion (2:3, March/April 1965), Gonick wrote again, insisting that the United States was losing the war and that its fundamental error was trying to impose its own regime on the country. It was the same policy that the United States was pursuing in the Congo, Laos and British Guiana. Gonick mused on the possibility of a Chinese intervention in Vietnam and ended by calling for negotiations and the establishment of a coalition government of communist and noncommunist elements. In response to readers' requests for more information, later the same year (2:4, May/June) Gonick published part one of a series of articles entitled "What Every Canadian Should Know About Vietnam," outlining the history of French colonialism and the course of the national liberation struggle in that country.

Five eventful years later, following the Tet offensive, the fall of US President Lyndon Johnson and the announcement of a new American policy of Vietnamization, Gonick (6:7, February/March 1970) recalled *Dimension's* role in helping to provide a Canadian voice against the Vietnam War and noted that opinion in Canada and elsewhere had decisively turned against the war. As with so many others of his generation Gonick's involvement in the antiwar movement was personal as well as political. Writing on the threshold of the conclusion of the Paris Peace Accords (9:4, March 1973), he observed that Vietnam "was a living experience, my first real contact with world events . . . It shattered my romance with liberalism and liberal democracy." He observed that despite the setbacks of the US, that imperialism was still strong and that the Left had to fortify itself against the ongoing struggle against imperialism in Indo-China and the rest of the world. Significantly, he added that the anti-imperialist struggle should include Canada.

The antiwar movement of the 1960s was the moral equivalent of the fight against fascism in Spain during the 1930s. Indignation against American atrocities against the Vietnamese sometimes reached high pitch. In 1967 (4:4, May/June), popular Canadian author Farley Mowat expressed his own disgust and anger in the pages of *Dimension*, asserting that "the American presence in Vietnam and the undeclared war being waged there by the United States constitutes one of the most blatant acts of aggression the world has seen since the destruction of Hitler's Third Reich." Mowat even went so far as to assert that photos of war atrocities emanating from Americans were not the result of candour but of a sadistic pleasure. A less intemperate and internationalist perspective was brought to bear on the war by John Warnock (6:5, October/November 1969) on the occasion of Ho Chi Minh's death. Entitled "The Lessons of Ho Chi-Minh," Warnock's piece extolled Ho Chi Minh's patient political work, stress on building consciousness, lack of dogmatism and emphasis on political struggle rather than purposeless violence.

Vietnam was the focal point of *Dimension's* internationalism in its early years. But the journal was keenly aware of the relationship between the struggle there and the spread of political unrest globally during the 1960s. In a note dating from 1965 (3:1, November/December), Gonick made

322

connections between the Watts riots in Los Angeles, the anticolonial reaction to the Unilateral Declaration of Independence in Southern Rhodesia and the national liberation struggles in South Africa, Mozambique and Angola. "In 1965," he claimed, "we [the world] went over the edge."

In the same issue of the magazine anthropologist W.E. Wilmott criticized the American foreign policy of containment in the face of a rising tide of anticolonial and nationalist revolts whose source was internal discontent directed against colonial oppression. A year later (3:5, July/ August 1966), a book review of Franz Fanon's *Wretched of the Earth* by George Haggar introduced readers of *Canadian Dimension* to some sense of the psychological and sociological roots of anticolonial revolutions according to this celebrated third-world thinker. Haggar underlined Fanon's stress on the dialectic connection between colonial racism and violent revolution in Africa and elsewhere in the Third World. He pointed to Fanon's emphasis on the peasant base of such revolts and the dangers of the subsequent emergence of a corrupt nationalist bourgeoisie which likely would undermine the revolutionary process.

It is widely appreciated that *Canadian Dimension* was one of the most important voices of Canadian left nationalism in these years. However it should be borne in mind, for all *Dimension*'s nationalism, that Gonick was a product of what may be described as Berkeley internationalism, an influence which marked his approach throughout his editorship of the magazine. As a reflection of this more cosmopolitan outlook, we find in the pages of *Dimension* during the sixties articles on imperialism by William Appleman Williams and Eugene Genovese, the two most important historians of the US of the last generation. Reviewing American history from the perspective of its involvement in Vietnam, Williams saw Vietnam as part of America's long transition from a territorial to an overseas empire. According to Williams, this process saw the integration of American ideas of freedom and democracy with the crucial imperatives of economic empire. For Williams, Vietnam represented a roadblock in the way of this globalizing progress. Remarking on the counterculture of the day (4:3, March/April 1967), this former naval lieutenant concluded that in the wake of this tragic history "it is small wonder that some young Americans emigrate to the land of LSD. It is no wonder that many of them contract out of the American Empire." Two years later (6:1, April/May 1969), Genovese offered *Dimension* his assessment of the struggle between global capitalism and the revolutionary forces battling against it. On the one hand, capitalism and imperialism were maintaining themselves through war, militarism and consumerism. The forces of revolution suffered from the absence of democracy in the Soviet Union, fragmentation of the Left, a lack of good theory and the resort to adventurism. It was urgent that the revolutionary Left build its capacity for theory and its ability to organize.

Dimension did embody a Canadian perspective on international affairs that differed from that of the United States. But that did not make that perspective simply anti-American. Rather, the essence of *Dimension's* viewpoint was that of a North American internationalism, something which could scarcely be found in the United States. From that perspective the journal was to report on and analyze revolution and imperialist counterrevolution across more than five decades and still counting. Indeed, it is not too much to say that the content of the magazine on these questions constitutes a history of our times.

The contributions of these two great American historians were feathers in the cap of the still-fledgling new journal. But more important for *Dimension* in the long run was the debut of Jim Petras as a regular contributor. Petras was a fellow graduate student with Gonick at Berkeley and taught for many years at the State University of New York at Binghamton. In the course of his career Petras has been the author of some seventy books and over six hundred scholarly articles. An acknowledged expert on contemporary Latin America, Petras has a deep understanding of world capitalism and imperialism as well as the revolutionary movements fighting against it, especially in the Americas. From the late sixties into the 2000s Petras's contributions to *Dimension* constituted the bedrock of the journal's internationalist analysis and perspective.

Petras's first article (3:3-4, March-June 1966) dealt with the US invasion of the Dominican Republic in 1965, which prevented the elected president Juan Bosch from resuming the presidency following a military coup two years earlier supported by landlords and the Catholic Church. A counter-coup led by progressive elements of the army as well as the working class attempted to restore Bosch to office. Fearing another Cuban Revolution, US President Johnson sent thirty thousand American marines into the island to block the popular reinstallation of Bosch. Petras explained the American action as part of an overall American design to maintain its control over Latin America in the face of growing popular revolutionary movements. Especially notable was Petras's linking American intervention to the power of the US sugar lobby which included luminaries like Roland Harriman, Adolphe Berle and Abe Fortas, the latter named by Johnson to the US Supreme Court.

In a follow-up article (4:2, January/February 1967), Petras documented the progress of these popular movements in Latin America by providing readers with an overview of the guerilla insurgencies in Guatemala, Colombia, Venezuela and Peru. While each had their specificity Petras noted their common basis in peasant organizing and armed resistance. Such a strategy of rural insurrection had emerged in the face of American military and economic aid designed to block revolution developing in the towns.[1] In 1969 (5:8, February), Petras attempted to theorize the overall relationship between imperialism and revolution in third world countries. Imperialism, he wrote, rested on the relationship between a hegemonic imperialist power and various subimperialist entities through which it was able to exercise a flexible and multidimensional control. Focusing on possible sites of resistance in such countries, Petras noted the weakness of trade unions and parliamentary politics. Indeed, mass migration to the cities actually weakened the capacity to organize. In such places mobilizing in the place of residence and throughout neighbourhoods was more effective than trying to create organized resistance at the worksite. Mobilization in the indigenous rural communities rather than in the towns was best of all.

The revolution stalls: the 1970s

The Vietnam War remained a major preoccupation in the pages of *Dimension* during the decade of the 1970s. An update on Vietnam by University of Oregon graduate student Jeffrey Freed at the beginning of that decade (6:7, February/March 1970) insisted that the Tet Offensive had driven the Americans from the countryside. In fact the situation was more complicated. While beginning a drawdown of its troops on the ground, the US was attempting to reoccupy the rural areas through a campaign of accelerated pacification, which included its murderous computer-driven Operation Phoenix, designed to terrorize rural supporters of the NLF and the Communist Party. Freed asserted that in the Paris peace talks then underway that the DRV and NLF would insist that the Americans leave Vietnam and that the Thieu military dictatorship be replaced by a coalition government. The danger was that the Soviets, seeking détente, would try to force the Vietnamese to compromise, as they had at the time of the Geneva Conference (1954). As events turned out the Soviets proved constant in their support of the DRV. Rather naively Freed insisted that the DRV and NLF could count on China.

In 1975 (10:8, June), a former Canadian nurse in Vietnam and antiwar activist, Claire Culhane, authored an article on "Women and Vietnam." This was part of a special issue of *Dimension* commemorating International Women's Year. The issue marked the real debut of the magazine's increasing concern for the rights of women, gays and people of colour. Culhane began by noting the "delightful irony" that 1975 was the year of women as well as that of "victory for sisters in Vietnam, Cambodia and Laos." That year in fact spelled the collapse of the American-backed regimes in Indo-China and the triumph of communist-led national liberation movements. Her article underlined the suffering women had endured during the American imperialist war. She dwelt particularly on the heroism of women in North Vietnam under the stepped-up bombing campaigns launched by Nixon as a last-gasp effort that tried unsuccessfully to bring the DRV to its knees. In her visit to North Vietnam Culhane incidentally noted how the war had accelerated the breakdown of the gender division of labour and speeded up the building of socialism.

In the wake of the communist victory the United States tried to cover its tracks. It made great play over the fate of Vietnamese orphans threatened with being forced to live under Communism as well as the exodus of refugees known as boat people from the country. The Canadian government and media enthusiastically joined this propaganda game. Culhane had no time for such ploys, pointing to the fact that many of those fleeing had in fact compromised themselves by cooperating with the former regime and the Americans. Her harshest condemnation was reserved for the Canadian government, which, she rightly pointed out, had been deeply complicit in the American war in Indo-China. As regards Canada's complaint that the DRV was violating human rights she observed with reference to the indigenous people of Canada that "we are witnessing a government which persistently denies human rights to its own citizens" while it rushes "mercy planes" to rescue "children from another land."

The global implications of the American defeat in the Vietnam War was dealt with most trenchantly by James Petras. A year after the fall of Saigon (11:8, November 1976), Petras and coauthor Robert Rhodes asked whether the US was really in decline. It was not simply a matter of the US withdrawal from Indo-China but also the OPEC oil crisis, competition from Europe and Japanese and American lack of competitiveness which led to such questions. The answer of Petras and Rhodes was a resounding no to the notion of a decline of the American empire. According to them, the US military was being renewed, US finance capital was extending its reach, there was no internal working-class opposition to the rule of the capitalist class and economically powerful Japan remained a subordinate ally of the US in Asia and American capitalism. They contended that US power was mainly challenged by the European and Japanese working classes determined to maintain their historic standards of living rather than from third-world revolutions whose class basis was relatively weak. In retrospect this assessment seems to hold up in the short run although it took no account of the longer-term implications of declining competitiveness. In this light Petras was shortly afterwards forced to change his mind about American decline.

Petras's gloomy outlook with regard to the possibilities for real change in the Third World may have been shaped by the overthrow of the socialist government of Chilean President Salvador Allende by a military coup (1973). This was presaged by a pessimistic report (9:4, March 1973) by a Montreal Gazette reporter, Glen Allen, on the Chilean situation a few months before the coup. Allen did a series of interviews with working- and middle-class residents of Santiago. Noting the improvements that the Popular Unity government had brought, Allen also remarked on the sense of discouragement, persistent impoverishment, economic shortages and splits between progressives in Chile. In a postscript he wrote: "In the past half year Allende has spent so much time in the valley of the shadow of defeat he might as well be paying rent on it." But in an article ironically titled "The Crimes of Allende" (9:7-8, November/December 1973), Petras eulogized Allende's achievements including widespread nationalization of the economy, expropriation of the landlords, redistribution of income and the development of popular political power. Allende was brought down by sabotage and terrorism backed by the United States. Petras acknowledged some of the mistakes of Allende but underscored the failure of the Chilean Communist Party to mobilize resistance and the positive role in this respect of the radical Left and grassroots activists.

The reactionary counteroffensive: the 1980s

The overthrow of Allende in Chile in the 1970s proved the harbinger of things to come. The decade of the 1980s was marked by the installation of neoliberalism, Reagan-era rollbacks of revolutionary advances in Grenada, Nicaragua, El Salvador, Angola, Mozambique and Afghanistan, massive increases in American military spending and at the end of the decade the foundering of the Soviet Union. Explaining or criticizing the failures of socialist governments provoked head-scratching in the editorial offices of *Dimension*. That history was taking an unwelcome turn was first suggested by an editorial on the Soviet invasion of Afghanistan (14:6, May 1980). Despite the fact that the US and Pakistan were actively organizing the *mujahideen* as a counterrevolutionary force and that Soviet troops had been invited in by the existing government, *Dimension* argued that no good could come from Soviet military support for the Babrak Karmal regime. The invasion was launched more to protect the strategic interests of the Soviet Union than on behalf of social progress. *Dimension*'s prediction that it would do more harm than good to Afghanistan proved prophetic. But how this squared with the well-attested fact of Soviet military and economic aid to Cuba, Nicaragua or for that matter the liberation movements in Africa which were deeply appreciated by the recipients was not explained as it might have been. Perhaps such views could not be squared. The negative view on the part of *Dimension* was rather fostered by memories of the Soviet invasion of

Hungary and Czechoslovakia, which had proved disastrous for socialism.

A tone of defiance is evident in a report on Chile published in the magazine in 1982 (16:3, May). While the Western media claimed that Pinochet and the so-called Chicago Boys had imposed a stable and popular counterrevolutionary and neoliberal regime on the country which was firmly under control, Brent Knazen (later to become an Ontario Court Judge) claimed that strikes, demonstrations and armed resistance by the extreme Left were continuing. A certain defensiveness is likewise evident in CD's response (14:8, August 1980) to the exodus of some 120,000 refugees from Cuba in 1980, which was depicted in the Western media as a failure of socialism. An editorial noted that this flight was being encouraged by the United States not only to discredit the Cuban revolution but also to try to stem a rising revolutionary tide in the Central American and Caribbean republics of Nicaragua, El Salvador, Guatemala and Grenada. It noted the concurrent hypocritical deportation of Haitian refugees from the US. While it exploited the propaganda value of the Cuban exodus, Washington had placed all sorts of obstacles in the way of legal immigration from Cuba to the US. The editorial admitted the problems of the Cuban bureaucracy and economy and the persecution of homosexuals. But it insisted that the revolution was still popular despite the exodus and continuing American sabotage and boycotts.

A similarly defensive tone can be found in the article by anthropologist Kathleen Gough (16:3, May 1982) on the situation in Vietnam. Gough reports on the austerity and economic failures experienced by Vietnam following the American war. While accepting that these disappointments were in part due to bureaucratic control and poor planning, she also attributed them to the American economic boycott and the hostility of China and ASEAN.

Real alarm was *Dimension's* reaction to the US marines' invasion of Grenada in 1983, an event which constituted the first step in the process of renewed direct US intervention in third-world conflicts after its defeat in Vietnam. An editorial in December of that year (17:6) demanded that the US leave Grenada. The invasion was interpreted as a first toward American intervention in revolutionary Nicaragua. This initial response to the Grenada invasion was followed by interviews with two Canadian workers, Dianne Brand and Barbara Thomas, who provided a vivid first-hand account of the events which allowed the American invasion. Facilitating the American move was a split within the Marxist New Jewel Movement, which led to the arrest and killing of leader Maurice Bishop. The civil conflict which followed allowed the marines to invade in the name of protecting American lives. Susan White described in detail US post-invasion plans to reinstall a capitalist economy on the island (18:1, March 1984).

Restoration of American control of Latin America and punishment of the revolutionary regimes in Cuba, Nicaragua and Vietnam was only a part of a larger program. In an editorial published already in the spring of 1981 (15:5, April), *Dimension* had laid out the full American agenda under Reagan. The new president was launching a second Cold War which included massive new military spending, a comprehensive program of counterinsurgency in the Third World and a neoliberal economic agenda. An interesting follow-up story with regard to Reagan's star- or space-war program appeared in the mid-eighties (20:2, April 1986) as physicist Dirk Leemans and community educator Bob Luker speculated on the existing possibilities of using space technology to fight counterinsurgency wars in Third World countries. In doing so they anticipated by many years the development of GPS and the use of drones, which have become so important to the current American war against terror in the Middle East.

In 1986 the Reagan administration sought to use the sale of arms to Iran, which was illegal, to continue to fund the Contras seeking to overthrow the Sandinistas in Nicaragua. In the wake of this scandal or tempest in a teapot Petras undertook a serious evaluation of the foreign and domestic performance of the Reagan administration (21:5, September 1987). Reversing himself from an earlier view, Petras now saw the United States as definitely in economic decline and its empire tottering. Industrial capital was being transformed into fictitious forms. Under such circumstances the ranks of Reagan advisors were being filled by so-called lumpen-intellectuals who were prepared to champion military adventures and terrorist counterinsurgency as a way of holding on to global power. As the end of the decade approached, a *Dimension* editorial in the July/August 1989 issue (23:5) attempted to weigh up the state of world politics in the wake of the growing détente in the Cold War. It noted that both the Soviet Union under Gorbachev and the United States under Reagan/Bush were attempting to revitalize themselves. Perhaps the Soviet Union could do so by pursuing its own democratization. Meanwhile China appeared to be embarked on the capitalist road. But a decade of neoliberalism under Thatcher and Reagan should hardly be a recommendation to China, especially evident in the growing levels of inequality and signs of ecological crisis. The only hope with respect to the capitalist world, the editorial concluded, was a rising tide of opposition to militarism and neoliberalism.

The 1980s had been characterized by an imperialist counter-offensive including staggering increases in US military spending, the beginning of space-based weapons deployment and counterinsurgency. The Soviet Union was tottering on the edge of ruin or renewal. In the face of this uncertain prospect the same 1989 issue of *Dimension* sought to celebrate the idea of revolution in honour of the bicentennary of the French revolution. It recalled the French revolution's epochal event which, in the face of current political and intellectual reaction, signified the ability of the mass of humanity to transform history. The memory of the Revolution of 1789 continues to inspire revolutionaries in Central America, Asia and Africa.

In his assessment of the impact of the Sandinista revolution (23:5, July/August 1989), Petras pointed out that the pluralist character of the revolution had enabled it to attract the broadest international constituency of any parallel upheaval in the post-1945 period. Its influence was being felt in concurrent movements in the neighbouring states of El Salvador, Guatemala and even Honduras. While the persistence of the Vietnam syndrome ruled out direct intervention by the American military in Central America, Petras did note that economic difficulties and external pressure were endangering the Sandinista Revolution. His piece was paired with one by Canada's preeminent Cuba scholar, John M. Kirk (23:5, July/August 1989), assessing thirty years of the Cuban revolution. In the context of the underdeveloped world Kirk argued that Cuba had done well over the thirty years since its revolution. If one compares the island to Mexico, Venezuela or Brazil, for instance, it is clear that any balanced assessment had to fall in Cuba's favour. In contrast to these other countries there are no death squads, or political assassinations, or elemental food riots on the island. Furthermore, its provision of universal employment, health care and education is a model from which the whole world can take example.

Neoliberal imperialism in the nineties

The new decade began badly with further victories for imperialist counterrevolution. Having celebrated ten years of the Sandinista revolution in 1989, the next year *Canadian Dimension* was forced to write what seemed to be its obituary as the revolutionary government went down to electoral defeat at the hands of a conservative coalition headed by the liberal Violeta Barrios de Chamorra. The editorial (24:3, April/May 1990) explained that the Nicaraguan people had voted for the right-wing not because they opposed the revolution but because they were exhausted after a decade of struggling against counterrevolutionary invasion and economic blockade backed by the United States. Nicaraguans had voted for the privilege of eating and, indeed, their very survival. The editorial expressed the hope that the Sandinistas would preserve their organizational structure and be able to fight and win future parliamentary victories. *Dimension's* hope was realized in 2006 when the Sandinista leader Daniel Ortega returned to power. However, the radicalism of the new Sandinista regime was much circumscribed, given the ongoing suspicion and hostility of the United States. The revival of American influence in its Caribbean backyard was signalled by the return to power of the president of Haiti, Jean-Baptiste Aristide (1994), who had been ousted three years earlier in a military coup. As pointed out by Paul Graham (28:6, December/January 1994–95), Aristide returned to Haiti at the instance of a Clinton Administration in Washington eager to demonstrate its commitment to electoral democracy. Posing as a friend of such democracy Washington had reinstalled Aristide in power with so many conditions that Aristide would be able to do nothing to help his people.

The new decade was also marked by the final collapse of the Soviet Union (1991). In an article written shortly before its final dissolution

(24:4, June 1990), Petras noted that the end of the Soviet empire was opening the gates to imperialism in Central America and Eastern Europe. The Contra war against the Sandinistas and the invasion of Panama represented the opening moves in a bid to restore American hegemony over the region. In Eastern Europe the decline of Soviet influence opened the way for an American drive to capture resources and labour power in the region. America's allies in Europe were going along for the ride. They bet that America's commitment to militarism would further weaken its debilitated economic competitiveness. Indeed, the US's recent successes in Nicaragua and Panama had emboldened it, preparing the way for new American military adventures. Meanwhile the US lacked any strategy to address its growing inability to compete in international markets. Any idea by progressives that the decline of the Soviet Union and the end of its rivalry with the US would open up a political space for the Left in the West was a pipe dream, Petras asserted. At the same time America's drive to the east was laying the basis for a new capitalist elite and social inequality to emerge in Eastern Europe.

Following up on Petras, University of British Columbia historian Colin Gordon commented on the significance of the Gulf War (1991) in which an international coalition organized by the triumphant United States expelled Sadam Hussein from Kuwait. Gordon (25:3, April/May 1991) focused on the disparity between the growing economic weakness of the United States and its increasingly aggressive foreign policy: "this novel combination of American interests and American weakness does not bode well for the future of a 'new world order.'" What remains to be seen, he concluded, "is whether as the economic power of the US slips its willingness to use force will fall accordingly or increase in desperation." James D. Graff, who taught at the University of Toronto, took a more optimistic view of the possibilities for peace, at least in the Middle East. According to Graff (25:8, December 1991), with its victory in the Cold War and against Saddam Hussein it is in the interest of Washington to force Israel to compromise. US interests require that it should dictate such a policy to the Israelis. Professor Graff evidently did not understand that in this case it was the tail that wagged the dog, with the Israel lobby issuing the commands.

The demise of the Soviet Union spelled bad news for Cuba. During the 1980s the island had experienced a certain amount of real growth with the ongoing support of the Soviet Union. With the Soviet collapse Cuba was left to its own devices and many expected the collapse of the socialist experiment as it had in Nicaragua. In a report to *Dimension* (26:4, June 1992) Dawn Raby denied that Cuban socialism faced imminent collapse. Times in Cuba had now become quite difficult, but the Cuban people wanted reform and democratization of the system rather than its overthrow. Raby was to be proven right.

Mordecai Briemberg's review (28:6, December/January 1994–95) of a Canadian film on the Gulf War and its aftermath dating from mid-1990s took an openly and refreshingly accusatory stance not toward the US but the Canadian state. While complimenting the filmmaker, Martin Duckworth, for giving the Iraqis a voice in explaining the tragedy inflicted on them by American aggression, Briemberg criticizes him for casting the film in terms of a nostalgia for Canada's role as Middle East peace-keeper — a role invented by the former minister of external affairs and prime minister Lester Pearson. Briemberg flatly asserted that, far from the Canadian role being one of peacekeeping, it had helped to prepare for the US-Israel control over the whole area. This review marks the start of an increasingly critical view of the imperialist dynamic behind Canadian foreign policy in *Dimension*.

The momentum of the imperialist counteroffensive was suddenly broken by a revolt of the impoverished peasants of Chiapas, the south-ernmost state of Mexico, in 1994. *Dimension* published a text entitled "The Reality" by the leader of the revolt, anonymous Subcommander Marcos of the Zapatista Army of National Liberation (30:4, July/August 1996). Marcos invoked the example of Che Guevara as the true inspiration of the struggles against oppression throughout the Americas. John Warnock (31:3, May/June 1997) surveyed these growing populist struggles in Bolivia, Brazil, Venezuela, Ecuador and Argentina in the wake of the movement in Chiapas while James Petras focused on the revival of the Latin American peasantry as a revolutionary force in the 1990s. During the previous period of counterrevolution peasants had responded to their growing economic difficulties by migrating to the cities. But in the late nineties peasant movements were resurgent in Colombia, Bolivia, Mexico and Paraguay. The Movement of the Landless (MST) in Brazil took its distance from the old Left, which was in a state of decay. The MST rooted its activities in democracy, collective leadership, mass mobilization and direct action. Marxism was fundamental to its ideology but so, too, was popular religiosity and communitarian practice. According to Petras (31:3, May/June 1997), the current global crisis had two aspects: collapsing communism and crisis-ridden neoliberalism. Ryan Thiessen (32:2, March/April 1998) surveyed the re-energized Colombian guerrilla insurgency, which was advancing despite drug wars and government supported terrorist campaigns and murders orchestrated with the complicity of the US. The rising tide of optimism about Latin America was reflected in a review of a newly-published biography of Che Guevera by John Lee Anderson (31:6, November/December 1997). While complimentary, Asad Asami notes that Anderson missed the broad historical context including the fact that Che was not the "new socialist man" that Anderson makes him out to be but, rather, part of Latin America's anti-US guerrilla tradition which included Augusto Sandino in Nicaragua, Camillo Torres in Colombia and Turcios Lima in Guatemala. The increasingly buoyant mood with respect to Latin America brought forth a piece by James Petras (32:5, September/October 1998) on that other socialist martyr, Salvador Allende. Based on personal acquaintance, Petras testified to the Chilean leader's openness, democratic instincts, internationalism and deep understanding of his country. Allende's understanding of the relationship between parliamentary and nonparliamentary politics provides an important lesson for today's socialist leaders, Petras reflected, as does Allende's integrity, which led him to pursue a legislative agenda based not on social-democratic sell-outs but on a thorough-going socialist agenda.

In the January/February 1999 issue (33:1) Petras addressed the concept of globalization, which had become the ideological buzzword of the decade. According to Petras, contemporary globalization retained many of the key features of the earlier phases of globalization: the driving forces are centred in the imperial state and the multinational corporation and banks, backed by the international financial institutions. What was significantly different was the scale, scope and speed of the circulation of capital and commodities, particularly financial flows between deregulated economies. Technological changes, especially in communications, were a prime factor in shaping the high velocity of movements of capital but scope and scale of movement of capital and commodities were due less to technological than to political changes. The demise of socialism in the former communist countries of Europe and Asia, the conversion of nationalist-populist third-world regimes to unregulated capital and the demise of the welfare state in the West opened vast areas for accumulation of profits and new markets for sales and investment. These political victories were central to the advance of globalization in relation to the period immediately following World War II, and certainly in relation to the interwar period. These processes are essentially imperialist, Petras insisted. The term globalization was invented by Western propagandists and ideologues to make it seem an inevitable and positive process.

In a subsequent article (38:6, November/December 2004) Petras evaluated the relative strength of the different imperialist powers by studying their multinational corporations. He found the US to be still overwhelmingly dominant with its control of 45 per cent of the top five hundred global corporations, Western Europe holding only 28 per cent and Asia only 18 per cent trailed behind. The three regional power blocs of the US, Europe and Asia controlled 91 per cent of the biggest multinational corporations. Overwhelmingly, then, "globalization" should be seen as a derivative of the power of the multinational corporations based in these power blocs to move capital and to control trade, credit, financing and entertainment. US and European capital have become increasingly interpenetrated. Despite this, Petras held out the possibility of growing tension between the US and Western Europe as a result of increasing differences over the Middle East.

The new century

Walden Bello (35:2, March/April 2001) announced the dawn of the new century for *Canadian Dimension* with his description of the rise of the antiglobalization movement. According to him, the previous year would probably go down as one of those defining moments in the history of the world economy. Of course, the structures of global capitalism appeared to be solid. Many in the global elite were congratulating themselves for containing the Asian financial crisis and trying to exude confidence about launching a new round of trade negotiations under the World Trade Organization (WTO). What the world witnessed, nevertheless, was a dramatic series of events that might, in fact, lead to that time when, as the poet said, "all that is solid melts into thin air." It began on November 30 to December 1, 1999, when the Third Ministerial of the WTO collapsed in Seattle and continued with a succession of protests all over the world against globalization. Reacting to the anarchist-inspired outbursts at the Quebec Summit of the Americas in April 2000 (35:4, July/August 2001), Ken Kalturnyk accepted the need for a violence from below as a response to violence above. But he also called for such actions to be related to real political goals and to be based on democratic decison-making.

In the lead-up to the Iraq war, an article by Perry Anderson (39:3, May/June 2005) denounced the project as a naked display of American unilateralism which could only foster rather than suppress anti-Western terrorism. As a preemptive strike it could only undermine respect for international law. On a lighter note (39:1, January/February 2005) Saul Landau pointed out that Bush's evangelically-guided imperialism in the Middle East was rooted in the beliefs of earlier US presidents. Notably, William McKinley's decision to seize the Philippines was similarly inspired: "I went down on my knees and prayed to Almighty God for light and guidance." American conquest of the islands cost two hundred thousand Filipino lives and led one critic to point out that: "G is for guns/That McKinley has sent/To teach Filipinos/What Jesus Christ meant." In his keynote address at a *CD* benefit in 2004 (39:1, January/February 2005), Noam Chomsky saw reason for hope in the unprecedented worldwide mobilization of public opinion against the invasion of Iraq. By 2005 Petras was able to point to the failure of the United States to pacify Iraq in the face of mounting guerilla resistance. In "The Empire in Year 2005" (39:2, March/April 2005) he also pointed to the growing weakness of the economic foundations of American imperialism and its lack of capacity to launch attacks elsewhere.

A bitter dispute broke out in the *Canadian Dimension* collective over the role of the pro-Israel lobby in determining American foreign policy toward the Middle East. It arose as a result of the publication of articles by both James Petras and Edward Herman on the overwhelming power of the Zionist lobby group AIPAC in American politics. While focusing on rich and powerful Zionist Jews, Petras (36:3, May/June 2002) castigated the moral blindness of much of the Jewish community with regard to the fate of the Palestinians. The subsequent course of the debate was summarized by editorial collective member Terry Murphy:

> *In a strongly-worded attack, editorial board member Abbie Bakan accused Herman and Petras of shifting the focus of the Left away from the strategic interests of US imperialism in the Middle East and fuelling anti-Semitism by their focus on the role of "rich Jews" in the formation of US foreign policy. Herman and Petras separately replied that Bakan was guilty of exaggeration and misrepresentation and that her claim of racism was indefensible. As Herman questioned, "Is a critique of the Cuban refugee terrorist network or an Italian mafia syndicate 'anti-Cuban' or 'anti-Italian'?" For his part Petras pointed to the empirically verifiable public records of organizations such as the American Israel Public Affairs Committee and the Conference of Presidents of Major American Jewish Organizations as evidence for his argument.*

In "Unusual Sensitivities" (36:4, July/August 2002), *Dimension* collective member Mordecai Briemberg placed the reasons for the ferocity of accusations against Herman and Petras in an unanalyzed fear of a second Jewish Holocaust. "Concerns about fuelling anti-semitism," he wrote, "should be addressed to the Israeli government, not directed against progressives who wish to analyze the structures and practices of Israeli state lobby forces within our own political system. People who are silenced out of fear, or people who rise above that fear only to face the indignity of smears and punishment are a seed-bed for the explosion of hate. But this does not trouble the power-holders of Israel who have demonstrated by their past record they were willing, and remain willing today, to sacrifice the security of Jews elsewhere in the world for their own colonial adventures and racist fantasies."

The Israeli occupation received continuous attention in *CD*. In "Unholy Alliance: Christian Zionists and the Israeli/Palestinian Conflict" (37:2, March/April 2003), Michael Welton reported that there are over two hundred different evangelical organizations in the US and Canada committed to Christian Zionism. They applaud the settlement movement and resist any move by US and Canadian governments, international agencies and civil society associations to press Israel for the implementation of UN Resolution 242, that Israel leave the occupied territories. "These groups have immense power," he wrote, "pumping their ideas and political strategies into American culture through church life, rallies, prophetic Bible conferences, tours to Israel, films, magazines, videos, pamphlets, web sites, well-heeled lobbies and insider political trading."

Daniel Freeman-Malory's "Organizing the Canada-Israel Alliance" (40:6, November/December 2006) described the bipartisan foreign policy alignment with the US, including far more explicit support for Israel than Canada exhibited in the past. The article provided an account of the organizations in Canada, tied to their US senior partners, especially the United Israel Appeal Federations Canada (UIAFC), American-Israel Public Affairs Committee (AIPAC) and the Canadian-Jewish Political Action Committee, their growth, practices and increasing influence in domestic politics and foreign policy.

Articles by Independent Jewish Voices (39:1, January/February 2005) and Edwin Janzen (40:5, September/October 2006), among others, promoted a Canadian boycott, divestment and sanctions campaign to thwart the occupation. Meanwhile, pointing out the parallel between Palestinians and the indigenous peoples of North America, Susan Abulhawa (42:2, March/April 2008) declared that "Palestinians are the natives of the land that was called Palestine until 1948 when Jewish foreigners changed its name to Israel."

The first decade of the new century saw the consolidation of populist or leftist regimes in many countries in Latin America. American hegemony over the region seriously eroded. *Dimension* reported and analyzed these developments by publishing articles on Mexico, Venezuela, Cuba, Colombia, Brazil and Bolivia. The revolutionary process in Bolivia became a particular focus of attention. James Petras (38:1, January/ February 2004) traced the evolution of the leadership of the revolutionary movement from the class-conscious, Marxist-led tin miners in the 1950s to the coca unions, the community-based urban coalitions of unions, consumers, street vendors and unemployed of the present. Susan Spronk and Jeffrey Weber (39:3, May/June 2005) sketched the growing social polarization between these elements and the Bolivian oligarchy over the control of water, hydrocarbon and mineral resources. *Dimension* noted the popular victory reflected through the election of Evo Morales as Bolivian president (2006) and the subsequent nationalization of the country's oil and gas resources (40:4, July/August 2006). At the forefront of the struggle in Bolivia was the peasantry. Petras (39:4, July/August 2005) painted a broad canvas of the peasant movements in Bolivia and throughout the countries of Latin America. The import of heavily subsidized foods and other inputs from abroad reduced prices and bankrupted peasants while the development of agro-exports led to the dispossession of the same small farmers. Dispossession meant not only loss of income but loss of family and community as well more often than not. Growing rural discontent was being led by a new generation of leaders who were better educated and independent of urban elites and party machines.

The changes sweeping Latin America were reflected in an article by *CD* collective member Greg Albo (39:2, March/April 2005) who reported on the Caracas Encounter in Defense of Humanity of early December 2004 attended by over 350 delegates from fifty-two countries. The Encounter was a public assertion of the emergence of a Cuban-Venezuelan political pole in Latin American politics against American imperialism and, with hardly a word being said, a challenge to the centre-left governments of the southern zone regarding their political accommodation to neoliberalism. The conference could be seen as an effort to re-form a revolutionary tendency across Latin America and a development that would be the real sign of a resurgence of the Latin American Left. The changes in Latin America as reflected in *Dimension* were not all positive. Two stories focused on the American-inspired second coup against the elected president of Haiti Jean-Baptiste Aristide (2004) and the occupation of the island by a UN military and police force subservient to the US.[2] *Dimension* ranged further afield with reports on the US occupation of Afghanistan and the development of the Taliban insurgency and on the growth of the Naxalite movement in India.[3]

The most striking new development in *Canadian Dimension* has been the spate of articles and editorials with titles like "Haiti: A Very Canadian Coup"(40:2, March/April 2006), "Canada Out of Afghanistan and Haiti" (40:3, May/June 2006), "Canada's Military Lobby" (40:4, July/August 2006), "Blood on Our Hands" (44:3, May/June 2010) and "Bad Neighbors: Canadian Mining Companies in Latin America" (45:1, January/February 2011). Greg Albo (40:6, November/December 2006) explained this in terms of the deeper integration of global capital and concurrent buildup of and cooperation between the security and global military apparatuses of the Canadian state and other capitalist states. But others have argued that Canada's increasingly aggressive foreign policy is not simply the result of the increasing integration of global capitalism. On the contrary, Jerome Klassen and Todd Gordon, for example, argue that Canada has become an imperialist state in its own right.[4] *Dimension* from its inception argued that Canada was a dependency of the United States and rejected the argument that it was itself an imperial power. In the November/December 2006 issue of *CD* (40:6), Cy Gonick finally grappled with the question of Canadian imperialism: "Canada an imperialist state? Yes, I would say — but only as a second-tier member of US-led collective imperialism. The American empire works through other states, including the Canadian state, and in this sense the Canadian state is complicit in imperialism and Canadian capital certainly benefits from imperialism."

In the last decade *Dimension* has been consistent in its focus on how Canadian mining companies have been exploiting Latin American workers, disrupting local communities and causing damage to the environment. Among the articles devoted to this theme see in particular "Barrick's Gold" by Ricardo Acuna (40:6, November/December 2006), "Goldcorp in Honduras" by Dawn Paley and "Canadian

Capital in south Asia" by Harsha Wallia (41:3, May/June 2007). In 2011 *Dimension* produced a special issue on Canadian mining in Latin America and Africa with an introduction by Cy Gonick titled "A Global Mining Powerhouse" (45:1, January/February 2011).

Conclusion

The valiant struggle of the Vietnamese, which was the catalyst of the revolts of the sixties, was the inspiration for the creation of *Dimension*. Entering the fifth decade of publication Anthony Black (34:4, July/August 2000) argued that the increasingly aggressive imperialism of the United States demonstrated that American involvement in the Vietnam War was no aberration. Black further argued that it was the Vietnam Peoples War above all that defeated the US and forced it to retreat. In his review of a new edition of Daniel Singer's *Prelude to Revolution*, a work which described the uprising in Paris in May, 1968, Herman Rosenfeld (37:2, March/April 2003) concluded that, despite the changes wrought by neoliberalism, there were lessons to be drawn from the 1960s for the possibility of revolution today:

- Young radicals, whether in the antiglobalization movement or other social-justice movements, need to find ways to use their energy, dynamism and fresh insights, to address the interests and struggles of the working class, and to familiarize themselves with and help apply Marxist theory to the present context.

- The working class — even the so-called "affluent workers" — retains the potential to challenge the system. Its seeds are there in the everyday lives we live: in our alienated, oppressive and precariously held jobs; in the difficulties we face in developing healthy communities and families, and in the declining prospects for our children and environment.

- In order for the working class to have any chance of developing its capacities to build a different kind of society, it needs access to a critique of the system — couched in its terms and integrated into its everyday experiences and struggles in the workplace and communities. Without this it is impossible to translate its concerns into a movement for fundamental change.

As if on cue, the Occupy movement arose just as *Canadian Dimension* entered its fiftieth year, a fitting bit of historical synchronicity. As remarked upon in a *CD* editorial (46:1, January/February, 2012), "Occupy Wall Street began as a single event and turned into one of the most significant mass movements in recent North American history. Above all, the occupations changed the nature of public debate. Deficit and austerity, previously the focus of political discourse, were forced to give way to talk of inequality, taxing the rich and freeing the state from control of the banks and industry. Conservative and liberal pundits alike now have to confront the failure of neoliberal capitalism."

CHAPTER 14
A Journey from Israel to Palestine
Mordecai Briemberg

It was nearly four years after *Canadian Dimension's* first issue that the subject of Israel appeared in its pages. And it was many years later before Palestine and Palestinians assumed a place of importance at the table of discussion. This long journey of "rediscovery" of the land and people of Palestine, unearthed from a superimposed Israel, is not unusual in Canadian progressive circles. But the fact that *Canadian Dimension* made that journey, and arrived where it is today, is an achievement to acknowledge and welcome.

1967 War

Prior to 1967 there were articles in *CD* centred on Jews (Gad Horowitz comparing the mosaic in Canada and the US), and articles about anti-semitism and hate literature, from Alberta to the Soviet Union. In a twenty-five-page supplement on "Canadian Foreign Policy — The Decade Ahead," the only reference to the Middle East was a passing comment on "Suez" and Canada's role in reconciling intra-imperial differences. No comment, certainly no critique of the British, French, Israeli invasion of Egypt seeking to crush pan-Arab nationalism.

For *Canadian Dimension* writers Israel's well-planned war of conquest was presented as a war of desperate "defence." Joe Flexer wrote that Israel faced "destruction and the physical annihilation of her people" (4:5, July/August 1967). And in the following issue, under the heading "Israel is not Vietnam," Cy Gonick wrote Israeli settlers never came as "exploiters of Arabs [but to] rediscover themselves as full human beings . . . Surely there can be no regret that Jews will never again allow themselves to be slaughtered as they did under the Nazis" (4:6, September/October 1967).

From this beginning *Canadian Dimension* began a definite and sustained, though not always direct move away from reflexive "defence" of Israeli actions and "denial" of its initiative and ambitions. Indeed in the very next issue, responding to a critical letter from a reader, after Cy Gonick repeated his earlier comment about resisting the danger of extermination, he immediately added a comment that points in a new direction: "On the other hand, the current Israeli policy of settling the conquered lands is equally foolish and, moreover, reprehensible" (5:1, November/December 1967). If "foolish" grows out of persisting concern for the self-interest of the Israeli state, "reprehensible" opens the door to concern for the well-being of Palestinians. And in the evolution of the magazine that concern occupies more and more space. This most often has taken the form of seeking an end to the Israeli occupation of lands conquered in the 1967 war as the precondition for the formation of an independent Palestinian state on the 1967 territories presently occupied by Israel.

In that context *Canadian Dimension* has brought to light and denounced Israeli ongoing war-making and war crimes, publicized and supported activists engaged in solidarity struggles for Palestinian human rights, and pinpointed networks and mechanisms in Canada and elsewhere that supporters of Israeli state policies use to discredit and silence critics of Israeli practices and policies. But before reviewing these and other important positive contributions of *Canadian Dimension* in greater detail, it is necessary to recognize a worm within the apple of a "Palestinian state" in the 1967 occupied territories.

Partition

To be sure, *Canadian Dimension* is far from alone in its reach for a second partition of Palestine. After all, the imperial schemes of partition of Mandate Palestine have a long history, in which Canada — and most prominently Lester Pearson — played important parts. Moreover the

345

Palestine Liberation Organization (PLO) itself turned onto this path in the late 1970s, and with the Oslo agreement of 1993 formally sanctified a "two-state" agreement as the terminus of its journey. In these circumstances it is not so surprising that the memory of an alternative objective quickly fades.

But not for everyone.

It is much to the credit of *Dimension*, that it published (35:3, May/June 2001) the text of a February 2001 talk by Azmi Bishara. Azmi Bishara, a Palestinian citizen of Israel, was a founder of the political party Tajamu' (in Arabic), under whose banner he campaigned and was elected to the Israeli parliament (Knesset). The speech originally appeared in a wonderfully stimulating, now sadly defunct magazine, *Between the Lines*, produced in Jerusalem by two collaborating editors, one Palestinian and one Jewish Israeli, Toufic Haddad and Tikva Honig-Parnass, a publication that *CD* highly recommended to its own readers.

Bishara titled his talk "Apartheid Consciousness and the Question of Palestine." Originally presented a dozen years ago, it now resonates so closely with current discussions of one single democratic state for Palestinians and Jews, that it would be both useful and appropriate for the magazine to republish it, as a contribution to a discussion that is gaining momentum.[1] Here is a brief excerpt from that text:

> [T]he commonly used conceptual perception of "occupied territories" to be solved by a "Palestinian state" is not a very good tool to understand what is going on here . . . Many Israelis, particularly those . . . who consider themselves supportive of the Palestinian cause, deluded themselves into thinking that the Palestinians are not struggling for freedom, liberation and equality or any of these "western values," but are struggling for a state. I call this "state fetishism." According to this system of thinking Palestinians should sacrifice everything in order that they can have their own prisons and their own police force.
>
> In fact the national charter of the Palestine Liberation Organization of 1965 and 1968, equivalent to the charter

of the African National Congress in South Africa, made
no mention of a state. Many of its articles make mention
of "liberating Palestine," but not one word is said about a
"Palestinian state" . . .

Oslo has proven that it is impossible for the Zionist
movement to give up the lands occupied in 1967 . . . Now
if Zionism cannot do this, then the "two state solution" can
more accurately be described as the "Tale of Two States"
There will be no two states . . . If we begin to understand
and perceive the situation from the perspective of an
"apartheid regime" — something that still remains to be
done — and not within the limiting framework of the
"1967 occupation," we will start thinking of strategies that
lead to liberation of two nationalities in one state.

Exploring these strategies needs to be the central focus of future discussions. But much can be learned already from the accumulated commentary that *CD* has published since 1967. So let us turn to that.

Since 1967

Israel's abuse of Palestinians under its rule has been documented in the magazine, and exposed for its cruelties. But sometimes a "cartoon" is the most incisive, and *CD* has used these as well. One of my favourites is a drawing by Bill Schorr. Two Israeli soldiers, helmeted and with rifles pointing forward, stand behind a small child, facing his mother poking her head out the front door, mouth agape. "We caught him throwing stones . . . so we're gonna bulldoze your house."

Israel's international role has been more shadowy for most, but *CD* has cast its light here too. The first to bring forth evidence, in a letter, was Claire Culhane, a courageous opponent of the US war, who worked in Vietnam. She informed readers of meeting in Germany a group of young Israelis being sent to Saigon for three months to "teach judo combat tactics." She says she tried to convince them to disobey orders (8:3, November/December 1971). Contributor Bryon Smith undertook an analysis of Israel's counterrevolutionary involvements in Central America

347

(17:3, July 1983). He documented Israel as an arms supplier for several repressive dictatorships in the world, and the central arms source during the 1970s for dictatorships in El Salvador, Guatemala and Nicaragua. Human rights efforts in the US had had some effect in restricting that government's direct aid for these dictatorships, and Israel was "acting as a US surrogate." Smith also demonstrated the significant stake the Histadrut, the Israeli "trade union" federation, had in the arms industry through "SOLTAM," the major armaments company it owned.

Jack Colhoun draws on several Israeli and other sources to document the "Israeli-South African Collaboration" (21:3, May/June 1987) — from economic to military, including nuclear arms development — during the global campaign of boycott, divestment and sanctions to end South African apartheid.

Israel's nuclear arms policy and arsenal has been discussed in *CD*, mainly centred on the brave Israeli nuclear technician and whistle-blower Mordechai Vanunu. He had worked at Israel's Dimona nuclear reactor, documented weapons production, and taken photos and information to England where they were published in the *Sunday Times*. Israel soon lured Vanunu to Italy where he was kidnapped, shackled, transported to Israel, sentenced in a secret trial and imprisoned for eighteen years, more than eleven of them in solitary confinement, as explored in "A Man for the Time" (23:1, January/February 1989) and "Vanunu's Truth" (31:2, March/April 1997).

And of course Israel's role as a partner in the imperial control of the Middle East region as a whole has been analyzed in *CD*. One brilliant example was Tom Naylor's dissection of Israel's Orwellian-named "Peace for Galilee," their 1982 ruthlessly destructive and deadly invasion of Lebanon. Detailed, informed and analytical, Naylor's work exposed the grandiose ambitions of conquest, with Israel and the US aiming to reshape the Middle East in their interest (17:2, May 1983). One reader's "disappointment, dismay and disgust . . . in [Naylor's] attempt to blacken the Israelis, but more seriously to reflect on Jewish morality . . . [a] thinly veiled demonstration of anti-Semitism" led him to cancel his subscription "forthwith" (17:4, September 1983).

This effort to dismiss political criticism by simply labelling it "anti-Semitic" (or "new anti-Semitism" as the rebranding goes) and thereby sidestepping the responsibility of responding with substantive arguments, is a standard device of devotees of Israel. It is a ploy to divert discussion, blacken critics and ultimately to silence all but Israel's cheerleaders. So how has *CD* dealt with charges of anti-Semitism/new anti-Semitism?

Anti-semitism, "new anti-semitism" and hate . . .

Canadian Dimension has not been hesitant in supporting individuals and organizations against whom such slanders have been levelled. See, for example, Sid Shniad's "B'nai Brith uses human rights complaint to squelch criticism of Israel" (41:5, September/October 2007). And Richard Sanders, expert on the Canadian war-making industry, wrote "Banning Art: blaming the victim and rewarding Canadian war exporters" (43:3, May/June 2009). He took to task the president of Carleton University, Roseanne Runte, for banning student use of a poster showing an Israeli AH-64 attack helicopter shooting at a child in Gaza, promoting "Israeli Apartheid Week." She said the posters "were deemed . . . to incite hatred," although this precise helicopter was one of Israel's major weapons in its 2008–2009 bombardment of Gaza, killing 1,400 people — over 400 of them children. Sanders reported that at least fifty Canadian military industries "manufacture key components" for the helicopter depicted in the poster and "two other major US weapons exported to Israel, namely F-15 and F-16 warplanes." Yet the same president refused the request of fifty-six professors at her university to sign a condemnation of Israel's violation of human rights caused by the bombing of a Gazan university.

Beyond support of those abused by false accusations of spreading "hate" and "anti-semitism," *CD* has delved more deeply into the philosophical concepts and historical trends important to grasp if one aims for a secure footing on this slippery terrain. Helpful in this regard are two articles by Yakov M. Rabkin (43:6, November/December 2009; 44:1, January/February 2010). He carefully distinguished Zionism, the political philosophy guiding Israel, from religious tenets of Judaism. Rabkin argued that "Zionism has been a rebellion against traditional

Judaism," to the extent that Theodor Herzl, the founder of Zionism, "considered anti-Semites 'friends and allies' of his movement." For both considered Jews a "distinct people or race," not a "transnational and extraterritorial . . . identity centred on the Torah," as religious Jews saw themselves. As well, both anti-Semites and Zionists worked to "transfer the Jews from their countries of origin." For the Zionists the goal was to "establish political and economic control over the land [of Palestine], if need be by force."

The familiar accusation that criticism of Israel is an attack on Jews, most often a direct expression of anti-Semitism, is at the very least a practice that nurtures anti-Jewish hatred. Yakov Rabkin countered this smear with the argument that it is the conflation of Israel and Jews that "implicates Jews around the world into what Israel is and does . . . [and so] predictably foments anti-Semitism and breeds anti-Jewish violence . . . Conversely [when] Jews speak against Israeli action . . . that flies in the face of the anti-Semitic canard of world Jewish conspiracy."

The evolution of Christian Zionism, which pre-dates Jewish Zionism, and its size, which outnumbers Jewish Zionists, was the focus of a very important article by Michael Welton, published almost a decade earlier (37:2, March/April 2003). Welton described Christian Zionism's theological origins, its current organizational forms, and political influence. He commented on how the founding of the Israeli state in 1948 "fuelled [Christian Zionists] with tremendous nervous energy," a sign "history was moving rapidly towards the final events." In the words of Jerry Falwell, quoted in Rabkin's article, 1948 was the "most crucial event in history since the ascension of Jesus to heaven . . . Without a State of Israel in the Holy Land, there cannot be the second coming of Jesus Christ, nor can there be a Last Judgement, nor the End of the World." Welton added that for Christian Zionists Israeli 1967 conquests also were an antidote for a "U.S. mired in Vietnam apparently losing."

But surely the actions of the Israeli state are of concern to more than Christians and Jews. Or are they? Sometimes it appears the answer is "no."

More Palestinian voices will help part the heavy clouds of suspicion and racial prejudice that still cast doubt upon the common humanity

Palestinians share with us all. Needed are more voices like those of the three hip-hop artists DAM interviewed in "Hip Hop Palestinian Style" (44:3, May/June 2010), the passionate and analytical *cri de coeur* of Susan Abulhawa's "Our home and native land: Palestine" (42:2, March/April 2008) and the "Urgent call to world civil society" circulated by prominent figures of Palestinian civil society (36:3, May/June 2002).

The journey from Israel to Palestine also has been normalized by being integrated into the magazine as a whole: from discussion of musical, literary, and artistic creativity, to feminist, queer and labour activism; from cover features to editorials to regular short announcements of solidarity activities. And importantly, analysis of and support for the Palestinian struggle has appeared with increasing frequency over the years.

Activism

The two on-going international Palestinian solidarity campaigns — the educational campaign centring on Israeli Apartheid and the Boycott, Divestment and Sanctions campaign — have been actively supported by *Canadian Dimension*. The magazine has also advocated for change in Canada of government policy on Israel and Palestinian rights.

A divisive question for the magazine has been whether analysis and critique of the organization and activities of the pro-Israeli lobby, particularly including that part of the lobby based in the Jewish community, is necessary or counterproductive for building an effective Palestine solidarity movement. This was debated in three issues 36:3 (May/June 2002), 36:4 (July/August 2002) and 36:6 (November/December 2002). While a lot of the discussion focused on the situation in the US, *CD* has published more substantial analysis of the lobby in Canada written by the late David Noble, "The New Israel Lobby in Action (39:6, November/December 2005) and Daniel Freeman-Maloy's "Organizing the Canada-Israel Alliance" (40:6, November/December 2006).

David Noble, both in analysis and in action, also demonstrated how to integrate resistance to Zionism with resistance to other reactionary trends. See his two articles "Private Pretensions: The Battle for Canadian Universities" (39:5, September/October 2005) and

"Reviving the Radical Critique of Religion" (40:1, January/February 2006). Perhaps the highlight of skillful and essential "weaving of strands" has been Tim McCaskell's feature article "Queers Against Apartheid: From South Africa to Israel" (44:4, July/August 2010). He reasoned carefully from direct experience, spanning countries and decades, how sexual liberation is bound up with liberation from racism and the colonial projects that generate it.

Generations

Canadian Dimension began its long journey to Palestine by viewing the landscape in 1967 from the perspective of the Israeli state. This didn't go without angry comment at the time. Stan Gray raged, "I can't stomach the Zionism" (6:8, April/May 1970), and Edward Herman called *CD*'s "treatment of Israel very bad — indefensible and wholly unrealistic sentimentality" (7:4, October/November 1970).

Since then *CD*, as I have tried to document, has markedly shifted to become a voice of support for Palestinian people's rights, a voice for deepening critiques of the dominant Zionist trend that has shaped Israeli state practices, and an opponent of efforts of Israeli boosters to silence and sanction those with whom they disagree. This has happened over a period of time that can be characterized as generational, as the founders of *CD* willingly incorporated younger people with different starting points and trajectories on this question. At least so I hypothesize.

As one very preliminary and simple exploration of that hypothesis I composed a set of questions, and simultaneously posed them to Cy Gonick and Ed Janzen. Cy has been the driving force of *CD* from the beginning, and wrote several of the first articles and has remained engaged throughout the "journey from Israel to Palestine." Ed Janzen, an active member of the *CD* collective for many years, coming from a different cultural milieu and a younger generation, became engaged with the Palestinian liberation struggle and Israel in the twenty-first century. To close this chapter here are some of their comments framed in response to my questions.

Following are the words of Cy Gonick:

I joined up as a member of a labour Zionist movement in 1948. I was twelve years old. My interest then had nothing to do with Israel per se, but with the kibbutz, which I understood to be an experiment in communistic living and economy. I was interested in that. At that time and for a few years after, the Jewish community in Winnipeg, as I experienced it, was very divided about Israel. As unlikely as that would seem today, probably most were actually antagonistic to the founding of the state, seeing it as possibly upsetting their increasingly comfortable existence in the diaspora. That changed dramatically with the Six-Days War. My initial position was expressed in an article in CD titled "Israel is not Vietnam" and in a subsequent long exchange with one of our readers. There, looking back at it now, my intent was to defend Israel's right to exist as a Jewish state while surrounded by Arab states determined to crush it. I even defended the Jewish Agency's land acquisition policies prior to 1948. I interpreted its actions in Suez in 1956 supporting western imperialism as the price it had to play to retain US and French support against hostile neighbouring states. Similarly, I interpreted its military action against Egypt, Syria and Jordan in the Six-Days War as a defensive action to avoid being crushed by Arab states that were amassing troops on its borders. While I argued that these actions would ultimately fail to win a secure place for Israel in the Middle East, there were no other available options. I also noted that establishing Jewish settlements in the conquered lands was a disaster in the making and "reprehensible."

After I visited Israel in the summer of 1968 (I spent most of that visit on a kibbutz) I was invited to speak to a Winnipeg Jewish audience about my views on Israel . . . The line I presented there was, in retrospect, very moderate but it raised a storm of protest as I was denounced one after another by virtually every leader of the community and I have never been asked by them to speak on the subject since. The message was that while for Jews the establishment of the state was The Great Return, for Palestinians it was The Great Invasion and that the struggle there was between two legitimate nations over the rights to the same small strip of land.

It's interesting to me that in contrast to the Six-Days War, I can barely remember the 1973 Yom Kippur War — except for the resulting oil embargo launched by members of OPEC in retaliation against US decision to resupply the Israeli military for its extensive losses during the war launched initially by Egypt and Syria, later joined by Iraq. This indicates to me that by then I had lost whatever emotional attachments to Israel that still remained from the time of my youth . . . And I have been entirely alienated from the Jewish community for over forty years.

By then, my sense of Israel was entirely focused on the occupation. I was one of the founders of Independent Jewish Voices a few years back and a supporter of the movement against Israel Apartheid.

Following are words of Ed Janzen:

I grew up in both a religious (Mennonite) family, and a very academic one too. My first images of Israel were the colourful maps in the back of my Bible (for a kid, the only interesting part!) and maps and images of archaeological artifacts . . . [As an undergraduate] I still knew relatively little about Israel in its twentieth-century form. But I had friends who were well versed in Palestine solidarity politics and history, and my involvement in the student press and student politics quickly led me in that direction.

[I]t was with great interest that I discovered the Israel/Palestine conflict, especially how anyone who criticized Israel quickly stirred the wrath of a group of people whose

354

politics were mostly right-wing and whose thinking was
very problematic, even in many cases genuinely crazy and
stupid. But their passion about the subject was screaming
virulent, and I was amazed at how wildly they threw
about accusations of anti-Semitism . . . So, witnessing
how criticism of Israel drove these doltish right-wing Israel
apologists genuinely bonkers — dependably, every last
time — my instincts (the journalist's "nose for a story,"
perhaps?) told me there was work to be done, here, for
anyone willing to do it.

Reading and learning about the Israel/Palestine conflict
was peeling back the layers of an onion — each one a
demonstrably false claim or myth about Israel's inherent
goodness. I was simply astounded how a brutal little war
of independence in which one people stole the lands and
rights of another could be and had been completely rewritten
into a narrative of glorious independence, vindication
from the shame of the Holocaust, "progressive" civilization
against the benighted Arab world, and so forth. I was also
astounded how widely this narrative was accepted with few
or no questions, especially in North America.

I believe that at root the conflict stems from various
strains of anti-Semitic thinking among the nations of Europe
and North America. The creation of a Jewish state always
appealed to white European racists, from Hitler (at least in
his thinking prior to his shift toward a "Final Solution") to
Churchill to Lord Balfour (the influence of whose infamous
"Balfour Declaration" is well known). Leaders like these saw
a Jewish state as a fine way to impel Jews to leave Britain,
Germany, wherever, leaving those countries' cities, clubs,
beaches, etc., thus cleansed of a "foreign element" perceived
by them to be troublesome, subversive, or simply distasteful.
And many Jews, including Jewish leaders, opposed Zionism
for the same reason (as well as for other reasons, too, in
some cases).

Today, the mother lode of support for a Jewish state comes from the American religious Right, or "Christian Zionists." Religiously speaking, these people and their organizations are anti-Semitic in the truest sense, insofar as they believe that the End Times are imminent and that God will destroy any Jews who do not convert to Christianity and banish their souls, deservedly, to Hell for eternity. Zionist these Christians may be, but by no measure are they "pro-Jewish."

One of the great things about having been active on Palestine solidarity has been the political "spinoffs" it produced in my thinking. Learning about apartheid via books, films, etc., as well as cooperation between CanPalNet-Winnipeg and other activist organizations (Friend of Grassy Narrows, for example), taught me a great deal about the ugliest colonialist chapters of Canada's history, about what being Canadian really means. This may seem odd or ass-backwards — learning about Israel first and my own country second — until you consider how poorly educated the majority of Canadians are regarding pretty much all matters Aboriginal.

This is what makes the Israel/Palestine conflict so important: It really does represent a decision about the kind of world in which we wish to live. Will it be a world ruled by white supremacy and colonization, or one in which indigenous peoples are able to govern themselves and enjoy the same rights and freedoms as everyone else?

Some people say that Israel must be brought into compliance with the various relevant UN resolutions on the matter. I agree that it should, but I'm not sure that a resolution will come on such terms. I feel that the process of resolving the conflict will be far muddier, and will happen as a result of social and geopolitical changes in the region.

PART VII

DIMENSIONS OF POLITICAL ECONOMY

CHAPTER 15
Beyond Economic Nationalism: Clashes with Canadian Capitalism

Greg Albo and Chris Bailey

Assessing capitalist development in any particular state immediately confronts the limit that capitalism always exists as a world market. Adam Smith, the eighteenth-century founder of modern political economy, first made the claim that *The Wealth of Nations* (1776) was limited by the extent of the market — already long constituted as a world market with the great plunder of "the discoveries" and the Atlantic slave trade. But it was Karl Marx, writing in the nineteenth century, who clarified the issue, observing that capital strives "to tear down every spatial barrier to intercourse, i.e., to exchange, and conquer the whole earth for its market."[1] If the production of use-values and labour-processes are always concrete, local and embedded in the political relations of states, the pursuit of exchange-values through the circulation of capital universalizes capitalist social relations across the world market.

The accumulation of total social capital, as the movement of value in Volume 2 of Marx's *Capital* is referred to, is always the accumulation and internationalization of particular forms of capital — money capital (loans and financial assets), productive capital (foreign direct investment — FDI) and commodity capital (traded goods). Multinational corporations organize these flows in a series of interconnected labour processes and value chains. This forms the basis for the interpenetration of national and foreign capitals and the spread of capitalist social relations. As a consequence, capital accumulation in any particular place (or national space) entails a specific insertion into the international division of labour and the world market, formed into an imperialist chain from the dominant imperial centres to the weakest links in the periphery. States do not exist as mere appendages to the flows of value: their national and local economic policies are central to the international movement of capital via exchange rates, tariff policies, export finance, regulations over capital movements and so forth. The state is, as Marx put it, "the form of organization which the bourgeois necessarily adopt for internal and external purposes, for the mutual guarantee of their interests and property."[2]

As capitalism developed in the twentieth century, an additional — somewhat contentious — thesis gained prominence in Marxian political economy. As world commodity exchanges increase in their complexity and volume, a "nationalization" occurs through, on the one hand, the formation of an ever more intricate inter-state system and, on the other, capitalist states extending their range of activities and sophistication to provide the physical and administrative infrastructures that undergird ever more massive fixed capital complexes and extensive circuits of capital. State economic policy thus occupies, irrespective of the particular economic doctrine guiding policy-makers, an increasingly prominent role in facilitating accumulation. An aphorism from *The Communist Manifesto* has gained in its theoretical and political salience over time: "Though not in substance, yet in form, the struggle of the proletariat with the bourgeoisie is at first a national struggle. The proletariat of each country must, of course, first of all settle matters with its own bourgeoisie."[3]

The nationality of states and the internationalization of capital

The contradiction between the nationality of states and the internationalization of capital is, then, a constitutive feature of capitalism and a point of concentration of class struggles. It is the basis, however, of much confusion and division in economic analysis and strategy.

In the liberal ideology that dominates intellectual discourse in Canada, it is the Smithian theme of "truck, barter and exchange" that pervades explanations of Canadian history. From the colonial fur trade to the modern tar sands, it is individual entrepreneurs — even when commanding huge bureaucratic corporations — responding to market incentives that forged the commercial empires that converted the Canadian wilderness into today's post-industrial economy.[4] The conventional texts used to teach the history of capitalist development in Canada have all had this theme — W.T. Easterbrook and Hugh Aitken into the 1980s, and Kenneth Norrie and Doug Owram since the 1990s.[5] The hegemony of this narrative is such that it even informs Canadian social democracy. From the initial *Social Planning for Canada* (1935) through the periodical *Canadian Forum* to current ideologues for a "third way," it is the market that is given analytical weight, if supported by the Canadian state promoting the "defensive expansion" of Canada and social reforms.

For the emerging New Left in Canada in the 1960s, such a political economy of Canada would hardly do. It left to the side — even to this day — the colonial occupation of Aboriginal peoples and territories, the exploitation of workers, the location of the Canadian state within the British and American empires and much else.[6] From the outset, *Canadian Dimension* (*CD*) launched a more critical view of Canadian capitalism drawing upon the thematics of Marx, if still often crossed with Smithian notions. This meant closer scrutiny of the unequal relations of power and exploitation between workers and corporations, indigenous peoples and settlers, men and women, endless consumption and nature, Quebec and English Canada and between Canada and the US empire. These inequalities had to be assessed, a good portion of the New Left argued, in terms of the uniqueness of Canadian capitalism and its particular dependence on the US. It followed that Canada needed to disengage from the American empire via a national political front to avert a spiral of deindustrialization and decline.

But for others Canadian capitalism was located within the core zone of advanced capitalism and, for reasons of geography and economic calculus, a close ally of the American state. The particular Canadian issues of democratic sovereignty and social inequalities were no different in kind from those facing other core states. The central political question was whether political forces could be marshalled that could push beyond the limits of the social democratic management of Canadian capitalism to form an explicitly anticapitalist political pole and platform.

The critical analysis of the political economy of Canada has had, of course, many other themes and variations over the last fifty years. But the economic consequences and the political import of the ownership and production patterns of Canada's place in the world market remains a fundamental division in the interrogation of Canadian capitalism. CD's archive of essays provides unique insight into the Canadian New Left — where it has been, what it is, where it yet needs to go.

The 1960s: Economic nationalism and public ownership

In postwar Canada, these debates held a special prominence. The twin crises of depression and war completed Canada's transition from alignment within the British empire to the American one — a conversion also of financing development from British portfolio capital to US direct investment. Postwar reconstruction in Canada, moreover, integrated capital markets and labour processes across a series of sectors that began forming a North American economic bloc.

The closer ties to the US appeared, to Canada's political and business elites, to be enormously beneficial to Canada. The pace of economic growth over the period produced an unprecedented boom, with unemployment staying low into the 1970s. The spread of Fordist mass production facilitated a new basis for value production in the manufacturing sector in Canada and "catch-up" to US productivity levels. Many of the leading firms were American multinational corporations (MNCs). Their investment in branch-plants in key sectors, such as steel, autos, defence and others, aided by Canadian and US government policies for integration, gave them a prominent position in Canadian industry. Indeed, the value flows between the two countries became critical to Canadian development. Canadian trade with the US, for example, grew to occupy the vast bulk of trade, built around resource exports but with defence and automotive goods manufacturing also prominent. Like other zones of the world, Canada relied on imports of American manufacturing and capital goods, typically leaving Canada in a current account deficit with the US. This deficit, in turn, was covered by imports of US capital, especially in the form of long-term Foreign Direct Investment (FDI), which eventually consolidated into American majority ownership of Canadian production capacity that was unique among states.

Canada's new place in the postwar configuration of the world market meant that any economic turbulence, domestic or international, quickly registered instability of the Canadian dollar (uniquely allowed to float in terms of the American dollar standard of the Bretton Woods fixed exchange rate system). Not only were US MNCs a central feature of capital accumulation in Canada, the Canadian state and economic policy now revolved around US policies — fiscal policies in terms of expenditures and taxation, monetary policy in terms of interest rates, commercial policies in terms of regulatory standards, and so forth. Keynesianism in Canada did not directly mirror the US policy framework, but there was an unmistakable structural dependency of US policy initiative and Canadian response. At the time, the leading liberal political economist in Canada, Harold Innis, worried about the new forms of imperialism emerging with the rise of American power.[7] By the 1960s, the issue was shaking key nodes of power in the Canadian state. First, it destabilized the Conservative Diefenbaker government over the "Coyne Affair," with the sitting Governor Bank of Canada pushed out and the benefits of American foreign capital inflows reasserted. In turn, Walter Gordon as Liberal Minister of Finance was driven from office over his policies to increase national control over industry in favour of maintaining more "American-friendly" financial policies.

Postwar integration with the US generated caution from political elites and even sharp division in the 1960s (unlike the boosterism that would characterize the elite response to free trade in the 1980s). On the left it was also — and remains so — a matter of considerable tension. Political economists have invented any number of terms to summarize Canada's national capitalism and its relation to the American empire — rich dependency, continentalism, staples-led Keynesianism, periphery of the core, American satellite, permeable Fordism, among others. As far back as the Socialist Party of Canada, there were warnings of a lack of national control over industry, and the key strategic document for social democracy in Canada, *Social Planning for Canada*, cautioned that "even when we socialize industry it will be difficult to rid ourselves of the annual tribute to the foreign investor."[8] David Lewis and Frank Scott's *Make This Your Canada* (1943) was but one of a series of texts to pose the question of national control of the Canadian economy.

For the Communist Party of Canada, American FDI held great strategic significance. US FDI in Canada represented imperialist capital blocking democratic sovereignty and the consolidation of state monopoly capitalism. The Canadian road to socialism, as in other national states, had to pass through a "national-democratic" stage. A flurry of books and pamphlets — *Canadian Independence and a People's Parliament: Canada's Path to Socialism* (1954) and *Lenin and Canada* (1970) — pitched the theme of a "popular front" of people's organizations in alliance with smaller national capitals against the monopolies to gain national and then democratic control of the Canadian economy.

Any critical publishing project in Canada in the early 1960s could not avoid engaging this political terrain. Indeed, under the publishing leadership of Cy Gonick, *CD* became a focal point of dispute over the economic consequences of FDI for national development, sovereignty and advance toward socialism. A debate centred, in other words, on whether a project of economic nationalism could unify the nationality of capital and the nationality of the state.[9]

The dialogue started, not surprisingly, in the first issue of *CD* and set out (in Keynesian terms) a focus on ownership of the Canadian economy that dominated policy and political debate in the magazine for almost two decades. In "Foreign Investment in Canada" (1:1-2, October/November 1963), Scott Gordon observed that "foreign control of Canadian industry is rapidly emerging as a matter of the highest importance in Canadian political and economic discussion." For Gordon, Canada had long relied on foreign capital for development, had few burdens yet and several advantages from foreign ownership, and mainly suffered from an inefficient industry structure and the undue influence of Washington on Canadian industry and policy. In this way, Gordon argued, foreign ownership was particularly a "political problem." As such, there was a need for a "deliberate policy of Canadianizing the ownership . . . of our industry" and enactment of "legislation against further growth of foreign ownership.".

If Gordon set out some of the problems being raised by FDI in Canada, he offered little in the way of an alternate economic strategy and seemed to affirm, by implication if nothing else, the policy departures of Walter Gordon to increase Canadian ownership. The critical views emerging within industrial economics at the time about the linkage between nationality of the ownership of firms and their economic behaviour were, moreover, completely ignored. But essays that soon followed by H.C. Pentland, Charles Taylor and Gonick — three prominent radical academics — laid out more critical assessments of FDI replete with dire warnings about FDI and bolder ambitions for economic policy.

Writing at the end of the early 1960s recessionary cycle and policy instability ("A Plan for a Canadian Owned Economy," 1:8, September/ October 1964), Pentland attributed the problems of "distortion of the Canadian economy, political dependence and burden of dividend payments" to the foreign ownership of industry. Foreign capital is now unnecessary to fund development as Canadian savings are now adequate, and now perpetuates a cycle of foreign ownership, economic stagnation and political fragmentation. Pentland suggested several Keynesian failings from FDI: in a recessionary phase, foreign capital inflows displace domestic savings and do not expand planned investment; the flow of capital inward keeps exchange rates high, penalizing exports; and large current account deficits become self-sustaining. What was needed, Pentland argued, was a new national policy centred on a programme for Canada to drive up and "finance its own investment and repatriate its foreign-owned assets."

Charles Taylor went further with his view of foreign ownership as a general political problem for Canada: "We must choose: either we do something as an independent power or become annexationists" ("Alternatives to Continentalism," 3:5, July/August 1966,). For Taylor Canada was a "bicultural" country limited by its continental economy. American capital invests in natural resources to export back into the US, but also hops over the tariff barrier to set up "as duplicate in miniature of the American economy" resulting in an inefficient branch-plant manufacturing sector. This was, in good part, due to the parent company forcing its foreign subsidiaries to operate and limited their linkages in the host economy. The Gordon strategy of encouraging minority Canadian ownership was, for Taylor, "absurd" and a "Canadian designed economy" could only come via "public ownership and planning, with mobilization of Canadian investment resources in government hands" But a pan-Canadian Left lacked a "political vehicle for . . . [this] model of Canadian development." Taylor elaborated his views a year later in a controversial essay, "Nationalism and Independence" (4:3, March/April 1967), where he tied his previous stance directly to neomercantalist contentions: "The political economy of independence concerns principally a nation's foreign trade position . . . The major problem of Canadian independence is therefore the problem of developing a more favourable balance of trade." As this was due to the branch-plant economy, Taylor put forward a strategy to address the branch-plant economy — reducing the proportion of foreign direct equity investment, partly from a phased reduction in tariffs that lessen incentives for branch plants; guidelines and disclosure requirements for foreign subsidiaries; and extensive investment, via a Canadian Development Corporation, in public entrepreneurship. But if a year earlier the Canadian Left lacked a political instrument, "a new political alliance . . . is already being attempted by the New Democratic Party."

In the following issue, Gonick took the analysis a step further in drawing the implications of "Canada within the American Empire." In "The Political Economy of Canadian Independence" (4:4, May/June 1967), he departed from Pentland and Taylor both in terms of analysis of the uniqueness of the Canadian case and the anticapitalist implications of Canadian independence. "Canada is a small regional economy within the continental North American economy . . . [And] we should bear in mind that capitalism is an international system rather than a national system." The staples theory explains, he argued, a "kind of imperial relationship." The key agent in the current period is the US MNC which structures a similar dependent relationship with other parts of the world with the same linkages between foreign ownership and trade via intra-firm transfers. Indeed, a web of dependency forms via innovation blockages, branch-plant inefficiencies, transfer pricing, strategic resource calculation and so forth. The activist policies of liberal and even social democratic nationalists lack support "within the ruling circles of Canada . . . [as] Canadian business is thoroughly integrated into the continental economic structure."

For Gonick, the anti-corporate conclusion seamlessly followed: "Within the framework of a corporation-centred market economy, continentalism is necessary because independence is impossible." Here, too, Gonick departed from previous interventions, for an independent Canadian economy "is impossible without socialism . . . giving socialism a relevance it has not had for over 30 years. But this will only occur when the issue of Canadian independence dominates the politics of this country." The alternate program Gonick proffered built on Pentland and Taylor in widening the case for mobilization of internal savings, reorienting Canadian international policies and state funding, and pushing for more nationalizations and public ownership. But it differed from them in suggesting an explicit left united front strategy — "a new organization is needed to mobilize the majority nationalist sentiment in the country . . . [to] create a new political environment in which socialism could ultimately emerge as a real possibility in Canada."

If all three were calls for a radical political intervention, framed in terms of economic nationalism and public ownership, partly through the NDP but backed by other movements for democracy, the echoes of the CP's popular democratic front strategy were unmistakeable. But for an emerging New Left this meant a commitment to participatory democracy and not the command planning and democratic centralism of the Soviet Union. These were, clearly, some of the analytical seeds that would form the Waffle Movement. The analysis gained, moreover, wide political cachet when the US government forwarded guidelines for US MNCs at the end of 1965 that applied extra measures on their subsidiaries to improve the American balance of payments situation. According to sharp assessments from Eric Kierans ("The Political Economy of Guidelines," 3:3-4, March/June 1966) and Gonick ("Guidelines and Counter-Guidelines," 3:3-4, March/June 1966), these measures directly compromised the autonomy of the Canadian state. For Kierans, Canada "must orient our economic policy as to encourage the growth and development of large-scale Canadian enterprises" while for Gonick, this was cause for economic planning and "widespread public ownership."

The debates over FDI were not the only issues drawing a radical rethink of Canadian political economy. A series of other essays in the 1960s focused on poverty, unemployment, wages and technological change. At the outset, this was put in terms of firmer Keynesian state intervention, as in an opening editorial on "Poverty in Canada" (1:6, May/June 1964): "In Canada today the two major problems are the elimination of poverty and the provision of steady growth and full employment . . . [A]ny general economic policy must take into account the two facts of the 1960s which overshadow all others in their economic implications — automation and the large numbers of new entrants in the labour force . . . They also mean that the work week will decline to perhaps 30 hours by 1975 . . . [T]he adjustments they require will be painful unless they are averted by conscious government effort." But the limits of orthodox Keynesian policies also began to be explored. Raymond Franklin, for example, introduced the American debate on monopolies through Paul Baran and Paul Sweezy's *Monopoly Capital* (1966). Its Marxian critique of the "waste" produced by Keynesian responses to stagnation, soon became a standard reference point ("Marxism in an Affluent Society," 4:3, March/April, 1967; "American Capitalism and Its Liberal-Left Critics," 6:1, April/May 1969).[10] Gonick's essays also progressively drew a linkage between capitalism as a mode of production, social inequalities and the limits of Keynesianism that could not be absolved by a change in the nationality of ownership ("Labour and Inflation," 3:6, September/October 1966; "Poverty and Capitalism," 6:5, October/November 1969).

Foreign ownership and foreign capital, however, remained an obstacle that could not be evaded. It became all but inevitable that a political project centred on economic nationalism would form. The 1968 report of the Liberal government's *Taskforce on Foreign Ownership and the Structure of Canadian Investment*, for example, offered up many of the economic arguments against FDI that *CD* had been espousing. (The chief author, Mel Watkins, had, in fact, already been publishing in *CD*.) In a *CD* symposium favourable to the report, Ken Wyman agreed with the concerns of FDI on Canadian technological capacity and the "extra-territoriality" of US policies to Canada via US MNCs, but noted the failure to use a Canadian state investment fund "as a means of buying back Canadian companies" ("A Report from the Tip of the Iceberg?" 5:4, April/May 1968).[11]

With the formation of the Waffle Group inside the NDP, and the publication of the Waffle Manifesto in 1969, left economic nationalism took an explicit political form linking the challenge of FDI to forming an *independent and socialist* Canada.[12] The Manifesto received immediate endorsement by *CD*. A confrontation within the NDP, and across the Canadian Left, over a program of economic nationalism linked to nationalization of industry could not be avoided (Gonick, "The 'Waffle Manifesto,'" 6:5, October/November 1969).

The 1970s: The energy and economic crises

The politics of economic nationalism soon intersected with the limits of Keynesian economic policy, but for a quite different reason than economic ownership. Suddenly, the unprecedented postwar boom erupted into another great crisis of capitalism. Across the 1970s, economic growth in the core capitalist countries was cut in half. Even as unemployment doubled and then tripled from postwar lows, inflation accelerated, surging toward double-digit rates. Like the great crises of the late nineteenth century and the 1930s, the entire world market entered a period of turmoil, with debt crises and wild swings in currencies illustrating both the depth and the breadth of the global slump. The buildup of the capital stock over the expansion meant, moreover, that productivity gains within the old Fordist technologies were reaching their technological limits. In other words, the conditions for both the production and extraction of surplus value had sharply deteriorated.

Each crisis of capitalism takes a specific historical form, and in the 1970s this meant "stagflation" — slow growth and high inflation in the context of a decline in profits and productivity. The unprecedented strike wave from the late 1960s to the end of the 1970s was the most visible sign of the crisis as the distributional struggle intensified over which classes and groups would bear the burden of the crisis. Unlike the 1930s, Keynesianism, in the narrow sense of monetary and fiscal policies, had far less in its policy arsenal to offer in the new circumstances. Rather than being the point of social compromise between capitalists and workers over the distribution of higher levels of economic growth in stable markets, Keynesian policies became the point of concentration of class struggle. A radical shift in the balance of class forces in favour of the capitalist classes to restructure and internationalize capital, free market forces and raise the rate of exploitation was one strategy for exit. This was the neoliberal option that would take hold in the 1980s. The crisis first played out in the 1970s, however, as a radicalization of politics, nationally and internationally, to deepen democracy and increase social control over capital within national states.[13] Each national labour movement seemed to be coming to terms, as in the edict of the *Communist Manifesto,* with its own national bourgeoisie.

In Canada, economic developments followed the stagflation narrative. But two features of the crisis in Canada stood out. In attempting to sustain real wages, Canadian workers led the entire Western working class in days lost due to strikes — a militancy that would continue into the 1980s and prompt a thorough rethinking of ruling class strategies. The social pressures for a dramatic recasting of Canada economic policy was also coming from a second source: after a period of "catch-up" with American levels, Canadian productivity was showing signs of weakness and failure to develop innovative capacities in emerging industrial sectors. In other terms, structural economic weakness from resource dependence and truncated manufacturing capacity now raised fundamental questions of relative economic decline. After more than two decades of policy incrementalism centred on managing the dollar, Canadian economic policy began to run through a panoply of new policies — wage controls, a consumer price watchdog, a state energy company, foreign investment reviews, monetary growth targets and a host of others. A major turning point in world capitalism thus intersected with the particular crisis of Canadian capitalism. The Canadian state had no clear idea on how to address either.

Across the pages of *CD* in the 1970s, these events reshaped the debate between national developmentalism or anticapitalism. On the one hand, a strategic debate unfolded over how public ownership might displace foreign ownership, with the development of the tar sands raising the need for a national energy policy; on the other, the crisis of capitalist production and the intensification of class conflict opened space for explicitly socialist reforms.

In the political and economic turbulence of the 1970s, the analysis of FDI in Canada took shape within dependency theory. Watkins, Kari Levitt and John Warnock, for example, all sharpened the critique of Canadian capitalism from within the perspective of the Waffle movement. Watkins argued that "the contradictions of capitalism and its exemplary institution, the multi-national corporation, are increasingly evident in a world polarized along class and racial lines . . . Socialism is the positive negation of the multi-national corporation." With Canadian resources under foreign control, "Canada permanently put herself into a satellite condition" ("Attacking America's 'International' Corporations Multi-Nationally," 7:4, October/November 1970). Warnock reasserted the long-standing critique that Canadian FDI was largely funded out of Canadian savings; that the returns to foreign capital outstripped net new American investment; and that this export of capital was also the export of jobs ("Unemployment and Foreign Ownership: A Cause or a Solution?," 7:8, April 1971). Levitt provided the most thorough-going application of dependency theory's metropole-satellite metaphor to Canadian FDI in her bestselling book, *Silent Surrender* (1970). But she turned here to look "Beyond Foreign Ownership" (8:6, March/April 1972) "as the repatriation and restructuring of economic institutions, at present largely controlled by foreign capital," was also opening political space for a more participatory socialism, including nationalization of key industries but also such things as "a vast socialisation of personal transportation in our great metropolitan areas, with free transportation by Metro."[14]

The innovative radical economist Stephen Hymer also had his roots in the dependency critique, having worked on the Watkins report. But his analysis ("The Multinational Corporation," 8:6, March/April 1972) took off from the general internationalization of capital and a highly original analysis of MNCs (set out in 1979 in his *The Multinational Corporation*). In an extended essay, prefaced by an introduction by Gonick, Hymer argued that the MNC was the key vehicle in the integration of metropole and hinterland, changing the patterns of regional interdependence. In this, American capital was in the lead, but common to any MNC was how "it spreads capital and technology . . . [and] centralized control by establishing a vertically integrated network in which different areas specialize in different levels of activity." Earlier than others, Hymer identified MNCs with an increase in centralized planning capacity alongside decentralized international production networks that expanded their tactical flexibility. This thesis preceded the much later theme of globalization, including that the "centralizing tendencies of multinational capital implies a world hierarchy of cities." For Hymer, the growth of MNCs did not imply a need "to build up a national capitalist class to defend the national interest," but rather the need to build national planning capacities and regional coordination with other democratizing states.

In line with dependency theory's focus on breaking reliance on resource extraction for export markets, foreign control of the Canadian resource sector became an area of particular unease across the Canadian Left in the 1970s. James Laxer's essay, "Alienation of Canada's Resources: An Overview" (7:6, January/February 1971), set out key themes — American capital, Canadian resources — that would occupy *CD* for decades. Although the dependence on the US could be traced back to the gutting of Ontario forests in the nineteenth century, the Truman government's 1952 Materials Policy Commission, *Resources for Freedom* (Paley Report), established the agenda "on the part of the US to gain access to the resources of its allies and satellites, the world over. US investment in resource-rich countries would be followed by the dependence of those countries on US manufacturing — all to the benefit of American business and American security." INCO and the nickel industry was a powerful example of this situation as nickel exports supplied the US military, and profits flowed to American investors. But foretelling of the future was the energy sector where American supply shortfalls were leading Canada to form a continental energy policy. Laxer warned that such "an energy deal with the US would lead to economic underdevelopment for Canada. Further, it would lead to an economy with a high rate of unemployment as a permanent feature, and finally, it would mean the end of Canadian sovereignty in basic economic questions." Laxer concluded that shifting to Canadian ownership would not change Canada from being "a resources producing hinterland for US capitalism".[15]

Two further essays came to much the same conclusions. From his increasing alienation from the Liberal Party, Eric Kierans became, perhaps, the most vocal "resource nationalist." In 1973, his report for the Manitoba NDP government ("The Kierans Report on National Resource Policy in Manitoba," 9:5, May 1973) presented a careful analysis of the profits of resource companies operating in Manitoba, detailing the extent of profits and the limited royalties being imposed by the province. In his view, national developmental prospects in Canada depended upon "state capture" of an increasing proportion of resource rents and converting these, in a classical import-substitution industrial strategy, into support for increased nationally controlled processing and manufacturing capacity. For his part, Gonick contended that the economic and energy crises and the symptoms of decline in the American empire were intensifying the US "scramble for resources" as initially advocated in the Paley Report. As with Gonick (and the political conclusion of the Waffle), Canadian corporations were all too happy to build pipelines and hydroelectric plants that deepened Canadian dependency ("The American Empire: The Long Descent," 9:7-8, September/October 1973).

The 1973 "oil shock" placed the energy sector, across the world, at the centre of intense political struggles (Rob Dumont and John Warnock, "The ABCs of Oil," 9:7-8, September 1973; Michel Bosquet, "The Energy Crisis," 10:1, April 1974). For *CD*, the oil sector became a preoccupation (if quite distinct from the linkage between fossil fuels and global warming today). Already in 1971, the National Energy Board turned down a request to export additional natural gas to the US, amidst growing US concerns for energy supplies. This gave impetus to development of the Mackenzie Valley pipeline to draw gas from the Arctic Ocean to American markets via a mixture of Canadian and American energy consortiums, with American capital playing a preponderant role. In an exhaustive survey of the proposals, Warnock warned of the consequences for the environment, Aboriginal peoples along the route and the reinforcement of a pattern of "mercantile colonial exploitation" of Canadian resources ("The Mackenzie Valley Pipeline," 9:1, October 1972).

From here, a dissection of the Canadian oil industry ensued, parallel to the federal government's 1970s *Energy Policy for Canada*. Jim Laxer's *The Energy Poker Game* (1970) and *Canada's Energy Crisis* (1974)[16] served as the starting points for a long review by John Richards (eventually leading to his own influential book on these issues with Larry Pratt, *Prairie Capitalism*, 1979). The oil crisis was seen to be a result of the OPEC cartel and the oil giants, with American geopolitical strategies intricately interconnected with the crisis. Laxer's thesis followed from these premises but further asserted that Canadian energy policies were an adjunct to US control over the Canadian economy and a central contributor to what he saw as the "deindustrialization" of the Canadian economy. Richards's assessment differed from Laxer's on the degree to which the US could engineer the oil price spike, the failings of the Saskatchewan NDP to offer an alternate energy strategy and whether cheap energy should be an objective of socialist policy ("Reviewing the Energy Crisis," 10:4, September 1974).[17]

In contrast, Pratt pointed out that the joining of forces between the governments of Canada, Alberta and Ontario with Gulf and Imperial Oil to subsidize (partly via taking an equity position) Syncrude's development of the tar sands "stands in the great traditions of Canadian state capitalism . . . [t]he use of public moneys to underwrite the costs of massive resource-extraction projects controlled by foreign capitalists" ("Syncrude: The Canadian State as Agent of Foreign Corporations," 10:7, March 1975.) This would turn into the theme of Pratt's book *The Tar Sands: Syncrude and the Politics of Oil* (1976). In his review, Ed Shaffer noted the extensive subsidies — no-strike agreements, government infrastructure, tax concessions, guaranteed prices and more — necessary for tar sands development ("The Political Economy of Alberta Synthetic Crude," 12:1, February 1977). For both, Syncrude was symptomatic of the economic strategy of American imperialism (and its Canadian supports) to lock in a continental energy supply in the threat of a continued global oil crisis. Shaffer extended this analysis in a subsequent essay, and eventually to his own book, *Canada's Oil and the American Empire* (1983). Shaffer contended that Peter Lougheed's "state capitalism" project linked an urban professional elite, a new industrial class formed in Syncrude, Alberta Energy and other Alberta companies in the broad oil sector, and the multinational oil companies — "joint-ventures with private companies . . . to use public funds in a way that supports private profit" ("Oil and Class in Alberta," 13:8, June 1979).

The wider economic crisis also received a great deal of consideration, largely through Gonick's continued exploration of the limits of

Keynesianism managing the class contradictions of capitalism. These essays amounted to less an examination of the sources of the crisis (a debate figuring prominently in the international Left), and much more of an interpretative guide to the economic events and class struggles breaking apart the old Fordist postwar order. Fittingly, this began with essays in 1971 examining growing unemployment and the crisis in US economic policy. By the early 1970s, it was hard to overlook that Canada had a permanent unemployment problem that had been growing even across the postwar boom. For Gonick, this resulted from the "satellite structure of the economy, with its heavy emphasis on resources, [that] explains why Canadian booms and busts are usually much more severe and longer in duration than those of . . . other mature industrialized nations" ("The Scourge of Unemployment: 10 Lessons in Capitalist Economics," 8:1, June 1971). This meant that Keynesian policies were more limited in their impact in Canada, largely working through the "automatic stabilizers" which had emerged with the increased size of government expenditures.

But a new contradiction had also emerged with the rise of chronic inflation and even higher rates of unemployment doing little to control a wage-price spiral. This was, Gonick argued, a new contradiction of capitalism and the Nixon and Canadian governments were beginning to experiment with "wage-price guidelines" at the expense of tying "the working class to its existing share of the national income." In the case of Nixonomics, the contradictions emerging in Keynesianism were overlaid with the decline of US competitiveness from the burdens of empire and military spending such that a "spectre of open economic conflict among the capitalist nations of the world" was looming ("Nixonomics in Ten Easy Lessons," 8:3, November 1971). This was drawing Canada deeper into integration with the US, but also toward new economic policies targeting working-class incomes to raise corporate profits.

With the deceleration of economic growth and the acceleration of inflation, the distributional conflicts over which class would bear the burden of the economic crisis intensified.[18] In day-to-day economic indicators, this appeared as a wage-price spiral. In "Plumptre's Complaint,"(9:7-8, September 1973), Gonick and Fred Gudmundson contended that the Food Prices Review Board headed by Beryl Plumptre was limited in addressing the crisis in food prices as it would take on the extensive monopolization and thus pricing power of the wholesale and retail components of the food system. This led, not surprisingly, to union militancy in an effort, as Gonick demonstrated across a series of articles in 1974 as the crisis took hold, to keep real wages from falling behind inflation in the context of economic turmoil and the pricing power of the monopolies attempting to sustain profits ("Wildcats, Prices and Profits," 10:2, June 1974). Alternation between stagnation and inflation characterized monopoly capitalism.[19]

In Canada, the oil shock did not immediately trigger a radical cut in growth rates, but rather a surge in accumulation from the strength of commodity prices and exports ("Investment Boom . . . and Bust," 10:3, July 1974). But Gonick argued that this also was unleashing an inflation rate approaching double digits and a rise in the Canadian dollar. In other words, a "boom in resource development designed to supply American requirements of raw materials . . . that squeezes out the domestic manufacturing sector of the economy . . . The Keynesian revolution has not replaced the anarchy of the market." Canada could not, moreover, insulate itself from an economic crisis that was, like all major capitalist turning points, worldwide in its impact, with the erosion of American competitiveness and the dollar at the centre of the turmoil. The paradox being that US MNCs helped undermine the American economy via their internationalization and spread of US technology via their branch plants, and yet could still gain by US government efforts to reverse capital outflows ("Inflation and the Coming Crisis," 10:4, September 1974).

In contrast to the hopeful early years of *CD* for economic policy, Gonick bluntly commented that "[o]ne of the victims of the present shambles of world capitalism is the economic theory of John Maynard Keynes" ("The Current Crisis Marks the End of the Keynesian Era," 10:5, November 1974). But rather than the hope in social democratic circles circulating that incomes policy and a more participatory industrial relations could offer a solution to the crisis, or the views of impending collapse ever being projected by Trotskyists and communists, Gonick drew the more sober conclusion that a possible and likely "avenue of escape is a savage attack on the living standards of working people."

Indeed, the Canadian state attempted to contain the growing class conflicts through new forms of state intervention into wage-setting, such as the Anti-Inflation Board, running from 1975 to 1978, that raised enormous dissent from the Left and the union movement, and occupied the pages of CD from 1976 to 1977. Wage controls, followed by efforts to form tripartite institutions, were meant to stabilize prices and wages and, in turn, boost corporate profits. But Gonick warned "that in its present state of illegitimacy, Trudeau's anti-inflation board could be defeated by a strictly trade union strategy. But [the AIB's] defeat . . . does not in itself constitute a resolution of the economic crisis" ("Socialists and Wage Controls," 11:4, March 1976). Similar critiques were raised against the CLC's 1976 Labour Manifesto for Canada and its support for tripartite bargaining with the government. This produced the scathing assessment from Gil Levine that "the leaders of organized labour in Canada appear to be moving away from the concept of democratic control at the plant level to advocating a system of corporatism" ("Comments on the CLC Manifesto: A Pertinent Viewpoint," 11:7, October 1976).

By the end of the 1970s it was quite clear that the crisis was still working itself out and more radical measures were on the agenda. Across the pages of CD in the 1970s, this led to extensive coverage of the socialist turn in Third-World liberation struggles but also the possibilities for more radical forms socialization of industry and state intervention in the core capitalist countries. Indeed, workers' control, following the analysis of Andre Gorz in his Strategy for Labor (1968), figured more prominently than restrictions on FDI as the central strategic theme of CD.[20] But it was also quite possible to see the crisis radicalizing a new right without the Left being able to respond. In surveying the wreckage of the 1970s crisis, Gonick warned that with the "decline of US power," the options for Canada were few without new technological breakthroughs with the possibility of a "long decline" for another decade ("Why Prosperity Is Not Around the Corner," 14:1, July/August 1979). It was not clear, Gonick proposed in a follow-up essay, that the driving up of interest rates by the US Federal Reserve, with the "monetarists having their day," could offer an alternate route to recovery after pushing the world into a steep recession. This pattern, however, would dolefully be followed as "Canadian policy-makers — the middle-managers of a regional satellite — will accommodate themselves to every twist and turn of the American policy" ("Notes on the New Economic Crisis," 14:4-5, 1980).[21]

The 1980s: Free trade and neoliberalism

The decisive turning point in the history of capitalism that the 1970s now mark can be seen in retrospect. In prospect, however, the rise and then suffocating hegemony of the New Right and neoliberalism could not. From the Volcker economic shock of 1981–83 that brought to a close the strike wave of the 1970s, through to the Reagan boom that followed, a new era of "deregulation, privatization and free trade" emerged. This political-economic shift cut across the core capitalist countries, including the social democratic heartland of northern Europe, and took hold in the global South. The political initiative for the neoliberal restructuring of capitalism was to be found in North America.

When the Liberals initially returned to power, however, the Trudeau government, under pressure to respond to a persistent economic crisis, flirted with a nationalist industrial policy in the early 1980s. The policy encompassed new state regulations over natural resources, plans for "mega-projects" and, notably, the creation of the National Energy Programme (NEP) with plans to expand the state-controlled Petro-Canada. The NEP met strong opposition from both Canadian and US capital. Both had become wary of a potential statist turn of the Liberals, as well as the broader implications of the NEP for continental economic integration. Fearing that nationalist economic policy might trigger a pro-tectionist backlash from the US, Canadian capital moved to defeat the program and, further, to "disable permanently such interventions by the state."[22] The strategy for "disabling" would come via a bilateral free trade agreement between Canada and the US, alongside a major restructuring of the Canadian economy from recession, the introduction of the new "post-Fordist" production systems of flexible technologies and workers, and the unprecedented internationalization of Canadian capital. The political demarcations of the postwar period continued but they took on new colourations. The centre-right economic policies of continentalism now embraced neoliberalism; and the politics of economic nationalism also became code for a defence of Keynesianism against market liberalism. The ensuing debates were among the most divisive and polarized in Canadian history, and filled the pages of *CD* across the 1980s.

At the outset, the centre-left grudgingly accepted the economic nationalism of the Trudeau government for taking steps towards a national industrial strategy.[23] For many prominent figures such as Mel Hurtig, Walter Gordon, James Laxer and Mel Watkins, the NEP marked a hopeful first step in the gradual delinking of the Canadian "hinterland" economy from the US "metropolis," and the development of a Canadian-owned and -controlled energy sector. Watkins, for example, came out strongly in support of the NEP, and Laxer would go even further in suggesting that Trudeau had come to understand the challenges facing Canada more than other leaders. These views seemed to skip back to the 1960s — nationalist economic intervention in itself a good in challenging the logic of branch plants and continentalism.

But the divisions of the 1970s over the development of the Canadian oil and gas sector could not be concealed. Gonick, for example, although sympathetic to the nationalizations, read the NEP as foremost about building Canadian capitalism. "[T]here is nothing," he argued, "anti-imperialist about the NEP . . . Petro-Canada is no threat to Canadian capitalism. Like Ontario Hydro and other crown corporations, it will be used to expand capitalist accumulation, not hinder it." Instead, the crucial question was of public ownership and democratic control: what "distinguishes Socialism and Capitalism is not form, but content and process" ("NEPMEN and other Nationalists," 15:7, August/September 1981). Julian Sher added that although the NEP was pro-capitalist in nature, it was still important to counter US attacks against the NEP and other forms of political economic interference in Canadian affairs ("NEP — Is it all Gloom and DOME?" 16:7-8, January 1983).

The NEP was one of several interventionist proposals that included a Major Projects Task Force, calls for a National Manpower Board, and burgeoning tripartite bodies at the provincial level, especially in Quebec. This led the editors to put together a second special feature on corporatism,

"Towards a Corporatist Canada" (15:3, December 1980), in this case extending beyond wage controls to the range of tripartite bodies forming. "Corporatism may not resolve the conflicts of capitalist society," CD warned, "but it does serve to demobilize the working class." The emergent economic policy was dissected in an essay by Gonick (that would then become a core to his book *The Great Economic Debate*, 1987). Here Gonick argued that the policies of economic nationalism were less about national control than a move from Keynesian demand management to the supply side "to help restructure Canada's floundering manufacturing industry . . . as it develops a stake in specialized high technology industries geared for the world market" ("The New 'Supply Side' Economics," 15:4, February 1981).

Although the nationalist economic phase of the early 1980s was short-lived, the political struggle between continentalist and nationalist forces entered a decisive stage. The pushback against the statist NEP from business associations was but one of a series of skirmishes ushering in neoliberalism. Numerous essays in CD across the 1980s make for a remarkable catalogue of neoliberalism birthing in Canada — privatization (1980), plant closures (1981), concessions bargaining (1982), monetarism and Canadian banks (1983), shock therapy (1984), stagnation (1985), unemployment (1986), government cuts (1987), the global economic casino (1988), financialization and interest rates (1989) and more. The massive report of the Royal Commission on the Economic Union and Development Prospects for Canada in 1985 laid out a comprehensive continental and neoliberal strategy for the overhaul of the Canadian state system and an all-inclusive free trade agreement (FTA) with the US. The Commission was the perfect vehicle to craft a new ruling-class strategy for Canada: appointed in 1982 by the Liberal government, chaired by long-time liberal nationalist Donald MacDonald and reporting to the newly elected Conservative government of Brian Mulroney.[24] It came in for special attention.

In an opening appraisal of the Commission and its centrepiece free-trade proposal, Jim Turk raised the prospect that a deeper process was in fact evolving — a process that would soon become known as globalization. The traditional branch-plant dependency of Canada on the US was being succeeded by a more wide-ranging dependence on transnational corporations ("Free Trade with the United States: The Implications for Canada," 19:4, September/October 1985). For Turk, the rise to prominence of TNCs was the product of a "massive worldwide corporate reorganization and rationalization . . . Governments, including Canada's, have been pressed by the TNCs to develop economic strategies compatible with this corporate thrust. This means abandonment of policies based on the priority of the domestic economy in favour of a policy of export-oriented development. Coupled with this, there has been intense pressure to eliminate restrictions on the mobility of capital to minimize impediments to the TNCs global reorganization." Gonick elaborated that the reconstruction of the policy architecture proposed by the MacDonald Commission included deregulation, decreased corporate taxes and a smaller welfare state, and cuts to anything else that was seen to restrict and distort the operation of market forces. These policy changes, he argued, needed to be seen as a response to increasing global competitiveness. The core recommendation of free trade with the US, moreover, constituted a dramatic shift toward a more export-oriented development strategy on the part of Canadian capital. Gonick presciently warned that the FTA would come with heavy social costs, especially for medicare and unemployment insurance, and the further loss of political sovereignty and capacity for national economic policies ("The Twisted Mind of Donald McDonald & Co.," 19:6, January/February 1986).

The critical assessments of the likely consequences of free trade for Canada came fast and furious in the pages of *CD* after 1986 — on the impacts on First Nations and women, on rationalization pressures on wages and branch plants, on water and labour law and included the special report issue in 1987 (21:7, November/December). From today's vantage, these appraisals have fared much better than the anodyne free trade predictions of the neoliberals on rising incomes, increasing productivity, greater democracy and policy autonomy and improved social programs. The resistance to free trade at the time, however, as Gonick and Jim Silver observed, had only lukewarm support from the NDP and a desperate lack of a campaigning strategy on the part of the labour movement. The various anti-FTA forces, moreover, could not agree on any political economic alternative to the FTA ("Fighting Free Trade," 23:3, April/May 1989).

A common assessment of many contributions, as the FTA moved from proposal to implementation in 1989, was that strategies of economic intervention of all kinds were now confronting a more hostile climate. The Canadian economy faced increasing exposure to global market pressures and, as the pages of CD consistently warned, free trade reinforcing resource dependence in the absence of a compensatory industrial strategy. This had implications for programmatic alternatives in the campaigns against the FTA. GATT-Fly (a popular coalition of church groups opposed to the FTA), for example, developed a proposal for self-reliance that rested upon three key principles: Canada should produce essential goods and services domestically; the government must ensure goods and services are affordable; and Canada should continue foreign trade, but limit it to a secondary role in the overall industrial strategy ("Building Self-Reliance: The Alternative to Free Trade," 21:5, September 1987). Further, GATT-Fly argued for "any form of control [over capital] which is democratic, and which accepts the goals of self-reliance, is valid. This includes family owned and worked enterprises, marketing and consumer cooperatives, worker co-operatives, and even private enterprises provided that the employees have organized themselves, are granted trade union rights and have a substantial input into management decisions."

For others, the FTA was a more radical marker of the maturing of Canadian capitalism and a reminder of the indispensible role of the state in constructing neoliberalism. As Greg Albo and Donald Swartz argued, Canadian capital was all but unanimous in its support for free trade with its own interest in penetrating the US market. The FTA "is about *freeing capital* from the political obstacles which impede its restructuring" ("Why the Campaign Against Free Trade Isn't Working," 21:5, September 1987). With capital accumulation increasingly internationalized, and significant fractions of Canadian capital actively championing the cause of continental integration, it was no longer plausible to expect a direct antagonism between national capital with unique national interests and foreign capital (as was still animating

381

much of the common front of opposition to the FTA). The attempted anti-FTA cross-class coalition lacked willing partners on the part of big or even small business. An alternative strategy in this new period had to develop a "more comprehensive class based critique . . . and a political process of mobilization which includes the building of an oppositional program and culture for the longer term."[25]

The challenges of alternative strategies had already been raised, of course, particularly as NDP policies began to waft away from traditional Keynesian regulatory concerns to allowances for market-led policies (Errol Black, "James Laxer on the NDP: A Hodge-Podge of Contradictions and Dead-End Solutions," 18:2, May 1984). Leo Panitch's forceful case for "The Need for a New Socialist Movement" (18:3, June 1984) emerged in this context of the breakup of the old political certainties. Arguing with clarity and force on the political drift of social democracy and the cracks breaking apart the old Leninism, Panitch contended that "it may be misleading to think of the current malaise of capitalist as a crisis at all . . . [as] the vacuum left by the collapse of Keynesian-welfare state reformism is filled by resignation or the tenets of market populism." The challenge is less the question of the crisis than "to advocate proposals for the overcoming of the weakness of socialist forces."[26]

The 1990s: Debating globalization

The 1990s were even more unrelenting in the advance of global capitalism as one world-changing event followed another — the end of the Soviet Union, the turn to the "socialist market" model in China, the formation of the World Trade Organization and the European Union, and the adaptation of the new technologies in workplaces enabling unprecedented international production networks. The political realignment of social democracy under the sign of the "Third Way" lent credence to the claim that neoliberalism had emerged as the natural order of things. This was, to be sure, a decade of consolidation of a new global economic architecture undergirded by a US global hegemony without rivals.

In Canada, the new economic architecture entailed the 1994 extension of the FTA to Mexico in the continent-wide North American Free Trade

Agreement (NAFTA), and the sweeping redesign of the Canadian welfare state by the Liberal government through the cuts engendered by the 1995 Canada Health and Social Transfer (CHST). These changes offered the political space to the hard-right governments of Mike Harris and Ralph Klein in Ontario and Alberta respectively to break the old Ontario-Quebec compact and forge an east-west alliance spreading neoliberal policies across the provincial and local landscapes.

The post-FTA transformations renewed, for a period, the old dependency world-view that Canada was a resource hinterland adjunct to the US empire. But the limits of positing a relation between an "autonomous state" and its "national economic system," as mediated by the political competition between elites and popular forces, was also exposed. Neoliberal globalization made it more difficult to identify MNCs as "external" to the national community, unilaterally taking decisions that should properly reside with nationally controlled capitals as part of the "national community." Globalization clarified that it is the accumulation and internationalization of capital, irrespective of the nationality of shareholder ownership, which takes precedence in capitalism — a position that Hymer and Gonick had already broached in the pages of CD in the early 1970s. Both domestic and foreign capital invested in Canada served to integrate Canadian workers and resources into a value chain of international accumulation. National states like Canada, moreover, reorganized their policy and administrative structures to facilitate the internationalization of capital irrespective of the nationality of ownership. NAFTA was, to cite the most prominent Canadian example, a central institution of the new imperialism, and positioned Canada as a core power and key ally of the American empire. Coming to grips with the new "globalization" in this meaning took many turns in the CD debates of the 1990s.

The spotlight initially — and quite naturally — was on the impact of the FTA on Canadian industry. Bruce Campbell, for instance, closely tracked the first years of free trade, guided by the thesis that the FTA would lead to a levelling of wages and benefits in Canada as Canada's branch-plant economy converted into a warehouse economy ("In the Image of the Eagle: Remaking Canada Under Free Trade," 24:2, March

1990). A year later, Campbell maintained that a key factor in the made-in-Canada recession was the Mulroney government's policy of high interest rates driving up the Canadian dollar to make Canada more attractive to US FDI. The increased competition from the FTA meant, moreover, "massive corporate restructuring: takeovers, mergers, foreign control, production shifts, plant closures, consolidation, downsizing, business failures" ("Goin' South: 2 Years Under Free Trade," 25:1, January/February 1991). In the context of increasing competition to attract capital investment, governments are pressured to "relax social and environmental standards, lower taxes, etc., in other words to tax less and spend less." With these trends continuing to accelerate and NAFTA now just over the horizon, a year later Campbell drew as bleak a conclusion as any that has appeared in *CD* on the political economy of Canada: "Canada is disintegrating under this free trade driven trans-formation. North-south trade and financial flows are growing far faster than east-west flows. The national economy is breaking down into regions increasingly disconnected from each other as they integrate along a north-south axis . . . Big business clamours for a decentralized Canada whose supreme mandate is to ensure competitiveness and provinces that compete with each other to offer the most attractive business conditions" ("Free Trade: Year 3," 26:1, January/February 1992; "Free Trade — Abrogation to Rebuild the Nation," 27:1, January/February 1993).

Alternative political strategies to trade liberalization became a pre-occupation in the anti-NAFTA opposition, now led by the Council of Canadians (formed in 1985) and the Pro-Canada Network (formed in 1988 and later renamed as the Action Canada Network), in the early 1990s. The list of charges trumpeted against NAFTA in the pages of *CD* were many and telling: as no solution to Mexico's development problem; the elimination of production guarantees for the auto sector allowing for continental rationalization in the long run; the new "rules of origin" as incapable of monitoring Mexico's export processing zone; the locking out of state control of Canadian oil and gas production while guaranteeing supply to the US; the disproportionate impact of employment losses on women from industrial rationalization of light-manufacturing sectors;

and the undermining of the agricultural marketing board structure. There was, however, also a parallel case being made for fair as opposed to free trade. For example, Canadian-content rules to guarantee national production were proposed to stem unemployment and capital flight to low-wage sunbelt and maquiladora production zones. The CAW also forwarded a proposal for the reregulation of trade and investment that would force industries to conform to national environmental and health standards as well as Canadian-content rules ("Hard Times, New Times," 27:6, November/December 1993).

As in the 1980s, a big push occurred during the 1993 election campaign to challenge the neoliberal policies of the Conservatives and defeat NAFTA. Once again, *CD* was at the centre of contentions on how to defeat NAFTA and challenge global capitalism. Early on Campbell and John Fryer argued that successful opposition to free trade involved globalizing the left, and "insisting that 'global competitiveness' must not be imposed at the expense of Canadian working men and women, or of workers in less developed countries" ("Worse Than Canada-US FTA," 24:6, September 1990). For some, the immediate task was blocking NAFTA or, failing that, pushing a Liberal minority government to renegotiate the worst features. In the course, new social movements against corporate capitalism might continue to build (Tony Clarke, "We Must Build a Strong Social Movement," 26:8, November/December 1992). For others, what was unfolding was a global restructuring of the capitalist economy, of which free trade is merely a part. Gail Bauman and Andy Shadrack suggested that any "tactics and long term strategy, especially the upcoming Canadian federal elections, must include total repudiation of GATT, World Bank, and IMF policies as they are now constituted. Without a more balanced exchange of resources between the various peoples and regions of the planet and a marked de-escalation in military spending the current global crisis will only continue to worsen" ("Free Trade Not the Main Villain," 26:5, July/August 1992). And for Howard Brown the long-term capitalist crisis called for a maximalist "demand for abrogation [as the FTA] diverts working people down the dead-end path of national capitalist reform" ("Free Trade Abrogation is a Diversion," 27:3, May/June 1993). In the event, the election of a Liberal majority government that ended up fully supporting NAFTA and pursuing neoliberal policies pointed to the harder times yet to come.[27]

At times in the 1990s, the epitaph "free trade" carried the entire indictment against neoliberalism for the Left in Canada. But there were other lines of analysis. The importance of the restructuring of the auto sector to the Canadian economy, for example, was already receiving prominence in the 1980s from the discussion of the world car and the new industrial relations that came with the "transplants" (Sam Gindin, "The World Car: Who's Behind the Wheel?" 15:5, April 1981; Don Wells, "'Teamwork' and the New Industrial Relations," 22:1, February 1988). Herman Rosenfeld and the CAW further took apart the "Japanese model" of production gaining favour from corporations and progressives alike. In Canada, flexible production meant the "Team Concept," and Rosenfeld warned that the changing work practices could not be met by trying to find a common "interest between the workers and the corporation." Rather, the education and militancy of members had to be vehicles to confront the new "corporate offensive" ("CAW Opposes the Team Concept," 24:2, March 1990; "Team Concept at CAMI," 27:1, January/February 1993).

Others addressed the particular features of neoliberalism in Canada. One focus was the Bank of Canada as monetarism mutated into wider deregulation of the banking sector. Already in the 1990s a number of post-Keynesian essays charged that changes in bank regulation, reserve requirements and a shift of government borrowing away from the central bank were fuelling an unsustainable financial asset expansion that would lead to massive public bailouts (George Crowell, "Reforming the Bank of Canada," 29:5, October/November 1995; William Krehm, "Megabank Bust," 32:4, July/August 1998).

But even more attention was paid to the fixation on fiscal deficits and the potential for "participatory budgeting" to offer both practical alternative economic paths and to forge a disparate opposition into union-social movement coalitions. Gideon Rosenbluth, the doyen of Keynesian economists in Canada, for example, forcefully laid out the left social democratic case that "deficits" had served as neoliberal justification for government cutbacks. There were any number of fallacies to austerity — misguided credit ratings, the consequences of foreign debt obligations, unneeded tax cuts. Even NDP governments had failed "to introduce innovation in fiscal policies" in adopting conservative economic policy ("Deficitphobia," 27:3, May/June 1993).[28] For John Loxley, this led to an extensive engagement with the "Alternative Federal Budget" process, an initiative that received considerable — if critical — support in *CD* ("A Way Out of the Economic Wasteland?" 26:3, April/May 1992; "Pondering the Alternative Budget," 29:3, June/July 1995; Linda McQuaig, "Alternative Federal Budget," 31:1, January/February 1997). For Gonick and Todd Scarth, the AFB, in the context of neoliberal consolidation, was "far and away the most ambitious project attempted by the Canadian Left in many years" in combining an anti-neoliberal agenda with community capacity-building ("A People's Budget," 30:2, April 1996). But like so many of the other projects to emerge out of the serial coalitions of the 1990s, the democratic imprint of alternate budgeting soon dissipated.

Since the late 1970s, *CD* had been highlighting the world economic crisis, with important contributions on structural adjustment policies coming from Loxley ("Saving the World Economy," 18:5, July/August 1984) and James O'Connor on "The Changing Face of World Capitalism" (22:4, June 1988). By the 1990s this required a careful delineation of the form, content and spatial variation of the "globalization" of capitalism. In the late 1990s, *CD* undertook important surveys of the different paths by which Russia, Mexico, South Africa and Cuba became integrated into the world market (33:3, May/June 1999). These world-historic shifts inevitably gave rise to divergent assessments of the contradiction between the "new" globalization of capital and the "old" nation states.

For Andrew Jackson, globalization posed the problem of how to restore "wage-led" economic growth against the way the world market was now configured: "The expansion of the 1990s, like previous expansions since the 1960s, was fueled by a massive growth of debt . . . The roots of the tendency to stagnation are complex, but they lie in some basic structural features of the deregulated global economy. In a fiercely competitive world driven by massive flows of both real and financial capital, different countries are driven to seek growth by increasing exports, restraining wages and other costs, rather than expanding their own economies. This results in competitive austerity" ("The Global Financial Crisis," 33:1, January/

February 1999). But for James Petras, there was a need to confront the "globalist ideology." "Contemporary globalization," Petras continued, "retains many of the key features of the earlier phases of globalization: the driving forces are centred in the imperial state and the multi-national corporation and banks, backed by the international financial institutions . . . The scope and scale of movement of capital and commodities however, are due less to technological than to political changes" ("Globalization: A Socialist Perspective," 33:1, January/February 1999).

These were but some of the efforts to break down the new patterns of power and accumulation with globalization. Melding the many oppositions into a contentious social movement confronted formidable obstacles in union setbacks, the eclipse of the radical Left and the marginalization of all social alternatives from political discussion. As Gonick bluntly put it: "In this environment social democratic governments can do nothing, not even maintain the welfare state. Unable to confront Capital in the midst of all the restructuring taking place, they implement their own version of neo-conservative economics" ("Reinventing the Left," 28:5, October/November 1994; "Forum: Political Renewal: What's Left?" 28:6, December 1994).

Another track in the face of bleak prospects was to insist, as CD had repeatedly done in the past, that a battery of socialist ideas remained viable, but entailed a rethinking of economic strategy as democratization and not simply of "national" control of corporations via state ownership. As Albo framed the challenge: "Left alternatives to globalization are not so much a choice between international and national strategies, or between reflation and community economic development . . . They are about our democratic capacity to deliberate collectively as social equals about the type of society we want and the solidaristic — rather than competitive — forms international relations might take. They are about our capacity to devise alternative development consistent with sustaining national and local ecosystems and develop self-management in workplaces" ("Breaking the Mold," 31:3, May/June 1997).

The 2000s: From antiglobalizationization to an age of austerity

The antiglobalization movement grew with amazing speed out of such sentiments — "there is an alternative." From its initial origins in the opposition to the FTAs in North America in the 1980s, the movement was an emerging anticapitalist force by the early 2000s. The Asian financial crisis and the bursting of the new economy bubble at the end of the 1990s gave particular weight to its critique, as expressed by Jim Stanford, of an unregulated global casino and the power of MNCs ("Dispatches from a Meltdown," 35:3, May/June 2001). The movement was, however, extremely heterogeneous with many competing analyses of the global economy and alternatives to free trade. If arguments for national ownership of corporations remained an important pulse within antiglobalization discourse, they rested alongside spirited struggles against neoliberalism and the new powers being concentrated in supranational bodies like the WTO and IMF to defend global capitalism. If the US remained the central pivot for the world market, it increasingly shared space with China and other emerging markets. These powerful economic and state forces in the making of global capitalism sparked a debate of considerable range and insight into the questions of "empire" and the "new imperialism."

For more than a decade *CD* had monitored the ever more radical commitment of the Canadian state to neoliberal politics and the internationalization of capital at the expense of the democratic content of liberal democracy. An essay from a stalwart of the antiglobalization movement, Walden Bello of Focus on the Global South, registered a resurgent political optimism at the outset of the new decade in the growing and common "opposition to the expansion of a system that promoted corporate-led globalization at the expense of social goals like justice, community, national sovereignty, cultural diversity, and ecological sustainability" ("2000: The Year of Global Protest Against Globalization," 35:2, March 2001). Another of the central figures of the antiglobalization movement, Tony Clarke of the Polaris Institute, elaborated the critique against WTO efforts to extend its free trade framework ("Will the WTO Survive Hong Kong?" 39:6, November/December 2005), as did a forum on "Perspectives on the Free Trade Area of the Americas" (37:6, November/December 2003).

But despite its many provocative interventions, the antiglobalization movement could not stall — never mind reverse — the internationalization of capital accumulation. The belligerent assertion of American supremacy over geopolitics with the "war on terror" after 2001 radically shifted the political-economic terrain (Walden Bello, "The Multiple Crises of Global Capitalism," 37:1, 2003). Although the antiglobalization movement fused into the massive global antiwar protests of February 15, 2003, it soon faltered and all but collapsed in North America. The fragments of the movement dissolved, almost as quickly as it emerged, into an anarchist-tinged "anti-power" political program centred on eco-localist economic development, on the one hand, and the most practical reform politics of defending as best as one could existing state programs, on the other.

In Canada, the opposition to globalization was entangled with particular worries about the "hollowing out" of corporate Canada as MNCs operating in Canada reorganized at the expense of their Canadian subsidiaries under the competitive pressures of NAFTA. As a result of the restrictions on industrial policy and foreign-ownership monitoring in the agreement, investments in Canada and Canadian companies were vulnerable to the economies of scale and cost advantages of producing in the US and Mexico ("Forum: NAFTA at 10," 38:2, March/April 2004). For economic nationalists, the long-standing concerns over political capacities to pursue national economic policies were clearly in doubt. For Steven Clarkson, the challenge was to go "post-global" and reestablish the institutional conditions which might yield a "progressive competitiveness agenda": "A social-democratic, post-globalist agenda would turn back to the state as the prime instrument for altering the competitive conditions for capital. Market competition based on high technical quality, rather than low labour costs, would necessitate large public expenditures to rebuild an infrastructure that had degenerated because of the false economies inflicted by two decades of single-minded budget cutting. A quality-based economic strategy would also require highly skilled personnel able to carry out demanding work tasks" ("Going Post-Global: Reshaping the Canadian State," 36:6, November/December 2002). Watkins, in contrast, echoed the warnings in his essays in *CD* from decades past that lifting regulations on foreign ownership did nothing to promote Canada's manufacturing competitiveness while sacrificing policy autonomy. In opposition to such corporate globalization, Watkins (drawing upon

Bello) suggested that the "time has come to talk about delinking from the global economy, of lessening the links — not enhancing them — of opposing mergers, acquisitions and takeovers" ("Hollowing-Out," 42:1, January/February 2008).[29]

Other antiglobalization strategies moved from "delinking" from the world market through trade and capital controls to various strategies of "localism." David Morris opined that "policymakers have created rules that value mobility over community, competition over co-operation, inequality over equality, absentee ownership over local ownership, selling abroad over selling to our neighbours, doing well over doing good" ("Defending Community in the Age of Globalization," 32:3, May/June 1998). Wally Seccombe pitched a turn to community economic development as "[n]othing undermines the self-reliance of communities like capitalist globalization . . . If a nation's economic destiny is controlled by external forces, its political sovereignty is compromised. This does not mean that we cannot trade with others; it means that we must take steps to restore a measure of self-reliance." For Seccombe, community economic development represented the seeds of an anti-statist and participatory approach to socialism: "As vehicles of citizen action, community agencies are everything that centralized state bureaucracies cannot be — innovative problem solvers, need-driven, small-scale, decentralized and locally responsive" ("Community Economics of Nanny State?" 34:2, March/April 2000).

It is not clear how a turn to localism, however, does not just accommodate the reproduction of capitalist social relations on a smaller — national or local — scale. The critique of corporate globalization and the concentration of capital certainly suggested more radical conclusions. A world order of "infinite war," "global capital" and "empire" begged for a more thorough interrogation of the new imperialism. Just months after 9/11, CD offered a series of outstanding essays that did just that — Ellen Wood on "war without boundaries" Petras on the Pentagon's "blowback," Aijaz Ahmad on "perpetual war," Yildiz Atasoy on the coming reorganization of the world economy, as a sample (35:6, November/December 2001). The following year Petras detailed the "The Imperial Counter-Offensive" (36:2, March/April 2002) and offered that the "decline of "indirect" imperial control over the impoverished and devastated Third World states required a "new imperialism" in the form of a vast expansion of US MNCs and wars of "recolonization" of the global South. If for Petras the new imperialism stemmed from terminal US decline, for Gindin it meant confronting the "American-led internationalization" behind the reassertion of US economic power. For Canada, Gindin claimed, "at least since the free-trade debates it is no longer possible to talk about a Canadian business class oriented to national economic development. Every major sector of business is now dominated by an international, or, more accurately, continental perspective" ("Challenging Globalization," 36:4, July/August 2002).

Gindin's intervention called for a more sober and radical appraisal of Canada's role in global accumulation and place in the international state system. The thesis of a more aggressive Canadian imperialism guided two remarkable *Dimension* issues documenting the internationalization of Canadian mining buttressed by a more assertive Canadian state — "Canadian Mines the South" (41:3, May/June 2007) and "Canadian Mining Companies Invade the Global South" (45:1, January/February 2011). Gonick placed these developments within *CD* themes on Canada and the world market since the 1960s. In critically assessing the old notion of "Canada as the world's richest dependency," Gonick pointed out the ways that Canadian capital had become more dynamic in key sectors outside resources, such that "Canadian multinational corporations have developed ambitions far exceeding what could be achieved within the boundaries of this country. They see themselves as players on the global scene and, in particular, players on the North American scene." Canada was, indeed, an imperialist state, but as a "second-tier member of U.S.-led collective imperialism" ("*Is* Canada an Imperialist State?" 40:6, November/December 2006).

It was also necessary to show how the Canadian state had reorganized its political doctrines, organizational structures and operations as part of its new imperialism ambitions. For Albo, Canada was the American empire's most loyal ally. In order to "sustain global accumulation, there has been a consistent increase in the relative power of the international and coercive apparatuses of the [Canadian] state. The 'economic security' of NAFTA has for business interests become directly linked to 'North American security' and thus 'imperial security'" ("Empire's Ally: Canadian Foreign Policy," 40:6, November/December 2006). It was misleading, these articles all maintained, to judge the political economy of Canada as one of a peripheral state: Canada was an important, if secondary, imperialist power with its own economic interests to assert, and aligned with the objectives of the US state in the making of world order.[30]

The 2008 global economic crisis rocked the entire world market and provided vindication of themes that many authors in *CD* had long championed. The contradictions of neoliberal economic policy, for instance, were clearly exposed. Some on the Left saw this as a revalidation of Keynesianism. Radhika Desai and Alan Freeman pushed for a careful assessment of the more radical implications of Keynes's ideas for economic reforms ("Keynes and the Crisis," 43:4, July/August 2009). Panitch and Gindin, however, argued for a more careful perspective on the role of US economic authorities to manage the crisis as other states "recognized the U.S.'s central bank as the world's central bank and cooperated with it in coordinating internationally repeated provision of liquidity to the banks. As in the previous instances of financial crises during the 1980s and 1990s, this reproduced and extended the American state's leading role in managing global capitalism." The US had, they stressed, considerable leeway to manage the crisis by "virtue of the weakness of its working class" ("Perspectives on the US Financial Crisis," 42:4, July/August 2008).[31] Gonick contended that the capitalist classes remained hostile to programs of redistribution and state intervention. Keynesian policies could, at best, offer "a short-term solution to the crisis. Socialists need to think beyond Keynes. With capitalism now so thoroughly discredited, this is the time for bold proposals" ("The Return of Mr. Keynes," 43:2, March/April 2009).

The global economic crisis appeared, for a brief moment, to foretell neoliberalism's demise. The initial surge of the Occupy movement, Idle No More and anti-austerity protests looked to be the executioner. But as the crisis dragged on, it was necessary to consider — as Gindin, Stanford and Marjorie Cohen did in a roundtable — how the financial crisis was being contained and the persistence of stagnation across the world market ("The Global Economic Crisis," 46:1, January/February 2012). For Michael Hurley and Gindin, the turn to austerity also meant "a reduction and privatization in public services on a scale not seen before" that the Left had to formulate new strategies to confront ("The Assault on Public Services," 45:6, November/December 2011). The turn to austerity confirmed warnings going back to the 1980s of the antidemocratic tendencies of the New Right in the new authoritarian measures being taken up by the state. *CD* was one of the fora in Canada to warn from the outset of the crisis that neoliberalism could be reconstructed and a phase of perpetual austerity ushered in.

However different the circumstances, a revisit to a dilemma of the Canadian Left that seemed to haunt the pages of *CD* since the 1960s could not be averted. Social democratic parties like the NDP were nowhere setting out an alternative agenda. Yet, the Left and unions had few political resources to strike out on an independent course of action. In a remarkable essay at the height of the antiglobalization movement, Gindin put the issue rather bluntly: "'Anti-capitalism' is not itself an alternative, but it points towards a new political project which is oriented to creating an alternative. To demand the currently impossible, and to actually be realistic about this rather than only utopian, involves figuring out what 'anti-capitalism' means and where it leads" ("The Terrain of Social Justice," 35:4, July/August 2001). But at the outset of the crisis it was difficult to identify, as Albo reported, the "organizational capacities to forge an alternate approach to the crisis" and push beyond the network and anti-power politics of the antiglobalization movement. "For a brief moment, it seemed as if a decentralized 'network politics' — a 'movement of movements' — would provide, if not a map for the future, a renewed political capacity for the Left. But apart from episodic demonstrations and annual social-justice fairs, the networks have broken apart more often than they have provided new organizational nodes. There has been almost a complete lack of organizational grounding in the day-to-day struggles of working-class communities, workplaces and unions" ("Ways Forward," 43:3, May/June 2009).

Over the last decade, the organizational grounding for the critical political economy of *CD* has been located in the project of "eco-socialism"

("Focus: Climate Change," 45:2, March/April 2011; "Degrowth Focus," 46:2, March/April 2012). The vision of eco-socialism in the 2010s appears, at first glance, radically different from the political economy of industrial policy in the 1960s. It is the continuity of attempting to grasp the emerging threads of the new struggles of an age of austerity and weave them together with the old demands for a new democratic order that remains intact.

CD and the next Left

The pages of CD have animated the debates of the Left in Canada for decades like no other venue. This has not been by offering a single — or even consistent — line of analysis. Instead, the central concerns of the Left have been engaged across a plurality of topics and perspectives — the limits of Keynesianism; democratic control over national and local spaces; Keynes-plus strategies for socializing investment and industrial policy; the inequalities spawned by globalization and financialization; and projects small and visionary for radical democratization.

The limitations of the Left in Canada over the last half-century have meant, however, that the analysis of Canadian capitalism in CD has been overtly situational. The emblematic CD intervention has tended toward tactical concerns over the latest turn in Canadian capitalism: what might be possible in the way of reforms given the existing balance of political forces? Strategic economic debate, apart from the volleys over FDI and economic planning in the first decade has been, at best, sporadic. This judgment must be made even in the contentions over the Waffle Manifesto and its fallout in the 1970s or resistance to regional integration in the 1990s. The cumulative building of an anticapitalist analysis matched by a programmatic intervention has been, it needs noting, far less than might have been expected.[32] But, to be fair, this is a charge that could be made against the entire Canadian Left (with Quebec not exempted on the matter).

This is not to slight the numerous CD themes that have entered into the conventional arsenal of the Left. For one: that democratic control and sovereignty over economic development in Canada does not rest in the hands of the First Nations, Quebecois or Canadian peoples. The working classes and ecology of Canada have been left exposed to the hyper-exploitation and environmental abuse of Canadian and foreign capital buttressed by the Canadian state. CD also bears recognition for sustaining the hard-won theme that neoliberalism is not simply the result of the mistaken policies of Canadian elites best reversed by a return to Keynesianism and a "fairer capitalism" — a contention that, remarkably, is still plumped by many progressive research centres. From the adoption of monetarism by the Bank of Canada in the 1970s through to the signing of the FTA and NAFTA, CD contributors have maintained that a fundamental turning point in the development of Canadian capitalism had transpired.

These two themes — the empty shell of Canadian democracy and the hardening of the Right and the state since the 1980s to implement "free markets" — underscore a corollary CD contention. Social democracy, as practiced by the NDP and its sister organizations in the Socialist International, provides a key support for neoliberalism today. A wide "popular front," stretching from the radical Left to the NDP to a potential coalition with the Liberal Party (as advocated by much of the social movement leadership and even unions like CAW/Unifor over the last two decades), is a reform alternative with little prospect of advance.

This is, to be sure, a difficult, if necessary, analysis to defend in Canada. It does not provide consolation in steady incremental progress toward a program of legislated social justice; or in the accumulation of social resistances — led by an organized vanguard or by autonomous actions of loose civil-society networks — crystallizing in a dramatic moment of institutional breakdown and political rupture. CD has carried, instead, the uncomfortable case: that a new national political organization of the left has to be built; that strategic and particular interventions need reconsidering; and that the Left needs to struggle in, against and apart from the state (Sam Gindin, "The Fightback Against Globalization Must Begin at Home," 38:6, November/December, 2004). This is no way a claim that, for most contributors, the socialist vision of Marx, Luxemburg and Gramsci should be discarded. Quite the contrary: their declaration for radical democracy turned against capitalist institutions has gained in relevancy. But it is an assertion that the socialist project must be fully contemporary for its time — calibrating the changes in techniques of production and communications and integrating the transformations in global social relations.

The precise meaning of this project in the *CD* milieux has mutated significantly across the decades. From its first decade being fixed on confronting foreign capital by building up public ownership and a new national policy, an agenda of socio-ecological transformation has been central to the last. The parameters of this project have been set widely, ranging across various conceptions of localism, mutualism, communism and others. There is not — nor could there have been — a *CD* school of political economy that fit neatly into the boxes of left-nationalism, Leninism, euro-communism and so forth. This has its strengths. No orthodoxy today is capable of synthesizing the challenges of a post-capitalist project for Canada or, for that matter, elsewhere.[33]

Here it is the tenacity that has characterized the *CD* enterprise that impresses: the unflagging resolve that capitalism directly violates the equality claims of liberal democracy and is incapable of meeting the human needs of all. In the face of innumerable political conversions to faith in capitalism and the market (not least by Canadian social democracy), the contribution of *CD* lies in fidelity to its banner "the world can be changed." This is the imperative of the question of "what can be done" in present circumstances, yet never shying from the socialist one of "what needs to be done."

It is an urgent task of the coming decades to sustain the critique of the irrationalities produced by a capitalist world market, and the particular ecological destructiveness of Canadian capitalism. The ceaseless and unchecked production for exchange-value has again given rise to a "great crisis of capitalism" and an age of permanent austerity. What social forces and political organization can reverse this trajectory and contribute to an advance toward socialism? This returns to the question of strategy.[34] *CD* is likely to continue to make a vital contribution to addressing that question and to the making of the next New Left in Canada.

PART VIII

THE REGIONAL AND URBAN DIMENSION

CHAPTER 16
The Home Province:
Canadian Dimension and Manitoba
Alvin Finkel

The Doer New Democratic government chose to accept nearly all
of the regressive amendments to the Manitoba Labour Relations
Act *introduced by the Filmon government. It also rejected the*
recommendation of its own appointed Minimum Wage Chairman,
John Godard, a professor of business, who argued that the standard
approach of adding an arbitrarily chosen hourly increase to the
minimum wage should be rejected in favour of a system that ties the
minimum wage to a universal standard of just pay, like Statistics
Canada's Low-Income Cut-Off. Instead, the Doer government chose
the two-bits-an-hour route. And, when assembly-line workers at Motor
Coach Industries, a large bus manufacturer, chose to go on strike
despite threats of plant closure and relocation to the south, the premier
intervened on the side of the company, urging workers to accept a
humiliating contract.

— Canadian Dimension *Editorial (37:2, March/April 2003)*

In its first five years, *Canadian Dimension* focused on pan-Canadian
and international concerns, barely betraying the identity of its place of
publication. By the 1970s, however, *CD* expanded its coverage of provincial and municipal issues, social movements, cultural production and
iconic individuals. Unsurprisingly, because the journal was planned by

Winnipeg-based editors and Manitobans produced a disproportionate number of the articles relative to their weight in the Canadian population, more than any other source the pages of *Canadian Dimension* offer the most thorough point of reference of Manitoba's history from a left-wing perspective.

A three-part feature section in the July 1969 issue commemorated the Winnipeg General Strike's fiftieth anniversary. Its contents reflected the willingness of *CD* to engage both socialist and "moderate" views. This became less common after the Waffle challenge clarified the huge divide within left-of-centre thinking in Canada, including Manitoba. An interview with Fred Tipping, a member of the Strike Committee that led the strikers, spoke of the gains that workers make when they unite to fight the bosses and bourgeois governments (6:2, July/August 1969). By contrast, economist H.C. Pentland provided an excellent analysis of the different ways in which the business elite, on the one hand, and the union leaders, on the other, regarded the strike as an unwise strategy for labour. A general strike, he noted, makes capitalists "close ranks and fight like jungle beasts for their class interests." Rather more radical analyses of the strike that created a permanent sense of class grievance in Winnipeg appeared in the issue marking the seventy-fifth anniversary of the strike (28:3, May/June 1994).

The issue following the first General Strike accounts announced the victory of the Manitoba NDP in the provincial election in June, 1969, to *CD* readers. Cy Gonick wrote that "the centre position was vacant and the vacuum could be filled by the NDP because, over the years the NDP has melted into the conservatism of Manitoba" (6:3-4, August/September 1969). He was optimistic that, while the new government was not radical, it would demonstrate an openness to innovation that would benefit Manitobans. Gonick urged the NDP government to tackle the widespread poverty in Manitoba and not to be shy of public instruments to achieve this goal. The modest editorial omitted an interesting detail: Cy was one of the elected MLAs, defeating Tory Finance Minister Gurney Evans in a mixed working-class/middle-class seat that had never been fertile ground for the NDP before. But the outlines of that editorial presaged the position that *CD* would generally take regarding NDP governments in Manitoba. They were not radical, but they would take at least some steps that the Conservatives and Liberals would be loath to take. Nonetheless, the magazine's attitude, as we shall see, differed somewhat with regards to each of the three runs at power that the NDP has had in Manitoba so far.

Within months, *CD* was already demonstrating its disillusionment with the NDP administration of Edward Schreyer. The February/March 1970 issue, which placed Schreyer on the cover, had a long feature by University of Manitoba economics graduate student Harold Chorney about the Manitoba Development Fund, a Tory-created instrument to use public money in the form of grants and loans to lure private investors to Manitoba. The Fund was shovelling taxpayers' dollars to private companies with few job guarantees. Its most notorious grant promised $100 million to Churchill Forest Industries, a mysterious group of European investors, to develop a sawmill and pulp and paper mill in The Pas. Chorney noted that although most of the money promised by the Conservatives to the obscure investors had yet to be dished out when the NDP came to power, Schreyer, who had once opposed the CFI project altogether, now supported the deal, announcing a renegotiation with the principals that gave no greater protection to the investment of the people of Manitoba. The CFI story would be followed up several times in *Dimension*; when the project had gone bust, Gonick provided an account of the NDP caucus discussion on the project (10:5, November 1974), in which he denounced "the Schreyer administration's refusal to act in a principled and responsible manner in those crucial 18 months" during which the NDP government handed tens of millions to CFI that would never be recovered.

While *CD* found some reasons to praise the Schreyer government, particularly the implementation of public auto insurance, mostly the magazine noticed growing conservatism within the administration, especially in its second term, and an unhealthy contempt for party democracy. I reported on the 1970 and 1971 provincial conventions (7:5, December 1970; 9:2-3, January 1973), observing the ways in which cabinet ministers attempted to neuter the party. My efforts were unappreciated by Lily Schreyer, the wife of the premier. She tore her copy of the December

1970 issue into hundreds of pieces and mailed it to Cy, commenting, "with friends like these, who needs enemies?"

But *CD*'s Manitoba coverage in the 1970s went well beyond discussions of its frustrations with the provincial NDP. In 1970, when I was employed as *CD*'s full-time assistant editor, we ventured beyond the earlier academic political pieces in the magazine to also include some journalistic pieces that included voices from the streets. In a special double issue, we produced a Manitoba section of nine articles to coincide with Manitoba's centennial as a province. For the first time, the neocolonial regime under which Manitoba Natives lived was featured prominently in *CD* with two articles. Stanley Ryerson commemorated Louis Riel's historic role in the period before the province was established in his article, "Riel vs. Anglo-Canadian Imperialism" while Heather Robertson's "100 Years After the Treaties" focused on neocolonial relations imposed on First Nations by both the Canadian and Manitoba governments (7:1-2, June/July 1970). This issue also had articles on the corporate elite of Winnipeg, the province's cultural elite, and the so-called Citizens' Committees of a small group of developers who controlled Winnipeg's civic politics. Also featured was a set of interviews that I conducted with a range of people in Winnipeg and Selkirk which illustrated how different groups of Manitobans responded to the lavish government-sponsored events that marked the centennial, and their hopes for change during Manitoba's centennial. While the wife of a construction company president on exclusive Wellington Crescent in Winnipeg planned to attend a slew of events and wished only for the overthrow of the NDP government, a pensioner in Winnipeg's North End would attend no events because he could not afford bus fare to get to them.

The Winnipeg North End's past and present were celebrated in a variety of articles in *CD* over the years. Myra Haas's "On the Street Where I Live—Excerpts from an Unpublished Novel" (10:4, September 1974) celebrated Selkirk Avenue, with its variety of ethnic eateries and shops and its friendly denizens who all seemed to know each other. But a later issue presented several articles with a grittier view of the area. Both a photo essay by John Paskievich, "North End Winnipeg," and an article by George Melnyk on the continued degradation of his old neighbourhood despite eight years of an NDP regime complicated the *gemeinschaft* portrayed by Haas for the area (12:4-5, September 1977). But poems and celebrations of such North End institutions as Kelekis restaurant and The Good Earth served to balance the critical insights of Paskievich and Melnyk.

Over the years, as North Winnipeg changed from an area of modest bungalows owned by working-class residents mainly of eastern European descent to an area where those small homes were bought by slumlords who then rented them to First Nations migrants to Winnipeg, the portrait of the area in CD became bleaker. Still, there remained an emphasis on the resilience of North Enders, with emphasis now on residents' efforts to create cooperative institutions that reflected Native values and provided an alternative to the Native gangs that scooped up young people whose lives were marked by racism, limited opportunities and complicated family relationships. Esyllt Jones (30:1, February/March 1996), for example, wrote about the group Community United for Change, of which she was a member. Initiated by community development workers, its members were mostly single moms, many without paid work, and their key priority was to repel the johns who crept in from better-off parts of the city and who accosted all women, whether they were in the sex trade or not. The constant, noisy presence of the johns in their cars was a reminder of the class, race and sexual prejudices within Winnipeg of which the area residents were victims who intended to resist their oppressors. Jones, a student and single mom who chose to live in the North End primarily to enjoy cheap accommodation, had been the victim of several house break-ins and admitted that she did not feel that she or her son were especially safe in the slums. But she drew strength from the determination of her fellow community members to create a better life for themselves and their offspring.

Jim Silver, writing of "Winnipeg's North End, Yesterday and Today," (44:6, November/December 2010) wrote that, "Many in Winnipeg do not venture into today's North End; most are largely ignorant of life in the North End; it has ever been thus." Like Jones, Silver suggested that the initiatives occurring in the North End to counter gang violence, unemployment and hopelessness sprung from the grassroots. While the NDP provincial government of the period after 1999 was sympathetic to the social origins of North End destitution and crime and supported some community initiatives meant to house people better, and to promote education, employment and community solutions to criminal activity, its fiscal conservatism limited such support.

Articles dealing with both the plight and resistance of Aboriginal communities, both within Winnipeg's North End and throughout the province — rare in *CD* before the centennial issue — became common fare in the 1980s. In the summer issue of 1984 (18:4), two articles dealt with Native efforts in Manitoba to attack neocolonialism and disempowerment. One was an article by Ustun Reinert on Métis self-government initiatives while the other was an interview with Robert Daniel, coordinator of Anishinabe, which was tackling the problem of "stolen children" from Native communities by placing children for adoptions on reserves. Then, in December 1985 (19:5), Murray Dobbin raised the controversial issue, "Why Pardon Riel" and provided an analysis of the position of the Métis in the twentieth century.

Coverage of both the victimization and fightback of Native peoples in Manitoba continued in the years that followed. Journalist Lisa Priest provided a summary of her book on the murder of Helen Betty Osborne, a young Native woman who was raped and murdered by young men in The Pas in 1971 (23:4, June 1989). While Priest focused on a conspiracy of silence in the white community that protected the murderers for many years, *CD* also published the reactions of three Native women to Priest's account, all of whom documented Native women's efforts to organize to fight both racism and sexual oppression. In September 1990 (24:6), Tanya Lester documented a national story that had focused on NDP MLA Elijah Harper's use of the Meech Lake debate to highlight federal inaction regarding the poverty of Native peoples. Lester took the story beyond the single individual to describe "How Manitoba's Aboriginal People Stopped Meech."

In recent issues, *CD* coverage of Manitoba has returned to a focus on both the destitution and fighting spirit of Native communities. Helen Falding (45:2, March/April 2011) documented the poor health of the community of ten thousand people in Island Lake owing to poor living conditions that the federal government largely ignored. Deadly outbreaks

405

of H1N1 flu and whooping cough highlighted the desperate conditions of life of the people who live along the shores of Island Lake and Red Sucker Lake, half of whom had no plumbing. Two years earlier (44:1, January/February 2009), Jim Silver outlined the work of Aboriginal organizations in Winnipeg's inner city. The March/April 2010 issue (44:2) interviewed Native gang leaders in the area, who demonstrated that despite being written off by the media and by some organizations within their communities, they had a social historical understanding of why their gangs existed and what changes were necessary within their communities to eradicate the need for gangs.

A recurring issue in *CD*'s examination of European colonialism in northern Manitoba has been the devastating impact of Manitoba Hydro's hydroelectric projects in Northern Manitoba. Scientist Cass Booy first raised the issue in the July 1973 issue (9:6), expressing his disappointment that the Schreyer government, which had initially appeared willing to reconsider its Tory predecessor's determination to flood the stable and indeed wealthy First Nations community of South Indian Lake, folded to Manitoba Hydro and business pressure to approve the project. Three decades later, Peter Kulchyski, Native studies professor and Aboriginal rights activist, produced several articles on Manitoba Hydro's continuing colonial assumption that First Nations in northern Manitoba had no right to stand in the way of the Crown corporation's ambitious plans to continue expanding its dam-building projects. It began with his piece, "Manitoba Hydro: How to Build a Legacy of Hatred" (38:3, May/June 2004), which accused Hydro and its political masters of subordinating the interests of Northern Native communities to southerners' desire for cheaper energy for industrial and residential purposes.

A lively debate ensued when the chief and a councillor of the Nisichawayasihk Cree Nation replied to Kulchyski's article, insisting that they had wrested significant concessions from Manitoba Hydro and suggesting that Kulchyski needed to recognize that the Cree in the North could no longer supply their needs solely through hunting (39:1, January/February 2005). Kulchyski, unrepentant, suggested that the chief and councillor had, at least in part, embraced the views of colonial administrators. "In fact, what the twentieth century proved is that hunting, long predicted to be outdated, is a resilient, flexible, sustainable way of life that offers rewards of an incalculable sort." Later that year (39:6, November/December 2005), Kulchyski was back with a report on Natives in Grand Rapids setting up a camp to publicize their demand for compensation for a Manitoba Hydro project.

The gradual amplification of coverage of Native struggles in Manitoba over the years fit in with the magazine's embrace after the 1960s of issues of race, gender, lifestyles and environment that went beyond the initial narrow focus of CD. Initially articles on women's liberation were of a generic sort and only rarely homed in on particular places and specific struggles. But an article by Meral Somer in July 1985 (19:3), an issue which featured a variety of articles on the Howard Pawley NDP regime in Manitoba, provided the sometimes diverging views of three prominent Manitoba feminists on "Women and the NDP." Though all three were disappointed with the government's limited progress on files of importance to women, Roberta Ellis, chairperson for the Manitoba Advisory Council on the Status of Women, gave the government some credit for its willingness to lay charges against wife abusers and their spending on daycare. Union leader Leslie Spillett, by contrast, regarded the government's overall performance as "pitiful," including their daycare program. She pointed out that the government was "fiscally conservative" and had done little to promote pay equity. By contrast, Susan Hart (20:1, March 1986) who would later be elected president of the Mantoba Federation of Labour, called Manitoba's 1985 pay equity legislation "gutsy," while decrying its application only to public sector workers, from which it excluded municipalities and school boards.

Beginning in the 1980s, tributes to Manitoba feminists, both those well known nationally and internationally and those known mainly to local activists, often appeared in CD. In the March 1987 issue (21:1), Ken Hughes paid tribute to author Margaret Laurence, while Brenda Austin-Smith extolled Milly Lamb, "activist, teacher, scholar, literary critic, writer and friend" in the March 1992 issue (26:2). Lamb and Laurence had worked together on political struggles in the 1940s, and though Lamb was known to few outside of Winnipeg leftist circles and her students, her tireless efforts to promote feminism, peace and socialism made her a role model for many Winnipeg leftists of several generations.

CD articles often dealt with the struggles of women workers, including nurses and other workers in the medical field. Both strikes and the consciousness of unions and workers more generally were a constant theme in the magazine, and for Manitoba, the relationship between the unions and the NDP was also frequently commented on. While *CD* was generally more positive towards the more interventionist Pawley administration of the 1980s than the second Schreyer government, it was hardly uncritical. It took particular aim at Pawley's sticking to his promise to the business community in Manitoba not to follow Quebec in passing an anti-scab law. As compensation, it offered final-offer selection as an alternative for striking workers dealing with intransigent management. The Manitoba Federation of Labour split on the issue at its annual convention though government supporters won the vote. *CD* warned in an article by Peter Kennedy (19:6, January/February 1986) that subsequent right-wing governments might use the legislation to end strikes and force weak settlements on workers. *CD's* forecast proved prophetic when the Filmon government, in the 1990s, introducing a slew of anti-labour legislation, included forcing strikers to vote on a supposed final offer from management when management requested one. Errol Black discussed the Tory assault on workers (30:5, September/October 1996) in an article entitled "The Manitoba government declares war on workers and trade unions,"

While *CD* was often similarly prophetic on other Manitoba issues, it occasionally slipped up big time. When a tired Schreyer administration offered the Manitoba electorate nothing new in 1977, Sterling Lyon's Progressive Conservatives took office after Lyon promised not to undo the social and economic reforms of their predecessors. "We do not perceive the new Tory administration in Manitoba destroying most of what the NDP has introduced in Manitoba," *CD* editorialized confidently in December, 1977 (12:8). But two issues later came a report of ruthless government cuts to social programs, a selling-off of profitable Crown corporations established by the NDP, and attacks on working people's rights to overtime pay, job safety and minimum wages. Canada's first neoliberal government had slipped in under *CD*'s radar and it would be more cautious afterwards about assumptions regarding the continuation of a postwar welfare state consensus, however conservative, in Manitoba.

Indeed, *CD* charted the tragic embrace of neoliberalism by the Manitoba NDP and its consequences for that party's performance after it returned to power in the province in 1999. As the party led by Gary Doer won its third consecutive election in 2007, Cy Gonick made clear that the latest iteration of the NDP lacked the reformist zeal, however cautious, of either the Schreyer or Pawley administrations. "The man doesn't have a socialist bone in his body, a characterization he would enthusiastically endorse" (41:4, July/August 2007). Though the Manitoba business community continued ritualistically to support the Conservatives over the NDP, they spoke positively of the Doer regime and its emphasis on tax cuts and business-favourable labour and agricultural policies. Almost the only praiseworthy achievement of the Doer years was the government's agreement to support a protected area on the east side of Lake Winnipeg as it planned its hydroelectric development policies. Gonick made clear that even that achievement had only been made possible by a long-fought battle of Indigenous peoples and environmentalists.

In September 2011, as Doer's successor, Greg Selinger, battled for a fourth consecutive term for the NDP, Gonick elaborated on the consequences of the status quo policies that both Doer and Selinger had pursued. Manitoba's child poverty rates remained the highest in Canada, and social allowances had declined, after inflation, since the NDP had regained power in 1999. Selinger had given a modest lift to the minimum wage but only after pressures from a well-organized coalition of labour, church and anti-poverty groups. While the NDP still expected the less well-off in Manitoba to give them their votes, the party had largely succumbed to conservative business views of how to organize the provincial economy and for whose benefit.

Manitoba's cultural production was becoming less conservative over time and beginning with the centennial issue *CD* began, at least occasionally, to pay tribute to various Manitoba authors, artists and musicians who either embraced left-wing political views or who broke the cultural mold in other ways. Kelly Clark, whose cover designs and layout had for years made *CD* incredibly attractive for a low-budget magazine, received a twenty-four-page spread on his art (14:8, August 1980). A special issue on "Our Winnipeg" (44:1, January/February 2010), edited by filmmakers Noam Gonick and Guy Maddin, and writer Ria Julien, paid tribute to the Manitoba Theatre Centre's legendary director John Hirsch as well as to Winnipeg artists. But in line with the broader understanding of culture that *CD* had developed after its early years, the special issue also shone a spotlight on such Winnipeg institutions as Bar Italia and the left-wing hangout Mondragon Bookstore and Coffeehouse, which featured not only books and coffee but an excellent restaurant and fair-trade store, with the entire operation run as a worker coop. The cultural coverage was not all cheery. In the April 1978 edition (13:1), Manitoba artist Trudie Heiman lamented the poor representation of women in the arts in the province. And in September 2001 (35:5), Paul Phillips regretted that Winnipeg's iconic Folk Festival, originally a haven for every kind of traditional music, had lost its way and become "a multi-stage pop concert festival with a few folk performers thrown in for flavour."

No doubt, with its base in Winnipeg, *CD*, despite its valiant efforts to cover events throughout the province, seemed to give outsize coverage to the capital city where indeed an increasing majority of Manitobans lived. But the presence of Brandon's Errol Black on the editorial collective insured that Manitoba's second city also received a reasonable share of Manitoba pieces within the magazine. While Black also reported on province-wide issues and phenomena, he provided over the years both historical and present-day issue-based articles. His article, "Would You Hire This Man?" (17:2, May 1983) documented the interference of Brandon's business elite along with the Lyon government in trying to dictate who and what could be presented in university classrooms in the city. In July of the same year (17:3), Errol Black and Tom Black wrote a historical piece on the East End Community Centre, which they viewed as representing "working class socialism on a small scale." Black's "The Struggle Against Eaton's Moves to Manitoba" in the March 1986 magazine (20:1) reported Eaton's threats to close down half of its Brandon operation to spite the Manitoba government for imposing a first contract that Eaton's, which nevertheless adamantly refused to open its books, swore it could not afford.

Just as culture was better represented in *CD* as the years passed, the environmental movement and its concerns picked up more coverage from the 1980s onwards. An article by Ken Gibbons (19:3, July/August 1985) gave the Pawley government a B on intentions and C on environmental actions, noting that the predecessor Lyon regime rated an F on both scores. Gibbons commended the NDP on its handling of the Garrison River diversion project and for establishing collection depots to recover waste, but condemned its continued aerial spraying with toxic chemicals to deal with Manitoba's gazillions of mosquitoes. In April/May 1995 (29:2), *CD* supported protests against the granting of an environmental licence to Louisiana Pacific to clear-cut a huge area of forest lands and build the world's largest oriented strand board operation. Writer Don Sullivan sympathized with demands of First Nations for co-management of the resource, and protection of trapping areas as well as culturally significant places.

The loving but critical glimpses and full portraits of Manitoba that *CD* provided, especially from members of the editorial collective that produced the magazine in later years, make that magazine a documentary treasure of everything that a left-winger might want to know about Manitoba over the past fifty years. Interestingly, while the magazine's views about what constituted politics and therefore what deserved inclusion in a change-oriented journal demonstrated a greater plasticity over time, the underlying notions about what was right and what was wrong about Manitoba maintained an amazing continuity over half a century.

CHAPTER 17
Work and Change in Atlantic Canada
Angela Day

As each new obstacle arose — injunctions, imprisonments, the cumulative hardships of maintaining a family on the $10 to $20 a week strike pay month after month — the families grew more militant in their determination to gain the only thing that could improve the previous pattern of their lives — the UFAWU [United Fishermen and Allied Workers Union]. As one Mulgrave woman said, "We know we have to go hungry to get anything that's worth fighting for."

— Larry Katz (8:1, June 1971)

In many ways, the East Coast is an enclave of forgotten history. It's the location of a history that persists, but we're rarely represented in national papers, textbooks or magazines. Instead, our stories are woven through journeys out west, large families and kitchen parties.

Struggle is writ large here, but is absorbed by the sound of the waves, rarely making it onto the national agenda — unless it involves some degree of quaintness or a disproportionate level of violence.

The last fifty years of *Canadian Dimension* stories depict some of these hidden histories. They cover stories that most younger generations of Atlantic Canadians are unfamiliar with, such as the 1971 fishermen's strike in Nova Scotia; the politics behind the rise of the Irving empire in New Brunswick; and Newfoundland's union struggles.

A key theme in all of the articles is working-class life in a resource-based economy. Outward migration, the collapse of the fisheries, the closing of coal mines and steel factories, and a strong culture of resistance are all symptomatic of an economy focused on export-based resource extraction.

While the world is changing rapidly, the socio-economic climate remains eerily similar in 2012 to that of the 1970s.

In 1966 New Brunswick began facing significant economic reforms, leading to centralization of power, modernization of state services, and increased taxes in what *CD* writer Richard Wilbur called "20th Century Reform" (3:4, March/June 1966). Of course, this trend could arguably be seen as a movement towards a more egalitarian and functioning province, but according to Wilbur, this centralization did not have these intentions, nor this effect. While many business owners were not in favour of the reforms due in part to higher taxes, K.C. Irving, at the beginning of his economic reign in NB, was mildly affected, and thus didn't block the reforms.

By 1969, again according to Wilbur (6:3-4, August/September 1969), the reality in New Brunswick was such that "no government can survive for long if it ignores or bucks K.C. Irving." Already, Irving controlled the region's pulp and paper; public transportation; and the media:

"The CBC is perhaps the only media outlet that remains beyond Irving's direct control, but even here, as I can attest, any mention of Irving in a broadcast immediately brings requests for copies of the scripts from the industrialist's legal representatives in Saint John and Halifax."

That said, *The Mysterious East* and *The 4th Estate* were both Maritimes-based alternative publications with, as a *CD* writer explained, "slender populations and slender resources" (8:1, June 1971). The writer proceeded to say that what "*The Mysterious East* has done, and nothing else really matters, is to break the Irving monopoly." Alas, the Fredericton-based magazine only lasted for a few years, starting in 1969 and going out of print in 1972.

The other publication, the *4th Estate*, was published out of Halifax by a group of journalists from 1969 to 1977, and receives much more praise in the 1971 *CD* article — "with all the punch and topicality that a

413

popular newspaper should have." The thrust of the *4th Estate* was a focus on slum housing — "naming landlords, printing pictures of their homes, and in two cases publishing a picture of a landlord's retail business." More than three decades later, with rapid gentrification and skyrocketing rents incongruous with the city's few jobs, Halifax could use such a publication.

Perhaps the most notable battle on the East Coast emerged in the 1970s, covered in "Maritime Fisherman vs. Leviathan," by Larry Katz (8:1, June 1971). Katz states that "after almost three months of picketing the facts of the strike became known, and Nova Scotia may now be facing the severest confrontation between government and labor that it has ever witnessed." Fishermen worked ten to twelve days at sea, with two days off between trips, all year round. They received a so-called minimum wage of $4/day, but they were required to pay room and board, resulting in as little as $2 for a ten-day trip. The companies tried to starve the fisherman back to work, but they were "already used to deprivation." In a beautiful motion of solidarity, and rare demonstration of national interests in the region, the National Farmer's Union supplied produce for the striking families. The fight was deemed "heroic and protracted" by Katz.

The confrontation was centred on the demand for recognition of the workers' union of choice — the United Fishermen and Allied Workers Union (UFAWU). The Canadian Labour Congress (CLC) didn't support this demand, saying they would rather leave Nova Scotia than support the UFAWU. Various restrictions were forced on strikers during talks resulting in an agreement between the workers and the companies seven months later, without their key demand being met.

The story of the (in)famous fishing strike is one of few in the sixties and seventies that highlights the roles of women in Maritime history. According to Katz, "the strike had an . . . effect on family relationships. As the women became actively involved, they too began to realize they were an integral part of the struggle."

In Lori Vitale Cox's 1996 article, she explains that women were hit especially hard by the fishing crisis, and writes "In the Bay [St. Lawrence], women have been the first ones to sense what has been going on and they have been at the centre of the struggle." The article then describes the Bay

St. Lawrence Women's FishNet, a way for women who were concerned about the fishery crisis to connect and take action.

A review of all of the articles illustrates that this system has been carefully architected — low wages plus resource extraction equals profit for a select few, and this "development" via a capitalist lens. In 1971, Richard Wilbur took a crack at explaining the "planned underdevelopment" in the Maritimes, which he looks at systematically, via an examination of the different resource bases, and how they were quickly depleted by rapid extraction (7:7, January/February 1971). Jobs were more of a focus than natural resources, but when the natural resources were gone, so were the jobs.

It wasn't just foreign private enterprise driving the region's political economy, however. Over decades, the province of Nova Scotia and the federal government have both clearly showed that the preservation of Maritime culture, resources and diverse local economy is not a priority. Perhaps the clearest example of this is in the 1984 story "The State Versus The Woods Harbour 15 & 1043" (Grady and Sacouman, 18:3, June 1984), which describes a standoff between the Department of Fisheries and Oceans (DFO) and the people of Woods Harbour, Nova Scotia, who were "defending their community and way of life." The battle was over inshore vs. offshore fishing, where a community member said "state capital [was] being used to salvage the biggie, while even the most successful of the little guys [were] being drowned."

While raw, this story is also an inspiring glimpse into the strength of communities. As one Mulgrave woman said, "We know that we have to go hungry to get anything that's worth fighting for." Then and today, this is one of the unfortunate realities of life on the East Coast — people end up fighting for things they shouldn't need to fight for.

Of course, the fishing crisis wasn't limited to Nova Scotia — it was also fierce in Newfoundland, where at one point, in "Fish and the Fisherman" (13:2), McCurdy writes: "the resource seemed limitless, and it became the nerve centre of a whole way of life."

History would tell that resources are never limitless. Although Newfoundlanders practiced "occupational pluralism," which consisted of making a living in diverse ways — fishing, logging, sealing, gardening and fur trapping — overfishing quickly ensued. Overfishing was not necessarily a result of the local communities' fishing practices, but also by an array of offshore "foreign fleets."

In this context of economic insecurity, Newfoundland fishermen and their families battled for unionization to try and hold onto their livelihood. With the leadership of a "radical priest," Father Desmond McGrath, they formed the Newfoundland Fishermen, Food and Allied Workers union (NFFAW), a formation that happened over a cold winter of "meetings in kitchens and school rooms along the northwest coast." Beyond financial gains, McCurdy said the greatest accomplishment of the NFFAW was an establishment of pride in Newfoundland's fishing industry.

Meetings in kitchens are not relics of the past, though. In "Resources, Struggles and Human Development in Atlantic Canada" (19:1, March/ April, 1985), Jim Sacouman said, "'making do' continues as a way of life in the region . . . Perhaps in no other region of Canada are there as many unemployed and underemployed socialists and feminists working towards equality in their own locales."

The precariousness of the Atlantic economy led to significant outward migration over decades, continuing today with workers heading off to Ontario, Alberta, British Columbia and elsewhere in search of a decent wage. In a particularly poetic article about migration in the region, Susan Perly described the setting: "the generation about to go mixes with the generation that has already been" (13:2). The article weaves in the story of a Cape Breton band called Every Buddy, whose songs evoke the experience of the local Everyman, always somewhere between home and away.

Like any written history, there are still stories within these stories that merit written exposure — particularly the voices of African Nova Scotians, and the Mi'kmaq, which are not always explicit on these pages.

That said, during the Burnt Church standoff, CD provided an effective counterweight to Eurocentric stories told by government actors and mainstream media. In "The Media, The Marshall Decision and Aboriginal Representation" (36:4, July/August 2002), Paul Fitzgerald examined the media response to the Burnt Church conflict and Aboriginal representation, providing a thorough critique of the way Aboriginal groups were portrayed. The media's lack of focus on the Marshall decision, which clearly upheld Native fishing rights, was a way of vilifying the Aboriginal community of Burnt Church. This article is another example of east coast resource wars, yet intensified by colonialism.

Little Prince Edward Island got a touch of limelight in the fifty years of coverage. In 1987, Mary Boyd illustrated how, to create jobs — PEI also has a higher than average unemployment rate — Litton Industries was awarded a federal contract to build thirty-nine air defense, anti-tank system units for the military (21:4, July/August 1987). Social justice groups were outraged, although the local NDP players as well as key labour unions were notably mute. Boyd wrote, "the Island experience proved that this trend towards militarization can be overcome by greater mobilization and solidarity among groups." Litton didn't end up in PEI (although it did end up in NS).

This region is always referred to as a have-not place. And, in many ways that's true. But, having little is what makes people create here — whether that's music, art, community or change. We don't wait for things to come, because we know they won't. And, if fifty years of coverage says anything, it says that if we need something, we'll fight for it.

CHAPTER 18
The "Next Year" Province:
Canadian Dimension and Saskatchewan

James N. McCrorie

The NDP's relationship with labour can be understood best by looking at its relationship with business. . . . NDP administrations . . . delivered four things they could claim to be brought about better than other political parties: (a) astute oversight over capitalist economic development; (b) sound and honest public administration; (c) domestication of the labour and social movements; and (d) cautious and incremental improvements to the welfare state.

— Larry Haiven (37:2, January/February 1999)

Canadians are a people of the Shield. We settle in the river valleys and hug the coastlines. Only in the north and on the prairies have we dared spread out — in modest numbers and at considerable risk. The land encompassed by the province of Saskatchewan has always been central to the history and political economy of the prairie region and beyond. Beginning in the seventeenth century, the French and British colonial powers fought to marry the region to their metropolitan needs and colonial ambitions. Following Confederation, the political economy of the region was quickly converted from a fur staple to a wheat economy, providing central Canada with a captive, expanding, noncompetitive market for Canadian manufactured goods and commercial services.

Throughout the twentieth century, the region in general, and

Saskatchewan in particular, revolted against the "national policy" — one that defined the "national interest" in central Canadian terms, at times to the disadvantage of the region. Today, the political economy of the region and province has expanded beyond the "wheat economy" to challenge, if only momentarily, the hegemony of central Canada. The question follows: how has *Canadian Dimension* captured and dealt with this legacy and what is becoming of it?

As Alvin Finkel notes in his contribution to this book, *CD* focused on pan-Canadian and international concerns during its first five years of publication. When it turned its attention to Saskatchewan it did so forcefully. Three articles among the first about the province are outstanding: Lorne Brown's "A Hinterland Rebels" (8:8, August 1972), the late John Gallagher's "Moose Jaw: Moscow of the Prairies" (9:7-8, November/ December 1973) and James Harding's "Saskatchewan Waffles" (10:1, April 1974).

Brown's article deals with a succinct history of the Saskatchewan Farmers' Movement. With the commencement of agricultural settlement in the last two decades of the nineteenth century, the agrarians were quick to discover that the rules of the political economy had not been made for them. If they were offered free land and the chance to till it, it was eastern financial, merchant and industrial capital that "farmed the farmers." Over time, the agrarians revolted and Brown did a commendable job describing the scope and consequences of this rebellion. During the first half of the twentieth century, the agrarians challenged financial, commercial and industrial capital by building cooperatives and credit unions. In the political arena, they eventually rejected the "old line parties" and placed their faith in the CCF. The formation of the first "socialist" government in 1944 was arguably their crowning achievement. Over time, however, Brown concluded, the NDP became a political party with "no understanding of socialism, let alone any attachment to it." He speculated that new socialist formations might arise and it is the 1973 split of the Waffle from the NDP that is ably dealt with by Gallagher and Harding.

Harding's "Saskatchewan Waffles" is the more comprehensive of the two. The split of the Waffle from the NDP took place at a convention held in Moose Jaw on October 18, 1973. Harding offered a comprehensive coverage of the convention, reporting that two tendencies emerged from the debate. One he labeled "populace" and the other "vulgar marxist." His final conclusion about the Waffle was not flattering. "Although the Saskatchewan Waffle has . . . contact with the larger population, which may be its saving grace, it has all the components of becoming a non-NDP reformist party at its inception. . . . I think the most accurate way to describe the Saskatchewan Waffle may be social democrats in a hurry."

John Gallagher's report was more optimistic. In his words: "Despite its parochialism, its frailty and isolation, its apparent inability to yet deal with ideological and organizational questions in anything more than a fuzzy way, the Saskatchewan Waffle does offer hope for the growth of a socialist left." It was a hope that never materialized. The 1944 provincial election is correctly remembered as the one in which the first socialist government was elected in North America. What is so often overlooked is that it was an election in which metropolitan ideological hegemony triumphed over the celebration of the hinterland. Both the incumbent Liberals and the opposition CCF campaigned on a platform of "industrialization." They did so in the belief that agriculture and rural life alone could never provide a sustainable future for the province.

CD has not explored and captured the consequences of this moment as well as it might have. That notwithstanding, it has assembled an impressive stable of contributors, many with academic credentials and records of scholarship. They include Ron Bourgeault, Joyce Green, John Conway, Alvin Finkel, Larry Haiven, the late Ed Mahood, Martin Robin, Bob Sass, the late Ray Sentes and John Warnock. Other notable contributors over the years include Barb Byers, Murray Dobbin, Barbara Evans, John Ferguson, the late Fred Gudmundson, Dennise Henning, Don Kossick, Stephen Larose, Barry Lipton, Glen Makahonuk, Don Mitchell, Terry Pugh, Darrin Qualman, Mark Stobbe, Bernadette Wagner, Winona Wheeler and Victoria Wotherspoon.

A third of the articles deal with the NDP: its electoral triumphs and failures, and the Party's consistent and continuing move to the right. This, despite the strong influence the Waffle enjoyed in shaping party policy at the 1972 provincial convention.[1] But as J.J. Jons (John Gallagher) reports in "No More Smiles" in the same issue, the Party's right wing captured all the important party offices, leaving a left-wing program in the hands of those opposed to it.

In a recent review of David McGrane's *New Directions in Saskatchewan Public Policy*[2] (*CD* 45:3, 2012), John Warnock pointedly documents the NDP's policy shift to the right, catering to business interests and avoiding the demands of the labour and women's movements. Taken together, the articles on the NDP have two things in common. All document the drift away from any pretense of "socialism" to the quiet acceptance of capitalism. None explain why. The rest of the articles are scattered over a wide range of topics and concerns: trade union issues, the environment, occupational health and safety, mining, pulp mills, the meat packing industry and the changing character of agriculture.

To the extent that the strategy of industrialization is dealt with, two articles deserve mention. Alvin Finkel's "Saskatchewan: The Great Depression" (7:4, October/November 1970) described the process of "de-industrialization" in towns like Moose Jaw, where Robin Hood Mills, Gulf Oil, Prairie Bag Plant and Moose Jaw Sash and Door closed operations. Equally devastating were the closure of the CPR car repair shop and the reduction of crews in the running trades. Where growth has taken place is in the resource sector. An insightful article by the Saskatoon Resources Study Group (8:2, August 1971) on the Prince Albert Pulp Mill and the one scheduled for operation in Meadow Lake examined the degree to which taxpayer risk and financial support was co-opted by the Liberal Government to create a favourable environment from which foreign capital could extract profit.

Barbara Evans's article "Women's Role in the Rise of the Saskatchewan Farmers Movement and Early CCF" (21:3, May/June 1973) reminds readers that farm women were not merely homemakers. They played an important role in the process of production and an active role in the development and shaping of agricultural and social policy. Indeed, the first public call for universal, publicly funded medicare came from the women's section of the Saskatchewan Grain Growers' Association in 1913. What is puzzling is the absence of articles on the current struggles. There is no mention, for example, of the work and accomplishments of a recent advocacy group known as Saskatchewan Working Women.

A number of articles offer insight to current struggles among aboriginal peoples. Winona Wheeler's and Denise Fleming's "What's Up at the First Nations University of Canada" (40:1, January/February 2006), and Stephen Larose's "After the Coup" (41:5, September/October 2007), describe and examine the struggle within the Federation of Saskatchewan Indians to shape and control the future of postsecondary education for aboriginal peoples. Bob Sass's "Mary's Story" (29:4, August/September 1995) concerning racism and the dismissal of Mary Pitawakanak from the secretary of state's office in Regina, along with Ron Bourgeault's "The Killing of George LaChance" (31:3, May/June 1997) and the rape and murder of Pamela George in Regina by two white, middle class youth (*31:1*, May/June 1992) are moving and troubling case studies of rampant racism within the province. But they are not complemented by articles that address the larger issue of the destruction of aboriginal and Métis life and culture nor the place and future of Indian and Métis peoples in Canadian society.

Questioning the tendency of socialists to dismiss the concerns of ecologists as being anti-technological, the late Ed Mahood — twice a federal NDP candidate for Saskatoon — wrote: "The assumption underlying such reasoning is that developments in science and technology are neutral and free of ideology. The view is clearly erroneous. Science and technology are an integral part of the society in which they exist. No science or technology is separate from the social relations of that science or technology . . . At present, virtually all research and development are financed and controlled by large corporations and are used for capitalist ends, that is, to strengthen and perpetuate capitalism" (13:6, March 1979). Mahood invited the reader to consider a question: Would our approach to uranium mining and nuclear power be different in a socialist society? Mahood's answer was unequivocal. It must be.

Longevity is not the good fortune of progressive and left-wing magazines in Saskatchewan. *Next Year Country* and *Prairie Fire* have long since vanished. There remains much in the life of the province that deserves to be more fully explored. Over the past fifty years, *Canadian Dimension* has earned a reputation for publishing informed and enlightened opinion, sound reporting and solid scholarship. It has an obligation to "carry on."

CHAPTER 19
Canadian Dimension and the "other" Ontario: Radical Reportage through Rour Transformative Decades

Bryan Evans

Economic crises of this order have one redeeming feature. They create the potential for a new kind of unity within the labour movement as people begin to recognize that the existing fragmentation leads nowhere but to disaster. They also shatter the old belief that politics is something that happens only at election time. Whether the labour movement and the political left can break out of old patterns to effectively defend the living standards of working people and mount a campaign around a radical economic program will be severely tested over the next few years.

— Cy Gonick and Leo Panitch, "Wage Controls" (11:3, 1976)

In *Radical Rag: The Pioneer Labour Press in Canada,*[1] Ed Finn observed that the labour-left press had historically been independently engaged in open debates that often criticized union leaders. Through the early postwar years, union newspapers focused on the economic concerns of their members and said little about political questions or engaged in debate. They reflected the cultural and political context of the Cold War. Consequently, the political reach and effectiveness of this medium was limited. By the 1960s, a new wave of radical journalism emerged which revived the earlier tradition of autonomous, critical reportage and analysis that went beyond economism and embraced the new social movements and presented issues through the lens of left political economy and cultural analysis. *Canadian Dimension*'s founding in 1963 expressed this new wave more than any other "new model" magazine in Canada. Its scope of reportage positioned it to provide critical comment and analysis on a wide range of struggles through four decades of profound change in postwar Ontario. Moreover, as a radical magazine, *CD* would cover places and events mainstream media would either ignore completely or, perhaps worse, spin in more business-friendly and conventional terms. Thus *CD* gave voice to a rich and diverse array of radical activists and analyses. The writers sojourning through the pages of *CD* from 1963 to now compose a "who's who" of the Canadian radical Left.

This chapter identifies the key episodes in *CD*'s coverage of Ontario from 1970 to 2012. It should be noted that *CD*'s reportage through the sixties was more concerned with national liberation movements and anti-imperialist struggles, as well as the growing expressions for Quebec sovereignty. Ontario did not loom large though reportage of a more national scope clearly held relevance for Ontario's left and labour movement. Writing in the mid-1960s, for example, Ed Finn observed a new militancy arising within the Canadian labour movement after decades of quiescence and the emergence of a "new left" within both the trade unions and the universities (2:4, May/June 1965). This was a political trend that would receive serious expression in *CD*'s pages in the decade to follow. In part, the relative paucity of earlier Ontario coverage stemmed from *CD*'s deliberate concern to be less Ontario-centric in that it believed it had a responsibility to cover regions that received little if any attention from the mainstream. Given *CD*'s limited resources and the reach and scope of the Toronto-based big media, it was a wise choice. But with the election of an NDP government in Ontario, and the subsequent shift to the right, it was necessary to provide more space to events in Canada's largest province.

The tumultuous 1970s: A renewed wave of Left-Labour militancy

CD's reporting of labour struggles during the decade reflected enduring themes which are as prominent today as then. Job security, pensions, working conditions and, astonishingly absent from the debate today, the question of who owns the economy and for what purpose, was central to lived workplace struggles. The decade of the seventies witnessed a profound policy and ideological shift as inflation overtook unemployment as the central concern of government. The macro-economic crisis would engender stagflation and a reconsideration of the postwar Keynesian consensus. A series of articles analyzed the causes of inflation and the Canadian government's turn to wage controls in 1975 to suppress it. A particularly superb essay by Cy Gonick and Leo Panitch parses the political content of the wage control policy and which economic interests it would benefit (11:3, February 1976). Gonick, in a subsequent editorial, wrote: "failure to mount an effective counter-offensive will involve a massive defeat" (11:4, March 1976). The counter-offensive would come in the form of Canada's first and only national general strike, on October 14, 1976. But its effectiveness politically was minimal as no ongoing mobilization or political program ensued from this single action. Gonick's suggestion would prove prescient in ways hardly imagined.

The struggles at Brantford's Texpack and Sudbury's INCO in the late 1970s loomed significantly in the pages of *CD*. In both cases, large foreign-owned multinational corporations sought significant concessions from their workers. The Texpack strike symbolized a much larger problem — that of Canadian underdevelopment and dependency on US multinational branch plants combined with inadequate regulation of foreign capital and sectional division within the trade unions. But the events in Sudbury through the late 1970s, including a nine-month strike, were defining struggles presenting transformative potential and lost opportunity.

Job security and pensions were the key issues in Sudbury as elsewhere. Dave Patterson, then president of USWA Local 6500, would later lead a grassroots left working-class insurgency to become Steelworkers director for Ontario and that despite the opposition of Steelworkers head office to strike action. The Sudbury labour movement issued a demand for the public ownership of the resource industry. The slogan was "Nationalize nickel: Public ownership and public control." The left-nationalism of the Waffle had real roots in segments of the working class. But, reflecting an enduring theme that is more pronounced in 2012 than in 1977, the

425

New Democratic Party was divided in its support for public ownership. A moment of remarkable militancy was ultimately lost.

These struggles signalled the end of the long-post war boom and the political compromises forged between capital, labour and the state. The most important political development was the emergence of the left-nationalist Waffle within the NDP to challenge social democracy and conservative trade unionism. A key chapter in the story of the Waffle's impact on the NDP was written at the Ontario Convention of the NDP in October 1970. This was the convention at which Stephen Lewis was selected to replace Donald MacDonald as Ontario NDP leader. In his report from the convention (7:4, October 1970), Cy Gonick wrote that "The Waffle movement reached its peak at the October Ontario NDP convention." The Waffle showed remarkable organizational and policy strength at the convention. The Ontario Waffle Manifesto nearly passed as a policy resolution. Waffle policy resolutions on energy, housing and women's rights were accepted by the convention and, most threatening to the party establishment, a third of the newly elected provincial executive were Wafflers. Gonick concluded his report with this perceptive statement: "The NDP was boring and dull before the Waffle. The Waffle has made the NDP exciting. How it will retain the delicate balance of simultaneous autonomy from and involvement in the party remains to be seen." It was precisely on the ostensible grounds that the Waffle was operating as a "party within a party," that is, as an independent organization within the NDP, that in Orillia, Ontario, on June 24, 1972, the ONDP's provincial council, at the behest of ONDP leader Stephen Lewis, voted to order the Waffle to either disband or to leave the NDP. This was fourteen months after the twenty-eight-year-old neophyte Waffle leader, Jim Laxer, had come second to David Lewis on the final ballot at the federal leadership convention. In a signed *CD* editorial, "The Lewises vs the Waffle," Gonick offered a highly critical opinion of the NDP's intolerance of dissenting opinion:"in one breath claiming that dissent is tolerated in the NDP and in the next breath that dissenting groups shall be denied the means that are necessary to make their dissent effective" (8:7, June 1972). Predictably, this led to a heated exchange between Gonick and Ontario NDP President Gord Vichert in the next issue of the magazine.

In a special 1980 issue, CD presented Robert Hackett's definitive post-mortem essay on the history of the Ontario Waffle. Despite winning the Ontario party's leadership with the support of most of the Waffle delegates, Steven Lewis would soon characterize calls for nationalization as "pointless" (15:1-2, October/November 1980). It was a harbinger of the later rejection of the Sudbury miners' call for public ownership and public control and perhaps the entire project of social democratic moderation and electoralism. The ONDP's fortunes surged in 1975, as it became the official opposition, reflecting a broader popular mood for social change in the context of economic stress. It was the first electoral signal that the pragmatic, centrist, "red"-Tory province was beginning to wobble.

The 1980s: Turning back the Left-Labour insurgency

Capital's efforts to offload its crisis onto the working class continued to roll into the 1980s. Cy Gonick captured the economic context in several pieces that noted the stagnation of wages in the context of a level of corporate profits drifting ever higher amidst widespread plant closures. His observations were provident and foreshadowed the decades of employment income stagnation to follow. Moreover, his words could have been written today as highly profitable corporations now, as then, shutter doors, destroy working class lives and communities, and relocate in the never-ending search for larger profit margins and shareholder dividends. CD continued to document working-class resistance. The political and economic polarization of the 1970s caused a deepening working-class politicization and militancy that went well beyond the boundaries of sectional interests. This spilled over into the 1980s and was acutely expressed in the internal politics of the United Steelworkers of America where an ongoing trend of rank-and-file militancy produced a new generation of radical challengers who explicitly rejected the Cold War old guard of their union. Sudbury's Dave Patterson and Hamilton's Cec Taylor personified this new wave of leadership that challenged the Cold Warriors' shibboleths. But, as the decade progressed and the conservatives reorganized, labour's Prague Spring would soon end.

The tide was turning and in certain respects CD's Ontario reportage began a turn toward a new range of issues including several noteworthy contributions on occupational health and safety (OHS) by Stan Gray, Jim Brophy and Marg Keith; Ontario's adoption of pay equity legislation; struggles for affirmative action; and anti-racism campaigns.

As with the 1970s, CD's coverage of Ontario captured the moments but there was little macro-analysis of a more conceptual or theoretical nature. The most glaring absence in reportage was the absence of any analysis of the historic 1985 "accord" signed between the Liberals and NDP that consigned the Conservatives to opposition for the first time in forty-two years. As with its efforts to tell the stories of places and regions rarely heard from in the mainstream, minimizing copy space for electoral contests was, and is, a generally wise approach. But given the historic significance of this particular election, and various reforms that were negotiated into the agreement, a noteworthy gap in critical left reportage remains.

The 1990s: Ontario's neoliberal decade and the mess left

The decade of the 1990s was the most tumultuous in Ontario's postwar history. The deepest recession since the Great Depression saw unemployment rise to the double-digit range and a million Ontarians subsisted on social assistance. The incremental ascent of neoliberalism that had begun in the 1970s now rapidly ascended.

The election of Ontario's sole NDP government in September 1990 began with great promise but soon the groundwork was laid for a turn to neoliberal restructuring. Naturally, one of CD's first articles in 1990 assessed the prospects of the NDP. It was prescient. Initial optimism was tempered by sober reflection. Was there any reason to believe this government would be any different from other NDP governments? A series of articles dealt with how the NDP might implement its platform, including public ownership of auto insurance, employment equity and labour law reform. But through it all there was a cautionary message of uncertainty respecting which political voices the new government would ultimately listen to. And consistently, CD analysts suggested that the only assurance there was to keeping the NDP anchored to its program and political base was to keep trade unionists and the social movements mobilized and pressing in from outside of the Legislature. Indeed, a series of articles marking the NDP's first year in government shared the common observation that the government was drifting away from its political base and program on virtually all fronts. Fiscal restraint and partnership with business were emerging as the new centre of politics in Ontario's brief experiment with social democracy. The turn to the Social Contract, in 1993, marked a shift to fiscal conservatism and a fracturing of the NDP's base in the trade union movement. Not surprisingly, the final eighteen months of CD's Ontario coverage exclusively dealt with the implosion of the NDP government and the fraying of its electoral base.

The 1995 election saw an explicitly New Right party arrive in government. Ontario's history of a politics of the pragmatic centre was definitively over. Oddly, given the magnitude of this shift, CD did not provide any substantive analysis of the election campaign or the results. But the next eight years of the Common Sense Revolution provided substantial fodder for CD journalists, particularly Geoff Bickerton and Bryan Palmer among others, to report and assess. From 1996 through to the end of the decade, CD's Ontario coverage was overwhelmingly concerned with resistance, in particular undertaking a critical analysis of the Days of Action (DOA) which initially held tremendous promise for a deepening of class-based struggle but ultimately shriveled and disappeared. In 1999, the Harris-led Conservatives won a second majority.

It was evident on June 28, 1995, that the pragmatic centrist "One Ontario" politics which had prevailed since the mid-1940s were truly dead when a thousand protestors rushed the doors of the Legislature as Harris's cabinet was sworn in. The early opposition caused Jason Ziedenberg to consider the possibility that the unabashed class warfare that characterized the Conservative program would cause a regeneration of the atrophied Ontario Left (30:2, April 1996).

The Days of Action, seven in total, suggested profoundly powerful new alliances were possible. But the strategic fissures within the labour movement created by the NDP's turn to austerity reemerged. Who would lead the resistance to Harris and what were to be the political objectives? Would the emerging opposition recoalesce around electoralism and the NDP as the pro-NDP "pink-paper" unions urged, and be led by the unions, or would it be a broad-based alliance that included trade unions but also social movements working as equals to build an extraparliamentary common front? Geoff Bickerton's critique of the Pink group proposed that if social democracy was to rebuild in Ontario, it could only do so through broad-based political mobilization (30:2, April 1996).

Building a political understanding the Days of Action figured prominently in *CD*. A May Day special edition (30:4, July/August 1996) covered the Hamilton and Kitchener-Waterloo DOAs. The Hamilton action of February 24, 1996, saw more than a hundred thousand demonstrators come out — up to that point the largest labour rally in Ontario history. Mobilization was everywhere. The London DOA had happened the month before and within a couple of days of the Hamilton action, fifty-five thousand Ontario government workers would be on strike — another labour first, as this would be the largest strike against a single employer in Canadian history. And Ontario's teachers, among the most militant unionists in the province, were moving toward their own confrontation with the government. Indeed, the last time the Ontario labour movement had seen such mobilization was in 1976 in response to wage controls (30:2, April 1996). Bryan Palmer celebrated the revival of a class politics and mobilization writing: "there is no mistaking the class grievances at the centre of the oppositional current. Labour is leading, and trade unions and working class politics are undeniably central to the escalating protests . . . class is the knot that ties it all together" (30:2, April 1996). Again, the role of the "Pink" unions in slowing the mobilization was seen as undercutting a rare moment when the working class had the potential to transform the political landscape.

The movement reached its zenith with the Toronto DOA of October 25 and 26, 1997, with 250,000 taking part in the demonstration that now surpassed that in Hamilton as the largest in Canadian history. But even here, despite the appearance of broad unity, the cracks in the labour movement emerged over the strategic role of the DOAs. But this did not dilute the historic significance of what was underway. Sam Gindin saw two defining characteristics in the emerging new politics. First, it named where real power lay — the banks and private corporations. And, second, it mobilized a broad popular social movement in defence of social rights (31:1, February 1997). But even as teachers briefly struck in late 1997, it was becoming evident that the transformative potential of the DOAs was fading. The teachers retreated as their inter-union solidarity cracked. Gindin wrote that their struggle might well have been the lynchpin to bringing down the Harris government, but only if the movement had escalated into a general strike. That had been the objective for many DOA activists (32:1, January/February 1998). But, political and ideological division worked to direct the DOA movement into a political dead end. In assessing the Days of Action, Bryan Palmer bluntly criticized the trade union "hierarchy" for ensuring the anti-Harris movement would be "overcome with doubt and demoralization." Ultimately, the DOAs, Palmer asserted, were nothing but empty symbolism unless the objective was for the mobilization to culminate in a general strike (32:5, September/October 1998).

Thanks to *CD* an analysis that was both left and independent could be presented. Seasoned analysts such as Bickerton, Gindin and Palmer, among others, could voice a perspective that would likely not have found such an open medium. Of course, the election of 1999 saw the Conservatives returned with a second majority. The popular vote for the Conservatives had hardly shifted. As the decade closed, the final word was Bickerton's, who mused that the way forward in confronting a second term majority for Harris was to reassemble the coalition of unions and social movements that had worked so well, at least initially, in launching the Days of Action. That never did materialize as resistance turned sharply to a strategy of strategic voting and the formation of a Liberal-Labour defensive alliance (33:4-5, Fall 1999).

CD's Ontario coverage through the nineties went beyond the DOA mobilizations. Articles covered diverse issues including greening the economy, Ontario's abrogation of human rights, and the casualization of academic work. But it was the King Learian rise and demise of the extraparliamentary anti-neoliberal resistance that clearly captured the imagination of contributors. The 1999 election was simply not covered in any meaningful depth. As noted earlier, *CD* was reluctant to narrowly define politics in electoral terms alone, but this was not simply another bourgeois election with predictable outcomes. That Harris won a second term, given the unprecedented polarization, was itself noteworthy; but, more importantly, the 1999 election witnessed a shift in the substance of resistance. Significant elements of labour fully embraced strategic voting as the next phase in the struggle. This meant the beginning of a new alliance with the Ontario Liberals. The movement toward a more transformative program was gone.

The twenty-first century: From Common Sense Revolution to pragmatic neoliberalism

Perhaps because resistance had clearly faded, CD's coverage of Ontario politics broadened significantly in these years. Notably, commentary and analysis of indigenous struggles, most prominently the Six Nations struggle to reclaim First Nations' land around Caledonia, and artistic/cultural projects, received significant exposure. Other subjects included policing, Queer politics, migrant workers, youth activism and the significance of 9/11 in transforming the political environment.

The Ontario Coalition Against Poverty (OCAP) now resumed the counteroffensive against the last gasps of the Common Sense Revolution. On June 15, 2000, a thousand antipoverty protestors assembled at Queen's Park. What ensued was a police riot. For the previous eighteen months a mood of resignation had dominated the Ontario Left. OCAP's action, and many to follow, demonstrated the ember of resistance had not been extinguished. Bryan Palmer's superb account, "The Riot Act: Reviving Protest in Ontario," was a must-read (34:5, September/October 2000). This was politically important given that the October 27, 2000, "Rebuilding the Left" conference came to nothing. David McNally, a convenor of the OCAP Allies Network and prominent Marxist intellectual, provided much of this reportage (35:1, January/February 2001). McNally argued for the unity of struggles, writing that since 9/11 the need for such unity was urgent.

Once again the pages of CD were completely quiet with respect to the election of October 2003, where the Progressive Conservative Party, now led by Ernie Eves, was defeated and the Liberals under Dalton McGuinty won a huge majority, with the NDP losing official party status. Given that several unions had endorsed strategic voting, effectively supporting the Liberals over the NDP, greater insight into the significance of these developments from a left perspective would have been valuable.

In 2011, with the financial crisis reengineered into a crisis of the public sector, austerity loomed. Ontario's finance minister had set out a seven-year austerity agenda. Sam Gindin and Michael Hurley warned in *CD* that this crisis "provided political and economic elites with an opportunity" to shrink and privatize public services on an unprecedented scale. With private-sector unions virtually destroyed, only the public sector remained as a centre of trade union strength (45:6, November/December 2011). As with the Days of Action, different forms of struggle would be required. And before the year was out, Occupy Wall Street, which began as a single event, had become a global movement of resistance. It is fitting to close this overview with reference to a *CD* editorial on the Occupy "moment," which stated the "critical question is where to go from here" (45:6, November/December 2011). Indeed, that is the enduring question. In 2012, as Ontario turns to an unprecedented agenda of public sector austerity, it will fall to *Canadian Dimension,* as one of a very few spaces for critical and radical journalism, to document the struggles to ensue and tell the stories of the Ontario of workers — both public and private —, of students, of First Nations, of single-industry communities, and of all the diverse people who inhabit, not the Ontario of finance capital, stock dividends and wealth management, but the "other" Ontario.

CHAPTER 20

Canadian Dimension Covers British Columbia: Power, Promises and Pulp Fiction

Frank Tester

The characterization of B.C. politics is unique in Canada. Generalizations about B.C. which derive from experiences in other Canadian regions are, at least, folly, at most, as we have seen here, disastrous. The political economy of B.C. lends itself to highly polarized, highly class conscious political tendencies of both right and left.

— J.F. Conway, "The British Columbia Election . . ." (6:5, October/November 1969).

Canadian Dimension's coverage of BC politics generates an emotional tug-of-war suggesting a landscape of lofty peaks and deep valley bottoms. The results are embarrassingly euphoric, suddenly sobering. Not unlike the complexity of Quentin Tarantino's 1994 classic film, *Pulp Fiction*, the entanglements of BC political history and culture, revealed by those writing for *CD*, call for deeper explanation.

BC has a workforce organized into one of the largest — and at times, the most militant — labour movements in the country. The neoliberal logic of the 1980s, nineties, and 2000s reveals how badly its interests have been compromised. In 1982 (16:4, June), North made it clear that middle-class unions — the BC Teacher's Federation and the BC Government Employees Union — had taken hit after hit from the province, applying to public services what the lash of so-called market-driven necessity had already doled out to its working-class counterparts. BC's early labour history — useful in understanding this trajectory — was perhaps too little explored in the pages of *CD*.[1] However, the CCF/NDP got plenty of attention from *CD*, the party, as John Conway (6:5, October/November 1969) noted, coming in 1952 within one seat of putting a CCF government in the provincial legislature.

Had they succeeded, the province might have been spared twenty years (1952–1972) of right-wing hucksterism, boosterism, favouritism, talk and "doodling." This is how Martin Robin, former Simon Fraser University professor and personal friend of Dave Barrett, writing in a 1966 edition, colourfully coined "Wacky" Bennett's penchant for puttering with little more than his own imagination in mind. Robin's review of Paddy Sherman's book *Bennett* (3:6, September/October 1966) was lively to the point of being a Rick Mercer rant.

If labour history was neglected, the history of BC's entry into Confederation was not. In 1971 (8:3, November), it got a thorough and largely apolitical work-over from Hugh Keenleyside; at first glance, a curious contributor to *CD*. Keenleyside, a left-leaning liberal and public servant, was chair of the BC Power Corporation and BC Hydro from 1960 to1969. An advocate for Aboriginal rights, in the mid-1940s he reportedly refused to run for federal office unless a coalition of the CCF and Liberals would set the stage for "a truly liberal or socialist government."[2]

Coverage by *CD* makes it clear that the provincial NDP has often delivered both, commencing with Dave Barrett, who gave the province public auto insurance and, at the same time, a minister of labour, Bill King, who in 1975, ordered forty-five thousand striking workers back to work. The "sometimes socialist rhetoric" of the NDP, increasingly divorced from its roots in labour activism and wrapped in liberal humanitarianism only a social worker could feel good about, rankled just about everyone covering the province for *Canadian Dimension*, including Goldberg (25:8, December 1991; 34:2, March/April 2000), Kuehn (26:1, January/February 1992), Larkin (20:8, February 1987), Persky (12:7, 1977) and Yankel (10:4, September 1974).

Union activity in relation to BC's tumultuous contemporary political history gets lots of attention from *CD*. So do the internal union struggles of the 1970s and early eighties. These include: an anonymous 1972 article, "What happened at Kitimat" (9:2-3, January 1973), telling the tale of union members defecting from the United Steel Workers of America to the newly-minted Canadian Aluminum, Smelter and Allied Workers' Union; an often-debated relationship with the NDP covered in another anonymous article on labour conventions (12:7, 1977); Paul York's article on struggles between moderate and more radical elements within the BC Federation of Labour (13:6, March 1979); and Terry Glavin's coverage of dissension within the BC Government Employees Union over contract negotiations (16:6, October/November 1982). Dissension "all over the place" stars the beguiling behaviour of International Woodworkers of America's Jack Munro. Munro brought the "almost general strike" of 1983 to a grinding halt by negotiating a "tin pan agreement" with Bill Bennett's Social Credit Government. This treachery gets plenty of attention from Jackie Larkin (18:1, March 1984), writing in a special edition devoted to Operation Solidarity. An editorial, "Solidarity's Work: Far From Over" (18:1, March 1984), peered optimistically into a future of more of the same. Unfortunately, the militant socialism and defiance of the 1960s, seventies and early 1980s had become, by the mid to late 1980s, something of a whimper.

Popular revolt was not, in the late sixties and early seventies, restricted to organized labour. The complex fate of Simon Fraser University's (SFU's) Political Science, Sociology and Anthropology (PSA) Department, renouncing "research for governments and corporations" and its intention to pursue, instead, "research for the community, for unions and especially for the poor and powerless" was skillfully treated by Sharon Yandle (6:7, February/March 1970); an analysis that would leave Jean-Paul Sartre beaming from ear to ear. Years later, Mordecai Briemberg (40:2, March/April 2006), a once-upon-a-time PSA assistant professor, does a thorough job of "dishing" SFU Professor Hugh Johnson's attempt in his book, *Radical Campus: Making Simon Fraser University*, to paint over the mindless stupidity of an administration dedicated in the early seventies to making SFU yet another (yawn) handmaiden of corporate malfeasance.

Making sense of social and political organizing in BC requires paying prodigious attention to the environmental movement. Commencing in the 1990s, *CD*'s coverage of BC politics focused more on social movements. In a province dominated for decades by the forest industry, and with a landscape guaranteed to capture the most romantic of imaginations, BC is a stage for contemporary issues gnawing at capitalist logic. However, until the late eighties, with the exception of a footnote in an anonymous article (9:6, July 1973) covering demands by the Pulp and Paper Workers Union of Canada that a labour contract contain a clause prohibiting members from operating equipment violating pollution laws in the province, the emergence of the environmental movement got threadbare attention from *CD*. Greenpeace was born in a BC kitchen, September 1971. *CD* was not there. The anonymous author of the 1973 piece about the Pulp and Paper Workers Union wrote — in a notable understatement — that "during 1969, the eco movement expanded through B.C. communities with the speed and force it has done everywhere." The rise in BC of an "aesthetic consciousness" and level of environmental activism among a generation of well-schooled — and predominantly middle-class — activists complicates BC politics to a degree unparalleled elsewhere in the country. How this sensibility meshed with working-class realities (and the anguish of recognizing that it doesn't fit well) got increasing attention from *CD*. In "Fight Back" (36:4, July/August 2002), Kimball Cariou took this on in his account of opposition to Premier Gordon Campbell's neoliberal response to the recession of 2001.

Kim Goldberg, Nanaimo poet and regular contributor to *CD*, reported on Gordon Campbell's May 17 decimation of the NDP in the July/August 2001 edition (35:4); an outcome that left a mob of Liberals staring at each other in the BC legislature, looking through the crowd for two seats occupied by the opposition. It was a dismal outcome she had nicely predicted in "Premier Dosanjh: Lights Out for the NDP?" (34:2, March/April 2000). Campbell's Liberals then took the bloody sword of neoliberal logic to the BC economy. Cariou's subsequent coverage of resistance to this carnage beamed with the possibility of working-class solidarity. Unfortunately, earlier coverage of Operation Solidarity in the fall of 1983 (17:5, November) suggested limits to the organized resistance Cariou wanted to celebrate in 2002. Cariou (36:4, July/August 2002) noted that the Liberal budget of January 2002 proposed cutting all ministry budgets by an average of 25 per cent, eliminating 11,700 jobs — a third of the public service, freezing spending on health and education, cutting funding to all women's centres, and contained a list of slashing that went on and on. He noted that protest rallies in Victoria and Vancouver drew tens of thousands. The Liberals were not impressed. They carried on.

Cariou, editor of *People's Voice* — a weekly newspaper published by New Labour Press and with an editorial policy in line with the Communist Party of Canada — used class analysis as an analytical lens. His contributions to *CD*, from July 2002 to October 2004, opened a Pandora's box of problems, suggesting the profoundly populist politics of a province mired in the myth of opportunity. The reality of differences between working- and middle-class unions, the role of Green politics, and the changing nature of labour in the province, invited a reexamination of the content of class relations. Cariou's coverage of opposition to Campbell's early 2000s neoliberal agenda recalled a longing for working-class and socialist solidarity, sought on the pages of *CD*'s early coverage of BC political life (1:1-2, September/November 1963). Cariou noted that: "Unfortunately, few believe that the B.C. working class is ready to walk off the job *en masse.*" Goldberg, while covering the same events also focused on grassroots and community examples of social change in articles such as "Courtney's World Community Film Festival" (34:6, November/December 2000), "Reclaiming the Airwaves" (35:5, September/October 2001), "B.C. Youth Say 'Check Your Head'" (36:1, January/February 2002) and "Media Democracy Day" (36:4, July/August 2002).

In covering opposition to Campbell's 2002 budget, readers were taken back to *the* BC political event of the 1980s — Operation Solidarity — where working-class solidarity got a thorough, and some would say fatal, workout. The malfeasance of the Social Credit government led by Bill Bennett, son of "Wacky" Bennett, came in what Bill Tieleman, a communication consultant for the NDP, called "Bills, Bills, Bills" (17:5, November 1983). Bennett's response to the recession of the early eighties, a neoliberal agenda on steroids, was taken right from the handbooks of the World Bank and International Monetary Fund. He proposed legislation to eliminate rent controls and allow landlords to evict tenants without cause. It stripped school boards of budgetary control, increased the sales tax and gave the minister of education direct control over courses offered by the BC Institute of Technology, making sure the interests of capital would be well served. Changes to the *Medical Services Act* were to allow doctors to opt out of medicare. Private-sector employers were to be empowered to negotiate standards for employment lower than those set by government. The province's Human Rights Commission was on the chopping block. *CD* covered it all.

Socreds had trod here before. When they took power from the NDP in 1975, they targeted social assistance, led by "give 'em shovels" Vander Zalm. The minister of social services and future premier set out to eliminate every vestige of NDP initiative he could lay his hands on. This included the Community Resource Boards set up by the NDP to decentralize the delivery of mental health services. Stan Persky and Michele Brunet's (10:3, July 1974) coverage of attempts by the NDP to create community-based psychiatric services is likely the most detailed and critically-insightful article dealing with BC politics and policies published by *CD*. Persky appeared in print three years later with an engaging verbal cartoon taking Bill Bennett and, one by one, his flock of used car salesmen "come cabinet ministers to task for meanness, fraud and a farcical handling of provincial affairs" (12:7, 1977).

As already noted, time and time again, a longing for — and failure to achieve — solidarity among working (and even working-class) people in BC, and the failure of progressive politics haunted the pages of *CD*. It is a theme with deep roots, mindful of an earlier theme — "free enterprise" vs. socialism — captured by Conway's coverage (6:5, October/November 1969) of the decimation of the NDP with Tom Berger at the helm in the spring election of 1969. It's a concern that gave way to hand-wringing by several *CD* contributors, over a party compromised in attempts to achieve political office.

Nowhere was this tension better illustrated than in the 1991 election of Mike Harcourt's New Democrats. Larry Kuehn, former head of the BC Teacher's Federation, noted in "BC — No 'New Jerusalem'" (26:1, January/February 1992) that British Columbians had just elected a premier given to "wealth creation" and *not* to achieving social justice through redistribution. The result? According to *CD*'s Kim Goldberg (25:8, December 1991), it was a "sort-of socialist" solution to the worst excesses of the Vander Zalm theatrics of the late 1980s, with a fate that was, as Goldberg saw it, rather predictable.

Wealth creation? Perhaps, but what about the logging, and the Clayoquot Sound controversy; an issue brewing, along with a long list of other forest issues in the province, since the late 1970s. These contradictions were outlined nicely in an article written by the Friends of Clayoquot Sound (23:5, July/August 1989), as CD increasingly opened its pages to popular forms of resistance. Harcourt's welfare liberals set the NDP up for no end of trouble with BC environmentalists. The contribution of the forest industry to BC's coffers, its organization and management, the often reactionary role played by the IWA in BC political life, conflicts with environmentalists, and attempts to heal these — all received critical analysis in *CD* starting back in 1971 with an article by Robert Williams, "British Columbia Timber! Ripping Off B.C.'s Forests" (7:7, January/February) and more recently with articles by Gordon Bailey, "Touch Wood: British Columbia Forests at the Crossroads" (28:5, October/November 1994); Chris Genovali, "Your Child May be an Eco-terrorist" (32:2 March/April 1998); Gabriel Haythornthwaite, "The Clayoquot Legacy: the future of environmental activism" (33:1, January/February 1999); Gill Yaron, "The Corporatization of B.C.'s Forests" (34:1, February 2000), and numerous contributions by Kim Goldberg.

Cariou's article (36:4, July/August 2002) on resistance to the Campbell government's draconian budget of 2002 pointed to populist (and pragmatic) sentiments undermining working-class solidarity in BC for its entire post-Confederation history. This was evident in coverage given by committed *CD* socialists writing about Operation Solidarity in 1983, and in the emergence of the BC Green Party; a cacophonic collection of irreconcilable ideological sentiments treating the environment as some kind of political glue. Annett (17:5, November 1983) described this admixture of colourful (but green) political aspirants coalescing to form the Green Party of British Columbia in February of 1983, as "socialists, environmentalists, New Age hippies and small businessmen." They were immediately, without policies, cast into a provincial election. Their newly-minted leader, Adrienne Carr — as Annett notes — declared that "a party only needs solid policies if it gets elected."

This "right of centre populist organization" is not without its own political intrigue. Carr, who along with her husband Paul George founded the Western Canada Wilderness Committee in 1980, stayed as leader until 1985. When she stepped down the position of leader was eliminated in favour of three party spokespersons. In 1993, after years of internal conflict, twenty-one-year-old Stuart Parker became leader. Goldberg (34:4, July/August 2000) noted with approval Parker's efforts to expand "the party's constituency until it included significant representation from youth, anti-poverty activists, Native sovereigntists and the Afro-Canadian community (to which Parker himself belonged), as well as fledgling ties with labour." But in March 2000, as Goldberg notes, Carr engineered a coup backed by Greens intent on making environmental issues *the* focus of party organizing.

CD's coverage of the disintegration of progressive politics in BC in the 1990s was thorough. The Green headache given the NDP reached migraine proportions when Mike Harcourt's version of welfare liberalism walked into the woods on Vancouver Island's west coast. In "Meet The New Boss" (26:2, March 1992), Goldberg outlined the conundrums of a dithering Harcourt government. Never one to shy away from pointing out the strengths — and failings — of BC unions, Goldberg also suggested that the "fossilized brain cells powering the IWA leadership" needed to put woodworkers alongside environmentalists protesting the province's export of raw logs.

Glenn Clarke, Harcourt's minister of finance, oversaw the NDP government's purchase of over two million shares in forest company MacMillan Bloedel in February of 1993, making its interests and commitments more than obvious (27:5, September/October 1993). The NDP ran headlong into a storm of environmental protesters hell-bent on saving Clayoquot Sound on Vancouver Island's west coast from a blizzard of buzzing chainsaws. Eight hundred fifty-six people were arrested; three hundred on one day alone — August 9, 1993. It's a controversy with ideological and political implications that perhaps got too little analysis from *CD*;

Shadrack and Bauman's article, "Colour the fightback green: desperately seeking democracy (The political Left)" (29:3, June/July 1995) being a notable exception.

After Harcourt's departure, Glenn Clarke, now Premier, pitted the interests of working people in the forest industry against a new generation of activists. The party's understanding of economic growth in relation to the environment and employment revealed a take on class relations and capital accumulation little changed since the Winnipeg general strike of 1919. Under Clarke and Dave Zirnhelt, minister of forests, environmentalists became, as CD recorded, "eco-terrorists," "economic terrorists," and "enemies of BC," with Greenpeace cast as an organization funded by the US forest industry (32:2, March/April 1998). Stephen Harper, dealing with opposition to the Northern Gateway pipeline proposal, could hardly have done better.[3] On this one, CD gave voice where many socialists fear to tread; writers like Goldberg and Genovali put themselves in touch with political and social sensibilities resonating with new — and different — circumstances and a new generation of social activists. As previously noted, the election of April 2001 reduced the NDP to two seats.

In BC, the fate of government employees, teachers and others who are part of organized labour, as well as many who are not, suggests the merit of reexamining familiar Marxist notions of class. Events since 2008 might return us to basics. There are two classes increasingly in conflict: those who own the means of production — albeit assisted by a comparatively small administrative elite — and those who have nothing to sell but their labour. Investments, pension funds, professional credentials and even wages have muddled this distinction. But it persists.

The question is: "What do we have in common?" CD's coverage of British Columbia suggests the central importance of the question. Both David Harvey, Marxist geographer and cultural theorist, and Fredric Jameson tackle this head on; contemporary class interests in relation to the modern machinations of capital accumulation.[4] In *Representing Capital: A Reading of Volume One*, Jameson concludes that the category of unemployment is central to a reading of *Capital*. We might extend this to a better appreciation of underemployment gleaned from an enlightened reading of *Capital*; an experience that has many of my well-qualified

— and some would say "middle-class" — students turning up behind the counter as baristas at Starbucks all over Vancouver. Jameson goes so far as to suggest that social class cannot be defined, that it is "at one and the same time a sociological idea, a political concept, a historical conjecture, an activist slogan, (and that) a definition in terms of any one of these perspectives alone is bound to be unsatisfactory." Perhaps our interest in living sustainably and ensuring a future for our children can be defined. That being the case, a close reading of fifty years of *CD* reporting on British Columbia suggests that now is a good time to interrogate what, as working people, our interests really are, and how, in relation to the machinations of capital, we might — all of us — best exercise them.

CHAPTER 21
Alberta
Trevor W. Harrison

The erosion of individual rights, the hardening of a conservatism that advocates state paternalism and the primary of all big power, whether military, police or private marks the drift of public policy in Alberta.

("Alberta: The totalitarian drift," 3:5, July/August 1966)

Reading nearly fifty years of *Canadian Dimension*'s eye on Alberta is both sobering and heartening. Sobering because one realizes how little the province's political culture and economy changed during that period, but heartening to see how often the magazine was in the vanguard of critically examining several important issues — and, one wonders, perhaps signaling in a small way the political shift that in 2015 saw a New Democratic government elected in the province.

Two large, interconnected themes run through *CD*'s examinations of the province: its authoritarian politics and, since the large oil discoveries of the late 1940s, the petroleum industry's dominance in the political and economical life of Alberta. The first of these themes — Alberta's political culture — was the subject of *CD*'s very first targeted article on Alberta, written by Robin Mathews (3:5, July/August 1966). Mathews's cogent description of Alberta as a largely one-party, totalitarian state, buttressed by a corporatist relationship between government and business, aided and abetted by a compliant media, remains as accurate as it was when written. Likewise, Mathews's detailing of threats to academic freedom bear chilling resonance with today.

While the overall pattern of Alberta politics has remained until recently, the scale has of course changed; and as Alberta's economy has developed, new issues have arisen or have become foregrounded. When Mathews wrote the inaugural piece, Alberta's tar sands remained only a gleam in some petroleum engineer's eye. It was only the next year that the Great Canadian Oil Sands project began, over time transforming the nature of capitalist production in Alberta with consequences for Canada as a whole; thus, the second of the major themes — tar sands development — that has framed *CD*'s critical examinations of the province.

In 1971, Peter Lougheed's Progressive Conservatives replaced the Social Credit government, in office for thirty-six years. In 1973, the Yom Kippur War broke out, setting off the OPEC Crisis. At the world-historical level, these events began a long and steady march towards higher oil prices and intensified Middle East conflict. For Alberta, these events added weight to the opening that same year of the Syncrude plant north of Fort McMurray, beginning the kind of massive, if frequently volatile, petroleum-based economic growth that we still see today. In turn, this development also solidified Conservative political control in the province.

Abigail Poot's 1973 article (9:7-8, November/December) termed the agreement between the Conservative government and the Syncrude consortium a "sweetheart" deal in which the government assumed all the risks and the private owners the vast majority of the profits. But Poot also situated the deal within a broader discussion of public policy, specifically that of Canadianization, then prominent, touting the idea of Alberta owning and developing its own resources: "[T]he Alberta government should develop the oil sands itself and take ALL profits. The risks are a myth" [capitals in original]. Finally, Poot concluded: "[W]ith this deal the Lougheed government will effectively hand the economy into the hands of four American oil companies. We have entered the Syncrude era." No truer words were ever uttered.

Poot's article was followed by others examining Alberta's changing political economy. Ed Shaffer favourably reviewed Larry Pratt's book *Tarsands*,[1] noting the book's critical look at the costs of Alberta's intensified pace of

445

development, specifically its class implications and impacts on Aboriginal peoples (12:1, January 1977). In 1979 (13:8, June), Shaffer provided his own critical examination of Alberta's oil-based development strategy, describing the Lougheed Conservatives as engaging in a form of "state capitalism." Shaffer went further, however, to situate Alberta's development strategy within broader theories of industrial growth, notably Harold Innis's staples approach, arguing that oil-led industrialization would ultimately slow economic growth. Finally, like Pratt, Shaffer identified changes in Alberta's class structure associated with the economic changes. In particular, he argued that the surpluses accrued as a result of the oil boom had been siphoned off to create a new class, an "industrial bourgeoisie." Shaffer's article concluded with words that would become all too prescient:

[I]t is certain that this industrialization will have all the
evils associated with capitalist development — boom and
bust, over-expansion in some sectors, under-expansion
in others, urban blight and the degradation of the
environment. The benefits will accrue to the new ruling class
while the relative position of the workers, farmers and small
businessmen will continue to decline.

Shaffer's critique was written at a pivotal time. As in 1973, events in the Middle East hugely impacted Alberta's fortunes. In early 1979, the Shah of Iran was deposed, setting the stage for another sudden rise in world oil prices. Just as Shaffer had predicted, however, staples production left Alberta vulnerable. Uneven development meant that Alberta had few other substantial industries to fall back upon when the price of oil collapsed two years later. Tar sands expansion stopped dead in its tracks, while conventional oil-rigs elsewhere pulled up and headed south to what they hoped would be greener pastures. Likewise, laid-off workers left the province or sought Unemployment Insurance, walking away from mortgaged homes. House prices dropped, food banks proliferated and government revenues dropped sharply.

Predictably, the collapse of oil prices in the early 1980s set in motion a series of conflicts that CD once more dutifully recorded. One such conflict

446

was between capital and labour. Barb Livingstone detailed Alberta government attacks on private sector construction workers and public employees (18:2, May 1984). Two years later (20:5, September/October 1986), Jim Selby wrote an exposé of the strike by United Food and Commercial Workers at the Gainers' meat packing plant in Edmonton. The strike, bitter and violent, precipitated by the growth of the transborder meat industry and the specific actions of Peter Pocklington, then owner of the Edmonton Oilers and a former candidate for the federal Progressive Conservative party leadership, continued throughout the summer and fall of 1986.

A second conflict that manifested itself openly during this time was between global capital and Aboriginal nations. Throughout much of Canada, after the 1960s, economic growth increasingly meant exploiting — recolonizing — the northern regions, areas Aboriginal peoples still inhabit in large numbers. In Alberta, this period of renewed exploitation first involved oil, but — spurred by the downturn in world oil prices — led in the early 1980s to efforts at diversifying the province's economy through forestry development in the north.

Failing to heed past lessons, however, Alberta's elite decided not to abandon staples production or foreign-based private ownership; instead, they doubled down on another staple, forestry. In the mid-1980s, the Alberta government provided another sweetheart deal, this time to the Japanese forestry giant Diashowa, to cut down and ship Alberta's raw forest products to foreign markets. As recorded by Dale Stelter in March 1991 (25:2), the result was conflict with Alberta's Lubicon Cree, a band whose traditional land claims go back to the 1930s; an issue revisited by Christopher Genovali (31:2, March/April 1997) in his discussion of the growing environmental costs of tar-sands development and its impact on the band whose claims remain, sadly, unresolved today; and examined regarding indigenous peoples at large by Clayton Thomas-Müller in 2008 (42:2, March/April).

By 1991, of course, a larger narrative of conflict between Aboriginal peoples and Canadian governments was being written throughout Canada, in Quebec and elsewhere. In southern Alberta, the ethos of capitalist development ran into opposition with Aboriginal peoples over the proposed Oldman River dam project. As recorded by Cy Gonick in 1991 (25:8, December), however, such conflicts also highlighted another growing issue, the environment, that has become more prominent in the years since.

Meanwhile, Alberta's economic woes continued, by the early 1990s threatening the governing Conservative party. In the fall of 1992, Premier Don Getty — who had replaced Lougheed as premier in 1985 — announced his resignation and was quickly replaced by Ralph Klein. As detailed by Alvin Finkel (28:5, October/November 1994), Klein's elevation to premier represented the collapse of Alberta's regional bourgeoisie.

Diversification of the Alberta economy, which Lougheed regarded as dependent on state financing and involvement as an offset to the central-Canadian bias of Canadian finance, has simply failed to occur. The Alberta economy is even more dependent on the health of its energy sector than it was when the Social Credit regime was toppled.

As Finkel also noted, the Klein revolution — as it soon became known — also saw Alberta revert to its authoritarian impulses. Under the guise of dealing with a debt crisis — echoes heard elsewhere since — the Klein government set about restructuring Alberta in line with the demands of foreign capital. Attacks on labour, combined with draconian cuts in spending to public services and a messianic zeal for privatization and deregulation, became the order of the day. Symbolic of the Klein government's approach early on was the privatization of Alberta's lucrative liquor control board, as detailed by Dean Neu (29:1, February/March 1995).

As the Klein revolution picked up steam it also gathered an array of critics.[2] Laurie Adkin followed Neu's article in spring 1995 with a discussion of the growing resistance in Alberta "mainly from liberal-democratic and social-democratic journalists, a handful of academics, and activists" to what Adkin (29:2, April/May 1995) referred to as "folksy fascism." Shades of Mathews's article of thirty years earlier, Neu in April 1996 (30:2) returned with an examination of the efforts by some members of Alberta's economic and political elite to silence academic criticism of the government. A historically centred piece by Tim Rourke (43:4,

448

September/October 1996) further expanded on Alberta's entrenched authoritarian political culture.[3]

The Klein period coincided with a major shift in Alberta's place within Canada. Free trade after 1988 gave Alberta both enormous economic clout and greater latitude to use it. But this period also saw the rise of the Reform Party under Preston Manning, son of Alberta's former Socred premier, Ernest Manning, thus beginning the process of transforming Canada's old Tory Conservative party into the right-wing pseudo-populist version that governs in Ottawa today. Beginning with Finkel, several writers for *CD* recognized the dangers to Canada in the politics being brewed in Alberta. Said Rourke: "Take note, Canadians, that the latest right wing wave sweeping our country is largely directed and financed from Alberta . . . Alberta's political reality is a disgrace that endangers the entire country."

While the Klein government was gaining accolades in the business community for its economic prowess, critics denounced Alberta's growing democratic, social[4] and environmental deficits, and warned that the province's apparent economic prosperity was itself threatened by the government's development model. As a result of these concerns, labour, academic and other progressive elements within Alberta society began working together to explore alternatives, as detailed by Geoff Bickerton (31:6, November/December 1997) and later by Kristine Owram (38:5, September/October 2004) in her discussion of the emergence of Parkland Institute as a prominent, vocal critique of current government policies.

This is perhaps a good point to review how far Alberta has come in the years since writers for *CD* began critically examining it. To read *CD*'s critical opus of the province is, on one level, sobering. Authoritarianism, including threats to academic freedom[5] and human rights, and the problems of economic underdevelopment, including environmental destruction, remain constant themes. To read Ian McKenna's examination of labour strife at Tyson Foods, for example (40:1, January/February 2006), is to travel back in time to the Gainers strike of twenty years earlier.

Yet, to read two more recent articles (2006 and 2009) by Petr Cizek (40:4, July/August 2006; 43:1, January/February 2009) sandwiching a previously mentioned 2008 article by Thomas-Müller (42:2, March/

April 2008) — all dealing with the economic, social and environmental problems of tar sands development — is to be heartened, realizing that *CD* has been, and continues to be, in the forefront of critically examining issues ahead of their mention by the more mainstream media. Take, for example, the first of these articles, in which Cizek revisits an old theme, the development of Alberta's tar sands, but with an additional twist — a scathing indictment of Canada's best-known environmental groups (Pembina, World Wildlife Foundation, the Sierra Club) for accepting donations from large American foundation grants — and then raises anew the need for Canadian economic sovereignty.

Or take the second of Cizek's articles, in which he dismisses calls by former premier Peter Lougheed and others for a moratorium on new tar sands projects, because — as Cizek argues — simply winding down tar sands production is ineffective to deal with the problem of greenhouse gases and global warming; indeed, it is a false solution. Instead, Cizek calls for the complete shutting down of the projects already in place.

Over its fifty years, *CD* has popularized critical studies in political economy, while — at the same time — never stooping to dumb-down the issues. As witness the case of Alberta, it has consistently and boldly dealt with issues — Canadian sovereignty, human rights, the environment — well ahead of their recognition or discussion by other media. This is *Canadian Dimension*'s legacy — one to be cherished as the magazine embarks on its next half century.

PART IX

THE SOCIALIST DIMENSION

CHAPTER 22
The Urban Dimension
David Hugill

In the spring of 1969 the *William and Mary Law Review* published a sym-´
posium on the urban crisis in the United States. American cities had been
shaken by unrest throughout the preceding decade and the special issue
brought together a series of "outstanding figures" to assess the meaning
of these events. Maxwell Cohen, Dean of the Faculty of Law at McGill
University, was the only contributor invited to offer an international
perspective. His article opened with a frank acknowledgement that no
society — "even the preferred among the nations" — had been immune
to the upheavals of the 1960s. In the US, however, they had created a
rupture of such "explosive" proportions that it had begun to menace the
very "mutual reliances" that "must reinforce . . . a democratic order."[1]
This differed sharply from the situation in his native Canada, Cohen
continued. There, disturbances had been largely confined to a few student
agitators unwilling to go beyond "break-ins, sit-ins, character assassination, group insults, and violent demands for participation." There was no
reason to expect that anything other than stability would persist north of
the border, not least because the country had only a "minor race question" to contend with.[2]

Cohen is certainly right to observe that challenges to the "Canadian
idyll" in the 1960s bear little resemblance to the fiery fightbacks
that engulfed places like Watts, Newark and Detroit. But his remarks
also cloak the Canadian urban experience in a mantle of innocence.

Narratives of American brutality — from Custer's crusades to the siege of Fallujah — have long served as a foil against which Canadian pretensions of harmony have been constructed. It is not surprising, then, that a certain image of the American metropolis as a powder keg of racial tension has often worked to relieve Canadians of the burden of scrutinizing the fault lines of our own shared existence. Assumptions about the comparative calm of Canadian urban life assure us that the *real* barbarians remain contained on the nether side of the forty-ninth parallel — *Bowling for Columbine* all over again.

The best critical analysis militates against such self-congratulation. Evidence that our cities remain spaces of stark inequity grounded in longstanding forms of structural exclusion is always abundant, but the pervasiveness of what Yasmin Jiwani calls "discourses of denial" demands that the task of chipping away at mythologies of national innocence be an ongoing enterprise.[3] The monumental incapacity of mainstream organs of knowledge production to offer anything close to a sustained pattern of critical self-reflection means that such efforts fall to alternative entities, like *Canadian Dimension*. What follows, is an effort to evaluate how well the magazine has done this job, with a particular focus on its coverage of urban issues.

Boom urbanism

The years that followed the Second World War were a period of unprecedented economic growth in Canada. The protracted postwar boom facilitated massive transformations of the country's urban landscapes as cities were remade by a powerful wave of suburban development and a profound reorganization of the inner city.[4] Growth on the fringe coupled with efforts to build urban centres that were in step with the needs of a modern city. Processes of "urban renewal" became de rigueur and municipalities began converting huge swaths of city space into a series of tabulae rasae onto which the ambition of a new urbanism could be written.[5] Such reclamations allowed planners and elites to justify the destruction of districts deemed undesirable, halt the devaluation of downtown rents, and rebuild the urban core as an attractive site for investment.[6] *Canadian Dimension* was born in interesting urban times.

Yet urban analysis is sparse in the magazine's first decade. By the late 1960s, to be sure, contributors like R.W.G. Bryant and Inno Vatter (6:1, April/May 1969; 7:7, January/February 1971) were taking aim at the homogeneity and sterility of the new landscapes, bemoaning the emergence of colonies of "ticky-tacky boxes" on the fringe and commerce-oriented high-rises in the core but largely sidestepping the broader political economy that was driving their production. Not until the mid-1970s did a serious indictment of the politics of urban development appear in *Dimension*'s pages. It was here, in comprehensive articles by Sarah Berger (8:8, August 1972) and G. Barker (9:2-3, January 1973), that the magazine first began to show how an unquenchable thirst for accumulation was vitally connected to the reshaping of Canadian urban life. These interventions trace, among other things, the rise of super-profitable development corporations and deliver a searing critique of the state's broad failure to alleviate housing shortages in an equitable manner. They show that once the building boom opened serious opportunities for profit making, mega-developers (alongside their partners in big finance) began to wield an unprecedented influence on the industry and argue that the meteoric rise of big builders like Trizec and Bramalea can be explicitly linked to public policy. Cited as one piece of evidence is CMHC's 1970 "innovation" program, which sought to overcome the bureaucratic hurdles of publicly administered housing builds by investing huge blocks of capital in the "laboratory" of the market. Berger argues that the scale of planned projects and the state's aversion to particular kinds of risks virtually ensured that only big players would be able to compete for the contracts. The result, she shows, was that developers accumulated staggering levels of profit while the state was left with problem-ridden housing projects and a series of unmet objectives. Importantly, however, it is precisely such failures that would be mobilized by various governments to justify their withdrawal from the construction of housing. The signal contribution of these *Dimension* critiques is that they give readers a clear basis to refuse such hollow rationalizations.

Yet it must be said that while these early critiques are developed in a thorough way, other fundamental urban contradictions are strikingly underconsidered in *Dimension*'s early years. One that stands out is an inattention to the ways that official renewal efforts were laden with a range of problematic commitments. Clear critiques of the cultural and economic shortsightedness of urban agendas are in abundant supply but there is little mention of how such efforts were employed to deal with "problem" populations. Renewal almost always meant removal and the question of *who*, precisely, was to be removed is revealing of broader dynamics. Areas slated for demolition were not the leafy enclaves of the bourgeoisie but low-income districts deemed chaotic or unseemly and renewal offered an opportunity not only to be rid of these spaces but also to discipline their "undesirable" inhabitants.

Reform and reaction

The 1970s and 1980s were also a time of significant urban transformation in Canada. Widespread deindustrialization worked to sap inner cities of their working-class character. "New" generations of middle-class professionals began an epochal "return" to the city. And urban regions became far more diverse as the last traces of overt racial discrimination were eliminated from Canadian immigration law. Postwar patterns of urban development were also renegotiated and by the early 1970s the "slash and build" spirit of renewal had begun to be countered by demands for the production of more "livable" cities.[7] The pursuit of such objectives contributed to the emergence of new reform coalitions, many of which drew their support from segments of the "new" middle classes that opposed wrecking-ball forms of renewal and the "large, anonymous projects" that followed in their wake.[8] The introduction of downtown-bound expressways intended to cut large swaths through city centres, for example, was a fierce rallying point in a number of communities. Such struggles had a decisive influence on the political culture of several cities as they brought together the interests of more social-democratically inclined currents with conservative counterparts. The new coalitions would soon begin to have an influence in municipal politics as reformers chipped away at the hegemony of business-led political blocs. Nominally progressive groups backed by strong community organizations came to power in Toronto, Vancouver, Montreal, Quebec City and elsewhere at various points throughout the 1970s and 1980s, securing some genuinely progressive developments. Nevertheless, reformers that won office were often constrained and tended to yield to more conservative forces. By the early 1990s, *Dimension* contributors were still adding to a steady stream of analysis that chronicled these capitulations. Malcolm Reid (27:6, November/December 1993) showed how Quebec City's *Rassemblement populaire* movement brought Mayor Jean-Paul L'Allier to power only to discover that he was more committed to a bid for the Winter Olympics than to neighbourhood democracy. Henri Lustiger-Thaler and Eric Shragge (29:6, December/ January 1995–96) observed that the Montreal Citizens' Movement, which had relied on grassroots support to get elected, tended to cater "to the needs of business" and yield a great deal of control to municipal technocrats. Such about-faces were partially reflections of the challenge of *actually* governing, but they also showed that most reform movements remained tepidly liberal in orientation. These broad failures opened an important discussion in *Dimension*'s pages about the consequences of grassroots participation in the formal urban political sphere.

Reform-inflected politics, however, were not hegemonic in this period and reactionary currents continued to wield influence in urban settings. The social upheavals of the 1960s had delivered a degree of liberality, to be sure, but they also provoked a backlash that found expression in political formations, public institutions and the press, well into the 1980s. In this context, several constituencies — especially LGBT communities, sex workers and people of colour — were routinely scapegoated. One of *Dimension*'s distinct contributions in this period was its provision of robust analysis from the front lines of these battles. Reports from Toronto, for example, demonstrate that the ethnically homogenous police force responded to urban transformation by amplifying its repression. "Some segments of the force have responded to the new Toronto by embracing a paranoid, racist, sexist and homophobic ideology in which they are the lone battlers for civilization — small-town, Protestant Ontario — against immigrants of all colours, lesbians and gays, Jews and even Catholics," wrote Ken Popert and Brian Mossop (15:8/16:1, December 1981). This perception of a "civilizational" struggle ensured that those identified as threats would be the primary targets of aggressive policing. Toronto-based *Dimension* writers showed how queer people (particularly in the city's emergent gaybourhood) and people of colour (particularly, but not exclusively, in the city's West Indian communities) were frequently singled out for police violence. In the former case, they reported on a sustained pattern of homophobic violence that included a staff sergeant's attempt to get gay teachers fired, the publication of a racist and homophobic internal newsletter, the death of a gay man in custody, tacit tolerance of an annual "Halloween pogrom" in which "thousands of suburban youths" attacked gay people on parts of Yonge Street, and raids on bathhouses that led to mass arrests and a major fightback. In the latter case, they showed how people of colour have had a fraught relationship with Toronto police. Lennox Farell, a high school teacher and Trinidadian migrant, used an extended biographical piece to look back at this period and recount how such targeting has been a definitional part of his life since he arrived in Canada (34:2, July/August 2000). He describes being dragged off a subway car, harassed for his involvement in antibrutality organizing, and the visceral humiliation of being routinely stopped and searched.

In general, then, *Dimension*'s assessment of the limits of urban reform politics serves as an important check on a tendency to retell the history of this era in overly rosy tones. It is interesting to note, however, that the best analysis comes from contributors involved in various kinds of queer rights struggles; we hear little from immigrants, people of colour and urban Aboriginal people in these first decades of the magazine's publication. My point here is not at all that *Dimension* was ignorant on questions of racism, Aboriginal struggle or migrant justice. Indeed, the magazine has consistently committed considerable coverage to antiracist and Indigenous struggle but what is largely absent in this phase of its development is an attempt to give explicitly urban forms of Canadian racism the comprehensive treatment that they deserve. There is robust analysis of Black Power struggles in the United States as well as Indigenous land struggles in rural Canada, but few attempts to come to grips with how racialized patterns of exclusion were unfolding in the Canadian metropolis. Of course, this would be largely reversed in the

decades that would follow as *Dimension* began to devote serious attention to urban racism, publishing interventions by an impressive range
of activists at the fore of struggles against it.

Urban neoliberalism

The rise of neoliberal orthodoxies from the 1980s on provoked a comprehensive rescaling of capitalist relations. The restructuring of urban
regions as self-contained "competitive units" began to undermine earlier
arrangements where cities functioned primarily as the centripetal cores
of national economies. The necessity of engaging in an ever-intensifying
inter-local competition for investment has driven urban governments to
take on an increasingly entrepreneurial hue and marketing local place
as globally connected has moved to the fore of urban priorities.[9] It has
become important, in this climate, for cities to go to great lengths to prove
their cosmopolitan bona fides. In places like Toronto ethnic plurality has
been reimagined as a competitive advantage while the city's diversity and
skilled migrant labour pool have become core elements of a regional sales
pitch.[10] More centrally, perhaps, the view that attracting a capable and
transnational "creative class" is key to the economic vitality of cities has
gained broad acceptance among municipal elites and engendered a new
emphasis on providing amenities capable of luring them in. Planners and
boosters have sought to construct a new urbanism accented by architec-
tural showpieces and international culture festivals as they've adhered
closely to the "creative city script." *Dimension* has been relatively attuned
to the significance of these shifts. The publication of three consecutive special issues on Canadian cities in 2004 (38:4, July/August; 5, September/
October; 6, November/December), for example, helped unravel the cultural and ethical poverty of Richard Florida–inspired "competitive city"
policy development (well before the "creative class" was a household
phrase). Importantly, too, these issues appeared at a time when the formal
political classes had begun to muse publicly about the importance of a
"new deal" for Canadian cities. *Dimension*'s coverage reminds readers that
any such deal — important as its infrastructural commitments might be —
remains firmly in line with a vision of urbanity that places international
competitiveness far above spatial and infrastructural justice.

This revelatory work is of vital importance because the hard edges of the "competitive city" can be easily lost in the dazzling lights of cultural revival and marketed diversity. The ways in which the reconstruction of downtown districts has worked to obliterate the "spaces of the poor" can easily be rendered opaque by the rhetoric of urban investment.[11] *Dimension's* coverage, particularly from the late 1990s on, consistently showed how the neoliberalization of urban space has, in fact, reinforced and consolidated polarity; it helps us understand why in several Canadian cities spaces of elite consumption continue to butt up against spaces of acute deprivation (Vancouver being the paradigmatic example) while in others, perhaps even most, zones of poverty and prosperity have been increasingly segregated from one another. Startling data from Toronto, analyzed at some length in Tanya Gulliver's (42:6, November/ December 2008) cover story, for example, reveals that Canada's largest city has grown starkly segregated between amenity-rich high-income corridors and a vast wilderness of precarious existence, spread broadly across the city.

Yet processes of neoliberalization invite contestation and the places where they have been most aggressively pursued are also where the most robust forms of opposition have sprung up. Accordingly, *Dimension's* best coverage of the Canadian "neoliberal moment" tends to come from the two places where neoliberal statecraft was practised in its most "gloves off" form, namely Mike Harris's Ontario and Gordon Campbell's British Columbia. It is through coverage of the activities of grassroots groups like the Ontario Coalition Against Poverty (OCAP) that the magazine was able to illustrate for its readers the life-and-death stakes of the neoliberal state's assault on the urban poor. *Dimension* could not have ignored the massive marches and roving city-wide strikes that brought the Harris regime's assault on labour into sharp relief, but it is worth asking whether the intensity of the attack on Ontario's very poor would have appeared so prominently in its pages if groups like OCAP hadn't agitated so successfully. Reports like Bryan Palmer's (34:5, September/October 2000) analysis of the June 15 riots at Queen's Park brought attention not only to the plight of the dispossessed but also offered an opportunity to observe the degree of repression that the state was willing to pursue in order to crush a persistent adversary. Dramatic moments like these, however, were flashpoints in a far more comprehensive pattern of repression that emerged in the mid-1990s. The adoption of revanchist "safe streets" policing in various jurisdictions mobilized bylaws and criminal sanctions that empowered authorities to punish the urban poor. The Harris Tories, among the most aggressive practitioners, introduced, for example, sanctions on "aggressive panhandling" in an explicit effort to rid Ontario of dangerous urban villains, like the "squeegee kid." Contributors, like Samir Gandesha (34:1, February 2000) and Al Pope (38:1, January/February 2004), tended to agree that the ascendance of this sort of policing was an inevitable public policy response to expanded immiseration and retrenched entitlement. Pope even suggests that they had the effect of completing Campbell's program of effectively criminalizing poverty by transferring social problems to police. The abandonment of comprehensive efforts to find "political solutions" to intensified urban poverty, Gandesha pointed out, meant that political elites would have to find new ways to explain the persistence of these problems. The obvious strategy, he continues, was to redefine such problems as moral in nature — created by welfare cheats, multiculturalism, single mothers and a lack of discipline, for example — and to recalibrate the solution as laying down the moral law. The promotion of a certain form of urban authoritarianism, in other words, became a tactic for dealing with new vulnerabilities created by the retrenchment of social provision.

The urban present

Readers of *Canadian Dimension* are well aware that Canadian cities remain sites of concentrated injustice. They are places where a growing army of international migrants swell the ranks of precarious wage-labour; where people in the bottom ranks of the sex trade are disproportionately criminalized and harassed; where street and day homelessness abound; where detox facilities are funding-starved and safe-injection alternatives are menaced with closure; where Aboriginal people are vastly overrepresented in indexes of social suffering; and where infrastructural deficits spiral out of control, to offer just a few examples. These and other specifically urban crises have been considered at length in the magazine's pages and its readers have certainly benefited from an increased attention to cities as a critical site of political contestation. We need publications like *Dimension* to help us work through these and other challenges. But we also need to remind ourselves that Canadian cities are profoundly integrated into broad transnational patterns of violence and dispossession, not self-contained units somehow removed from broader circuits of transnational injustice. Thus in spite of the steady stream of popular rhetoric that describes Canadian cities as the drivers of national prosperity it is critical to remember, as Stefan Kipfer and Kanishka Goonewardena (38:4, July/August 2004) have pointed out in *Dimension*'s pages, that these urban units are not all "free standing sources of innovation, productivity and growth." Rather, urban elites are the beneficiaries of a broad exploitation of resources from around the world. Efforts to broker new kinds of urban justice thus need to be doubly focused. On the one hand they must challenge inequity at home and on the other they must make the link between the reproduction of certain forms of Canadian prosperity and the international violence that they necessarily imply. Undermining enduring narratives that allow us to imagine our cities as cosmopolitan examples or innocent bystanders in a complicated world must be at the very centre of these efforts. This is the task for *Dimension*'s next fifty years of urban analysis.

CHAPTER 23
The Socialist Dimension

Bryan Palmer[1]

Canadian Dimension was born in the shadows of a fading Cold War and in the metaphorical equivalent of a solar eclipse of conventional left-wing politics. Appearing in 1963, the Cy Gonick–edited, Winnipeg-based magazine appeared two years after Montreal's *Our Generation Against Nuclear War*, founded by Dimitri Roussopoulos, and three years before *This Magazine is About Schools*, in which Toronto's Bob Davis and George Martel figured centrally. For decades these founding journals of the Canadian New Left continued to promote ideas, debates and the struggles expressive of a politics that resonated with the sensibilities of the 1960s. *Dimension* is the only member of this trio of publications that survives in anything approximating its original form.

Gonick's first editorial, "Introducing Ourselves," (1:1-2, September/ November 1963) echoed somewhat Tom Hayden's 1962 "Port Huron Statement," accenting "the terrifying (and terrified) world in which we were born," situating this "new and independent journal of fact and opinion" within the thought of a "postnuclear generation of leftish thinkers." Like Hayden, Gonick insisted that the youth of the 1960s were shedding the disillusionment of their predecessors; they were insistent that "the good society" could be attained, and that reason was their guide to action. Again, very much in the spirit of Hayden's "Port Huron Statement," there was a rejection of commercialism and the superficial-ities evident in the mass media's depiction of contemporary life and politics. "We are tired of the old frame of reference," wrote Gonick, who proclaimed the intention to "challenge the assumptions of the cold war and of the free enterprise economy" as well as analysis of "the problems of communist society." As much as the NDP would be a focal point of early *CD* articles, the magazine was emphatic that it "affiliated with no political party and with no organization," Gonick taking pains to stress that, "We aim to be critical and provide a forum for the discussion of meaningful alternatives, not to patronize any party or organization." Socialism was not mentioned in this opening editorial statement.

For fifty years, *Dimension* has negotiated the difficult terrain of being Canada's main forum for discussion, debate and exchange of left-wing thought. An examination of its first half-century provides something of a weather vane of left opinion, the articles, editorials, letters, reviews, graphics and even advertisements and cartoons charting the ways in which different decades have spawned new perspectives and nurtured shifts in the ways left discourses and practices have been structured. Always straddling the ultimate purpose of changing Canada and the global relations within which it is situated, *Dimension* has had one foot firmly planted in an understanding that it is primarily a *venue* for discussing how to actually get to that other world that leftists think is possible, with another foot more uncertainly situated in the always-shifting terrain of what to do to achieve such fundamental transformation. To explore this tension, it is appropriate to first examine at length how *Canadian Dimension* has addressed the broad politics of the Left. This substantive background can then be used to develop more discrete accounts of the evolving particularities of the magazine's always critical engagement with the Co-operative Commonwealth Federation and New Democratic Party (CCF/NDP) traditions and the different ways in which it has contributed to the analysis and realization of socialism.

A new venue for the discussion of left politics: Fifty years of Canadian Dimension

In 1965 (3:1, November/December), Stan Gray, who would later in the decade become a preeminent New Left leader in Quebec, provided *Dimension* readers with a guide to the "new left/old left" divide. The graphic heading the essay illustrated a rigid linear demarcation between a bearded youth gazing across an urban working-class alleyway, and a jacket-and-tie clad counterpart, eyes fixed on Ottawa's Parliament Buildings. Gray detailed the activities of the Student Union for Peace Action (SUPA), seeing its activities as the expression of "the birth of a new left in Canada, a new left which borrows many ideas from the parallel American development and which has the potential of channelling the growing idealism and radicalism of Canadian youth into a social movement capable of transforming Canadian society." Community organizing and participatory democracy, counterposed to electoral politics, were the animating approaches promoted in Gray's article.

The framework was almost entirely that of youth radicalization in the United States, referencing Students for a Democratic Society, the Student Nonviolent Coordinating Committee and the Northern Student Movement. Gray also noted that, while originating among students, the American New Left was extending its reach into civil rights struggles in the South and into poor and working-class neighbourhoods in Chicago, Newark and Cleveland. When Gray addressed the Canadian scene he did so negatively, rejecting forcefully the notion that the NDP had any chance of functioning as a left lever in the social transformation of Canada. "[A]s long as Canadian radicals persist in their commitment to the NDP (or to changing the NDP in a leftward direction) there will be no radical politics that is relevant to basic social change in Canada," Gray insisted, concluding bluntly, "Any radicalism that has any prospects of being relevant to Canada in the 1960s must be built outside the NDP."

Stan Gray was a red-diaper baby, reared in a Communist Party family. By the end of the 1960s he would be veering back to something of his roots, especially in the stress on the working class (as opposed to youth or students) as the vehicle of fundamental social transformation. Soon he would be involved in shop-floor struggles and trade unionism in Hamilton, Ontario (18:3, June 1984; 38:6, November/December 2004). *Dimension* was never simply a product of red-diaper babies, but there were indeed other New Leftists who came out of Old Left backgrounds. James Laxer was one, and along with SUPA activist Arthur Pape he provided another commentary on the New Left as it saw itself in the mid-1960s.

In a 1966 *CD* essay (3:6, September/October 1966), Laxer and Pape shared a great deal of Gray's understandings, including the stress on youth radicalization, a rejection of Canada's established electoral parties as possibilities of change, and a positive assessment of what they called radical democracy and community decision-making. What distinguished Laxer and Pape from Gray, however, was their accent on the necessity of reinvigorating a flagging Canadian nationalism: at the heart of their view of the New Left was the clarion call to fight for Canadian economic independence from the escalating encroachments of American Empire.

One of *CD*'s great strengths is that it has been a forum for debate and exchange. It has never shied away from controversy, or from presenting conflicting views on issues central to left politics. The Gray and Laxer/Pape articles, as well as much else that appeared in the mid-1960s in *Dimension* and that made it clear how much New Left ideas were animating an ongoing youth radicalization, were responded to in the pages of the magazine by Old Left figures like the Co-operative Commonwealth Federation journalist/MP Douglas Fisher. Fisher (3:6, September/October 1966) found the New Left devoid of curiosity, unwilling to listen, unlikely to organize, and fundamentally uninterested in the actualities of mainstream politics and the nuts-and-bolts workings of the economy. A distrust of leaders, avoidance of responsibilities, and disdain for parliamentary procedure characterized a New Left that, for Fisher, likes "the idea of the 24-hour day, caring every hour of the day, being available all day, but abhorring office hours." For the New Left, Fisher suggested cavalierly, the "exploiters" are everywhere, composed of the "middle-class, the politicians, the men and women who staff schools and government departments — all bureaucrats." Fisher asked one young Company of Young Canadians volunteer in 1966 if, in her intention to work with Inuit and aboriginal peoples, she was inclined to talk to any "experts" in the field. As she wrinkled her nose and replied, "Never. They've been oppressing the Indians and Eskimos for a century. They'll be my enemy," Fisher had heard enough to write the New Left off his script of who was worth treating seriously on the political spectrum.

More substantive and engaging critiques of the New Left emerged from Old Leftists whose Marxism and oppositional politics marked them apart from Fisher, with his almost instinctual social-democratic revulsion at the cultural gulf separating youth radicals and followers of parliamentary icons like Tommy Douglas. University of Montreal professor Charles Taylor was a Montreal-born veteran of the first British New Left of the late 1950s. Sir George Williams University professor Eugene D. Genovese had been drubbed out of the Communist Party in the early 1950s, but remained sufficiently Marxist to find himself a refugee from the American university system's anticommunism.

Taylor, an associate editor of *Canadian Dimension* at the time, pilloried what he labelled the "obscurantism, egocentric pseudo-existentialism, and abstract moralizing" of young, largely student, radicals (5:6, September/October 1968). Targeting the American New Left's attraction to the thought of Herbert Marcuse, profiled in *CD* in 1968, Taylor questioned such theory's "blithe unconcern with what rebellion is *for*, as long as it's stridently enough against." He also deplored Marcuse's ruling out "the possibility that a paroxysm of rebellion could destroy the discipline and character-form of one civilization without building those of another, higher one." The result would only be "disillusionment and despair: a binge of agitation followed by a prolonged hang-over" (7:3, August/September 1970). At the time of Taylor's withering 1970 assault on Marcuse's utopian thinking, the New Left rebellion at Sir George Williams had left the university community deeply divided over allegations of systemic racism raised by black, largely West Indian, students; its computer centre torched; and upwards of ninety students arrested. Taylor was attacking Marcuse, but his angry article was as much about student radicalism's tactics as it was with the philosophical foundations of the New Left. Two years earlier, in 1968 (6:1, April/May), Genovese, writing on New Left strategies opposing the war in Vietnam, echoed such repudiations, doing so out of fundamentally Old Left premises. Genovese deplored the New Left's "flamboyant revolutionary rhetoric," rejected its "appeals to stand and die" as well as its "regressions into the public display of four-letter words" and its "psychologically self-serving allusions to the lonely plight of those who have to make 'existential decisions'." Attacking imperialism and its global carnage, rejecting the values, activities and very existence of "the ruling class," and aware of what he called "the classic dilemmas of Western Leninism and Social Democracy," Genovese was adamant that, "The nihilist tendency on the Left . . . has to be put down, if we are to move an inch. In particular, those who urge the destruction of the universities or of their disruption so as to provoke military occupation must be seen for what they are — not as misguided and impatient comrades, but as the advocates of a politics and a world view with which socialists have no more essentially in common than we do with those of the ruling class."

Struggles of the New Left

For some, then, the New Left unleashed, in Genovese's *Dimension* words, "A War on Two Fronts." *CD* editor Cy Gonick was more measured in his developing perspectives on the New Left, but was never as enamoured of the SUPA-variant of Canada's youth revolt as Stan Gray. In 1966 (4:1, November/December), Gonick suggested that the Canadian New Left was as much myth as reality. For Gonick, Canadian New Leftists, with "a few outstanding exceptions," lacked numbers behind them, had failed to develop either organizations or coherent commitments, and were limited in their practice to summer projects. Gonick's long 1965 essay, "Strategies for Social Change" (4:1, November/December 1966), spent far more time discussing what he regarded as the schizophrenia of the NDP than it did addressing the New Left. Congealed within the NDP, Gonick suggested, were "two striking different political programmes." The majority within the NDP, according to the *CD* editor, adhered to a moderate politics of welfare enhancement and economic planning, eschewing socialism and confining its reform orientation to managing capitalism. Gonick's critique of this hegemonic politics, comprising piecemeal, incremental tinkering with the system of exploitation and oppression, was for all of his skepticism about the New Left quintessentially New Leftist in its premises.

Drawing on Erich Fromm, rather than Marx, Gonick condemned the ways in which the modern quest for material goods monopolized "men's energies and creativities." "Homo consumes," insisted Gonick, compensated for an inner emptiness "by continuous and ever-increasing consumption." Responsibility for this systemic degeneration of human social relations lay with modern competitive capitalism and the powerful business corporation, whose tentacles reached from the public domain into the private corners of everyday life. Moreover, in the context of the Cold War, corporations were invariably structured into the military-industrial complex. The power and ongoing strength of United States capitalism lay in its global dominance, shored up by its military capacity to protect markets and resources and resist communist encroachment on territories whose pliant integration into the American Empire was, by the 1960s, essential to the contours of international relations. This was also pivotal to the affluence and consumer contentment that dulled the appetite for opposition and resistance in Canada and the United States. In all of this Gonick argued, as had Hayden in "The Port Huron Statement," that specialized institutions such as the educational system, the churches and the mass media played central roles, cultivating ideologies of acquiescence. Even the trade unions, Gonick claimed, had been made into something other than the vehicles of discontent and protest evident in their origins. They were now "an accepted part of the industrial system," and in their developing status as a "vested interest" they performed "a controlling function within the framework of the prevailing society."[2]

Gonick melded this fundamentally New Left critique of the Establishment and its meanings to an Older Left understanding of the necessity of struggling for a socialist Canada. Socialist institutions, he insisted, had to be built within organizations of teachers, university faculty, social workers, the professions, student organizations, churches, even bodies like home and school associations and, above all, in "the trade union movement and, yes, the New Democratic Party." As part of this agenda, moreover, Gonick twinned this struggle for socialism to the project of making Canada more economically independent of the monolith of global capital, the United States. Thus, "A socialist Canada," in Gonick's vision, could not sever all ties with the American Empire, but it would never be realized unless tangible efforts were made to "eliminate the corporate links which act as the instruments of continental integration." Within a decidedly economic framework, Gonick articulated, as early as 1965, a view of Canadian socialism as achievable only through "a far greater degree of economic independence" from the United States.

The irony of this kind of left politics evolving from engagement with the ideas of the American New Left and then generating calls for Canadian independence would be obvious by the end of the 1960s. James Laxer's influential 1969 *CD* article, "The Student Movement and Canadian Independence" (6:3-4, August/September 1969), negotiated the creative tensions in this process with claims that the "powerful impact of American radicalism on the development of the Canadian [New Left] movement" had stunted the politics of youth radicalism north of the forty-ninth parallel. In the aftermath of 1968 and its Paris, Belgrade, Mexico City, Rome and Berlin uprisings, which for Gonick represented a "stunning" expression of the birth of a "new international left" (5:6, September/October 1968), Laxer's claims that the Canadian student movement bore "the stamp of its American influence[s]," including undue attention to questions of marginal relevance in Canada, such as "the race question," certainly seem, in retrospect, narrow, even parochial. *Dimension* nevertheless continued to provide a wide range of creative commentary on developments relating to 1960s happenings that reflected the left politics of the era, including politically attuned analysis of the folk-song movement and its displacement by rock music. One such 1969 analysis was provided by former Communist Party member, *Guardian* executive editor, and later advocate of the 1970s Maoist-oriented New Communist Movement, Irwin Silber (6:3-4, August/September 1969). It concluded that rock music rejected "society's most sacred values." Rather than a political program, it provided, in classic New Left fashion, "the torment, the brutalization, the anger, the cynicism of a generation which hungers for faith — and trusts no one." Unlike the folk music that it succeeded, and that was in many ways rooted in the politics of the Old Left, 1960s rock was not "marching music." But it was an aesthetic, according to Silber, "suitable for the disaster that is today's America."

Finally, *Canadian Dimension*'s tumultuous ride through the 1960s resulted in copious comment on a plethora of topics, many treated earlier throughout this volume. Among the subjects addressed in ways that deepened understanding of left politics in Canada were labour, war and peace, poverty, civil disobedience, culture and the arts, imperialism, sport, schooling and higher education, health, prisons, economic issues and race.

La belle province

None, however, stood out more than the particularities of Quebec's experience within Canadian Confederation. From Gonick's first editorial in 1963, the magazine had promised "critical reviews and translations from the French-Canadian press," (1:1-2, September/November 1963), singling out Quebec as in a special region within the Canadian mosaic. Over the course of its first seven years of publication, approximately thirty articles addressed Quebec, with contributing editors, correspondents and editorial board members (designations of such individuals changed over time) such as G. David Sheps, Charles Taylor, E.J. Smith, Gad Horowitz, Hubert Guindon and Stan Gray providing ongoing commentary detailed elsewhere in this volume, much of which framed francophone nationalism and socialism together. This prepared the way for a reasoned discussion of the politics of the Front de libération du Québéc (FLQ) and the repressive atmosphere that overtook Canada in 1970 with Pierre Elliott Trudeau's declaration of the *War Measures Act*. Counter views, such as that expressed in Michael Nemiroff's "Revolutionary Consciousness in Quebec: A New Parochialism" (6:7, February/March 1970), were also aired.

Even Charles Taylor's contribution to the discussion on Quebec, while railing against the New Left and its "absurd" solutions, nonetheless recognized that the October Crisis revealed "alienation too profound for the system to contain." If Andre Larocque urged English Canadian readers to defend left values by refusing to accept the suspension of democracy, insisting that "Trudeau's army marches not in the defense of principles but to protect the power of a minority against a power that must find its roots in the working class of English Canada," Taylor saw the unfolding and dramatic clash of the *independentistes* and federalist authority as "bad news for the Left" (7:5-6, December 1970).

Taylor perhaps provided the most pressing challenge to the New Left sensibilities that were always evident in the pages of *CD* over the course of the 1960s. In 1969 (5:8, February), he offered a lengthy "Socialist

Perspective on the 1970s," in which he called on *Dimension* readers to reject the bumbling, antiquated "old-guard" leadership of Canada's mainstream parties as well as the seemingly more hip and up-to-date "'swinging' technologically literate alternative" that, as much as it promised change *à la Trudeau*, was also bankrupt.

If Taylor acknowledged that within the CCF-NDP tradition too many punches had been pulled in the socialist critique of capitalism, he himself, as Gonick noted in reply, failed to adequately address what was wrong with the old social-democratic Left and its Canadian party. Democratization, with which Taylor was much concerned, was simply not enough, Gonick suggested, and indeed, as we shall see in discussion of the NDP and the Waffle later in this essay, it would not be lived up to very convincingly among New Democrat "heavies." Such social democratic traditionalists thought New Left critics needed to be silenced and driven out rather than listened to and integrated into the leadership of the NDP. When Ed Broadbent responded to Taylor, moreover, he sounded rather like the offspring of a shotgun marriage of a utopian socialist of the early nineteenth century and a curiously truncated Trotskyist of the late 1960s, mouthing a transitional program that lacked a sense of what *the transition* was leading toward.

Broadbent (5:8, February 1969; 6:2, July 1969) advocated laws which "recognize the fundamental right of worker's citizenship" on the utopian socialist side, and, in his program of transition, insisted on legislation "compelling employers to open their books," providing "complete disclosure" of all "information relevant to the running of an enterprise." Alongside funds being made available to the unions to hire research staffs "comparable to that possessed by management," such laws would apparently "remove all rights of control from those who own companies or who own shares in companies." In Broadbent's parliamentary road to socialism, capitalism could seemingly be legislated into giving up its capacity to exploit the working class, and democratic socialism would be the result. This 1969 Taylor, Gonick and Broadbent exchange was essentially a debate within the NDP, but it brought into relief the extent to which the New Left/Old Left divide that *Canadian Dimension* had originally appeared out of was itself now being rethought.

What was most evident in this end of the 1960s/beginning of the 1970s climacteric was the sense that the New Left was fading and a shift in the politics of the Left was occurring. Larocque signalled this in his clarion call to English Canadian readers of *Dimension* (7:5-6, December 1970) to support and recognize what was happening in Quebec, which extended through the FLQ in ways that went well past the clandestine organization and its limited, if galvanizing, practices. "The Left in Quebec can succeed only if it continues, harder than ever, to penetrate working-class districts," wrote Larocque, suggesting that the René Lévesque–led Parti québécois (PQ) had done precisely this in an April 1970 election, and that the francophone province's union struggles, citizen's committees and community organizations were now the primary sites of left-wing activism. One of Canada's leading Marxist historians, and a committed voice of the right of national self-determination for the Québécois, Stanley Ryerson, reiterated this point years later in a 1977 article, "An Opening in Quebec" (12:2, April). The detonating quality of the October Crisis, he wrote in retrospect, was its "concealed component: *class struggle.*" Ryerson concluded his article insisting that in Lévesque's Parti québécois government, with its advocacy of independence, "the door is ajar at least for fresh approaches and new initiatives from neighborhoods and union locals and all manner of people's groupings."

Changing labour and everything else

This note of a turn to the working class, to organizing the poor, and to creating structures of politics beyond the seemingly anarchic and often rhetorical/performative substance of what an American contributor to *Canadian Dimension*, Staughton Lynd, called the "guerrilla warfare" of 1967–1970 (11:6, Summer 1976), would be apparent throughout the 1970s. "The revolutionary process cannot be set in motion merely by the ardour of our convictions," lectured Silber as early as the summer of 1970 (7:3, August/September). "It is still true that only a revolution based in the working class is capable of destroying capitalism and developing socialism." David Lewis Stein and Alvin Finkel lent implicit credence to Silber's more angular formulations by questioning the staying power of 1960s New Left cultural phenomena like the Yippies and urban communes (7:3, August/September 1970).

Lynd, writing in 1976 (11:6, Summer), noted the exhilarating capacity of the New Left to "blow the minds" of masses of youth, but stressed that it also "failed to create permanent organizations" and that it had yet to "reach the home-owning, union-belonging, over thirty" set. Concluding that 1960s youth radicalism was "strong on vision," but much weaker when it came to sustaining institutions and forums for continuing and deepening radical dissent, Lynd asked if anyone could really imagine the coming of socialism without "the prior creation of people's organizations, institutions of dual power, a labor party" and the like.

All of this fit well with *Dimension's* 1970s coverage of Toronto's Just Society Movement (7:1-2, June/July 1970), an organization of poor people chronicled in the magazine's pages by George Ford and Steven Langdon. International figures such as André Gorz were also featured, discussing workers' control and urban revolutionary initiatives that reached past the limitations of trade unions and addressed ways of confronting and challenging capitalist domination (8:1, June 1971; 10:4, September 1974). Labour had, of course, figured centrally in *CD* in the 1960s. Ed Finn, a maverick journalist, left-wing social democrat, and staffer in the Canadian Brotherhood of Railway, Transport, and General Workers, authored a number of *Dimension* articles on the militant upsurge of young Canadian workers in the mid-1960s. He continued to write for the magazine for years. But over the course of the 1970s the coverage of labour — historical, theoretical and contemporary — more than quadrupled, with almost ninety separate discussions appearing during the decade. In 1972 (8:7, June) *Canadian Dimension* focused on "Why Canadian workers are in Revolt," while a 1979 issue on "The Battle for the Workplace" (14:3, December), contained articles by Gonick on the work process, labour historian Craig Heron writing on workers' history, sociologist Graham Lowe offering comment on the rise of modern managerial techniques, Joan Kuyek and Bill Burns discussing what it was like to work for Bell Canada and political economist Wallace Clement outlining how labour resisted the strategies of management. University of Regina political scientist Lorne Brown provided perhaps the most influential statement on labour in his lengthy and

473

groundbreaking 1973 overview of Canadian working-class history (later reproduced as a *Dimension* pamphlet), "Breaking Down Myths of Peace and Harmony in Canadian Labour History" (9:5, May). It was in the 1970s, moreover, that historians of work and workers such as Gregory S. Kealey, David Frank, Ian McKay and Nolan Reilly first contributed to *CD*.[3]

Being had determined consciousness

The 1970s saw the imposition of wage and price controls, a one-day Canadian Labour Congress–sponsored general strike, and an outbreak of working-class militancy. Embittered class conflicts and the jailings of trade union leaders associated with the Common Front in Quebec and Jean-Claude Parrot of the Canadian Union of Postal Workers stamped the decade with a sense of urgency and resistance. Breakaway unions raised the issue of independence within the labour movement and the constraints of American domination of large "international" unions. Confederation of Canadian Unions head Kent Rowley and United Steelworkers of America spokesman Lynn Williams squared off against one another in *Dimension's* pages (9:6, July 1973).

Also indicative of the shift in left politics associated with the 1970s was increasing attention to feminism and to aboriginal issues. In the case of women's liberation, destined to be seen as fundamental to a rethinking of socialism, *Dimension* contributor Nancy Lubka opened discussion in 1970 with an important overview (7:1-2, June/July). Much followed, culminating in a special issue on women (10:8, June 1975) that included Claire Culhane on "Women and Vietnam," Shelly Gavigan on the prosecution of Henry Morgentaler, Margaret Randall on Cuban women, Kay Macpherson on aspects of the legacies of the 1960s and much more by writers as varied as Margaret Benston, Deborah Gorham, Dorothy Livesay and Marlene Dixon.

Native peoples also came increasingly to the fore in the pages of *Canadian Dimension,* with the government's Indian policy (especially after the 1969 Trudeau-Chrétien "White Paper") and the nature of aboriginal wage labour, as well as the history of indigenous dispossession and the reserve system, discussed. Aboriginal militancy was front and centre in Canada by 1974. The occupation of Kenora's Anicinabe Park by members of the Ojibwa Warriors Society and the American Indian Movement–sponsored cross-country native people's caravan to Ottawa protested the alienation of aboriginal land and the abysmal conditions of living indigenous peoples in Canada experienced. Acts of resistance like these were showcased in two 1974–1975 issues of *Dimension*. (10:5, November 1974; 10:6, January 1975). The political economy of Northern development and its impact on First Nations was increasingly addressed (8:7, June 1972; 11:2, October 1975).

These were but some of the subjects broached and broadened by *Canadian Dimension* in the 1970s. The magazine's conception of itself as a venue for debate and discussion on the Left had widened considerably. Longstanding topics such as imperialism and international struggles against it, the state of the labour movement (addressed in a regular 1980s column by the research director of the Canadian Union of Postal Workers, Geoff Bickerton), and the Quebec question jostled with new understandings of matters such as sexual identity, prison culture and mental health. Indeed, in the 1980s it would arguably be the addition of articles on gay and lesbian challenges to heterosexism that challenged the left consensus of *Dimension* most decisively. "Talking sex," the title of a 1986 article by Jackie Larkin (20:2, April) — who contributed a semi-regular feminist column throughout the mid-1980s — morphed easily into the beginnings of what would, in our times, come to be known as queer politics.[4]

Especially significant was the unprecedented Solidarity uprising in British Columbia in 1983. A general strike had been threatened in opposition to a massive Social Credit legislative assault on public-sector workers, particularly government employees and teachers, and a generalized attack on welfare provisioning, leaving women, children, aboriginal people and the poor at the mercy of state-initiated cutbacks to a wide array of social services. Contributors such as Jackie Larkin, Sharon Yandle, Harry Rankin, Cynthia Flood and myself, among others, commented on the movement, chronicling its exhilarating rise and dissecting its deflating fall (18:1, March 1984; 18:2, May 1984). One of *CD*'s most talented resident poets, Tom Wayman, eventually provided an epic evaluation of the abrupt, sell-out–like, cheek-by-jowl settlement reached on the Kelowna patio of BC premier Bill Bennett. Acting for the province's workers, and arbitrarily deciding for them that nothing was to be gained by future struggle, International Woodworkers of America *lider máximo* Jack Munro dashed the hopes of hundreds of thousands of west coast workers and their supporters by ending what had undoubtedly been the most vibrant labour uprising in British Columbia's post–World War II history. Wayman vilified Munro in verse, his "The Face of Jack Munro" first appearing in *Dimension* (20:1, March 1986).

Also centrally important in the 1980s, a decade in which nuclear weapons were proliferating and "star wars" threatened, was *CD's* coverage of the peace movement and its debates over strategy and tactics. Contributions from Kathleen Gough, Eric Shragge and David Mandel, Reg Whitaker, David Langille and an interview with the European Nuclear Disarmament (END) campaigner E.P. Thompson (16:5, July/August 1982; 16:7, January 1983; 17:5, November 1983; 17:6, December 1983; 18:1, March 1984; 19:1, March/April 1985; 19:2, May/June 1985; 18:6, December 1984) highlighted the importance of war and peace in the early-to-mid-1980s. These concerns spilled over into controversies and exchanges over the question of Soviet expansionism later in the decade (21:2, April 1987) and the apocalyptic possibilities of World War III (21:3, May/June 1987).

The peace movement that *CD* addressed so fulsomely in its pages was complemented by increasing attention to ecology, both initiatives aimed directly at the preservation of the earth and its resources. James Harding and John Warnock were among those whose writings on ecology signalled a new awareness of one of the more destructive features of capitalist political economy, and this consciousness was increasingly reflected in *Dimension* editorials (15:6, July 1981; 15:7, August/September 1981; 24:4, June 1990). In 1985 one such *CD* statement asked simply, "How Many Bhopals?" while the same issue contained two articles on the way famine had disfigured the developing world (19:1, March/April 1985). By the end of the 1980s the politics of environmentalism were one area where there seemed a sense of urgency among Canadians, and Harding, Dorothy Smith and others made the case for left-leaning *Dimension* readers that this was "*the* major concern" that needed to be addressed in the politics of opposition (23:1, January/February 1989; 23:8, November/ December 1989).

Achieving its age of majority, *Canadian Dimension* rightly paused to consider its history, a twentieth anniversary issue in 1984 (18:5, October/ November) featuring a reflection by editor Cy Gonick, Reg Whitaker's summing up of the Trudeau era, commentaries on Canadian and Quebec nationalism by Danny Drache and Pauline Vaillancourt, an interview with aboriginal militant George Erasmus, Varda Burstyn's account of "the age of women's liberation," my assessment of where the working class was going and Marv Gandall's remembrances of where it had been. A twenty-fifth anniversary number appeared in 1988 (22:2, March/April). In an editorial entitled "Sanitizing the 60s," *Dimension* reiterated not only its New Left origins, but its sense of pride in those beginnings. Convinced that "The last thing the establishment wants to see is a re-emergence of the astonishing energy, enthusiasm and social consciousness of the 60s," *CD* declared with conviction and continuity, "We were brazen and brave and we shook them badly despite our mistakes. We'll do it again" (22:8, November/December 1988).

There was less confidence throughout the 1990s, especially early in the decade, when the fallout from the collapse and implosion of the Soviet Union and the ideologically-mounted assertions of the ultimate victory of the free enterprise system ran rampant in the mainstream culture. Environmentalism remained a topic covered extensively and enthusiastically, with "sustainable development" drawing much attention. Global warming was introduced to *CD* readers as early as 1990 (24:3, April/May 1990) and articles on ecofeminism and deep ecology linked environmental, feminist and social justice concerns (23:6, September 1989; 23:4, June 1991).

Also prominent in *Dimension's* pages was feminist accent on the personal dimension of politics. This was highlighted in 1989 (23:2, March), where the cover depicted a naked androgynous body sprawled on a bed labelled "Socialist" at the end and "Feminist" along one side, with an equally ambiguous unclothed figure sitting, hands draped over head, on the floor. Captioned "Going to Bed with your Politics," the graphic was a subtle, but carefully posed, depiction of *potential* fissures in the gender relations of progressive politics. Gone were the days when heterosexual bedroom scenes and bodies *en déshabillé,* clearly gendered and sexualized, could be presented as they were in a 1968 *Dimension* cartoon (5:6, September/October): a male radical, a book labelled "Mao" at his side, touches the exposed breast of his smiling naked female companion and states, "I'm going to call this one 'Marx' and this one 'Lenin'!" As *Dimension's* editorial collective debated the strengths and weaknesses of Gad Horowitz's Personal/Political column, which might run under titles such as "Amazon Fantasy Troubles Continue," (22:8, November/December 1988), or as Varda Burstyn, Gary Kinsman and Roberta Hamilton explored issues such as pornography, the erotic and the personal, the magazine ran an appeal under the bolded title, "Desperately Seeking Socialist Sex!" announcing that it was "looking for writers on the topic of socialist sexuality." The resulting outpouring of essays on how the personal was indeed political helped to reorient socialist thought (24:6, September 1990; 24:7, October 1990; 25:4, June 1991; 25:8, December 1991).

Solidarity and fragmentation

At the same time that there was acknowledgement in *Dimension* quarters that the issues of relevance for the Left were expanding, there was recognition of the possibility of losing one's political moorings. Articles questioning the abandonment of basic left commitments began to appear in *CD* (24:8, December 1990; 28:5, October/November 1994), and Gonick thought out loud about how the political climate of the 1990s was being narrowed to the protection of the very "welfare state we used to sneer at for its obvious flaws and limitations." He suggested that the vibrant social movements of the moment, such as those associated with women and the environment, had little to do with traditional socialist appeals and were in conflict with traditional left perspectives and priorities, which Gonick claimed were "too limited and limiting." Seeming to opt for "radical democracy," Gonick discovered that with the "profusion of leftward identities" evident in *Canadian Dimension* it was more and more difficult to hold to old certainties, many of which clustered under the umbrella-like panacea of 'socialism'. A year later (29:2, April/May 1995) a *CD* editorial commenced, "Today the Left everywhere appears feeble and aimless." This gloom and doom resonated in suggestions that the Old Left project of, in David Mackenzie's words, building "a competitive political party" of alternative, one that fused labour and social democracy in a forceful opposition, had been derailed in single-issue campaigns and coalitions of dispersed social movements.

As was often the case in *Dimension*'s history, events tended to overtake the crisis of political consciousness that seemed to sweep over the Left in the early-to-mid 1990s. Ontario's Common Sense Revolution, led by the resurgent right wing of central Canada's Conservative Party, brought Mike Harris to power in 1995. Like Bill Bennett in British Columbia in 1983, he launched an all-out attack on the public sector and the welfare state. "The Counter Revolution," in Jason Ziedenberg's account (30:2, April 1996), was helping to "regenerate the Ontario Left." As the Canadian Autoworkers Union showed signs of militant revival, helping to lead a series of industrial-political one-day general strikes and protests known as the Days of Action, CD editorialized "Organize, Educate, Resist: Strike!" (30:4, July/August 1996; 30:6, November/December 1996; 31:1, January/February 1997).

As I suggested in "Showdown in Ontario: Build the General Strike," and as Joe Flexer confirmed in a later assessment, "Days of Action or DOA?" this class struggle was derailed as the trade union tops turned the taps of protest mobilization off at the eleventh hour. No sooner had the Days of Action wound down, however, than Harris was at it again, precipitating an unprecedented walkout of the provincial teachers' unions (30:3, May/June 1996; 31:5, September/October 1997; 32:1, January/February 1998; 32:5, September/October 1998). *Dimension* editorials were now emblazoned, "Seizing the Moment." The magazine entered the new millennium editorially with a commentary on some chosen "keywords": capitalism, class, progress, globalization, work, culture, the environment, democracy and socialism (33:6, December 1999). The list reflected the continuity and change at the core of the *Canadian Dimension* project, with a part of this vocabulary reaching back to the origins of the publication in

1963, while other words signalled concerns that resonated more directly with the world as it was constituted in 2000.

Food for socialist thought

For the next dozen years, as it approached 2013 and its fiftieth anniversary, *Dimension* continued on this path. In the aftermath of the 1999 World Trade Organization protests in Seattle, the magazine defined itself as part of the "rebellion and renewal" that animated progressive politics in Canada and globally (34:2, March 2000). As it entered its fifth decade in 2003, *CD* proclaimed itself "an avowedly radical, anticapitalist magazine" and, proud of its continuity, asked, "Who would have thought that an independent Canadian magazine dedicated to the struggle against the capitalist system and to secure a better world would still be around after 40 years" (37:1, January/February 2003; 37:5, September/October 2003). Commissioned articles commemorating *CD*'s first forty years of publishing included Leo Panitch's insistence that the magazine had been decisively important in the "continuing vitality and relevance of . . . socialist renewal," Cy Gonick's two-part reminiscence of "the *CD* story (so far)," my own account of the ways in which Canadian class struggles had paralleled the development of the magazine from the 1960s into the 2000s, and wide-ranging exchanges on the women's movement (Myrna Wood, Dorothy Smith, Tammy Findlay) and nationalism and sovereignty in Quebec and Canada (Jocelyne Couture, Daniel Salee, Pierre Dostie, James Laxer, Ricardo Grinspun, Steven Staples and Marjorie Griffin Cohen).[5] These contributions flagged *Dimension*'s longstanding concerns.

But as Gonick's outline of the *diversity* of topics that, by the 1980s, had come to be addressed in the pages of *CD* revealed, the forum for left debate was ever widening. Politics might be approached through a discussion of an upcoming election and the challenges it posed for the Left, or a brief for proportional representation as "a new strategy for the Left" (34:6, November/December 2000). Anticapitalist and antiglobalization protests drew much commentary, from discussions of the mobilization potential of the 2000 World Social Forum in Porto Alegre to the tactics of the Black Bloc (which the *CD* editorial collective distanced itself from decisively) in the G20 demonstrations in Toronto in 2010 (35:2, March/

April 2001; 44:5, September/October 2010). Social movements like the Ontario Coalition Against Poverty became the focal point of discussions revolving around the dismantling of welfare, state repression and the necessity of class-struggle solidarity with all dispossessed people (34:5, September/October 2000; 37:3, May/June 2003). The magazine continued to debate left nationalism in Canada, as in a forceful statement on the "mistaken return" of this politics by Paul Kellogg that was replied to by the *CD* collective (37:2, March/April 2003).

The peace movement refused to die as a subject of discussion, with imperialist aggression and its foes remaining a major focus of longstanding *CD* writers like the prolific James Petras. "Indian Country" was the subject of many and varied contributions, culminating in issues devoted almost entirely to native peoples, their resiliency, their contributions and their struggles (43:1, January/February 2009; 44:2, March/April 2010). Women, the environment and a staple of *Dimension* discussion, political economy, were central to the publication's pages. But more space was now also devoted to queer politics, which dominated special issues (43:4, July/August 2009; 44:4, July/August 2010), to racisms of various kinds, and to health, media and culture.

Food was now clearly very much on the progressive agenda, almost unimaginable as a topic of discussion in the 1960s and 1970s outside of the longstanding and obvious accent on famine and dearth as consequences of monoculture, agribusiness and other capitalist and imperialist deformations. One issue of *CD* (42:4, July/August 2008) contained analysis of the global crisis around food, a critical rethinking of the "green revolution," an account of ethically-grown soybean products in Atlantic Canada, and a revealing discussion of the "slow cooking" movement that was generating different kinds of relationships between producers and consumers and within cities. No longer was it possible to proclaim that you are only what you eat; now you could become what you might be through eating differently.

When a *Dimension* editorial of 2012 (46:1, January/February) declared its support for the Occupy movement, it subtitled its endorsement, "We Plant Ourselves and Stand Firm," noting that this experiment in participatory democracy extended the politics of the 1960s. But it struck a new note demarcating such continuities, suggesting that when the 250,000 Indignados ("Outraged") of Barcelona assembled in their Occupy moment, they "came with gardening systems for long-term urban cultivation. They were ready to stay." This was part of the movement to think globally and act locally that Canada's oldest and only surviving New Left magazine had been promoting for some time. In 2011 *Dimension* boasted that it had published four food theme issues over the last decade (45:4, July/August 2011).

All of this and much, much more provided *CD* readers with a steady diet of old themes and fresh, new tastes of what constituted the possibilities of a better world. Two staples nonetheless continued to figure decisively in *Dimension's* agenda: agitation and accounting. Looking at the magazine's always-mercurial relationship to the New Democratic Party, on the one hand, and positioning of itself with respect to socialism, on the other, completes an understanding of the ways in which *CD* both stayed its particular course of origins and branched out in new directions.

Dimension and the New Democrats

Canadian Dimension, as a quintessentially New Left journal, began publication in 1963 declaring that it owed allegiance to no political party. Yet it was not difficult to discern in the magazine's first years of publication that it was constantly wrestling with the meaning of Canada's social democratic tradition. Covering the Quebec NDP's constitutional convention, Ed Smith stressed the absence of leading francophone socialists, such as Michel Chartrand, who remained unconvinced that the party could ever "think in French." Smith also noted that the majority of NDP delegates were "either well-dressed representatives of Montreal's English and Jewish neighbourhoods or CLC trade unionists sent by their affiliated organizations" (2:5, July/August 1965). Disappointment and skepticism, then, coloured *CD's* approach to the NDP, but the centrefold of Canadian social democracy was not a body politic from which the publication could avert its gaze for too long.

One reason for this was evident in James Harding's attempt to address the NDP through *historical* appreciation of its origins. Harding, reared in a social-democratic Saskatchewan family, looked to the CCF's 1933

Regina Manifesto, which, he pointed out was a socialist document that stressed both the necessity of planning and the critical importance of economic power. Both of these factors, Harding felt, had been slighted by the New Left in its accent on a kind of social activism that commenced, not with intellectual engagement, but with pragmatic contact with the dispossessed, out of which could emerge participatory forms of democracy. Against the tendency to see the New Left and the NDP polarized in "unproductive debate," Harding looked to the CCF legacy, in its most clearly socialist variants, to "establish the beginnings of a common heritage for radicals of the old and young generations in Canada." Yet for all of his positive intent, Harding ended up critical of both the New Left and the New Democrats. New Leftists, with whom Harding sympathized, needed to extend their appreciation of an economic analysis of the Canadian class system, transcending their "obsession with community tactics." New Democrats, whose "social philosophy" had atrophied to the point that they could only conceive of social transformation in the limited vision of "reforming capitalism into welfare capitalism," had, however, lost the spirit of the Regina Manifesto that the New Left needed to recover. Social justice, Harding concluded, was not possible in Canada "without a new political federation" (4:1, November/December 1966).

Yet in the same issue, as we have seen, Gonick insisted that the NDP was one of the many venues that the New Left must be active in, creating new approaches to, and awareness of, socialism. *Canadian Dimension* soon initiated a province-by-province survey of the state of the NDP. More than two years before the drafting of the Manifesto for an Independent Socialist Canada, W.D.G. Hunter, an economist and future president of the McMaster University Faculty Association, introduced this overview with a blistering denunciation of the NDP's soft-pedalling of the importance and necessity to stand firmly against the United States takeover of the Canadian economy. It amounted to nothing less than an anticipation of the Waffle, and concluded that "the New Democrats must disabuse themselves of the idea that socialism is an impossible stance in the modern age." Hunter thought the NDP's future was crystal clear, pointing out in mid-1967 that its job was to "infiltrate the trade unions with progressive socialist ideas; to rally to the cause of true nationalism and militant socialism wherever it may arise in the Third World; to encourage and stimulate the greatest possible measure of popular dissent from elite politics; to mobilize mass support for the inevitable struggle to rid the country of American dominated capitalism." This was an almost made-in-*Dimension* agenda, and not surprisingly Hunter called on the NDP "to lead the country into a new era as the party of the New Left." But his questioning as to whether New Democrats had "the courage and commitment to accept the challenge" was echoed in a variety of ways, some pro and some con, by other comments on the *realpolitik* of the NDP in its particular provincial settings (4:5, July/August 1967). Vancouver's Walter D. Young, later to be an academic commentator on the NDP, thought *CD*'s account of the social democratic party in British Columbia a "fantasy," writing in a letter that socialism would never be achieved as long as it was straitjacketed in a political fundamentalism, "expressed in the tiresome battle cries of the depression, and concerned exclusively with 'the workers' — whoever they may be." "Workerism," Young suggested, was merely sidelining all youthful criticism of old-guard socialists as right-wing.

For his part, NDP Nanaimo MP Colin Cameron replied directly to *Dimension* editor Cy Gonick, whom he dismissed as a young whipper-snapper alienated from the "world of reality, safely ensconced in" a "cosy little hut in the groves of Akademe" (5:1, November/December 1967). Cameron castigated Gonick for not validating the apparently essential social democratic principle that social change can only come about through persuading the mass of people to vote into positions of political power representatives who will then transform society through democratic, parliamentary procedures. Cameron's way to change was contrasted with the only other alternative: "The other way is by violent upheaval. There is no third way." At the same time that New Leftists associated with *Dimension* were calling for the NDP to reassess the path to fundamental social change, then, powerful guardians of social democracy's legacy were insisting that this road was clearly and correctly marked, that it could not be rerouted, and that any deviations would be treated as heretical detours, tarred with the Cold-Waresque brush of violent revolutionism, dressed in the now-discernible garb of youth radicalism.

An earlier contribution by Cameron (4:6, September/October 1967), on an ostensibly new program for the NDP, would have put most New Leftists to sleep, its penchant for tinkering with the economy through legislative non-events destined to induce little more than a yawn. Worse, Cameron's insistence that "the fact of foreign ownership as such" was not something the NDP need be concerned with, but that it was the behaviour of foreign companies that warranted monitoring and regulation, would have angered many in *Canadian Dimension* circles. The magazine was now a forum promoting Canadian independence, the most striking statement of which was the May/June 1967 issue (4:4). The cover of this issue, adorned with a red maple leaf, carried "An Open Letter To Canadian Nationalists," while its pages bristled with statements by *CD* mainstays Gonick and Horowitz on "The Political Economy of Canadian Independence" and "On the Fear of Nationalism."

The NDP came to power in Manitoba in 1969 and, irony of ironies, Gonick achieved a narrow electoral victory as a New Democratic Party candidate, defeating the Progressive Conservative incumbent in Winnipeg's Crescentwood riding by a mere 273 votes. As Gonick explained in a *CD* editorial (6:3-4, August/September 1969), a series of fortuitous developments paved the way to the New Democrats' Manitoba 1969 win. A combination of Liberal and Conservative Party collapse and irrelevance, combined with NDP accommodations to the status quo (Gonick described the new social democratic premier, Edward Schreyer, as "more of a conservative than he is a radical") produced a breakthrough, not for socialism, but for a "minimal program" that could, if properly carried out, "have its own dynamic in stimulating further change." Gonick would prove to be something of an accidental tourist in the parliamentary arena, serving one term before deciding not to run again, and being as much a thorn in the side of his own ruling party as he was a staunch opponent of the Liberals and Conservatives. In the end he stood very much alone in the Manitoba Legislature, being the only provincial NDP member to endorse the Waffle Manifesto.

Dimension would proclaim 1969 "The Year of the Waffle!" (6:6, December/January 1969–70). The Waffle was led by *CD* contributor James Laxer and a leftward-moving, formerly mainstream economist,

Mel Watkins, who had worked with the Liberal Minister of Finance, Walter Gordon. It originated as a caucus within the federal NDP, one marked by its obvious New Left concerns with the American domination of the Canadian economy and its insistence that New Democrats take an active stand in favour of "an independent socialist Canada." Laxer and Watkins rallied to their cause a half-dozen prominent British Columbia NDPers, Nova Scotia NDP leader Jeremy Akerman, and *Dimension* editor Cy Gonick. They also galvanized a significant cohort of youthful feminists and radicals, especially in Ontario, the subject of probably the most detailed discussion of the Waffle to date, Robert Hackett's issue-length "Pie in the Sky: A History of the Ontario Waffle," that appeared in a 1980 *CD* (15:1, October/November). The trade union tops in established "international" unions saw the Waffle's Labour Committee as a fifth column marching in step with the threateningly nationalist breakaway movement disrupting the longstanding hegemony of mainstream, American-based labour organizations. They had a scare thrown into them by the Wafflers. The 1969 publication of the Waffle's Manifesto for an Independent Socialist Canada occurred on the eve of a national NDP convention, held in Winnipeg, and the radical document managed to garner considerable support, endorsed by 35 per cent of the delegates and dominating convention proceedings.

As Gonick reported, this did not change what the NDP was, but it did convince many youthful and rebellious New Leftists to prolong their connection with Canadian social democracy (6:3-4, August/September 1969; 6:5, November 1969; 6:6, December/January 1969–70). Although the Waffle could claim the direct support of only three thousand of the NDP's official membership of fifty thousand, it managed to give David Lewis a respectable run for his leadership money at a 1971 convention. It took Lewis four ballots to defeat his Waffle challenger, Jim Laxer, in the run off for federal head of the Party, the elder statesman of Canadian social democracy finally tallying 1,046 votes to the outspoken New Leftist's 612. From this point on the NDP hierarchy moved to squelch the Waffle threat: feminist voices were muffled, powerful labour bureaucrats muscled student radicals to the sidelines, and New Left New Democrats were castigated as "a cancer" and "social misfits" by Old Left

Party loyalists. By 1972–1973 the Waffle had been driven into retreat and, indeed, out of the NDP. The writing had been on the NDP wall as early as the 1971 Winnipeg convention, with Waffle women silenced by procedural rulings, their angry protests drowned out by union-affiliated delegates breaking into a chorus of "Solidarity Forever" as embittered radicals flung venomous shouts of "Sieg Heil" in the direction of the podium (7:8, April 1971; 8:1, June 1971).

Gonick closed the door on the Waffle experiment in the pages of *Dimension* in 1972, his sad post-mortem dripping with defeat: "The Liberals have coopted the nationalist issue because it has been shorn of its socialist content. David Lewis sounds like an angry Trudeau or a petulant Stanfield. Maybe his driving fist and his outraged indignation will be enough to win a few more seats for the NDP in the upcoming federal election. Somehow it doesn't seem to matter" (8:6, March/April 1972; 8:7, June 1972; 8:8, August 1972). Insistent that the NDP no longer agitated for fundamental reform and that "the days of the Regina Manifesto are long past," *CD* saw radicalism inherent in many aspects of Canadian life: among natives, women and workers militant voices rang out, and social movements addressing ecology and radical nationalist aspirations gave the magazine's board members cause for great hope. Yet there was no party of socialism on the horizon, and *CD* was "convinced that none will be formed until we come to terms with the inherent limitations of social democracy and make the break with it" (12:6, 1977).

The rise and fall of the Waffle convinced many young radicals and *CD* contributors that the project of reorienting the NDP to its radical, CCF, Regina Manifesto roots was a dead end. Long, reflective historical *Dimension* articles by Gonick and his chief editorial associate, Alvin Finkel, reiterated this realization, confirmed in a number of other 1970s articles that addressed the NDP's shortcomings on women's issues, labour, and other matters. John Gallagher summed things up nicely in a 1975 account of the NDP convention (11:1, July/August 1975) that saw Ed Broadbent defeat Rosemary Brown for the Party leadership. Despite a rhetoric of radicalism, Gallagher insisted that the social-democratic Party brass, always in control, "moved in a conservative direction every time." Wishing those socialists who remained in the NDP with the intention of "reforming it from inside" the best of luck, Gallagher concluded bluntly and decisively: "The NDP isn't a socialist party and it never will be." For almost a decade, as Gonick later recalled, "*CD* pretty well ignored the NDP" (37:5, September/October 2003).

As Canada moved from the 1970s to the 1980s, the economic context was one of malaise (stagflation and recession) and the political setting dominated by a resurgent conservatism that would soon give birth to the ideological onslaught of neoliberalism. "Big government" was decried as an infringement on the sacrosanct "freedoms of the marketplace." Attacks on workers and unions escalated, the poor were scapegoated and criminalized, the public sector denigrated, and the social safety net provided by the post–World War II welfare state weakened, many of its components either eliminated or starved for state funds.

Dimension editorialized on the eve of a 1980 federal election that the NDP, led by "Edusual" Broadbent, posed no "credible alternative to Liberal-Toryism/Tory-Liberalism." Replacing the incompetencies and inconsistencies of governments led by Joe Clark or Pierre Elliott Trudeau with an admittedly more intelligent team of New Democrats would not, according to *CD*, provide solutions to the economic crisis. More important than a few more NDP seats in the election was "the ability of the working class and its allies to organize and effectively fight for jobs, workplace control, stable living standards and a rational energy policy and *against* a further erosion of social services and healthcare, and further takeovers by multinationals" (14:4-5, March 1980). There were those, like future Canadian Association of University Teachers boss Jim Turk, who insisted that as constrained as the possibilities of the Left were inside social democracy "its prospects outside the NDP [were] even worse" (14:7, June 1980). But this view, in the early 1980s, seemed displaced by an orientation to grassroots organizing and advocacy of social movements. Struggles like the Solidarity uprising in British Columbia which, as we have seen, *Dimension* both supported and covered in detail, largely took place outside of any overt orientation to the NDP.

By the mid-1980s, however, *Dimension*'s tone with respect to the NDP shifted. "The NDP is not just another party," the magazine editorialized in 1985 (19:2, May/June). "Its roots in Canadian social-ist history, its ties with Canada's reformist labour movement, and its working class and progressive electoral base all shape its development and potential." Recognizing that the NDP would not "challenge capital-ism or its authoritarian state," *CD* nonetheless insisted that it could be "forced to defend existing gains and used to win new ones." In part this new orientation had been conditioned by the reactionary and recession-ary drift of the political economy, and the electoral victory of Manitoba New Democrats in 1981. This necessitated, as Errol Black suggested in kicking off a *Dimension* issue devoted to assessing the record of social-democratic provincial governance, a reassessment of parliamentary alternatives in an age of conservatism. In Ontario the politics of the period saw an informal (and quite stunted) NDP-Liberal "alliance," but Leo Panitch (19:3, July/August 1985) suggested that this compromised politics, into which the New Democrats "stumbled . . . in an entirely ad hoc manner," contributed to the "counterweight" offsetting the reactionary consequences of the Mulroney federal Conservatives and their international and domestic policies. Panitch promoted a "popular frontism," in which he argued that for both the sake of the NDP and future socialist advance, it would have been preferable for "the NDP-Liberal negotiations" to yield "a real coalition with NDP Ministers in the Cabinet," rather than simple agreement on reforms already consist-ent with the platform of the Ontario Liberal Party.

In conjunction with a flurry of *CD* articles addressing the possibility of NDP breakthroughs in the parliamentary logjam in Quebec, where Lévesque's Parti québécois was moving decidedly to the right under the pressures of economic crisis, such developments brought Canadian social democracy back into the pages of *Canadian Dimension*.[6] On the eve of the "free trade" election of 1988, *Dimension* saw "many reasons to support the NDP federally." It called on New Democrats to reject the Meech Lake Accord, which would, with its constitutional procedure of freezing change until agreement was reached by all provinces and Ottawa, "stand in the way of the NDP's ever making any improvement in the rights of Canadians as members of groups." And it pressed on Broadbent and his Party the need to oppose strongly free trade and all that it entailed (21:5, September 1987).

Some disagreed, and they ploughed through their *CD* archives to point out that since the 1960s *Dimension* had tortured itself with the hope that the NDP was some kind of answer to those who wanted social change in Canada. Ulli Diemer told the magazine to "stop kidding ourselves about the NDP" and recognize that it was an "electoral machine interested in nothing more than bringing in a few reforms to make capitalism more humane and more efficient" (23:8, November/December 1989). In the early 1990s this faith in what a minimalist contribution the NDP could make, when and if it came to power, had worn less than thin. Bob Rae's Ontario New Democrats actually made the leap into government with their September 1990 victory; but they found themselves on the short end of a proverbial pecuniary pickle, David Peterson's Liberals having run up a deficit that put Rae and his neophyte cabinet up against the restraint wall.

The result was cutbacks and a so-called Social Contract that tore up collective agreements in the public sector and engendered anger and resentment among quarters traditionally aligned with or resigned to the New Democratic Party as their chosen parliamentary voice. Things only worsened with the mid-1990s. A Conservative Common Sense Revolution divided the trade unions into two camps. The more militant sector, led by the powerful Canadian Automobile Workers with civil servant unions largely onside, began to question the NDP's value as an electoral arm of the labour movement. *Dimension's* mid-to-late 1980s cautiously optimistic assessment of social democracy's prospects soured accordingly. "We are dealing with a government that wants to place itself firmly in the middle when no middle ground exists," wrote feminist Kerry McCuaig (25:7, October/November 1991).

Throughout the 1990s, in spite of continuing support for some NDP governments in power, *Dimension's* approach to the pragmatic politics of a rightward-moving Canadian social democracy was increasingly critical, distancing from rather than aligning with New Democrats.[7] John F. Conway (28:5, October/November 1994) wrote of Roy Romanow's governing Saskatchewan NDP in terms of "betrayal." In the same *CD* issue, Gonick concluded: "The NDP is not worth renewing." As *Dimension* contributors debated and discussed left mobilization and its relationship to the NDP in 1999 few had any stomach for slugging it out in the old-guard party of social democracy, either at the provincial or federal levels.

This did not change all that much as the new world order marched into the new millennium, and the magazine saw little to cheer about in Jack Layton's NDP, poised as it was between the past and the third, Blairite, way of abdication (37:2, March/April 2003; 40:2, March/April 2006). "We can elect all the NDP and social democratic governments we want," Greg Albo wrote (37:4, July/August 2003), pointing out that since 1990 the European Union had managed to elect twelve of them, but the end product was still little more than a political attempt to manage capitalism more effectively. It is difficult to see in the pages of recent issues of *CD* much enthusiasm for the NDP and possibilities for the Left within it. Socialism, as the vexed relationship of the magazine to Canada's social democratic party has made abundantly clear, is neither a priority nor a politics that has gained much traction within the NDP. Indeed, the history of the NDP over the course of *Dimension*'s fifty years is nothing if not an undeniable backing-away from the difficult project of building socialist possibility in Canada.

Dimension: From "Canada's Independent Journal of Fact and Opinion" through "A Socialist Magazine" to "A Publication for People Who Want to Change the World"

What's in a name? Not, to be sure, everything, but almost certainly something. *Canadian Dimension*, a New Left magazine, was originally wary of labelling itself socialist. It wanted to distance itself from both the old Left of the Stalinized communist parties as well as the old social-democratic Left associated in Canada with the CCF/NDP tradition. But by the sixth issue of *CD* socialism, albeit of a new kind, was being embraced by *Dimension*, defined as a radical "analysis and critique of the mechanisms and institutions of capitalism, projections of new societies, and actions and policies designed to move the old society into the new" (1:6, May/June 1964). It is largely in this sense that *CD*'s founder and perennial editor, Cy Gonick, would conclude that "helping to build the socialist movement has always been *Canadian Dimension*'s single largest project." (37:5, September/October 2003). But for all of this continuity, the magazine has shifted gears over its fifty-year life-span, and its orientation to socialism has necessarily evolved.

In the 1960s *Dimension* was a central player in moving the New Left towards a non-vanguardist socialism, one rooted in the history and traditions of Canada where, in Gad Horowitz's contributions, it was acknowledged, "a Tory past [might] contain the seeds of a socialist future" (2:4, May/June 1965). Not all *CD* editorial board members, contributors and readers agreed with the Horowitzian dialectic, but there was no denying the importance of a fusion politics in the socialism of the magazine, where potent strains of English- and especially French-Canadian nationalism were seen as nurturing the possibility of a radical rejection of capitalism and the embrace of socialist alternative. *Dimension* promoted the Waffle's vision of an "Independent Socialist Canada." But *Dimension's* socialism was also informed by the discontents of historical surveys of Stalinism, of the limitations and disappointments of Arab and African socialism, and of the mechanical tendencies inherent in Scandinavian socialism (2:1, November/December 1964; 2:2, January/February 1965; 2:5, July/August 1965; 5:8, February 1969). As much as Marx, Lenin and Mao appeared — often as iconic images — in the pages of *Dimension*, there was little appetite for vanguardist models of organizing (6:6, December/January 1969–70). James Harding, a frequent contributor to *Dimension* in the 1960s, dismissed one socialist opponent as a "reductionist, mechanist, vulgar, maoist Marxist" (7:5, December 1970), seeing in those who espoused grand, deterministic theories of revolution the alienated antithesis of socialist alternative that had been nurtured in parts of the 1960s New Left."

The Waffle debacle seared into *Dimension's* being a sense that socialism could never be merely about reform of capitalism through expansion of the welfare state. As the fiscal crisis of the state imploded in the 1970s, *Dimension* was increasingly willing to proclaim itself "a socialist magazine" and explore what socialism in the Canadian context meant: the Quebec question, party formation within a context of democratic but non-reformist socialism, feminism, national independence and international solidarities were all discussed, and their relationship to socialism explored. Having given up on social democracy, bemoaning the lack of a party of Canadian socialism, *Dimension* was nonetheless not, for the most part, drawn to those small groups of Maoist and Trotskyist inclinations that emerged out of the cauldron of the 1960s. "The recruit and destroy operations of some small left groups find no sympathy here," declared *Dimension* somewhat dismissively in a 1978 issue exploring Eurocommunism (13:4, November/December). The attraction to Eurocommunism proved short-lived, however, and while it resulted in a number of forceful exchanges in *CD* over the nature of socialist organization, it failed to translate into the sought-after leap into an invigorated practice.

The 1970s wound down with *Dimension* editorializing about socialism's contradictions, debating the future of the Left (13:8, June 1979). Over the course of the next decade *CD* dedicated itself to reviving a debate about political alternative, reestablishing "the seemingly abandoned notion of socialism as a VISION — a vision of a better future" (16:6, October/November 1982). The magazine sponsored a centenary celebration of Marx's death in 1983 and, in the same year, explored the collapse of revolutionary Maoist organizations, addressing the ways in which women had come to reject the "patriarchal attitudes and discriminatory practices" that pervaded society as a whole, but that had affected left groups as well (17:3, July 1983; 17:5, November 1983). Out of this disarray of the revolutionary Left, Leo Panitch (18:3, June 1984) initiated what would be one of the first of a decades-long parade of left forums in the pages of *CD*, calling for a "new socialist movement" to be forged out of the ashes of social-democratic reformism and the self-destruction of the Canadian far Left. Amidst the politico-moral bankruptcy of the Right, and the inability of capitalism to steer the ship of political economy out of its ongoing crisis, Panitch saw signs that the limitations of past socialist practice were inducing "a degree of non-sectarianism on the Canadian Left which probably surpasses anything since World War One."

Insistent that Social Democratic, Communist, Trotskyist and Marxist-Leninist initiatives had all "played themselves out," Panitch echoed *CD*'s earlier accent on socialist vision, and eschewed the necessity — long a staple of party formation on the Left — of defining a program of policies as the first step in creating institutions of socialism. Instead, Panitch called on independent socialists to rally together to build their organizational, reading, cultural and social skills, intervening in popular struggles in ways that would highlight socialist goals and collective practices. In the process, Panitch suggested, new languages and behaviours would surface, and go a long ways towards overcoming "arcane Marxist disputations" and "sexist practices" that had killed something of socialist possibility throughout the mid-twentieth century.

In the next issue of *Dimension* (18:4, 1984), the magazine listed a number of principles that it felt were fundamental to the socialist ideal: economic democracy, social ownership and workers' control; full democratic rights for all social groups and the right to organize autonomously; women's liberation; national self-determination; international relations of peace, cooperation and solidarity. CAW Research Director Sam Gindin contributed to this push (22:1, February 1988), calling for socialism to be put on labour's agenda by supplementing the economistic militancy of Canadian workers with a new pamphleteering culture of agitation and organization. A spirit of ecumenical socialist pluralism dominated the publication in the late 1980s, with olive branches extended to the Communist Party and celebrations of the supposed "spring winds of democratic change" blowing "over the Soviet Union, thawing away the authoritative ice that has frozen the country into a [sic] straight jacket" (21:1, March 1987; 22:4, June 1988).

Thaws there were aplenty, to be sure, but by 1989–1990 it would be apparent that the Chinook winds that blew across the terrain of actually existing socialism carried with them a destructive charge of capitalist restoration. With the collapse of the Soviet Union, revolutionary socialism may well have been given a new lease on life, but it was purchased with the Left's free-fall from grace. It became, in the context of the 1990s and into the new millennium, more and more difficult to promote socialism as an alternative to capitalism, whose ideological hegemony was, in spite of its recurring crises, never more secure. History, defined as a Cold War contest between the superpowers of East and West, had supposedly ended in the unambiguous victory of "free-market individualism."

Dimension resisted this ideological onslaught, but necessarily was affected by it. A 1990 editorial (24:2, March) asked if there was a future for socialism, answering positively, concluding that, "the democratization of the Soviet Union and Eastern Europe is less likely to produce a new lease on life for capitalism, as it is a socialist society that successfully combines economic efficiency and social justice." This prediction could not have been more wrong, but *CD*'s optimism about future possibilities resulted in articles assessing the changing situation in the Soviet Union and its Eastern European satellites, and where the Canadian Communist Party was going.[8]

What to do? The answer to this question became even more complicated as the once-Soviet Union collapsed. At the end of 1991, a *CD* editorial on "The Soviet Collapse" (25:7, October/November 1991) referred to "the extent of the disaster for Soviet socialism, and indeed, for socialism world wide." The precipitous implosion of the aging Stalinist state, suggested *Dimension*, should induce a sense of modesty in any who considered themselves socialist. Latin Americanist James Petras (26:8, November/December 1992) thought there were "reasons to be prudently optimistic," but there was no mistaking the extent, within the mainstream culture, of how difficult it was to fly the red flag in the mid-1990s. In a statement on "Stealth Rhetoric" and being "intimidated into speechlessness" (27:1, January/February 1993), *Dimension* deplored the signs of left surrender, called on "progressives" to "speak clearly about working people's rights without apologizing for sounding like old-time Marxists," and suggested that "a creeping hesitancy" to speak up as socialists must be resisted. But it was not long before even *Dimension* jettisoned its "Socialist Magazine" tag, substituting for this statement of political clarity a more ambiguous by-line: "For People Who Want to Change the World." *CD* editorials, in a future that would bask in the shadow of the youthful rebelliousness that exploded in the 1999 Battle of Seattle World Trade Organization protests, talked less and less about socialism. Instead *Dimension* committed itself to "progressive social change," expressing confidence that spirited Canadians would "revitalize the political life of our country" (34:2, March 2000).

In 1999-2001 *Dimension* provided a forum for broad discussions about how such a revitalization might take place. The starting point was Sam Gindin's proposal (35:1, January/February 2001) that what was needed was a structured anticapitalist movement. Developing out of 1990s struggles against Mike Harris's Common Sense Revolution in Ontario, and convinced that the NDP's "narrowly electoral" vision was insufficient, Gindin called for "something less than party" but "more than coalitions." Understanding that such a structured anticapitalist movement needed resources, organizers and agitational speakers and writers, and that it would necessarily have to be embedded in regional peculiarities, Gindin clearly saw his proposal as a transitional vehicle, one that, if successful, might lead to the formation of a committed party. But, in his desire to regroup the Left and to bridge longstanding divisions that he no doubt thought stale and unproductive, Gindin was essentially calling for old debates to be shelved in the interests of building an activist movement animated by select, but quite general, principles. Tellingly, the accent in this generalized anticapitalist politics was on egalitarianism and democratization, as well as analysis of globalization, neoliberalism and political economy. Insisting that taking capitalism on meant thinking and dreaming in big, alternative ways, Gindin nonetheless avoided the "S" word: socialism was never mentioned.

Among the contributors to the debate and discussion that grew out of Gindin's proposal in the pages of *Canadian Dimension* were David McNally, Herman Rosenfeld and Jayme Gialola, Himani Bannerjii, Greg Albo, John Clarke, Ken Kalturnyk, Joe Roberts, Donald Swartz, Cy Gonick, John Warnock, Judy Rebick, Leo Panitch and David Camfield (33:2, March/April 1999; 33:6, December 1999; 34:2, March/April 2000; 34:4, July/August 2000; 34:6, November/December 2000; 35:1, January/February 2001; 35:2, March/April 2001). For all the useful discussion and advances registered (hundreds came to conferences in Toronto, Vancouver and elsewhere), however, it proved difficult to transcend some of the differences that separated people on the Left. The structured anticapitalism movement that had seemed so promising as a new century dawned soon faded. It would periodically resurface, however, in Gindin's call for popular workers' assemblies (41:2, March/April 2007), and in Thom Walkman's understanding that a critical Left could be renewed and rebuilt through the promotion of a left culture, which was always an important component of how the structured anticapitalist movement was conceived (43:3, May/June 2009). Perhaps sensing that something was being lost in the turn to an anticapitalist movement that avoided discussion of socialism, *CD* editor Cy Gonick penned a lengthy 2001 statement, "A Democratic Socialist Vision for the 21st Century" (35:2, March/April 2001). He stressed that the growing anticapitalist movement needed a utopian vision.

Indeed, it was difficult to keep socialism out of the pages of *Dimension*, even if contributors such as Leo Panitch often had to title their essays, "What Happened to Socialism?" (37:5, September/October 2003). Environmentalism was increasingly discussed in terms of eco-socialism (41:6, November/December 2007; 44:5, September/October 2010). Coverage of the Porto Alegre, Brazil, World Social Forum brought socialism back into the pages of the magazine, and from Venezuela, where he worked with the Hugo Chavez government, Michael Lebowitz wrote of the revival of twenty-first-century socialism. Lebowitz, a veteran New Leftist, saw this contemporary socialism as stressing above all else "the centrality of human development." He insisted that the Bolivarian Revolution had rekindled hope in the possibilities of socialism, of building a society based on relationships of solidarity. Yet the forces arrayed against twenty-first-century socialism were also great and threatening. The choice, Lebowitz insisted, in Luxemburgist terms, was actually no choice at all: socialism or barbarism (42:6, December 2008; 45:3, May/June 2011).

Canadian Dimension's cover girl in 2011, however, was not Rosa Luxemburg, but the "Determined, Defiant, [Brigette] DePape" (45:4, July/August) a parliamentary page who had the pluck to smuggle onto the floor of the Senate a "Stop Harper" sign that she then proceeded to silently hold up in the middle of Governor General David Johnston's throne speech. DePape promptly lost her job, but gained an iconic status in left-liberal circles for having the temerity to voice the growing progressive, populist antagonism to Stephen Harper and his threatening right-wing agenda. As *CD* editorialized in the aftermath of the 2011 federal election — which gave Harper a coveted majority and ushered Canada into an era of unbridled, mean-spirited, Reform Party–originating conservatism as comfortable slashing social services as it was saying no to sensuality and science — *CD*'s understanding of what needed doing was "organizing a broad and publicly visible opposition to Conservative policies and developing innovative ways to mobilize the substantial segment of the of the electorate that is disaffected — mostly poor and working people (45:4, July/August 2011).

In this context, socialism was clearly a receding concern in the magazine's pages. When, in 2008, *Canadian Dimension* put together a pamphlet *Toolkit for a New Canada*, comprised of ten articles, many of which had already appeared in past issues, the term "socialism" was nowhere to be seen on the pages of the agitational primer. Nonetheless, the socialist *Dimension*, always a left publication that occupied those spaces at the interface of activism and analysis remained, and Gonick was resolute in addressing the impending environmental crisis in terms that were unmistakably eco-socialist (45:4, July/August 2011).

Shifting with the times, and embracing and assessing alternatives to capitalism differently, depending on the particular historical circumstances, *Canadian Dimension* has, for half a century, been a sounding board for the relevance, renewal, and revolutionary possibilities of socialism. In a country such as Canada, where the vise-grip of an enervated social democracy has long existed to squeeze such potential into the constricted and misshapen limitations of the parliamentary road to non-socialism, *Dimension*, for all that it reflects the changing fortunes of the Left, serves as a steady beacon of debate and discussion that always brightens the prospects of breaking the chains of capitalist hegemony. It has proven a rare place where both thinkers and doers associated with the socialist movement have been given free reign to think in ways defiantly counter to the ethos of the marketplace, to challenge not only the multi-layered hold of the profit system over our minds, bodies and aspirations, but to question socialist shibboleths as well. The great English socialist, author and craftsman William Morris used to address working-class audiences in the 1880s, concluding, "It is to stir you up not be contented with a little that I am here to-night." *Dimension* has been pursuing this fundamentally socialist project for fifty years. Its tonight has lasted decades; and its prod against contentment with a little has proven to be quite a lot.

PART X

DIMENSIONS OF IDENTITY

CHAPTER 24
CD and Feminism:
Chronicle of a Movement Defining Itself

Stephanie Ross[1]

What we need . . . is a dialogue that recognizes both our collective identity with women and our ties to class. . . . Feminism envisions a direction of desirable change, but as socialists we need a theoretical perspective from which to assess and develop feminist strategies for action. Marxism as an analytical tool insists on the centrality of class and sees class struggle as the cornerstone of change. How, then, can we develop feminist analysis without losing this class dynamic? In adding a gender dimension to that of class, are we dealing with parallel systems, a synthesis of Marxism and feminism, and extension of Marxism to incorporate feminist theory, or the reverse of this? And because all theory is reflected in practice, how do we reconcile the differences between socialists and feminists in their modes of organizing . . . ?

— *"Socialism and Feminism,"* Editorial, 19:4, September 1985

Over its fifty years, *Canadian Dimension* featured some of Canada's most well-known and thought-provoking feminists, activists and scholars, often in the early stages of their careers. The majority of these contributors straddled the line between academia and activism, fittingly for a magazine that has made such a dedicated effort to mobilize knowledge in ways that activists can use in their struggles. In a 2010 journal article,[2] historian Joan Sangster credited *CD* with being one of a handful of magazines emerging in the 1960s that provided a space for socialist feminists in the face of a labour movement only very slowly beginning to embrace basic principles of gender equality and a feminist movement often dominated by the concerns of middle-class women. *CD*'s coverage of feminism was most vibrant when the feminist movement itself was vital, engaged in concrete struggles and actively debating the best strategic ways forward.

Maintaining that feminist voice in *CD*, however, was often a challenge. The magazine's sustained coverage of feminism only really began after 1975, a full twelve years after its inception. This issue was raised by the magazine itself in 1985, when the collective wrote: "what is missing from the magazine is a consistent, strong, feminist presence that says this magazine is about and for women as well as men, that the 'revolution' is not disconnected from women's collective vision" (19:4, September 1985). Nor was this voice singular. As in the movement in general, there was always debate over what it means to be a feminist and how the struggle for gender equity relates to other quests for social justice. Consideration of how feminist issues were covered and framed in *CD*'s pages over the years provides a fascinating chronicle of the complexity of the wider feminist struggle in Canada as well as of the Canadian Left's engagement with that struggle. *CD*'s exploration of a series of debates within feminism — about work and class, race, racism and white privilege, reproductive rights, sexuality, sexual violence and the issue of male allies — indicated a commitment to engage activists in thoughtful discussion, to challenge unspoken assumptions and to work through sometimes uncomfortable disagreements. However, given the current fragmented state of the feminist movement in Canada, *CD*'s role in informing strategic debates in its next fifty years is an open question.

Patriarchy and capitalism / Feminism and socialism

Unsurprisingly, given its mandate as an "independent forum for left-wing political thought and discussion," one of *CD*'s earliest recurring themes was the relationship and tensions between socialism/Marxism and feminism as both analysis and politics. This issue weighed on the minds of many feminists whose experience in various New Left movements had left them deeply dissatisfied. In 1975 (10:8, June), a writer referred to only as SSF — "a long-time activist in the Women's Education Press" — posed the problem this way:

> *Socialist women found that . . . traditional Marxist models*
> *for examining societies, however useful, were inadequate.*
> *The realm of work that women have been traditionally*
> *assigned has been designated by many Marxists as the*
> *private or personal sphere, which lay outside the major battle*
> *lines of our economic system — wage labour versus capital.*

The stance that women's oppression was somehow tangential or secondary to the operations of capitalism was challenged early and often in *CD*'s pages. Indeed, analyses of the inextricable links between patriarchy and capitalism can be counted among *CD*'s most developed theoretical contributions to feminist struggle. In "Women's Impossible Dream" (10:8, June 1975), Sandra Henneman located the seeds of capitalist exploitation and the gendered division of labour at work in the socialization of young boys and girls into sex-role stereotypes. Learning how to look and act like proper "girls" and "boys" was not just about reproducing unequal gender roles in personal life; instead, "He has to learn how to be boss, and she has to learn how to be bossed." Women's training to concern themselves with their appearance and to not seem smarter than their boyfriends was part and parcel of becoming suitable for employment in "the lowest end of the wage scale, the dead end jobs," "jobs whose real importance is degraded by low wages, condescending attitudes, repetition, dullness, jobs that can be done without much applied brain power, but with lots of patience." Marlene Dixon's[3] extensive (if jargon-laden) piece in the same issue, "Women's Liberation: Opening Chapter Two," mapped out the relationship between gender oppression and capitalist exploitation as one in which capital, able to count on women's unpaid domestic labour for social reproduction, could accumulate more surplus value because both men's and women's wages could be lower. Meg Luxton's pioneering work on domestic labour (12:7, Winter 1977) revealed the complex forms of physical, intellectual, organizational and emotional labour involved, and showed how the conditions under which it was conducted

— unpaid, unvalued and in personal relationships of both love and dependence — made it tension-ridden and oppressive. For Myrna Wood (5:5, June/July 1968), "Male domination of women and the family" was "[t]hat primary, essential opiate of the working class" and worked to create personalities that could fit into — or at least cope with — capitalist work. In this way, women's oppression at work and at home was seen as a crucial part of the generation of profits and the reproduction of capitalism as a mode of living itself.

Socialist feminists writing in *CD* insisted that patriarchy underpins the spread and pervasive power of industrial capitalism, and its resistance is therefore an essential part of resisting capitalism itself. Socialist feminist critique was not about dividing the left, but rather about making the struggle against both capitalism and patriarchy more effective. On the one hand, socialists had to attend to gender inequality:

> [t]he predicament of working class women is the most
> potentially revolutionary to society because it spans
> production and reproduction, class exploitation and sex
> oppression. They need each other, they need the support of
> male workers; their fight at work connects immediately to
> their situation at home. Their organization and militancy
> is vital not only for women's liberation but for the whole
> movement for progress in society ("SSF" 10:8, June 1975).

By the early 1980s, this view that socialism had to involve women's liberation was explicitly integrated into the magazine's editorial line (see "Reproductive Choice," 17:5, November 1983). The editorial "Feminism and Socialism" (19:4, September/October 1985), penned by the women on the editorial collective but representing the views of the whole board, emphasized the need to explore that area where the bonds of "class solidarity" conflict with those of "sisterhood," particularly since women experienced oppression at the hands of "the very same husbands, lovers, with whom they are supposed to share this sense of [class] solidarity." These personal relations constituted a real barrier to effective socialist political work.

On the other hand, there were many warnings that a feminism not grounded in the struggle against capital was potentially empty, easily coopted by piecemeal reforms for the benefit of only the most privileged women and used in a process of creating "new gradations among the underprivileged" ("SSF," 10:8, June 1975). Dixon (10:8, June 1975) highlighted the "class contradictions" of the mass feminist movement and the limits, in her view, of "a multi-class, single-issue series of reformist campaigns." Feminists had to "realize that it is not enough to struggle for particular reforms, important though they be. We must understand the relationships of all the structural elements — economic, legal, social and sexual — on women's condition, lest we find our few improvements twisted against us and serving the interests of the middle class reform movements" ("SSF," 10:8, June 1975). This insight did not make it any easier for feminists, socialist or otherwise, to sort out how to engage in particular feminist campaigns, as we shall later see.

The call for understanding the interpenetration of patriarchy and capitalism, and for socialists to integrate this analysis into their political and personal practice, did not obviate the need for women to develop their own separate spaces for discussion, support and strategizing. Unequal gender relations, even "male supremacy" (10:8, June 1975), pervaded New Left organizations, unions and political parties, and produced contradictions between stated commitments to gender equality and the reality of women fetching the coffee and printing the flyers. Much of this reality emerged in analyses of the labour movement or the NDP. Despite many feminist contributors' very close links to these organizations, they were unafraid to critique them in CD's pages. In her 1971 article "Sexism Prevailed at the NDP Convention" (8:1, June), Varda Kidd (later Burstyn) describes a convention in which women speakers and their issues were repeatedly marginalized. A resolution for gender parity in party decision-making bodies was "railroaded." Delegates goaded women speakers at the microphones with injunctions to "go back to the kitchen where you belong" and the "suggestion" that "what you really need is a good fuck."4

Krista Maeots challenged the more polite reasons NDP delegates gave for rejecting the allocation of a designated percentage of leadership with a sharp critique of the "liberal myth" of meritocracy, arguing that, as socialists, "you manipulate the structures of your party to attain that goal [of gender parity], you don't manipulate people to fit existing structures" (7:8, April 1971). The issue of "how little room men are willing to give women politically" (8:1, June 1971) was also discussed by Judy Darcy in 1983, who pointed out that, despite much significant progress, "[t]he predominantly male union leadership . . . is fundamentally threatened by the power and demands of trade union women and the women's movement" (17:4, September 1983). An extensive discussion of the collapse of two far-left organizations in 1982–83 — "In Struggle! and the Workers Communist Party" — pointed to the central role that sexism played in their disintegration, when the women collectively began to say no to the subordination and narrowing of women's issues and the unequal division of labour in which "men [were] thinking and elaborating the revolutionary theory, women [were] doing all the shit work, the typing, the translation and all that jazz" (17:5, November 1983).

These experiences pointed to the need for women's self-organizing, separate from men and male-dominated organizations of the Left. Despite their leftist commitments, "women [had to] stop subordinating their struggle for their own liberation to the 'general' socialist struggle" (8:1, June 1971). Women's self-organizing, often misunderstood as a form of separatism,[5] was instead a process for developing women's political capacity for struggle in the midst of hostile and resistant institutions. This strategy and its results were well described by Linda Briskin in 1990 (24:1, January/February), where she documented the way that the "convergence of feminism and rank and file unionism" in the form of the "new structures . . . generated by women unionists on the margins of tradition union organization" had led to transformations in the definition of "real" union issues and internal processes. As Darcy pointed out in 1983 (17:4, September), "those victories . . . have come about *only* as result of women organizing and fighting for them, refusing to take NO for an answer — either from the trade union leadership or from their union brothers." However, there were also voices arguing that affirmative action initiatives in the unions were actually signs of defeat rather than victory, since women's equal representation had to be "forced" on their union brothers (Bail, 17:4, September/October 1985).

CD's identification with socialist feminism, as well as its commitment to pull established left and working-class organizations to the Left, meant that it provided a consistent forum for feminist analyses of work, workplaces, unions and economic policy, particularly in the 1980s and 90s as feminist activism around these issues was building. Contrary to the concerns voiced by Farid and Kuyek (10:8, June 1975), for whom the women's liberation movement was hopelessly bourgeois and of little real relevance to "pragmatic" and "exhausted" working-class women who "consider the demands of the women's movement to be unrealistic in the context of Canadian society," Canadian feminism evolved to push the economic demands of working-class women to the forefront. As Meg Luxton argues, despite the assertion that feminism was a middle-class movement, "union-based, working-class feminism . . . has been a key player in the women's movement" in Canada.[6] This working-class women's activism was amply documented in the pages of *CD*, crucially so since, as Luxton claims, such activism has otherwise been "hidden" from mainstream accounts of feminism. From the 1970s on, pay equity (McDonald, 14:6, May 1980; Sandford, 20:1, March 1986; Bakker, 21:1, March 1987; Moorcroft, 39:2, March/April 2005), employment equity and access to good jobs (Kennedy, 18:3, June 1984; Wood, 18:4, 1984), child care (Lange, 14:8, August 1980; Morrison, 20:5, September/October 1986; Ferguson and Kass, 26:3, April/May 1992), workplace sexual harassment (Burstyn, 15:3, December 1980; Kadar, 18:3, June 1984; Gray, March/April 1985) and parental leave were covered regularly, as were the experiences of particular groups of women workers (in nursing, services and banks, on farms, in the fisheries and in northern resource towns).[7]

CD also featured critical analyses of established labour movement strategies and positions whose gendered implications were often overlooked. In October 1988 (22:7), in a response to Herman Rosenfeld's review of Don Wells's book *Empty Promises*, feminist scholar Dorothy Smith provided a gendered perspective on "new management strategies" like "quality of working life" initiatives. While agreeing that QWL strategies don't empower workers (as their proponents claim) and do undermine "the traditional social relations on the job" that "have been the foundation of union organization," Smith pointed out that this "traditional foundation was also thoroughly sexist," based on a gendered division of labour in which women were allocated jobs with the least skill and responsibility and the lowest pay. Smith's research suggested that work circles and multitasking had broken the occupational trap for women, allowing them to gain a wider set of skills and to qualify for better jobs. Similarly, law professor Judy Fudge made the case for adopting new kinds of bargaining strategies that would address the (gendered) polarization of labour markets and workplaces (26:3, April/May 1992; 27:2, March/April 1993). In her searing critique of the gendered foundations of the postwar labour legislation, Anne Forrest argued that the law assumed large, male-dominated workplaces in the industrial and resource sectors, resulting in a "male model of rights and bargaining practices" that (has) made successful organizing and collective bargaining in female-dominated sectors like private services nearly impossible (29:1, February/March 1995).

As neoliberal globalization tightened its grip on Canada through the 1980s and nineties, *CD* highlighted feminist economic analyses of the specific impact of these political-economic transformations on women. *CD* published feminist perspectives on the federal government's economic policies, including the budget, free trade (21:8, Jan 1988; 26:5, July/ August 1992), cutbacks (28:2, March/April 1994; 29:2, April/May 1995) and privatization (40:3, May/June 2006). These authors emphasized the importance to women in general, and poor, working-class and minority women in particular, of the social wage, those government-financed programs that supplement workers' money wages and protect working-class living standards. In January 1992 (26:1), Isa Bakker (rightly) predicted that free trade would substantially weaken the social wage. As free trade would lead to lower corporate taxes, privatizations and service cutbacks, not only would "workers and their dependents shoulder more of the tax burden and get a more meager social wage in return," but women in particular, especially those who "head up single parent households or are elderly . . . will be hit the hardest by Canada's emulation of the less generous, less universal, and more regressive" US system. The "triple threat" of cuts to women — as consumers of public services, producers of services via good public sector jobs and providers of unpaid care in the home

— continues today, making *CD*'s socialist feminist analysis as relevant as ever (28:2, March/April 1994).

Reproductive rights: A bedrock of women's liberation

Dimension's pages also offer a glimpse into an era many Canadians either would rather forget or know very little about: when abortion was a crime and reproductive rights were considerably restricted. However, *CD* asserted often that women's right to control their own bodies was "a basic demand of the women's movement" (10:7, March 1975) and "every bit as important a part of the socialism we want to build as say, workers' right to control the workplace" (17:5, November 1983). *CD*'s coverage of reproductive-rights struggles was a chronicle of the very gradual and grudging acknowledgement of women's autonomy as well as of the powerful backlash faced each step of the way. Fifty years on, with the US in the midst of a major regression in reproductive rights policy and the former Harper Government having given its tacit approval to backbenchers pushing for Criminal Code changes that would lead to abortion's recriminalization,[8] *CD*'s pages remind us what was — and is — at stake, for both women's freedom and socialism.

It is worth noting that *CD*'s first article on an explicitly feminist topic, in the July 1968 issue (5:5), was "Abortion and the Liberation of Women" by Myrna Wood. In it, Wood reviewed the proposed changes to the Criminal Code (passed in 1969) that would decriminalize birth control and reform access to abortion. She argued that class inequalities would restrict access to birth control and therefore continue to make abortion necessary. However, the Liberal government's amendments would be "useless": they would define as "legal" only those abortions approved as necessary for the physical or mental health of the mother by hospital-based therapeutic-abortion committees (TACs) dominated by "conservative, moralistic doctors." Any abortions that took place outside of this state-mandated process would remain illegal. *CD* commentators hammered away at the TAC system's contradictions and the way that it increased access for only the most privileged women, not least because hospitals were not required to have TACs or to offer abortion services (17:5, November 1983).

By the 1970s, reproductive rights organizing reached a fever pitch, and it therefore had a sustained presence in the magazine. *Dimension* actively championed Dr. Henry Morgentaler when he was imprisoned in March 1975 for defying the Criminal Code by performing abortions in his free-standing clinic in Montreal. Although a jury had acquitted him, refusing to enforce what they considered an unjust law, the Quebec government appealled and the Quebec Court of Appeal overturned the jury's decision. Margie Gordon and Shelley Gavigan, then law students at the University of Saskatchewan, decried "the blatant . . . legal persecution" of Morgentaler and expressed deep skepticism that the class- and gender-biased courts could be used effectively as a tool of women's liberation (10:8, June 1975).[9] *Dimension* again focused on reproductive rights in its November 1983 issue (17:5), in the wake of the opening of Morgentaler's clinic in Winnipeg[10] earlier that year and the conflicts which arose around it. Repeated police raids of the clinic in June 1983 led to Morgentaler, another doctor and five staffers being charged with conspiracy to commit an illegal abortion, mobilizing choice supporters to demonstrate at the legislature. Perhaps indicative of the prevailing attitude on abortion rights in the upper reaches of the legal profession, Manitoba's chief justice had signed an anti-abortion petition, and Manitoba Crown Attorney Mike Baryluk declared "any woman who wants an abortion should be given a razor blade" (17:5, November 1983). The Manitoba government, an NDP government led by Howard Pawley and containing several prominent pro-choice feminists, refused to intervene, whether to pressure the federal government to change the law or to encourage the attorney-general to drop the charges. The Manitoba Federation of Labour also withdrew from the Coalition for Reproductive Choice when the latter harshly criticized the NDP's inaction, due to "pressure from MFL affiliates." The Manitoba situation highlighted deep divisions within the broad Left over reproductive choice, but also mobilized new individuals and organizations (Labour People for Choice, Manitoba Doctors for Reproductive Choice, and Lawyers for Choice) to join the fight. Parallel developments were happening in Toronto, as the Ontario Coalition for Abortion Clinics (OCAC) invited Morgentaler to open a clinic there as part of a movement-building strategy to challenge the federal law (32:2, March/April 1998).

In contrast to some earlier contributors who characterized reproductive choice as primarily a middle-class women's issue (Farid and Kuyek, 11:1 July/August 1975) or a limited single-issue campaign (Dixon, 11:1 July/August 1975), *CD*'s editorial collective argued that winning the right to reproductive choice would "represent more than just another reform" because it indicated "a significant break with the patriarchal domination of women by man . . . a denial of the notion . . . of woman who has an obligation to perform reproductive and mothering roles for men" (17:5, November 1983). Women's freedom was central to any future socialist society.

However, critical reflection on what was gained — and not — from the 1988 Supreme Court of Canada decision that declared the abortion provisions of the Criminal Code unconstitutional was also in order, not least on the relationship between short-term reforms and long-term (radical/revolutionary) transformation. Concerns were raised about the long-term effects of strategic choices that had been made to conduct the struggle in particular ways. Ruth Corobow, a former staffer at Morgentaler's Winnipeg clinic, made the case that the private, for-profit clinic model, around which so much civil disobedience had been organized, actually exposed women to "anti-choice violence" (in the form of running a protesters' gauntlet) and constituted a "divisive obstacle in our working together towards secure, non-profit, community-based, safe, insured, women-centred, comprehensive health care than includes abortion" (23:2, March 1989). Dorothy Smith also considered the "class experience" of pro-choice and other kinds of activism, importantly recognizing that many pro-life activists were working class. She highlighted an unresolved problem for the Left which continues to resonate today, and well beyond the feminist movement:

> *The New Right mobilizes divisions of race, class, gender*
> *and sexuality among the economically exploited. It drives*
> *a wedge between the mass of working people and a*
> *socialist intelligensia. What . . . does the Right know about*
> *empowering the powerless that we don't? (23:4, June 1989)*
> *In other words, had the abortion rights struggle been*

watered down, in both message and constituency, for
expediency's sake? And, as Gordon and Gavigan wondered
in 1975, was it really possible to expect that the fight for
genuine reproductive freedom could ever truly be won in
the courts or legislatures of "a society dedicated to the
perpetuation of capitalism and its inevitable companion,
sexist ideology" (10:8, June 1975)?

Others acknowledged that choices had been made to focus on reform, and that the struggle was unfinished. The editorial collective emphasized the "landmark" nature of that "long-sought-after victory," but also the importance of broadening demands to include the economic and social conditions in which meaningful choices could be made, as well as expanding arenas of struggle beyond legislatures or courts to ensure that "rights in principle" became "rights in practice" (23:2, March 1989). As Carolyn Egan, one of the founding members of OCAC, later put it, "[t]he struggle for abortion rights [was] only one part" of a broader agenda of choice that included "a whole range of women's demands" in order "truly to have choices in our lives":

The right to safe and effective birth control in our own
languages and our own communities, the right to funded
child care and parental leave, the right to decent jobs, the
right to love freely and openly as lesbians, an end to forced
or coerced sterilization, the right to have the children we
choose to have and, of course, the right to full access to free
abortion (32:2, March/April 1998).

While agreeing with this view, Miriam Jones and B. Lee took on the issue of immediate reforms versus long-term transformation faced by all left movements in their response to Ruth Corobow (23:5, July/August 1989). For them, the decision to defend the Morgentaler clinics was a product of the fact that "we cannot choose the overall political and ideological environment under which we fight," nor can we wait for the "perfect conditions" to make change. In the end, while the fight for overall social transformation had not yet been won, stages in a struggle should not be confused with their overall goals. Ultimately, the abortion rights struggle had allowed for movement building, by developing "strong links . . . between labour, health, feminist, and so many other community groups" and thus creating the basis for broad-based coalitions to fight for the broader socialist-feminist agenda.

Intersectionality and the diversity of women's experiences

CD's sustained focus on the relationship between gender and class was ahead of its time, and presaged feminist scholarship's turn to intersectionality in the 1990s. Johanna Brenner explains that intersectionality is an analytical strategy that examines how "multiple, crosscutting institutionalized power relations defined by race, class, gender, and sexuality" create distinct social locations that "shape experience and identity."[11] One of the first such pieces, "Who speaks for working-class women," by Z. Farid and J. Kuyek (10:8, June 1975), challenged the universalization of middle-class women's problems and concerns in the feminist movement and pointed to working-class women's distinct position within class relations as shaping the conditions for their gendered liberation. But the magazine did not limit itself to class issues, and engaged early and extensively with other dimensions of women's identities, including race, aboriginality, age, disability and sexuality. Throughout, CD contributors and editorial boards showed themselves remarkably sensitive to the different experiences of and inequalities between women, and to the need to resist middle-class solutions as addressing all women's needs and interests.

Coverage of the situation of Aboriginal peoples in Canada and Quebec, and particularly of Aboriginal women, featured intersectional analysis. Aboriginal women's experiences of gender oppression were depicted as profoundly shaped by racism and economic marginalization, both of which subjected them to particularly high levels of poverty and violence. The implications of this for both feminism and the movement for Aboriginal self-determination were full of tensions. As Doris Young and Ustun Reinart wrote in 1988 (22:2, March/April), Aboriginal women had "remained outside of the mainstream women's movement

. . . because they needed to struggle against racism, and for an economic base." However, their experiences in male-dominated Native organizations and communities were also of relative marginalization. Violence within Aboriginal communities was one such difficult issue. Despite its commitment to Aboriginal self-government, *CD* did not shy away from publishing strong feminist positions on cases that divided the Aboriginal activist community. In one prominent case, a woman from the Long Plain First Nation in Manitoba had gone on a hunger strike to protest Anishinabe Child and Family Services' refusal to intervene when she reported complaints from her children that they were being abused by their father — who was also the chief. The Aboriginal Women's Unity Coalition of Winnipeg went public with the dispute in defiance of the Assembly of Manitoba Chiefs (AMC), which had tried to address the matter internally.[12] This public challenge to their own community leaders was no small gesture since, as Marilyn Fontaine-Brightstar wrote (26:2, March 1992), "All too often oppressed people refuse to address conflicts of power within their own ranks in the interest of maintaining solidarity." Just as socialist feminists insisted to their male comrades that a revolution against capitalism that was patriarchal was no revolution, so too did Aboriginal women problematize the notion that genuine self-government could be based on relations of sexual exploitation and violence within the community.[13]

The diversity of women's experiences, problems and movements was also reflected in *CD*'s coverage of international issues and commitment to anti-imperialism. In the 1970s and eighties, *CD* featured reports from front-line struggles in the Cold War battlefields of South East Asia, Africa and Latin America, in which women played a crucial if under-recognized part. Canadian antiwar activist Claire Culhane chronicled the role of Vietnamese women in military defence against US occupation forces (10:7, March 1975). Readers encountered women activists in Cuba (10:7, March 1975; 14:1, July/August 1979), South Africa (13:1, 1977), Nicaragua (19:6, January/February 1986; 20:1, March 1986; 20:3, May 1986, a three-part series on women in the revolutionary war effort), Nairobi (19:6, January/February 1986), Palestine/Israel (23:4, June 1989), and then, in the midst of the collapse of the Soviet

Union, Russia (24:3, April/May 1990) and East Germany (29:2, April/May 1995).

However, the feminist movement itself was increasingly riven by tensions through the late 1980s and early 1990s, particularly as activists tried to make sense of the political implications of intersectionality and a more nuanced understanding of privilege and oppression for feminist organizations, for the relationships between differently situated women, and for the role of male allies. The National Action Committee on the Status of Women went through a painful period of self-examination about the inequalities between white and racialized women beginning in the early 1990s, as did many community-based feminist organizations like Nellie's Place in Toronto.[14] CD did not shy away from airing such tensions in its own pages (although this was perhaps relatively underexplored, given its importance). While these exchanges were often painful, they exemplified the larger debates in the movement and served to push the Left to develop a more nuanced understanding of the dynamics of oppression and basis of solidarity.

The question of racism and inequality in the feminist movement was one such difficult conversation. In August 1993 (27:4), CD published "A Tale of Three Sisters" by then-writer and filmmaker (and now professor) Judy Haiven. In it, she recounted a sequence of events that occurred to her during the 1993 NAC conference in Saskatoon (her hometown): she offered a lift to two NAC delegates, women of colour she didn't know, and her two-year old son responded with fear, tears and screams when he saw them. The subsequent interactions were awkward and tense: Haiven's attempts to explain why her child would not have encountered black people in Saskatchewan were full of acknowledged missteps. The women of colour seemed mistrustful and unsatisfied with her explanations. Haiven later heard the story retold at a NAC workshop in which she and her child (unnamed) were characterized as racists. Haiven's reflections on the incident led her to a more generalized set of reflections. She challenged the way that, for her, accusations of racism were "ripping apart" progressive and women's organizations at a time when women's organizations were at risk from the Mulroney government's cuts to granting programs. She argued that "[w]ere the real enemies of women and the oppressed trying to think of ways to neutralize the popular opposition, they could scarcely have concocted a more effective scheme than 'confronting our own racism.' If there were somebody planning all of this, we'd call them an evil genius." While she acknowledged that progressives had to "recogniz[e] and confront ... our place in a racist society," she questioned whether "the question of race within progressive organizations" was really "the primary contradiction" needing to be faced. Instead, she wondered whether, in the face of difficult-to-personify systemic racism, it was simply "easier to attack the white face on the barricade next to you than the faceless enemy that deprives you of full equality." Finally, she pointed to what she saw as the construction of a hierarchy of oppression, evidenced by her perception that the women of colour didn't seem cognizant of or interested in the racism experienced by Aboriginal women.

Knowing how controversial such an analysis would be, *CD*'s editorial collective published Haiven's piece with a disclaimer, noting that "all [its] members . . . found aspects of this article to be objectionable." However, "because we believe it expresses a point of view held by more than a few activists, but which never finds its way into print," they published so as to "stimulate a debate on the nature of racism in Canada's progressive movements." That debate was soon taken up by Sunera Thobani, then the newly elected — and first woman of colour — president of NAC, in the January 1994 issue (28:1). She acknowledged that dealing with racism, one's own previously unexamined assumptions, and the reactions of others is both "very difficult and very painful . . . particularly when you have to recognize oppressive aspects in your own behaviour." However, for Thobani, Haiven's references to "black women['s] . . . alleged ignorance of aboriginal issues" or "divisions which exist between people of colour" only served "to silence any kind of further anti-racist work." Instead, feminists had to face up to the inequalities of power amongst them, and "recognize that the power you have in society is not an individual power" but one conferred or denied through processes of structural privileging or oppression. Thobani emphasized the complexity of an intersectional analysis of relative power, "because not all white people have the same level of power," but that this had to be understood in the context of a "white supremacist society." Though many of Thobani's insights about privilege have become commonplace in contemporary antiracist feminism, reading this exchange reminds us of the very long, challenging process of refining feminist thought and practice and of the rough exchanges that took place. The editorial collective summed up its position on the way forward in September 1992:

> [W]omen of colour and aboriginal women . . . have openly confronted . . . the assumptions, issues, and leadership of (predominantly) white, relatively privileged women of the feminist movement. This has resulted in controversy and splits. This is to be expected in any movement, and is not unhealthy if this helps activists clarify issues and chart a way forward. But for this to happen, both sides must be willing to listen to one another. Traditional leaders of the women's movement must be willing to make room for the issues, priorities and ideas brought to the movement by aboriginal women and women of colour. And all concerned have to remember who the real enemy is. ("The Rising of the Women," 26:6, September 1992)

The question of men's relationship to feminism, and their responsibility to challenge the various manifestations of patriarchy, was also the subject of much debate in CD's pages. The magazine featured discussions of men's engagement with patriarchy, masculinity and feminism through the 1980s,[15] foreshadowing the rise of studies of masculinity as the proper subject of feminist analysis concerned with the concept and dynamics of gender. However, the debate became more urgent in the years following the Montreal Massacre in December 1989 (although, strangely, no clear editorial analysis of the events was forthcoming until Joyce Green's excellent essay on behalf of the collective in 2005). On the one hand, many men engaged in a sober soul-searching, particularly as the antifeminist and misogynistic nature of the Massacre was clear to those who wished to see (although many in the broader population did not, preferring to see the incident as the work of a crazy individual).[16] Other men problematized the idea of "male violence against women" and what it implied about men's responsibility in general. In his 1992 piece, "Dances with Guilt" (26:1, January/February), Ulli Diemer criticized what he described as a "we're all guilty" paradigm that had come to dominate the thinking of progressive men. For Diemer, "this line of thinking . . . actually encourages men who really are violent to evade responsibility for their violence" as it allows an essentialist recourse to men's violent "nature." Other nonviolent men were paralyzed by guilt and unable to sort out what to do. In a laudable attempt to direct men's analysis to their own actions and complicity in patriarchy, "the line between violence and behaviours which, though wrong, are not violence" was blurred. While not intending "to absolve non-violent men from the responsibility of taking action against violence," and while also holding that "[m]en also have a special responsibility to act against violence precisely because there are men who are violent," Diemer argued that, both politically and personally, taking responsibility was not the same as accepting blame.

The question of men's role in feminist struggles against violence was taken up from a different angle by Brenda Austin-Smith in "A man's place," appearing in the same January 1992 issue as Diemer's piece. For Austin-Smith, the problem was not the depth of guilt but the shallowness of men's activism, as evidenced in their participation in the White Ribbon Campaign (launched in 1991). She noted the frustration of observing the ease with which men could attract positive media for engaging an issue on which women had been organizing relentlessly and in obscurity for decades. This also "fuel[led] the suspicion that some men may find it easier to wear a shred of white ribbon in token support of an end to male violence, and enjoy the attendant praise, than to take concrete steps in their lives and in their communities to really end it." However, while recognizing how "galling" it was that "that Brian Mulroney considers himself a man who can wear a white ribbon with a clear conscience," and that "feminist anger" at the reality that "only when men become involved in an event or movement will anyone take it seriously" was justified, Austin-Smith recognized the White Ribbon Campaign as a genuine and positive attempt of men who "took to heart feminists' directive that men take responsibility not just for their own violence, but for the violence perpetrated by other men." The editorial collective also soon weighed in, entitling the next issue's editorial "Rooting out male violence" (27:2, March 1993). Although Diemer's piece was not explicitly mentioned, it is difficult to imagine it was not in part a response, since the editorial responded to many of his points. What follows is an impressive structural analysis of the causes and purposes of violence against women and other oppressed groups as "a mechanism for enforcing inequality between sexes, racial groups and social classes." Although individual men are not all perpetrators of violence against women, they benefit (to greater or lesser extents) from a system that constructs rigid gender identities and expectations and pays men "wages" for masculinity,[17] not least as compensation for other forms of powerlessness they experience due to class and racial inequalities. As such, CD's stand has long been that men themselves had to take responsibility for transforming the patriarchy, at both the macro- and micro-level, that they themselves benefit from.

Taking stock: Reflecting on the women's movement

Undoubtedly, CD's coverage of women's and feminist activism has risen and fallen over the years. This is at least in part an index of the fortunes of the feminist movement itself over the past fifty years. In 1980, CD's editorial collective was noting that, "after a decade or more of activism [in the late 1960s and 1970s], it looks as though another period of dormancy is upon us" (14:6, May 1980). By 1992, however, the collective was speaking of a strongly entrenched and militant feminist movement whose achievements, though incomplete, were many (26:6, September 1992). By 2003, they were asking "What ever happened to the Women's Movement?" (37:5, September/October). These pieces point to a key fact: movements are cyclical, and the "doldrums" are important moments to take stock of achievements, contradictions and the capacities for revival in the next period of struggle.

On the one hand, CD is replete with real victories that have made a qualitative difference in women's lives. As Nancy Peckford summarized in her analysis of the twenty-five years since Canada's signing of the UN Convention on the Elimination of All Forms of Discrimination Against Women, we have witnessed

> *significant reforms to marriage and property law; increased*
> *awareness and penalties for the perpetrators of violence*
> *against women; recognition of the right of Aboriginal*
> *women to maintain their status regardless of who they*
> *married;*[18] *adoption of employment equity legislation for the*
> *public service; and decriminalization of abortion in order to*
> *enhance women's reproductive choice. ("25 Years: Ready or*
> *Not?," 40:2, March/April 2006)*

CD's pages also depict "the growth of a feminist consciousness among trade union women" ("Women and Labour," 19:5, Dec 1985) and the impressive progress of those women in taking on major roles in their organizations.[19] Legislative victories like proactive pay equity in Ontario were incredibly important if contradictory advances in reducing the effects of systemic workplace discrimination. These were rightly attributed to a powerful and effective women's movement ("The Rising of the Women," 26:6, September 1992).

On the other hand, after 1996, *CD*'s coverage of explicitly feminist issues noticeably thinned out, particularly compared to the impressive regularity of coverage in the 1980s and nineties, partly reflecting the real challenges faced by the feminist movement itself. Impressive mobilizations by feminists in Quebec and Canada (in the form of the Women's Marches Against Poverty in 1995 and 1996,[20] and the 2000 World March of Women) could not avert the deterioration. As Sunera Thobani put it in a 2007 interview, she no longer believed there was a "strong national feminist movement" in Canada, the causes of which were both internal and external. Internally, "divisions between different visions of what feminism is and can be, and which groups had been represented in the national women's movement and which had been excluded" had taken their toll, but, more importantly for Thobani, so had the "massive budget cuts and the restructuring of the Canadian welfare state in the 1990s," which meant that the many women's organizations dependent on state funding could no longer survive.[21] Despite persistent and crucial local organizing, the feminist movement was in disarray by the mid-2000s, and a trend to "unstructured, ad hoc and less formal groupings" first noted by Kay MacPherson in 1975 (10:8, June) persisted.

In 2003 (37:5, September/October), the magazine asked various generations of feminists "Whatever Happened to the Women's Movement?" Their collective diagnoses noted a series of key problems that continue to plague the movement and make sustained engagement in CD's pages more challenging. Many feminist victories were unevenly distributed. The growing representation of women in business, the professions and educational institutions masked the feminization of poverty, persistence of pay and occupational inequalities, and various forms of violence, contributing to the hegemonic view that feminism was no longer needed. Dorothy Smith agreed with Thobani that differences within the movement — important though they were to work through — had created obstacles to unity that no movement could be expected to easily overcome. Myrna Wood rightly pointed out that single-issue struggles often resulted in women's organizations taking on service provision, which created a deepening dependency on state funding and a resulting depoliticization as service provision became an end in itself and restrictions of advocacy to maintain charitable status took their ideological toll. As various forms of activism faded or localized, university-based Women's Studies departments increasingly became the centre of gravity of feminist education. Wood and Tammy Findlay noted the growing elitism and inaccessibility of jargon-filled feminist theory, separate from the practical concerns of most women. These assessments reflected cautions raised over the decades in CD's pages, and identified the real and continuing challenges for revitalizing the contemporary feminist movement.

In 2007, CD reestablished a feminist column, "Feminist Ramblings" (taking up the role that "Half The Sky . . . And Then Some" played in the 1980s), written by Bernadette Wagner, which regularized CD's feminist commentary again for some time. Wagner's first column (41:2, March/April) examined the Harper government's 2006 cuts to Status of Women Canada offices and research programs, a further blow to the institutional equality apparatus built by second-wave feminism. Wagner went on to write about such topics as work, food and aging from a feminist perspective.

From 2010 on, looking to connect with a new generation of feminists, *CD* began to cover the activism of the pan-Canadian network RebELLEs, a movement that brings together activists to deepen analysis, catalyze feminist energies and organize decentralized but coordinated protests (44:6, November/December 2010). As Sarah Granke and Lissie Rappaport put it, "young womyn are the next generation of feminists who are going to fight — with love and with rage. As young womyn we need to learn from and work with our elders while also forming our own feminist analysis and priorities for action." This issue of the magazine reflects strongly the concerns and orientations of third-wave feminism. In this view, there is no one-size-fits-all approach to women's liberation. Rather, there is a much more decentralized approach to feminist strategy, and intersectionality and analysis of privilege and oppression in the movement that is taken for granted, as evidenced in the discussion at RebELLES gatherings in Montreal (2008) and Winnipeg (2010). The RebELLES network asserts a feminism that is "radical, antihierarchical, anticapitalist, anticolonialist, and antipatriarchal; assertive, grassroots, action-oriented, diverse, disruptive, dissident, explosive, welcoming, colourful, celebratory and fun," learning from both the lessons "and errors" of previous generations (Barbara Legault, "RebELLEs: Feminists Fighting with Love and Rage," 44:6, November/December 2010). These commitments represent important advances over second-wave feminism, and show that the difficult debates amongst feminists discussed earlier have been in some ways transcended. However, the important victories of second-wave feminism, whether in the form of legislative rights or institutional transformation, involved particular kinds of coordinated strategic interventions that developed and applied leverage on the centres of economic and political power. As these victories come under attack, it is unclear that they can be effectively defended through the decentralized forms of resistance that are more typical of third-wave feminism. However, these are the kinds of strategic debates that *CD* could and should feature. It will be interesting to see how, on the one hand, this contemporary generation of feminists will engage with the insights of the socialist feminist tradition so well represented in the magazine and, on the other hard, whether *CD* can become for them what it was for those on the front lines in the previous five decades.

Conclusion

CD's engagement with feminism since the late 1960s reflected the struggles that characterized the impact of feminist ideas and practices in the academy, in progressive movements and in personal lives and relationships. Because feminism sought to undo centuries-old patriarchal practices that implicated all our institutions and our own subjectivities, the process of that undoing inevitably involved conflict and controversy. The articles and debates that appeared in *CD*'s pages provide a chronicle of a movement defining itself, and often at odds with itself. Historically, the pivotal role played by many *CD* contributors in the feminist struggles taking place in the economic, political and cultural spheres renders their contributions of particular significance, and the magazine truly provides a living archive of a vibrant and dynamic era.

Although clearly influenced primarily by socialist feminist analysis, *CD* never asserted a clear editorial policy line on the "correct" approach to feminist issues. However, what this openness allowed was a full airing of the real intellectual, political and emotional challenges that needed to be worked through for feminist commitments to gender equality to take root and become "common sense" on the Left. It also helped that strong and powerfully articulate feminist voices were always present, able to challenge the limits of defensive reactions to difficult issues. And *CD* also allowed for iconoclastic thinkers to puncture what superficial consensus may have developed, always requiring its readership to deepen and make more complex its understanding of gender politics.

Yet as feminism's centre of gravity shifted in the mid-1990s from the streets and communities and into the academy, the gap in grounded feminist political analysis became more evident. For the strength of *CD*'s feminist contributors was that they were speaking to movement activists as much as to academics, and contributing to the development of strategic analysis, of what is to be done to push forward the cause of gender equality. As the movement has fragmented and faded, so too has *CD*'s sustained contribution to understanding the nature of patriarchy, the relationship between capital, property and the oppression of women, the intersection between personal and political liberation, the role of men in the women's movement, and feminist strategy. As Canada moves into an age of increasing repression, austerity and conservatism — one in which the various institutions built to support women's equality are rapidly being dismantled — it remains to be seen whether this will lead to a renewed and sustained feminist activism. Only in a context of renewal of the feminist movement will *CD*'s drive to explore and understand the fundamental roots of patriarchy in our culture[s] and in the capitalist system regain the traction and influence it once had. Let that day arrive soon.

CHAPTER 25
The Personal Dimension

Dennis Pilon

Introduction — the Left and the personal dimension

It is a query we've all heard at some point: "Can I ask you a personal question?" It gets asked because there is a line between our fully public selves and whatever we might not wish to divulge to just anyone. Just where that line is or what might constitute "personal" for any given person is not fixed. It used to be that asking people how much money they made was considered to be too personal a question — now some could care less. But there is always something. In this sense, "personal" is understood as private. Yet this does not exhaust our possible understanding of the personal dimension. Personal can mean direct and experiential, as in the expression "up close and personal." What happens to us in our individual day to day lives is personal in a way that the headlines or events occurring in various local, national or world stages may not be. And finally when we evoke the "personal" it hints at something more than abstract knowledge or ideas — it suggests an intimacy of impact, of emotion. To "take it personally" means to take it to heart, to open oneself up to feelings: hurt, joy, excitement and much else. For these reasons, the personal dimension, unlike so many arenas of debate on the Left, cannot be neatly parsed as it traverses all these fields — private, experiential, emotional — simultaneously. To "get personal" means risking something: the exposure of our unfinished selves.

The personal is like a hanging thread, to pull on it risks an unravelling that cannot be effectively gauged in advance.

Since its founding, *Canadian Dimension*, like much of the Left, had first a fumbling then uneven relationship with all things "personal." Ignored in its first five years of existence, personal themes emerged sporadically by the late 1960s, then more consistently in the 1970s, only to fade out again in mid-1980s, to return in a more biographical form from the 1990s on. If there are consistent themes to *CD*'s ruminations on the personal they are sex and death, perhaps because so many people have some experience of both. In reviewing the various contributions, what comes through is how hard it is to go there — to the personal — how divisive it can be, but also how moving. We often hear how "the Left" has ignored this or that issue, but that does not appear to be the case for *CD*. As issues rose in public consciousness, they also increasingly appeared in the magazine. In some cases, *CD* appeared behind the curve, coming to feminism only in the 1970s, but in others it was well ahead, as with sex and sexuality. Throughout the period examined here the work that is consistently excellent is biography. The personal is about stories, and they are fascinating: sexual abuse, uncomfortable sexual fantasies, particular struggles or just lives lived. At different times, *CD* has tried to push the boundaries of left commentary on the personal, as with Gad Horowitz's experimental and controversial advice column in the late 1980s. But mostly *CD* has seemed satisfied to remain topical on the personal dimension, changing with the times, reflecting both the uneasiness and occasional boldness of the general public itself in dealing with personal issues.

It should be underlined upfront that old left reticence over the "personal" is easy to understand and not entirely without foundation. The dominant tropes of the North American ideology have long used an abstract individualism precisely to obscure power, particularly the collective power of capital and the need for collective action to oppose it. This politics of personhood can be wielded in a number of ways. An "anyone can make it" rhetoric sustained by anecdotal stories of individual success says failure is largely personal, rather than structured in unequal social relations rooted in class, race, gender and much else. Or another approach puts the stress on talent, arguing that some people are just smarter or prettier and that explains their personal success, as if these attributes too are not given their power socially. Either way, social and contextual influences on an individual are downplayed in favour of their unrestrained agency — and their sole responsibility for whatever results. In the face of such a one-sided ideological broadside, it is perhaps not surprising that the Left has tipped things a bit far toward the structural side of the debate over how the world works and what affects individual fates, sometimes losing sight of the individuals in the story.

And there are other possible reasons for left reticence about the personal. The generations embracing personal openness from the 1960s on had a very different life trajectory from the generations that preceded them. The Old Left formed out of the 1930s and 1940s was influenced by an economic insecurity that often exposed the personal lives of individuals to state scrutiny and public shame. A measure of personal privacy for the poor and working class and their ability to avoid the prying eyes of their "betters" — be they the church, community or the state — was itself a great victory that accompanied increased economic opportunities. In this sense, avoiding the personal was a sign of respect.

Another factor influencing the neglect of the personal might be the oppositional stance of the Left itself. Acknowledging the personal draws us into relationships we on the Left might prefer to stand apart from. After all, the Left often rejects the current world and its oppressions and seeks to shape a new one. But we are a part of the current world nonetheless. The "personal" implicates us in the very relations we seek to subvert and overthrow. It raises difficult questions for us as individuals. How far are we personally responsible for sustaining what we oppose? Are we doing enough to challenge and change it? Could or should we do more? The personal goes to the heart of how we cope with the contradictions of acting *in* while still acting *to* change the world, something we might sometimes prefer to ignore. And regularly someone or something comes along to call into question the trade-offs we have accepted or normalized. This is not just "touchy feely" stuff. Battles over the personal have arguably been defining moments for many in their engagement with the Left, pushing some middle-class activists back to the more comfortable spaces of their privilege, or encouraging reaction from a working class that feels personally threatened while lacking the space or privilege to explore those feelings. On the other hand, for others, personal encounters, challenges and conflicts have politicized them, pushed them in more radical directions, and moved them to action and personal sacrifice.

Ironically, as a magazine *Canadian Dimension* itself was designed to hook readers with a strong personal appeal — in this case, the individual reader's sense of what it meant to be Canadian. Though "Canadian" is clearly a collective noun, it is experienced and given meaning by individuals. In a magazine that argued that a Canadian dimension to politics was important to the Left and to the North American experience (e.g., we're not Americans), readers were encouraged to see their personal experiences and understanding of the world as related to this larger political project. Arguably, Canadian national identity-making as a left project was the dominant "personal" theme of magazine's first decade. Later what was considered personal would expand considerably. Why did *CD* take up the personal dimension as it did over the past fifty years? It was probably due to the particular configuration of the magazine's editorial board at any given time, the initiatives of particular individuals, the larger flow of events (e.g., the women's movement, gay marriage), or simply randomness. As will be shown, there was little personal terrain that was actively ignored by *CD*. If the magazine failed, it was more in terms of its depth of coverage, which perhaps was not surprising for a magazine primarily devoted to political economy.

Over fifty years, *CD* has explored the personal dimension in a number of ways. Different articles have attempted to analyze how people experience oppression/inequality on a personal level, or critiqued bad social theories that purport to explain personal behaviour, or explored the personal angle in popular culture like movies, music and books. Different contributors have attempted to relate the personal experiences of different identities: gender, race, sexuality; or the magazine has featured people recounting their own personal experiences of something. As a fetish of "personal empowerment" arose in the 1970s and 1980s, *CD* writers critically assessed the counterculture, psychology and alternative lifestyle fads. And throughout this period, *CD* featured biographies of international leftists, obituaries of key Canadian activists and testimonial accounts from people about their efforts to make the world a better place. The personal dimension has also had its share of heated debate, particularly where some might transgress accepted left opinion or the goals of different movements collided (e.g., the women's and sexual liberation movements). These changes will be explored in four distinct, though sometimes overlapping, periods of the personal dimension in *CD*.

Introducing the personal — 1963–73

CD first got personal in 1968 with "Reflections on a Proletarian Puberty or A North End Place in the Sun" (5:4, April/May), a humorous poke at the gaps between left principle and practice from journalist Larry Zolf. By his recollection of Winnipeg's North End, Zolf faced all the usual oppressors: sadistic teachers, slum landlords, oppressive bosses, etc. But his real problem was that there was no one to champion his cause against them because they were all card-carrying socialists of one hue or another. Though he regarded himself a man of the Left, Zolf got off some good lines about left hypocrisy:

> . . . *never trust a man who's a socialist in principle and a capitalist in practice because his hypocrisy will do you in. Never trust a man whose doctrinal purity is more important than the people around him whom it may affect. Never trust a man who has absolute truth because you and he will have absolutely nothing to talk about . . . Never trust a man who proposes overall solutions for the needy but never feels the need to meet, talk and live with them . . .*

Zolf's humorous self-reflection would prove to be an exception in *CD*. As a rule, the personal dimension was seldom funny.

More typically, *CD* began its exploration of the personal dimension in the late 1960s and early 1970s sociologically from the perspective of the omniscient observer, analyzing how social problems manifest in personal lives, or reviewing academic or popular works on personal issues, or reporting on events that touched on the personal aspects of lives. Over time *CD*'s explorations of the personal would shift to a more first-person perspective, with contributors drawing from their own stories or experiences, through columns, interviews, biography and obituaries, though examples were few in this early period.

An early example of this sociological approach can be found in Nancy Lubka's "The Ins and Outs of Women's Liberation" (7:1-2, June/July 1970), a fairly straightforward introduction to the late 1960s feminist movement and its rationale, goals and divisions, including an analysis of the differences between middle- and working-class women, and the key role of students in challenging male dominance in the new Left. A similar "overview" approach can also be found in Lysiane Gagnon's "Growing Up Poor in Quebec" (7:5, December 1970), which introduced readers to the stark economic inequality between French and English within Quebec, Evelyn Shapiro's exposure of the poor treatment of Winnipeg's elderly in her review of Simone de Beauvoir's *Coming of Age* (9:6, July 1973) and Paul Delaney's reviews of various books grappling with sexual liberation (8:3, November 1971; 9:2-3, January 1973). Despite its seemingly glib title, in "Jocks of the World Unite! Jocks Lib, USA" (7:7, January/February 1971), Bruce Kidd shed a serious light on what little power amateur athletes had (and still have) in American college athletic programs, and how they were often subject to macho, mean-spirited coaches and program administrators who could destroy both their potential professional careers and their health.

In addition to promoting new ways of seeing personal life, *CD* expended considerable energy debunking what it saw as biased treatments of these issues as well as the many fads and pseudoscientific theories that emerged in this period purporting to explain individual behaviour. In 1968 Myrna Wood wrote a long letter to *CD* that contained an incisive class analysis of the limits of then recent reforms relating to birth control (5:5, June/July 1968). She argued that, despite the reforms, poor and working-class women would still have limited access to birth control and even less to abortion because of the class and gender dynamics that exist between upper-middle–class male doctors and their female working-class and poor patients. But, for Wood, the problem wasn't merely one of doctors and patients, it extended to the state, which kept women ignorant about their bodies and failed to pursue research relevant to women's health. Later Jackie Larkin would expand on this critique in her assessment of the 1970 Status of Women Report (7:7, January/February 1971). Larkin argued that the report basically called for more opportunities for women to be like men, rather than talking about fundamentally reorganizing society.

As more and more women demanded equality in late 1960s, popular culture theorizing about the "nature" of human societies increased. With hindsight, the relationship between the two seems pretty obvious. As women challenged their traditional social role, various kinds of "science" (always authored by men) purported to find evidence that traditional gender roles were "natural." A host of books emerged — Desmond Morris's The Naked Ape, Konrad Lorenz's On Aggression — arguing that male dominance and female submission were genetically reproduced through a long period of evolution and could not — indeed, should not — be altered. A number of CD contributors weighed in, exposing the thinly-veiled sexism masquerading as science.[1]

A more difficult critical project involved how to respond to the emerging counterculture movement of the late 1960s. In "Yippies: Defining a Revolutionary Life Style" (7:3, August/September 1970), David Lewis Stein reported on his time with the group, attempting to capture the spontaneity of its activities, its lack of formal structure, and its roots in mind-altering drugs and "feelings" rather than reason. Though sympathetic to their efforts to unify all the political outsiders at the time — blacks, women, drug users, sex radicals — he ultimately judged their efforts a failure. He concluded that the Yippies were allies to radicals in Canada but could not be our leaders — our context was just too different. Irwin Silber was less generous. While allowing that a genuine counterculture had emerged, and that it was challenging previously dominant assumptions about right and wrong, good and bad, and what constituted the "good life," Silber complained that the counter culture was often apolitical or antipolitical, dismissive of the welfare-state gains made by previous progressive movements, and not necessarily anticapitalist (7:3, August/September 1970). In the end he judged the counterculture to be largely a middle-class event, appealing to their class privilege and experience. Specifically he highlighted a number of its more problematic themes: hyperindividualism, mysticism, diversions (like drugs), escapist utopianism, selling the revolution and an indifference to state institutions that working-class people still needed. Silber's analysis would prove astute on most counts, particularly into the 1970s. But his inclusion of sexual liberation and sensitivity training as distractions to the Left indicated a gulf between old and new Left that would require much more work to bridge.

More positive yet still critical assessments of counterculture experimentation also appeared in *CD*. In "Whither Commune-Ism?" (7:3, August/ September 1970), Al Finkel wrote about the decline of a housing commune in Regina, highlighting the challenges of communal living; e.g., cash flow problems, waxing and waning member enthusiasms, personality conflicts, etc. But unlike Silber, Finkel distinguished between hippies and communards, suggesting that the former were prepared to "live and let live" with capitalism while the latter wanted to create something different. Yet, as members related to Finkel, trying to living cooperatively in a capitalist society proved very difficult to do even with the best intentions. Instead of challenging the routinized mode of living they associated with capitalism, the amount of work involved in just keeping the commune going created its own form of routinized living.

Drug experimentation also received some positive coverage in *CD* in the early 1970s. June Callwood wrote an editorial for the magazine in 1970 endorsing the recommendations of the LeDain Commission, which had called for an end to treating drug use as a crime (7:3, August/ September 1970). Entitled "The Right to Own Yourself," Callwood questioned whether we needed the state to protect us from our choices around drugs. Later, Gad Horowitz (writing under the name L.S. Drey) recounted his own experimentation with mind-altering drugs in "Psychedelic Experiences I Have Known" (8:6, March/April 1972), arguing that such drugs basically break down socially and psychologically constructed rules of behaviour and social interaction. Curiously, given the times, the piece managed to be neither pro- nor anti-drug in that it did not promote drugs as *the* answer or a danger. Instead Horowitz saw them as a window into what he was really fascinated with, which was how our conscious and subconscious interact, in some ways to help us cope, but in others to limit our understanding/acceptance of ourselves. In the end, he seemed to suggest that we could learn a lot about ourselves through/with drugs, but to do so would require critically examining the experiences, rather than just "blowing our minds."

Horowitz's contribution is notable for a few other reasons. Though Stein's piece on the Yippies also drew from his personal experience rather than invoking an omniscient sociological perspective, Horowitz's examination of his drug use revealed a personal dimension not previously seen in *CD*: feelings. Horowitz talked about how the drugs made him feel, even how they sometimes made him feel uncomfortable. His piece was also remarkable for its unforced humour. In discussing how people often speak in code, unconsciously referring to something else, he used this example:

> Here is a fictional example of code: Pierre and Margaret
> Trudeau are at a cocktail party. They are in conversation
> with a guest who slips into his patter a remark about having
> read in the newspaper the story of a young girl of twenty
> who was locked up with aged degenerates in the back ward
> of an insane asylum. Now what could he have meant by
> that? Pierre, being cool, would receive the message, but
> give none in return. Or would there be some karate? (8:6,
> March/April 1972).

By the end of this early period of the personal dimension, *CD* embarked on the biographical approach to the personal it would rely on heavily in the future, though with just two examples here. In "N. Bethune: National Hero" (9:5, May 1973), David Frank set out how the Chinese had to teach Canadian officialdom about why Bethune is revered abroad but not at home. In "Canadian Workers: A Message from Kent Rowley" (9:4, March 1973), the longtime labour activist recounted his life experience from the 1930s on working in so-called "international" unions controlled by their Cold War American counterparts, particularly how US unionists aided American foreign policy and helped squelch labour militancy at home and abroad. Here the personal is marshalled to make the case for Canadian-controlled unions and separation from the American-controlled "internationals."

Reckoning with the personal — 1973–83

Up to 1973 the personal dimension, to the extent it showed up in *CD*, appeared as a special focus, as an "added feature" to what might be characterized as the real stuff of the magazine: political events, political economy, organizing, etc. From 1973 on, various writers attempted to grapple with how best to integrate the personal into the political itself, not as a side issue or afterthought, but as an integral part of political work. Debate over what would become known as "identity politics" emerged in this period, fuelled by the women's movement and surprising degree of attention to sexuality. The personal really does become political in the 1970s for *CD*, but in a host of (sometimes contradictory) ways.

The dividing line was a brilliant essay by Sue Negrin, "Begin at Start: Some Thoughts on Personal Liberation" (9:4, March 1973). Negrin argued that personal liberation and social change were inextricably linked: dropping out to find yourself wasn't really an option, nor was burying yourself in some future-oriented revolutionary cause. Instead, she made the case that we need to find the balance between being in the present, engaged in our own personal oppression/liberation, without losing connection to the larger social world and struggles. But what made Negrin's case so compelling was the personal voice she used. Unlike so many previous analyses that touched on the "personal" she spoke from her own personal experience as mother, a spouse and an activist, rather than from some kind of omniscient and "objective" left perspective. In various sections of a long essay, Negrin highlighted the complexity of personal bonds, the shaping role of relations of dependency and domination, and how we are implicated in both. Negrin noted how as a wife she was dependent on her husband, while as a mother her children were dependent on her. In saying this, she was not saying that there is no difference between oppressor and oppressed. Instead she claimed:

> I'm just replacing melodramatic simplicity (whether the
> mustachioed landlord or capitalist pig) with the more difficult
> conflict and contradictions of reality. Because it is these
> that we really have to comprehend if we're going to be free.

No more simple good and evil — we are all bad guys (9:4, March 1973).

In other words, if we don't change ourselves, our efforts to change to world will simply reproduce the domination we have internationalized. Yet Negrin was not merely arguing that the personal is political, she was also arguing the opposite. As such she challenged the idea that one can simply explore personal consciousness on one's own, divorced from social reality; an approach she argued would lead to alienation and isolation. Instead she argued that:

> *the political is personal — because all the consciousness in the world, if not used toward social change, isn't enough to bring about personal change.*

Yet Negrin was not unaware of how difficult this work is, and how much the Left had been flailing in its efforts to respond. Her critique was both prescient and unstinting, and sadly would remain relevant for decades to come. The Left, she complained, tended to subdue the personal under a schematic grid that crowded out how complex people are and could produce totalitarian results. In her opinion, in practice, too much of the new Left of her day was an "in crowd" that spoke in code, seemingly leaving their personal selves at the door of any event, and unable to communicate with others who were not up on the code:

> *This aloofness from the real world has also contributed to a dangerous sense of omniscience. The tyranny of virtue of the New Left makes Robespierre pale by comparison — little judges of correct revolutionary behaviour.*

Still, writing at a point where the debate over "dropping out" versus "joining in" was raging, Negrin had seen both sides and tried to argue for a new way of seeing the dispute:

> *When I first conceived of this [article], I was mostly*

thinking in terms of the necessity for personal solutions. I
was reacting to the gung-ho Movement days of "collectives"
and "masses" and political "organizing," of scorn for
individual needs. But now after being away from organized
politics and the emotional density of the city, I find that
the dangers of the personal solution are much more on my
mind.

In other words, the need for individual autonomy should not give way
to atomization.

In the end, Negrin argued that personal work required "context, validation, group energy." Though uncomfortable with a term like "social structure," she admitted that something like it clearly exists and should exist
to give individuals a social context, something that is simultaneously
enabling, restricting, and freeing. As she said:

With no cultural base, I'm a faceless tourist shopping
for souvenirs, atomized, "unique" to the point of social
extinction. Only with an organic relationship to a vital
society, can I develop true individuality (autonomy).

Though Negrin effectively named the problem, *CD* writers would continue to struggle about how to effect the balance and integrate their personal and political commitments. Jim Harding was clearly struggling with
this issue as he followed R.D. Laing's mid-1970s Canadian tour (10:2,
June 1974). Impressed with what he'd read of Laing's radical psychology,
his encounters with Laing and his followers were disillusioning, leaving
Harding to vacillate between arguing for the need for engagement on
an individual level while also offering a critique of its limits. Later Cliff
Andrew would go undercover for *CD* with "Come Alive" (15:5, April
1981), one of the many pseudo-psychology group-therapy sessions that
flourished in the late 1970s and early 1980s, offering even more pointed
criticism of the seemingly expanding market for "personal empowerment." Andrew attended a day-long session with others he characterized
as an alienated middle class looking for a "meaningful experience [as

a] highly individualistic, inward-turning self seeking [and] self discovery." Besides recounting the manipulative techniques deployed by the facilitators to influence people, Andrew complained that such "personal development centres" stressed the individual's personal responsibility for both their problems and their solutions. Here *CD* highlighted how the personal dimension could be exploited for profit and cast as a very reactionary space.

More positively, *CD* ran a number of stories where writers explored how their personal experiences radicalized them or awoke in them a new appreciation of the need to "get personal." Bruce Kidd had long written for *CD* on sports matters but in 1977 delved into his own personal story in "Left Runner" (12:4-5, September 1977). Kidd had been a national Canadian track and field star in the 1960s, lauded by social and media elites. But when he used a public speech to touch on some of the systematic problems with amateur sport, specifically how it operated and the pressure it put on young athletes, the reaction was swift and blunt: "my status as a golden haired boy changed overnight." Kidd's fall from elite grace forced him to ask some tough questions, eventually radicalizing his understanding of the link between sport, commercialization and capitalism. Pat Smart was brought up short by a different kind of shock: the sudden death by suicide of Waffle activist Krista Maeots (13:5, January/February 1979). Smart wondered how it was possible to know so much about some people, to be so involved in activism with them, but not be aware, as in the case of Maeots, of the enormous personal pain and suffering that they were going through. Smart lamented how people, herself included, could get caught up in the activity, the divisions and disagreements, and somehow lose track of the individual people.

A great deal of *CD*'s personal self-reflection in the 1970s was driven by the activism of the women's movement. Contributors took on women's erotic art (11:4, March 1976), the lack of family law reform (12:4-5, September 1977), and the shifting representations of women in popular culture, particularly movies (14:6, May 1980). Tanya Lester gave these concerns concrete expression in her article "Growing Up Female: The High School Woman's Career" (14:6, May 1980). She recounted from her own experience how young women in high school were steered toward marriage and away from a career in a host of subtle and not-so-subtle ways. While she supported what the women's movement was doing generally, she argued that they needed to place more emphasis on younger women, specifically to make more resources and support available to them in high school.

More attention to women in CD eventually brought the conversation back to men, in contradictory and controversial ways. In "Why Men Don't Raise Children" Michael Welton offered a fairly straightforward critique of the conventional breakdown of parenting roles in the nuclear family; e.g., how men's work is valued while women's work is not, along with some suggestions for how this might be challenged (12:3, July 1977). What emerged from all this was a sense that men had a great deal of personal work to do in terms of understanding why they acted as they did. Yet as Welton himself later noted in a review essay of various books on "male liberation," not everyone saw an increasing focus on male self-reflection as positive (13:6, March 1979). Indeed, some feminists argued that this once again turned attention back to men at the expense of women. Ultimately Welton was not convinced by the critics, responding that men couldn't wait until male/female equality was achieved to start addressing their feelings and reaching out to others. Of course, the two goals were not mutually exclusive and CD kept up both foci. Later in 1979 Welton would critically review the pornographic magazine *Swank*, what he thought it said about the men who purchased it and the society that condoned it (14:1, July/August 1979), while in 1980 Jonathan Barker reported on the progress of a men's group that met biweekly to explore their emotions and issues men didn't typically deal with (14:6, May 1980).

Another personal arena given space in CD was sexuality, specifically the emerging gay and lesbian movement and its struggle for basic civil rights. CD's positive coverage of this issue in the early 1980s was laudable, given the movement's marginalization from mainstream society and the social democratic left at the time. However, CDs first foray involved a book review of interviews with gays and lesbians in 1974. Reviewers Dick Held and Mike Hunt (in retrospect, clearly naughty pseudonyms) complained that the book exploited its subjects, over-focusing on their looks and demeanor and suggesting that to be gay means one can be nothing else (10:1, April 1974). The reviewers, themselves gay and a couple, preferred to see gay sex as an activity rather than an identity. However, they recognized that those interviewed liked their "labels and boxes" and admitted that this was understandable as a strategy to create a group identity and give people on the outs a sense of belonging. After that, the issue disappeared until 1980 when Robin Metcalfe wrote to ask why *CD* wasn't showing more support for the emerging gay and lesbian movement (14:4-5, February/March 1980). A response wasn't long in coming.

In June 1980 Brian Mossop told a very personal story of becoming a gay activist in "Confessions of a Commie Fag" (14:7, June 1980). After joining the Communist party in 1967, and coming out as gay in 1974, Mossop eventually dedicated more and more of his activism to gay liberation, a choice that eventually led to his expulsion from the CP. For Mossop, being gay was less an identity than a new way of living. As he put it, to come out meant you would never marry, never have kids, never be part of a conventional family. In response, gays and lesbians created a self-chosen community of social support, divorced from the nuclear family model. If gays and lesbians could do it, he asked, why couldn't everyone else? His point was that the Left tended to see gay rights as a civil-rights issue. But politically Mossop thought gays represented a challenge to our whole way of living, one the Left should take seriously. Later Mariana Valverde would make this challenge more explicit in "Heterosexism: A Challenge to the Left" (17:1, March 1983). Mossop returned to the pages of *CD* with Ken Poppert to explain how the Toronto bathhouse raids of 1979 and 1981 radicalized a large group of gays and lesbians, sending hundreds into the streets to violently confront the police, after community efforts to gain redress through conventional political channels failed (15:8/16:1, December 1981). Mossop also explained in very plain and non-sensational terms how a gay bathhouse operated and the code of conduct typically observed by the patrons (15:8/16:1, December 1981).

CD continued in this period to highlight the personal impact of political events and decisions: the use of drugs to pacify the elderly (15:7, August/September 1981), the impact of stress on workers (14:7, June 1980), the historic wrongs inflicted on different groups of immigrants

(14:7, June 1980) and the alienation of those no longer needed in the workforce (15:7, August/September). In one special issue, a number of contributors focused on the problem of class identity (17:1, March 1983), the lack of working-class culture (17:4, September 1983), and the hidden injuries of class (17:1, March 1983). And the personal stories were gripping and inspirational, ranging from the experience of a woman escaping torture in post-coup Chile (14:4-5, February/March 1980), to the unusual career path of working-class cartoonist Roy Careless (15:8, December 1981), to the assassination of third-world liberationist Walter Rodney (14:8, August 1980), to the curious experience of a child whose communist father turned out to be a spy for the RCMP (12:4-5, September 1977). And yet, for some inexplicable reason, the personal dimension in CD faded as the 1980s advanced. From 1984 to 1986, only one personal contribution was made: Errol Black's idyllic recollection of childhood in his "The River, Growing Up by the Assiniboine" (20:7, December/January 1986–87).

Negotiating the boundaries of the personal — 1987–2004

From the late 1980s to the new millennium the personal dimension became an increasingly politicized space. Sex and gender would dominate discussions of personal behaviour and many contributors would struggle to remake themselves in light of feminist and other critiques. But negotiating the boundaries of this new personhood would prove more difficult than social critics and even earnest activists would have imagined. Contributors to CD would come back to this theme again and again — how do we become different men and women? Male violence, remaking heterosexual sex, and the continuing pressures on women were key themes in this period, with important contributions from Gad Horowitz, Roberta Hamilton and Brenda Austin-Smith. The period also witnessed a significant increase in personal stories, testimony from individuals about how they tried to grapple with these challenges and contradictions.

Not surprisingly, given the previous two decades of feminist critique, the question of appropriate and inappropriate gender roles continued to dominate discussion of the personal dimension in CD, with a number of contributors attempting to get at the roots of negative male behaviour. In "Socialist Sexuality: Male Reflections on the Roots of Pornography" (23:4, June 1989), Brian Murphy argued that male self-hate was at the root of male violence toward others and society's intolerance of sexual diversity. Men needed to engage in "relentless self examination and candid revelation" and remake the act of sex altogether. Even progressive men harboured anti-women views in some ways, according to Murphy, because of their conventional male socialization. John Stoltenberg echoed these themes in "How Men Have (a) Sex" arguing that a dominating male identity and male sexual practices were inextricably linked (25:1, January/February 1991). Vic Seidler put it a bit differently in "Redefining Masculinity" when he talked about how men perform masculinity, specifically by denying fear and not sharing their intimate selves (25:8, December 1991). Editorials and book review choices in this period also reflected this theme of male violence and male identity (26:2, March 1992; Editorial, "Rooting Out Male Violence," March 1992; 27:2, March/April 1993).

Not everyone signed on to the male identity equals domination equation. Ulli Diemer argued in "Dances with Guilt" that the indiscriminate use of collective guilt against men would be counterproductive, specifically suggesting that the broad claims being made that all men were violent would actually prevent effective action on male violence (26:1, January/February 1992). Steve Maynard delved into some of these complications in his review of *Male Order: Unwrapping Masculinity*, from the emerging field of gender studies (24:7, October 1990). Mark Etkin wrote about how a specific group of men in Winnipeg were trying to address these issues more concretely through weekly encounter sessions in "The Men's Movement" (25:1, January/February 1991). And changes in women's gender behaviour came under scrutiny as well in Charlynn Toews's "Why Women Smoke," where she reviewed the research on how changing gender expectations were contributing to greater stress for women and increases in female smoking rates (25:1, January/February 1991).

CD writers also explored emotional and sexual relationships, particularly aspects thought to be taboo. Roberta Hamilton wondered why there was such a scarcity of caring in capitalist society, specifically linking traditional possessive heterosexual monogamy to a constructed scarcity in love (23:2, March 1989). Later Hamilton would provide answers from her own experience in a remarkably candid exposition of her inability to sustain an open relationship (25:7, October/November 1991). It was one thing to theorize new kinds of relationships, it was another to act on them. CD also featured a fascinating exchange amongst readers about some of their "unprogressive" sexual desires. "Anonymous" wrote a long letter detailing "The Erotic Power of Patriarchal Fantasies," in his case involving submission/dominance role-playing (24:6, September 1990). Anonymous went to great lengths to assure readers of his commitment to women's liberation yet he remained "turned on" by pretending to dominate them sexually. And though he underlined how he and his female partner acted on these desires under strict rules and regularly discussed how they felt about it, the topic was clearly out of sync with a great deal of popular feminism. Later a "Woman from Toronto" wrote to defend sex-fantasy role-playing but complained that she couldn't talk about it with her feminist friends because of what she called their "puritanical streak" (25:4, June 1991).

Reconciling thought with deeds, aspirations with desires, new goals with old learned behaviours — this would increasingly become the project of the 1990s. To somehow capture the complexity of the whole person that was enmeshed in capitalist social relations, with its attendant patriarchal, racialist, heterosexist, etc., residues, was a huge challenge. Just fashioning a new set of prescriptive behaviours didn't appear to be working — personal change was harder than that. And different movements disagreed about just what the goals of liberation should be, particularly the women's movement and the emerging sexuality liberation groups. For CD, the floodgates had been opened by the introduction of an unusual and innovative advice column in 1987, authored by University of Toronto political philosophy professor Gad Horowitz. "Personal/Political" was unlike anything CD, or arguably any left magazine, had done before, and it generated both support and condemnation precisely because it openly addressed these emerging tensions about just how to individually navigate through the politics of personhood in a progressive way.

Gad's column was an unusual move for *CD*. Left magazines didn't typically offer personal "advice" — that was stuff of mainstream magazines and newspapers and their obsession with the individual and individual problem-solving. But by the mid to late 1980s the Left had been infused with enough "personal empowerment" and "holistic thinking" that some kind of serious alternative to "Dear Abby" seemed appropriate. The column itself was also unique: Gad made up all the letters based on a therapy practice he had established in Toronto and then answered them in his own direct and engaging style. Wherever the Left seemed unwilling to go, Gad went there. Basically, he used his fictionalized letters to give voice to the anxieties many progressives were feeling on an individual level: being too wealthy to be on the left, straight-male negotiations of sex with women, worries about not making an original contribution with graduate work, suppressed feelings of "not-niceness," uneasiness with a lesbian partner's interest in dominance/submission sex-role fantasies, spending too much time with books, boredom with family home life, etc. Gad's responses drew from critical academic work in sociology and psychology, radical approaches to psychotherapy and psychoanalysis, as well as his own broad experience of life as well as his therapy practice. Often his responses did not go where his progressive audience expected. He told "wealthy" to get a sense of humour, and "straight male" to forget feeling guilty for the sins of other men (21:6, October 1987). He told "graduate" that no one is really that original — we all build on collective knowledge (21:7, November/ December 1987). He told "not nice" that it was okay to feel that way sometimes (21:8, January 1988). And he told "lesbian partner" that she should engage her lover about her desires, rather than just dismissing them (22:3, May 1988). He counseled "books" and "boredom" to break with their dependent relationships, to get out of their heads and into their bodies more often (22:1, February 1988; 22:6, September 1988).

Gad's columns sparked controversy amongst letter-writers and *CD*'s editorial committee, particularly for his advice aimed at women, leading to a special board meeting to discuss the concerns of female members of the collective. In a published report of the meeting in the March 1989 issue of *CD*, the concerns basically amounted to different readings of the letters and the perception that Gad was "flippant, condescending and even defensive" in response to his critics, several of whom took *Dimension* to task for engaging Gad to undertake an advice column as it pertained to women, questioning his ability as a male to understand the context of women's reality. But in reading Gad's columns and his responses to critics one sees that he usually admitted that the situations he created in his letters were open to multiple readings and many possible responses. Yet he also stood his ground in suggesting that an individual negotiation of the world was much more complex than simply taking a position on an issue. And Gad *was* cheeky. His column "The Canadian Multi-Dimensional Questionnaire" was actually a very funny and challenging essay on gender and sexuality, dressed up as a reader survey (22:4, June 1988). From his early explorations of psychedelic drugs, to his advice column, to his long-running Horowitz paragraph, Gad has continually popped up in *CD* like a trickster, tweaking accepted views and transgressing recognized boundaries.

The special meeting came to no conclusion about what to do with Gad's column. Coincidentally at the same time Gad informed *CD* that he did not have time to continue with it. But the end of the advice column did not stem the flow of the issues it had opened up. In truth, Gad was only giving voice to a widespread reexamination of the role of subjectivity across the left. Roberta Hamilton addressed this in "Left Personal Dilemmas," arguing that how people feel about themselves is important, that personal dilemmas should be taken more seriously by a Left that claimed it wanted a more caring society (23:2, March 1989). She suggested the need for a language that could more easily move between class analysis and emotions, from an abstract, huge capitalist totality to the personal and intimate perceptions of an individual. Without this focus, she argued, the Left would never understand why so many individuals might react to change by simply protecting what was most immediate to them. Brenda Austin-Smith weighed in on the debate in "The Uses of Subjectivity," nicely summing the traditional left concerns with individualism and subjectivity but noting that the recent challenges of identity politics could not be ignored (27:3, May/June 1993). Her key concern was the danger of treating subjectivity as a kind of private property. The challenge, she argued, was to utilize this rich resource of difference without giving up on collective action.

Austin-Smith and others would take up the challenge of combining subjectivity and collective action in a series of interviews with activists about the difficulties they faced in doing their work. In "Taking Politics Seriously" and "Coping with an Activist Life," Austin-Smith interviewed people about the toll that their political work had taken on their personal lives and relationships (27:4, August 1993, 27:5, September/ October 1993). In "Feminist Mothers, Feminist Daughters" a number of women interviewed each other about how they had influenced the young women in their lives (28:1, January/February 1994). More personal testimony from different people about their life and left experiences began appearing in *CD* at this point. Contributions ranged from "Hannah"'s harrowing story of her own long-term sexual abuse by an uncle (24:8, November/December 1990); to David Ellis's moving discussion of the social pressures that led his father to live his life in the closet (28:5, October/November 1994); to Lori Vitale Cox's inspiring account of her grandma's life and radicalism and how it influenced her to join the Left (30:3, May/June 1996); to Brenda Austin-Smith's personal experience with a miscarriage and her frustration with the social silence surrounding it, due to what she called the "ideology of pregnancy" (32:3, May/June 1998); to Lennox Farrell's story of coming to Canada and battles with racial profiling (34:4, July 2000). This period also witnessed one of the rare ruminations in *CD* on personal spirituality where Margaret Adair, citing no less a figure than Marx, argued that a spiritual commitment can help ground people and better connect with others (26:2, March 1992).

Death seemed an increasing occasion to reflect on the personal in the magazine, perhaps reflecting the aging of *CD*'s first generation of contributors. Obituaries appeared for international leftists like C.L.R. James, I.F. Stone, Ralph Miliband, Rudolph Bahro and Paul Sweezy (23:5, July/ August 1989; 23:6, September 1989; 35:3, May 2001), as well as Canadian progressives like Mary Pitawanakwat, P.K. Nambiar, Claire Culhane, Alf Jackson, Glen Makahonouk, Pat McEvoy, Stanley Ryerson and Jack Scott (29:5, Oct/November 1995; 30:2, April 1996; 30:6, November/December 1996; 32:1, January/February 1998; 32:2, March/April 1998; 32:3, May/ June 1998; 32:4, July/August 1998; 35:2, March 2001).

The age of storytelling — 2004–present

The personal dimension faded out briefly as *CD* entered the new millennium only to return strongly by mid-decade. Perhaps unwilling to wait for radicals to die before honouring them, *CD* began featuring biographical pieces of longtime leftists who were nonetheless still active, as well as autobiographical accounts of left artists, academics and movement organizers. The new century also witnessed *CD* writers still grappling with the complexity of identity and its contradictions.

The personal, autobiographical accounts covered a range of experience, from "Judy"'s involvement with a squat in Vancouver, to Susan Thompson's explanation of how she became a left Canadian nationalist, to Varda Burstyn's gripping account of her radicalization living in Chicago in 1967–68, to Melissa Gibson's account of "Growing into Filipino" and how it helped her understand the politics of migration between Canada and the Philippines (38:1, January/February 2004; 39:1, January/February 2005; 39:2, March/April 2005; 40:2, March/April 2006). A special issue dedicated to art and culture featured biographies and examples of work by Shirley Bear, Rick Slye and others (41:4, July/August 2007). Academics like Peter Kulchyski, Bryan Palmer, Mel Watkins, Taiaiake Alfred and Joseph Roberts shared their stories about becoming politically aware and how it influenced their research and activism (39:3, May/June 2005; 39:5, September/October 2005; 40:6, November/December 2006; 41:1, January/February 2007; 41:3, May/June 2007). Other academics, activists and political figures — Jack Warnock, Francoise David and Roland Penner — were featured in biographical, autobiographical or review pieces (39:6, November/December 2005; 41:2, March/April 2007; 43:1, January/February 2009). Death also spurred a lot of story-telling, with obits covering Bernelda Wheeler, James Grafff, Betty Mardiros, June Callwood, David Brophy, Andre Gorz, Jim Littleton, Gil Levine, Robin Wood, David Noble, Ralph Akiwenzie, David Orton and Marion Yeo (39:6, November/December 2005; 40:2, March/April 2006; 41:4, July/August 2007; 41:4, July/August 2007; 41:5, September/October 2007; 42:1, January/February 2008; 43:2, March/April 2009; 44:1, January/February 2010; 44:4, July/August 2010; 45:2, March/April 2011; 45:3, May/June 2011; 45:4, August 2011; 45:6, November/December 2011).

Actual debates over personal identity faded in this most recent period but did not completely disappear. Gay marriage faced a critique from some queer activists that argued that seeking state recognition for queer relationships was conformist and anti-community. In 2004 I entered this debate in "The Freedom to Choose: Gay Marriage and its Radical Other" arguing that "gay" had never been a sutured identity, free from other complicating identity markers (38:1, January/February 2004). In doing so, I drew from my own mixed-up set of identity commitments — working class, male, left wing, gay, etc. — to highlight how something like gay marriage offered a way to bring together all the parts of who I was. Another testament to the complexity of personal identity was Richard Wagamese's "The Night John Lennon Died" (44:1, January/February 2010), where he recounted how a childhood of foster homes meant he had no "Indian heroes" and instead drew his from mainstream society. He recounted how, in his twenties:

> *I was a loner for the most part and music was my constant companion. Along with books there never seemed to be anywhere important to go or anyone important to see. My heroes were on my shelves and they never disappointed me or jilted me in favor of brighter more ebullient companions.*

John Lennon's death in 1980 hit him hard. Despite our labels, or how we appear to others on the outside, there is no accounting for just who might move us in important ways. As Wagamese noted, "John Lennon wasn't Native but he was a tribal person and he was a hero of mine."

Finally, the question of love came in for a humorous and self-deprecating treatment from Peter Kulchyski, who complained that "nothing works." Here, by "works," he was referring to those seeking a neat formula for a successful relationship (46:1, January/February 2012). In his experience, he had seen every kind of combination succeed and fail, and had tried most of them.

Conclusion

It is hard not to see the decline of debate over the personal dimension as some kind of retreat, as if despite all the heart-wrenching debate over years on the issue has somehow fallen away. Are we facing the end of the personal dimension? It is possible that the need to highlight the "personal" may have ebbed for a different reason — it has become more integrated into our general analysis and critique of society, it may be a victim of its own success? And yet there is still more work to do. Ours is still a society that tries to rationalize and compartmentalize human intellect from emotion and feelings. As Marx once noted, capitalism seeks to turn quality into quantity, to convert the unique into something that can easily be exchanged. As such, we will continue to struggle to bring together all the complex parts of our individual selves in a society that would tear them asunder. People telling their stories remind us of that and help us to see openings to do it.

The hard work *CD* and its contributors have done over five decades exploring the personal dimension has been as important as any revolution or specific issue covered by the magazine. The traditional neglect of the personal dimension came at a significant cost for the Left. People are not just ideas and beliefs — they are embodied experiences and feelings too, and those can be difficult to sort out, understand and change. In a telling exchange of views in the August/September 1995 issue of the magazine Colleen Fuller and Elsa Scheider wrestled with the issue of the hurt feelings and counter-hostility that can emerge as people speak from their personal experience of oppression, sometimes implicating those around them as part of their problem. Fuller felt dominant groups had to learn to take the criticism but Scheider felt that responding in such situations was more complicated, clouded by personal experiences and our society's inability to handle conflict productively. Regardless of who was right or wrong, the exchange underlined a real challenge for a Left that wanted to tackle oppression — feelings might get hurt, and that could have consequences for ourselves and our movement.

If the impact of "feeling bad" was underestimated by the Left, then "feeling good" was too often ignored as well. As Roberta Hamilton complained (quoting Sheila Rowbotham) the problem with the Left was the unstated feeling that no one should have any fun (23:2, March 1989). Some efforts to address this have emerged. In 2008 Joyce Green and others organized a musical event to "honour our activists" and "celebrate *Canadian Dimension*" (43:1, January/February 2009). Increasingly, leftists are recognizing that fun, love and celebration should not just be frills, squeezed in when convenient, but essential components of our activist work.

ENDNOTES

CHAPTER 1

1. Daly, Margaret, *The Revolution Game*, New Press, 1970, p. 29.
2. Palmer, Bryan, *Canada's 1960s*, University of Toronto Press, 2009, p. 338.
3. Palmer, Bryan, *Canada's 1960s*, University of Toronto Press, 2009, p. 278.

CHAPTER 2

1. Stanford, Jim. "A Cure for Dutch Disease: Active Sector Strategies for Canada's Economy." Canadian Centre for Policy Alternatives, April 4, 2012. Online: http://www.policyalternatives.ca/publications/reports/cure-dutch-disease.
2. L. Martin, "Rebranding Canada," *Globe and Mail*, October 18, 2011.

CHAPTER 3

1. Denis, Serge. *Le long malentendu: Le Québec vu par les intellectuels progressistes au Canada anglais 1970-1991*. Montréal: Boréal, 1992.
2. Bourque, Gilles. "Between Nations and Society," in Michel Venne (ed.) Vive Québec. Toronto: Lorimer, 2000.

CHAPTER 4

1. Robertson, Heather. *Reservations are for Indians*. Toronto: J. Lewis & Samuel, 1970.
2. Cardinal, Harold. *The Unjust Society: The Tragedy of Canada's Indians*. Edmonton: M.G. Hurtig Ltd., 1969.
3. Cumming, Peter A., and Neil H. Mickenberg, Eds. *Native Rights in Canada*. Toronto: Indian and Eskimo Association of Canada, 1972.
4. Berger, Thomas R. *Northern Frontier, Northern Homeland*, Vol. II. Ottawa: Supply and Services Canada, 1977.
5. National Indian Brotherhood. *Indian Control of Indian Education*. Ottawa: National Indian Brotherhood, 1972.
6. Nielsen, Erik (Chair). *Report of the Ministerial Task Force on Program Review*. Ottawa: Supply and Services Canada, 1986.
7. Knight, Rolf. *Indians at Work: an Informal History of Native Indian Labour in British Columbia, 1858–1930*. Vancouver: New Star Books, 1978.
8. Penner, Keith (Chair). *Report of the Special Committee of Parliament on Indian Self-Government*. Ottawa: Supply and Services Canada, 1983.
9. Royal Commission on Aboriginal Peoples. *Report of the Royal Commission on Aboriginal Peoples*. Ottawa: Indian and Northern Affairs, 1996.

10. Widdowson, Frances, and Albert Howard. *Disrobing the Aboriginal Industry: The Deception Behind Indigenous Cultural Preservation*. Montreal: McGill-Queen's University Press, 2008.

CHAPTER 5

1. The phrase is Don Sullivan's from his piece "Divine Intervention" (28:4, August/September 1994).

2. See her particularly trenchant "Mac-Blo's Tree" (26:3, April/May 1992), for example.

3. Personal communication.

4. For example, "Canada's most censored story," by Tina Harrison, then director of Canadians for the Ethical Treatment of Food Animals, 26:7, October 1992, and more recently Jo-Anne McArthur's photo essay, 48:1, January/February 2014.

5. The phrase is from Ted Benton and Simon Redfearn, "The Politics of Animal Rights—Where Is the Left?" *New Left Review*, p. 215 (January–February 1996), p. 48.

6. Martin Lukacs, "Indigenous rights are the best defence against Canada's resource rush," *The Guardian*, April 26, 2013, http://www.theguardian.com/environment/true-north/2013/apr/26/indigenous-rights-defence-canadas-resource-rush.

7. For *CD*'s coverage, see Dale Stelter, "Lubicons Fight Uphill Battle," 25:2, March 1991.

8. For *CD*'s coverage, see Jenny Wilton and Liam Barrington-Bush, "From Ontario to Oaxaca: How To Kick a Mining Company Out of Your Community," 47:3, May/June 2013.

9. See for example Petr Cizek, "Northern Pipe Dreams, Northern Nightmares," 39:2, March/April 2005.

CHAPTER 6

1. Innis, Harold A. *Essays in Canadian Economic History*. Toronto: University of Toronto Press, 1956.

2. Resnick, Philip. "Canadian Defence Policy and the American Empire." In Ian Lumsden, ed. *Close the 49th Parallel: The Americanization of Canada*. Toronto: University of Toronto Press, 1970.

3. See, for example, Cuff, R.D., and J.L. Granatstein. *Canadian-American Relations in Wartime*. Toronto: Wakkert, 1975. Also Eayrs, James. *In Defence of Canada: Appeasement and Rearmament*. Toronto: University of Toronto Press, 1965.

4. Warnock, John W. *Partner to Behemoth: The Military Policy of a Satellite Canada*. Toronto: New Press, 1970.

5. Aitken, Hugh G.J. 1961. *American Capital and Canadian Resources*. Cambridge: Harvard University Press, 1961.

6. Other important and influential studies included Hugh Aitken et al., *The*

American Economic Impact on Canada (1959), Hugh Aitken's *American Capital and Canadian Resources* (1961), Richard Caves and Richard Holton's *The Canadian Economy* (1961) and the Twentieth Century Fund study, *Canada: An Appraisal of Its Needs and Resources* (1965).

7. Wilson, George W. et al. *Canada: An Appraisal of Its Needs and Resources.* Toronto: University of Toronto Press, New York: Twentieth Century Fund, 1965.

8. See Wilson et al., 1965: pp. 219–46.

9. Warnock, 1970.

CHAPTER 8

1. Labour Canada. 2011. "Union coverage in Canada, 2011." Online: http://www.hrsdc.gc.ca/eng.labour.labour_relations/info_analysis/union_membership/2011/unionmembership2011.shtml#fn2.

CHAPTER 9

1. On the CUCND and SUPA, see Myrna Kostash, *Long Way from Home: The Story of the Sixties Generation in Canada.* Toronto: Lorimer, 1980, 3–30; Doug Owram, *Born at the Right Time: A History of the Baby Boom Generation.* Toronto: University of Toronto Press, 1996, 218–233; Bryan D. Palmer, *Canada's 1960s: The Ironies of Identity in a Rebellious Era.* University of Toronto Press, 256–278, and Michael Maurice Dufresne, "'Let's Not be Cremated Equal': The Combined Universities Campaign for Nuclear Disarmament, 1959–1967," in M. Athena Palaeologu, ed., *The Sixties in Canada: A Turbulent and Creative Decade.* Montreal: Black Rose Books, 2009.

2. Anderson's contributions to the strategy and orientation, largely through *New Left Review*, of the British New Left should not be underestimated; Gerd-Rainer Horn considers him as "perhaps the most important Marxist theoretician to emerge from Britain in the second half of the twentieth century." Gerd-Rainer Horn, *The Spirit of '68: Rebellion in Western Europe and North America, 1956–1978.* Oxford: Oxford University Press, 2007, p. 235.

3. John Cleveland, "'Berkeley North': Why Simon Fraser Had the Strongest 1960s Student Power Movement," in Palaeologu, ed., *The Sixties in Canada*, 203. It is worth noting, of course, that students were drawn to non-campus issues from the outset. See Roberta Lexier, "'The Backdrop Against Which Everything Happened': English-Canadian Student Movements and Off-Campus Movements for Change, *History of Intellectual Culture*, pp. 7, 1 (2007).

4. Barbara Godard, "Quebec, the National Question and English-Canadian Student Activism in the 1960s: The Rise of Student Syndicalism," in Palaeologu, ed., *The Sixties in Canada*, pp. 303–304.

5. Historian Sean Mills sees the events around McGill as reflective of the sentiments and unity of the May–June events in France that grew to challenge the French state. Sean Mills, *The Empire Within: Postcolonial Thought*

and Political Activism in Sixties Montreal. Montreal: McGill-Queen's University Press, 2010, pp. 147–148.

6. For an account of the events in the context of 1960s Montreal see Sean Mills, *The Empire Within,* pp. 104–108.

7. Sheps pointed specifically at the Internationalists, which became the Communist Party of Canada (Marxist-Leninist).

8. This is the conclusion of John Cleveland, "Berkeley North," p. 231.

9. On the SFU events see Cleveland, "Berkeley North," and Hugh Johnston, *Radical Campus: Making Simon Fraser University,* (Vancouver: Douglas & McIntyre, 2005), especially p. 121 (on Yandle), and pp. 293–329 (on the PSA affair). Also see former PSA instructor Mordecai Briemberg's review of *Radical Campus* in *Canadian Dimension,* 40:2, March/April 2006.

10. The work under review was Howard Adelman and Dennis Lee, *The University Game.* Toronto: Anansi, 1968. It included an article by Gonick, "Self-Government in the Multiversity," republished from *Canadian Dimension,* 3:3–4, March/June 1966.

11. Pat Mooney, *Seeds of the Earth: A Private or Public Resource?* Ottawa: Inter Pares for the Canadian Council for International Co-operation, 1979.

12. Krista Maeots, *Ottawa Citizen,* cited by Robin Mathews, "The Americanization of Canadian Universities," *Canadian Dimension,* February, 1969.

13. Robin Mathews and James Steele, eds., *The Struggle for Canadian Universities.* Toronto: New Press, 1969. On Steeles, Mathews and the Canadianization movement see Jeffrey Cormier, *The Canadianization Movement: Emergence, Survival, and Success.* Toronto: University of Toronto Press, 2004.

14. Robert Adolph, "Reflections of a New Canadian Professor," *Canadian Dimension* 7:4, October 1970. The issue of American professors tended to die with the rapid decline in university hiring in the 1970s, as was explained by Antonio R. Gualtieri, "Nationalism and Canadian Graduate Schools," *Canadian Dimension* 10:7, March 1975. Mathews attempted to maintain the campaign, turning his criticisms on those, such as Laxer, who no longer shared his concerns. Robin Mathews, "Intellectual Life in Canada," *Canadian Dimension* 18:5, October/November 1984.

15. Steven High, "More about Youth," *Canadian Dimension* 21:8, January 1988. There was a brief acknowledgement of the student movement in Kevin Dearing's "Students Take on the Corporate Agenda," *Canadian Dimension* 28:5, October/November 1994.

16. This was republished in Adelman and Lee, *The University Game.*

17. See also, Jim Silver and Jeff O'Malley, "The Attack on Higher Education," *Canadian Dimension* 17:2, May 1983.

18. This issue includes articles by Claire Polster, David Noble, Arthur Schafer, Marc Spooner and Tanya Shaw on the consequences of privatizing research

at Canada's universities, as well as case studies on Mansanto by Jim Sanders and on military research by Paul A. Hamel. The article on Monsanto referred to the attempts by the University of Manitoba to censor the film *Seeds of Change*. Further information, as well as the video, is available at http://www.seedsofchangefilm.org. On the "Olivieri Affair" with the company Apotex see the report commissioned by the Canadian University of University Teachers: Jon Thompson, Patricia A. Baird, and Jocelyn Downie, *The Olivieri Report*. Toronto: Lorimer, 2001.

CHAPTER 10

1. Canadian Health Coalition. "Canadians' Views on Public Healthcare Solutions," October 2011. Online: http://healthcoalition.ca/wp-content/uploads/2011/11/NANOS-EN.pdf.

2. Canada. Commission on the Future of Health Care in Canada. "Building on Values: The Future of Health Care in Canada. Online: http://publications.gc.ca/collections/Collection/CP32-85-2002E.pdf.

3. Canada. National Council of Welfare Reports, "The Dollars and Sense of Solving Poverty." Online: http://publications.gc.ca/collections/collection_2011/cnb-ncw/HS54-2-2011-eng.pdf.

4. Wilkinson, R.G, K.E. Pickett *The Spirit Level: Why More Equal Societies Almost Always Do Better*. New York: Penguin Books, 2009.

CHAPTER 11

1. Dauverne, Mia and John Turner, "Police-reported Crime Statistics in Canada, 2009," *Juristat* 30:2 (2010).

2. Garland, David. *The Culture of Control: Crime and Social Order in Contemporary Society*. Chicago: University of Chicago Press, 2001. Hannah-Moffat, Kelly, "Prisons that Empower: Neo-liberal Governance in Canadian Women's Prisons," *The British Journal of Criminology* 40, 2000, pp. 510–551. O'Malley, Pat, "Volatile and Contradictory Punishment," *Theoretical Criminology* 3, 1999, pp. 175–196.

CHAPTER 12

1. The magazine's closest ideological partners being sixties New Left and counterculture publications like *Ramparts, Root and Branch* and *The Berkeley Barb*.

2. See Frantz Fanon, *The Wretched of the Earth*. New York: Grove Press, 1963.

3. Immanuel Wallerstein, Giovanni Arrighi and Terence K. Hopkins, *Anti-Systemic Movements*. London: Verso Books, 2012.

4. For a full explanation of wage differentials between white and racialized Canadians, including income levels for new and second-generation immigrations, see Grace-Edward Galabuzi and Sheila Block, "Canada's Colour Coded Labour Market: The Gap for Racialized Workers," Canadian

Centre For Policy Alternatives, March 2011.

CHAPTER 13

1. Petras, "Revolution and Guerilla Movements in Latin America," 4:2, January/February 1967.

2. Yves Engler, "The Politics of Money: Haiti and the Left," 39:6, November/December 2005, and "Haiti — the Job of Nations," 44:2, March/April 2010.

3. David Camfield, "Bleeding Afghanistan," 41:2, March/April 2007, Arundhatii Roy, "Guerrilla Regeneration," 44:4, July/August 2010, and Dhruv Jain, "A New Spring Thunder Over India," 44:4, July/August 2010.

4. Jerome Klassen, "Canada, Globalization, Imperialism: Rethinking Canada's Role in a Neo-Liberal World." York University, PhD Diss., 2007, and Todd Gordon, *Imperialist Canada*. Winnipeg: Arbeiter Ring Publishing, 2010.

CHAPTER 14

1. Among several others currently advancing this discussion are the following: Abunimah, Ali. *One Country*. New York: Metropolitan Books, 2006; Pappe, Ilan, "Blueprint for a one state movement: a troubled history" in *Gaza in Crisis: Reflections on Israel's War Against the Palestinians*, by Noam Chomsky and Ilan Pappe. New York: Penguin, 2010; Massad, Joseph, "The Compulsion to Partition", online: http://www.aljazeera.com/indepth/opinion/2012/08/201285124456911263.html. Loewenstein, Antony and Ahmed Moor (Eds). *After Zionism: One State for Israel and Palestine*. London: Saqi Books, 2012.

CHAPTER 15

1. Karl Marx, *Grundrisse* (New York: Vintage 1973), pp. 539, 542.

2. Karl Marx, *A Contribution to the Critique of Political Economy* (New York: International Publishers, 1970 [1859]), p. 80.

3. Karl Marx and Frederick Engels, *The Communist Manifesto* (London: Verso 1998 [1848]), p. 49.

4. See Michael Hart, *A Trading Nation: Canadian Trade Policy from Colonialism to Globalization* (Vancouver: UBC Press, 2003).

5. W.T. Easterbrook and Hugh Aitken, *Canadian Economic History* (Toronto: Macmillan 1956); Kenneth Norrie and Doug Owram, *A History of the Canadian Economy* (Toronto: Harcourt 1991). The main dissenting text is R.T. Naylor, *Canada in the European Age, 1453–1919* (Montreal: McGill-Queen's University Press 2006).

6. For this turn in analysis see: Wallace Clement and Glen Williams, eds., *The New Canadian Political Economy* (Montreal: McGill-Queen's University Press 1989); and the journal *Studies in Political Economy*.

7. Harold Innis, *Changing Concepts of Time* (Toronto: University of Toronto Press, 1952).

8. League for Social Reconstruction, *Social Planning for Canada* (Toronto: University of Toronto Press, 1975 [1935]), p. 55.

9. A theme of the most significant critical books of this period: Frank and Libby Park, *Anatomy of Big Business* (1962); Stanley Ryerson, *Unequal Union* (1968); Kari Levitt, *Silent Surrender* (1970).

10. Also see: F.W. Park, "The Price of Dependence," 4:3, March/April, 1967; Melville Watkins, "Monopoly — Will We Have to Nationalize?" 6:2, July 1969.

11. W.H. Pope offered up a more developed plan, in line with the Left-Keynesian thinking of J.K. Galbraith, to address foreign capital and the "controlled sector": "An Economic Program for the Seventies," 6:2, July 1969.

12. Reprinted in: Patricia Cormack, ed., *Manifestos and Declarations of the Twentieth Century* (Toronto: Garamond, 1998). Discussions on socialism in Canada had already figured in *CD*: Anthony Mardiros, "Socialism in Canada: Is it Relevant? 1:6, May/June 1969; James Laxer, "The Socialist Tradition in Canada," 6:6, December/January 1969–70; and numerous debates over a socialist program for the NDP.

13. As seen in the growing Marxist analysis of Canada in the 1970s that eventually gave birth to the periodical *Studies in Political Economy* in 1979. In the pages of *CD*, this came in the form of reviews of the collections edited by Gary Teeple, *Capitalism and the National Question in Canada* (1972) and Leo Panitch, *The Canadian State* (1977) in: C.B. Macpherson, "Marxism in Canada: New Beginning," 9:7-8, 1973; Watkins, "Canada, the State and Political Economy," 13:1, 1978.

14. Levitt along with Watkins and Gonick also commented on the Gray Report's failure to address the power structures of MNCs, technological dependency and nationalization. Instead, the report narrowed the issue of FDI to corporate performance and advocated a screening process for new investments, which would become the basis for the Foreign Investment Review Agency. See: "Three Socialists Analyse the Gray Report," 8:4-5, January 1972.

15. This was part of a wider debate on Canada's place in the world market notably with: Robert Laxer, *Canada Ltd.* (1973); Steve Moore and Debbi Wells, *Imperialism and the National Question in Canada* (1975); John Warnock, "Imperialism and the Canadian Left," 11:4, March 1976; Wally Clement, *Continental Corporate Power* (1977).

16. Laxer's own contributions on this in *CD* being: "Continental Energy: A Proposal," 6:8, April/May, 1970; "Imperial Oil Calls the Tune," 11:8, November 1976.

17. Such a policy, for Richards, could be found in the formation of the Public Petroleum Association of Canada, led by many of the leaders of the now-defunct Waffle movement, and its calls for extensive nationalization of the fossil fuels sector ("Organizing Around Oil," 11:4, March 1976).

18. Rick Deaton early on linked the developing economic impasse to a fiscal crisis of the state and contended (in a theme that remains crucial today) that: "Building political alliances in the between workers in the public sector and users of social public services is a necessity [via] qualitative collective bargaining demands." See: "Fiscal Squeeze," 9:4, March 1973.

19. A theme various authors picked up on in discussing the crisis of unemployment in a focus on unemployment in various issues in the late 1970s (as in, 12:8, 1978).

20. Gorz himself made a contribution on workers' control in 1971 from a speech in Toronto. See: Andre Beckerman, "An Organizer's Guide to Workers' Control," 8:7, June 1972; Leo Panitch, "The Importance of Workers' Control," 12:3, July 1977.

21. Themes further developed in Gonick's books, drawing upon his CD essays, *Inflation or Depression* (1975) and *Out of Work* (1978).

22. Leo Panitch, "Globalization and the State," in Ralph Miliband and Leo Panitch, eds., *Between Globalism and Nationalism: Socialist Register 1994* (London: Merlin, 1994), p. 79.

23. Debates well summarized in Glenn Williams, "On Determining Canada's Location Within the International Political Economy," *Studies in Political Economy* 25, 1988.

24. Stephen McBride, *Paradigm Shift: Globalization and the Canadian State* (Halifax: Fernwood, 2005). Shaffer, Pratt and others picked up their debate from the 1970s on the NEP in a forum on "What Energy Policy?" (16:2, March 1982). Much of the subsequent writing on energy in CD in the 1990s was on the way free trade changed national controls over energy and in the 2000s on the ecological challenges posed by the tar sands.

25. Themes also picked up by Panitch, "The Only Way Out of the American Empire," 22:4, June 1988; and Claude Denis and Len Guenther, "The NDP, GATT-Fly and Free Trade," 22:6, September 1988.

26. He further expounded these ideas in "A Socialist Alternative to Unemployment," 20:1, March 1986; and Sam Gindin also made the case for "Putting Socialism on Labour's Agenda," 22:1, February 1988. This was part of the massive outpouring of research on Canada since the 1970s and surveyed in Wallace Clement and Glen Williams, eds., *The New Canadian Political Economy* (Montreal: McGill-Queen's University Press, 1989).

27. The best summary of these issues being: Stephen Clarkson, *Uncle Sam and Us: Globalization, Neoconservatism and the Canadian State* (Toronto: University of Toronto Press, 2002); Wallace Clement and Leah Vosko, eds., *Changing Canada: Political Economy as Transformation* (Montreal: McGill-Queen's University Press, 2003).

28. These were themes extended by Sid Shniad, John Loxley and Errol Black and Robert Chernomas well, as the "politics of balanced budgets" restructured the entire Canadian state system ("The Politics of Canada's Debt Crisis,"

27:5, September/October, 1993; "Balanced Budget Legislation or Bad Budget Legislation?" 29:5, October/November 1995; "Jobs? Jobs? Jobs?" 31:5, September/October 1997).

29. For a contrary assessment see: William Carroll and Jerome Klassen, "Hollowing Out of Corporate Canada? Changes in the Corporate Network since the 1990s," *Canadian Journal of Sociology* 35:1 (2010), p. 2.

30. This became the basis for the book with Jerome Klassen, *Empire's Ally: Canada and the War in Afghanistan* (Toronto: University of Toronto Press, 2013).

31. This was also a thesis of their book, *The Making of Global Capitalism* (London: Verso, 2013). It also figured in the *Socialist Register* volumes, edited by Leo Panitch, Greg Albo and Vivek Chibber, *The Crisis This Time* (2011) and *The Left and the Crisis* (2012). The first reviewed by Mel Watkins in "From Corporation to Crisis," 47:2, March/April 2013.

32. See: Ian McKay, *Rebels, Reds, Radicals: Rethinking Canada's Left History* (Toronto: Between the Lines 2005); Thom Workman, *If You're in My Way, I'm Walking: The Assault on Working People Since 1970* (Halifax: Fernwood 2005).

33. For important recent interventions suggesting the variety of approaches: Michael Lebowitz, *The Socialist Alternative* (New York: Monthly Review Press 2010); Robin Hahnel, *Economic Justice and Democracy* (New York: Routledge 2005); E.O. Wright, *Envisioning Real Utopias* (London: Verso 2010).

34. Leo Panitch, Greg Albo and Vivek Chibber, eds., *Socialist Register 2013: The Question of Strategy* (Halifax: Fernwood, 2012).

CHAPTER 18

1. See, for example, John Warnock, "Saskatchewan NDP Policy Swings Left" (7:3, August/September 1970).

2. McGrane, David (ed.), *New Directions in Saskatchewan Public Policy*. Regina: Canadian Plains Research Centre Press, 2011.

CHAPTER 19

1. Verzuh, Ron. *Radical Rag: The Pioneer Labour Press in Canada*. Ottawa: Steel Rail Publishing, 1988.

CHAPTER 20

1. For this history, see Benjamin Issit, *Militant Minority: British Columbia's Workers and the Rise of the New Left, 1948–1972* (Toronto: University of Toronto Press, 2011).

2. Grant, Shelagh. "Hugh Llewellyn Keenleyside, Commissioner of the Northwest Territories, 1947–1950," *Arctic* 43:1, 1989.

3. See, for example, Dawn Paley, Sandra Cuffe, "Resistance to Pipelines Heats Up in Northern BC," *Canadian Dimension* 45:2, March/April 2011.

4. See, in particular, David Harvey, *The Enigma of Capital and the Crises of Capitalism* (Oxford: Oxford University Press, 2010); and Fredric Jameson, *Representing Capital: A Reading of Volume One* (London: Verso Books, 2011).

CHAPTER 21

1. Larry Pratt, *The Tar Sands: Syncrude and the Politics of Oil.* Edmonton: Hurtig, 1976.

2. See Gordon Laxer and Trevor Harrison (eds.), *The Trojan Horse: Alberta and the Future of Canada.* Montreal: Black Rose; and Mark Lisac, *The Klein Revolution.* Edmonton: NeWest Press.

3. Alberta's authoritarian past, with warnings for the present, was also explored in Lyle Dick and Ron Frohwerk, "State repression and sexual minorities," *Canadian Dimension* 43:4, July/August 2009.

4. While several writers detailed an array of social problems arising during this period, Fraser Bell's discussion of homelessness, "Down and out in Calgary," *Canadian Dimension* 31:1, February 1997, is worth specifically noting.

5. See, for example, Anthony Hall, "The Alberta disadvantage in higher education," *Canadian Dimension* 41:5, September/October 2007.

CHAPTER 22

1. Maxwell Cohen, "Civil Disobedience, Dissent and Violence — A Canadian Perspective," *The Urban Crisis: A Symposium.* New York: De Capo Press, 1971, p. 92.

2. Cohen, "Civil Disobedience," p. 93.

3. Yasmin Jiwani, *Discourses of Denial: Mediations of Race, Gender, and Violence.* Vancouver: University of British Columbia Press, 2006.

4. David Ley, "The New Middle Class in Canadian Central Cities," *City Lives and City Forms: Critical Research and Canadian Urbanism*, eds. John Caulfield and Linda Peake. Toronto: University of Toronto Press, 1996, p. 15.

5. Lee, Jo-Anne, "Gender, Ethnicity, and Hybrid Forms of Community-Based Urban Activism in Vancouver, 1957–1978: The Strathcona Story Revisited," *Gender, Place and Culture* 14:4 (2007), p. 381.

6. Stefan Kipfer and Jason Petrunia, "'Recolonization' and Public Housing: A Toronto Case Study," *Studies in Political Economy* 83.

7. Ley, "The New Middle Class," pp. 15–16.

8. Ley, "The New Middle Class," p. 15.

9. Neil Brenner and Nik Theodore, *Spaces of Neoliberalism: Urban Restructuring in Western Europe and North America.* Oxford: Blackwell, 2002, p. 20.

10. Julie-Anne Boudreau, Roger Keil and DouglasYoung, *Changing Toronto: Covering Urban Neoliberalism.* Toronto: University of Toronto Press 2009, p. 34.

11. Boudreau, Keil and Young, *Changing Toronto*, p. 20.

CHAPTER 23

1. Thanks to Sean Carleton for his help in researching this article.

2. See also *CD* 1:3, December 1963/January 1964.

3. See, for example, 9:5, May 1973; 12:3, Jul 1977; 12:6, 1977; 13:2, 1978.

4. See, for example, 14:7, June 1980; 15:8, December 1981; 17:1, March 1983; 17:4, September 1983; 20:2, April 1986; 22:3, May 1988; 23:5, September 1989; 23:7, Oct 1989; 23:8, November 1989.

5. See, for example, 37:5, September/October 2003; 37:6, November/ December 2003.

6. See, for example, 20:6, November 1986; 21:7, October 1987; 19:4, September/October 1985; 19:6, January/February 1986; 22:1, February 1988.

7. See, for example, 27:2, April 1993; 27:5, September/October 1993; 27:6, November/December 1993; 28:1, January/February 1994.

8. See, for example, 24:4, June 1990; 24:5, July/August 1990; 24:6, September 1990; 24:8, Nov/December 1990; 25:6, September 1991.

CHAPTER 24

1. Thanks to Hans Rollman for his very helpful research assistance in preparing this chapter.

2. Joan Sangster, "Radical Ruptures: Feminism, Labor, and the Left in the Long Sixties in Canada," *American Review of Canadian Studies* 40.1 (Spring 2010), pp. 1–21.

3. Dixon, a Marxist-Leninist and sociologist who taught at the University of Chicago and McGill University in the late 1960s and early seventies, was later the leader of the US-based Democratic Workers' Party.

4. Dixon (10:8, June 1975) described similar sexualized verbal violence in US New Left organizations like Students for a Democratic Society: the "all-time favorite . . . statement regarding the rebellion of women in the movement" at Berkeley was "let them eat cock."

5. For the important distinction between "separatism" as a goal and "separate organizing" as a strategy of women's empowerment in mixed-gender organizations, see Linda Briskin, "Union Women and Separate Organizing," in L. Briskin and P. McDermott (eds.), *Women Challenging Unions: Feminism, Democracy and Militancy* (pp. 89–108). Toronto: University of Toronto Press, 1993.

6. Meg Luxton, "Feminism as a Class Act: Working-Class Feminism and the Women's Movement in Canada," *Labour/Le Travail* 48, Fall 2001.

7. *CD* articles on specific groups of women workers, their conditions and organizing strategies include: Jane Armstrong, "VISA Workers Crack the Banks," 20:3, May 1986; Rosemary Tugwood, "Women in Northern Resource Towns," 23:5, July/August 1989; Errol Black, "Manitoba Nurses Strike," 25:3, April/May 1991; Katherine MacDonald, "Farm Women, Farm Crisis," 24:7, October 1990; S. Papernick and Nini Jones, "Organizing

Women in the Service Industry," 30:1, February/March 1996; and Lori Vitali Cox, "Women in the Atlantic Fishery," 30:1, February/March 1996.

8. The House of Commons Motion 312, which would have struck a committee to investigate the scientific evidence that established the beginning of life, was defeated on September 26, 2012, by a vote of 203–91.

9. However, given two more juries' acquittal of Morgentaler in 1976, the newly elected Parti Quebecois government decided that the Criminal Code's abortion provisions were unenforceable in Quebec and ceased its prosecutions of Morgentaler.

10. Morgentaler also opened his Toronto clinic in 1983, and was subject to police raids there as well.

11. Johanna Brenner, "Intersections, Locations, and Capitalist Class Relations: Intersectionality from a Marxist Perspective," in J. Brenner, *Women and the Politics of Class* (pp. 293–324). New York: Monthly Review Press, 2000.

12. In the end, the AMC organized a Special Assembly on Family Violence and Community Healing, which proposed a variety of changes to existing self-government policies and practices.

13. See also Doris Young and Ustun Reinart, "How Powerful We As Native Women Really Are," 22:2, March/April 1988; Nahanni Fontaine, "Aboriginal Women's Perspective on Self-Government," 36:6, November/December 2002; Anna Hunter, "The Violence Indigenous Women Face," 39:2, March/April 2005; and Lois Moorcroft, "Raising our Voices against Violence," 40:2, March/April 2006.

14. For an account and analysis of the conflict at Nellie's Place from two members of the Women of Colour Caucus, see Ruth Magaly San Martin and Lisa Barnhoff, "Let Them Howl: The Operation of Imperial Subjectivity and the Politics of Race in One Feminist Organization," *Atlantis* 29:1 (Fall/Winter 2004), 77–84.

15. For instance, see Michael Welton, "All About Men," 13:6, March 1979; Jonathan Barker, "The Men's Group," 14:6, May 1980; Bruce Kidd, "Goon Masculinity," 21:1, April 1987.

16. See, for example, Josh Freed, "Soul Searching in Montreal and Canada," 24:2, March 1990; Vic Seidler, "Redefining Masculinity," 25:8, December 1991.

17. This concept comes from David Roediger's *The Wages of Whiteness*, in which he demonstrates that the US white working class was "compensated" for their class subordination by being able to enjoy economic and social elements of white supremacy and therefore divided from their black working-class counterparts.

18. However, the status of their children, particularly when their father is not named, remained an issue for far longer; see Native Women's Association of Canada, "Loss of Indian Status: A Foremost Aboriginal Issue," July/August 2005: 15–16.

19. Briskin's article "Women, Unions and Leadership," 24:1, January/February 1990, features CLC President Shirley Carr and Saskatchewan Federation of

Labour president Barb Byers. Women also progressively took on leadership roles in the NDP, as depicted in the discussion of Judy Rebick's run for the presidency of the Ontario NDP (20:4, July/August 1986). Although Rebick lost the election, she did so to another woman, Gillian Sandeman.

20. See Marianne Roy, "Women's March Against Poverty," 30:3, May/June 1996.

21. Sharmeen Khan, "The Fight for Feminism: An Interview with Sunera Thobani," *Upping the Anti* 5, October 2007. Online: http://uppingtheanti. org/journal.article/05-the-fight-for-feminism.

CHAPTER 25

1. See, for example, Louis Feldhammer (6:6, December/January 1969-1970), and Sherill Cheda (9:4, March 1973).

ABOUT THE CONTRIBUTORS

Greg Albo teaches political economy at York University, is co-editor of the *Socialist Register*, and has been a regular contributor to *Canadian Dimension*.

Brenda Austin-Smith is an Associate Professor and teaches Film Studies at the University of Manitoba. Among her publications are articles and essays on film and effect, cinema memory, melodrama, and adaptation. She is co-editor, with George Melnyk, of *The Gendered Screen: Canadian Women Filmmakers*. She is an active member of her union, and has been a member of the *CD* collective since 1991.

Chris Bailey is a PhD Candidate in Political Science at York University. Bailey's doctoral research compares the different strategies of neoliberal education restructuring in Ontario and British Columbia. Bailey graduated with a Master's Degree in Political Science from the University of New Brunswick.

Evan Bowness is a PhD student at UBC's Institute for Resources, Environment and Sustainability where his research focuses on community-based urban agriculture. He teaches criminology courses and courses on social inequality at the Department of Sociology, University of Manitoba.

Mordecai Briemberg is a Rhodes scholar, a former university professor and, above all, a political activist for more than fifty years in Vancouver, BC. He has been continuously active in antiwar work, in Palestine solidarity activities, and in advocating in defense of free speech. He edited the book *It was, It was not - Essays and Art on the War against Iraq*, published in 1992. For thirty years he was a member of the RedEye collective of Vancouver Cooperative Radio.

Elizabeth Comack is a professor in the Department of Sociology at the University of Manitoba. Specializing in the sociology of law and feminist criminology, Elizabeth has published twelve books, including: *Criminalizing Women: Gender and (In)justice in Neo-Liberal Times*, *Locating Law: Race/Class/Gender/Sexuality Connections*, *"Indians Wear Red": Colonialism, Resistance, and Aboriginal Street Gangs*, and *Racialized Policing: Aboriginal People's Encounters with the Police*.

Angela Day is a PhD candidate in the department of Geography and Planning at the University of Toronto, and currently teaches part-time at Saint Mary's University in Halifax, NS.

Bryan Evans is an Associate Professor in the Department of Politics and Public Administration at Ryerson University. His publications include *Shrinking the State* (co-authored with Dr. John Shields), *Transforming Provincial Politics: The Political Economy of Canada's Provinces and Territories in the Neoliberal Era* (edited with Charles W. Smith) and *Social Democracy after the Cold War* (edited with Ingo Schmidt).

Alvin Finkel is professor emeritus of Athabasca University in Canadian history. A prolific author, his books include *Social Policy and Practice in Canada: A History*, *Our Lives: Canada After 1945*, *The Social Credit Phenomenon in Alberta*, *History of the Canadian Peoples*, *The Chamberlain-History Collusion* and *Working People in Alberta: A History*. Alvin served as assistant editor of *Canadian Dimension* in 1970–71.

Cy Gonick founded *Canadian Dimension* in 1963 and has been involved in the magazine since then as publisher and coordinating editor. He taught political economy for several years at the University of Manitoba and subsequently at the University of Winnipeg. He has written several books and edited still more.

Peter Graefe teaches in the Department of Political Science at McMaster University. His research focuses on the politics of economic and social development in Quebec.

Judy Haiven is an Associate Professor in the Management Department at the Sobey School of Business at Saint Mary's University in Halifax. She researches and writes in the areas of industrial relations, women and work and equity in the workplace and the wider community. She joined the *CD* collective in 2013.

Larry Haiven is a professor in the Management Department of the Sobey School of Business at Saint Mary's University in Halifax. He is an active researcher, writer and frequent commentator in areas of industrial relations, industrial conflict, labour markets and labour law. He is also a research associate of the Canadian Centre for Policy Alternatives.

Trevor W. Harrison is a Professor of Sociology at the University of Lethbridge and Director of Parkland Institute, a research network housed on the University of Alberta campus. He is best known for his studies in political sociology, political economy and public policy. He is the author, co-author or co-editor of nine books, numerous journal articles and book chapters and is a frequent contributor to public media.

Henry Heller is professor of history at the University of Manitoba. He is the author of *The Cold War and the New Imperialism* and *The Struggle for the American Mind: Intellectual Capitalism and Higher Education*. He has been a member of the *Canadian Dimension* collective since 1986.

David Hugill is an urban researcher and post-doctoral fellow in the Department of Geography at Simon Fraser University in Vancouver. He is the author of *Missing Women, Missing News: Covering Crisis in Vancouver's Downtown Eastside* and has been a member of *Canadian Dimension*'s editorial collective since 2011.

Peter Kulchyski is a Professor of Native Studies at the University of Manitoba and a long term activist around indigenous land rights. Among his many publications are *Like the Sound of a Drum, The Red Indians* and *Aboriginal Rights are not Human Rights*. He is currently active with hydro-affected communities in northern Manitoba and is working on a book about Northwest Territory Mountain Dene struggles for justice.

Andrea Levy has a PhD in History from Concordia University. An independent scholar, journalist and activist, she is a coordinating editor of *Canadian Dimension* and has been a member of the magazine's editorial collective since 1998. She is the author of EcoSide, a regular column on vanishing biodiversity and other environmental tragedies. She is also a member of the editorial board of the Quebec-based French-language journal *Les Nouveaux cahiers du socialisme*.

James N. McCrorie (1936–2013) was born and raised in Montreal. His early work on the Saskatchewan farmers movement, *In Union is Strength*, was followed by numerous academic books, articles and papers covering Canadian, Scottish, Chinese and Russian rural policies. McCrorie founded the Sociology Department at the University of Regina in 1965 and later ran the Canadian Plains Research Centre.

James Naylor is a historian of Canadian labour and radical movements and teaches at Brandon University in Manitoba. He is the author of *The Fate of Labour Socialism: The Co-operative Commonwealth Federation and the Dream of a Working-Class Future*.

Bryan D. Palmer, former editor of *Labour/Le Travail*, is a social historian of labour and the Left, and a contributor to *Canadian Dimension* since 1983. He has published widely in Canada, the United States, the United Kingdom, Latin America, Europe, and Asia with translations of his books and articles appearing in Greek, Spanish, Portuguese, French, Italian, and Korean. His most recent publication, a two-volume collection of essays, is entitled *Marxism and Historical Practice*. He also has an upcoming book on the history of Toronto's poor and out-of-work in the 19th and 20th centuries.

Dennis Pilon teaches in the Political Science department at York University. His research and activism has focused extensively on democratic reform. He has been a member of the *Canadian Dimension* editorial collective since 2002.

Joseph Roberts helped to build the social science faculty at the University of Regina in 1966, where he worked for the remainder of his academic career. His research has focused on the struggle for socialism, campaigns for peace and social justice and environmental issues.

Stephanie Ross is an Associate Professor of Work and Labour Studies in the Department of Social Science and co-director of the Global Labour Research Centre at York University. Her research and teaching focuses on public sector unionism, union renewal and democracy in working-class and social movement organizations. With Larry Savage, she has edited two books, *Rethinking the Politics of Labour in Canada* and *Public Sector Unions in the Age of Austerity*. She is also president of the Canadian

Association for Work and Labour Studies. Stephanie was a member of the *CD* collective from 2010 to 2014.

Arthur Schafer is Founding Director of the Centre for Professional and Applied Ethics at the University of Manitoba. He is also a Professor in the Department of Philosophy and served as Head of the Section of Bio-Medical Ethics in the university's Faculty of Medicine. He has published widely in the fields of moral, social, and political philosophy, is National Research Associate of the Canadian Centre for Policy Alternatives and has written dozens of articles for *The Globe and Mail, Toronto Star, The Winnipeg Free Press, The Medical Post* and *The Sunday Times* (London). Schafer has also appeared frequently in the media, on both radio and television.

Frank Tester teaches international social development studies, social policy and social theory in the School of Social Work at the University of British Columbia. He is best known for his work with Inuit youth and Elders in the Canadian eastern Arctic. Frank is a recipient of the Gustavus Myers Award for the Study of Human Rights in North America and the Erminie Wheeler-Voegelin Prize for the book *Tammarniit (Mistakes)* co-authored with Peter Kulchyski.

John W. Warnock is retired from teaching sociology and political economy at the University of Regina. He is the author of a number of books, including *The Politics of Hunger, Free Trade and the New Right Agenda, The Other Mexico, Saskatchewan: The Roots of Discontent and Protest* and *Creating a Failed State: The US and Canada in Afghanistan.* He has a special interest in farming and resource industries and is the author of *Selling the Family Silver: The Oil Industry in Saskatchewan.* He lives on a farm near Bulyea, Saskatchewan.

 **Mel Watkins** is Editor Emeritus of *This Magazine* and a long time political activist. He is Professor Emeritus of Economics and Political Science, University of Toronto and a recipient of the John Kenneth Galbraith Prize of the Progressive Economics Forum for his contribution to economics and social justice. His scholarly writings focus on the role of staple exports in Canadian economic growth. He blogs for rabble and the Progressive Economics Forum and has published over the years in *Canadian Dimension*.

 **Christopher Webb** is a PhD Candidate at the University of Toronto where he researches labour and development in Southern Africa. He has written for the *Review of African Political Economy*, the *Journal of Peasant Studies*, *Amandla! Magazine* and *Africa is A Country*. He worked as publishing assistant at *Canadian Dimension* from 2008 to 2010.

INDEX